AMERICAN HISTORY Beginnings to 1877

myWorld
INTERACTIVE

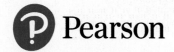 Pearson

Boston, Massachusetts   Chandler, Arizona
Glenview, Illinois   New York, New York

To start, download the free Pearson BouncePages app on your smartphone or tablet. Simply search for the Pearson BouncePages app in your mobile app store. The app is available for Android and IOS (iPhone®/iPad®).

Activate your digital course videos directly from the page.

To launch the videos look for this icon.

1. AIM the camera so that the page is easily viewable on your screen.
2. TAP the screen to scan the page.
3. BOUNCE the page to life by clicking the Bounce icon.

Cover: Tall Ship Festival - shaunl/Getty Images

ISBN-13: 978-0-32-896502-1
ISBN-10: 0-32-896502-2

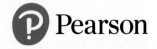

AUTHORS

Program Authors

James West Davidson

Dr. James Davidson is coauthor of *After the Fact: The Art of Historical Detection* and *Nation of Nations: A Narrative History of the American Republic*. Dr. Davidson has taught at both the college and high school levels. He has also consulted on curriculum design for American history courses. Dr. Davidson is an avid canoeist and hiker. His published works on these subjects include *Great Heart*, the true story of a 1903 canoe trip in the Canadian wilderness.

Michael B. Stoff

Dr. Michael Stoff received his Ph.D. from Yale University and teaches history at the University of Texas at Austin. He is the author of *Oil, War, and American Security: The Search for a National Policy on Foreign Oil, 1941–1947*, coauthor of *Nation of Nations: A Narrative History of the American Republic*, and coeditor of the *Manhattan Project: A Documentary Introduction to the Atomic Age*. Dr. Stoff has won numerous grants, fellowships, and teaching awards.

Contributing Author

Jennifer L. Bertolet

Jennifer Bertolet is a Professional Lecturer at George Washington University where she teaches American History courses, among them Introduction to American History. She received her Ph.D. from George Washington University. In addition to teaching, she has served as an education consultant, a subject matter expert for online teaching and learning, and as a historian and policy consultant specializing in Indian policy and environmental issues.

TEACHER REVIEWERS

Ruth Castro
Inglewood USD
Inglewood, California

Colleen Eccles
Instructional Coach and PDLT
Samuel Ogle Middle School
Bowie, Maryland

Piper Hudmon
Content Specialist/Secondary Social Studies
Muscogee County School District
Columbus, Georgia

Dana L. Roberts, Ed. S
Academic Coach and Gifted Lead Coordinator
Lindley Middle School
Mableton, Georgia

Anthony Zambelli
San Diego Center for Economic Education
San Diego, California

PROGRAM CONSULTANTS

ELL Consultant
Jim Cummins Ph.D.
Professor Emeritus, Department of Curriculum,
 Teaching, and Learning
University of Toronto
Toronto, Canada

Differentiated Instruction Consultant
Marianne Sender
In-Class Resource Teacher
Renaissance @ Rand Middle School
Montclair, New Jersey

Reading Consultant
Elfrieda H. Hiebert Ph.D.
Founder, President and CEO of TextProject, Inc.
University of California, Santa Cruz

Inquiry and C3 Consultant
Dr. Kathy Swan
Professor of Curriculum and Instruction
University of Kentucky
Lexington, Kentucky

PROGRAM PARTNERS

NBC Learn, the educational arm of NBC News, develops original stories for use in the classroom and makes archival NBC news stories, images, and primary source documents available on demand to teachers, students, and parents. NBC Learn partnered with Pearson to produce the topic opening videos that support this program.

Campaign for the Civic Mission of Schools is a coalition of over 70 national civic learning, education, civic engagement, and business groups committed to improving the quality and quantity of civic learning in American schools.

Constitutional Rights Foundation is a nonprofit, nonpartisan, community-based organization focused on educating students about the importance of civic participation in a democratic society. The Constitutional Rights Foundation is the lead contributor to the development of the Civic Discussion Quests for this program.

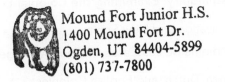

Mound Fort Junior H.S.
1400 Mound Fort Dr.
Ogden, UT 84404-5899
(801) 737-7800

CONTENTS

CONTENTS

TOPIC 5
The Early Republic (1789–1825)

TOPIC 6
The Age of Jackson and Westward Expansion (1824–1860)

TOPIC 7
Society and Culture Before the Civil War (1820–1860)

CONTENTS

TOPIC 8
Sectionalism and Civil War (1820–1865)

ACCESS MORE ONLINE
videos, audio, etext, interactivities, games, worksheets, and more!

TOPIC 9
The Reconstruction Era (1865–1877)

DIGITAL RESOURCES

Core Concepts

These digital lessons introduce key concepts for all of the social sciences and personal finance.

Culture
Economics

Geography
Government and Civics

History
Personal Finance

Landmark Supreme Court Cases

How has the Supreme Court interpreted the law of the land? Find out in these online multimedia lessons.

TOPIC 5
Lesson 4 *Marbury v. Madison*
Lesson 6 *McCulloch v. Maryland*
Lesson 6 *Gibbons v. Ogden*

TOPIC 6
Lesson 3 *Worcester v. Georgia*

TOPIC 8
Lesson 2 *Dred Scott v. Sandford*

TOPIC 9
Lesson 4 *Plessy v. Ferguson*

Topic Videos NBC LEARN

Begin each topic with a front seat view of history.

TOPIC 1
Austin Celebrates His Heritage

TOPIC 2
John Smith, Jamestown and the Roots of America

TOPIC 3
Benjamin Franklin and the Fight for Independence

TOPIC 4
James Madison, The Federalist Papers

TOPIC 5
William Clark, Mapping the American Frontier

TOPIC 6
Narcissa Whitman and the Journey West

TOPIC 7
Lucy Larcom, Weaving Opportunity

TOPIC 8
Robert E. Lee, The Marble Man

TOPIC 9
Born into Slavery

Lesson Videos

Preview key ideas from the lesson in these videos.

TOPIC 1
Lesson 1 Maya and Aztec Civilizations
Lesson 2 Native American Culture Regions of North America
Lesson 3 New Technologies and Exploration
Lesson 4 The Columbian Exchange

TOPIC 2
Lesson 1 Northern Borderlands of New Spain
Lesson 2 France, the Netherlands and the Fur Trade
Lesson 3 Religious Freedom in New England
Lesson 4 The Middle Colonies
Lesson 5 The Southern Colonies

Lesson 6 Colonial Cultural Achievements
Lesson 7 Colonial Government

TOPIC 3
Lesson 1 Causes and Results of the French and Indian War
Lesson 2 Taxation and Mercantilism
Lesson 3 The Boston Tea Party
Lesson 4 The Declaration of Independence
Lesson 5 Winning Independence

TOPIC 4
Lesson 1 The Articles of Confederation

Interactive Primary Sources

Go to the original sources to hear voices from the time.

DIGITAL RESOURCES

Biographies

Read about the people who made history.

TOPIC 3
Lesson 2 King George III
Lesson 2 Abigail Adams
Lesson 2 John Adams
Lesson 2 Samuel Adams
Lesson 2 Mercy Otis Warren
Lesson 2 Patrick Henry
Lesson 2 George Washington
Lesson 2 Crispus Attucks
Lesson 3 Thomas Jefferson
Lesson 4 Patrick Henry
Lesson 4 Benjamin Franklin
Lesson 5 Haym Solomon
Lesson 5 Marquis de Lafayette
Lesson 5 Wentworth Cheswell
Lesson 5 Bernardo de Galvez

TOPIC 4
Lesson 2 Gouverneur Morris
Lesson 2 James Wilson
Lesson 4 Alexander Hamilton
Lesson 4 James Madison
Lesson 4 George Mason

TOPIC 5
Lesson 1 Alexander Hamilton
Lesson 3 John Marshall
Lesson 5 Henry Clay
Lesson 6 James Monroe
Lesson 6 Daniel Webster

TOPIC 6
Lesson 1 John Quincy Adams
Lesson 1 Andrew Jackson
Lesson 1 Alexis de Tocqueville
Lesson 2 John C. Calhoun
Lesson 2 Daniel Webster

TOPIC 7
Lesson 4 Charles Finney
Lesson 4 Theodore Weld
Lesson 4 William Lloyd Farrison
Lesson 4 Frederick Douglass
Lesson 4 Charles Remond
Lesson 4 Sojourner Truth
Lesson 4 Harriet Tubman
Lesson 4 Robert Purvis
Lesson 5 Susan B. Anthony
Lesson 5 Elizabeth Cady Stanton
Lesson 5 Margaret Fuller
Lesson 5 Lucretia Mott
Lesson 5 Charley Parkhurst

TOPIC 8
Lesson 2 Abraham Lincoln
Lesson 2 John Brown
Lesson 3 Jefferson Davis
Lesson 3 Robert E. Lee
Lesson 4 Ulysses S. Grant

TOPIC 9
Lesson 3 Hiram Rhodes Revels

21st Century Skills

Learn, practice, and apply important skills using these online tutorials.

Analyze Cause and Effect
Analyze Data and Models
Analyze Images
Analyze Media Content
Analyze Political Cartoons
Analyze Primary and Secondary
  Sources
Ask Questions
Avoid Plagiarism
Being an Informed Citizen
Categorize
Compare and Contrast
Compare Viewpoints
Compromise

Consider and Counter Opposing
  Arguments
Create Charts and Maps
Create Databases
Create a Research Hypothesis
Develop a Clear Thesis
Develop Cultural Awareness
Distinguish Between Fact and
  Opinion
Draw Conclusions
Draw Inferences
Evaluate Existing Arguments
Evaluate Web Sites
Generalize

Generate New Ideas
Give an Effective Presentation
Identify Bias
Identify Evidence
Identify Main Ideas and Details
Identify Trends
Innovate
Interpret Sources
Make Decisions
Make a Difference
Make Predictions
Organize Your Ideas
Participate in a Discussion or
  Debate

Paying Taxes
Political Participation
Publish Your Work
Read Charts, Graphs, and Tables
Read Physical Maps
Read Special Purpose Maps
Search for Information on the
    Internet
Serving on a Jury Sequence

Set a Purpose for Reading
Share Responsibility
Solve Problems
Summarize
Support Ideas With Evidence
Synthesize
Take Effective Notes
Use Content Clues
Use Parts of a Map

Voting
Work in Teams
Write an Essay
Write a Journal Entry

Interactivities

Explore maps one layer at a time to see how events unfolded over time, go on
a gallery walk to examine artifacts and primary sources, analyze data, and explore
key historical sites and objects in 3-D!

INTERACTIVE MAPS

North American Geographic Regions Topic 1
Native American Culture Regions of North America
    Topic 1 Lesson 2
Routes of Exploration and Trade Topic 1 Lesson 3
The Columbian Exchange Topic 1 Lesson 4
European Settlements in North America, 1750 Topic 2
Spanish Explorers and Settlements in North America
    Topic 2 Lesson 1
Lands Controlled by Colonial Powers, 1660 Topic 2
    Lesson 2
The New England Colonies Topic 2 Lesson 3
Comparing the Thirteen Colonies Topic 2 Lesson 5
The Triangular Trade Topic 2 Lesson 7
Key British Colonies, 1775 Topic 3
Major Battles of the French and Indian War Topic 3
    Lesson 1
**Opinions of Delegates to the Constitutional
    Convention** Topic 4
Ratification of the Constitution Topic 4 Lesson 4
U.S. Expansion During the Early Republic Topic 5
Foreign Affairs Under Washington Topic 5 Lesson 1
Expansion and Exploration Topic 5 Lesson 4
Indian Lands Lost by 1810 Topic 5 Lesson 5
The War of 1812 Topic 5 Lesson 5
Westward Expansion of the United States Topic 6
Tariffs and Trade Topic 6 Lesson 2
Selected Native American Groups, 1820 Topic 6
    Lesson 3
Southern Native Americans on the Trail of Tears
    Topic 6 Lesson 3
The Erie Canal Topic 6 Lesson 4
The Oregon Trail Topic 6 Lesson 5
The Settlement of Texas Topic 6 Lesson 6

The Growth of the West to 1860 Topic 6 Lesson 7
Two Different Economies Topic 7
The Underground Railroad Topic 7 Lesson 4
Early American Music and Literature Topic 7 Lesson 6
States in the Civil War Topic 8
The Union's Strategies to Win the Civil War Topic 8
    Lesson 4
The Battle of Vicksburg Topic 8 Lesson 6
Key Battles of the Civil War Topic 8 Lesson 6
Reconstruction Topic 9
Change in Southern Industry Topic 9 Lesson 4

INTERACTIVE CHARTS

Reasons to Explore Topic 1 Lesson 4
Social Classes in New Spain Topic 2 Lesson 1
Thomas Hooker Topic 2 Lesson 3
Education in the Colonies Topic 2 Lesson 6
Influences on Colonial Government Topic 2 Lesson 7
Effects of the French and Indian War Topic 3 Lesson 1
Crisis on the Frontier Topic 3 Lesson 2
**Advantages & Disadvantages of the British and
    Colonists** Topic 3 Lesson 3
The Great Compromise Topic 4 Lesson 2
Federalists Versus Antifederalists Topic 4 Lesson 4
Methods of Amending the Constitution Topic 4
    Lesson 6
A Controversial Tax Topic 5 Lesson 1
Jefferson's Goals and Policies Topic 5 Lesson 3
Political Parties in the Age of Jackson Topic 6
    Lesson 1
Disagreements Over the Bank Topic 6 Lesson 2
Different Ways of Life in the South Topic 7 Lesson 3
Lives of Free and Enslaved African Americans Topic 7
    Lesson 3

Interactivities (continued)

Opposing Views on Slavery Topic 7 Lesson 4
Resources in the North and the South, 1860 Topic 8 Lesson 3
Abraham Lincoln and Jefferson Davis Topic 8 Lesson 3
The Cycle of Poverty Topic 9 Lesson 3

INTERACTIVE GALLERIES
Housing and the Environment Topic 1 Lesson 2
The Economy of the Middle Colonies Topic 2 Lesson 4
The Arts in Colonial America Topic 2 Lesson 6
Important People of the American Revolution Topic 3 Lesson 2
Thomas Paine's *Common Sense* Topic 3 Lesson 4
Interactive Declaration of Independence Topic 3 Lesson 4
Notable People of the American Revolution Topic 3 Lesson 5
Delegates to the Constitutional Convention Topic 4 Lesson 2
The First Amendment Topic 4 Lesson 6
Early American Leaders Topic 5 Lesson 2
Expansion of Federal Powers Topic 5 Lesson 6
New Transportation Methods Topic 6 Lesson 4
New Technology: The Steamboat Topic 6 Lesson 4
Oregon Country Topic 6 Lesson 5
The Defenders of the Alamo Topic 6 Lesson 6
The People of California Topic 6 Lesson 7
The Steam Locomotive Topic 7 Lesson 2
Changes in American Schools Topic 7 Lesson 5
Painting America Topic 7 Lesson 6
Uncle Tom's Cabin Topic 8 Lesson 1
The Effects of The Kansas-Nebraska Act Topic 8 Lesson 2
The Dred Scott Case Topic 8 Lesson 2
The Hardships of Soldiers Topic 8 Lesson 5

Photography and the Civil War Topic 8 Lesson 5
Lincoln and Reconstruction Topic 9 Lesson 1
Reconstruction-Era Political Groups Topic 9 Lesson 3

INTERACTIVE GRAPHS
The Downfall of the Southern Economy Topic 9 Lesson 1

INTERACTIVE TIMELINES
Foreign Aid Plays a Role Topic 3 Lesson 5
Influences on the Constitution Topic 4 Lesson 3
Changing Voting Rights in Early America Topic 6 Lesson 1
Choosing a Presidential Candidate Topic 6 Lesson 2
Texas: From Settlement to Statehood Topic 6 Lesson 6
New Inventions Improve Life Topic 7 Lesson 1
The Early Women's Rights Movement Topic 7 Lesson 5
Early Battles of the Civil War Topic 8 Lesson 4
Oppression of African Americans Topic 9 Lesson 4

INTERACTIVE ILLUSTRATIONS
How an Astrolabe Works Topic 1 Lesson 3
A Southern Colonial Plantation Topic 2 Lesson 5

INTERACTIVE CARTOONS
The Fugitive Slave Act Topic 8 Lesson 1
The Massacre of New Orleans Topic 9 Lesson 2

INTERACTIVE 3D MODELS
Aztec Temple Topic 1 Lesson 1
Plymouth Plantation Topic 2 Lesson 3
The Covered Wagon Topic 6 Lesson 5
Early Textile Mill Topic 7 Lesson 1
The Cotton Gin Topic 7 Lesson 3
The Battle at Gettysburg Topic 8 Lesson 6

Maps

United States: Political
United States: Physical
World: Political
Africa: Political
Africa: Physical

Asia: Political
Asia: Physical
Europe: Political
Europe: Physical
North and South America: Political

North and South America: Physical
Australia, New Zealand, and Oceania: Political-Physical
The Arctic: Physical
Antarctica: Physical

SPECIAL FEATURES

All of these resources are found right here in your student textbook.

Quest

Ask questions, explore sources, and cite evidence to support your view!

Primary Sources

Excerpts from original sources allow you to witness history.

SPECIAL FEATURES

All of these resources are found right here in your student textbook.

Primary Source Quotations

Quotations in the text bring history to life.

SPECIAL FEATURES

All of these resources are found right here in your student textbook.

Analysis Skills

Practice key skills.

Biographies

Read about the people who made history.

Charts, Graphs, Tables, and Infographics

Find these charts, graphs, and tables in your text. It's all about the data!

SPECIAL FEATURES

All of these resources are found right here in your student textbook.

Charts, Graphs, Tables, and Infographics (continued)

Timelines

Maps

Where did this happen? Find out with these maps.

ACCESS MORE ONLINE
videos, audio, etext, interactivities, games, worksheets, and more!

ENGLISH-LANGUAGE ARTS HANDBOOK

As you explore United States history in this course, you will read informational texts and primary sources. For this course and in other courses and beyond, you will need to think critically about the texts you read to absorb information and be able to express your thoughts about world events, past and present. You will need to communicate your ideas through writing (summaries, arguments, informative essays, and narratives), speaking (debates and one-on-one and small group discussions), and by giving presentations.

This Handbook will give you some tools for reading critically and expressing your ideas. The Quests and other activities in this program give you opportunities to write and speak about your ideas and create projects that will help you practice these skills.

> ▶ **INTERACTIVE**
>
> The 21st Century Skills Tutorials, found online, support many of the skills discussed here. Go online to find a Quick Reference, video of the skill being modeled, and more.

READING

Analyze Informational Text

Reading nonfiction texts, like a magazine article or your textbook, is not the same as reading a fictional story or novel. The purpose of reading nonfiction is to acquire new information. It's something that you, and the adults around you, do all of the time.

Process What You Read When you read informational text, it helps to know what to look for and what questions to ask yourself as you read. Use the chart below as a guide when you read.

	Look for	Questions to Ask	For More Help
Central Ideas and Details	• Central ideas or claims • Supporting details or evidence	• What is the subject or main point of this text? • What details support the main point? • What inferences do you need to make? • How does the author develop a few central ideas throughout a text?	▶ **Skills Tutorial** • Identify Main Ideas and Details • Draw Inferences • Summarize **Analysis Skill** Identify Central Issues and Problems
Word Choice	• Unfamiliar words and phrases • Words and phrases that produce a certain effect on a reader	• What inferences about word meaning can you make from the context? • What tone and mood are created by word choice? • What alternate word choices might the author have made?	▶ **Skills Tutorial** • Draw Inferences
Text Structure	• Ways the author has organized the text • Ways sentences and paragraphs work together to build ideas • Clue words signaling a particular structure	• Does the text have a specific structure? • For instance, is it structured by sequence or chronology? By comparisons and contrasts? By causes and effects?	▶ **Skills Tutorial** • Identify Evidence • Analyze Cause and Effect • Sequence • Compare and Contrast

Evaluate Arguments

One important reason to read and understand informational text is so you can recognize and evaluate written arguments. When you think of an argument, you might think of a disagreement between two people, but the word has another meaning, too. An argument is a logical way of presenting a belief, conclusion, or stance. A good argument is supported with reasoning and evidence and will often address opposing claims. Study the model below to see how the writer developed an argument about restrictions against African Americans after the Civil War.

These two sentences express the conclusion that Conservative Democrats in the South tried to restrict the rights of African Americans, including their right to vote.

This paragraph offers evidence for the conclusion by describing one way southern states restricted African American voting rights.

These sentences explain how literacy tests were used to keep African Americans from voting.

This paragraph explains how southern states allowed poor and illiterate whites to vote while using poll taxes and literacy tests to prevent African Americans.

New Legislation Restricts African American Rights

As federal troops withdrew from southern states, Conservative Democrats found new ways to keep African Americans from exercising their rights. Many of these were laws specifically intended to prevent African Americans from voting.

Over time, many southern states passed poll taxes, requiring voters to pay a fee each time they voted. As a result, poor freedmen could rarely afford to vote.

States also imposed literacy tests that required voters to read and explain a section of the United States Constitution. Since most freedmen had little education, such tests kept them away from the polls. Election officials also applied different standards to black and white voters. Blacks who were able to read often had to answer more difficult questions than whites on literacy tests.

Still, many poor whites could not have passed any literacy test. To increase the number of white voters, states passed grandfather clauses. These laws stated that if a voter's father or grandfather had been eligible to vote on January 1, 1867, the voter did not have to take a literacy test. No African Americans in the South could vote before 1868, so the only effect of the grandfather clauses was to ensure that white men could vote.

▶ INTERACTIVE

Go online for these interactive skills tutorials:
- Evaluate Arguments
- Consider and Counter Opposing Arguments
- Support Ideas With Evidence

Analyze Visuals

Another key component of understanding informational texts is being able to understand visuals like the maps, graphs, charts, and photos in your student text. Study the chart and the example to help you analyze some common types of visuals in your social studies text.

	Look for	For More Help
Maps	• Read the title. • Read the key. • Study the locator globe, scale bar, and compass rose. • Apply the key and labels to the map.	▶ **Skills Tutorial** • Use Parts of a Map • Read Physical Maps • Read Political Maps • Read Special-Purpose Maps
Graphs and Tables	• Read the title. • Use labels and key. • Look for patterns or changes over time.	▶ **Skills Tutorial** • Read Charts, Graphs, and Tables • Create Charts and Maps
Photographs	• Identify the content. • Note emotions. • Read captions or credits. • Study the image's purpose. • Consider context. • Respond.	▶ **Skills Tutorial** • Analyze Images • Analyze Political Cartoons

Example

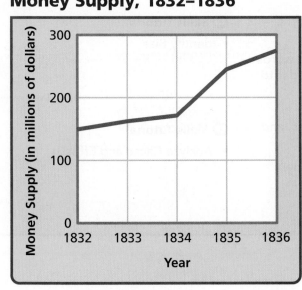

Money Supply, 1832–1836

❶ What is the title of the graph?

❷ Read the labels. What does the x-axis, or the horizontal edge of the graph, show? What does the y-axis, or the vertical side of the graph, show?

❸ How much did the money supply increase between 1832 and 1836?

❹ What is a likely cause for this change?

Analyze Primary and Secondary Sources

A primary source is an account or a document from someone who saw or was part of what is being described. A secondary source is information recorded later by someone who was not part of it. You will encounter many primary and secondary sources throughout your textbook and in Quests and other activities. Study these questions and the model primary sources that follow to help you unlock the meaning of these sources.

	Questions to Ask	For More Help
Determine the Author's Purpose	• Is the source written mainly to convey information, like a textbook? • Or is its purpose to persuade you to think a certain way, like an opinion piece in a newspaper?	▶ **Skills Tutorial** • Analyze Primary and Secondary Sources • Analyze Media Content • Draw Inferences
Determine the Author's Point of View	• What is the author's point of view? • Is the author's point of view shaped by subjective influences such as feelings, prejudices, or experiences? • Is the author's point of view shaped by his or her field of study?	▶ **Skills Tutorial** • Analyze Primary and Secondary Sources • Compare Viewpoints
Compare Viewpoints	• How is the author's point of view different from that of other authors' writing on the same subject? • Does the author avoid including certain facts that would change his or her point of view?	▶ **Skills Tutorial** • Compare Viewpoints
Analyze Word Choice	• Does the author use words in a neutral, factual way? • Does the author use loaded words that try to persuade the reader to think a certain way?	▶ **Skills Tutorial** • Identify Bias
Analyze Interactions	• How have individuals, events, and ideas influenced each other? • What connecting words signal these interactions (next, for example, consequently, however, etc.)?	▶ **Skills Tutorial** • Analyze Cause and Effect

Primary Sources Models As white settlers moved west into the interior of North America, they settled in lands that American Indian groups had settled for centuries. American Indians reacted in different ways to this new threat. The Cherokee Nation hoped to use the courts to stay on their land. They also rejected a treaty signed by several Cherokees giving up Cherokee land.

Study the excerpts and call-outs to help you better understand each author's purpose, word choices, and point of view.

The "we" is Ross and other Cherokee leaders.

Redress means to set something right. The Cherokee hoped that President Van Buren would set things right between the United States and the Cherokee Nation.

The author is choosing words with negative meanings to describe the treaty.

The author is a chief of the Cherokee Nation who was present at the negotiations between the United States and Cherokee governments.

Van Buren became President after Jackson. The event described in the primary source took place at the beginning of the Van Buren administration.

Forced infers that the Cherokee did not leave their land willingly.

Meeting with President Van Buren

On the 4th of March (1837), Mr. Van Buren assumed the presidential chair. On the 16th of March, we addressed the new president, stating to him fully our position and wishes, reviewing the circumstances which had occurred, and the hopes we entertained of receiving redress at his hands. We entreated the president to examine for himself into the grounds upon which we rested our charge, that the document called a treaty was fraudulent and equally an imposition upon the United States and upon ourselves.

—Letter from John Ross, the principal chief of the Cherokee nation, to a gentleman of Philadelphia

The Cherokee

The Cherokee also tried to hold out. They were still on their land in 1836 when Jackson left office. A small group of Cherokee agreed to become citizens of North Carolina. As a result, they were allowed to stay. Other Cherokee hid in remote mountain camps.

Finally, in 1838, President Martin Van Buren forced the Cherokee, who had not made agreements with North Carolina and those who were not in hiding, to move. The United States Army forced more than 15,000 Cherokee to march westward.

Support Your Analyses with Evidence

Historians and other writers make assertions, or claims, about events. Before accepting a claim as fact, however, look carefully at the evidence the author provides. Study the chart and the model secondary source to learn more about how to use evidence to support your ideas.

	Look for	Questions to Ask	For More Help
Support Your Analyses With Evidence	• The subject of the passage • Any assertion or claim that something is true • Appropriate evidence to support the claim • How well the evidence supports the claim, either explicitly or by inference	• What is the passage about? • Are there claims that something is true? • If so, what language supports the claim? • Does the evidence support the claim? • Did the author convince you that the claim was correct?	▶ **Skills Tutorial** • Identify Evidence • Support Ideas With Evidence

Model Secondary Source
Look for evidence in this model passage. Do you think the main point is supported by the evidence?

The writer claims that Vanderbilt used ruthless tactics.

The writer offers evidence of what Vanderbilt did when the owners of one railroad refused to sell to him.

The writer shows that Vanderbilt was able to accomplish his objectives by using these ruthless tactics.

Vanderbilt sometimes used ruthless tactics to force smaller owners to sell to him. In the early 1860s, he decided to buy the New York Central Railroad. The owners refused to sell. Vanderbilt then announced that the New York Central passengers would not be allowed to transfer to his trains. With their passengers stranded and business dropping sharply, the New York Central owners gave in and sold their line to Vanderbilt.

WRITING

Using the Writing Process

Writing is one of the most powerful communication tools you will use for the rest of your life. A systematic approach to writing—including planning, drafting, revising, editing, rewriting, and proofreading—will help you strengthen your writing.

Prewriting: Plan Your Essay

1. **Choose a topic.** Often your teacher will provide you with a topic. Sometimes, you will be able to choose your own topic. In that case, select a topic that you care about and that you think will be interesting.

2. **Narrow your focus.** Most writers begin with too broad a topic and need to narrow their focus. For example, you might start off knowing you want to write about the Civil War. You will need to narrow your focus to a single battle or a cause of the war in order to write a meaningful essay.

3. **Gather information.** Collect facts and details to write your essay. Research any points you want to include that you are unsure about.

4. **Organize your ideas.** Writers often find it useful to create an outline to help them plan their essay. You need not create a formal outline, but you'll at least want to jot down your main ideas, the details that support them, and the order in which you will present your ideas. A graphic organizer, such as a Venn diagram or concept web, can help you organize your ideas. Here is a graphic organizer for a paper on the causes of the Civil War:

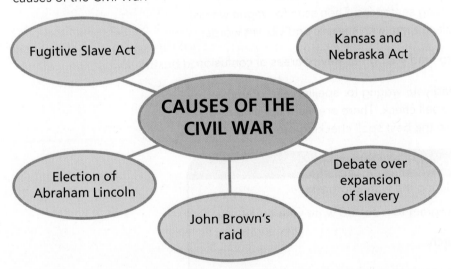

5. **Write a thesis statement.** A thesis statement focuses your ideas into a single sentence or two. Your thesis statement should tell your reader what the essay is about.

Drafting

1. **Maintain a clear focus.** If you find that your writing is starting to get off track, go back to your thesis statement.

2. **Elaborate for interest and emphasis.** Give details about each point in your essay. For instance, if you are writing an essay about the causes of the War of 1812, give details and specific examples.

3. **Provide evidence.** Evidence is key to convincing an audience. Provide factual, concrete evidence to back up your ideas and assertions.

Revising, Editing, and Rewriting

1. **Add transition words.** Clarify cause-and-effect relationships with words such as *because* and *as a result*. To compare or contrast ideas, use linking words, such as *similarly, both,* and *in contrast* and *yet.* Use words such as *first, next,* and *finally* to help readers follow a sequence.

2. **Focus on addressing your purpose.** Be sure that your essay addresses your purpose for writing. For a problem-solution essay, that means anticipating and responding to opposing arguments. For a cause-and-effect essay, stress the way one event leads to the next.

3. **Focus on your audience.** Check that you have not left out any steps in your essay and that your audience can follow your thinking. Make sure that your writing will hold your audience's interest.

4. **Review organization.** Confirm that your ideas flow in a logical order. Write your main points on sticky notes. Reorganize these until you are satisfied that the order best strengthens your essay.

5. **Revise sentences and words.** Look at your sentence length. Vary it to include both short and long sentences. Then scan for vague words, such as *good* or *nice*. Replace them with specific and vibrant words.

6. **Peer review.** Ask a peer to read your draft. Revise areas of confusion.

Proofread

Always proofread your writing for spelling and grammar errors. Do not simply rely on spell check. There are many spelling errors that slip by even when you use the best spell checking programs.

Use Technology

Technology has many uses during the writing process:

☑ Use a word processing program to plan and write your essay.

☑ Use the Internet for research.

☑ Use email and other online tools to collaborate with classmates.

☑ Create slides, charts, graphs, and diagrams for presentations.

☑ Share you writing with others through a blog or website.

▶ **INTERACTIVE**

Go online for these interactive skills tutorials:
- Identify Main Ideas and Details
- Organize Your Ideas
- Write an Essay

Write an Argument

In addition to evaluating other writers' arguments, you also need to be able to express arguments of your own, in writing and speaking. An argumentative, or persuasive, essay sets forth a belief or stand on an issue. A well-written argument may convince the reader, change the reader's mind, or motivate the reader to take a certain action.

In this program, you'll practice writing arguments in some Document-Based Inquiry Quests and Writing Workshops, with support in your 🗐 **Active Journal**. Use the checklist to help you write a convincing argument.

An Effective Argument Includes
☑ a precise claim
☑ consideration of alternate claims, or opposing positions, and a discussion of their strengths and weaknesses
☑ logical organization that makes clear connections among claim, reasons, and evidence
☑ valid reasoning and evidence, using credible sources and accurate data
☑ a concluding statement or section that follows from and supports the argument
☑ formal and objective language and tone
☑ error-free grammar, including accurate use of transitions

▶ INTERACTIVE

Go online for these interactive skills tutorials:
- Evaluate Arguments
- Consider and Counter Opposing Arguments
- Support Ideas With Evidence

Write Informative or Explanatory Essays

Informative/explanatory texts present facts, data, and other evidence to give information about a topic. Readers turn to these texts when they wish to learn about a specific idea, concept, or subject area, or if they want to learn how to do something.

An Effective Informative/Explanatory Essay Includes

- ☑ a topic sentence or thesis statement that introduces the concept or subject

- ☑ an organization (such as definition, classification, comparison/contrast, cause/effect) that presents information in a clear manner

- ☑ headings (if desired) to separate sections of the essay

- ☑ definitions, quotations, and/or graphics that support the thesis

- ☑ relevant facts, examples, and details that expand upon a topic

- ☑ clear transitions that link sections of the essay

- ☑ precise words and technical vocabulary where appropriate

- ☑ formal and objective language and tone

- ☑ a conclusion that supports the information given and provides fresh insights

INTERACTIVE

Go online for these interactive skills tutorials:
- Organize Your Ideas
- Compare and Contrast
- Analyze Cause and Effect
- Develop a Clear Thesis
- Draw Conclusions
- Support Ideas With Evidence

Suppose you are writing an essay comparing and contrasting the beliefs of Thomas Jefferson and Alexander Hamilton. You might start by creating a Venn diagram like this one to help you organize your ideas. You would then fill it in with facts, descriptions, and examples.

Jefferson and Hamilton

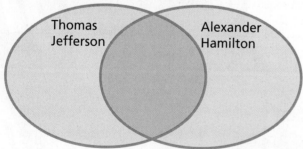

Thomas Jefferson

Alexander Hamilton

Write Narrative Essays

A narrative is any type of writing that tells a story. Narrative writing conveys an experience, either real or imaginary, and uses time order to provide structure. Usually its purpose is to entertain, but it can also instruct, persuade, or inform.

An Effective Narrative Includes
✅ an engaging beginning in which characters and setting are established
✅ a well-structured, logical sequence of events
✅ narrative techniques, such as dialogue and description
✅ a variety of transition words and phrases to convey sequence and signal shifts from one time frame or setting to another
✅ precise words and phrases, relevant descriptive details, and sensory language that brings the characters and setting to life
✅ a conclusion that follows naturally from the story's experiences or events

Model Narrative This passage is the beginning of a story by Edgar Allan Poe, a famous American author in the mid-1800s. Notice how it begins by grabbing the reader's attention with an assertion that the speaker is not mad. Notice how the author uses exclamation points to draw attention to his words

> True!—Nervous—very, very dreadfully nervous I had been and am; but why will you say that I am mad! The disease had sharpened my senses, not dulled them. Above all was the sense of hearing acute . . . How then, am I mad! Hearken! and observe how healthily—how calmly I can tell you the whole story.
>
> —*The Tell-Tale Heart*, Edgar Allan Poe

▶ INTERACTIVE

Go online for these interactive skills tutorials:
- Sequence
- Draw Conclusions
- Write an Essay
- Write a Journal Entry

Find and Use Credible Sources

You will often need to conduct research using library and media sources to gain more knowledge about a topic. Not all of the information that you find, however, will be useful—or reliable. Strong research skills will help you find accurate information about your topic.

Using Print and Digital Sources An effective research project combines information from multiple sources. Plan to include a variety of these resources:

☑ **Primary and Secondary Sources:** Use both primary sources (such as interviews or newspaper articles) and secondary sources (such as encyclopedia entries or historians' accounts).

☑ **Print and Digital Resources:** The Internet allows fast access to data, but print resources are often edited more carefully. Plan to include both print and digital resources in order to guarantee that your work is accurate.

☑ **Media Resources:** You can find valuable information in media resources such as documentaries, television programs, podcasts, and museum exhibitions.

☑ **Original Research:** Depending on your topic, you may wish to conduct original research, such as interviews or surveys of people in your community.

Evaluating Sources It is important to evaluate the credibility and accuracy of any information you find. Ask yourself questions such as these to evaluate sources:

☑ **Authority:** Is the author well known? What are the author's credentials? Does the source include references to other reliable sources? Does the author's tone win your confidence? Why or why not?

☑ **Bias:** Does the author have any obvious biases? What is the author's purpose for writing? Who is the target audience?

☑ **Currency:** When was the work created? Has it been revised? Is there more current information available?

Using Search Terms Finding information on the Internet is easy, but it can be a challenge to find facts that are useful and trustworthy. If you type a word or phrase into a search engine, you will probably get hundreds of results.

> **Did you know?**
>
> Beware of online encyclopedias. They can be a good starting place for information, but their contributors are not required to fact-check their submissions.

However, those results are not guaranteed to be relevant or accurate. These strategies can help:

☑ Create a list of keywords before you begin using a search engine.

☑ Enter six to eight keywords.

☑ Choose unique nouns. Most search engines ignore articles and prepositions.

☑ Use adjectives to specify a category. For example, you might enter "ancient Rome" instead of "Rome."

☑ Use quotation marks to focus a search. Place a phrase in quotation marks to find pages that include exactly that phrase.

☑ Spell carefully. Many search engines correct spelling automatically, but they cannot catch every spelling error.

☑ Scan search results before you click them. The first result isn't always the most useful. Read the text before making a choice.

Avoiding Plagiarism
When you conduct research, you must give credit for any ideas or opinions that are not your own. Presenting someone else's ideas, research, or opinion as your own—even if you have phrased it in different words—is plagiarism. Plagiarism is the equivalent of stealing. Be sure to record your sources accurately so you can identify them later. When photocopying from a source, include the copyright information. Include the web addresses from online sources.

Quoting and Paraphrasing
When including ideas from research into your writing, you will need to decide whether to quote directly or paraphrase. You must cite your sources for both quotations and paraphrases. **A direct quotation** uses the author's exact words when they are particularly well-chosen. Include complete quotations, without deleting or changing words. Enclose direct quotations in quotation marks. **A paraphrase** restates an author's ideas in your own words. Be careful to paraphrase accurately. A good paraphrase does more than simply rearrange an author's phrases, or replace a few words with synonyms.

Formats for Citing Sources
When you cite a source, you acknowledge where you found your information and give readers the details necessary for locating the source themselves. Always prepare a reference list at the end of a research paper to provide full information on your sources in a list of sources called a bibliography.

▶ **INTERACTIVE**

For more help, find these interactive skills tutorials on your Realize course:
- Search for Information on the Internet
- Evaluate Web Sites
- Take Effective Notes
- Avoid Plagiarism

Did you know?

A citation for a book should look like this: Pyles, Thomas. *The Origins and Development of the English Language.* 2nd ed. New York: Harcourt, 1971. Print. A citation for a website should include this information:
Romey, Kristin. "Face of 9,500-Year-Old Man Revealed for First Time." *National Geographic,* Jan. 2017. *news.nationalgeographic. com* Web. 20 Jan. 2017.

Write Research Papers

You will often need to conduct research in the library or on the Internet for a project or essay. In this program, you will conduct research for Quest projects and some Writing Workshop assignments. Before you begin, review the information in Using Writing Process as well as in Find and Use Credible Sources. Then follow these additional tips to help you make the most of your research.

1. Narrow or Broaden Your Topic
Choose a topic that is narrow enough to cover completely. If you can name your topic in just one or two words, it is probably too broad. Topics such as The Progressive Era are too broad to cover in a single report. When you begin to research, pay attention to the amount of information available. If there is way too much information, narrow your focus.

You might need to broaden a topic if there is not enough information available. A topic is too narrow when it can be thoroughly presented in less space than the required size of your assignment. It might also be too narrow if you can find little or no information in library and media sources. Broaden your topic by including other related ideas.

2. Generate Research Questions
Use research questions to focus your inquiry. For example, instead of hunting for information about the Revolutionary War, you might ask, "How did France influence the outcome of the Revolutionary War?" or "What events marked turning points in the Revolutionary War?" As you research your topic, continue to ask yourself questions. Follow your new questions to explore your topic further. Refocus your research questions as you learn more about your topic.

INTERACTIVE

Go online for these interactive skills tutorials:
- Ask Questions
- Create a Research Hypothesis
- Synthesize

3. Synthesize Your Sources
Effective research writing is more than just a list of facts and details. Good research synthesizes—gathers, orders, and interprets—those elements. These strategies will help you synthesize effectively:

☑ Review your notes. Look for connections and patterns among the details you have collected.

☑ Organize notes or notecards to help you plan how you will combine details.

☑ Pay close attention to details that emphasize the same main idea.

☑ Also, look for details that challenge each other. For many topics, there is no single correct opinion. You might decide to conduct additional research to help you decide which side of the issue has more support.

SPEAKING AND LISTENING

Discuss Your Ideas

A group discussion is an informal meeting of people that is used to openly discuss ideas, readings, and issues. You can express your views and hear those of others. In this program, you'll participate in Discussion Inquiry Quests and many one-to-one, group, and teacher-led discussions. You'll work with different partners on many topics and issues. Use Keys to Effective Discussions to help you be an active participant.

Keys to Effective Discussions

☑ Come to discussions prepared, having studied the required material and/or read relevant background information.

☑ Build on others' ideas and express your own ideas clearly.

☑ Be sure that your comments directly contribute to the topic, text, or issue under discussion.

☑ Give specific evidence for the points you wish to make.

☑ Follow rules for civic discussions, including letting everyone have a chance to speak and listening carefully to others' points of view.

☑ Pose and respond to specific questions and issues with elaboration and details.

☑ Be prepared to demonstrate your understanding of the different perspectives people have put forth during the discussion.

☑ Acknowledge the views of others respectfully, but ask questions that challenge the accuracy, logic, or relevance of those views.

▶ INTERACTIVE

Go online for these interactive skills tutorials:
- Participate in a Discussion or Debate
- Support Ideas With Evidence
- Work in Teams

Give an Effective Presentation

Many of the Quests in this program will require you to give a presentation to your teacher and classmates, and sometimes even to a wider audience. These presentations will be good practice for the presentations you will need to give in school and in professional settings. You can speak confidently if you prepare carefully and follow this checklist.

Keys to Effective Presentations

- ☑ Prepare your presentation in advance and practice it to gain comfort and confidence.
- ☑ Present your claims and findings in a logical sequence so that your audience can easily follow your train of thought.
- ☑ Use relevant descriptions, facts, and specific details.
- ☑ Consider using nonverbal elements like hand gestures and pauses to emphasize main ideas or themes.
- ☑ Use appropriate eye contact, adequate volume, and clear pronunciation.
- ☑ Use appropriate transitions (for example, *first, second, third*) to clarify relationships.
- ☑ Use precise language and vocabulary that is specific to your topic.
- ☑ Provide a strong conclusion.
- ☑ Adapt your wording to your purpose and audience. Use formal English for most presentations, but try to sound natural and relaxed.
- ☑ Include multimedia components such as you see in this chart to clarify information.

▶ INTERACTIVE

Go online for these interactive skills tutorials:
- Give an Effective Presentation
- Create Charts and Maps
- Support Ideas With Evidence

Maps	Graphs/Charts/Diagrams	Illustrations/Photos	Audio/Video
Clarify historical or geographical information	Show complex information and data in an easy-to-understand format	Illustrate objects, scenes, or other details	Bring the subject to life and engage audiences

Effective Listening

Active listening is a key component of the communication process. Like all communication, it requires your engaged participation. Follow the Keys to Effective Listening to get the most out of discussions, presentations by others, lectures by your teacher, and any time you engage in listening.

Keys to Effective Listening

☑ Look at and listen to the speaker. Think about what you hear and see. Which ideas are emphasized or repeated? What gestures or expressions suggest strong feelings?

☑ Listen carefully to information presented in different media and formats—including videos, lectures, speeches, and discussions—so you can explain how the information you learn contributes to the topic or issue you are studying.

☑ Listen for the speaker's argument and specific claims so that you can distinguish claims that are supported by reasons and evidence from claims that are not.

☑ Listen to fit the situation. Active listening involves matching your listening to the situation. Listen critically to a speech given by a candidate for office. Listen with kindness to the feelings of a friend. Listen appreciatively to a musical performance.

▶ INTERACTIVE

Go online for these interactive skills tutorials:
- Identify Bias
- Identify Evidence
- Distinguish Between Fact and Opinion
- Evaluate Existing Arguments

The Early Americas and European Exploration

(Prehistory–1600)

GO ONLINE
to access your
digital course

 VIDEO

 AUDIO

 ETEXT

 INTERACTIVE

 WRITING

GAMES

WORKSHEET

ASSESSMENT

Go back over 10,000 years

to **PRESENT-DAY ALASKA.** The first people to live in North America are arriving from Asia. Over time, American Indians spread across North and South America and learned how to use the environment to make their lives easier.

Explore
The Essential Question

How much does geography affect people's lives?

Throughout history people have been affected by the geography that surrounds them. How did early American Indians and people around the world use the land on which they lived?

Unlock the Essential Question in your 📓 Active Journal.

Read

about the different civilizations that lived in the Americas, about the Middle Ages, and European exploration.

Watch

 NBC LEARN

BOUNCE TO ACTIVATE ▶ VIDEO

Austin Celebrates His Heritage.

Learn how one boy investigates who he is.

The Temple of the Cross is in an ancient Maya city called Palenque in modern-day Chiapas, Mexico.

The Early Americas and European Exploration

(Prehistory–1600)

Learn more about the early Americas and European exploration of the world by making your own map and timeline in your 📙 Active Journal.

ARCTIC/SUBARCTIC

NORTHWEST COAST

INTERACTIVE

Interactive Timeline

What happened and when?

People learn to farm. . . Impressive civilizations form in the Americas. . . Europeans learn about lands they never knew existed. Explore the timeline to learn what was happening before 1600.

CALIFORNIA/ GREAT BASIN

GREAT PLAINS

EASTERN WOODLANDS

SOUTHEAST

SOUTHWEST

10,000 years ago people from Asia migrate and settle in North America.

TOPIC EVENTS

500   700

WORLD EVENTS

c. 600
Islam is founded.

1095
The First Crusade begins.

Where did some early American Indians live?

Before European explorers arrived in the Americas, many different cultures thrived in the Western Hemisphere. Locate the regions on the map where the Eastern Woodlands and Great Plains cultures lived.

Who will you meet?

Hiawatha, who helped organize an alliance of the Iroquois nations

Christopher Columbus, the first European explorer to reach the Americas

Ferdinand Magellan, a Portuguese explorer whose crew sailed around the world

1492
Christopher Columbus arrives in the Americas.

900
The Maya abandon their cities.

c.1300
The Aztec create a civilization in central Mexico.

| 900 | 1100 | 1300 | 1500 |

1307
Emperor Mansa Musa strengthens the empire of Mali.

c. 1430
Gutenberg uses movable type.

1520
Magellan reaches South America.

Quest

The Easter Mutiny

Quest KICK OFF

The year is **1520**, and Ferdinand Magellan is trying to sail around the world. During the journey, members of his crew revolt against Magellan and lead a mutiny on Easter Sunday.

How reliable is Antonio Pigafetta's account of the Easter Mutiny?

How do the different accounts of the Easter Mutiny differ? Find out as you explore how point of view can affect our understanding of a person or event.

▲ Antonio Pigafetta

1 Ask Questions

Start by considering the language Pigafetta used in his account. Get started by making a list of questions you would want to ask about how to judge word choices and tone. Write the questions in your 📓 Active Journal.

2 Investigate

As you read the lessons in this topic, look for **Quest CONNECTIONS** that provide information on how different points of view can affect how we evaluate information. Capture notes in your 📓 Active Journal.

3 Examine Primary Sources

Next explore primary sources about the Easter Mutiny. They will help you learn about the different ways people remembered the events. Make notes about the sources in your 📓 Active Journal.

Quest FINDINGS

4 Write Your Essay

At the end of this topic, you will write an essay in which you examine the reliability of Pigafetta's account. In your essay, be sure to clearly state your view in a strong topic sentence, use logical organization, and support your conclusion with evidence and relevant facts.

LESSON 1

The Early Americas

BOUNCE TO ACTIVATE ▶ VIDEO

GET READY TO READ

START UP

Examine the photo of the Maya temple. What does this pyramid tell you about Maya society?

GUIDING QUESTIONS

- How did people first reach the Americas?
- How would you describe the early civilizations and cultures of the Americas?
- What are some of the greatest achievements of early civilizations in the Americas?

TAKE NOTES

Literacy Skills: Summarize

Use the graphic organizer in your 📓 Active Journal to take notes as you read the lesson.

PRACTICE VOCABULARY

Use the vocabulary activity in your 📓 Active Journal to practice the vocabulary words.

Vocabulary		Academic Vocabulary
glacier	city-state	according to
settlement	causeway	complex
surplus	quipu	
civilization	terrace	

Like other early people around the world, the first Americans left no written records to tell us where they came from or when they arrived. However, scientists have found evidence to suggest that the first people reached the Americas sometime during the last ice age.

Who Were the First Americans?

According to geologists, the Earth has gone through several ice ages. The last ice age occurred between 100,000 and 10,000 years ago. During that time, thick sheets of ice, called **glaciers**, covered almost one third of the Earth. In North America, glaciers stretched across Canada and reached as far south as present-day Kentucky.

Early Peoples Spread Across a Continent Glaciers locked up water from the oceans, causing sea levels to fall and uncovering land that had been under water. In the far north, a land bridge joined Siberia in northeastern Asia to present-day Alaska.

Most scientists think that bands of hunters, tracking herds of grazing animals, reached North America by way of this land bridge.

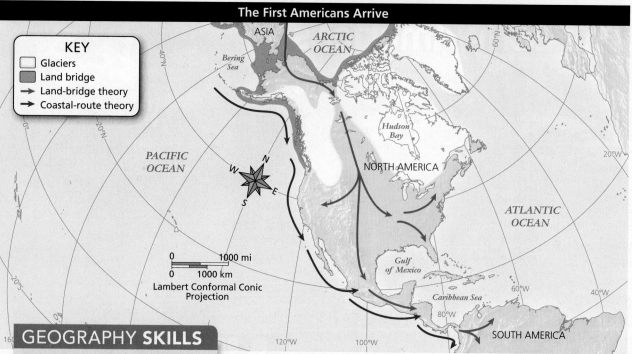

The First Americans Arrive

KEY
- ☐ Glaciers
- ⬛ Land bridge
- → Land-bridge theory
- → Coastal-route theory

ASIA
Bering Sea
ARCTIC OCEAN
Hudson Bay
PACIFIC OCEAN
NORTH AMERICA
ATLANTIC OCEAN
Gulf of Mexico
Caribbean Sea
SOUTH AMERICA

0   1000 mi
0   1000 km
Lambert Conformal Conic Projection

GEOGRAPHY SKILLS

This map depicts both the land-bridge and coastal-route theories of North American migration.

1. **Movement** What were the two ways the first Americans may have arrived from Asia?

2. **Identify Supporting Details** What route do scientists who disagree with the land-bridge migration theory believe early Americans followed?

Other scientists disagree. They think that the first Americans crossed the icy Arctic waters by boat, reaching North America by sea.

Once these early hunters reached the Americas, they had to keep moving in search of food. Slowly, over thousands of years, they spread across North America, Central America, and South America. The physical environments where they settled varied widely. American Indians adapted to the physical environments of mountain plateaus, dry deserts, fertile plains, lush woodlands, and thick rain forests. In adapting to these varied environments, American Indian groups developed many different customs.

Adapting to and Modifying Environments About 12,000 years ago, the last ice age ended. Glaciers melted. The land bridge between Siberia and Alaska disappeared.

About the same time, some kinds of large animals died out. This forced hunting bands to adapt to new conditions. Smaller animals, wild berries, nuts, grains, and fish became a larger part of their diets.

About 5,000 years ago, people in the Americas learned to grow crops such as corn, beans, and squash. Farming modified the environment and brought great changes to those who practiced it. Farmers no longer had to keep moving to find food. Instead, they stayed in one place and began to build permanent **settlements**, or small communities. As farming methods improved, people produced more food, which in turn allowed the population to grow.

Academic Vocabulary

according to • *prep.,* as stated by

✓ READING CHECK **Understand Effects** How did farming affect communities in the Americas?

The Olmec

Farming was a key advance for early societies in the Americas. In time, some farming communities in the Americas grew enough **surplus**, or extra, food to support large populations, and the first cities emerged.

Cities marked the rise of the first civilization in the Americas. A **civilization** is a society—or a people sharing a language, territory, and economy—that has certain basic features. Among these are cities, an organized government, different social classes, a **complex** religion, and some method of record keeping.

The earliest known civilization in the Americas was that of the Olmec in present-day Mexico. The Olmec lived in the lowlands along the Gulf of Mexico about 3,500 years ago. Scientists have found huge stone heads carved by the Olmec. Some were 10 feet tall and weighed several tons. Smaller figures showed creatures that were part human and part animal.

Olmec farmers supplied nearby cities with food. There, powerful leaders built stone temples. The Olmec left few written records, but they did make many advances. They studied the stars and developed a calendar to predict the change of seasons and mark the passage of time.

☑ **READING CHECK** **Identify Supporting Details** What features of Olmec society indicate that it was a civilization?

The Maya

The Olmec influenced many later peoples, including the Maya. The early Maya lived in the rain forests of what are today Honduras, Belize, Guatemala, and southern Mexico. About 3,000 years ago, they began clearing the rain forest and draining swamps to create farmland.

Maya farmers were able to produce great harvests of corn, enough to feed large cities. As the Maya population grew, city-states began to spring up from Central America to southern Mexico. A **city-state** is a political unit that controls a city and its surrounding land. Trade flowed along a network of roads that linked inland city-states and the coast. City-states often waged war with one another for land, riches, and access to trade routes.

Maya Social Classes Nobles also held great power in Maya society. The most powerful nobles were the kings, who also served as high priests.

Academic Vocabulary

complex • *adj.*, composed of two or more parts

Analyze Images The Olmec, a tropical civilization, left behind many carvings of giant stone heads. They are generally thought to be portraits of Olmec rulers. **Use Visual Information** How can you tell that this object is made of stone?

Analyze Images Like the Maya, the Aztec also built temples and palaces atop huge stone pyramids. **Infer** What position in society might the person at the top of the pyramid hold?

Other nobles also became priests. Priests held great power in Maya society. Only priests, the Maya believed, could perform the ceremonies needed to bring good harvests or victory in battle. Priests conducted these ceremonies in temples built on top of huge pyramids.

Still other nobles served as warriors and government officials. Near the bottom of Maya society were laborers and farmers, who grew corn, squash, and many other crops. Below them were slaves, most of whom were prisoners of war or criminals.

Achievements in Mathematics and Astronomy Maya priests had to know exactly when to honor the many gods who were thought to control the natural world. Every day, priests anxiously studied the sun, moon, and stars. They learned much about the movement of these bodies.

Based on their observations, priests made great advances in astronomy and mathematics. They learned to predict eclipses and created a relatively accurate, 365-day calendar. They also developed a system of numbers that included the new concept of zero.

Then, around 900 CE, the Maya abandoned their cities. Historians are not sure why. Perhaps they did so because of warfare, a drought—or both. The rain forests swallowed up the great Maya temples and palaces. Although Maya cities decayed, the Maya people survived. Today, more than 2 million people in Guatemala and southern Mexico speak Mayan languages.

INTERACTIVE

Aztec Temple

☑ READING CHECK **Infer** Why did city-states form as the Maya population grew?

The Aztec

Long after the Maya cities were abandoned, a new civilization arose to the northwest. Its builders were the Aztec. The early Aztec were nomads, people who moved from place to place in search of food. In the 1300s, the Aztec settled around Lake Texcoco (tays KOH koh) in central Mexico. From there, they built a powerful empire.

Tenochtitlán On an island in the middle of the lake, the Aztec built their capital, Tenochtitlán (tay nawch tee TLAHN). They constructed a system of **causeways**, or raised roads made of packed earth. The causeways linked the capital to the mainland.

▲ The Aztec used astronomy to develop a calendar. This calendar is carved from stone.

The Aztec learned to farm the shallow swamps of Lake Texcoco. In some places, they dug canals, using the mud they removed to fill in parts of the lake. In other places, they attached floating reed mats to the lake bottom with long stakes. Then, they piled mud onto the mats to create farmland. Aztec farmers harvested several crops a year on these *chinampas*, or floating gardens.

With riches from trade and conquest, Tenochtitlán prospered. Its markets offered a wide variety of goods. "There are daily more than 60,000 people bartering and selling," wrote a Spanish visitor in the 1500s.

Religion Like the Maya, Aztec priests studied the heavens and developed complex calendars. Such calendars gave them the ability to tell their people when to plant or harvest.

The Aztec paid special attention to the god who controlled the sun. They believed that each day the sun battled its way across the heavens.

Analyze Charts Aztec society was hierarchical, meaning some groups have more power than those below them. **Draw Conclusions** What does the organization of Aztec society tell us about Aztec values?

Aztec Society

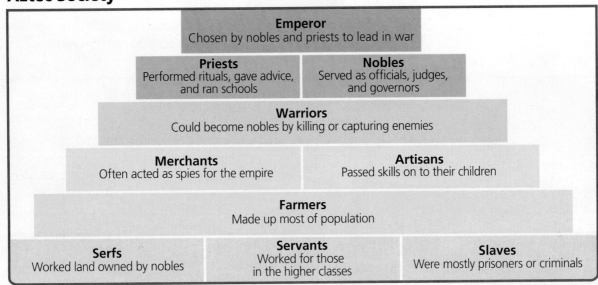

Emperor
Chosen by nobles and priests to lead in war

Priests
Performed rituals, gave advice, and ran schools

Nobles
Served as officials, judges, and governors

Warriors
Could become nobles by killing or capturing enemies

Merchants
Often acted as spies for the empire

Artisans
Passed skills on to their children

Farmers
Made up most of population

Serfs
Worked land owned by nobles

Servants
Worked for those in the higher classes

Slaves
Were mostly prisoners or criminals

At its height, the Aztec empire is thought to have been made up of more than 400 small states and some 5 to 6 million people. It covered a territory of more than 80,000 square miles.

They compared the sun's battle to their own, calling themselves "warriors of the sun." They believed that the sun required human sacrifices in order to rise each day. The Aztec therefore killed thousands of prisoners each year to please this powerful god.

A Powerful Empire By 1500, the Aztec ruled a huge empire. It stretched from the Gulf of Mexico to the Pacific Ocean and included millions of people. The Aztec took great pride in their empire and their capital. "Who could conquer Tenochtitlán?" boasted an Aztec poet. "Who could shake the foundation of heaven?"

The Aztec world was far from peaceful, however. Heavy taxes and the sacrifice of huge numbers of prisoners of war sparked many revolts. The Aztec waged war in part to capture more prisoners for sacrifice. Across the empire, people conquered by the Aztec were eager for revenge. Enemies of the Aztec would eventually help outsiders from distant lands destroy the Aztec empire.

☑ READING CHECK **Summarize** How did the Aztec benefit from digging canals?

The Inca

Far to the south of the Aztec, the Inca built one of the largest empires in the Americas. By 1500, their empire stretched for almost 2,500 miles along the west coast of South America.

An Impressive Capital The center of the Incan empire was the magnificent capital at Cuzco (KOOS koh), located high in the Andes in present-day Peru. Cuzco was a holy city to the Inca. All nobles in the empire tried to visit it at least once in their lifetimes. The city had massive palaces and temples made of stone and decorated with gold.

Analyze Images The remains of the ancient city of Machu Picchu show evidence of the incredible engineering capabilities of the Inca. **Infer** How might the buildings at Machu Picchu have looked when the Inca lived there?

At the center was the palace of the emperor, who was known as the Sapa Inca. The emperor was regarded as a god descended from the sun god.

From Cuzco, the emperor ruled more than 10 million people. They lived in varied environments, from coastal deserts to lowland jungles to the highlands of the Andes. The Inca had conquered the land through warfare.

The Incan empire was very well organized. The emperor was kept well informed about affairs in all parts of his empire. He sent high officials out to act as governors of his domain. The governors made sure that every person worked at least part of the time on projects for the state, such as road building, mining, and farming.

Incan Achievements To unite their empire, the Inca maintained a system of roads that covered more than 10,000 miles. Builders carved roads in rock cliffs and stretched rope bridges across deep gorges. Runners spread royal orders using the roads.

The runners carried with them a **quipu** (KEE poo). This was a cord or string with knots that stood for numbers or categories. The numbers might represent bags of goods that the government ordered from different parts of the empire. The quipu was also used by officials to keep records.

The Inca were skilled engineers. They built massive stone temples and forts. With only human labor, ropes, and wooden rollers, they moved stones weighing up to 200 tons. They also used their engineering skills to farm the dry, rugged mountain lands. They became experts at creating **terraces**—or wide, flat steps of land—out of the steep mountainsides. Sturdy stone walls kept rain from washing away the soil.

Analyze Images The Inca created a water system for the city of Machu Picchu using the natural stone from the mountains. **Use Visual Information** Why do you think the Inca designed the system in this way?

☑ READING CHECK Identify Main Ideas Why was a system of roads so important to the Inca?

☑ Lesson Check

Practice Vocabulary

1. How did a **surplus** of food lead to the first **civilizations**?

2. Why did the Aztec construct **causeways**?

Critical Thinking and Writing

3. Identify Cause and Effect How might the last ice age have helped hunters reach North America?

4. Identify Supporting Details What major impact did the development of farming have on the early settlers of the Americas?

5. Understand Effects How did the Aztecs' religious beliefs weaken their empire?

6. Writing Workshop: Generate Questions to Focus Research At the end of this topic, you will write a research paper on the question: How did a travel-related invention or improvement in one of the societies covered impact people's lives? Make a list of questions for this lesson that would need to be answered in order to write the paper. Record your questions in your ▱ Active Journal

Cultures of North America

BOUNCE TO ACTIVATE ▶ **VIDEO**

GET READY TO READ

START UP

Examine the photo of the Serpent Mound found in present-day Ohio. Why do you think the American Indians of the region constructed such a mound?

GUIDING QUESTIONS

- What early societies formed in North America?
- What are the human and physical characteristics of different regions of North America?
- What were the religious beliefs of American Indian groups in North America?

TAKE NOTES

Literacy Skills: Classify and Categorize Use the graphic organizer and your 📓 Active Journal to take notes as you read the lesson.

PRACTICE VOCABULARY

Use the vocabulary activity in your 📓 Active Journal to practice the vocabulary words.

Vocabulary		Academic Vocabulary
culture	diffusion	characteristic
adobe	potlatch	maintain
pueblo	clan	
culture region	Iroquois	
tribe	League	

Scholars have found evidence of complex societies in North America. Traders and migrating people carried foods, goods, arts, and beliefs from Central America and Mexico to the early peoples of North America.

Early North American Societies

These peoples developed many distinct cultures in North America. A **culture** is the entire way of life of a people. It includes their homes, clothing, economy, arts, and government.

Land and People of the Southwest At least 3,000 years ago, knowledge of farming spread northward. Gradually, farming societies emerged in what is today the American Southwest. Much of this region is desert, with little rainfall and hot summers. The early societies in this region included the Hohokam (hoh HOH kahm) and Anasazi (ah nuh SAH zee).

The Hohokam lived in present-day southern Arizona. About 2,000 years ago, they dug networks of irrigation ditches for farming.

The ditches carried water from the Salt and Gila (HEE luh) rivers to fields in the desert land, allowing farmers to grow corn, squash, and beans.

The Anasazi lived in the Four Corners region, where modern-day Colorado, Utah, New Mexico, and Arizona meet. Like the Hohokam, the Anasazi irrigated the desert in order to farm. They also created a network of roads to link dozens of towns. Traders traveled these roads, carrying cotton, sandals, and blankets woven from turkey feathers.

Anasazi Houses The Anasazi built large buildings with walls of stone and **adobe**, or sundried brick. When the Spanish later saw similar buildings in the early 1500s, they called them **pueblos** (PWEHB lohz), the Spanish word for "villages." (They also called the descendants of the Anasazi the Pueblo Indians.) About 1,000 years ago, some Anasazi villages faced attacks from warlike neighbors. To escape that threat, they built new homes along steep cliffs. Toeholds cut into the rock let people climb the cliff walls. Farmers planted their crops on land above the cliffs.

Mound Builders Far to the east, other farming cultures flourished in North America. Among them were the Mound Builders, various cultures that built large earth mounds beginning about 3,000 years ago. Thousands of these mounds dot the landscape from the Appalachian Mountains to the Mississippi Valley and from Wisconsin to Florida. What is now the eastern half of the United States had a wetter climate than the Southwest, and the Mound Builders were able to farm without irrigation.

The first mounds were used for burials. Later mounds were used for religious ceremonies. They were similar in function to the pyramid temples of the Maya.

The best-known groups of Mound Builders were the Hopewell and the Mississippians. The Mississippians took advantage of their moist climate to grow enough crops to feed large towns. Between 700 CE and 1500, the Mississippians built a city at Cahokia (kah HOH kee ah) in present-day Illinois. As many as 30,000 people may have lived there at one time.

READING CHECK Identify **Supporting Details** How did the Hohokam adapt to living in a desert region?

Analyze Images The Anasazi used stone and adobe to build this settlement in modern New Mexico. **Infer** Much of this settlement still stands, even though it was built more than 900 years ago. What does that tell you about Anasazi construction skills?

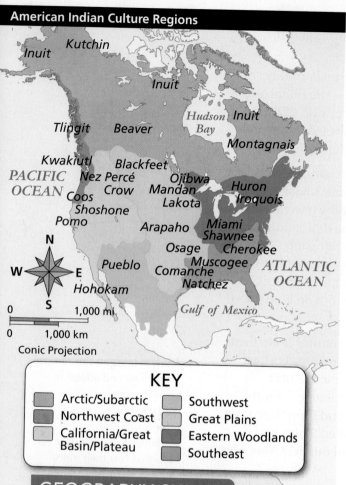

KEY

- Arctic/Subarctic
- Northwest Coast
- California/Great Basin/Plateau
- Southwest
- Great Plains
- Eastern Woodlands
- Southeast

GEOGRAPHY SKILLS

Groups of American Indians formed shared cultures in different geographic regions.

1. **Place** In what culture region did the Miami live?

2. **Infer** Why do you think few tribes lived in the Arctic/Subarctic region?

What Were the Cultural and Physical Characteristics of North America?

Like American Indian groups today, early American Indians included many different people with many distinct cultures. In North America alone, there were hundreds of American Indian languages spoken. American Indian cultures, too, varied greatly, much like the cultures of the people of Europe.

American Indian cultures were adapted to the many different physical environments of North America. The physical **characteristics** of the environment in each region influenced population distribution and settlement patterns, or where American Indians lived, right up to modern times.

A **culture region** is a region in which people share a similar way of life. Most culture regions shared similar physical environments. Each culture region was home to many different tribes. A **tribe** is a community of people who share common customs, language, and rituals. Members of a tribe saw themselves as a distinct people who shared a common origin. Tribal leaders often made decisions for the group.

Hunting, Gathering, and Fishing

American Indians developed a variety of ways to meet their basic needs for food, clothing, and shelter. In some culture regions, tribes hunted animals and gathered nuts, fruits, and vegetables that grew in the wild. Other tribes depended on the sea for food. They made boats out of animal skins or carved canoes out of trees. From their boats and canoes, they speared or netted fish or hunted marine animals such as seals, walrus, and whales.

Farming Other tribes lived mostly by farming, planting corn, beans, and squash. American Indian tribes farmed in many parts of North America, from the American Southwest to the Eastern Woodlands. Over time, farmers improved their crops. For example, more than 5,000 years ago, wild corn was tiny, about the size of a human finger. Indian farmers developed dozens of varieties of corn, including ones with larger ears.

Academic Vocabulary

characteristic • *n.*, a distinguishing trait, quality, or property

Trade American Indians traded with one another for goods not found within their own region. Trade networks linked people across large distances. Goods sometimes traveled more than 1,000 miles from where they were made.

In the Northwest, traders met near the Dalles on the Columbia River. Local Indians caught and dried salmon, which they exchanged for goods and produce from other places. More than goods were exchanged by the different groups. New ideas and skills also spread.

This process of spreading ideas from one culture to another is known as **diffusion**. Through diffusion, skills such as farming spread from one American Indian group to another.

INTERACTIVE

Native American Culture Regions of North America

Adapting to and Modifying Environments
American Indian cultures adapted to the physical features of different regions. These features influenced the kinds of food people raised, collected, or caught. Climate determined people's needs for clothing and shelter. Resources provided the materials they were able to use.

Climate and resources also affected organization. Where climates were harsh and resources limited, people struggled to find enough food and shelter. In such regions, people were often nomadic. They lived in small hunting bands. Each band included a number of families. In regions with more favorable climates and plentiful resources, people tended to live in larger groups and stay in one place for longer periods.

Cultures of the Arctic and Subarctic Regions
Frozen seas and icy, treeless plains made up the world of the Inuit, who lived in the Arctic region. The Inuit used all the limited resources of their environment. In the short summer season, they collected driftwood along the ocean shore, using it for tools and shelters.

Analyze Charts American Indians supported themselves by being resourceful. **Draw Conclusions** How did the foods American Indians ate influence their way of life?

Ways American Indians Supported Themselves

	FORAGING	FARMING	HUNTING
FOOD SOURCE	Fruits, nuts, seeds, roots, stems, and leaves from wild plants	Cultivated plants such as maize, beans, and squash	Wild game and fish
TOOLS AND TECHNOLOGY	Grinding tools for crushing seeds	Tools for clearing and cultivating: axes; hoes made with bone, shells, or stone	Tools such as spears and sharp points; trapping and netting food
INNOVATIONS	Baskets for storage	Methods for storing and preserving foods over winter months; irrigation methods	Techniques for drying meat and fish to balance the food supply over the winter
CULTURAL CHANGES	Mobility needed to find new food sources	Cultivating land required more labor but also created settlements and communities	Mobility needed when food resources became depleted
ADVANTAGES	No need to work in fields and risk fatal encounters with wild animals	Control over the food supply when growing conditions were favorable	Hunted animals provided clothing and shelter in addition to food
DISADVANTAGES	Poor weather could lead to shortages	Poor weather conditions could wipe out a harvest	Required a plentiful supply of wild game

For most of the year, the Inuit lived in pit houses, houses dug into the ground and covered with wood and skins. Lamps filled with seal oil kept their homes warm even in the bitter cold. Women made warm clothing out of furs and waterproof boots out of seal skins.

The Subarctic culture region consisted of a belt of forest stretching across North America south of the Arctic. This forest is made up mainly of conifers, or cone-bearing trees such as hemlock and spruce. People in the Subarctic lived where they could find food. Groups like the Chipewyan (chip uh WY un) were nomads, following large game like caribou. Physical characteristics of the environment influenced their settlement patterns. The Carrier, for example, settled near salmon streams, although they sometimes moved to other hunting sites.

Cultures of the California, Great Basin, and Plateau Regions The California region offers more forgiving climates, with mainly hot, dry summers and mild, wet winters. The physical features included mountains, coastal lowland, and interior valleys and deserts.

Over 200 different tribes called this region home. Along the Colorado River, land was irrigated to grow corn, pumpkin, and beans. In the Northwest, the Yoruk (YAWR uk) used redwood trees to build houses and canoes and caught the plentiful fish of that region. In central California, salmon and acorns were plentiful. People there hunted and gathered plant products instead of farming. With enough food nearby, people could spend time producing crafts. The Pomo wove watertight baskets out of grasses and reeds.

The Great Basin culture region consisted of mountains and valleys with a dry climate, with hot summers and cold winters. Many of the bands that lived here, like the Bannock, were small and nomadic. They traveled to find seeds, nuts, roots, and bulbs. The Northern Paiute (PY yoot) lived near lakes and marshes. Hunting, fishing, and farming often provided enough food for them to stay in one place.

The Plateau region, centered on the Columbia Plateau, has a cool and dry environment, but winter snows feed rivers flowing through the region. Surprisingly, numbers of hardy plants and animals thrive in the region. Among the people of the Plateau region were the Ute (YOOT) and Shoshone (shah SHOH nee). The American Indians of the region had few possessions beyond digging sticks, baskets, and tools and weapons needed for hunting.

Analyze Images The Inuit used caribou and seal fur to make warm clothing that would offer protection against extreme Arctic weather. **Infer** How might clothing worn by groups to the south have been different?

Cultures of the Northwest Coastal Region Elsewhere in North America the climate was kinder, which helped more complex cultures emerge. The people of the mountainous Northwest Coast enjoyed milder temperatures and abundant rainfall and food supplies. They gathered rich harvests of fish from the sea.

From nearby forests, they cut down tall cedar trees and split the trunks into planks for houses and canoes. With plenty of food, the people of the Pacific Northwest stayed in one place. They built permanent villages and prospered from trade with nearby groups.

Within a village, a family gained status according to how much it owned and could give away. Families sometimes competed with one another. To improve its standing, a family might hold a **potlatch**, or ceremonial dinner, to show off its wealth. The potlatch could last for many days. The family invited many guests and gave everyone gifts. The more goods a family gave away, the more respect it earned. However, people who received gifts at a potlatch were then expected to hold their own potlatches.

▲ This basket is representative of Great Basin American Indian artwork. It is made of grass roots, fern roots, and redbud roots.

Analyze Images The abundant forests of the Pacific Northwest provided the trees American Indians used to carve totem poles. The images on the poles often told stories from Indian creation stories. **Use Visual Information** Do you think the images symbolize animals or people?

▲ This stone head was made by a Mississippian artist. It dates to between 1200 and 1500 CE.

Cultures of the Southwest Region

The Southwest is a hot and dry region consisting of deserts, the southern Rocky Mountains, and the Colorado Plateau. People could survive only if they found water.

The Pueblo people used irrigation methods such as building dams and tanks to store water. They were able to grow corn and cotton on small farms. However, it wasn't all work in the desert. The Hohokam played games on ballcourts and made beautiful art with acid-etchings on shells.

Cultures of the Southeast Region

Many tribes lived in southeastern North America. This region is made up of coastal plains, the southern Appalachian Mountains, and rolling hills and valleys. It has hot summers, mild winters, and plenty of rainfall. Among the people of this region were the Natchez (NACH ihz). They benefited from the region's warm, moist climate. They hunted, fished, and farmed in the fertile Mississippi Valley.

The Natchez calendar divided the year into 13 months. Each month was named after a food or an animal that the Natchez harvested or hunted. Their months included Strawberry, Little Corn, Mulberry, Deer, Turkey, and Bear.

The ruler of the Natchez was known as the Great Sun and was worshipped as a god. The Great Sun's feet never touched the ground. Either he was carried on a litter or he walked on mats. Below the Great Sun were members of his family, called Little Suns.

Analyze Images The Nachez built ceremonial mounds to bury their dead and for other religious events. **Synthesize Visual Information** What do you think the Nachez may have done with the smaller mound atop the large mound?

Next came Nobles, then Honored People, and finally Stinkards, or commoners, who made up the majority of the people.

By law, Nobles had to marry Stinkards. Even the Great Sun chose a Stinkard as a wife. In this way, no one family could hold the position of Great Sun forever. In time, even descendants of a Great Sun became Stinkards.

Cultures of the Great Plains Region

The Great Plains were dry, open grasslands in the center of North America with very few trees, hot summers, and cold winters. Tribes like the Sioux (SOO) hunted wild animals to survive. The Sioux were nomads who followed the buffalo. They ate buffalo meat and used the hide to build tents. These tents were easy to carry when they were on the move. No part of the buffalo was wasted. They made spoons and cups out of the horns and weapons from the bones.

Cultures of the Eastern Woodlands Region

Like the peoples of the Southwest and Southeast, the peoples of the Eastern Woodlands were not nomads. Their culture region spanned what is today much of the Midwest and Northeast. This region includes coastal plains, the northern Appalachian Mountains, the Great Lakes region, and interior rolling hills and plains. The region receives plenty of rainfall, with warm summers and snowy winters.

The Iroquois (IHR uh kwoi) lived near lakes and streams. They cleared land for farming, which was mostly done by women. Their diet was based on the "Three Sisters": corn, squash, and beans. Algonquian (al GAHN kwee un) tribes lived near the ocean and along the Great Lakes. Many of them farmed as well. In some places the soil was too poor to farm. Instead, the Algonquian built boats for fishing. Like the Iroquois, they also used trees from the forests to make houses and tools.

☑ READING CHECK **Identify Cause and Effect** Why did the tribes who lived in the Southwest region irrigate the land?

INTERACTIVE

Housing and the Environment

Religious Beliefs

The many American Indian groups held a wide variety of beliefs. Yet, they shared some basic ideas.

Close Ties to Nature Whether hunting, fishing, farming, or gathering wild plants, many American Indians felt a close connection to the physical environment. Their prayers and ceremonies were designed to **maintain** a balance between people and the forces of nature. They believed that they must adapt their ways to the natural world in order to survive and prosper.

Many American Indians believed that the world was full of powerful, unseen forces and spirits. They honored those spirits, which were thought to act and feel like humans.

In the Pacific Northwest, many tribes relied on fishing. One such group was the Kwakiutl (kwah kee OOT ul). Each year when they caught their first fish of the season, they chanted this prayer:

Primary Source

"We have come to meet alive, Swimmer, do not feel wrong about what I have done to you, friend Swimmer, for that is the reason why you came, that I may spear you, that I may eat you, Supernatural One, you, Long-Life-Giver, you Swimmer. Now protect us, me and my wife."

—Kwakiutl Prayer of Thanks

Academic Vocabulary
maintain • *v.*, to keep in an existing state

Analyze Images
American Indians, such as the Kwakiutl, still fish for salmon using traditional methods. **Infer** Why are these people fishing from a plank instead of from the shore?

Analyze Images Pueblo Indians perform a dance in New Mexico. **Use Visual Information** What is the woman second from the right in this picture holding in her hands? Why might this be the case?

Special Ceremonies Kachinas were spirits represented by masked Indian dancers. The Pueblo believed kachinas could bring good harvests. At Pueblo festivals, the kachinas danced. Religious leaders prayed to the spirits and gave them gifts.

In the Southwest and the Southeast, many tribes held a Green Corn Ceremony when the corn ripened in the fall. The ceremony lasted for several days. It marked the end of the old year and the beginning of a new one. On the last day, a sacred fire was lit. Dancers circled the flames, and the people enjoyed a great feast. Women used coals from the fire to make new fires in their houses.

✓ READING CHECK **Draw Conclusions** What do you think American Indians might have assumed if there was a lack of rain?

The Iroquois League

The Iroquois (IHR uh kwoi) people of present-day New York State called themselves the People of the Long House. They took great pride in their sturdy dwellings, called long houses. A typical long house was about 150 feet long and 20 feet wide. Twelve or more families lived in a long house.

Women had a special place in Iroquois society. They owned all the household property and were in charge of planting and harvesting. When a man married, he moved in with his wife's family.

Women also had political power. They chose clan leaders. A **clan** is a group of related families. If a clan leader did not do his job well, the women could remove him from his position.

Quick Activity

Create a matching game. Match characteristics of different American Indian cultures to facts about their climate, resources, and lifestyles.

Analyze Images The Iroquois lived in wooden long houses that were built clustered together. The long houses were built of posts and poles covered with tree bark. **Draw Conclusions** Why would the cultures of the Great Plains have been unable to build long houses covered with tree bark?

The Iroquois included five nations that spoke similar languages: the Mohawk, Seneca, Onondaga (ahn un DAW guh), Oneida (oh NY duh), and Cayuga (kay YOO guh). Each nation had its own ruling council. Until the 1500s, the five nations were frequently at war.

Then, in the 1500s, the five Iroquois nations formed an alliance to end the fighting. According to legend, a religious leader named Dekanawida (deh kan ah WEE dah) inspired Hiawatha (hy ah WAH thah) to organize the alliance. It became the **Iroquois League**.

A council of 50 specially chosen tribal leaders, called sachems, met once a year. The council made decisions for the League. Here, too, women had a political role because they chose the sachems and watched over their actions.

The Iroquois alliance did not end the fighting. The Iroquois spoke a different language from the Algonquian tribes, their neighbors to the east and west. The two groups fought many wars over land and trade.

☑ READING CHECK Identify Supporting Details What role did women play in Iroquois culture?

☑ Lesson Check

Practice Vocabulary

1. What were the buildings in Anasazi **culture** made from, and what did the Spanish call them?

2. What role did women play in the **clans** of the **Iroquois League**?

Critical Thinking and Writing

3. Compare and Contrast What did the Anasazi and Hohokam do to adapt to their environments?

4. Identify Main Ideas How did harsh climates and warmer climates affect American Indian cultures differently?

5. Writing Workshop: Support Ideas with Evidence In your ▤ Active Journal, record details about the impact of trade networks on the peoples of North America.

Primary Sources

Constitution of the Iroquois Nations: The Great Binding Law

In the 1500s, the five Iroquois nations formed an alliance to end the frequent wars among them. A council of 50 tribal leaders met once a year to resolve issues. Women chose the leaders and monitored their actions. The oral constitution of the Iroquois Confederacy was called the Great Binding Law.

► Hiawatha speaks to members of the council at the creation of the Iroquois League.

When a leader or lord was selected to represent his tribe, the constitution required that this pledge be recited.

"We now do crown you with the sacred emblem of the deer's antlers, the emblem of your Lordship. You shall now become a mentor of the people of the Five Nations. The thickness of your skin shall be seven spans—which is to say that you shall <u>be proof against</u> ① anger, offensive actions and criticism. Your heart shall be filled with peace and good will and your mind filled with a yearning [longing] for the welfare of the people of the Confederacy. With endless patience you shall carry out your duty and your firmness shall be tempered [lessened] with tenderness for your people. Neither anger nor fury shall find <u>lodgement</u> ② in your mind and all your words and actions shall be marked with calm deliberation. In all of your deliberations in the Confederate Council, in your efforts at law making, in all your official acts, self interest shall be <u>cast into oblivion.</u> ③ Cast not over your shoulder behind you the warnings of the nephews and nieces should they chide you for any error or wrong you may do, but return to the way of the Great Law which is just and right. Look and listen for the welfare of the whole people and have always in view not only the present but also the coming generations, even those whose faces are yet beneath the surface of the ground—the unborn of the future Nation."

—Constitution of the Iroquois Nations: The Great Binding Law, Gayanashagowa

Reading and Vocabulary Support

① "Be proof against" means that these behaviors should not occur.

② "Lodgement" means to reside.

③ What does it mean to "cast into oblivion"?

Analyzing Primary Sources

Cite specific evidence from the source to support your answers.

1. **Cite Evidence** What behavior was a tribal leader told to avoid?

2. **Identify Supporting Details** According to the pledge, what were two things that the leaders were expected to focus on?

Be an Informed Citizen

Follow these steps to become an informed citizen.

INTERACTIVE

Being an Informed Citizen

1 **Learn the issues.** A great way to begin to understand the responsibilities of citizenship is to first find topics of interest to you. Next, become well informed about civic affairs in your town, city, or country. Read newspapers, magazines, and articles you find online about events happening in your area or around the world. Analyze the information you read to come to your own conclusions. Radio programs, podcasts, and social media are also great ways to keep up with current events and interact with others about issues.

2 **Get involved.** Attend community events to speak with others who know the issues. Become well informed about how policies are made and changed. Find out who to speak to if you would like to take part in civic affairs and policy creation. There are government websites that can help direct you to the right person. These websites will also provide his or her contact details.

3 **Take a stand and reach out.** Write, call, or meet with your elected officials to become a better informed, more responsible citizen. To be an informed voter, do research about candidates who are running for office. Start your own blog or website to explore issues, interact with others, and be part of the community or national dialogue.

Complete the graphic organizer below to help you become an informed citizen.

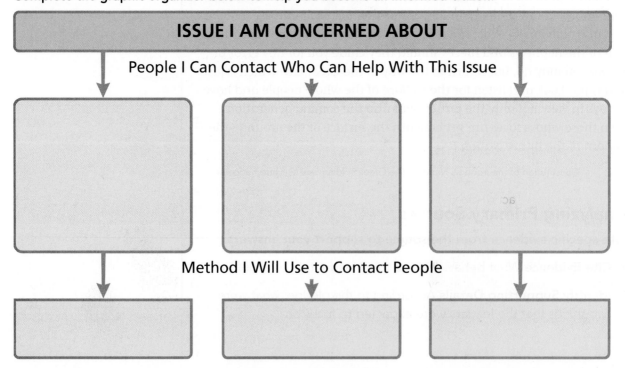

ISSUE I AM CONCERNED ABOUT

People I Can Contact Who Can Help With This Issue

Method I Will Use to Contact People

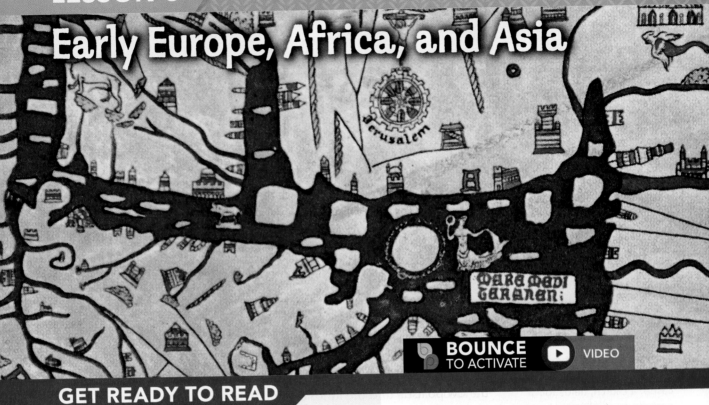

Early Europe, Africa, and Asia

BOUNCE
TO ACTIVATE   ▶ VIDEO

GET READY TO READ

START UP

Examine the map of the world from 1280. How does it differ from modern maps?

GUIDING QUESTIONS

- How did Europe change during the Middle Ages?
- Describe trade and technological innovations in the Muslim world, Africa, and East Asia.
- What was the impact of technological innovations on the Renaissance?

TAKE NOTES

Literacy Skills: Summarize

Use the graphic organizer in your 📓 Active Journal to take notes as you read the lesson.

PRACTICE VOCABULARY

Use the vocabulary activity in your 📓 Active Journal to practice the vocabulary words.

Vocabulary		Academic Vocabulary
feudalism	caravan	decline
manor	kinship	innovation
Crusades	Renaissance	
astrolabe		
Silk Road		

The period from about 500 to around 1500 is known as the Middle Ages. Many wars were fought, but the world also became more interconnected as trade grew and explorers traveled widely.

What Was Europe Like in the Middle Ages?

During the early Middle Ages, invasion and war were common. People in Europe had to find new means of defending themselves.

Feudalism A new kind of government evolved during the Middle Ages. Kings and queens divided their lands among warrior nobles. In return, nobles promised to fight for the ruler when asked. This system of rule by lords who ruled their lands but owed loyalty and military service to a monarch is called **feudalism** (FYOOD ul iz um).

At the top of feudal society stood the king and the most powerful lords. Next came the lesser nobles. Most people in feudal society were peasants who farmed the lord's lands and could not leave the land without the lord's permission.

Analyze Images A typical medieval manor included a castle, a church, fields for agriculture and livestock, and dwellings for serfs.
❶ Castle ❷ Church ❸ Serf home ❹ Fields ❺ Mill
Identify Cause and Effect Why was the mill placed along the river?

Feudal Life

Feudal life revolved around the **manor**, which included the lord's castle and the lands around it. Manor lands might include several villages. Each manor was self-sufficient. That is, people made almost everything they needed. Life for peasants was hard. Peasants were farmers who worked mostly by hand on small plots. They struggled to produce enough food just to survive.

By about 900, life began to change. Peasants used new methods of farming to produce more food. Warfare **declined** and trade began to grow. Slowly, people began to look beyond their isolated villages.

Religion in Medieval Europe

The most powerful force in medieval western Europe was the Roman Catholic Church. The Roman Catholic Church was the main branch of Christianity in western Europe. Like other branches of Christianity, it was based on the teachings of Jesus, who had lived centuries earlier. During ancient and early medieval times, the religion spread across Europe.

The Church ruled more than religious life. It owned large amounts of land and offered the only source of education. The clergy were often the only people who could read and write. Because of their efforts, much of the learning from the ancient world was preserved.

While Christianity was the main religion in western Europe, the region also had a strong Jewish community. The Jewish people's religion was Judaism, a religion centuries older than Christianity. It, too, had spread across Europe in ancient and early medieval times. While Jewish people played an important role in medieval Europe, they often faced persecution, or attacks because of their beliefs.

The Crusades

The pace of change in Europe increased between 1100 and 1300. This was in part because of the Crusades.

Academic Vocabulary
decline • v., to draw to a close

The **Crusades** were a series of wars fought by Christians to control the region then known as the Holy Land or Palestine, much of which is now Israel. This region included Jerusalem and the other places where Jesus had lived and taught. Muslims had controlled this region for centuries.

During the Crusades, tens of thousands of Christians journeyed to the Middle East. Fighting between Christians and Muslims continued for almost 200 years. Christians won some victories, and they ruled kingdoms in the region for more than 100 years. But in the end, they failed to keep control of the Holy Land.

Trade Grows The Crusades had important effects on Europe, however. Crusaders traveled beyond their villages and came into contact with other civilizations. In the Middle East, they tasted new foods, such as rice, oranges, dates, and new spices. They saw beautiful silks and woven rugs.

Europe had traded with the Middle East before the Crusades. However, returning Crusaders demanded more Asian foods, spices, and silks. Italian merchants could get high prices for such goods. They outfitted ships and increased trade with the Muslim world.

Technological Innovations in Navigation Trade brought new knowledge and with it, new technological **innovations**. From the Muslim world, Europeans acquired sailing skills and the magnetic compass. Muslims had adopted the magnetic compass from the Chinese. The magnetic needle of the compass always pointed north, which helped ships stay on course.

Another useful instrument was the **astrolabe** (As troh layb), which helped sailors determine their latitude while at sea. These new instruments let Europeans sail far out to sea, beyond sight of land. By 1500, Portugal had taken the lead in this new overseas travel.

✔ READING CHECK Identify Main Ideas How did the Crusades affect trade in the Middle Ages?

INTERACTIVE

How an Astrolabe Works

Academic Vocabulary
innovation • *n.*, a new method or idea

Analyze Images Many medieval Christians joined the Crusades to fight for control of territory in the Middle East. **Identify Supporting Details** What item hanging from the horse suggests a battle will occur?

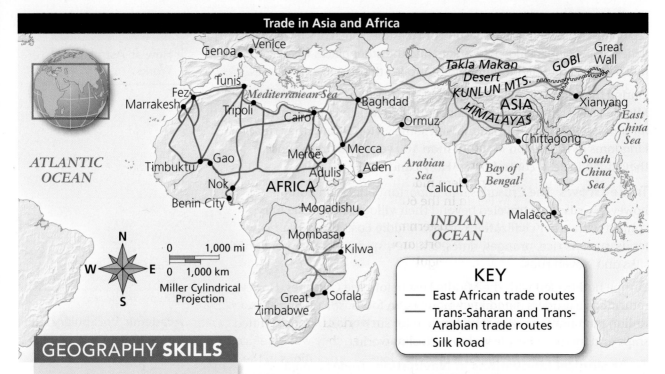

KEY
— East African trade routes
— Trans-Saharan and Trans-Arabian trade routes
— Silk Road

GEOGRAPHY **SKILLS**

Traders used routes such as the Trans-Saharan route and the Silk Road to transport goods to different places.

1. **Location** Which cities on the Trans-Saharan and Trans-Arabian trade routes were located on the Mediterranean Sea?

2. **Draw Conclusions** Which of the three routes probably had the least amount of trading? Why?

INTERACTIVE

Routes of Exploration and Trade

How Was the Middle East a Crossroads of the World?

Middle Eastern merchants played a large role in this growing trade. Linking Europe, Africa, and Asia, the Middle East was a major crossroads of the world.

Muslim Conquests and Inventions The growth of trade was also linked to the spread of a new religion. In the early 600s, a new religion, Islam, emerged in Arabia. A people called the Arabs lived in Arabia, in the southern Middle East.

Islam won many followers among the Arabs. Beginning in the 600s, Islam spread rapidly. Devout followers conquered North Africa and much of Spain. They conquered lands to the east, too, from Persia to India and beyond. Eventually, the Muslim world spread from South Asia to what is now Portugal and Spain. In many countries ruled by Muslims, however, there were also communities of Christians and Jewish people.

Islam expanded through trade and conquest. While some remained faithful to Christianity, Judaism, and other religions, many people in conquered lands chose to convert to the new religion.

Others were converted by force, or under the threat of crippling taxes. Elsewhere, Muslim merchants carried the new faith to people living along the trade routes of Asia and Africa.

Islam united Muslims from many lands and fostered the growth of trade. Muslims had a basic duty to make a pilgrimage, or journey, to the holy city of Mecca at least once in their lives. Every year, people from across the Muslim world traveled to Mecca.

Muslims from North Africa, Persia, Afghanistan, India, Spain, and West Africa crowded Mecca's dusty streets. They prayed in Arabic, the language of Islam. This regular travel encouraged trade among the Muslim lands.

People in the mainly Muslim Middle East developed many of the technologies we use today. Experiments with how light enters the eye led 10th century Muslim mathematician Ibn al-Haitham to invent the first pin-hole camera. A Muslim engineer invented the crankshaft, a key device in modern machinery, and the windmill was invented in Persia in the 600s to grind corn.

Navigating the Seas Middle Eastern merchants traded across a vast area. They sailed to ports around the Indian Ocean. Their ships used large, triangular sails that allowed captains to sail close to the direction the wind was blowing from.

Middle Eastern sailors had knowledge of wind and weather conditions in the Indian Ocean. As a result, merchants in ports around the region knew when the trading ships had to sail and when they would return. Middle Easterners made important technological innovations in the astrolabe, which, as you have learned, helped sailors find their way far from shore.

Middle Eastern merchants sold porcelains, perfumes, and fabrics from China. Jade and tea were popular, too.

The Spice Islands of Indonesia offered nutmeg, clove, and mace. Cloth, indigo, and sugar came from East Africa, as well as spices, salt, and slaves. Goods like textiles and spices traveled well. They quickly spread across the globe.

▲ The astrolabe helped sea captains determine the latitude of their ships.

Analyze Charts Trade routes made it possible for people in Africa and Eurasia to exchange goods with one another. **Identify Main Ideas** How did the exchange of goods and information between Africa and Eurasia benefit both regions?

Trade in Africa and Eurasia

AFRICA		EURASIA	
Domesticated camels enabled North African merchants to cross the Sahara. Caravans could include merchants, missionaries, pilgrims, and scholars.		Improvements in land and sea travel enabled goods and ideas to travel between East Asia, South Asia, the Middle East, and Europe.	
RESOURCES AND GOODS	**TECHNOLOGY AND EDUCATION**	**RESOURCES AND GOODS**	**TECHNOLOGY AND EDUCATION**
• Gold, copper, and salt • Ivory for artistic carving • Kola nuts for medicine; coffee beans prized as a stimulant	• Advanced metal forging techniques for toolmaking • Weaving techniques for patterned textiles • Education in mathematics, medicine, law, geography, history, and art at universities • Training in carpentry, fishing, and tailoring	• Spices for flavorings, perfumes, and medicines as well as European wines • Textiles including silk and wool • Copper, iron, and silver	• Techniques for making pottery, ceramics, glazes, glass, and lacquerware • Study in mathematics, medicine, and engineering; advances in agricultural and irrigation techniques • Architectural domes and arches in mosques, temples, and churches • Surgical instruments and techniques

Trade Along the Silk Road Some Middle Eastern traders traveled the overland routes that crossed the grasslands, mountains, and deserts of Central Asia and linked China and the Middle East. These routes had become known as the **Silk Road** because prized Chinese silks had been carried westward along them for more than 1,000 years.

Travel on the Silk Road was dangerous. Desert storms, hunger, and bandits were a constant threat. Traders formed **caravans**, or groups of people who traveled together for safety. Despite the dangers, trade along the Silk Road prospered.

By the 1400s, trade goods were flowing across a huge area. More than just silk was traded on the Silk Road. Everything from horses to spices and gems traveled along the route.

✓ READING CHECK **Identify Cause and Effect** What impact did the Silk Road have on trade?

African Trade and Cultures

Trade routes played a large role in Africa, too. Long-distance trade routes crossed the vast Sahara, the desert linking West Africa and North Africa.

A peaceful afternoon in a West African village might be pierced by sounds of a horn. Children would shout, "Batafo! Batafo!" Traders! Soon, a long line of porters and camels arrived. Villagers watched as the tired travelers unloaded sacks of salt or dried fish. Gold, fabrics, jewelry, and slaves were also part of the caravan.

Sea traders also spread navigation technologies throughout Africa and eventually to Europe. The lateen sail was a triangular sail that allowed ships to travel toward the wind.

Although historians cannot be certain, it is likely that North Africans adapted the astrolabe for sea travel, too. It was used by African, Arab, and Indian sailors and then adopted by Europeans.

BIOGRAPHY
5 Things to Know About

MANSA MUSA
Emperor of Mali c. 1280 -c. 1337

- He built an empire in West Africa that was known far and wide for its wealth.

- On his journey to Mecca, his caravan had more than 70,000 men and 80 camels, which carried 300 pounds of gold each.

- Historians say he might have been the wealthiest person to have ever lived.

- His empire was one of the largest in the world at that time.

- He built the Great Mosque in the city of Timbuktu, which still stands.

Critical Thinking What information indicates that Mansa Musa was rich and powerful?

Analyze Images This medieval map shows Mansa Musa on his throne. **Use Visual Information** What information does the image of Mansa Musa on his throne, holding a golden object, add to the map?

East African City-States Trade had long flowed up and down the coast of East Africa. Small villages that had good natural harbors grew into busy trading centers.

Gold from Zimbabwe (zim BAH bweh), a powerful inland state, was carried to coastal cities such as Kilwa and Sofala. From there, ships carried the gold, and prized goods such as hardwoods and ivory, across the Indian Ocean to Arabia, India, and China.

Wealth from trade helped local East African rulers build strong city-states. East African city-states gained wealth and power by trading people as well as goods. They traded enslaved people from the interior of East Africa to Arabs and other groups across the Indian Ocean.

Many rulers of these city-states became Muslims. In time, Muslim culture influenced East African traditions. The blend of cultures led to the rise of a new language, Swahili, which blended Arabic words and local African languages.

West African Trading Kingdoms A region of grasslands, called the savanna, covers much of West Africa. Several rich trading kingdoms emerged there. Among the best known were Mali and Songhai (SAWNG hy). The city of Timbuktu was the major trading center for both kingdoms. These West African empires gained power through warfare. They conquered neighboring peoples and took control of surrounding lands.

The kingdom of Mali rose in about 1200 and flourished for about 200 years. Like the rulers of East Africa's city-states, many rulers in West African kingdoms adopted the religion of Islam.

Mali's most famous ruler, Mansa Musa, was a Muslim. In 1324, the emperor made a pilgrimage to Mecca. On the way, he and his caravan stopped in Cairo, Egypt. His wealth in gold amazed the Egyptians.

Analyze Images African villages included huts with roofs made from grass. **Infer** What other material from the environment did Africans use?

In time, stories of Mansa Musa's immense wealth reached Europe. A Spanish map from that time shows Mansa Musa on his throne, holding a golden object:

Primary Source

"So abundant is the gold in his country that this lord is the richest and most noble king in all the land."

—Catalan Atlas, 1375

In the 1400s, Songhai emerged as the most powerful empire in West Africa. Muslim emperors extended Songhai's power and made Timbuktu into a thriving city.

Ways of Life in Africa Ways of life varied greatly across the huge continent of Africa. While powerful trading states flourished in some regions, most people lived outside these kingdoms. Many lived in small villages. They made a living by herding, fishing, or farming.

Family relationships were important in African cultures. Although family patterns varied across Africa, many people lived within an extended family.

In an extended family, several generations live in one household. An extended family usually included grandparents, parents, children, and sometimes aunts, uncles, and cousins. The grandparents, or elders, received special respect for their wisdom and knowledge.

Ties of **kinship**, or sharing a common ancestor, linked families. People related by kinship owed loyalty to one another. Kinship ties encouraged a strong sense of community and cooperation.

Religious beliefs varied widely across Africa. Yet, African beliefs reflected some common threads. Links among family members lasted after death.

Quest CONNECTIONS

Read the quote. Does the quote verify the information in Mansa Musa's biography? Record your findings in your ▢ Active Journal.

In their rituals and ceremonies, many Africans honored the spirits of their ancestors as well as the forces of nature. Powerful spirits, they believed, could harm or could help the living.

☑ READING CHECK **Summarize** How would you explain what an extended family is to a friend?

Chinese Trade and Technology

Africa had many different cultures and kingdoms. By contrast, in China, power was centered on one emperor. Chinese rulers were often suspicious of outsiders. Long distances and physical barriers separated China from Egypt, the Middle East, and India. This isolation contributed to the Chinese belief that China was the center of the Earth and the sole source of civilization. The ancient Chinese looked down on outsiders.

China Uses Technology to Increase Trade Chinese inventions changed shipbuilding around the globe. The Chinese invented the rudder, which made it easier to steer large ships. They created watertight compartments that went in the ship's hull to reduce the risk of sinking. They also probably invented the magnetic compass, which decreased the likelihood of getting lost on the open seas.

Analyze Images Historians believe the Chinese may have invented the magnetic compass. A later version is shown below. The rudder on this Chinese trading ship allowed the craft to be steered more easily. ❶ rudder ❷ compass ❸ watertight compartment **Infer** What do you think was located in the watertight compartments?

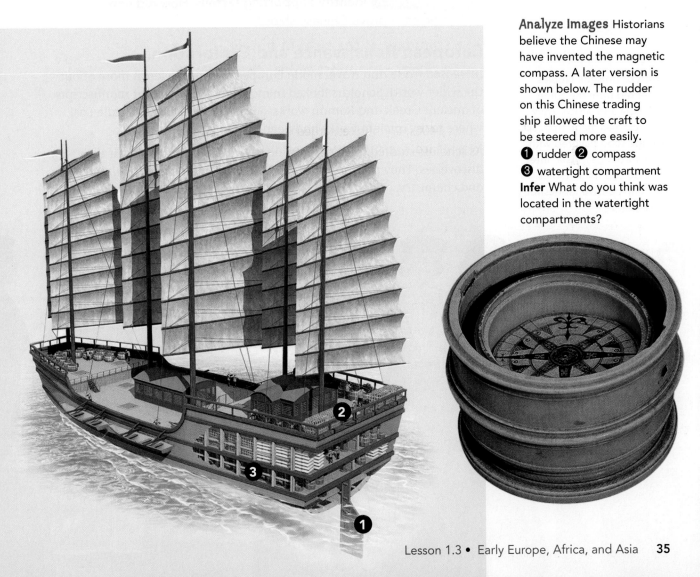

A young emperor who came to power in 1402 was eager to use these new technologies to increase trade. He ordered a huge fleet to be built and named Zheng He (JUNG HUH) to command it. Zheng He's fleet numbered more than 300 ships. It carried tons of trade goods. The largest ships were more than 400 feet long.

Zheng's fleet traded at ports in Southeast Asia, India, Arabia, and East Africa. At every port, Chinese traders carried on a brisk business. They expanded Chinese trade and influence across a wide region.

The Voyages End Zheng He's great fleet returned home with exotic goods and animals, such as giraffes, that the Chinese had never seen. However, China's overseas voyages soon ended. A new emperor decided that China had nothing to learn from the outside world. He outlawed most foreign trade. However, traders like Zheng He had spread Chinese technological innovations around the world.

The Chinese first invented paper in 105 CE. They also developed a printing press with movable type. The Chinese made advancements in timekeeping, developing several different kinds of clocks. They also invented gunpowder. Europeans later used gunpowder in handguns and cannons, which were based on Chinese designs.

✓ READING CHECK **Identify Supporting Details** How did new technologies improve Chinese ships?

European Renaissance and Exploration

Increased trade and travel made Europeans eager to learn more about the wider world. Scholars looked in monastery libraries for manuscripts of ancient Greek and Roman works. Some traveled to the Middle East, where many ancient works had been preserved.

As scholars studied ancient learning, they began to make their own discoveries. They produced new books on art, medicine, astronomy, and chemistry.

Analyze Images Nobles benefited from the trade with Asia and Africa. They wore clothes made from silk and ate food flavored with spices from East Asia. **Infer** Why do you think nobles chose expensive fabrics for their clothes?

This great burst of learning and technological innovation was called the **Renaissance** (REN uh sahns). It is a French word meaning rebirth. The Renaissance lasted from the late 1300s until the 1600s.

The Chinese had invented the printing press and movable type, or metal letters that could be used to print paper. However, the Chinese language required thousands of different letters, and movable type had little impact.

During the 1430s, a German printer named Johannes Gutenberg (GOOT un burg) is believed to have invented movable type without knowing that it had existed in China. Movable type was much more useful for printing in European languages, which used only 26 letters. Together, movable type and the printing press helped to spread Renaissance learning. Before movable type and the printing press, books were scarce and costly because each was copied by hand. With these technological innovations, large numbers of books could be produced quickly and at a low cost. Soon more people began to read, and learning spread more quickly.

▲ Moveable type made printed books available to many people and spread the knowledge of Renaissance thinkers and explorers.

A Search for New Trade Routes

During the Renaissance, trade brought new prosperity. European rulers began to increase their power. In England and France, kings and queens worked to bring powerful feudal lords under their control. In Spain and Portugal, Christian monarchs drove out Muslim rulers, who had governed there for centuries.

Rulers in England, France, Spain, and Portugal were eager to increase their wealth. They saw the great profits that could be made through trade. However, Middle Eastern and Italian merchants controlled the trade routes across the Mediterranean Sea. So, western Europe's leaders began hunting for other routes to Asia. European rulers also looked to Africa as a source of riches. Tales of Mansa Musa's wealth had created a stir in Europe, but no one knew the source of African gold.

Portuguese Voyages Portugal was an early leader in the search for a new trade route to Asia and for the source of African gold. In the early 1400s, Prince Henry, known as Henry the Navigator, encouraged sea captains to sail south along the coast of West Africa. Realizing that Portugal needed better navigators to accomplish the task, he set up an informal school to teach sailors techniques of navigation and the art of shipbuilding.

Under Henry's guidance, the Portuguese designed a new type of ship. The caravel (KAR uh vel) had triangular sails and a steering rudder. Caravels could be sailed closer to the direction from which the wind was blowing. Portuguese caravels stopped at many places along the coast of West Africa.

👆 INTERACTIVE

Seafaring Technologies

Portuguese Routes of Exploration

GEOGRAPHY SKILLS

This map shows the sea routes taken by Bartolomeu Dias and Vasco da Gama.

1. **Movement** Which Portuguese explorer stayed closer to land?

2. **Infer** Why do you think Vasco da Gama chose a route that did not follow the west coast of Africa?

EUROPE

PORTUGAL

Mediterranean Sea

ATLANTIC OCEAN

ASIA

INDIA

AFRICA

N
W   E
S

0   2,000 mi
0   2,000 km
Miller Cylindrical Projection

Cape of Good Hope

INDIAN OCEAN

KEY
→ Bartolomeu Dias, 1487–1488
→ Vasco da Gama, 1497–1499

They traded cloth, silver, textiles, and grain for gold and ivory. They also bought Africans who had been forced into slavery and sold them in Europe and elsewhere.

Further Exploration Slowly, Portuguese explorers ventured farther south, hoping to find a sea route around Africa to the rich spice trade of Asia. In 1488, Bartolomeu Dias reached the southern tip of Africa. The Portuguese pushed on to the East Indies, the islands of Southeast Asia and the source of valuable spices.

☑ READING CHECK **Understand Effects** What effect did movable type and the printing press have on learning?

☑ Lesson Check

Practice Vocabulary

1. Describe life on the **manor** in **feudal** Europe.

2. How did innovations such as the compass and **astrolabe** help sailors?

3. What happened in Europe during the **Renaissance**?

Critical Thinking and Writing

4. **Identify Supporting Details** What was the impact of the Roman Catholic Church in medieval western Europe?

5. **Identify Cause and Effect** What encouraged Muslims from different lands to trade with one another?

6. **Identify Cause and Effect** What advantages did Middle Eastern merchants possess that allowed them to take such a central role in the expansion of trade?

7. **Draw Conclusions** In what ways did trade between China and other civilizations have long-term effects worldwide?

8. **Writing Workshop: Find and Use Credible Sources** You will need more information to write your paper. List three credible sources of information you could use to write a research paper about improved technology for travel, such as the astrolabe.

European Exploration in the Americas

BOUNCE TO ACTIVATE ▶ VIDEO

GET READY TO READ

START UP
Study the replica of one of the ships Christopher Columbus used to reach North America. Write three questions you have about sea travel during that time.

GUIDING QUESTIONS
- Why did Europeans explore the Americas?
- What was the impact of European exploration of the Americas?
- How did European and American Indian interactions affect both cultures?

TAKE NOTES
Literacy Skills: Identify Cause and Effect
Use the graphic organizer in your 📙 Active Journal to take notes as you read the lesson.

PRACTICE VOCABULARY
Use the vocabulary activity in your 📙 Active Journal to practice the vocabulary words.

Vocabulary	Academic Vocabulary
colony	modification
turning point	despite
circumnavigate	
Columbian Exchange	

Many stories exist about early people from Europe or Asia sailing to the Americas. Yet, real evidence has been hard to find. Most experts agree that such voyages were rare, if they occurred at all. Unlike other possible early voyagers to the Americas, the Vikings left behind a detailed record of their voyages.

Contact with the Americas

In 1001, Viking sailors led by Leif Erikson reached the eastern tip of North America. Archaeologists have found evidence of the Viking settlement of Vinland in present-day Newfoundland, Canada. The Vikings did not stay in Vinland long and no one is sure why they left. However, Viking stories describe fierce battles with Skraelings, the Viking name for the Inuit.

Evidence suggests that Asians continued to cross the Bering Sea into North America after the last ice age ended. Some scholars believe that ancient seafarers from Polynesia may have traveled to the Americas using their knowledge of the stars and winds.

Analyze Images The Vikings were one of the first groups to travel from Europe to the Americas. Their boats were powered by sail and oars. **Draw Conclusions** What disadvantages do you see in using this type of boat for travel in the ocean?

Modern Polynesians have sailed canoes thousands of miles in this way. Still others think that fishing boats from China and Japan blew off course and landed on the western coast of North or South America.

Perhaps such voyages occurred. If so, they were long forgotten. Before 1492, the peoples of Asia and Europe had no knowledge of the Americas and their remarkable civilizations.

✓ READING CHECK Identify Supporting Details Why are we uncertain whether early people from Europe or Asia, other than the Vikings, sailed to America?

The Voyages of Columbus

Portuguese sailors had pioneered new routes around Africa toward Asia in the late 1400s. Spain, too, wanted a share of the riches. King Ferdinand and Queen Isabella hoped to keep their rival, Portugal, from controlling trade with India, China, and Japan. They agreed to finance a voyage of exploration by Christopher Columbus. Columbus, an Italian sea captain, planned to reach the East Indies by sailing west across the Atlantic. Finding a sea route straight to Asia would give the Spanish direct access to the silks, spices, and precious metals of Asia. The spice trade was a major cause for European exploration and a reason the Spanish rulers supported Columbus's voyage. They also wanted wealth from any source. "Get gold," King Ferdinand said to Columbus. "Humanely if possible, but at all hazards—get gold."

Crossing the Atlantic In August 1492, Columbus set out with three ships and about 90 sailors. As captain, he commanded the largest vessel, the *Santa María*. The other ships were the *Niña* and the *Pinta*.

After a brief stop at the Canary Islands, the little fleet continued west into unknown seas. Fair winds sped them along, but a month passed without the sight of land. Some sailors began to grumble. They had never been away from land for so long and feared being lost at sea. Still, Columbus sailed on.

Did you know?

Many streets in the United States have been named in honor of Christopher Columbus, such as this one in New York City.

On October 7, sailors saw flocks of birds flying southwest. Columbus changed course to follow the birds. A few days later, crew members spotted tree branches and flowers floating in the water. At 2 A.M. on October 12, the lookout on the *Pinta* spotted white cliffs shining in the moonlight. *"Tierra! Tierra!"* he shouted. "Land! Land!"

At dawn, Columbus rowed ashore and planted the banner of Spain. He was convinced that he had reached the East Indies in Asia. He called the people he found there "Indians." In fact, he had reached islands off the coasts of North America and South America in the Caribbean Sea. These islands later became known as the West Indies. For three months, Columbus explored the West Indies. To his delight, he found signs of gold on the islands. Eager to report his success, he returned to Spain.

Columbus Claims Lands for Spain In Spain, Columbus presented Queen Isabella and King Ferdinand with gifts of pink pearls and brilliantly colored parrots. Columbus brought with him many things that Europeans had never seen before: tobacco, pineapples, and hammocks used for sleeping. Columbus also described the "Indians" he had met, the Taino (TY noh). The Taino, he promised, could easily be converted to Christianity and could also be used as slaves.

The Spanish monarchs were impressed. They gave Columbus the title Admiral of the Ocean Sea. They also agreed to finance future voyages. The promise of great wealth, and the chance to spread Christianity, gave them a reason to explore further.

Columbus made three more voyages across the Atlantic. In 1493, he founded the first Spanish colony in the Americas, Santo Domingo, on an island he called Hispaniola (present-day Haiti and the Dominican Republic). A **colony** is an area settled and ruled by the government of a distant land. Columbus also explored present-day Cuba and Jamaica. He sailed along the coasts of Central America and northern South America. He claimed all of these lands for Queen Isabella of Spain.

Columbus proved to be a better explorer than governor. During his third expedition, settlers on Hispaniola complained of his harsh rule. Queen Isabella appointed an investigator, who sent Columbus back to Spain in chains.

Analyze Images This illustration shows Columbus meeting the Taino of the West Indies. His voyages benefited Spain but brought much misery to the world of the Taino. **Infer** How do you think the Taino might have reacted to Columbus's arrival?

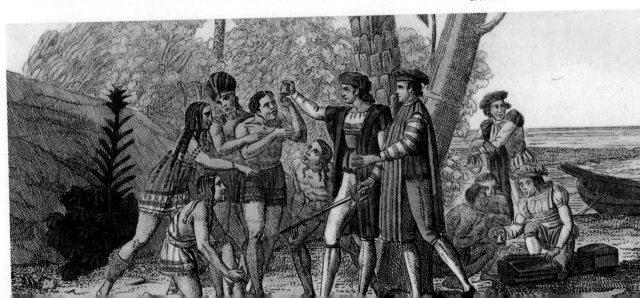

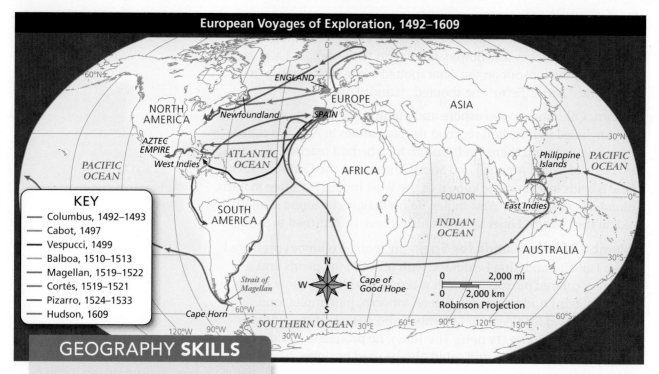

European Voyages of Exploration, 1492–1609

KEY
— Columbus, 1492–1493
— Cabot, 1497
— Vespucci, 1499
— Balboa, 1510–1513
— Magellan, 1519–1522
— Cortés, 1519–1521
— Pizarro, 1524–1533
— Hudson, 1609

GEOGRAPHY SKILLS

Many Europeans went on voyages of exploration in the 1400s, 1500s, and 1600s.

1. **Location** From which European country did most voyages of exploration originate?

2. **Infer** Why do you think Magellan was the only explorer to sail around the world?

In the end, the queen pardoned Columbus, but he never regained the honors he had won earlier. He died in 1506, still convinced that he had reached Asia.

The Impact of Columbus's Voyages Columbus has long been honored as the bold sea captain who "discovered America." Today, we recognize that American Indians had settled these lands long before 1492. Still, in at least one sense, Columbus deserves the honors history has given him. Europeans knew nothing of the Americas until Columbus told them about this "new world." His daring voyages marked the beginning of lasting contact among the peoples of Europe, Africa, and the Americas.

For a great many American Indians, contact had tragic results. Columbus and those who followed were convinced that European culture was superior to that of the Indians. The Spanish claimed Taino lands and forced the Taino to work in gold mines, on ranches, or in Spanish households. Many Taino died from harsh conditions or European diseases. The Taino population was wiped out.

For better or worse, the voyages of Columbus signaled a turning point for the Americas. A **turning point** is a moment in history that marks a decisive change. Curious Europeans saw the new lands as a place where they could settle, trade, and grow rich.

✓ READING CHECK **Identify Main Ideas** What reasons did Spain have for sending Columbus on his voyages?

Spanish Exploration Continues

After the voyages of Columbus, the Spanish explored and settled other Caribbean islands. They wanted to take advantage of the land Columbus had found, seeking gold, crops, slaves, and converts to Christianity for the Spanish crown. By 1511, they had conquered Puerto Rico, Jamaica, and Cuba. They also explored the eastern coasts of North America and South America in search of a western route to Asia.

In 1513, Vasco Núñez de Balboa (bal BOH uh) crossed the Isthmus of Panama. American Indians had told him that a large body of water lay to the west. With a party of Spanish soldiers and Indians, Balboa reached the Pacific Ocean and claimed the ocean for Spain.

The Spanish had no idea how wide the Pacific was until a sea captain named Ferdinand Magellan (muh JEL un) sailed across it. The expedition—made up of five ships and about 250 crew members—left Spain in 1519. Fifteen months later, it cut through the stormy southern tip of South America by way of what is now known as the Strait of Magellan and entered the Pacific Ocean. Crossing the vast Pacific, the sailors ran out of food:

Primary Source

"We remained 3 months and 20 days without taking in provisions or other refreshments and ate only old biscuit reduced to powder, full of grubs and stinking from the dirt which rats had made on it. We drank water that was yellow and stinking."

—Antonio Pigafetta, *The Diary of Antonio Pigafetta*

Quest CONNECTIONS

What fact from Magellan's biography helps you to verify the facts in Pigafetta's account? Record your ideas in your Active Journal.

INTERACTIVE

Reasons to Explore

BIOGRAPHY
5 Things to Know About

FERDINAND MAGELLAN
Portuguese Explorer 1480–1521

- He sailed around South America and spent 99 days crossing the Pacific Ocean.

- He became interested in sea exploration as a boy, when he worked for the family of Portugal's queen.

- He launched his journey because he was looking for the Spice Islands, which are off the coast of Indonesia.

- During the journey, members of his crew rebelled against him and tried to take over the fleet, but Magellan stopped them.

- Magellan died in battle before he reached the Spice Islands.

Critical Thinking Why do you think Magellan's crew rebelled against him?

INTERACTIVE

The Columbian
Exchange

Magellan himself was killed in a battle with the local people of the Philippine Islands off the coast of Asia.

In 1522, only one ship and 18 sailors returned to Spain. They were the first people to **circumnavigate**, or sail completely around, the world. In doing so, they had found an all-water western route to Asia. Europeans became aware of the true size of the Earth.

✓ READING CHECK Understand Effects Explain the significance of Magellan's voyage.

How Did the Columbian Exchange Affect the Rest of the World?

Academic Vocabulary
modification • *n.,* a change

The encounter between the peoples of the Eastern and Western Hemispheres sparked a global exchange of goods and ideas. Because it started with the voyages of Columbus, this transfer is known as the **Columbian Exchange**. The Columbian Exchange refers to a biological and cultural exchange of animals, plants, human populations, diseases, food, government, technology, the arts, and languages.

The exchange went in both directions. Europeans learned much from American Indians. At the same time, Europeans contributed in many ways to the culture of the Americas. This exchange also brought about many **modifications**, or changes, to the physical environment of the Americas, with both positive and negative results.

Changing Environments Europeans introduced domestic animals such as chickens from Europe and Africa. European pigs, cattle, and horses often escaped into the wild and multiplied rapidly. Forests and grasslands were converted to pastures. As horses spread through what would become the United States, Indians learned to ride them and used them to carry heavy loads.

Analyze Images Horses and other domesticated animals were introduced to the Americas by Europeans. Horses soon became part of American Indians' way of life. **Understand Effects** In what ways do you think horses helped American Indians?

THE COLUMBIAN EXCHANGE

Famines and starvation were common events in Europe during the Middle Ages. Famine affected native peoples of the Americas as well. As a result of the Columbian Exchange, newly arrived species made the food supply more abundant and diverse on both sides of the ocean.

CORN OR MAIZE

Previously unknown, corn became a dietary staple in Mediterranean, African, and Asian countries.

WHEAT AND RICE

Brought by Spaniards, wheat and rice grew well in the Americas. Rice was sometimes used as a substitute for corn.

FROM THE AMERICAS TO EUROPE, AFRICA, AND ASIA

- maize
- potatoes
- sweet potatoes
- beans
- peanuts
- squash
- pumpkins
- peppers
- pineapples
- tomatoes
- cocoa

FROM EUROPE, AFRICA, AND ASIA TO THE AMERICAS

- wheat
- sugar
- bananas
- rice
- grapes
- olive oil
- dandelions
- horses
- pigs
- cows
- goats
- chickens

SUGAR

Europeans brought both sugar cane and enslaved Africans to grow it to the Americas.

COWS AND PIGS

Cows and pigs were unknown in the Americas before Europeans brought them. Over time, American Indians added beef and pork to their diets.

Plants from Europe and Africa changed the way American Indians lived. The first bananas came from the Canary Islands. By 1520, one Spaniard reported that banana trees had spread "so greatly that it is marvelous to see the great abundance of them." Oranges, lemons, and figs were also new to the Americas. In North America, explorers also brought such plants as bluegrass, the daisy, and the dandelion. These plants spread quickly in American soil and modified American grasslands.

Tragically, Europeans also brought new diseases, such as smallpox and influenza. American Indians had no resistance to these diseases. Historians estimate that within 75 years, diseases from Europe had killed almost 90 percent of the people in the Caribbean Islands and in Mexico.

American Indian Influences on Europe, Africa, and Asia For their part, American Indians introduced Europeans, Africans, and Asians to new foods, customs, and ideas. After 1492, elements of American Indian ways of life gradually spread around the world. Sadly, disease also spread from the Americas to Europe and other parts of the world.

American Indians introduced Europeans to valuable food crops such as corn, potatoes, sweet potatoes, beans, tomatoes, manioc, squash, peanuts, pineapples, and blueberries. Today, almost half the world's food crops come from plants that were first grown in the Americas.

Europeans carried the new foods with them as they sailed around the world. Everywhere, people's diets changed and populations increased. In South Asia, people used American hot peppers and chilies to spice stews. Chinese peasants began growing corn and sweet potatoes. Italians made sauces from tomatoes. People in West Africa grew manioc and corn.

Analyze Graphs The Columbian Exchange affected people all over the world. **Identify Main Ideas** What were some positive consequences of the Columbian Exchange?

Quick Activity

Plan a dinner party using food from the Columbian Exchange. Record your plan in your 🗐 Active Journal.

Analyze Images In the 1600s, European settlers traveled along the Mississippi River in canoes. **Synthesize Visual Information** What is one difference between this canoe and the boats the Vikings used?

European settlers often adopted American Indian skills. In the North, Indians showed Europeans how to use snowshoes and trap beavers and other fur-bearing animals. European explorers learned how to paddle Indian canoes. Some leaders studied American Indian political structures. In the 1700s, Benjamin Franklin admired the Iroquois League and urged American colonists to unite in a similar way.

Positive and Negative Consequences

Through the Columbian Exchange, Europeans and American Indians modified their environments and gained new resources and skills. At the same time, warfare and disease killed many on both sides. Europeans viewed expansion positively. They gained great wealth, explored trade routes, and spread Christianity. Yet their farming, mining, and diseases took a toll on the physical environment and left many American Indians dead. **Despite** these negatives, the Columbian Exchange shaped the modern world, including what would become the United States.

Academic Vocabulary

despite • *prep.*, in spite of; notwithstanding

☑ **READING CHECK** Summarize How would you define the Columbian Exchange?

☑ Lesson Check

Practice Vocabulary

1. What was the first Spanish **colony** in the Americas?

2. How did the **Columbian Exchange** affect Europe and the Americas?

Critical Thinking and Writing

3. **Use Evidence** How did European expansion in the Americas affect American Indians?

4. **Compare and Contrast** How did the expeditions of Vasco Nuñez de Balboa and Ferdinand Magellan differ?

5. **Summarize** the career of Christopher Columbus.

6. **Draw Conclusions** Why were American Indians so susceptible to European diseases, such as influenza?

7. **Writing Workshop: Develop a Clear Thesis** You should now choose the invention or improvement for your paper. Write a thesis in your 📓 Active Journal in which you address the question: How did a travel-related invention or improvement in one of the societies covered in this topic impact people's lives?

Christopher Columbus, Diary

During his voyage across the Atlantic Ocean, Christopher Columbus recorded his thoughts. In these excerpts, you will see that Columbus was concerned about his crew.

▶ When Columbus returned to Europe from his first voyage, he gave his journal, written during the expedition, to Queen Isabella.

Sunday, 9 September. Sailed this day nineteen leagues ①, and determined to count less than the true number, that the crew might not be dismayed if the voyage should prove long. ② In the night sailed one hundred and twenty miles, at the rate of ten miles an hour, which make thirty leagues. The sailors steered badly, causing the vessels to fall to leeward toward the northeast, for which the Admiral reprimanded them repeatedly.

Monday, 10 September. This day and night sailed sixty leagues ③, at the rate of ten miles an hour, which are two leagues and a half. Reckoned only forty-eight leagues, that the men might not be terrified if they should be long upon the voyage. . . .

Thursday, 11 October. Steered west-southwest; and encountered a heavier sea than they had met with before in the whole voyage. Saw pardelas ④ and a green rush near the vessel. The crew of the Pinta saw a cane and a log; they also picked up a stick which appeared to have been carved with an iron tool, a piece of cane, a plant which grows on land, and a board. The crew of the Nina saw other signs of land, and a stalk loaded with rose berries. These signs encouraged them, and they all grew cheerful. ⑤

After sunset steered their original course west and sailed twelve miles an hour till two hours after midnight, going ninety miles, which are twenty-two leagues and a half; and as the Pinta was the swiftest sailer, and kept ahead of the Admiral, she discovered land and made the signals which had been ordered.

Analyzing Primary Sources

Cite specific evidence from the document to support your answers.

1. Why was it a problem that the sailors accidentally steered the ship toward the northeast?

2. How do you think Columbus's crew felt when they saw land, after more than two months at sea? Explain.

Reading and Vocabulary Support

① A *league* is a unit of measurement equal to about four miles.

② Why do you think Columbus wanted his crew to believe they had traveled fewer miles than they had?

③ How many miles is 60 leagues?

④ A *pardela* is a type of bird.

⑤ Why do you think the crew was encouraged by all the signs of land they had seen?

Quest CONNECTIONS

Do you believe Columbus's account of his journey? Do the details he provides give credibility to his account?

☑ Review and Assessment

VISUAL REVIEW

Life in the Northwest and Eastern Woodlands Regions

NORTHWEST REGION
- Built permanent villages
- Traded with nearby groups
- Held potlatches

Cut down trees to make houses

EASTERN WOODLANDS REGION
- Farmed land
- Grew corn, squash, and beans
- Settled near water

Trade in Africa and Eurasia

TRADE, TECHNOLOGY, AND EDUCATION IN AFRICA, EUROPE, AND ASIA

Technology	Education
• Advanced metal-forging techniques for toolmaking • Weaving techniques for patterned textiles • Teaching in mathematics, medicine, law, geography, history, and art at universities • Training in carpentry, fishing, and tailoring	• Techniques for making pottery, ceramics, glazes, glass, and lacquerware • Study in mathematics, medicine, and engineering; advances in irrigation techniques • Architectural domes and arches in buildings • Surgical instruments and techniques

READING REVIEW

Use the Take Notes and Practice Vocabulary activities in your Active Journal to review the topic.

👆 **INTERACTIVE**

Practice Vocabulary using the Topic Mini-Games.

Write Your Essay

Get help for writing your essay in your 📘 Active Journal.

ASSESSMENT

Vocabulary and Key Ideas

1. **List** What were the early **civilizations** of Central and South America?

2. **Define** What is a **city-state**?

3. **Describe** What are some ways that American Indian **tribes** interacted with one another?

4. **Describe** life for most people living under **feudalism**.

5. **Check Understanding** What happened during the **Renaissance**?

6. **Identify** Who founded the first Spanish **colony** in the Americas?

7. **Explain** How did the **Columbian Exchange** change the relationship between the Eastern and Western Hemispheres?

Critical Thinking and Writing

8. **Identify Supporting Details** How did the Maya and Aztec civilizations use science and math?

9. **Compare and Contrast** How did the physical environment of the Chipewyan and Carrier affect settlement patterns?

10. **Identify Cause and Effect** What was the impact of the Crusades on the trading relationship between Europe and the Middle East?

11. **Identify Main Ideas** What were the political, religious, and economic reasons for Spanish exploration of North America?

12. **Revisit the Essential Question** How much did geography affect the lives of American Indians and European explorers?

13. **Writer's Workshop: Write a Research Paper** Using the notes you made in your 📖 Active Journal, answer the following question in a research paper: How did a travel-related invention or improvement in one of the societies covered in this topic impact people's lives?

Analyze Primary Sources

14. How would you describe the people who Christopher Columbus met?
    A. suspicious
    B. friendly
    C. angry
    D. religious

"As I saw that they were very friendly to us, and perceived that they could be much more easily converted to our holy faith by gentle means than by force, I presented them with some red caps, and strings of beads to wear upon the neck, and many other trifles of small value, wherewith they were much delighted . . . Afterwards they came swimming to the boats, bringing parrots, balls of cotton thread, javelins, and many other things which they exchanged for articles we gave them, such as glass beads, and hawk's bells; which trade was carried on with the utmost good will."

—from the diary of Christopher Columbus

Analyze Maps

15. Which letter represents the route of Bartolomeu Dias?

16. Which letter represents the route of Vasco da Gama? How did it differ from that of Dias?

17. What was the easternmost point of da Gama's sea route?

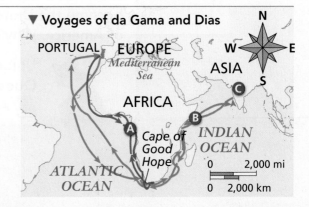

▼ Voyages of da Gama and Dias

European Colonization of North America (1500–1750)

GO ONLINE
to access your
digital course

▶ VIDEO

◀» AUDIO

📖 ETEXT

👆 INTERACTIVE

✎ WRITING

🎮 GAMES

📄 WORKSHEET

✓ ASSESSMENT

Go back five centuries

to the time of the **EUROPEAN COLONIZATION OF NORTH AMERICA**. Colonists from England came to North America for many reasons. Some wanted to practice their religions freely, while others were looking for economic opportunities or to start a new life.

Explore
The Essential Question

Why do people move?

North America is far from Europe. Despite this, about 400 years ago many people began to emigrate to the land that would one day become the United States of America. Why?

Unlock the Essential Question in your 📘 Active Journal.

◀ This engraving shows a busy seaport scene in Charleston.

Read

about the North American colonies and the people who lived and worked there.

Watch

VIDEO

Watch a video about the exploits of John Smith in North America.

European Colonization of North America (1500–1750)

Learn more about the British colonies in North America by making your own map and timeline in your 📓 Active Journal.

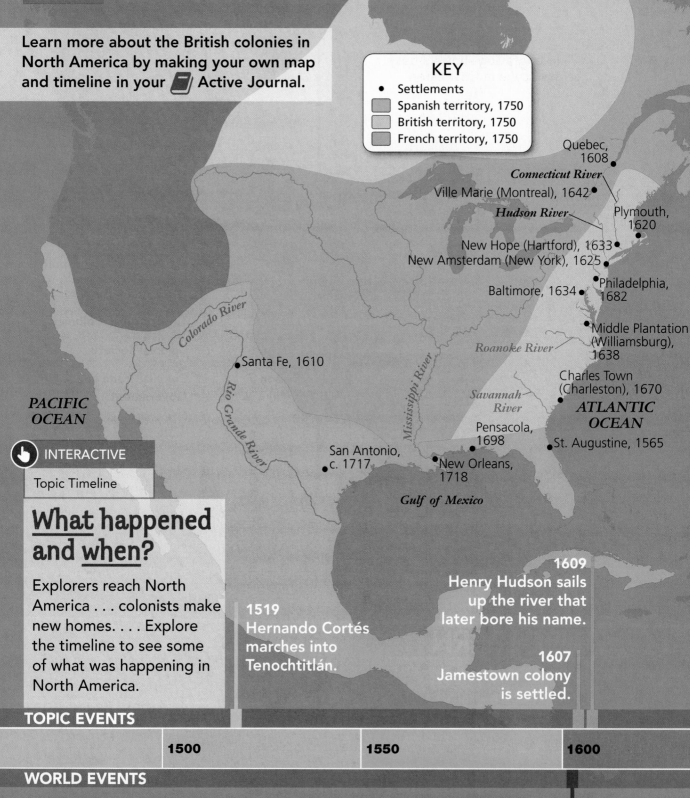

KEY
- • Settlements
- ▢ Spanish territory, 1750
- ▢ British territory, 1750
- ▢ French territory, 1750

Quebec, 1608

Connecticut River

Ville Marie (Montreal), 1642

Hudson River

Plymouth, 1620

New Hope (Hartford), 1633

New Amsterdam (New York), 1625

Baltimore, 1634

Philadelphia, 1682

Middle Plantation (Williamsburg), 1638

Roanoke River

Santa Fe, 1610

Charles Town (Charleston), 1670

Colorado River

Savannah River

Rio Grande River

Mississippi River

ATLANTIC OCEAN

PACIFIC OCEAN

Pensacola, 1698

St. Augustine, 1565

San Antonio, c. 1717

New Orleans, 1718

Gulf of Mexico

🖱 INTERACTIVE

Topic Timeline

What happened and when?

Explorers reach North America . . . colonists make new homes. . . . Explore the timeline to see some of what was happening in North America.

1519
Hernando Cortés marches into Tenochtitlán.

1609
Henry Hudson sails up the river that later bore his name.

1607
Jamestown colony is settled.

TOPIC EVENTS

1500	1550	1600

WORLD EVENTS

1602
Dutch merchants form the Dutch East India Company.

<u>Where</u> were the original British colonies?

These colonies, which later became the United States of America, were located on the East Coast of North America, along the Atlantic Ocean. Locate the British settlements on the map.

<u>Who will</u> you meet?

Anne Hutchinson, an outspoken believer in religious freedom

William Penn, who believed everybody was equal in God's sight

Benjamin Franklin, who used reason to improve the world around him

1620
The Pilgrims settle Plymouth colony.

1664
New Amsterdam is taken over by England and renamed New York.

1673
Father Jacques Marquette sails up the Mississippi River.

1681
William Penn founds Pennsylvania.

1712
The Carolinas split into North and South Carolina.

1650   1700   1750

1652
Dutch immigrants arrive in southern Africa.

1700
The French establish a fort in present-day Senegal.

1740
The population of China reaches 140 million.

53

Quest

Project-Based Learning Inquiry

Examining the Colonial Environment

Quest KICK OFF

The year is **1700**. You've just moved to one of the thirteen British colonies in North America and are looking to make a living. There are many possibilities! How do you decide what to do?

How did the environment influence the economy and population of the British colonies?

What impact did the environment have on the colonists who lived there? Explore the Essential Question "Why do people move?" in this Quest.

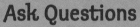

▲ Colonial silversmiths at work.

1 Ask Questions

The thirteen colonies were very diverse and had many different environments and natural resources. Get started by making a list of questions you'd like to ask to learn about the environments and natural resources of the colonies. Write the questions in your 📕 Active Journal.

2 Investigate

As you read the lessons in this topic, look for **Quest CONNECTIONS** that provide information on how the British colonists made a living. Capture notes in your 📕 Active Journal.

3 Conduct Research

Next explore primary sources from the colonial period. They'll help you learn more about how the colonists in North America lived. Capture notes in your 📕 Active Journal.

Quest FINDINGS

4 Create an ePortfolio

Assemble a digital portfolio with maps, graphs, charts, and/or models that describe how the physical environment of the colonies influenced economic activities and population distribution. This will help you determine what type of work you should do!

Spanish Colonization and New Spain

GET READY TO READ

START UP

Examine the image of Europeans meeting the Native American emperor Moctezuma. Why do you think they are wearing armor?

GUIDING QUESTIONS

- How did Spanish conquistadors defeat two American Indian empires?
- Why did Spain settle its colonies?
- What were the causes and effects of the transatlantic slave trade?

TAKE NOTES

Literacy Skills: Summarize

Use the graphic organizer in your 📕 Active Journal to take notes as you read the lesson.

PRACTICE VOCABULARY

Use the vocabulary activity in your 📕 Active Journal to practice the vocabulary words.

Vocabulary

conquistador   peninsular
pueblo   creole
presidio   mestizo
mission

Academic Vocabulary

shrewd
hesitate

"What a troublesome thing it is to discover new lands. The risks we took, it is hardly possible to exaggerate." Thus spoke Bernal Díaz del Castillo, one of the many Spanish **conquistadors** (kahn KEES tuh dorz), or conquerors, who marched into the Americas in the 1500s. When asked why they traveled to the Americas, Díaz responded, "We came here to serve God and the king and also to get rich."

Who Were the Conquistadors?

In their search for glory and gold, the conquistadors made Spain one of the richest nations in Europe. Spanish colonists followed the conquistadors and created a vast new empire in the Americas.

The rulers of Spain gave conquistadors permission to establish settlements. In return, conquistadors agreed to give Spain one fifth of any gold or treasure they captured.

Like other conquistadors, Hernando Cortés was eager to win riches and glory. He had heard rumors of a fabulously wealthy American Indian empire in Mexico. With only about 600 soldiers and 16 horses, Cortés set sail for Mexico in 1519 in search of gold.

Hernando Cortés kneels before the Aztec emperor Moctezuma. **Infer** What is the artist suggesting about this interaction between Moctezuma and Cortés?

The Spanish Destroy an Empire

Moctezuma (mok tuh ZOO muh), the Aztec emperor who ruled over much of Mexico, heard disturbing reports of a large house floating on the sea. It was filled with white men with long, thick beards. Aztec sacred writings predicted that a powerful white-skinned god would come from the east to rule the Aztec. The strangers were approaching Tenochtitlán (tay nawch teet LAHN), the Aztec capital, which is now Mexico City. Moctezuma decided to welcome them as his guests.

Cortés took advantage of Moctezuma's invitation. **Shrewdly**, Cortés had already begun to win the support of other Indians who resented Aztec rule.

One of his trusted advisers was an Indian woman the Spanish called Doña Marina. She gave Cortés valuable information about the Aztec and acted as a translator and negotiator. On November 8, 1519, Cortés marched into Tenochtitlán. The city was much larger than any Spanish city at that time. Thousands upon thousands of Aztecs turned out to see the astonishing newcomers riding horses. Díaz recalled:

Primary Source

"Who could count the multitude of men, women and children which had come out on the roofs, in their boats on the canals, or in the streets, to see us?"

—Bernal Díaz del Castillo, *True History of the Conquest of New Spain*

At first, Cortés was friendly to Moctezuma. Soon, however, he made the emperor a prisoner in his own city. Tensions mounted in Tenochtitlán over the next half year.

Finally, the Aztec drove out the Spanish. Their victory, however, was brief. Aided by people whom the Aztec had conquered, Cortés recaptured the city. In the end, the Spanish destroyed Tenochtitlán, and Moctezuma was killed. The Aztec empire had fallen.

The Inca Empire Falls

Another conquistador, Francisco Pizarro (pee SAHR oh), set his sights on the Incan empire. Pizarro sailed down the Pacific coast of South America with fewer than 200 Spanish soldiers.

Academic Vocabulary
shrewd • *adj.,* clever

In 1532, he captured the Incan emperor Atahualpa (ah tuh WAHL puh) and later executed him. Without the leadership of Atahualpa, Incan resistance collapsed. By 1535, Pizarro controlled much of the Incan empire.

Why the Spanish Won How were the Spanish able to conquer two great empires with only a handful of soldiers? First, the Spanish had superior military equipment. They were protected by steel armor and had guns. The Aztec and Inca relied on clubs, bows and arrows, and spears. Also, the Indians had never seen horses. They were frightened by mounted Spanish soldiers.

In addition, the American Indians did not fight as hard as they might have. The Aztec **hesitated** to attack at first because they thought the Spanish might be gods. Also, the Inca were weakened from fighting among themselves over control of their government.

Finally, many Indians died from European diseases, such as smallpox, measles, and influenza. Some historians believe that disease alone would have ensured Spanish victory over the Indians.

From the Spanish perspective, their interaction with the Aztec and the Inca resulted in great victories that brought wealth and power. The Spanish also saw the conquests as further proof of their natural superiority. The Aztec and Inca, of course, had a much different view of the same events. From their perspectives, the Spanish conquests were disasters that devastated their civilizations.

✓READING CHECK **Identify Supporting Details** What reasons can you identify that help explain why the Spanish conquered the Aztec and the Inca so easily?

Academic Vocabulary
hesitate • *v.*, to stop briefly because of nervousness

Analyze Images This 19th-century painting shows Pizarro capturing Atahualpa and slaughtering his followers. **Infer** Why did the artist include a Catholic friar in the scene?

Why Did the Spanish Explore Lands to the North?

The Spanish search for treasure reached beyond the lands of the Aztec and Inca. Moving north, conquistadors explored the Spanish borderlands. The borderlands spanned the present-day southern United States from Florida to California.

Juan Ponce de León (PAWN say day lay OHN) traveled through parts of Florida in 1513, looking for a legendary fountain of youth. Indians claimed that anyone who bathed in its magical water would remain young forever. Ponce de León found no such fountain.

An Expedition Proves Difficult Another explorer, Pánfilo Narváez (nahr VAH es), led an expedition that ended in disaster. In 1528, a storm struck his fleet in the Gulf of Mexico. Narváez and many others were lost at sea. The rest landed on an island in present-day Texas. Indians captured the few survivors and held them prisoner. Álvar Núñez Cabeza de Vaca (kah VAY suh day VAH kuh) assumed leadership of the small group.

Cabeza de Vaca, an enslaved African named Estevanico, and two others finally escaped their captors in 1533. The four walked across the plains of Texas, searching for a Spanish settlement. Finally, in 1536, they reached a town in Mexico. They had traveled by foot more than 1,000 miles through the Southwest.

The Search for Gold Continues From 1539 to 1542, Hernando de Soto explored Florida and other parts of the Southeast. In his search for gold, he reached the Mississippi River. De Soto died along the riverbank, without finding the riches he sought.

GEOGRAPHY SKILLS

Spanish explorers took several different routes through North America.

1. **Place** What impact might exploration of the Spanish borderlands have on the present-day United States?

2. **Use Visual Information** Which Spanish settlements on the map are still cities in the United States today?

Spanish Explorers and Settlements in North America

KEY
— Ponce de León, 1513
— Narváez/Cabeza de Vaca/ Estevanico, 1528–1536
— De Soto, 1539–1542
— Coronado, 1540–1547
▨ Spanish territory, 1530
⸸ Spanish missions, 1565–1776
● Other Spanish settlements, 1565–1776

0   500 mi
0   500 km
Lambert Azimuthal
Equal-Area Projection

The conquistador Francisco Coronado (koh roh NAH doh) heard legends about "seven cities of gold." In 1540, he led an expedition into the southwestern borderlands. He traveled to present-day Arizona and New Mexico. Some of his party went as far as the Grand Canyon. Still, the Zuni (ZOO nee) villages he visited had no golden streets.

The Spanish expeditions into the borderlands met with little success. Faced with strong Indian resistance in the north, Spain focused instead on bringing order to its empire in the south.

☑ READING CHECK Identify Cause and Effect What reasons did explorers have for traveling north?

Colonizing New Spain

The conquistadors set up colonies in many parts of the Americas. Spain had many reasons for colonization, or setting up colonies. One was the search for wealth. Settlements provided bases from which expeditions could set out in search of gold. Settlements could also create wealth through farming and trade. A second important reason for settlement was to spread Christianity by converting native peoples. A third reason was to satisfy a thirst for adventure and exploration. Sometimes, historians summarize the Spanish exploration and settlement of the Americas as motivated by "Gold, God, and Glory." Thousands of Spanish immigrants moved to Spanish settlements looking for opportunities the colonies offered, especially farming.

▲ Mission San Francisco de la Espada in San Antonio, Texas, was one of Spain's many religious settlements in the Americas. **Use Visual Information** What features do you see that distinguish this mission from a pueblo and a presidio?

At first, Spain let the conquistadors govern the lands they conquered. When the conquistadors proved to be poor rulers, the Spanish king took away their authority. He then set up a strong system of government to rule his growing empire. In 1535, he divided his American lands into New Spain and Peru. The northern borderlands were part of New Spain. The king put a viceroy in charge of each region to rule in his name.

A set of laws called the Laws of the Indies stated how the colonies should be organized and ruled. The laws provided for three kinds of settlements in New Spain: pueblos, presidios (prih SID ee ohz), and missions. Some large communities included all three.

Spanish Settlements Spain established many settlements in the Americas. Many of these Spanish settlements were built in a similar pattern. The **pueblos**, or towns, were centers of farming and trade. In the middle of the town was a plaza, or public square. Here, townspeople and farmers came to do business or worship at the church. Shops and homes lined the four sides of the plaza.

Spanish Territories in the Americas

KEY

Spanish territories, about 1750

40°N

20°N

St. Augustine

West Indies

Mexico City

Viceroyalty of New Spain

Caribbean Sea

EQUATOR

0°

PACIFIC OCEAN

N

Lima

Viceroyalty of Peru

Brazil

ATLANTIC OCEAN

W E

S

0   2,000 mi

0   2,000 km

Lambert Equal-Area Projection

Valparaiso

180°W

60°W

0°

20°S

40°S

160°E   160°W   140°W   120°W   100°W   80°W   60°W   40°W   20°W   0°   60°E

GEOGRAPHY SKILLS

Spanish territory covered Central America, part of North America, and much of the Caribbean islands and South America.

1. **Region** Into what two regions did Spain divide the lands it claimed in the western hemisphere?

2. **Infer** What language do you think is still spoken today in many of the countries that were claimed by Spain from the 1500s to 1750?

The Spanish took control of Indian pueblos and built new towns as well. In 1598, Juan de Oñate (oh NYAH tay) founded the colony of New Mexico among the adobe villages of the Pueblo Indians. He used brutal force to conquer the American Indians of the region. Don Pedro de Peralta later founded Santa Fe as the Spanish capital of New Mexico.

Presidios were forts where soldiers lived. Inside the high, thick walls were shops, stables, and storehouses for food. Soldiers protected the farmers who settled nearby. The first presidio in the borderlands was built in 1565 at St. Augustine, Florida. St. Augustine was the first permanent European settlement in what would become the United States. Its founding marked the beginning of the era of colonization in the future territory of the United States, which would continue until the United States declared independence in 1776.

The Legacy of Missions Like other Europeans in the Americas, the Spanish believed they had a duty to convert Indians to Christianity. They set up **missions**, settlements run by Catholic priests and friars whose goal was to convert Indians to Christianity. They often forced Indians to live and work on the missions.

In New Mexico, the Spanish tried to destroy any trace of traditional Pueblo Indians' religious practices and subjected them to severe punishments. This resulted in the Pueblo Revolt of 1680. The Pueblo Indians rose up against Spanish rule. They killed about 400 Spaniards and drove the others out of the region. The Spanish recaptured the region in the mid-1690s.

Missions gradually spread across the Spanish borderlands. The first mission in Texas was founded in 1659 at El Paso.

In 1691, Father Eusebio Francisco Kino (KEE noh) crossed into present-day Arizona. He eventually set up 24 missions in the area. The missions were a direct result of early Spanish colonization efforts. Over time, they had a significant impact in the Americas. By the late 1700s, a string of missions dotted the California coast from San Diego to San Francisco, and Spanish language and culture gradually spread with them.

INTERACTIVE

Social Classes in New Spain

☑ READING CHECK **Understand Effects** What do you think the long-term impact of Spanish colonization has been on the religion and language of Central and South America?

How Was Society Organized in New Spain?

The Laws of the Indies also set up a strict social system. People in Spanish colonies were divided into four social classes: peninsulares (puh NIN suh LAH rayz), creoles (KREE ohlz), mestizos (mes TEE sohz), and Indians.

Different Social Classes At the top of the social scale were the **peninsulares**. Born in Spain, peninsulares held the highest jobs in government and the Church. They also owned large tracts of land as well as rich gold and silver mines.

Below the peninsulares were the **creoles**, people born in the Americas to parents of Spanish origin. Many creoles were wealthy and well educated. They owned farms and ranches, taught at universities, and practiced law. However, they could not hold the jobs that were reserved for peninsulares.

Below the creoles were people of mixed Spanish and Indian background, known as **mestizos**. Mestizos worked on farms and ranches owned by peninsulares and creoles. In the cities, they worked as carpenters, shoemakers, tailors, and bakers. Over the course of Spanish colonization, mestizos came to be the largest class of people.

The lowest class in the colonies was the Indians. In the early years of Spanish colonization, Indians were the largest class. The Spanish treated them as a conquered people. Under New Spain's strict social system, Indians were kept in poverty for hundreds of years.

A Blend of Spanish and Indian Cultures The effects of colonization can be seen in the new way of life in New Spain that blended Spanish and Indian ways. Spanish settlers brought their own culture to the colonies. They introduced their language, laws, religion, and learning. In 1551, the Spanish founded the University of Mexico.

▼ Penisulares and their children, called creoles, occupied a higher position in society than Indians.

▲ The Spanish made beautiful jewelry and objects, such as this crucifix, out of the gold they mined in the Americas.

American Indians also influenced the culture of New Spain. Colonists adopted Indian foods, such as corn, tomatoes, potatoes, and squash. Indian workers used materials they knew well, such as adobe bricks, to build fine libraries, theaters, and churches. Sometimes, Indian artists decorated church walls with paintings of local traditions.

Harsh Treatment of American Indians

Spanish colonists needed workers for their ranches, farms, and mines. To help them, the Spanish government gave settlers encomiendas (en koh mee EN dahz), land grants that included the right to demand labor or taxes from American Indians.

Mines in Mexico, Peru, and other parts of the Americas made Spain rich. Treasure ships laden with thousands of tons of gold and silver sailed regularly across the Atlantic.

The Spanish forced American Indians to work in the gold and silver mines. In flickering light, Indians hacked out rich ores in narrow, dark tunnels. Many died when tunnels caved in.

These harsh conditions led one priest, Bartolomé de Las Casas (day lahs KAH sahs), to seek reform. Traveling through New Spain, Las Casas witnessed firsthand the deaths of Indians due to hunger, disease, and mistreatment. What he saw horrified him:

Primary Source

"The Indians were totally deprived of their freedom. . . . Even beasts enjoy more freedom when they are allowed to graze in the field."

—Bartolomé de Las Casas, *Tears of the Indians*

Many Spanish in New Spain did not share Las Casas's view or his values. So, he journeyed to Europe and asked the king of Spain to protect the Indians' civil rights. In the 1540s, the royal government passed laws prohibiting the enslavement of American Indians. The laws also allowed Indians to own cattle and grow crops. However, few officials in New Spain enforced the new laws or took the time to think about Indians' basic human needs.

☑ READING CHECK **Identify Supporting Details** What were some ways in which peninsulares were powerful?

The Transatlantic Slave Trade

The death toll among American Indians continued to rise. Faced with a severe shortage of workers, Spanish colonists looked across the Atlantic Ocean for a new source of labor.

Reasons for the Slave Trade Still seeking to protect American Indians, Bartolomé de Las Casas made a suggestion that had a lasting, tragic impact. His idea was that Africans be brought as slaves to replace forced Indian laborers. Las Casas argued that Africans were less likely to die from European diseases. He also claimed that Africans would suffer less because they were used to doing hard farm work in their homelands.

Las Casas's arguments encouraged the Atlantic slave trade, or the trade of enslaved Africans across the Atlantic to the Americas. In many parts of Africa, slavery had existed for centuries. Often, war prisoners were enslaved. Eventually, these enslaved people or their children might gain freedom. After the Americas were colonized, though, some Africans began to capture and enslave people and sell them to European traders. The traders then shipped the enslaved men, women, and children to the Americas. Most Africans who settled in the Americas did so against their will.

By the time he died, Las Casas had come to regret his suggestion. He saw that enslaved Africans suffered as much as the Indians. By that time, however, it was too late to undo the damage. Slavery had become a key part of the colonial economy.

Slave Trade Expansion Demand for African labor grew rapidly, mainly in the West Indies—including what are now Cuba, the Dominican Republic, and Puerto Rico—and in other parts of the Americas.

Analyze Charts Enslaved Africans were shipped to destinations in Europe, Asia, and the Americas. **Use Visual Information** Which region received the fewest enslaved Africans? Which received the most?

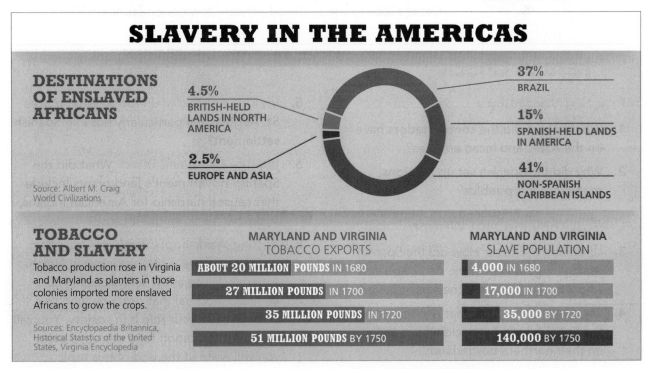

SLAVERY IN THE AMERICAS

DESTINATIONS OF ENSLAVED AFRICANS

4.5%
BRITISH-HELD LANDS IN NORTH AMERICA

2.5%
EUROPE AND ASIA

37%
BRAZIL

15%
SPANISH-HELD LANDS IN AMERICA

41%
NON-SPANISH CARIBBEAN ISLANDS

Source: Albert M. Craig
World Civilizations

TOBACCO AND SLAVERY

Tobacco production rose in Virginia and Maryland as planters in those colonies imported more enslaved Africans to grow the crops.

Sources: Encyclopaedia Britannica, Historical Statistics of the United States, Virginia Encyclopedia

MARYLAND AND VIRGINIA
TOBACCO EXPORTS

ABOUT 20 MILLION POUNDS IN 1680

27 MILLION POUNDS IN 1700

35 MILLION POUNDS IN 1720

51 MILLION POUNDS BY 1750

MARYLAND AND VIRGINIA
SLAVE POPULATION

4,000 IN 1680

17,000 IN 1700

35,000 BY 1720

140,000 BY 1750

Analyze Images Enslaved Africans search a river in Brazil for gold. **Use Visual Information** Who do you think the man on the right side of the image is?

Enslaved Africans were especially valued on sugar plantations in the West Indies and in the Portuguese colony of Brazil. A plantation is a large estate farmed by many workers. Sugar could not be grown on small estates because it required too much land and labor. Enslaved Africans often worked all through the night cutting sugar, which was then sold in Europe for a large profit.

Some scholars estimate that Europeans transported more than 10 million enslaved Africans across the Atlantic Ocean to the Americas between the 1500s and the 1800s. The vast majority came from West Africa.

☑ READING CHECK **Draw Conclusions** Why did Bartolomé de Las Casas's idea to use enslaved Africans to work on farms backfire?

☑ Lesson Check

Practice Vocabulary

1. What impact did the **conquistadors** have on the Aztec and Incan empires?

2. Why did the Spanish set up **missions, presidios,** and **pueblos**?

Critical Thinking and Writing

3. **Understand Effects** How did the Spanish search for gold impact the Aztec and Inca who were living in the Americas at the time?

4. **Identify Main Ideas** What two reasons did the Spanish have for deciding not to focus on their northern borderlands?

5. **Identify Implied Main Ideas** What makes St. Augustine a particularly notable Spanish settlement?

6. **Identify Cause and Effect** What did the Spanish government's land grants include that caused hardship for American Indians, and what hardship did it cause?

7. **Writing Workshop: Introduce Characters** Imagine you are a colonist living in North America. Write a few sentences in your 📓 Active Journal that describe who you are and what your role is in society. You will use this information for a narrative essay you will write at the end of this topic.

Bartolomé de Las Casas, *Historia Apológetica*

Bartolomé de Las Casas was a Spanish historian and writer who traveled to the island of Hispaniola 10 years after Christopher Columbus discovered it. He spent much of the next 20 years there, and in 1527 he wrote the *Historia Apológetica*, or Apologetic History. At the time, many Europeans felt the people of the Indies were not advanced. Las Casas disagreed.

▶ *Historia Apológetica* was one of many books Bartolomé de Las Casas wrote about the Indians.

The ultimate cause for writing this work was to gain knowledge of all the many nations of this vast new world. <u>They had been defamed by persons who feared neither God nor the charge, so grievous before divine judgment, of defaming even a single man and causing him to lose his esteem and honor.</u> ① From such slander can come great harm and terrible calamity, particularly when large numbers of men are concerned and, even more so, a whole new <u>world</u>. ② It has been written that these peoples of the Indies, lacking human governance and ordered nations, did not have the power of reason to govern themselves. . . . From this it follows that they have all proven themselves unsocial and therefore monstrous, contrary to the natural bent of all peoples of the world; and that He did not allow any other species of corruptible creature to err in this way, excepting a strange and occasional <u>case</u>. . . . ③

Not only have [the Indians] shown themselves to be very wise peoples and possessed of lively and marked understanding, prudently governing and providing for their nations (as much as they can be nations, without faith in or knowledge of the true God) and making them prosper in justice; but they have equalled many diverse nations of the world, past and present, that have been praised for their governance, politics and customs; and exceed by no small measure the wisest of all these, such as the Greeks and Romans, in adherence to the rules of natural <u>reason</u>. ④ This advantage and superiority, along with everything said above, will appear quite clearly when, if it please God, the peoples are compared one with another.

Reading and Vocabulary Support

① Las Casas says that the Spaniards had damaged the reputation of the Indians, ignoring God's wishes.

② What calamity do you think Las Casas might have been writing about?

③ Las Casas is summarizing the argument that Indians were monstrous and that God didn't usually allow this to happen to people.

④ Las Casas argues that Indians follow the laws of reason as much as any civilization has.

Analyzing Primary Sources

Cite specific evidence from the document to support your answers.

1. **Infer** What is Bartolomé de Las Casas's overall opinion of the people of the Indies?

2. **Draw Conclusions** What reason does Bartolomé de Las Casas give to suggest that the people of the Indies might not have a true nation?

The First French, Dutch, and English Colonies

BOUNCE TO ACTIVATE   ▶ VIDEO

GET READY TO READ

START UP

Study the engraving. How was shipping important for European colonization?

GUIDING QUESTIONS

- Why did Europeans explore North America's coast?
- Why did the French, Dutch, and English colonize North America?
- How did Virginia begin a tradition of representative government?
- In what ways did different groups in Jamestown interact with the environment?

TAKE NOTES

Literacy Skills: Sequence
Use the graphic organizer in your 📕 Active Journal to take notes as you read the lesson.

PRACTICE VOCABULARY

Use the vocabulary words in your 📕 Active Journal to practice the vocabulary words.

Vocabulary

northwest passage
coureurs de bois
alliance
charter
burgess

representative government
Bacon's Rebellion

Academic Vocabulary

pioneer
signify

European nations began to compete for riches around the world. Religious differences heightened their rivalry. Soon, there were competing religious views.

How Did European Rivalries Affect Exploration?

Until the 1500s, the Roman Catholic Church was the only church in Western Europe. That unity ended when a major religious reform movement sharply divided Christians.

Religious Reform In 1517, a German monk named Martin Luther publicly challenged many practices of the Catholic Church. Soon after, he split with the Church entirely. Luther believed that the Church had become too worldly. He opposed the power of popes. He also objected to the idea that believers could gain eternal life by performing good works. He said people were saved by faith in God.

Because of their protests against the Church, Luther's supporters became known as Protestants. The Protestant Reformation divided Europe. Soon, the Protestants themselves split, forming many different churches.

By the late 1500s, religion divided the states of Western Europe. Roman Catholic monarchs ruled Spain and France. A Protestant queen, Elizabeth I, ruled England. In the Netherlands, the Dutch people were mostly Protestant.

Religious Difference Leads to Rivalries As Europeans settled in the Americas, they brought their religious conflicts with them. Queen Elizabeth encouraged English adventurers to raid Spanish colonies and capture Spanish treasure fleets. Protestant England also competed with Catholic France for lands in North America.

Not all rivalries were religious. Both the Netherlands and England were Protestant. Still, they competed for control of land in North America and for economic markets all over the world, including Asia.

Reasons for the Exploration of North America Like Columbus, other Europeans continued during the 1500s to look for new ways to reach the riches of Asia. Magellan's route around South America seemed long and difficult. Europeans wanted to discover a shorter **northwest passage**, or waterway through or around North America.

Giovanni Caboto, an Italian sea captain whom the English called John Cabot, set out to find a northwest passage for the English. He was confident he had found such a passage, but he was mistaken. The "new-found land" that he thought he had discovered off the Asian coast in fact lay off the coast of North America. Today, Newfoundland is part of the easternmost province of Canada.

French Exploration The French sent another Italian captain, Giovanni da Verrazano (vehr rah TSAH noh), in search of a northwest passage. Verrazano journeyed along the North American coast from the present-day Carolinas to Canada. During the 1530s, Jacques Cartier (kar tee YAY), also sailing for the French, traveled more than halfway up the St. Lawrence River.

Mapping New Regions None of these explorers found a northwest passage to Asia. However, they did map and explore many parts of North America. The rulers of Western Europe began thinking about how to profit from the region's rich resources through colonization.

☑ READING CHECK **Use Evidence** What factors contributed to rivalries between English and Spanish explorers?

Analyze Images In his *Ninety-five Theses*, Martin Luther listed disagreements he had with the Catholic Church. **Identify Main Ideas** What was the political significance of the Protestant Reformation?

How Did New France Develop?

Samuel de Champlain (sham PLAYN) founded Port Royal, the first permanent French settlement in North America, in 1605. Three years later, he led another group of settlers along the route Cartier had **pioneered**. On a rocky cliff high above the St. Lawrence River, Champlain built a trading post known as Quebec (kwih BEK). The opportunity to create wealth through trade was one of the main reasons for French colonization in America. The French also wanted to surpass their rivals, the English. Many French settlers were looking for adventure and hoped to find their fortune in the New World.

Economic Activity in New France Unlike Spain's American empire, New France had little gold or silver. Instead, the French profited from fishing, trapping, and trading.

French colonists who lived and worked in American Indian lands beyond the French settlements became known as ***coureurs de bois*** (koo RUHR duh BWAH), or "runners of the woods." The French brought knives, kettles, cloth, and other items for trade with American Indians. In return, the Indians gave them beaver skins and other furs that sold for high prices in Europe.

Coureurs de bois established friendly relations with American Indian groups. Unlike the Spanish, the French did not attempt to conquer the Indians. Also, because *coureurs de bois* did not establish farms, they did not interfere with Indian lands. Indians taught the French trapping and survival skills, such as how to make snowshoes and canoes. Many *coureurs* married Indian women.

Academic Vocabulary

pioneer • *v.*, to develop or to be the first to do something

GEOGRAPHY **SKILLS**

Explorers from Europe took different routes to North America.

1. **Interaction** Why might you expect conflict to develop between the French and the English in North America?

2. **Infer** What might have motivated French explorers to search the interior of North America as they looked for a northwest passage?

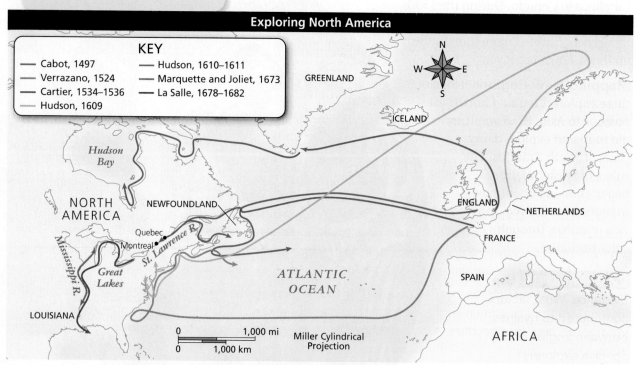

Exploring North America

KEY
— Cabot, 1497
— Verrazano, 1524
— Cartier, 1534–1536
— Hudson, 1609
— Hudson, 1610–1611
— Marquette and Joliet, 1673
— La Salle, 1678–1682

GREENLAND

ICELAND

Hudson Bay

NORTH AMERICA

NEWFOUNDLAND

Quebec
Montreal
St. Lawrence R.

Great Lakes

Mississippi R.

LOUISIANA

ATLANTIC OCEAN

ENGLAND

NETHERLANDS

FRANCE

SPAIN

AFRICA

0   1,000 mi
0   1,000 km

Miller Cylindrical Projection

Missionary Work Continues Catholic missionaries often traveled with fur traders. A missionary is a person who goes to another land to win converts for a religion. French missionaries tried to convert American Indians to Christianity. They also drew maps and wrote about the lands they explored.

Life was difficult, especially in winter. One French priest recalled traveling on foot through deep snow:

Primary Source

"If a thaw came, dear Lord, what pain! . . .
I was marching on an icy path that broke
with every step I took; as the snow softened . . .
we often sunk [sank] in it up to our . . . waist."

—Paul Le Jeune, quoted in *The Jesuits in North America*

Analyze Images American Indians brought furs to trappers in exchange for goods like knives, kettles, and cloth. **Infer** Why did Indians buy knives and kettles from Europeans?

Colonization Along the Mississippi River French trappers followed the St. Lawrence deep into the heart of North America. Led by Indian guides, they reached the Great Lakes. Here, Indians spoke of a mighty river, which they called Mississippi, or "Father of the Waters."

A French missionary, Father Jacques Marquette (mar KET), and a fur trader, Louis Joliet (joh lee ET), set out to reach the Mississippi in 1673. Led by Indian guides, they followed the river for more than 700 miles before turning back. Nine years later, Robert de La Salle completed the journey to the Gulf of Mexico. La Salle named the region Louisiana in honor of the French king, Louis XIV.

To keep Spain and England out of Louisiana, the French built forts in the north along the Great Lakes. Among them was Fort Detroit, built by Antoine de la Mothe Cadillac near Lake Erie. The French also built New Orleans, a fort near the mouth of the river. New Orleans grew into a busy trading center. French control of the network of waterways at the heart of North America gave the French a strategic advantage over the Spanish and the English.

French colonists imported thousands of Africans to work as slaves on plantations around New Orleans. Some enslaved Africans, however, joined with the Natchez Indians in a revolt against the French. The French put down the Natchez Revolt in 1729. Some enslaved Africans who fought on the side of the French received their freedom. In Louisiana, free and enslaved Africans together made up the majority of settlers.

Government in New France New France was governed much like New Spain. The French king controlled the government directly, and people had little freedom. A council appointed by the king made all decisions.

Did you know?

The Cadillac automobile, which was first built in Detroit, Michigan, is named in honor of Antoine de la Mothe Cadillac, explorer, trapper, and trader.

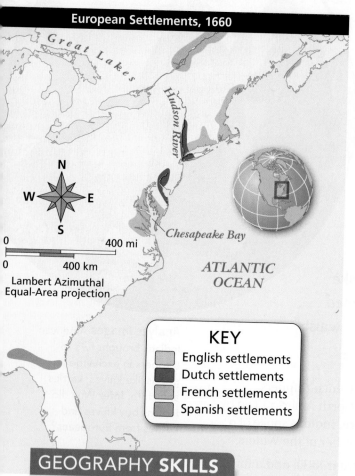

European Settlements, 1660

Great Lakes

Hudson River

Chesapeake Bay

ATLANTIC OCEAN

N · W · E · S

0 — 400 mi
0 — 400 km
Lambert Azimuthal
Equal-Area projection

KEY
- English settlements
- Dutch settlements
- French settlements
- Spanish settlements

GEOGRAPHY SKILLS

Four European colonial powers planted settlements in eastern North America.

1. **Movement** What form of transport does the map suggest the settlers relied on?

2. **Draw Conclusions** Based on the map, where would you expect each country's settlements to expand next? Why?

Louis XIV worried that too few French were moving to New France. In the 1660s, he sent about a thousand people to the colony, including many young women. New France still grew slowly. Winters were harsh, and the short growing season made farming difficult. Only about 10,000 settlers lived in the colony by 1680. Some lived on farms, while others chose to become *coureurs de bois*, living largely free of government control.

✓ **READING CHECK** **Summarize** How did both the French and American Indians benefit from one another?

Where Did the Dutch Establish New Netherland?

Like the French, the Dutch hoped to profit from their discoveries in the Americas by colonizing. In 1626, Peter Minuit (MIN yoo wit) led a group of Dutch settlers to the mouth of the Hudson River. Other Dutch colonists had already settled on Manhattan Island and farther up the Hudson River. Minuit bought Manhattan Island from local Indians. Minuit called his settlement New Amsterdam. The entire colony was known as New Netherland (now known as New York).

New Netherland was privately funded by the Dutch West India Company. Many colonists immigrated to New Netherland hoping to profit from the region's active fur trade.

From a tiny group of 30 houses, New Amsterdam grew into a busy port. The Dutch welcomed people of many nations, ethnic groups, and religions to their colony. A Roman Catholic priest who visited New Netherland in 1643 reported:

Primary Source

"On the island of Manhattan, and in its environs, there may well be four or five hundred men of different sects and nations: the Director General told me that there were men of eighteen different languages; they are scattered here and there on the river, above and below, as the beauty and convenience of the spot has invited each to settle."

—Father Isaac Jogues, quoted in *Narratives of New Netherland, 1609–1664*

The Dutch also built trading posts along the Hudson River. The most important one was Fort Orange, today known as Albany. Dutch merchants became known for their good business sense.

The Dutch enlarged New Netherland in 1655 by taking over the colony of New Sweden. The Swedes had established New Sweden along the Delaware River some 15 years earlier.

Trade Rivalries in the Region Dutch traders sent furs to the Netherlands. The packing list for the first shipment included "the skins of 7,246 beaver, 853 otter, 81 mink, 36 cat lynx, and 34 small rats."

The Dutch and French became rivals in the fur trade. Both sought alliances with American Indians. An **alliance** is an agreement between nations to aid and protect one another. The Dutch made friends with the Iroquois. The Huron (HYOO rahn) helped the French. Fighting raged for years among the rival Europeans and their American Indian allies.

Interaction With American Indians and the Environment Dutch and French settlement on the east coast of North America brought major changes to American Indians and the environment. As in New Spain, European diseases killed thousands of Indians, and rivalry over the fur trade increased among different European countries' American Indian allies. The scramble for furs also led to overtrapping. By 1640, trappers had almost wiped out the beavers on Iroquois lands in upstate New York.

The arrival of Europeans affected American Indians in other ways. Missionaries tried to convert Indians to Christianity. Indians eagerly adopted European trade goods, such as copper kettles and knives. They also bought muskets and gunpowder for hunting and warfare. Alcohol sold by European traders had a harsh effect on American Indian life.

INTERACTIVE

Lands Controlled by Colonial Powers, 1660

▼ The island of Manhattan, which Peter Minuit purchased from local Indians, eventually became one of the most valuable pieces of land in the United States.

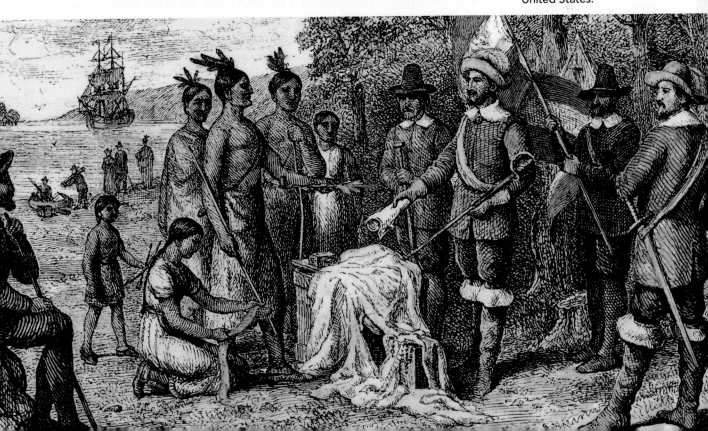

Europeans all waged warfare to seize Indian lands. As American Indians were forced off their lands, they moved westward onto lands of other Indians, which sometimes led to violence between Indian groups. The conflicts between American Indians and Europeans would continue for many years.

☑ **READING CHECK** Recognize Multiple Causes What were some results of the Dutch fur trade?

INTERACTIVE

The Early Years at Jamestown

Roanoke and Jamestown

England watched with envy as other European countries gained riches from their colonies in the Americas. Several ambitious English gentlemen proposed that England settle the Americas as well. With Queen Elizabeth's permission, Sir Walter Raleigh raised money to establish a colony in North America. In 1585, about 100 men set sail across the Atlantic. The colonists landed on Roanoke (ROH uh nohk), an island off the coast of present-day North Carolina. Within a year, however, the colonists had run short of food and were quarreling with neighboring American Indians. When an English ship stopped in the harbor, the weary settlers sailed home.

In 1587, Raleigh sent John White, one of the original colonists, back to Roanoke with a new group of settlers that included women and children. When supplies ran low, White returned to England, leaving behind 117 colonists. He planned to return in a few months. When he got back to England, however, he found the country was preparing for war with Spain. It was three years before he sailed back to Roanoke.

When White arrived, he found the settlement strangely quiet. Houses stood empty. Vines wound through the windows, and pumpkins sprouted from the earthen floors. On a tree, someone had carved the word CROATOAN, the name of a nearby island. No other trace of the colonists remained. White was eager to investigate, but a storm was blowing up and his crew refused to make the trip. To this day, the fate of the "Lost Colony" remains a mystery.

Analyze Images Archaeologists work on the ruins of James Fort at Jamestown. **Explain an Argument** What are the reasons for excavating James Fort?

Virginia

Jamestown Island

Jamestown Colony

James R.

Chesapeake Bay

ATLANTIC OCEAN

N
W   E
S

0   20 mi
0   20 km
Lambert Azimuthal
Equidistant projection

GEOGRAPHY SKILLS

The Jamestown colonists first settled upriver from the Chesapeake Bay.

1. **Location** Why might the colonists of Jamestown have chosen the location they did?

2. **Explain an Argument** What advantages and disadvantages are there to building a settlement near a river?

The Founding of Jamestown After the failure of Roanoke, nearly 20 years passed before England again tried to establish a colony in North America. In 1606, the Virginia Company of London, a private company, received a charter from King James I. A **charter** is a legal document giving certain rights to a person or company.

The royal charter gave the Virginia Company the right to settle lands along the eastern coast of North America. The charter also guaranteed that colonists of this land, called Virginia, would have the same rights as English citizens.

In the spring of 1607, a group of 105 colonists, funded by the Virginia Company, arrived in Virginia. They sailed into Chesapeake Bay and began building houses along the James River. They named their tiny outpost Jamestown after their king. Jamestown was the first permanent English settlement in what is now the United States.

Reasons for Colonization The settlers of Jamestown hoped to make a profit by finding gold or other riches. They also hoped to discover a water route to Asia. Furthermore, they wanted to claim the region for England.

One of the reasons they chose this particular location was security: they located their settlement in a place where Spanish ships would be unlikely to find them. If the Spanish did discover Jamestown, its location would make it more easily defensible against Spanish ships.

Governing the colony proved difficult. The Virginia Company had chosen a council of 13 men to rule the settlement. Members of the council quarreled with one another and did little to plan for the colony's future. By the summer of 1608, the colony was near failure.

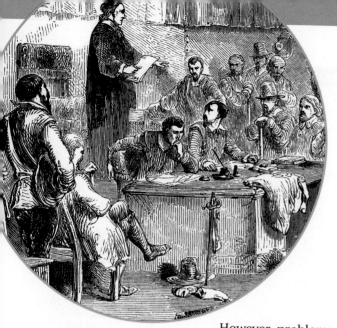

The Colonists Face Difficulties Another major problem the Jamestown colonists faced was starvation. Many colonists were not used to living in the wilderness and did not know how to take advantage of the plentiful resources. Furthermore, the colonists did not spend enough time producing food. Captain John Smith, a young soldier and explorer, observed that the colonists were not planting enough crops. He complained that people wanted only to "dig gold, wash gold, refine gold, load gold." As they searched in vain for gold, the colony ran out of food. Smith helped to save the colony. He set up stern rules that forced colonists to work if they wished to eat.

Analyze Images The House of Burgesses in Jamestown, Virginia, was the first elected legislative assembly in the English colonies. **Infer** How was government in the English colonies different from that in the Spanish or French colonies?

However, problems arose soon after John Smith returned to England in 1609. Desperate settlers cooked "dogs, cats, snakes, [and] toadstools" to survive. To keep warm, they broke up houses to burn as firewood. The colonists gradually learned to use the resources available in their environment to survive.

Tobacco Crops Help Jamestown's economy finally improved after 1612, when colonists began growing tobacco. Europeans had learned about tobacco from American Indians.

King James called pipe smoking "a vile custom." Still, the new fad caught on quickly. By 1620, England was importing more than 30,000 pounds of tobacco a year. At last, Virginians had found a way to make their colony succeed.

English immigrants to Virginia interacted with their environment by cutting down forests and planting the land with tobacco. Their interaction with the environment was different from that of other groups of immigrants to North America, such as the Dutch and the French, whose trading activity led to the near elimination of beaver populations in some areas.

✅READING CHECK **Draw Conclusions** What do you think could have happened to the Jamestown colonists had John Smith not forced them to work if they wished to eat?

How Did Colonists Improve Government?

For a time, the governors sent by the Virginia Company ran the colony like a military outpost. Each morning, a drumbeat summoned settlers to work at assigned tasks. Harsh laws imposed the death penalty even for small offenses, like stealing an ear of corn. Such conditions were unlikely to attract new colonists. As John Smith commented after his return to England, "No Man will go . . . to have less freedom there than here."

The House of Burgesses To attract more settlers, the Virginia Company took steps to establish a more stable government. In 1619, it sent a new governor with orders to consult settlers on all important matters. Male settlers were allowed to elect **burgesses**, or representatives to the government.

The burgesses met in an assembly called the House of Burgesses. Together with the governor and his council, they made laws for the colony. The first session met in July and August 1619.

The House of Burgesses **signifies** the beginning of representative government in the English colonies. In a **representative government**, voters elect representatives to make laws for them.

Political Rights and Responsibilities The idea that people had political rights was deeply rooted in English history. In 1215, English nobles had forced King John to sign the Magna Carta, or the Great Charter. This document said that the king could not raise taxes without first consulting a Great Council of nobles and church leaders. Over time, the rights won by nobles were extended to other people.

The Great Council grew into a representative assembly called Parliament. Parliament was divided into the House of Lords, made up of nobles, and an elected House of Commons. Only rich men had the right to vote, but now even monarchs had to obey the law.

Some Virginia Settlers Can Vote At first, free Virginians had even greater rights than citizens in England. They did not have to own property in order to vote. In 1670, however, the colony restricted the vote to free, white, male property owners.

Despite these limits, representative government remained important. The idea took root that settlers should have a say in the affairs of the colony. Colonists came to refer to the Virginia Company's 1619 frame of government as their own "Great Charter."

☑ READING CHECK **Identify Main Ideas** Why was the House of Burgesses created in Virginia?

Academic Vocabulary

signify • v., to indicate or be a sign of

Analyze Charts The population of the English colonies in America included a variety of European ethnic groups. **Draw Conclusions** What might account for the dramatic increase in the African American population of the Southern Colonies between 1700 and 1775?

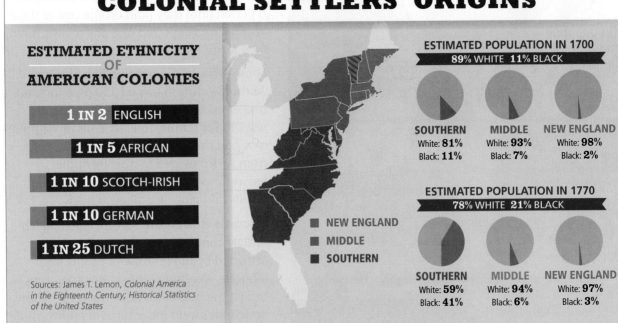

COLONIAL SETTLERS' ORIGINS

ESTIMATED ETHNICITY OF AMERICAN COLONIES

- **1 IN 2** ENGLISH
- **1 IN 5** AFRICAN
- **1 IN 10** SCOTCH-IRISH
- **1 IN 10** GERMAN
- **1 IN 25** DUTCH

Sources: James T. Lemon, *Colonial America in the Eighteenth Century; Historical Statistics of the United States*

- NEW ENGLAND
- MIDDLE
- SOUTHERN

ESTIMATED POPULATION IN 1700
89% WHITE 11% BLACK

SOUTHERN
White: **81%**
Black: **11%**

MIDDLE
White: **93%**
Black: **7%**

NEW ENGLAND
White: **98%**
Black: **2%**

ESTIMATED POPULATION IN 1770
78% WHITE 21% BLACK

SOUTHERN
White: **59%**
Black: **41%**

MIDDLE
White: **94%**
Black: **6%**

NEW ENGLAND
White: **97%**
Black: **3%**

Growth of the Jamestown Colony

During the early years of the Jamestown colony, only a few women chose to make the journey from England. Nor did enough workers come to raise tobacco and other crops.

Women in Jamestown The colony's first women arrived in 1608—a "Mistress Forrest" and her maid, Anne Burras. Few others followed until 1619, when the Virginia Company sent about 100 women to help "make the men more settled." This shipload of women quickly found husbands. The Virginia Company profited from the marriages because it charged each man who found a wife 150 pounds of tobacco.

Life for women was a daily struggle. Women had to make everything from scratch—food, clothing, even medicines. Many died young from hard work or childbirth. By 1624, there were still fewer than 300 women in the Jamestown colony, compared to more than 1,000 men.

Africans Arrive in Virginia Enslaved Africans were brought to Virginia early on. Records show that at least 15 black men and 17 black women were already living there by 1619.

Analyze Images A Dutch slave ship lands at Jamestown in 1619 with 20 African captives. **Infer** What features of this image do you think are realistic?

That same year, a Dutch ship arrived with about 20 Africans. The Dutch sold the Africans to Virginians who needed laborers to grow tobacco. The colonists valued the agricultural skills that the Africans brought with them. From the enslaved Africans' perspective, this was a journey into a brutal life of forced labor.

About 300 Africans lived in Virginia by 1644. Some were slaves for life. Others worked as indentured servants, or people who were pledged to work for a master for a period until they paid off the cost of their voyage, and expected one day to own their own farms.

Some Africans did become free planters. Anthony Johnson owned 250 acres of land and employed five servants to help him work it. For a time, free Africans in Virginia also had the right to vote. These newcomers from Africa helped to transform the environment of Virginia by cutting down forests and planting tobacco fields.

Bacon's Rebellion Meanwhile, English settlers continued to arrive in Virginia, attracted by the promise of profits from tobacco. Wealthy planters, however, controlled the best lands near the coast. Many newcomers were indentured servants.

When they finished their period of service, they looked for farmland. Often they pushed farther inland, onto Indian lands.

As in New England, conflicts over land led to fighting between some white settlers and Indians. After several bloody clashes, settlers called on the governor to take action against American Indians. The governor refused, in part because he profited from his own fur trade with Indians. Frontier settlers were furious.

Finally, in 1676, Nathaniel Bacon, an ambitious young planter, organized angry men and women on the frontier, including indentured servants. He raided American Indian villages, regardless of whether the Indians there had been friendly to the colonists or not. Then, he led his followers to Jamestown and burned the capital.

The uprising, known as **Bacon's Rebellion**, lasted only a short time. When Bacon died suddenly, the revolt fell apart. The governor hanged 23 of Bacon's followers. Still, he could not stop English settlers from moving onto Indian lands along the frontier, or the edge of the settlement.

Wealthy Virginians generally supported Governor Berkeley. They were alarmed that black and white indentured servants had joined together in a rebellion. In response, Virginia set up a system of laws replacing indentured servitude for Africans with a condition of lifelong slavery that would be passed on to enslaved Africans' children. As slavery expanded, free African Americans also lost rights. By the early 1700s, free African American property owners could no longer vote.

▲ Governor Berkeley faces angry colonists during Bacon's Rebellion in Jamestown.

READING CHECK Identify Supporting Details How did Virginia come to have a large African population?

☑ Lesson Check

Practice Vocabulary

1. What was the impact of the **Protestant Reformation** in Europe?

2. Why did the French and Dutch seek **alliances** with American Indians?

Critical Thinking and Writing

3. **Summarize** What did John Cabot, Giovanni da Verrazano, and Jacques Cartier all have in common?

4. **Use Evidence** What examples can you give to show that contacts between European colonists and American Indians had negative consequences?

5. **Infer** What do you think happened after Virginia law established lifelong enslavement for people of African origin?

6. **Writing Workshop: Introduce Characters** In your 📓 Active Journal, identify other people from colonial society that your character would interact with. Explain what these other characters do and how they know your character.

The New England Colonies

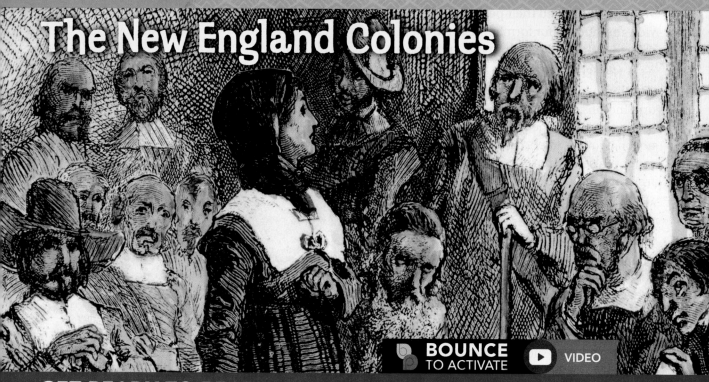

BOUNCE TO ACTIVATE   ▶ VIDEO

GET READY TO READ

START UP
Study the painting of a trial in the New England colonies. How do you think the men are reacting to the woman's words?

GUIDING QUESTIONS
- How did the desire for religious freedom lead to the settlement of the New England Colonies?
- Why was the Mayflower Compact significant?
- How were conflicts over religion and politics resolved in colonial New England?
- What were the reasons American Indians and settlers engaged in conflicts?
- How did the settlers of New England live?

TAKE NOTES
Literacy Skills: Compare and Contrast
Use the graphic organizer in your 📙 Active Journal to take notes as you read the lesson.

PRACTICE VOCABULARY
Use the vocabulary activity in your 📙 Active Journal to practice the vocabulary words.

Vocabulary		Academic Vocabulary
Pilgrim	Puritan	
persecution	General Court	resolve
Mayflower Compact	religious tolerance	virtue
	town meeting	

After two hard months at sea, the colonists on board the small sailing ship were relieved to see the shores of New England. Still, there were no European colonies for hundreds of miles.

Colonists Seek Religious Freedom
One of the voyagers, William Bradford, vividly remembered the situation:

Primary Source

"Being thus passed the vast ocean . . . they had now no friends to welcome them nor inns to entertain or refresh their weather-beaten bodies; no houses or much less towns to repair to. . . . And for the season it was winter, and they that know the winters of that country know them to be sharp and violent."

—William Bradford, *Of Plymouth Plantation*

Unlike the Jamestown colonists or the Spanish, these newcomers sought neither gold nor silver nor great riches. What they wanted most was to practice their religion freely. Years later, the founders of Plymouth became known to history as the **Pilgrims**, because they were religious people who traveled long distances to find a place where they could live and worship as they wanted.

Religion in Europe It was not easy for people to practice religion freely in Europe during the 1500s. As you have read, after the Protestant Reformation, Christians in western Europe were divided into Protestants and Roman Catholics. This division led to fierce religious wars. In France, for example, Protestants and Catholics fought each other for nearly 40 years. Thousands upon thousands of people were killed because of their religious beliefs.

Most European rulers believed that they could not maintain order unless everyone followed the ruler's religion. The religion chosen by the ruler was known as the established church. In England, for example, the established church was the Anglican church, or Church of England. In the 1530s, Parliament passed laws making the English monarch the head of the Church of England.

In England and other nations, people who did not follow the established religion were often persecuted. **Persecution** is the mistreatment or punishment of certain people because of their beliefs. Sometimes, members of persecuted groups had to worship secretly. If they were discovered, they might be imprisoned or even executed by being burned at the stake.

The Pilgrims One religious group in England that faced persecution were the people we now call the Pilgrims. At the time, they were known as Separatists. They were called that because, although they were Protestant, they wanted to separate from the Church of England.

The English government bitterly opposed the Separatists. William Bradford remembered what some Separatists had suffered.

▼ This replica of the *Mayflower* in Plymouth, Massachusetts, was a gift from Great Britain. British and U.S. sailors sailed it across the Atlantic in 1957.

Primary Source

"They . . . were hunted and persecuted on every side. . . . For some were taken and clapped up in prison, others had their houses beset and watched night and day . . . and the most were [glad] to flee and leave their houses."

—William Bradford, *Of Plymouth Plantation*

Quick Activity

In your 📓 Active Journal, write a letter from Pilgrims persuading other Separatists to join them on their journey across the Atlantic Ocean.

In the early 1600s, a group of Separatists left England for Leyden, a city in the Netherlands. The Dutch allowed the newcomers to worship freely. Still, the Pilgrims missed their English way of life. They were also worried that their children were growing up more Dutch than English.

✓ READING CHECK **Identify Main Ideas** Why did the Pilgrims want to escape England and establish their own colony?

Founding the Plymouth Colony

A group of Separatists decided to leave the Netherlands. Along with some other English people who were not Separatists, they won a charter to set up a colony in the northern part of Virginia. Like the colonists who followed them, the Pilgrims' enterprise was started and funded privately in the hopes that it would earn a profit. In September 1620, more than 100 men, women, and children set sail aboard a small ship called the *Mayflower*. The journey was long and difficult.

Academic Vocabulary

resolve • *v.,* to come to a firm decision

At last, in November 1620, the *Mayflower* landed on the cold, bleak shore of Cape Cod, in present-day Massachusetts. The passengers had **resolved** to settle farther south along the Hudson River, but the difficult sea voyage exhausted them. The colonists decided to travel no farther. They called their new settlement Plimoth, or Plymouth, because the *Mayflower* had sailed from the port of Plymouth, England.

A New Pledge to Govern the Colony Before going ashore, the Pilgrims realized that they would not be settling within the boundaries of Virginia. As a result, the terms of their charter would not apply to their new colony. In that case, who would govern them? The question was especially important because not all colonists on the *Mayflower* were Pilgrims. Some of these "strangers," as the Pilgrims called them, said they were not bound to obey the Pilgrims, "for none had power to command them."

▼ The *Mayflower* reached the coast of modern-day Massachusetts after a difficult journey across the Atlantic Ocean.

In response, the Pilgrims joined together to write a framework for governing their colony. On November 11, 1620, the 41 adult male passengers—both Pilgrims and non-Pilgrims—signed the **Mayflower Compact**. They pledged themselves to unite into a "civil body politic," or government. They agreed to make and abide by laws that ensured "the general Good of the Colony."

The Mayflower Compact established an important tradition of self-government. When the Pilgrims found themselves without a government, they banded together themselves to make laws. In time, they set up a government in which adult male colonists elected a governor and council.

Analyze Images Male passengers on the *Mayflower* sign the Mayflower Compact, which established a government for the colony at Plymouth. **Synthesize Visual Information** What do you think the artist was trying to show about the Pilgrims?

Thus, like Virginia's Great Charter, the Mayflower Compact strengthened the English tradition of governing through elected representatives. These representatives were expected to show the religious **virtues** that the Pilgrims valued and to make decisions for the common good. The colony at Plymouth thought that this type of government, rather than the monarchy that they knew in England, would best protect their religious freedom.

Religious Motivation and Creating a Tradition of Religious Freedom The Pilgrims were the first of many immigrants who came to North America in order to worship as they pleased. That did not mean that religious freedom spread quickly through England's colonies. Many settlers who wished to worship as they pleased still believed that only their own religious beliefs should be observed. Most of the English colonies set up their own established churches.

Still, the Pilgrims' desire to worship freely set an important precedent, or example for others to follow in the future. In time, the idea of religious freedom for all would become a cornerstone of American democracy.

Academic Vocabulary

virtue • *n.*, morally good behavior or character

✓ READING CHECK **Draw Conclusions** Why did the colonists at Plymouth believe that representative government would be the best way to protect their religious freedom?

INTERACTIVE

Plymouth Plantation

▲ The Wampanoag taught the Pilgrims to plant native crops at Plymouth. Here, re-enactors work the fields at Plimouth Plantation.

What Hardships Did Colonists Face in Plymouth?

The Pilgrims built their settlement on the site of an American Indian village that had been abandoned because of disease. The colonists even found baskets filled with corn that they were able to eat.

A Cold Winter in Plymouth However, the corn was not enough to get the Pilgrims through their first winter. The Pilgrims had failed to bring enough food with them, and it was too late in the season to plant new crops.

The harsh season was also difficult to survive because the Pilgrims had not had enough time to build proper shelters. During the winter days, the men worked to build houses onshore, while most spent nights aboard the *Mayflower*. Half the settlers had perished of disease or starvation by spring.

American Indians Offer Assistance In the spring, the Pilgrims began to clear land and plant crops. They also received help from neighboring American Indians. A Pemaquid Indian, Samoset, had learned English from earlier explorers sailing along the coast. He introduced the Pilgrims to Massasoit (MAS uh soit), chief of the local Wampanoag (wahm puh NOH ahg) Indians.

The Wampanoag who helped the Pilgrims most was named Squanto. As a young man, Squanto had been captured by an English expedition led by John Smith. Squanto lived for a time in England, where he learned to speak the language. As a result, he could communicate easily with the Pilgrims.

Squanto brought the Pilgrims seeds of native plants—corn, beans, and pumpkins—and showed them how to plant them. He also taught the settlers how to catch eels from nearby rivers. By treading water, he stirred up eels from the mud at the river bottom and then snatched them up with his hands. The grateful Pilgrims called Squanto "a special instrument sent of God."

In the fall, the Pilgrims had a very good harvest. Because they believed that God had given them this harvest, they set aside a day for giving thanks.

More than 200 years after the Pilgrims' first successful harvest, President Abraham Lincoln proclaimed a national day of thanksgiving. Americans today celebrate Thanksgiving as a national holiday.

✓ READING CHECK Identify Supporting Details How did American Indians help the Pilgrims?

Did you know?

Massachusetts was named for the Massachuset Indians.

Forming Massachusetts Bay Colony

The migration to Massachusetts Bay during the 1630s was led by a religious group known as the **Puritans**. Unlike the Pilgrims, the Puritans did not want to separate entirely from the Church of England. They wanted to simplify forms of worship. They wanted to do away with many practices inherited from the Roman Catholic Church. These included organ music, finely decorated houses of worship, and special clothing for priests.

Reasons for Immigration to Massachusetts The Puritans were a powerful group in England. Although some were small farmers, many were well educated and successful merchants or landowners.

Charles I, who became king in 1625, disapproved of the Puritans and their ideas. He canceled Puritan business charters and even had a few Puritans jailed.

By 1629, some Puritan leaders were convinced that England had fallen on "evil and declining times." They persuaded royal officials to grant them a charter to form the Massachusetts Bay Company. The company's bold plan was to build a new society based on biblical laws and teachings. John Winthrop, a lawyer and a devout Puritan, believed that the new colony would set an example to the world.

Some settlers joined the Massachusetts colonists for economic rather than religious reasons. In wealthy English families, the oldest son usually inherited his father's estate. With little hope of owning land, younger sons sought opportunity elsewhere. They were attracted to Massachusetts Bay because it offered cheap land or a chance to start a business.

A Greater Say in Government In 1629, the Puritans sent a small advance party to North America. John Winthrop and a party of more than 1,000 arrived the following year. Winthrop was chosen as the first governor of the Massachusetts Bay Colony.

Once ashore, Winthrop set an example for others. Although he was governor, he worked hard to build a home, clear land, and plant crops. There was discontent among some colonists, though. Under the charter, only stockholders who had invested money in the Massachusetts Bay Company had the right to vote. Most settlers, however, were not stockholders. They resented taxes and laws that were passed by a government in which they had no voice.

Winthrop and other stockholders saw that the colony would run more smoothly if a greater number of settlers could take part. At the same time, Puritan leaders wished to keep non-Puritans out of the government.

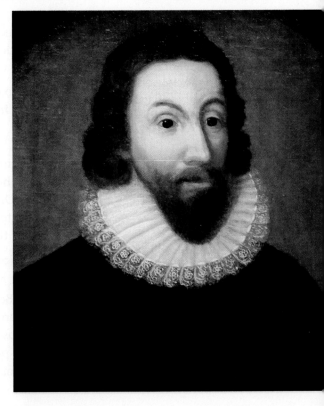

Analyze Images John Winthrop said his colony would be a "shining city upon a hill." **Draw Conclusions** How was John Winthrop important in the development of the United States?

Analyze Images Thomas Hooker led a group of settlers to set up a colony in Connecticut. **Identify Supporting Details** How did Hooker increase voting rights?

INTERACTIVE

Thomas Hooker

As a result, the colony granted the right to vote for governor to all men who were church members. Later, male church members also elected representatives to an assembly called the **General Court**.

✓ READING CHECK Identify Cause and Effect Why was the right to vote expanded in the Massachusetts Bay Colony?

Which New Colonies Formed Over Religious Differences?

The Puritan leaders of the Massachusetts Bay Colony did not like anyone to question their religious beliefs or the way the colony was governed. Usually, discontented colonists were forced to leave. Some colonists who left Massachusetts founded other colonies in New England.

A New Colony with Limited Government In May 1636, a Puritan minister named Thomas Hooker led about 100 settlers out of Massachusetts Bay. Pushing west, they drove their cattle, goats, and pigs along American Indian trails that cut through the forests. When they reached the Connecticut River, they built a town, which they called Hartford.

Hooker left Massachusetts Bay because he believed that the governor and other officials had too much power. He wanted to set up a colony in Connecticut with strict limits on government.

The settlers wrote a plan of government called the Fundamental Orders of Connecticut in 1639. It created a government much like that of Massachusetts, which relied on people to obey the law and seek the common good. There were, however, two important differences. First, the Fundamental Orders gave the vote to all male property owners. This included those who were not church members. Second, the Fundamental Orders limited the governor's power. In this way, the Fundamental Orders expanded the idea of representative government in the English colonies.

A New Relationship Between Religion and Government Another Puritan who challenged the leaders of Massachusetts Bay was Roger Williams. A young minister in the village of Salem, Williams was gentle and good-natured. William Bradford described him as "zealous but very unsettled in judgment." Some Puritan leaders probably agreed with this. Most people, including Governor Winthrop, liked him.

Williams's ideas, however, alarmed Puritan leaders. Williams believed that the Puritan church had too much power. In his view, the business of church and state should be completely separate, since concern with political affairs would corrupt the church. The role of the state, he said, was to maintain order and peace. It should not support a particular church. Finally, Williams did not believe that the Puritan leaders had the right to force people to attend religious services. Because of these political reasons, Williams sought to establish a new colony.

Williams also believed in religious tolerance. **Religious tolerance** means a willingness to let others practice their own beliefs. In Puritan Massachusetts, non-Puritans were not allowed to worship freely.

Puritan leaders viewed Williams as a dangerous troublemaker. In 1635, the General Court ordered him to leave Massachusetts. Fearing that the court would send him back to England, Williams fled to Narragansett Bay, where he spent the winter with Indians. In the spring of 1636, the Indians sold him land for a settlement. After a few years, the settlement became the English colony of Rhode Island.

In Rhode Island, Williams put into practice his ideas about tolerance. He allowed complete freedom of religion for all Protestants, Jews, and Catholics. He did not set up a state church or require settlers to attend church services. He also gave all white men the right to vote.

A Woman's Voice Calls for Religious Freedom Among those who fled to Rhode Island was Anne Hutchinson. A devout Puritan, Hutchinson regularly attended church services in Boston, where she first lived. After church, she and her friends gathered at her home to discuss the minister's sermon. Often, she seemed to question some of the minister's teachings.

Analyze Graphs This chart offers a snapshot of the people and economy of the New England Colonies. **Draw Conclusions** What does the graph of imports and exports tell you about the economy of the New England Colonies during the 1700s?

THE NEW ENGLAND COLONIES

TIMELINE
OF SETTLEMENT

1620 Plymouth Colony was settled by Pilgrims wishing to escape religious persecution in England.

1630 Massachusetts Bay Colony was settled by Puritans wishing to escape religious persecution in England.

1623 New Hampshire began as a group of coastal settlements.

1636 Connecticut was founded as a colony with strict limits on government power.

1636 Rhode Island was founded as a colony where church and state were separated.

PEOPLE
First settled by about 50 Pilgrims. Thousands came later. Most were Puritans who wanted to reform the Church of England. Persecution by King Charles I in the 1600s caused many to leave England.

ECONOMY

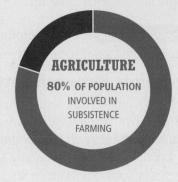

AGRICULTURE
80% OF POPULATION INVOLVED IN SUBSISTENCE FARMING

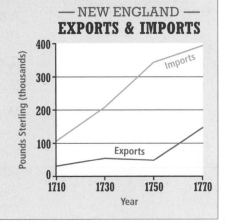

— NEW ENGLAND —
EXPORTS & IMPORTS

Imports

Exports

Pounds Sterling (thousands)

400 / 300 / 200 / 100 / 0

1710   1730   1750   1770

Year

- Hutchinson was born in England and moved to the American colonies in her early forties.

- She was one of many women of the time who was active in religious life.

- Hutchinson's understanding of how to use herbal remedies attracted neighbors to her home, where she spoke of her views.

- She was banished from Massachusetts for her beliefs, which were condemned by the Puritans.

- Hutchinson moved to New York after her husband died, and she was killed in an Indian raid a few years later.

Critical Thinking Why do we still remember Anne Hutchinson and what she did?

Hutchinson was very persuasive, and neighbors flocked to hear her. Her teachings and her popularity angered the Puritan leaders. They believed that Hutchinson's opinions were full of religious errors. Even worse, they said, a woman did not have the right to explain God's law. In November 1637, Hutchinson was ordered to appear before the Massachusetts General Court.

At her trial, Hutchinson answered the questions put to her by Governor Winthrop and other members of the court. Each time, her answers revealed weaknesses in their arguments. They could not prove that she had broken any Puritan laws or that she had disobeyed any religious teachings.

Then, after two long days of hostile questioning, Hutchinson made a serious mistake. She told the court that God spoke directly to her, "By the voice of His own spirit to my soul." Members of the court were shocked. Puritans believed that God spoke only through the Bible, not directly to individuals. The court ordered her out of the colony.

In 1638, Hutchinson, along with her family and some friends, went to Rhode Island. The Puritan leaders had won their case. For later Americans, however, Hutchinson became an important symbol of the struggle for religious freedom.

✔ **READING CHECK** **Identify Implied Main Ideas** What relationship did Roger Williams want to see between government and religion?

War Erupts Between Settlers and American Indians

From Massachusetts Bay, settlers fanned out across New England. Some built trading and fishing villages along the coast north of Boston. Port towns with good harbors were ideal for the fishing industry and also lured trading ships, building the area's economy. In 1680, the king would make some of these coastal settlements into a separate colony called New Hampshire.

Conflict Develops The first meetings between English settlers and American Indians did not foreshadow their future conflict. Some colonial leaders such as Roger Williams tried to treat American Indians fairly.

As more colonists settled in New England, they began to take over more American Indian lands. By 1670, nearly 45,000 English settlers were living in the towns in New England. Land was a resource, but as more people lived in the region, it became increasingly scarce. Fighting soon broke out between white settlers and Indian nations of the region.

King Phillip's War The largest conflict came in 1675. Metacom, also known by his English name, King Phillip, was chief of the Wampanoag. He watched for years as English towns were built on Wampanoag lands. "I am resolved not to see the day when I have no country," he told an English friend. Metacom's people attacked villages throughout New England.

Other Indian groups, from Rhode Island to Maine, soon allied themselves with the Wampanoag. They were determined to drive the English settlers off their land. Metacom and his allies destroyed 12 towns and killed more than 600 European settlers.

After more than a year of fighting, however, Metacom was captured and killed. The English sold his family and about 1,000 other Indians into slavery in the West Indies. Other Indians were forced from their homelands.

The pattern of English expansion followed by war between colonists and Indians was repeated throughout the colonies. It would continue for many years to come.

READING CHECK Identify Cause and Effect What was a significant cause of King Phillip's War?

INTERACTIVE

The New England Colonies

GEOGRAPHY SKILLS

Most of New England's major towns were located on harbors along the coast.

1. **Location** On what body of water was Hartford located?

2. **Infer** What do the locations of New England towns suggest about their economies?

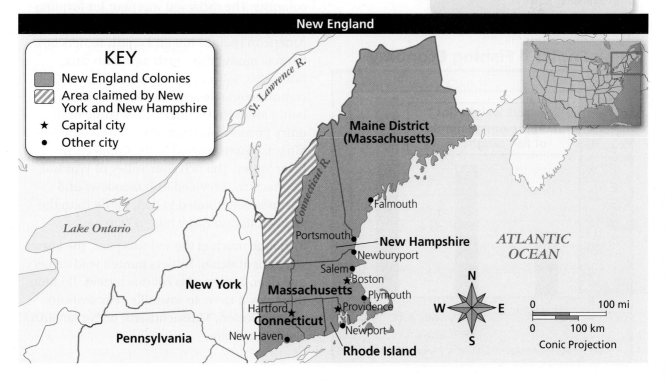

New England

KEY
- New England Colonies
- Area claimed by New York and New Hampshire
- ★ Capital city
- • Other city

St. Lawrence R.

Maine District (Massachusetts)

Connecticut R.

Falmouth

Portsmouth

New Hampshire

Newburyport

Lake Ontario

Salem

Boston

New York

Massachusetts

Plymouth

Hartford

Providence

Connecticut

New Haven

Newport

Pennsylvania

Rhode Island

ATLANTIC OCEAN

N W E S

0   100 mi
0   100 km
Conic Projection

Quest CONNECTIONS

Read the section called "The Environment Influences Economic Activity." In what ways was the environment helpful to people looking to make a living? In what way was it unhelpful? Record your findings in your 📖 Active Journal.

How Did People Live in the Towns of New England?

Puritans believed that people should worship and tend to local matters as a community. As a result, New England became a land of tightly knit towns.

At the center of many towns was the common, an open field where cattle grazed. Nearby stood the meetinghouse, where Puritans worshiped and held town meetings.

Religious Practice The Puritans took their Sabbath, or holy day of religious observance and rest, very seriously. On Sundays, no one was allowed to play games or visit taverns. The law required all citizens to attend Sunday church services, which would last all day.

During the 1600s, women sat on one side of the church and men on the other. African Americans and American Indians stood in a balcony at the back. Children had separate pews, where an adult watched over them.

The Importance of Local Government At **town meetings**, which were normally held in the meeting houses, settlers discussed and voted on local and church issues. They also chose ministers. Town meetings gave New Englanders a chance to speak their minds.

These early experiences encouraged the growth of democratic ideas in New England. Values such as self-government, individual choice, and the common good took root and thrived.

Still, Puritan laws were strict. About 15 crimes carried the death penalty. One crime punishable by death was witchcraft. In 1692, Puritans in Salem Village executed 20 innocent men and women as witches.

Analyze Graphs Fishing helped support the New England economy throughout the 1700s. **Synthesize Visual Information** Approximately how many fish were caught in 1731? Approximately how much did the catch that year weigh?

The Environment Influences Economic Activity New England was a difficult land for colonists. The rocky soil was poor for farming and required much labor. After a time, however, American Indians taught English settlers how to grow many crops, such as Indian corn, pumpkins, squash, and beans. Still, some communities relocated to take advantage of better lands. In the mid-1630s, cattle and dairy farmers who had settled in Dorchester, Massachusetts, moved to the Connecticut River Valley. The rich river valley at Windsor, Connecticut, provided lush meadows and pastures better suited to their cattle than the sandy soils and rocky hills of Dorchester.

Although much of the soil was poor, the forests were full of riches. Settlers hunted wild turkey and deer. Settlers also cut down trees, floating them down rivers to sawmills near seaports such as Boston, Massachusetts, or Portsmouth, New Hampshire.

New England Fishing Economy

Legend:
- Export weight (lbs.)
- Approximate number of fish caught

Y-axis: Units in millions (0–40)
X-axis: Year (1716, 1731, 1765)

SOURCE: The Fisherman's Cause, Christopher P. Magra

With miles of coastline and nearby raw materials, these and other New England towns grew into major shipbuilding centers. Because abundant timber meant that ships could be built more cheaply in New England than in England, New England sold many ships to English buyers.

New Englanders fished for cod and halibut. In the 1600s, people began to hunt whales. Whales supplied oil for lamps and other products. In the 1700s and 1800s, whaling grew into a big business.

The Puritans Leave a Lasting Legacy During the 1700s, the Puritan tradition declined. Fewer families left England for religious reasons. Ministers had less influence on the way colonies were governed. Nevertheless, the Puritans had stamped New England with their distinctive customs and their ideal of a religious society. The ideas of Pilgrims and Puritans, their virtues of hard work and thrift, their high regard for education, and their contributions to democratic thought still influence American values and American identity today.

▲ English settlers learned how to grow many crops, such as Indian corn, pumpkins, squash, and beans, from American Indians.

☑ READING CHECK **Identify Supporting Details** What values did Puritans associate with town meetings?

☑ Lesson Check

Practice Vocabulary

1. Why did many Europeans face **persecution** in the 16th century?

2. In what way were the **Puritans** different from the **Pilgrims**?

Critical Thinking and Writing

3. Identify Main Ideas Why did settling in Plymouth late in the year of 1620 pose significant problems for the Pilgrims?

4. Identify Cause and Effect What effect did population growth have on the conflict between colonists and American Indians?

5. Cite Evidence to support the claim that the New England Colonies promoted the ideals of democracy and self-government.

6. Writing Workshop: Establish Setting Write a few sentences in your 🗎 Active Journal to describe the setting where your character lives in the colonies. You will use them in your topic narrative essay.

William Bradford, *Of Plymouth Plantation*

William Bradford was one of the Pilgrims who sailed on the *Mayflower* and landed in Plymouth. He became one of the leaders of the colony, helping to write the Mayflower Compact and serving as governor. He wrote a journal called *Of Plymouth Plantation* in which he describes the story of the Pilgrims from 1608 to 1647. In this excerpt, he discusses the decision to move to North America.

◀ The signing of the Mayflower Compact

Reading and Vocabulary Support

① *Ye* was an early modern English word that means "the."

② How did Bradford describe the challenges he expected to face on the journey across the Atlantic Ocean?

③ *Providente* is a reference to God.

④ How does Bradford describe the thought process that went into the decision to move to North America?

All great & honourable actions are accompanied with great difficulties, and must be both enterprised [undertaken] and overcome with answerable courages. It was granted <u>ye</u> ① dangers were great, but not desperate; the difficulties were many, but not invincible [too powerful] ②. For though there were many of them likely, yet they were not cartaine [certain]; it might be sundrie [several] of ye things feared might never befale [take place]; others by <u>providente</u> ③ care & ye use of good means, might in a great measure be prevented; and all of them, through ye help of God, by fortitude [bravery] and patience, might either be borne, or overcome.

True it was, that such atempts were not to be made and undertaken without good ground & reason; not rashly or lightly as many have done for curiositie or hope of gaine, &c. But their condition was not ordinarie; their ends were good & honourable; their calling lawfull, & urgente; and therfore they might expecte ye blessing of god in their proceding. Yea, though they should loose their lives in this action, yet might they have comforte in the same, and their endeavors would be honourable.④

Analyzing Primary Sources

Cite specific evidence from the document to support your answers.

1. **Draw Conclusions** According to Bradford, what would the reward be for those who did not survive the journey to North America?

2. **Analyze Style and Rhetoric** How would you describe the tone of Bradford's journal entry?

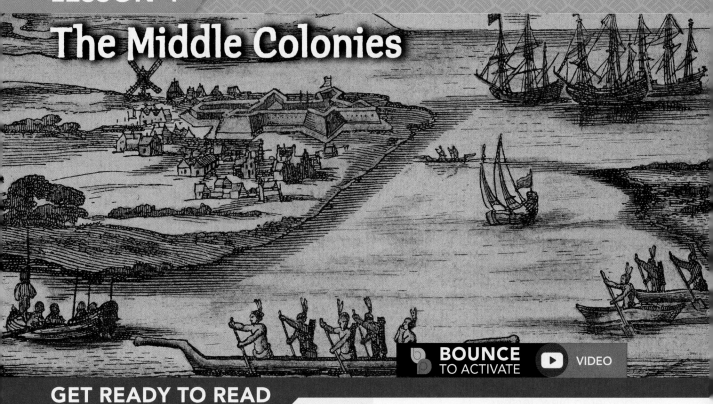

LESSON 4
The Middle Colonies

BOUNCE TO ACTIVATE ▶ VIDEO

GET READY TO READ

START UP

This engraving shows New Amsterdam in the 1660s, which later became New York City. What would a picture of the same area look like today?

GUIDING QUESTIONS

- What were the reasons the colonies of New York and New Jersey were established?
- Why were the colonies of Pennsylvania and Delaware established?
- How would you describe the economy of the Middle Colonies, and what was the relationship between the economy and the physical environment?

TAKE NOTES

Literacy Skills: Analyze Text Structure
Use the graphic organizer in your ▣ Active Journal to take notes as you read the lesson.

PRACTICE VOCABULARY

Use the vocabulary activity in your ▣ Active Journal to practice the vocabulary words.

Vocabulary
proprietary colony
royal colony

Quaker
Pennsylvania Dutch
cash crop

Academic Vocabulary
haven
commoner

By 1700, England had four colonies in the region just south of New England. These colonies became known as the Middle Colonies because they were located between New England and the Southern Colonies. The Middle Colonies had a greater mix of people than either New England or the Southern Colonies.

Why Did the Dutch Colony Become English?

Each of the colonies along the Atlantic coast had been established by different people for different purposes. Sometimes colonies were formed to escape political oppression or social tensions back home in Europe.

In the case of New Netherland, however, the conditions back home for the Dutch were stable and fairly prosperous. New Netherland was founded simply to take advantage of economic opportunities in North America.

INTERACTIVE

The Middle
Colonies

New Amsterdam The Dutch set up the colony of New Netherland along the Hudson River. They developed the fur trade and built settlements where fur-bearing animals were abundant. In the colony's early years, settlers traded with Indians and built the settlement of New Amsterdam into a thriving port. Located near good farmland and with a safe harbor for ships, New Amsterdam quickly became a center for commerce and trading valuable beaver skins.

Dutch officials also promoted agriculture. They granted large parcels of land to a few rich families. A single grant could stretch for miles. Owners of these huge estates were called patroons. In return for the grant, each patroon promised to settle at least 50 European farm families on the land. Patroons had great power and could charge whatever rents they pleased.

GEOGRAPHY SKILLS

The Middle Colonies lay between the New England Colonies and the Southern Colonies.

1. **Place** What colonies bordered New Jersey?

2. **Draw Conclusions** What geographic features of the Middle Colonies suggest that they were well placed for trade?

England Gains Control Many settlers lived in the trading center of New Amsterdam, which by 1664 had a population of about 1,500 people. They came from all over Europe. Most of them came for the economic opportunities, working as merchants or farmers, or in trades and crafts. Many were also attracted by the chance to practice their religion freely. African slaves were in demand as well. In the early years, they made up more than a quarter of the population of the town.

Dutch colonists were mainly Protestants who belonged to the Dutch Reformed Church. Still, they permitted members of other religions and ethnic groups—including Roman Catholics, French Protestants, and Jews—to buy land. "People do not seem concerned what religion their neighbor is" wrote a shocked visitor from Virginia. "Indeed, they do not seem to care if he has any religion at all."

Middle Colonies

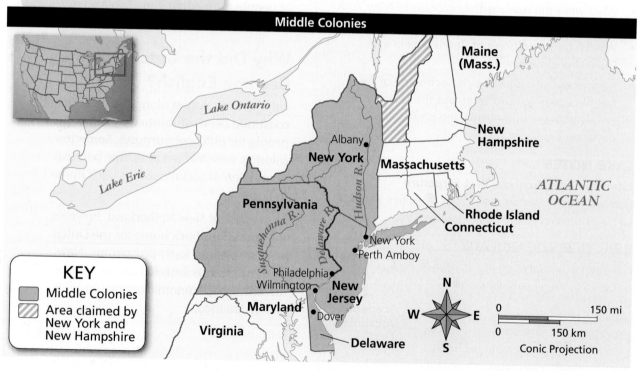

KEY

◻ Middle Colonies

▨ Area claimed by New York and New Hampshire

In fact, Peter Stuyvesant (STY vuh sunt), the governor of New Netherland, had been ordered not to interfere with other religions as long as they did not disturb the peace or restrict commerce.

The relationship between the English and the Dutch was complicated by their common interest in creating new colonies and expanding trade. In North America, the Dutch wanted to continue benefiting from New Amsterdam's economic growth. However, the English wanted New Amsterdam for themselves.

By 1664, the rivalry between England and the Netherlands for trade and colonies was at its height. In August of that year, English warships entered New Amsterdam's harbor. Governor Stuyvesant swore to defend the city. However, he had few weapons and little gunpowder. Also, Stuyvesant had made himself so unpopular with his harsh rule and heavy taxes that the colonists refused to help him. In the end, he surrendered without firing a shot.

King Charles II of England then gave New Netherland to his brother, the Duke of York. He renamed the colony New York in the duke's honor.

☑ READING CHECK Identify Cause and Effect Why did many people come to New Amsterdam?

New Jersey Forms Out of New York

At the time of the English takeover, New York stretched as far south as the Delaware Bay. The Duke of York decided that the colony was too big to govern easily. He gave some of the land to friends, Lord Berkeley and Sir George Carteret. They set up a proprietary (proh PRY uh tehr ee) colony, which they called New Jersey, in 1664.

A Proprietary Colony and a Market Economy In setting up a **proprietary colony**, the king gave land to one or more people in return for a yearly payment. These proprietors were free to divide the land and rent it to others. They made laws for the colony, but had to respect the rights of colonists under English law. This new system of colonization was different from most that had come before. Proprietary colonies placed vast lands and power in the hands of a few men loyal to the monarch. Earlier colonies had been financed by stock companies made up of a number of investors.

Like New York, New Jersey had fertile farmland and other resources that attracted people from many lands. Thousands of European settlers immigrated to New Jersey as a **haven** from war and poverty. Settlers came from Finland, Ireland, Scotland, Germany, and Sweden. English and Dutch settlers also moved there from New York.

Analyze Images This statue of Peter Stuyvesant stands in Stuyvesant Park in Manhattan. **Identify Implied Main Ideas** Why was Stuyvesant ordered to observe a policy of religious tolerance?

Academic Vocabulary

haven • *n.*, a place where people are protected from danger and trouble

In addition, some New England colonists, hoping to find better farmland, chose to relocate to New Jersey.

The proprietors of New Jersey encouraged the free enterprise system, which meant that government played a limited role in the economy. The free enterprise system benefited colonists. They could farm or run businesses without much control by the local government. Facing financial losses themselves, however, the proprietors eventually returned the colony of New Jersey to the English crown.

A Royal Colony In 1702, New Jersey became a **royal colony**, which is a colony under the direct control of the English king or queen. The colony's royal charter protected religious freedom and the rights of an assembly that voted on local matters. This charter could be viewed as a legal agreement between the monarch and settlers, binding to both.

Analyze Images New Jersey's fertile farmland attracted many colonists. **Compare and Contrast** How was farming in New Jersey different from farming in New England?

Despite these moves toward democracy, direct English rule tended to be harsh toward colonists. New Jersey's independent-minded settlers struggled to gain more influence over decisions that affected them.

✅ READING CHECK **Draw Conclusions** Why do you think the system in which government stays out of the way to let people run business with little control is called the free enterprise system?

How Did Pennsylvania Become a Colony?

West of New Jersey, William Penn founded the colony of Pennsylvania in 1681. Penn came from a wealthy English family and was a personal friend of King Charles II. At age 22, however, Penn shocked family and friends by joining the **Quakers**, one of the most despised religious groups in England.

The Quakers Seek Religious Freedom Like Pilgrims and Puritans, Quakers were Protestant reformers. Their reforms went further than those of other groups, however.

Academic Vocabulary
commoner • *n.,* a regular or average person

Quakers believed that all people—men and women, nobles and **commoners**—were equal in God's sight. They allowed women to preach in public and refused to bow or remove their hats in the presence of nobles. Quakers spoke out against all war and refused to serve in the army.

To most English people, Quaker beliefs seemed wicked. In both England and New England, Quakers were arrested, fined, or even hanged for their ideas. Penn became convinced that the Quakers must leave England. He took steps to found a new colony. Together with others, Penn purchased parts of New Jersey from their proprietors. Then he turned to the king for help.

Charles II issued a royal charter naming Penn proprietor of a large tract of land in North America. The king named the new colony Pennsylvania, or Penn's woodlands. During his time as proprietor, Penn took steps that aided the development of self-government in Pennsylvania. He proposed a constitution and a General Assembly. Later, he agreed to changes in the constitution and greater powers for the colonial assembly.

Showing Fairness to All Penn thought of his colony as a "holy experiment." He wanted it to be a model of religious freedom, peace, and Christian living. Protestants, Catholics, and Jews went to Pennsylvania to escape persecution. Later, English officials forced Penn to turn away Catholic and Jewish settlers.

Penn's Quaker beliefs led him to speak out for fair treatment of American Indians. Penn believed that the land in North America belonged to the Indians. He insisted that settlers should pay for the land. American Indians respected him for this policy. As a result, Pennsylvania colonists enjoyed many years of peace with their Indian neighbors. One settler remarked that, as Penn "treated the Indians with extraordinary humanity, they became civil and loving to us."

Analyze Images Painter Benjamin West imagined this scene of Penn signing the treaty with the American Indians. **Use Visual Information** How does the artist show peaceful relations among Penn, merchants, and Indians?

Quest CONNECTIONS

How was the environment of the Middle Colonies more favorable to workers than the New England colonies? Record your findings in your 📓 Active Journal.

Pennsylvania Expands Penn sent pamphlets describing his colony all over Europe. Soon, settlers from England, Scotland, Wales, the Netherlands, France, and Germany began to cross the Atlantic Ocean to Pennsylvania.

Among the new arrivals were large numbers of German-speaking Protestants. They became known as **Pennsylvania Dutch** because people could not pronounce the word Deutsch (doich), which means German. Many Pennsylvania Dutch had faced religious persecution in Europe, including the Amish and Mennonites. Because of their experiences in Europe, these German-speaking people were naturally attracted to the ideals of Penn's colony, in which people of different ethnicities and religions could live peaceably together. The ethnic diversity of Pennsylvania contributed to a developing American identity based on ethnic diversity.

Pennsylvania, like most other colonies, was created for a mix of political, economic, religious, and social reasons. Pennsylvania was like the New England colonies in the religious reasons for its creation.

Like New York, its political roots lay in a proprietor's ties to the king. Pennsylvania's social goals of harmony among different groups were similar to those of Rhode Island. Like most proprietors, Penn hoped to profit from his colony.

Enslaved Africans were also brought to the growing Pennsylvania colony. They made up about one third of all new arrivals between 1730 and 1750. Enslaved Africans were present in New York, New Jersey, and the New England Colonies as well, but in smaller numbers than in the Southern Colonies. Because of Philadelphia's location along the Delaware River, many worked as laborers in manufacturing and shipbuilding.

Delaware Is Born For a time, Pennsylvania included some lands along the lower Delaware River. The region was known as Pennsylvania's Lower Counties. Later, in 1704, the Lower Counties would break away to form the colony of Delaware.

✓ READING CHECK **Identify Main Ideas** Why did Quakers want to establish their own colony?

▼ A statue of William Penn stands atop Philadelphia's City Hall today.

Daily Life in the Middle Colonies

The majority of colonists made their living by farming. Farmers found more favorable conditions in the Middle Colonies than in New England. The broad Hudson and Delaware river valleys were rich and fertile. Winters were milder than in New England, and the growing season lasted longer.

A Thriving Economy On such promising land, farmers in the eastern counties of the Middle Colonies cleared their fields. They mostly chose to raise wheat, barley, and rye as a way to earn money. Wheat, barley, and rye were **cash crops**, or crops that were sold for money on the market and not consumed by the farmer's family. In fact, the Middle Colonies exported so much grain that they became known as the Breadbasket Colonies.

The Pennsylvania Dutch tended to settle the fertile interior lands. They altered the environment by clearing land and starting farms, turning these regions into rich fields that are still productive today.

Farmers of the Middle Colonies also raised herds of cattle and pigs. Every year, they sent tons of beef, pork, and butter to the ports of New York and Philadelphia. From there, the goods went by ship to New England and the South or to the West Indies, England, and other parts of Europe.

Farms in the Middle Colonies were generally larger than those in New England. Landowners hired workers to help with the planting, harvesting, and other tasks. Enslaved African Americans worked on a few large farms. However, most workers were farmhands who worked alongside the families that owned the land.

Aside from farmers, there were also skilled artisans in the Middle Colonies. Encouraged by William Penn, skilled German craftspersons set up shop in Pennsylvania. In time, the colony became a center of manufacturing and crafts. One visitor reported that workshops turned out "hardware, clocks, watches, locks, guns, flints, glass, stoneware, nails, [and] paper."

Settlers in the Delaware River valley profited from the region's rich deposits of iron ore. Heating the ore in furnaces, they purified it and then hammered it into nails, tools, and parts for guns.

▲ Farmers took advantage of the fertile land of the Middle Colonies by growing crops to sell at market.

INTERACTIVE

The Economy of the Middle Colonies

Home Life Because houses tended to be far apart in the Middle Colonies, towns were less important than in New England. Counties, rather than villages, became centers of local government.

The different groups who settled the Middle Colonies had their own favorite ways of building. Swedish settlers introduced log cabins to the Americas. The Dutch used red bricks to build narrow, high-walled houses. German settlers developed a wood-burning stove that heated a home better than a fireplace, which sent heat up the chimney and pulled cold air in through cracks in the walls.

Everyone in a household had a job to do. Households were largely self-sufficient, which meant that most things needed for survival—food, clothing, soap, candles, and many other goods—were made at home. As one farmer said, "Nothing to wear, eat, or drink was purchased, as my farm provided all."

Expanding Beyond Philadelphia In the 1700s, thousands of German and Scotch-Irish settlers arrived in Philadelphia. From there, many traveled west into the back country, the area of land along the eastern slopes of the Appalachian Mountains. Settlers followed an old Indian trail that became known as the Great Wagon Road.

Although settlers planned to follow farming methods they had used in Europe, they found the challenge of farming the back country more difficult than they had thought it would be. To farm the back country, settlers had to clear thick forests. From Indians, settlers learned how to use knots from pine trees as candles to light their homes. They made wooden dishes from logs, gathered honey from hollows in trees, and hunted wild animals for food. German gunsmiths developed a lightweight rifle for use in forests. Sharpshooters boasted that the "Pennsylvania rifle" could hit a rattlesnake between the eyes at 100 yards.

Analyze Charts Religious, economic, geographic, and ethnic differences distinguished the Middle Colonies from New England. **Use Evidence** Which colonial region would you rather live in? Why?

Comparing the New England and Middle Colonies

	NEW ENGLAND	MIDDLE COLONIES
MAIN REASON FOR SETTLEMENT	Avoid religious persecution	Economic gain
BUSINESS AND TRADE	Shipbuilding, shipping, fishing, forestry	Agriculture, skilled trades, shipping
AGRICULTURE	Mostly limited to the needs of the colonies	Fertile farmland produced export crops
ETHNIC DIVERSITY	Mainly English	English, Dutch, German, and Scotch-Irish
SETTLEMENT STRUCTURE	Close-knit towns	More scattered settlements
CULTURE AND SOCIETY	Religious uniformity; small family farms and businesses with few servants or slaves	Ethnic and religious diversity; larger farms and businesses need indentured servants

Analyze Images Members of a Dutch colonial family sit around their tea table in New York in the 1700s. **Synthesize Visual Information** How does this image show differences in colonial men's and women's roles?

Many of the settlers who arrived in the back country moved onto Indian lands. "The Indians . . . are alarmed at the swarm of strangers," one Pennsylvania official reported. "We are afraid of a [fight] between them for the [colonists] are very rough to them." However, officials did not step in to protect Indian rights. On more than one occasion, disputes between settlers and Indians resulted in violence.

READING CHECK **Identify Main Ideas** Why was so much of the Middle Colonies' economy based on farming?

☑ Lesson Check

Practice Vocabulary

1. What were the differences between a **proprietary colony** and a **royal colony**?

2. What were the **Quakers**' beliefs regarding equality?

Critical Thinking and Writing

3. **Identify Supporting Details** What did the term "free enterprise system" mean in New Jersey while it was a proprietary colony?

4. **Summarize** What did William Penn do to reflect the values of the Quaker religion in his colony?

5. **Draw Conclusions** How did the free enterprise system encourage the cultivation of cash crops in the Middle Colonies?

6. **Writing Workshop: Organize Sequence of Events** Make an ordered list of events in your 📓 Active Journal to show what happens to your character in your narrative essay. You will use this sequence of events when you write your narrative essay at the end of this topic.

The Southern Colonies

BOUNCE TO ACTIVATE

VIDEO

GET READY TO READ

START UP

Examine the image of the ships sailing in Charleston Harbor. What do the number of ships tell you about the city during the colonial era?

GUIDING QUESTIONS

- Why was Maryland was established?
- What were the reasons the Carolinas and Georgia were established?
- How would you describe the relationship between environments, settlement patterns, and economic systems in the Southern Colonies?
- How did slavery spread in the Southern Colonies?

TAKE NOTES

Literacy Skills: Classify and Categorize

Use the graphic organizer in your 📓 Active Journal to take notes as you read the lesson.

PRACTICE VOCABULARY

Use the vocabulary activity in your 📓 Active Journal to practice the vocabulary words.

Vocabulary

Act of Toleration   slave code

indigo   racism

debtor

Academic Vocabulary

deprive

quarters

In 1632, Sir George Calvert persuaded King Charles I to grant him land for a colony in the Americas. Calvert had ruined his career in Protestant England by becoming a Roman Catholic. Now, he planned to build a colony where Catholics could practice their religion freely.

Why Did Lord Baltimore Start a Colony?

Calvert named his colony Maryland in honor of Queen Henrietta Maria, the king's wife. Calvert died before the colony could get underway. His son Cecil, Lord Baltimore, pushed on with the project.

Settlers Come to Maryland In the spring of 1634, about 200 colonists landed along the upper Chesapeake Bay, across the Potomac River from England's first southern colony, Virginia. Maryland was truly a land of plenty. Chesapeake Bay was full of fish, oysters, and crabs. Across the bay, Virginians were already growing tobacco for profit. Maryland's new settlers hoped to do the same.

Remembering the early problems at Jamestown, the newcomers avoided the swampy lowlands. They built their first town, St. Mary's, in a drier location.

As proprietor of the colony, Lord Baltimore owned Maryland. It was his personal responsibility, not that of a company, to start the colony. He used private funds to do it. He appointed a governor and a council of advisers. He gave colonists a role in government by creating an elected assembly.

At first, settlers had to pay rent to Lord Baltimore. Few settlers came to Maryland, because most wanted to own their land. Eager to attract settlers, Lord Baltimore decided to make generous land grants to anyone who brought over servants, women, and children. Later he offered smaller farms, as well as great estates, to attract more settlers.

A few women took advantage of Lord Baltimore's offer of land. Two sisters, Margaret and Mary Brent, arrived in Maryland in 1638 with nine male servants. In time, they set up two plantations of about 1,000 acres each. Later, Margaret Brent helped prevent a rebellion among the governor's soldiers. The Maryland assembly praised her efforts, saying that "the colony's safety at any time [was better] in her hands than in any man's."

Acceptance of Other Religions To make sure Maryland continued to grow, Lord Baltimore welcomed Protestants as well as Catholics to the colony. Later, Lord Baltimore came to fear that Protestants might try to **deprive** Catholics of their right to worship freely. In 1649, he asked the assembly to pass an **Act of Toleration**. The law provided religious freedom for all Christians. As in many colonies, this freedom did not extend to Jews.

☑ READING CHECK **Identify Supporting Details** How did Lord Baltimore found the Maryland colony?

Who Settled the Carolinas and Georgia?

South of Virginia and Maryland, English colonists settled in a region that they called the Carolinas. In 1663, a group of eight English nobles received a grant of land from King Charles II. Settlement took place in two separate areas, one in the north and the other in the south.

Southern Colonies

GEOGRAPHY **SKILLS**

The Southern Colonies were bordered on the west by the Appalachian Mountains and on the east by the Atlantic Ocean.

1. **Location** Which of the Southern Colonies was the southernmost?

2. **Draw Conclusions** Why do you think the Southern Colonies did not extend past the Appalachian Mountains?

Academic Vocabulary

deprive • v., to take something away from

▲ The indigo plant is used to make blue dye.

Analyze Images This 1782 map shows a plan for Savannah, the first settlement of the Georgia colony. **Use Visual Information** What elements of the planned settlement can you identify?

The Carolinas Develop Differently In the northern part of the Carolinas, settlers were mostly poor tobacco farmers who had spread south from Virginia. They tended to have small farms. Eventually, in 1712, the colony became known as North Carolina.

Farther south, the proprietors set up a larger colony, Charles Town, where the Ashley and Cooper rivers met the ocean. The colony became known as South Carolina in 1719. Eventually, Charles Town's name was shortened to Charleston.

Most early settlers in Charleston were English people who had been living in Barbados, a British colony in the Caribbean. Later, other immigrants arrived, including Germans, Swiss, French Protestants, and Spanish Jews.

Around 1685, a few planters discovered that rice grew well in the swampy lowlands along the coast. However, they were unable to grow rich crops until Africans from rice-growing areas of Africa arrived in the colony. Before long, Carolina rice was a profitable crop traded around the world. Settlers farther inland in South Carolina later learned to raise **indigo**, a plant used to make a valuable blue dye.

Georgia Offers a Second Chance The last of England's Southern Colonies was carved out of the southern part of South Carolina. James Oglethorpe, an English soldier and social reformer, helped to found Georgia in 1732. He and the other trustees started and funded the colony privately. They wanted the new colony to be a place where **debtors**, or people who owed money they could not pay back, could make a fresh start. They also wanted to protect the colonies to the north from Spanish Florida. Like Penn, who had established Pennsylvania as a refuge for people of different religions, Oglethorpe established Georgia mainly for social reasons, as a refuge for debtors.

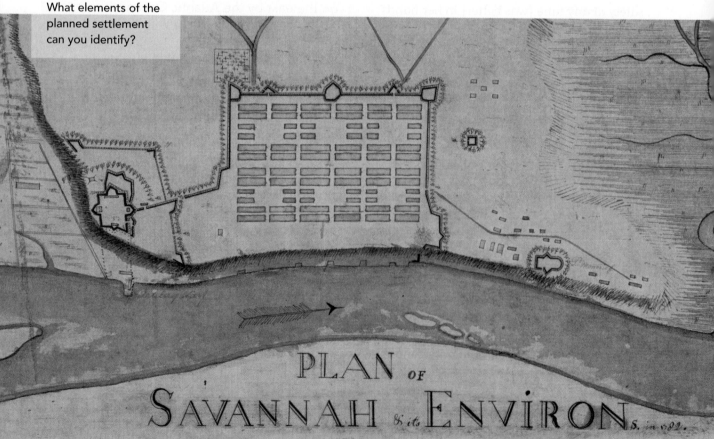

PLAN OF SAVANNAH & its ENVIRON

Under English law, the government could imprison debtors until they paid what they owed. If they ever got out of jail, debtors often had no money and no place to live. Oglethorpe offered to pay for debtors and other poor people to travel to Georgia. "In America," he said, "there are enough fertile lands to feed all the poor of England."

In 1733, Oglethorpe and 120 colonists built the colony's first settlement at Savannah, along the Savannah River. Oglethorpe set strict rules for the colony. Farms could be no bigger than 500 acres, and slavery was forbidden.

At first, Georgia grew slowly. Later, however, Oglethorpe changed the rules to allow large plantations and slave labor. After that, the colony grew more quickly.

Analyze Images James Oglethorpe founded Georgia in 1732. **Use Visual Information** How does the image portray Oglethorpe's arrival in America?

✓READING CHECK **Understand Effects** Why did South Carolina's economy come to depend on rice crops?

How Did Two Regions Develop Differently?

The plantation system developed in the Southern Colonies because of the headright. The headright was a grant of land for each settler who came to a colony, or for the person who paid to bring a settler. Wealthy settlers saw a chance to gain even more wealth by paying for farm workers and thus gaining ownership of large amounts of fertile, coastal farmland.

Although the plantation system developed first in Virginia, South Carolina planters turned to it as well. They wanted large numbers of workers for rice plantations. Few white settlers were willing to work in rice paddies. As in Virginia, planters turned to Africa for slave labor.

By 1700, most people coming to Charleston were African men and women brought against their will. Each time a planter bought an enslaved African, the planter gained more land. This system led to the expansion of slavery across the South.

Tidewater Plantations on the Coast The Southern Colonies enjoyed warmer weather and a longer growing season than the colonies to the north. Parts of Virginia, Maryland, and North Carolina near the coast all became major tobacco-growing areas. Settlers in lowland South Carolina and Georgia raised rice, indigo, and cotton. In these regions, physical characteristics of the environment, such as flat landscapes and fertile soils, resulted in a relatively dense population during the 1600s and 1700s.

● INTERACTIVE

Comparing the Thirteen Colonies

▲ Most enslaved Africans worked on large plantations with rich farmland where they grew crops of rice, indigo, tobacco, and cotton.

Colonists soon found that it was most profitable to raise tobacco and rice on large plantations. As you may recall, a plantation is a large estate farmed by many workers. The earliest planters settled along rivers and creeks of the coastal plain. Because these rivers and creeks rose and fell with ocean tides, the region was known as the Tidewater. The Tidewater's gentle slopes and rivers offered rich farmland for plantations.

Farther inland, planters settled along rivers. Rivers provided an easy way to move goods to market. Planters loaded crops onto ships bound for the West Indies and Europe. On the return trip, the ships carried English manufactured goods and other luxuries for planters and their families.

Most Tidewater plantations had their own docks along the river, and merchant ships picked up crops and delivered goods directly to them. For this reason, few large seaport cities developed in the Southern Colonies.

Academic Vocabulary

quarters • *n.*, living accommodations

Large Tidewater plantations often consisted of brick or framed mansions with nearby storehouses and **quarters** for enslaved workers. The mansions overlooked fields or paddies, and often, the nearest river. On these southern plantations, anywhere from 20 to 100 enslaved Africans and African Americans did most of the work. Most of these enslaved workers worked in the fields. Others were skilled workers, such as carpenters, barrel makers, or blacksmiths. Still other enslaved Africans and African Americans worked in the main house as cooks, servants, or housekeepers.

Only a small percentage of white southerners owned large plantations, yet planters set the style of southern living. Life centered around the planter's house, or the Great House. There, the planter's family lived in elegant quarters, including a parlor for visitors, a dining room, and guest bedrooms.

During the growing season, planters decided which fields to plant, what crops to grow, and when to harvest the crops. Planters' wives kept the household running smoothly. They directed enslaved cooks, maids, and butlers in the house and made sure daily tasks were done, such as milking cows.

In contrast to the lives of the planters, enslaved workers faced daily hardship. They were impoverished and denied basic rights. Their diets were often inadequate for the work they did. Their dwellings were rough and open to the weather. They faced diseases and other dangers.

Yet enslaved Africans played a crucial role on plantations. They used farming skills they had brought from West Africa. With their help, English settlers learned how to grow rice. Africans also knew how to use wild plants unfamiliar to the English. They made water buckets out of gourds, and they used palmetto leaves to make fans, brooms, and baskets.

The Backcountry Farther Inland

West of the Tidewater, life and the local economy were very different. Here, at the base of the Appalachians, rolling hills and thick forests covered the land. These physical characteristics of the environment would in turn influence where people lived and how they made a living in the region during the 1600s and 1700s. As in the Middle Colonies, this inland area was called the backcountry. Attracted by rich soil, settlers followed the Great Wagon Road into the backcountry of Maryland, Virginia, and the Carolinas.

Among the settlers who moved into the backcountry were Scotch-Irish and Germans, including German Moravians. The Scotch-Irish tended to be Presbyterian farmers and craftspeople. Many were escaping famine and harsh treatment under English rule in Northern Ireland, or were the children of such immigrants.

INTERACTIVE

A Southern Colonial Plantation

▼ Planters' wives kept the household running smoothly and directed the enslaved workers.

They built churches and started schools in their backcountry settlements. These immigrant groups transformed the environment by clearing the forests and creating fields where they grew crops such as wheat and building pens where they raised cattle and pigs.

The German immigrants to the backcountry, mostly Lutherans, sought good land at low cost. They often settled together in the same areas, speaking German and retaining German culture. The German Moravians were members of a Protestant group that sought to convert Indians to Christianity. They allowed women to preach and were pacifists. The Moravians kept careful records of backcountry life—including everything from the weather to fashions—that historians still use today.

The backcountry was more democratic than the Tidewater. Settlers there were more likely to treat one another as equals. Men tended smaller fields of tobacco or garden crops such as beans, corn, or peas. They also hunted game.

The distance of the backcountry from the coastline made trade difficult and prevented the development of a plantation economy. Instead of relying on income from cash crops, backcountry farmers had to be mostly self-sufficient. Surplus goods were sold or traded at local markets. Women cooked meals and fashioned simple, rugged clothing out of wool or deerskins. Another major difference between the backcountry and the Tidewater was slavery. Farms were smaller in the backcountry in part because of the hills and thick forests. Fewer enslaved Africans worked on these smaller farms, and most people were of European descent.

The hardships of backcountry life brought settlers closer together. Families gathered to husk corn or help one another build barns. Clustered in fertile valleys along the edge of the Appalachians, these hardy settlers felled trees and grew crops. By changing the environment, they in turn encouraged further economic development in the region.

Analyze Charts The Tidewater and the backcountry differed greatly in terms of physical environment, population, government, economy, and culture. **Understand Effects** How did the environment affect farming in each region?

☑ READING CHECK **Identify Supporting Details** Why was there less slavery in the backcountry than in the Tidewater region?

Life in the Colonial Tidewater and Backcountry

	TIDEWATER	BACKCOUNTRY
LOCATION	Coastal plains	Appalachian Mountains and their foothills
TERRAIN	Flat plain	Hilly, mountainous
POPULATION	Early English settlers and enslaved Africans	Scotch-Irish, poorer English migrants, Germans
ECONOMY	Large-scale plantation farming of cash crops for export	Small-scale subsistence farming, fur trade

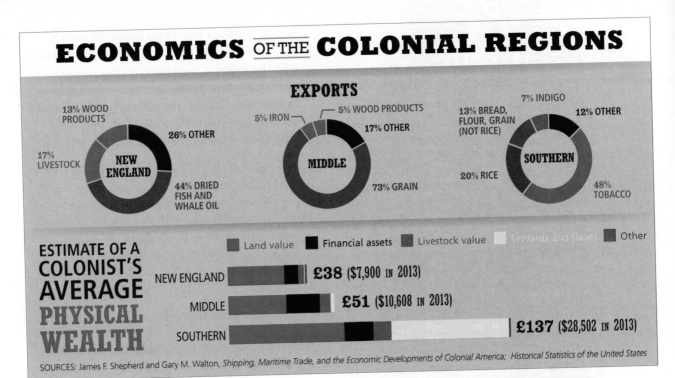

ECONOMICS OF THE COLONIAL REGIONS

EXPORTS

NEW ENGLAND
- 13% WOOD PRODUCTS
- 26% OTHER
- 17% LIVESTOCK
- 44% DRIED FISH AND WHALE OIL

MIDDLE
- 5% IRON
- 5% WOOD PRODUCTS
- 17% OTHER
- 73% GRAIN

SOUTHERN
- 7% INDIGO
- 13% BREAD, FLOUR, GRAIN (NOT RICE)
- 12% OTHER
- 20% RICE
- 48% TOBACCO

ESTIMATE OF A COLONIST'S AVERAGE PHYSICAL WEALTH

Legend: Land value | Financial assets | Livestock value | Servants and slaves | Other

NEW ENGLAND	£38 ($7,900 IN 2013)
MIDDLE	£51 ($10,608 IN 2013)
SOUTHERN	£137 ($28,502 IN 2013)

SOURCES: James F. Shepherd and Gary M. Walton, *Shipping, Maritime Trade, and the Economic Developments of Colonial America; Historical Statistics of the United States*

The Slave Trade Expands

In the early years, Africans in the English colonies included free people and indentured servants as well as enslaved persons. During the 1600s, even Africans who were enslaved enjoyed some privileges. The first enslaved Africans arrived in Virginia in 1619. For the next 50 years, since the African population was small, the status of Africans in the colony was not clearly established. Some enslaved Africans purchased their freedom. Several Africans during the 1600s, such as Anthony Johnson, became successful property owners. In South Carolina, some enslaved Africans worked without supervision as cowboys, herding cattle to market.

By 1700, plantations in the Southern Colonies had come to rely heavily on slave labor. Eventually, enslaved Africans made up the majority of the population in South Carolina and Georgia. They cleared the land, worked the crops, and tended the livestock. In order to maintain the supply of enslaved Africans, southern planters relied on a system of slave trading that stretched halfway across the globe.

Africans Are Enslaved As you have learned, in Africa and elsewhere around the world, slavery had been part of the social and economic system since ancient times. Usually, slaves were people who had been captured in war. Muslim merchants sometimes brought enslaved Africans into Europe and the Middle East.

Over a period of about 300 years, as the transatlantic slave trade grew, millions of Africans were enslaved. Slave traders from European nations set up posts along the West African coast. They offered guns and other goods in exchange for enslaved Africans.

Analyze Charts The economies of the three colonial regions depended on different resources. **Synthesize Visual Information** What two resources did the Southern Colonies possess in great abundance that increased their wealth over that of the New England and Middle Colonies?

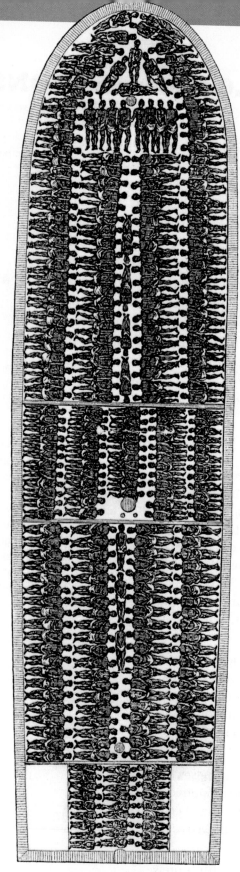

▲ Enslaved Africans were often crowded into extremely tight quarters during the Middle Passage across the Atlantic.

As the demand for cheap labor increased, Africans who lived along the coast made raids into the interior, seeking captives to sell to the Europeans. They marched their captives to the coast. There, the Africans were loaded aboard European ships headed for forced immigration to the Americas.

Sailing Across the Middle Passage In the 1700s, English sailors began referring to the passage of slave-trading ships west across the Atlantic Ocean as the Middle Passage. Below the decks of these ships, enslaved Africans were often crammed tightly together on shelves. One observer noted that they were "chained to each other hand and foot, and stowed so close, that they were not allowed above a foot and a half for each in breadth." The captives were allowed above deck to eat and exercise in the fresh air only once or twice a day.

Many enslaved Africans resisted, but only a few escaped. Some fought for their freedom during the trip. They would stage a mutiny or revolt. The slave traders lived in fear of this and were heavily armed. Other slaves resisted by refusing to eat or by committing suicide by jumping overboard to avoid a life of enslavement.

Records of slave-trading ships show that about 10 percent of Africans loaded aboard a ship for passage to the Americas died during the voyage. Many died of illnesses that spread rapidly in the filthy, crowded conditions inside a ship's hold. Others died of mistreatment. This slave trade lasted about 300 years. During that time, it may have caused the deaths of as many as 2 to 3 million Africans.

Human Rights Are Often Ignored As the importance of slavery increased during the 1600s, and particularly after Bacon's Rebellion in Virginia, greater limits were placed on the rights of enslaved Africans and African Americans. Colonists passed laws that set out rules for slaves' behavior and denied enslaved people basic human rights. These **slave codes** treated enslaved Africans and African Americans not as human beings but as property.

Analyze Images Some slave ships carried as many as 700 prisoners. **Use Visual Information** How does this image reflect the details described in the text?

Most English colonists did not question the justice of owning enslaved Africans. They believed that black Africans, as a racial group, were inferior to white Europeans. The belief that one race is superior to another is called **racism**. Some colonists believed that they were helping enslaved Africans by teaching them Christianity.

A handful of colonists spoke out against the evils of slavery. In 1688, Quakers in Germantown, Pennsylvania, became the first group of colonists to call for an end to slavery.

☑ READING CHECK Draw Conclusions Why did many colonists believe there was nothing wrong with slavery?

☑ Lesson Check

Practice Vocabulary

1. Which colony was set up as a refuge for **debtors?**

2. What is **racism?**

Critical Thinking and Writing

3. **Cite Evidence** What evidence supports the claim that the planters in the southern part of the Carolinas could not make rice a profitable crop on their own?

4. **Summarize** What was the Middle Passage like for most enslaved Africans?

5. **Understand Effects** Why was South Carolina the only English colony in 1700 where the majority of the population was made up of enslaved Africans?

6. **Writing Workshop: Organize Sequence of Events** Continue adding to your ordered list of events in your 📘 Active Journal to show what happens to your character in your narrative essay. You will use this sequence of events when you write your narrative essay at the end of the Topic.

Colonial Society

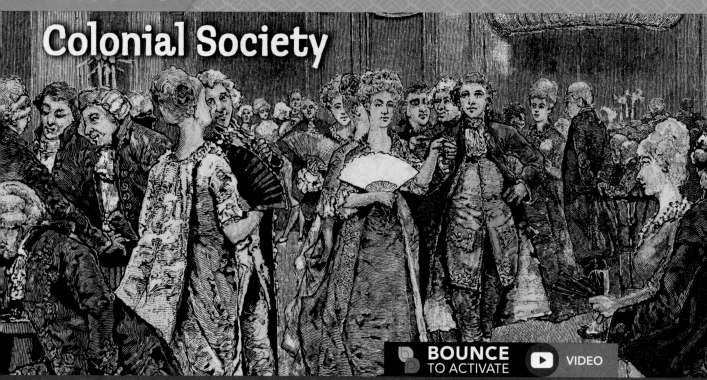

BOUNCE TO ACTIVATE ▶ VIDEO

GET READY TO READ

START UP

Examine the image of colonial men and women dancing. What does it tell you about colonial society?

GUIDING QUESTIONS

- How was colonial society structured?
- What impact did the Great Awakening have on colonial society?
- How would you describe education in the colonies?
- How did art, music, literature, and ideas have an impact on colonial society?

TAKE NOTES

Literacy Skills: Summarize

Use the graphic organizer in your 📓 Active Journal to take notes as you read the lesson.

PRACTICE VOCABULARY

Use the vocabulary activity in your 📓 Active Journal to practice the vocabulary words.

Vocabulary		Academic Vocabulary
gentry	apprentice	
middle class	dame school	tolerant
Gullah	Enlightenment	assumption
Great Awakening	libel	

For the most part, colonists enjoyed more social equality than people in England, where a person's opportunities in life were largely determined by birth. Still, class differences existed.

Colonial Social Classes

Like Europeans, colonial Americans thought it was only natural that some people rank more highly than others. A person's birth and wealth still determined his or her social status.

The Upper and Middle Social Classes At the top of society stood the **gentry**. The gentry included wealthy planters, merchants, ministers, successful lawyers, and royal officials. They could afford to dress in the latest fashions from London.

Below the gentry were the **middle class**. The middle class included farmers who worked their own land, skilled craft workers, and some tradespeople. Nearly three quarters of all white colonists belonged to the middle class.

They prospered because land in the colonies was plentiful and easy to buy. In addition, skilled work was in high demand and paid relatively well.

The Lower Social Classes
The lower social classes included hired farmhands and indentured servants. Far below them in status were enslaved Africans and African Americans.

Indentured servants signed contracts to work without wages for a period of four to seven years for anyone who would pay their ocean passage to the Americas. When their term of service was completed, indentured servants received "freedom dues": a set of clothes, tools, and 50 acres of land. Because there were so few European women in the colonies, female indentured servants often shortened their terms of service by marrying. Thousands of men, women, and children came to North America as indentured servants. After completing their terms, some became successful and rose into the middle class.

Working Life in the Countryside
From New Hampshire to Georgia, most colonists survived by farming. Men worked long hours planting crops, tending the fields, and raising livestock—pigs, cows, and other farm animals. Anything beyond what the family needed to live was taken to markets to sell. Families also traded crops and livestock with their neighbors for additional goods.

While men typically did much of the agricultural work, women often worked within the home. They worked hard taking care of the household and the family. By the kitchen fire, they cooked the family's meals. They milked cows, tended chickens and a vegetable garden, watched the children, cleaned, did laundry by hand, and made candles, cheese, and clothes.

Life was different in the backcountry, out beyond more settled lands. Wives and husbands often worked side by side in the fields at harvest time. No one worried whether harvesting was proper "woman's work."

Analyze Images Many middle-class colonists worked in small cottage industries such as silk making. **Synthesize Visual Information** What was life like for children in this household?

▲ A basket maker keeps Gullah traditions alive in Charleston, South Carolina.

One surprised visitor described a typical backcountry woman's activities: "She will carry a gunn in the woods and kill deer, turkeys &c., shoot down wild cattle, catch and tye hoggs, knock down [cattle] with an ax, and perform the most manfull Exercises as well as most men."

Working Life in Cities In cities, women sometimes worked outside the home. A young single woman from a poorer family might work for one of the gentry as a maid, a cook, or a nurse. Other women were midwives, who delivered babies. Still others sewed fine hats or dresses to be sold to women who could afford them. Learning such skills often required years of training.

Some women learned trades from their fathers, brothers, or husbands. They worked as printers, butchers, shoemakers, and silversmiths. A woman might take over her husband's business when he died.

Men often worked in trades, for example as coopers (who made and repaired wooden barrels), blacksmiths, and silversmiths. Most large towns in the colonies were seaports, where merchants and traders brought goods to and from Europe. As this trade grew, more men also took on jobs as bankers, lawyers, and businessmen.

Some educated men in the colonies became politicians. Others were pamphleteers, who wrote and distributed small booklets informing people on a subject. There were many doctors in the colonies, where illness was common. However, medical training varied. A surgeon might be a barber with little real medical training.

African Influences in the Colonies By the mid-1700s, the culture of Africans and African Americans in the colonies varied greatly. On rice plantations in South Carolina, enslaved Africans used methods from West Africa for growing and harvesting rice. For example, flat baskets holding the grains were shaken in the wind to separate the grains from leaves and other particles. Then a wooden mortar and pestle were used to clean the grains.

Language is another area where African influences were strong. In some coastal areas, enslaved Africans spoke a distinctive combination of English and West African languages known as **Gullah** (GUH luh). Parents often chose African names for their children, such as Quosh or Juba or Cuff.

In Charleston and other South Carolina port towns, some Africans worked along the dock, making rope or barrels or helping to build ships. Skilled craftworkers made fine wooden cabinets or silver plates and utensils. Many of their designs reflected African artistic styles. Although most Africans in these towns were enslaved, many opened their own shops or stalls in the market. Some used their earnings to buy their own and their family's freedom.

In the Middle Colonies and New England, the African and African American population increased during the 1700s. Africans and African Americans in the northern colonies included both free and enslaved people. Their numbers were much lower than in the Southern Colonies. However, they were still an important part of the population.

In some of the Middle Colonies, such as New York, there were even plantations that relied on slave labor. Often, these plantations produced grains and meat for sale to feed enslaved workers in the Southern Colonies or the West Indies.

INTERACTIVE

The Arts in Colonial America

✓ READING CHECK **Compare and Contrast** How was working life in the countryside similar to working life elsewhere? How was it different?

How Did Colonial Art, Literature, and Music Affect Society?

Colonists brought with them the artistic traditions of their homelands. New artistic styles also developed that reflected colonial society. Wealthy gentry decorated their homes with paintings of landscapes and religious art. Furniture, houses, and clothing were often decorated with intricate carvings or designs.

Art Reflects Colonial Society Paintings that celebrated important people of the time were especially popular works of art. Those who could afford it hired artists to paint portraits of their family members. These portraits showed off the family's importance and provided a valuable keepsake to be passed on for generations to come. Portraits also honored famous individuals and key events. One of the oldest surviving colonial portraits is of New Netherland Governor Peter Stuyvesant, painted in the 1660s.

Prints were also popular. Prints were made from engravings scratched into metal or carved into wood. Printmakers used the metal or wood with ink, paper, and a press to make a picture that could be easily reproduced. Many people had prints of famous figures, such as politicians or clergymen.

Many artists were self-taught. Few became wealthy from their work. They often traveled from town to town in search of people who wanted portraits done. The paintings they left behind are like time capsules. Much like photographs do today, they show how people dressed, what their tastes were like, and how their families lived.

American Literature Emerges Literature also developed in the colonies. The first colonial printing press was built in Massachusetts in 1640. It printed religious books and books for Harvard College. With the spread of printing, more colonists began to read.

Analyze Images This portrait of Peter Stuyvesant is one of the few colonial portraits that have survived. **Synthesize Visual Information** How did the painter try to please Stuyvesant?

Analyze Images A colonist plays the harpsichord, an instrument commonly featured in classical pieces of the period. **Infer** How many colonial homes do you think had a harpsichord? Why?

Colonists read reprints of European books and books by American writers. One of the most popular—and particularly American—types of stories was the captivity tale. In these stories, a white settler was captured by American Indians and had to overcome hardships in order to escape.

Colonial Music Music was another popular art form in the colonies. Colonists brought popular folk music from Europe. They sang and danced at weddings and other celebrations. Enslaved Africans brought musical traditions with them from Africa. These traditions combined with European traditions in musical forms such as work songs and spirituals, or religious songs.

Music was closely tied to religious life for many colonists. New organs appeared in churches. The hymns people sang grew especially popular during the Great Awakening.

☑ READING CHECK **Identify Supporting Details** What clues can we find about colonial lives in artwork such as paintings?

What Was the Impact of a New Religious Movement?

In the 1730s and 1740s, a religious revival, or movement, known as the **Great Awakening** swept through the colonies. Its drama and emotion touched women and men of all races, ethnic backgrounds, and classes.

Enthusiastic Preachers A New England preacher, Jonathan Edwards, helped set off the Great Awakening. In powerful sermons, Edwards called on colonists, especially young people, to examine their lives.

He preached of the sweetness and beauty of God. At the same time, he warned listeners to heed the Bible's teachings. Otherwise, they would be "sinners in the hands of an angry God," headed for the fiery torments of hell. The powerful sermons of preachers such as Edwards were one of the main causes of the Great Awakening.

In 1739, when an English minister named George Whitefield arrived in the colonies, the movement spread like wildfire. Whitefield drew huge crowds to outdoor meetings. An enthusiastic and energetic preacher, his voice would ring with feeling as he called on sinners to repent.

Quick Activity

Imagine three events that show important aspects of colonial life, and write newspaper headlines about these events in your 📓 Active Journal.

After hearing Whitefield speak, Jonathan Edwards's wife reported, "I have seen upwards of a thousand people hang on his words with breathless silence, broken only by an occasional half-suppressed sob."

The Great Awakening's Impact The colonies were made up of many different religious groups. There were Quakers, Puritans, Catholics, Presbyterians, and more. Each group had its own ideas about the proper relationship with God.

Some groups, like the Anglicans, disagreed strongly with Whitefield. Others, like the Baptists and Methodists, found new opportunities to expand during the Great Awakening as people revisited their faith.

The Great Awakening aroused bitter debate. People who supported the movement often split away from their old churches to form new ones. Opponents warned that the movement was too emotional. Still, the growth of so many new churches forced colonists to become more **tolerant** of people with different beliefs. Also, because the Great Awakening appealed to people in all of the colonies, from different classes and ethnic backgrounds, it brought colonists together for the first time. Ties formed during the Great Awakening helped establish the groundwork for future bonds among the colonies.

In the colonies, members of most churches controlled their parishes. The role parishes played in local communities made people think about the importance of self-rule—a key factor in the development of American democracy.

Analyze Visuals
Crowds of people gathered to hear sermons by English minister George Whitefield. **Infer** What does the artist suggest about the attitude of Whitefield's audience?

The Great Awakening contributed in another way to the spread of democratic feelings in the colonies. Many of the new preachers were not as well educated as most ministers. They argued that formal training was less important than a heart filled with the Holy Spirit. Such teachings encouraged a spirit of independence. People began to think differently about their political rights and their governments. They felt if they could figure out how to worship on their own and how to run their own churches, then they could govern themselves with those same virtues. Eventually, many colonists challenged the authority of colonial governors and the king.

☑️ READING CHECK Identify Main Ideas How did the Great Awakening change how people thought about themselves and their political rights?

Education in the Colonies

Among the colonists, New Englanders were the most concerned about education. Puritans taught that all people had a duty to study the Bible. If colonists did not learn to read, how would they study the Bible?

Public Schools in New England In 1642, the Massachusetts assembly passed a law ordering all parents to teach their children "to read and understand the principles of religion." They also required all towns with 50 or more families to hire a schoolteacher. Towns with 100 or more families also had to set up a grammar school to prepare boys for college.

In this way, Massachusetts set up the first public schools, or schools supported by taxes. Public schools allowed both rich and poor children to receive an education.

The first New England schools had only one room for students of all ages. Parents paid the schoolteacher with food. Each child was expected to bring a share of wood for the stove.

▼ In colonial New England, instructors taught students of all ages in a single classroom.

Private Education In the Middle Colonies, churches and individual families set up private schools. Because pupils paid to attend, only wealthy families could afford to educate their children.

In the Southern Colonies, people often lived too far from one another to bring children together in one school building. Some planters hired tutors, or private teachers. The wealthiest planters sent their sons to school in England. As a rule, enslaved African Americans were denied education of any kind.

Apprenticeships and Dame Schools Boys whose parents wished them to learn a trade or craft served as **apprentices** (uh PREN tis ez). An apprentice worked for a master to learn a trade or a craft. For example, when a boy reached the age of 12 or 13, his parents might apprentice him to a master glassmaker.

The young apprentice lived in the glassmaker's home for six or seven years while learning the craft. The glassmaker gave the boy food and clothing and taught him how to read and write. He also provided him with religious training.

In return, the apprentice worked as a helper in the glassmaker's shop and learned needed skills. Boys were apprenticed in many trades, including papermaking, printing, and tanning (making leather).

In New England, most schools accepted only boys. However, some girls attended **dame schools**, or private schools run by women in their own homes. Other girls, though, usually learned skills from their mothers, who taught them to cook, make soap and candles, spin wool, weave, sew, and embroider. A few learned to read and write.

The Growth of Colleges In 1633, Puritan John Eliot spoke of the need for Massachusetts to establish an official college. Institutions of higher learning were held up as a way to promote European culture in the Americas. As Eliot cautioned, "if we no[u]rish not L[e]arning both church & common wealth will sinke."

Harvard College, the first college in the colonies, opened in 1638 with ten students. The goal of the college was to educate future ministers. It was modeled after English schools, where students studied six days a week in Latin and Greek. It was open only to men.

By the late 1600s, however, Harvard graduates were moving away from the ministry. Some became physicians, public servants, or teachers. The College of William and Mary opened in Virginia to prepare men for the Anglican ministry. Yale College in Connecticut aimed to educate clergymen. Gradually, nine colleges opened over the following century and expanded their areas of study.

▲ Initially, colleges like Yale, shown here in a late-1700s engraving, were created to educate the clergy. Later, Yale expanded its offerings to other students.

✓ **READING CHECK** **Draw Conclusions** Do you think children were better educated in New England than they were in the other colonies? Why or why not?

 **INTERACTIVE**

Education in the Colonies

How Did New Ideas Influence the Colonies?

In the 1600s, European thinkers tried to question common **assumptions** and to base their understanding of the world on reason and logic. They developed theories and performed experiments to test them. In doing so, they discovered many of the laws of nature. The English scientist Isaac Newton, for example, explained the law of gravity.

The Ideas of the Enlightenment European thinkers of the late 1600s and 1700s also believed that reason and scientific methods could be applied to the study of society. They tried to discover the natural laws that governed human behavior. Because these thinkers believed in the light of human reason, the movement that they started is known as the **Enlightenment**. John Locke, an English philosopher, wrote works that were widely read in the colonies. He said people could gain knowledge of the world by observing and experimenting.

In the English colonies, the Enlightenment spread among better-educated colonists. They included wealthy merchants, lawyers, ministers, and others who had the leisure to read the latest books from Europe. Urban craftsmen also heard and discussed these ideas.

Benjamin Franklin's Thought and Inventions The best example of the Enlightenment spirit in the English colonies was Benjamin Franklin. Franklin was born in 1706, the son of a poor Boston soap and candle maker. Although young Ben had only two years of formal schooling, he used his spare time to study literature, mathematics, and foreign languages.

At age 17, Franklin made his way to Philadelphia. There, he built up a successful printing business. His most popular publication was *Poor Richard's Almanack*. Published yearly, it contained useful information and clever proverbs, such as "Early to bed, early to rise, makes a man healthy, wealthy, and wise."

Like other Enlightenment thinkers, Franklin wanted to use reason to improve the world around him. He invented practical devices that helped improve daily life. For example, Franklin suffered from poor eyesight, so he invented bifocal glasses to help himself—and countless others—see better. Franklin also invented a new kind of iron stove. It was set in the middle of a room instead of in a wall, and it kept houses warmer without filling them with smoke. Another one of Franklin's inventions, the lightning rod, protected buildings from catching fire in a storm because of lightning strikes. As a community leader, Franklin persuaded Philadelphia officials to pave streets, organize a fire company, and set up the first lending library in the Americas. Franklin's inventions and his public service earned him worldwide fame.

The Influence of Colonial Cities and Towns While most colonists lived on farms, towns and cities strongly influenced colonial life. Through the great ports of Philadelphia, New York, Boston, and Charleston, merchants shipped products overseas. Towns and cities also served as centers of a busy trade between the coast and the growing backcountry.

Culture flourished in the towns. By the mid-1700s, many colonial towns had their own theaters. Town dwellers found entertainment at singing societies, traveling circuses, carnivals, and horse races.

BIOGRAPHY
5 Things to Know About

Benjamin Franklin
Writer, Scientist, and Statesman (1706–1790)

- Franklin was born in Boston in 1706 and was one of the founding fathers of the United States.

- Even though he stopped going to school when he was 10 years old, he continued to educate himself and became a writer, scientist, inventor, and statesman.

- He moved to Philadelphia when he was 17 years old and later became a successful printer and publisher.

- Franklin helped create the city's first library, fire company, and police force. He also helped establish a postal service in the colonies.

- He famously (and dangerously) flew a kite in a lightning storm to show that lightning is electricity.

Critical Thinking Why do you think the creation of a library, fire company, and police force in Philadelphia was significant?

Analyze Images John Peter Zenger celebrates after a jury found that he had not committed libel. **Identify Implied Main Ideas** What important tradition did Zenger help establish?

In 1704, John Campbell founded the *Boston News-Letter*, the first regular weekly newspaper in the English colonies. Within 50 years, each of the colonies, except New Jersey and Delaware, had at least one weekly paper.

John Peter Zenger's Libel Trial The growth of colonial newspapers led to a dispute over freedom of the press. John Peter Zenger published the *Weekly Journal* in New York City. In 1734, he was arrested for publishing stories that criticized the governor. Zenger was put on trial for **libel**—the act of publishing a statement that may unjustly damage a person's reputation. Zenger's lawyer argued that, since the stories were true, his client had not committed libel. The jury agreed and freed Zenger. At the time, the case did not attract a great deal of attention. However, freedom of the press would become recognized as a basic American right.

☑ **READING CHECK** **Understand Effects** How did Franklin's inventions influence the daily lives of colonists?

☑ Lesson Check

Practice Vocabulary

1. Who were some of the people who were included in the **gentry**?

2. Why was John Peter Zenger found not guilty of **libel**?

Critical Thinking and Writing

3. **Infer** Women did not have access to certain jobs in the colonies. How was access to employment restricted for women?

4. **Understand Effects** How did the Great Awakening lead to greater religious tolerance?

5. **Draw Conclusions** Why do you think enslaved Africans were generally denied an education?

6. **Writing Workshop: Use Narrative Techniques** In your 🗐 Active Journal, identify and record some narrative techniques you can use to tell your story. You will use these techniques when you write your narrative at the end of the topic.

Colonial Trade and Government

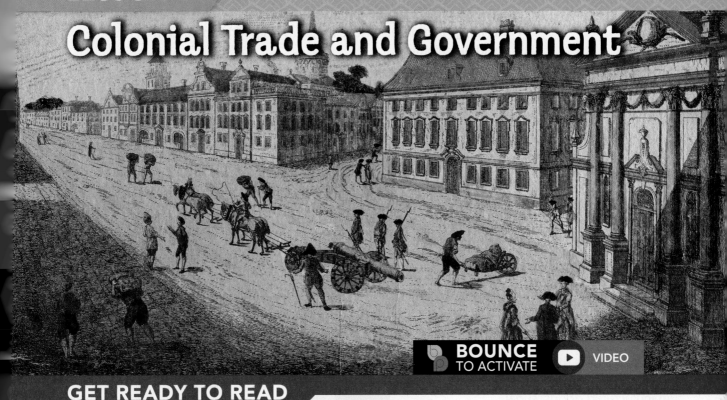

BOUNCE TO ACTIVATE ▶ VIDEO

GET READY TO READ

START UP

Examine the image of a busy street in Boston. What does it tell you about daily life in the British colonies?

GUIDING QUESTIONS

- How did mercantilism develop?
- What is the relationship between the slave trade and other forms of trade?
- How did governments and legal systems in the colonies develop?

TAKE NOTES

Literacy Skills: Draw Conclusions

Use the graphic organizer in your 📖 Active Journal to take notes as you read the lesson.

PRACTICE VOCABULARY

Use the vocabulary activity in your 📖 Active Journal to practice the vocabulary words.

Vocabulary		Academic Vocabulary
mercantilism	legislature	prosperous
export	Glorious Revolution	bribe
import	bill of rights	
Navigation Acts	English Bill of Rights	
Yankee		
triangular trade		

Like other European nations at the time, England believed that its colonies should benefit the home country. This belief was part of an economic theory known as **mercantilism** (MUR kun til iz um).

Mercantilism and the English Colonies

According to the theory of mercantilism, a nation could become strong by keeping strict control over its trade. As one English gentleman put it, "Whosoever commands the trade of the world commands the riches of the world."

Imports and Exports Mercantilists thought that a country should export more than it imported. **Exports** are goods sent to markets outside a country.

Imports are goods brought into a country. If England sold more goods than it bought abroad, gold would flow into the home country as payment for those exports.

The Navigation Acts Beginning in the 1650s, the English Parliament passed a series of laws governing colonial trade.

The **Navigation Acts** regulated trade between England and its colonies in order to ensure that only England benefited from trade with its colonies.

Under the new laws, only colonial or English ships could carry goods to and from the colonies. Colonists were banned from trading directly with other European nations or their colonies. The Navigation Acts also listed certain products, such as tobacco and cotton, that colonial merchants could ship only to England. In this way, Parliament created jobs for English workers who cut and rolled tobacco or spun cotton into cloth.

The Navigation Acts helped the colonies as well as England. For example, the law encouraged colonists to build ships for their own use and for sale to England. As a result, New England became a **prosperous** shipbuilding center. Also, colonial merchants did not have to compete with foreign merchants because they were sure of having a market for their goods in England.

Academic Vocabulary
prosperous • *adj.*, having success, usually by making a lot of money

Still, many colonists resented the Navigation Acts. In their view, the laws favored English merchants. Colonial merchants often ignored the Navigation Acts or found ways to get around them.

✓ READING CHECK **Identify Main Ideas** Why did England pass the Navigation Acts?

Trading Across the Atlantic

The colonies produced a wide variety of goods, and merchant ships sailed up and down the Atlantic coast. Merchants from New England dominated colonial trade.

GEOGRAPHY **SKILLS**

This map shows the routes of the triangular trade of rum and manufactured goods, sugar and molasses, and persons.

1. **Movement** Which region was the first destination for many enslaved Africans?

2. **Infer** Why did ships travel west from Africa?

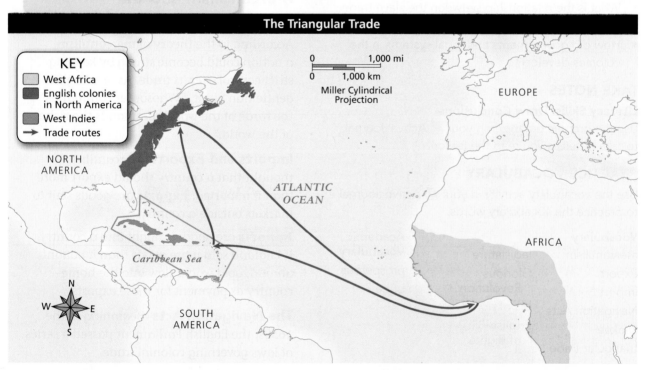

The Triangular Trade

KEY
- West Africa
- English colonies in North America
- West Indies
- → Trade routes

0   1,000 mi
0   1,000 km
Miller Cylindrical Projection

NORTH AMERICA

ATLANTIC OCEAN

EUROPE

Caribbean Sea

SOUTH AMERICA

AFRICA

N W E S

They were known by the nickname **Yankees** and had a reputation for being clever and hardworking. Yankee traders earned a reputation for profiting from any deal.

The Triangular Trade One colonial trade route was known as the **triangular trade** because the three legs of the route formed a triangle. On the first leg, ships from New England carried rum, guns, gunpowder, cloth, and tools from New England to West Africa. In Africa, Yankee merchants traded these goods for slaves.

On the second leg of the journey, ships carried enslaved Africans to the West Indies. This second leg of the voyage was known as the Middle Passage. With the profits from selling enslaved Africans, Yankee traders bought molasses—a dark-brown syrup made from sugar cane—and sugar. Ships then sailed back to New England, where colonists used the molasses and sugar to make rum for sale in Africa or Europe.

Merchants Disregard the Law Many New England merchants disobeyed the Navigation Acts and grew wealthy as a result. Traders were supposed to buy sugar and molasses only from English colonies in the West Indies. However, the demand for molasses was so high that New Englanders smuggled in cargoes from the Dutch, French, and Spanish West Indies, too. **Bribes** made customs officials look the other way.

▼ Ships leaving ports such as this one in Philadelphia were forced to sail to England because of the Navigation Acts.

✓ **READING CHECK** Identify Cause and Effect Why did many traders ignore the Navigation Acts?

What Were the Foundations of Representative Government?

Although each colony developed its own government, the governments had much in common. A governor directed the colony's affairs and enforced the laws. Most governors were appointed, either by the king or by the colony's proprietor. In Rhode Island and Connecticut, however, colonists elected their own governors. Representative government and institutions spread in the colonies for several reasons.

Elected Assemblies As you learned, the Virginia Company established an elected assembly, the House of Burgesses, to attract more settlers. This example, as well as the tradition of representative government established in the Magna Carta, led the colonies to create a **legislature** soon after founding. A legislature is a group of people, usually elected, that has the power to make laws. In most colonies, the legislature had an upper house and a lower house.

Academic Vocabulary

bribe • *n.*, something valuable that is given in order to get someone to do something

▶ **INTERACTIVE**

The Triangular Trade

The upper house was made up of advisers appointed by the governor. The lower house was an elected assembly. It approved laws and protected the rights of citizens. It also had the right to approve or reject any taxes or budget items the governor asked for. This "power of the purse," or right to raise or spend money, was an important check on the governor's power.

As colonial settlers founded new cities and towns, representative government and institutions grew. Most colonial cities and towns had their own city and town councils.

The Right to Vote Each colony had its own rules about who could vote. By the 1720s, however, all of the colonies had laws that restricted the right to vote to white Christian men over the age of 21.

In some colonies, only Protestants or members of a particular church could vote. All colonies restricted the vote to men who owned a certain amount of property. Colonial leaders believed that only property owners knew what was best for a colony.

Common Law The colonies followed English common law, or case law. Under common law, laws develop from the past rulings of judges. In applying laws, courts follow the idea that "like cases should be tried alike."

In the 1760s, William Blackstone published a book, *Commentaries on the Laws of England*. In it, Blackstone reviewed the entire history of English law. As a member of Parliament and a judge in England, he believed common law was the highest and best form of law.

Blackstone's ideas about common law took hold in the colonies. Common law was a body of laws that was valid independent of Parliament's acts. As such, it provided a basis for self-rule and an independent legal system once the colonies began to move toward independence.

Analyze Charts Colonial government in the English colonies was influenced by three important documents. **Identify Main Ideas** How did these documents influence the state and federal constitutions of the United States?

FOUNDATIONS OF AMERICAN DEMOCRACY

FOUNDING DOCUMENT

- Magna Carta
- English Bill of Rights
- Commentaries on the Laws of England

FUNDAMENTAL PRINCIPLES

- Government authority comes from the consent of the governed
- The power of government should be limited
- Government exists to protect individual rights and freedoms

INFLUENCE ON U.S. DOCUMENTS

U.S. Constitution
Bill of Rights
State constitutions
- Guarantee due process
- Establish rule of law
- Guarantee free elections and free speech
- Establish checks on government authority

The English Bill of Rights Colonists took great pride in their elected assemblies. They also valued the rights that the Magna Carta gave them as English subjects.

American colonists won still more rights due to the **Glorious Revolution** of 1688, when the English Parliament removed King James II from the throne and asked William and Mary of the Netherlands to rule. In return, William and Mary signed the English Bill of Rights in 1689. A **bill of rights** is a written list of freedoms the government promises to protect.

The **English Bill of Rights** protected the rights of individuals and gave anyone accused of a crime the right to a trial by jury. The English Bill of Rights also said that a ruler could not raise taxes or an army without the approval of Parliament. In addition, it strengthened the position of representative government and institutions in the colonies.

Liberties Are Restricted English colonists in the Americas often enjoyed more freedoms than did the English themselves. However, the rights of English citizens did not extend to all colonists. Women had more rights in the colonies than in England, but women colonists had far fewer rights than did free, white males.

In most colonies, unmarried women and widows had more rights than married women. They could make contracts and sue in court. In Maryland and the Carolinas, women settlers who headed families could buy land on the same terms as men.

African Americans and American Indians in the colonies had almost no rights. While so many colonists enjoyed English liberties, most African Americans were bound in slavery. The conflict between liberty and slavery would not be resolved until the 1860s.

 In most of the English colonies, women had the right to file suit in court.

☑ READING CHECK **Understand Effects** How did the English Bill of Rights promote freedom?

👆 INTERACTIVE

Influences on Colonial Government

☑ Lesson Check

Practice Vocabulary

1. What are **exports** and **imports**?

2. What did the **English Bill of Rights** do?

Critical Thinking and Writing

3. **Cite Evidence** What evidence in the reading suggests that molasses was critical to the success of the triangular trade?

4. **Draw Conclusions** How do you think colonial traders might have responded if England started to strictly enforce the Navigation Acts?

5. **Summarize** How did English laws contribute to the development of freedom and self-government in the American colonies?

6. **Writing Workshop: Use Descriptive Details and Sensory Language** Write notes in your 📓 Active Journal about descriptive details and sensory language that you can use in the narrative essay you will write at the end of the topic.

☑ Review and Assessment

VISUAL REVIEW

North American Colonial Powers

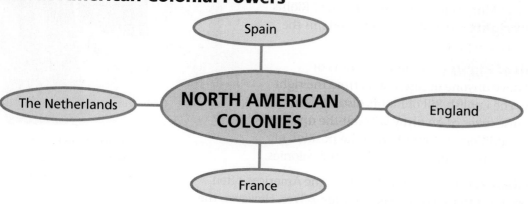

Spain

The Netherlands — **NORTH AMERICAN COLONIES** — England

France

NORTH AMERICAN ENGLISH COLONIES

New England Colonies	Middle Colonies	Southern Colonies
• Settlers sought religious freedom. • First settlements were at Plymouth and Massachusetts Bay. • New colonies formed over religious differences. • Fishing industry developed.	• First settlers were Dutch, but English took over. • First colony was New York; New Jersey, Pennsylvania, and Delaware formed later. • Land was fertile and had many natural resources.	• First settlement was Jamestown; settlers later arrived in Maryland, Carolinas, and Georgia. • Life was different on the Tidewater and in the backcountry. • The economy relied upon enslaved labor.

READING REVIEW

Use the Take Notes and Practice Vocabulary activities in your 📓 Active Journal to review the topic.

▶ INTERACTIVE

Practice vocabulary using the Topic Mini-Games

Quest FINDINGS

Create Your ePortfolio

Get help for creating your digital portfolio in your 📓 Active Journal.

ASSESSMENT

Vocabulary and Key Ideas

1. **Describe** What did the **conquistadors** in the Americas do?

2. **Define** Who were the **Pilgrims**?

3. **Describe** How did **racism** affect the way English colonists treated enslaved Africans?

4. **Identify Main Ideas** What was the significance of the **Great Awakening**?

5. **Recall** What set Pennsylvania apart from the other colonies?

6. **Explain** How did southern agriculture cause an increase in the number of enslaved Africans brought to America?

7. **Identify Supporting Details** What impact did religion have on the Puritans' approach to education?

Critical Thinking and Writing

8. **Use Evidence** Why were Cortés and his soldiers able to conquer the Aztec?

9. **Draw Conclusions** Why did the growth in the number of settlers in New England lead to war between the colonists and the Wampanoag-led alliance?

10. **Identify Cause and Effect** How did enslaved Africans boost the economy of South Carolina?

11. **Identify Main Ideas** Why did the Pilgrims form a government in which they governed themselves?

12. **Revisit the Essential Question** Why do people move? Explain using evidence from the topic.

13. **Writing Workshop: Write a Narrative Essay** Use the notes you made in your 📙 Active Journal to write a narrative essay in which you are a colonist describing daily life.

Analyze Primary Sources

14. The excerpt below is from a speech given during the Great Awakening. What do you think Edwards was trying to encourage people to do?
    A. Edwards wanted people to go to church more often.
    B. Edwards wanted people to convert to a new religion.
    C. Edwards wanted people to make sacrifices for God.
    D. Edwards wanted people to worship God to avoid his wrath.

"The wrath of God is like great waters that are dammed for the present; they increase more and more, and rise higher and higher, till an outlet is given; and the longer the stream is stopped, the more rapid and mighty is its course, when once it is let loose."
—Jonathan Edwards, "Sinners in the Hands of an Angry God."

Analyze Maps

15. Which letter represents Pennsylvania? Who founded the colony?

16. Which letter represents New Jersey? Which colony was to its south?

17. Which letter represents New York? Which colonies bordered it to the east?

▼ The Middle Colonies

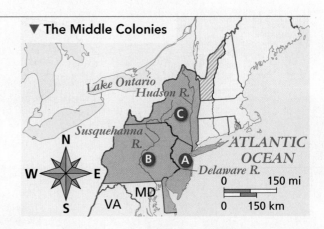

TOPIC 3

The Revolutionary Era
(1750–1783)

GO ONLINE
to access your
digital course

 VIDEO

 AUDIO

 ETEXT

 INTERACTIVE

 WRITING

 GAMES

 WORKSHEET

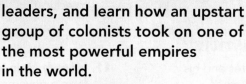 ASSESSMENT

Go back over 250 years

to **AMERICA IN THE LATE 1700s**. Why? Because you will see the birth of a new nation, get to know some of its greatest leaders, and learn how an upstart group of colonists took on one of the most powerful empires in the world.

Explore
The Essential Question

When is war justified?

In the late 1700s one war, called the French and Indian War, led to another war, the American Revolution. What were the causes of these wars?

Unlock the Essential Question in your 📔 Active Journal.

128

Watch

NBC LEARN

BOUNCE TO ACTIVATE ▶ VIDEO

Benjamin Franklin and the Fight for Independence

Learn about one of the nation's most accomplished founders.

Read

about the revolutionary people and events that led to the founding of the United States of America.

The Revolutionary Era
(1750–1783)

Learn more about the Revolutionary Era by making your own map and timeline in your 📖 Active Journal.

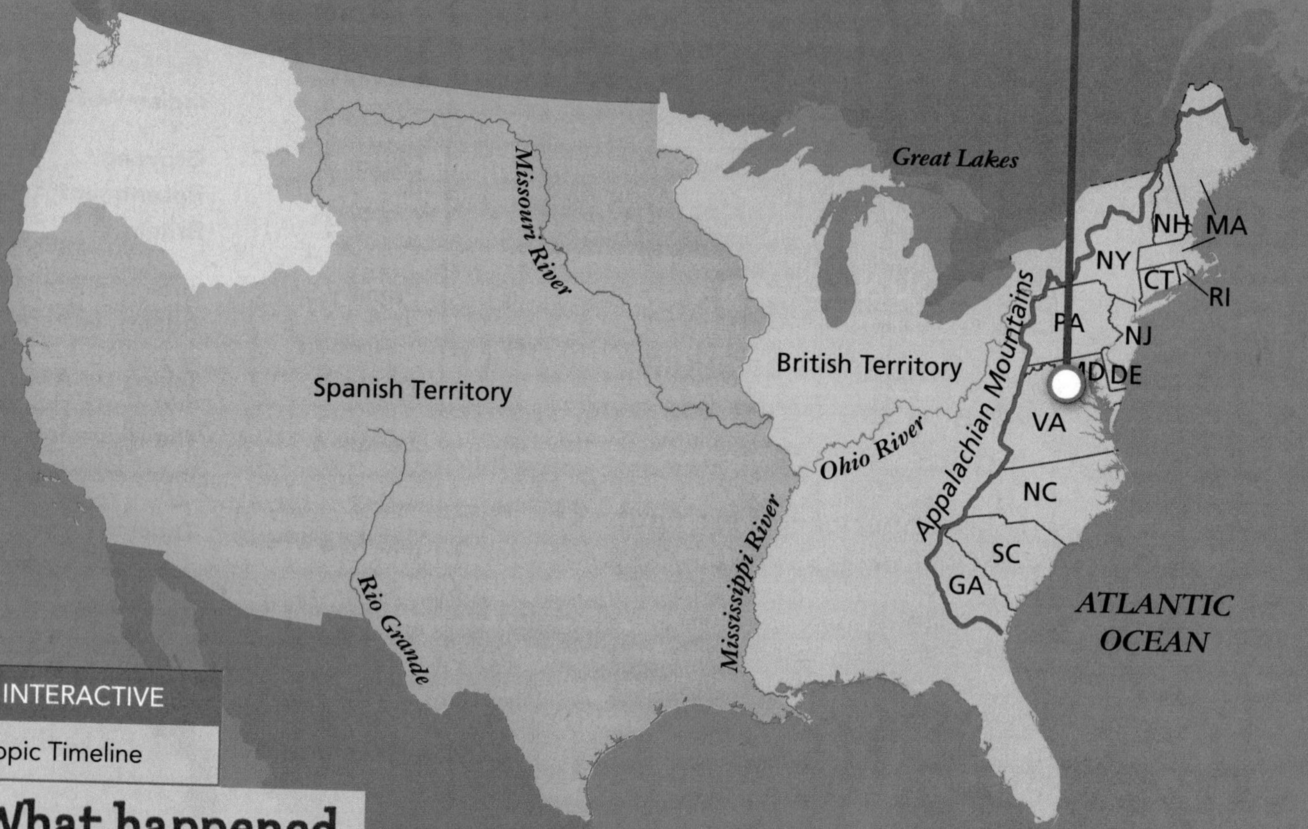

Great Lakes

Missouri River

British Territory

Spanish Territory

Ohio River

Appalachian Mountains

NH MA
NY
CT
RI
PA
NJ
MD DE
VA
NC
SC
GA

Mississippi River

Rio Grande

ATLANTIC OCEAN

👆 INTERACTIVE

Topic Timeline

What happened and when?

Colonists resented the British presence in their lives during the last half of the 1700s. Explore the timeline to find out why.

1754
The French and Indian War breaks out in North America.

1765
Parliament passes the Stamp Act, sparking protests by colonists.

1773
British Parliament passes the Tea Act.

1770
British troops fire on crowd in the Boston Massacre.

TOPIC EVENTS

| 1750 | 1760 | 1770 |

WORLD EVENTS

1762
Catherine the Great begins reign in Russia.

INTERACTIVE

Topic Map

Where was the American Revolution fought?

The British colonies stretched along the Atlantic seaboard. What were the names of the colonies?

Who will you meet?

Thomas Jefferson, writer of the Declaration of Independence

George Washington, General of the Continental Army

King George III of Britain

1775
British soldiers and colonial minutemen fight at Lexington and Concord.

1777
The American victory at Saratoga is a turning point in the war.

1781
The British surrender to the Americans at Yorktown.

1783
Britain recognizes U.S. independence.

1780

1790

1778
Captain James Cook explores the Hawaiian island of Kaua'i.

1783
Ludwig van Beethoven has his first composition published.

131

Quest
Project-Based Learning Inquiry

Choosing Sides

Quest KICK OFF

In **1776** the colonists were divided over a very important question: Should the colonies break away from Britain or stay loyal to the king? What would you have chosen? You may wonder . . .

How did colonists decide which side to support in the Revolutionary War?

Imagine you are living in the Chesapeake Bay region in 1776. You must decide whether to become a Patriot, become a Loyalist, or stay neutral. You will then write a blog documenting your decision-making process. Explore the Essential Question "When is war justified?" in this Quest.

1 Ask Questions

To make an important decision, you need to find reasons and facts that support one side or the other. Make a list of questions whose answers would provide reasons to help you decide. Write your questions in your 📓 Active Journal.

2 Investigate

As you read the lessons in the Topic, look for **Quest** CONNECTIONS about events and other facts that might be reasons for supporting one side or the other. Record notes in your 📓 Active Journal.

3 Conduct Research

Next begin your research by exploring primary sources from the Revolutionary Era. Capture notes in your 📓 Active Journal.

Quest FINDINGS

4 Write Your Blog

Now use your research and notes to decide whether to be a Patriot, a Loyalist, or a neutral colonist. Then write and produce your blog. Get help for writing your blog in your 📓 Active Journal.

LESSON 1

The French and Indian War

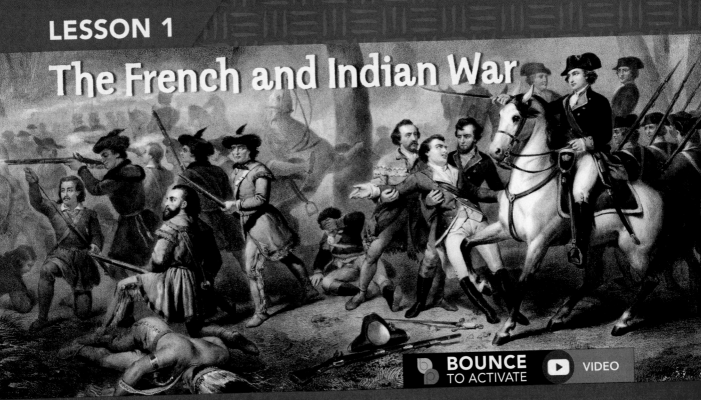

🔵 **BOUNCE** TO ACTIVATE   ▶ VIDEO

GET READY TO READ

START UP

Examine the illustration of George Washington at the Battle of Monongahela during the French and Indian War. Write what you would like to learn about his role in the war.

GUIDING QUESTIONS

- Why were Britain and France rivals in the mid-1700s?
- What role did American Indians play in the British-French rivalry?
- How did power in North America shift after the French and Indian War?

TAKE NOTES

Literacy Skills: Sequence

Use the graphic organizer in your 📔 Active Journal to take notes as you read the lesson.

PRACTICE VOCABULARY

Use the vocabulary activity in your 📔 Active Journal to practice the vocabulary words.

Vocabulary	Academic Vocabulary
ally	extensive
French and Indian War	devise
Albany Plan of Union	
Treaty of Paris	

By the mid-1700s, the major powers of Europe were locked in a worldwide struggle for empire. Britain, France, Spain, and the Netherlands competed for trade and colonies in far-flung corners of the globe. The British colonies in North America soon became caught up in the contest.

Why Did Europeans Fight Over North American Land?

The most serious threat came from France. It claimed a vast area that circled the English colonies from the St. Lawrence River west to the Great Lakes and south to the Gulf of Mexico. To protect their land claims, the French built an **extensive** system of forts. These forts blocked the British colonies from expanding to the west.

The Importance of the Ohio River Valley At first, most settlers in the British colonies were content to remain along the Atlantic coast. By the 1740s, however, traders were crossing the Appalachian Mountains in search of furs. Traders pushed into the forests of the Ohio Valley.

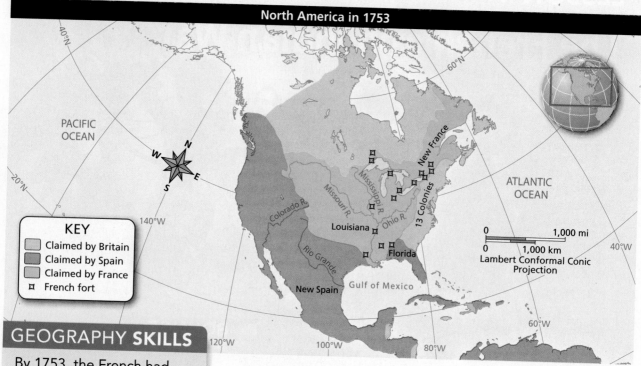

North America in 1753

PACIFIC OCEAN

New France

Mississippi R.

Missouri R.

13 Colonies

Colorado R.

ATLANTIC OCEAN

Louisiana

Ohio R.

Rio Grande

Florida

New Spain

Gulf of Mexico

KEY
- Claimed by Britain
- Claimed by Spain
- Claimed by France
- ⊞ French fort

0 — 1,000 mi
0 — 1,000 km
Lambert Conformal Conic Projection

GEOGRAPHY SKILLS

By 1753, the French had claimed a vast area of North America.

1. **Location** Why do you think the French built forts along rivers and lakes?

2. **Infer** Why were the French determined to prevent British colonists from moving westward?

Academic Vocabulary

extensive • *adj.,* covering a large area

Because of the abundance of wildlife, settlers tried to take over the profitable French trade with the Indians.

France was determined to stop the British from expanding westward. The Ohio River was especially important to the French because it provided a vital link between their claims along the Great Lakes and their settlements along the Mississippi River.

Ohio Valley American Indians Choose Sides American Indians had hunted animals and grown crops in the Ohio Valley for centuries. They did not want to give up the land to settlers, French or British. One American Indian protested to a British trader, "You and the French are like the two edges of a pair of shears. And we are the cloth which is to be cut to pieces between them."

Still, the growing conflict between Britain and France was too dangerous to ignore. Some American Indians decided that the only way to protect their way of life was to take sides in the struggle, or to become an ally with the British or the French. An **ally** is a nation that works with another nation for a common purpose.

The French expected the Indians to side with them. Most French in North America were trappers and traders. Generally, they did not destroy Indian hunting grounds by clearing forests for farms. Also, many French trappers married American Indian women and adopted their ways. As a result, France had built strong alliances with such American Indian groups as the Algonquins and the Hurons.

Most British settlers were farmers. These settlers usually ignored American Indian rights by felling trees and clearing land for crops. However, an English trader and official, William Johnson, helped gain Iroquois support for Britain. The Iroquois respected Johnson. He was one of the few British settlers who had an Indian wife, Molly Brant. She was the sister of the Mohawk chief Thayendanegea, known to the British as Joseph Brant. Both Joseph and Molly Brant became valuable allies for the British.

In the end, Britain managed to convince the powerful Iroquois nations to join with them. The British alliance was attractive to the Iroquois because they were old enemies of the Algonquin and the Huron. The war reignited old conflicts in the Ohio Valley between the Iroquois and the Algonquins and Hurons. Some groups, like the Shawnees, Delawares, and Mingos, formed alliances to push Europeans off their lands. More often, however, the alliances formed with the British and the French pitted Indian groups against each other in the fighting to come.

☑ READING CHECK | Identify Supporting Details Which American Indian groups sided with the British and which sided with the French as the war began?

Where Did the French and Indian War Begin?

Three times between 1689 and 1748, France and Great Britain fought for power in Europe and North America. Each war ended with an uneasy peace.

In 1754, fighting broke out for a fourth time. British settlers called the conflict the **French and Indian War** because it pitted them against France and its American Indian allies. The French and Indian War was part of a larger war called the Seven Years' War that involved conflicts not just in North America but also in Europe and Asia. In North America, the Ohio River Valley was at the center of the dispute. There, the opening shots of the war were fired by soldiers led by George Washington.

Washington Heads to Ohio
When Washington took part in the Ohio Valley conflict he was only 22 years old. He had grown up on a plantation in Virginia, the son of wealthy parents.

Gifted at mathematics, he began working as a land surveyor. His job took him to frontier lands in western Virginia.

▼ Many French living in North America were fur trappers who traded with American Indians for furs.

In 1753, the governor of Virginia sent Washington to deliver a letter to the French asking them to withdraw from the Ohio Valley. The French refused. After Washington returned from this mission, the governor of Virginia sent him west again. This time Washington's assignment was to build a fort where the Monongahela and Allegheny rivers meet to form the Ohio River (present-day Pittsburgh, Pennsylvania).

Washington led 150 men into the Ohio country in April 1754. Along the way, he heard that the French had just completed Fort Duquesne (doo KAYN) at the very spot where Washington hoped to build his fort.

Defeat at Fort Necessity Determined to carry out his orders, Washington hurried on. Indian allies revealed that French scouts were camped in the woods ahead. Marching quietly through the night, Washington launched a surprise attack and scattered the French. The Iroquois helped the British fight against the French, as well as the French allies, the Algonquins.

Washington's success was brief. Hearing that the French were about to counterattack, he and his men quickly built a makeshift stockade. They named it Fort Necessity. A force of 700 French and Indians surrounded the fort. Badly outnumbered, the Virginians surrendered. The French then released Washington, and he returned home.

British officials recognized the significance of Washington's skirmish. "The volley fired by this young Virginian in the forests of America," a British writer noted, "has set the world in flames."

✓ READING CHECK **Summarize** Why did Washington and his men fight the French?

Analyze Images
George Washington and his soldiers quickly built the makeshift Fort Necessity in the Ohio Valley to help defend themselves from the French. Shown here is a replica of the fort. **Cite Evidence** What clues in the photo show that Washington's troops built this fort quickly?

The Colonies Meet in Albany

While Washington was fighting the French, delegates from seven colonies gathered in Albany, New York. One purpose of the meeting was to cement the alliance with the Iroquois, who were willing to defend the British claim to the Ohio Valley. This alliance would help the British fight the French and their American Indian allies. Another goal of the meeting was to plan a united colonial defense.

The delegates in Albany knew that the colonists had to work together to defeat the French. Benjamin Franklin, the delegate from Pennsylvania, proposed the **Albany Plan of Union**. The plan was an attempt to create "one general government" for the British colonies.

Albany Plan of Union, 1754

Situation	Action	Plan
The British hoped to sign a treaty with the Iroquois and needed the cooperation of all colonies to enforce provisions of an American Indian treaty.	Seven colonies sent representatives to an Albany Congress to consider the need for a central governing body within the colonies.	The colonies (with the exception of Georgia and Delaware) agreed to unite under a governing body that would manage American Indian relations and conflicts between the colonies.

Outcome	Why It Failed
The Albany Congress adopted the plan, however individual colonial governments were unwilling to accept it.	With considerable competition among the individual colonies for power, territory, and trade, colonial governing bodies did not believe that a unified governing body would protect their interests.

Analyze Charts The Albany Plan of Union proposed a single government for the 13 colonies to defeat the French. **Drawing Conclusions** Why would competition among the colonies keep them from supporting a central governing body?

It called for a Grand Council made up of representatives from each colony. The council would make laws, raise taxes, and set up the defense of the colonies.

The delegates voted to accept the Plan of Union. However, when the plan was submitted to the colonial assemblies, not one approved it.

None of the colonies wanted to give up any of its powers to a central council. A disappointed Benjamin Franklin expressed his frustration at the failure of his plan:

Primary Source

"Everyone cries a union is necessary. But when they come to the manner and form of the union, their weak noodles are perfectly distracted."

—Benjamin Franklin, in a letter to Massachusetts Governor William Shirley, 1755

✔ **READING CHECK** Identify Main Ideas Why did the delegates from the colonies want to form a union?

British Defeats in the Ohio Valley

In 1755, General Edward Braddock led British and colonial troops in an attack against Fort Duquesne. Braddock was a stubborn man who had little experience at fighting in the forests of North America. Still, the general boasted that he would sweep the French from the Ohio Valley.

Surprise Attacks in the Forests

Braddock's men moved slowly and noisily through the forests. Although warned of danger by Washington and by Indian scouts, Braddock pushed ahead.

As the British neared Fort Duquesne, the French and their Indian allies launched a surprise attack. Sharpshooters hid in the forest and picked off British soldiers, whose bright red uniforms made easy targets.

Braddock himself had five horses shot out from under him before he fell, fatally wounded. Almost half the British were killed or wounded. Washington, too, was nearly killed.

Analyze Images The French and their American Indian allies ambushed General Braddock's forces in the forests as the soldiers made their way to Fort Duquesne in 1755. **Infer** What advantages did the American Indians and French have fighting in forests that Braddock's soldiers did not have?

British Setbacks at Lake Ontario and Lake George During the next two years, the war continued to go badly for the British. British attacks against several French forts failed. Meanwhile, the French won important victories, capturing Fort Oswego on Lake Ontario and Fort William Henry on Lake George. (Both forts occupied land that is now part of New York state.) All these defeats put a serious strain on the alliances with the Iroquois, who had been counting on the British to protect them from the French. The Iroquois faced increasing danger from enemy American Indian groups, who fought them for prisoners and goods.

☑ **READING CHECK** **Identify Supporting Details** Why were French attacks in the forests successful?

Quebec and New France Fall

In 1757, William Pitt became prime minister, meaning he was the new head of the British government. Pitt made it his first job to win the war in North America. Once that goal was achieved, he argued, the British would be free to focus on victory in other parts of the world. So Pitt sent Britain's best generals to North America. To encourage the colonists to support the war, he promised large payments for military services and supplies.

INTERACTIVE

Major Battles of the French and Indian War

Under Pitt's leadership, the tide of battle turned. In 1758, Major General Jeffrey Amherst captured Louisbourg, the most important fort in French Canada. That year, the British also seized Fort Duquesne, which they renamed Fort Pitt after the British leader. The city of Pittsburgh later grew up on the site of Fort Pitt.

The War Turns in Favor of the British The British enjoyed even greater success in 1759. By summer, they had pushed the French from Fort Niagara, Crown Point, and Fort Ticonderoga (ty kahn duh ROH guh). Next, Pitt sent General James Wolfe to take Quebec, capital of New France.

Climbing Cliffs to Attack Quebec Quebec was vital to the defense of New France. Without Quebec, the French could not supply their forts farther up the St. Lawrence River. Quebec was well defended, though. The city sat on the edge of the Plains of Abraham, on top of a steep cliff high above the St. Lawrence. An able French general, the Marquis de Montcalm, was prepared to fight off any British attack.

General Wolfe **devised** a bold plan to capture Quebec. He knew that Montcalm had only a few soldiers guarding the cliff because the French thought that it was too steep to climb. Late at night, Wolfe ordered British troops to row quietly in small boats to the foot of the cliff. In the dark, the soldiers climbed up the cliff and assembled at the top.

The next morning, Montcalm awakened to a surprise. A force of 4,000 British troops was drawn up and ready for battle.

Quickly, Montcalm marched his own troops out to join in battle. By the time the fierce fighting was over, both Montcalm and Wolfe lay dead. Moments before Wolfe died, a soldier gave him the news that the British had won. Wolfe is said to have whispered, "Now, God be praised, I will die in peace." On September 18, 1759, Quebec surrendered to the British.

The British Make Huge Gains The fall of Quebec sealed the fate of New France, though fighting dragged on in Europe for several more years. Finally, in 1763, Britain and France signed the **Treaty of Paris**, bringing the long conflict to an end.

The Treaty of Paris marked the end of French power in North America. By its terms, Britain gained Canada and all French lands east of the Mississippi River except New Orleans. France was allowed to keep only two islands in the Gulf of St. Lawrence and its prosperous sugar-growing islands in the West Indies. Spain, which had entered the war on the French side in 1762, gave up Florida to Britain.

In return, Spain received all French land west of the Mississippi. In addition, Spain gained the vital port city of New Orleans. Spain retained control of its vast empire in Central America and South America.

Academic Vocabulary

devised • *v.*, planned or invented a method of doing something

INTERACTIVE

Effects of the French and Indian War

Analyze Images After sneaking up a steep cliff under the cover of darkness, the British defeated the French on the Plains of Abraham the next morning and captured the capital city of Quebec. **Use Visual Clues** Why is the bird's-eye-view perspective helpful to understanding the action?

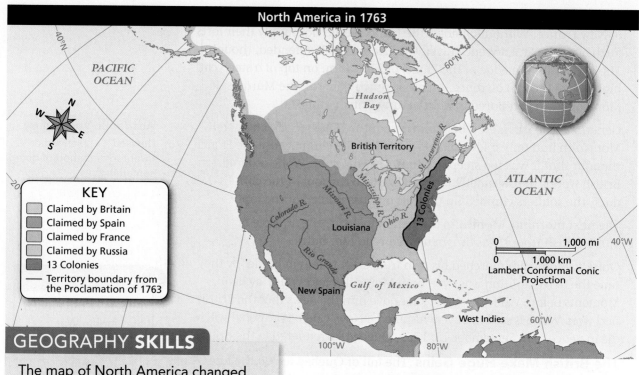

North America in 1763

PACIFIC OCEAN

Hudson Bay

British Territory

ATLANTIC OCEAN

Colorado R.

Missouri R.

Mississippi R.

Ohio R.

St. Lawrence R.

13 Colonies

Louisiana

Rio Grande

New Spain

Gulf of Mexico

West Indies

KEY
- Claimed by Britain
- Claimed by Spain
- Claimed by France
- Claimed by Russia
- 13 Colonies
- Territory boundary from the Proclamation of 1763

0   1,000 mi
0   1,000 km
Lambert Conformal Conic Projection

GEOGRAPHY **SKILLS**

The map of North America changed between 1753 and 1763, after the Treaty of Paris.

1. **Region** What caused the 13 colonies region to remain together after the French and Indian War?

2. **Draw Conclusions** What effect did the Treaty of Paris have on New Spain?

After years of fighting, peace returned to North America. Yet, in a few short years, a new conflict would break out. This time, the struggle would pit Britain against its own 13 colonies.

✓ READING CHECK **Recognize Multiple Causes** In what ways did Pitt help Britain win the war?

☑ Lesson Check

Practice Vocabulary

1. How did the **Albany Plan of Union** seek to involve the colonists in the **French and Indian War**?

2. Give two results of the **Treaty of Paris**.

Critical Thinking and Writing

3. **Summarize** Who fought the French and Indian War, and for what reason?

4. **Identify Supporting Details** What role did George Washington play in the French and Indian War?

5. **Revisit the Essential Question** When is war justified? Do you think the French and Indian War was justified? Why or why not?

6. **Writing Workshop: Consider Your Purpose and Audience** At the end of this Topic, you will write an essay to answer the question "Why was there an American Revolution?" Write a sentence in your 📖 Active Journal that tells what your purpose for writing will be and who you are writing for.

Identify Physical and Cultural Features

Follow these steps to identify physical and cultural features.

INTERACTIVE

Read Physical Maps

1 **Identify physical features.** Physical features include bodies of water, coastlines, mountains, valleys, and deserts. What are the main physical features shown on the map below?

2 **Identify cultural features.** Cultural features are features created by people, such as cities and towns, borders, buildings, roads, railroads, or canals. What is the main cultural feature on the western frontier shown on the map and mentioned in George Washington's report?

3 **Relate physical and cultural features.** Cultural features are often related to physical features. For example, a river (physical feature) can form a border between two countries (cultural feature). The natural landscape may determine where a city is built. People need water for drinking, cooking, and bathing. That is why so many early settlements were built near rivers or lakes. Bodies of water are a natural resource and a physical feature. People use that natural resource to meet their needs for living. Based on the map and the primary source, why was the fort George Washington built called Fort Necessity?

Secondary Source

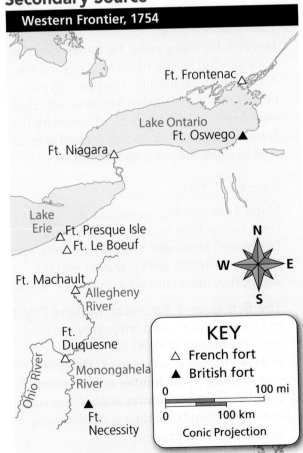

Western Frontier, 1754

Ft. Frontenac

Lake Ontario
Ft. Oswego ▲

Ft. Niagara

Lake Erie
Ft. Presque Isle
Ft. Le Boeuf

Ft. Machault
Allegheny River

N
W — E
S

Ft. Duquesne
Monongahela River

Ohio River

Ft. Necessity ▲

KEY
△ French fort
▲ British fort

0   100 mi
0   100 km
Conic Projection

Primary Source

. . .we received Intelligence that the French, having been reinforced with 700 Recruits, had left Monongehela, . . . Upon this, as our Numbers were so unequal, . . . (not exceeding 300) we prepared for our Defence in the best Manner we could, by throwing up a small Intrenchment, which we had not Time to perfect . . .

—George Washington and James Mackay of the Capitulation of Fort Necessity Williamsburg 19 July 1754

Growing Resentment Against Britain

BOUNCE TO ACTIVATE   ▶ VIDEO

GET READY TO READ

START UP

The illustration shows British troops searching a colonist's home. Explain in writing how colonists likely felt about such actions.

GUIDING QUESTIONS

- Why did the colonists oppose new taxes and feel that British law was increasingly oppressive?
- Who were the colonial leaders that emerged as tensions with Britain increased?

TAKE NOTES

Literacy Skills: Identify Cause and Effect
Use the graphic organizer in your 📓 Active Journal to take notes as you read the lesson.

PRACTICE VOCABULARY

Use the vocabulary activity in your 📓 Active Journal to practice the vocabulary words.

Vocabulary

petition
boycott
repeal
writ of
  assistance

committee of
  correspondence

Academic Vocabulary

prohibit
influential

By 1760, the British and their Indian allies had driven France from the Ohio Valley. Their troubles in the region were not over, however. For many years, fur traders had sent back glowing reports of the land beyond the Appalachian Mountains. The dense forests of the Ohio Valley offered new resources that were in short supply in the East, and with the French gone, British colonists wanted to head west to claim the lands for themselves.

Conflict Over Land

Many American Indian nations lived in the Ohio Valley. They included the Senecas, Delawares, Shawnees, Ottawas, Miamis, and Hurons. As British settlers moved into the valley, they often clashed with these Indians.

The British and American Indians Fight
In 1760, Britain made Lord Jeffrey Amherst military commander and governor general of its North American colonies. The British sent Amherst to the frontier to keep order. French traders had always treated American Indians as friends, holding feasts for them and giving them presents.

Amherst refused to do this. Instead, he raised the price of goods traded to Indians. Also, unlike the French, Amherst allowed settlers to build farms and forts on Indian lands.

Angry American Indians found a leader in Pontiac, an Ottawa chief who had fought on the French side during the French and Indian War. An English trader remarked that Pontiac "commands more respect amongst these nations than any Indian I ever saw." In April 1763, Pontiac spoke out against the British, calling them "dogs dressed in red, who have come to rob [us] of [our] hunting grounds and drive away the game." Pontiac led violent raids against British forts. Hundreds of British were tortured and killed, leading some officials to fear for the safety of colonists near American Indian land.

The British Secure the Frontier Later that year, Pontiac led an attack on British troops at Fort Detroit. A number of other Indian nations joined him. In a few short months, they captured most British forts in the Ohio country. British and colonial troops then struck back and regained much of what they had lost.

Pontiac's War, as it came to be called, did not last long. In October 1763, the French told Pontiac that they had signed the Treaty of Paris. Because the treaty marked the end of French power in North America, the Indians could no longer hope for French aid against the British. One by one, the Indian nations stopped fighting and returned home.

☑ READING CHECK **Identify Supporting Details** What arguments did Pontiac have against the British and settlers?

How Did the Proclamation of 1763 Fuel Resentment?

Pontiac's violent raids against British troops convinced officials that they should **prohibit** British subjects from settling beyond the western frontier for their own safety. To do this, the government issued the Proclamation of 1763. The proclamation drew an imaginary line along the crest of the Appalachian Mountains. Colonists were forbidden to settle west of the line. All settlers already west of the line were "to remove themselves" at once.

The Purposes of the Proclamation The proclamation was meant to protect British settlers in the western lands. To enforce it, Britain sent 10,000 troops to the colonies. Few went to the frontier, however. Most stayed along the Atlantic coast.

The proclamation also created four new places where colonists could settle. French Canada became part of the province of Quebec. Florida, once a Spanish colony, was divided into East and West Florida. British territories in the Caribbean became the province of Granada.

Quick Activity

Begin an online timeline of major events and ideas that led to the American Revolution. Add to it as you read. Explain each event and its significance.

INTERACTIVE

Crisis on the Frontier

Academic Vocabulary
prohibit • v., to refuse to allow; to forbid

▼ Chief Pontiac of the Ottawa incited other American Indian groups to fight the British and led an attack on British troops at Fort Detroit.

Colonists Disagree with the Proclamation The proclamation angered many colonists. They thought it was unnecessary and unjust. They did not think the British government had the power to restrict state settlements. Nor were they concerned with the rights of American Indians. After winning the French and Indian War, many colonists felt they had rights to the land.

Also, colonists now had to pay for the additional British troops that had been sent to enforce the proclamation. In the end, many settlers simply ignored the proclamation and moved west anyway. The proclamation remained most controversial in the west, where colonists clashed with American Indians. Some colonies, including New York, Pennsylvania, and Virginia, claimed lands in the west. The Proclamation would continue to cause problems up to the American Revolution from the tension it caused between the colonists and Britain.

GEOGRAPHY **SKILLS**

The Proclamation of 1763 prohibited colonial settlement west of the red line shown on the map.

1. **Location** Why would settlers resent the Proclamation border?

2. **Infer** How would people living in the Indian Reserve be affected if settlers ignored the Proclamation's border?

☑ READING CHECK **Identify Cause and Effect** What was the reasoning behind the Proclamation of 1763?

How Did Mercantilism Affect Taxation and Cause Resentment?

The Seven Years' War, which included the French and Indian War, plunged Britain deeply into debt. As a result, the taxes paid by citizens in Britain rose sharply. The British prime minister, George Grenville, decided that colonists in North America should help share the burden. In a mercantilist system, colonies were expected to serve the colonial power. Grenville reasoned that the colonists would not oppose small tax increases.

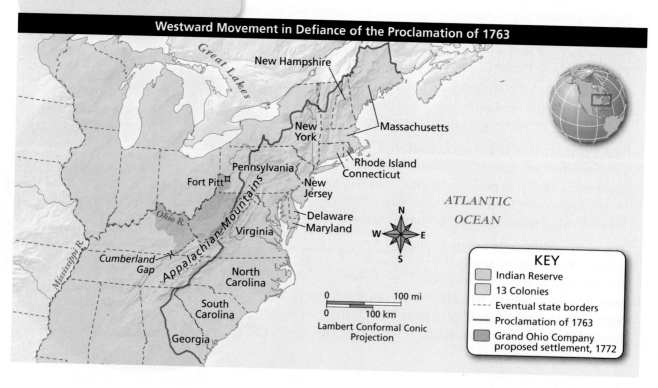

Westward Movement in Defiance of the Proclamation of 1763

New Hampshire
Great Lakes
New York
Massachusetts
Pennsylvania
Fort Pitt
Rhode Island
Connecticut
New Jersey
Ohio R.
Appalachian Mountains
Delaware
Maryland
Virginia
Cumberland Gap
Mississippi R.
North Carolina
South Carolina
Georgia

ATLANTIC OCEAN

N
W   E
S

0   100 mi
0   100 km
Lambert Conformal Conic Projection

KEY
- Indian Reserve
- 13 Colonies
- - - - Eventual state borders
- —— Proclamation of 1763
- Grand Ohio Company proposed settlement, 1772

The colonists, however, strongly resented these taxes. They argued that mercantilism was unfair because it limited trade and made goods more expensive. Many colonists also objected that the power to raise these new taxes was not granted by the English constitution. Grenville's policy led to the political and economic conflicts that would divide the colonies and England.

The Sugar Act Taxes the Colonies In 1764, Grenville asked Parliament to approve the Sugar Act, which put a new tax on molasses. The Sugar Act replaced an earlier tax, which had been so high that any merchant who paid it would have been driven out of business. As a result, most colonial merchants simply avoided the tax by smuggling molasses into the colonies. Often, they bribed tax collectors to look the other way.

The Sugar Act of 1764 lowered the tax. At the same time, the law made it easier for British officials to bring colonial smugglers to trial. Grenville made it clear that he expected the new tax to be paid.

✓ READING CHECK **Identify Main Ideas** What arguments did the colonists have against more British taxes?

Why Did the Stamp Act Anger Colonists?

Grenville also persuaded Parliament to pass the Stamp Act of 1765. The act placed new duties (taxes) on legal documents such as wills, diplomas, and marriage papers. It also taxed newspapers, almanacs, playing cards, and even dice.

All items named in the law had to carry a stamp showing that the tax had been paid. Stamp taxes were used in Britain and other countries to raise money. However, Britain had never required American colonists to pay such a tax.

Resistance to the Stamp Act When British officials tried to enforce the Stamp Act, they met with stormy protests from colonists. Lieutenant Governor Hutchinson's house in Massachusetts was looted by a mob. He was not the only official to feel the mob's anger. Some colonists threw rocks at agents trying to collect the unpopular tax.

In addition to riots in Boston, other disturbances broke out in New York City, Newport, and Charleston. In New York City, rioters destroyed the home of a British official who had said he would "cram the stamps down American throats" at the point of his sword.

The fury of the colonists shocked the British. After all, Britain had spent a lot of money to protect the colonies against the French. The British at home were paying much higher taxes than the colonists. Why, British officials asked, were colonists so angry about the Stamp Act?

Analyze Images British Prime Minister George Grenville wanted colonists to help share the burden of debt that Britain had incurred from the Seven Years' War. **Infer** How do you think colonists would react to sharing the expense of the Seven Years' War?

Quest CONNECTIONS

Look at the map. How would a disruption of trade with Britain affect colonists living in the Chesapeake Bay region? Record your findings in your 📖 Active Journal.

As one English letter-writer commented,

Primary Source

"Our Colonies must be the biggest Beggars in the World, if such small Duties appear to be intolerable Burdens in their Eyes."

—"Pacificus," *Maryland Gazette*, March 20, 1766

Lack of Representation in Parliament Colonists replied that the Stamp Act taxes were unjust and unnecessary. "No taxation without representation!" they cried. That principle was rooted in English traditions dating back to the Magna Carta.

Colonists insisted that only they or their elected representatives had the right to pass taxes. Since the colonists did not elect representatives to Parliament, Parliament had no right to tax them. Colonists were willing to pay taxes—but only if they were passed by their own legislatures. The colonists also felt that mercantilist policies like the Navigation Acts were unfair because they restricted their trade, which reduced colonists' income.

Peaceful Protests Lead Toward Revolution The Stamp Act crisis united colonists from New Hampshire to Georgia. Critics of the law called for delegates from every colony to meet in New York City. There, a congress would form to consider actions against the hated Stamp Act.

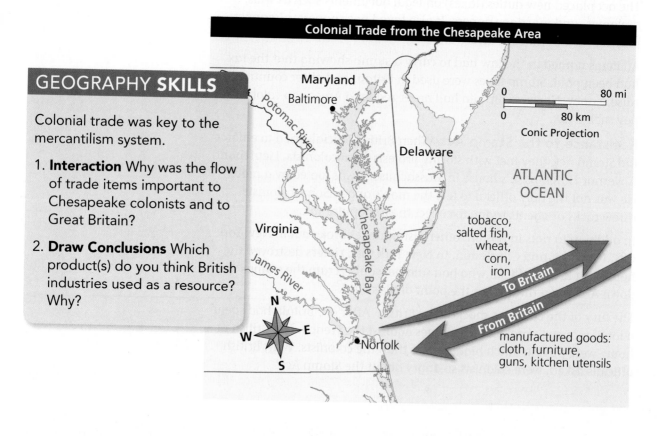

Colonial Trade from the Chesapeake Area

GEOGRAPHY SKILLS

Colonial trade was key to the mercantilism system.

1. **Interaction** Why was the flow of trade items important to Chesapeake colonists and to Great Britain?

2. **Draw Conclusions** Which product(s) do you think British industries used as a resource? Why?

In October 1765, nine colonies sent delegates to what became known as the Stamp Act Congress. The delegates drew up petitions to King George III, the British king, and to Parliament. A **petition** is a formal written request to someone in authority, signed by a group of people. In these petitions, the delegates rejected the Stamp Act and asserted that Parliament had no right to tax the colonies. Parliament paid little attention.

The colonists took other steps to change the law. They joined together to boycott British goods. To **boycott** means to refuse to buy certain goods and services. The boycott of British goods took its toll. Trade fell off by 14 percent. British merchants complained that they were facing ruin. So, too, did British workers who made goods for the colonies.

The colonists wanted the government to have less of a say over businesses and trade. They wanted a free-enterprise system, in which the market, rather than the government, determines what goods and services cost. British taxes, the colonists argued, unfairly restricted economic growth.

Finally, in 1766, Parliament **repealed**, or canceled, the Stamp Act. At the same time, however, it passed a law asserting that Parliament had the right to raise taxes in "all cases whatsoever."

✔ READING CHECK **Recognize Multiple Causes** What events led to the repeal of the Stamp Act in 1766?

How Did Colonists React to the Townshend Acts?

In May 1767, Parliament reopened the debate over taxing the colonies. George Grenville, now a member of Parliament, clashed with Charles Townshend, the official in charge of the British treasury.

Analyze Political Cartoons British officials held a "funeral" for the Stamp Act, which Parliament repealed in 1766. **Cite Evidence** What does this cartoon say about the artist's opinion of the Stamp Act?

"You are cowards, you are afraid of the Americans, you dare not tax America!" Grenville shouted.

"Fear? Cowards?" Townshend snapped back. "I dare tax America!"

The next month, Parliament passed the Townshend Acts, which taxed goods such as glass, paper, paint, lead, and tea. The taxes were low, but colonists still objected. The principle was the same: Parliament did not have the right to tax them without their consent.

Searches Without Reason Cause Unrest The Townshend Acts also set up new ways to collect taxes. Customs officials were sent to American ports with orders to stop smuggling. Using legal documents known as **writs of assistance**, the officers would be allowed to inspect a ship's cargo without giving a reason.

Colonists protested that the writs of assistance violated their rights as British citizens. Under British law, a government official could not search a person's property without a good reason for suspecting that the person had committed a crime. Yet the writs of assistance allowed persons and their property to be searched and even seized without reason in the colonies. Colonists angrily cited the words of James Otis of Massachusetts. Arguing against a British attempt to impose writs of assistance six years earlier, he had said:

Analyze Political Cartoons In this cartoon, colonists imagined punishing tax collectors by tarring and feathering them. **Draw Conclusions** What might the caption for this cartoon say?

Primary Source

"Now, one of the most essential branches of English liberty is the freedom of one's house. A man's house is his castle; and while he is quiet, he is as well guarded as a prince in his castle. This writ, if it should be declared legal, would totally destroy this privilege. Customhouse officers may enter our houses when they please . . . break locks, bars, and everything in their way. . . ."

—James Otis, February 24, 1761

Colonists Rebel Against British Economic Policies Colonists responded swiftly and strongly to the Townshend Acts. From north to south, colonial merchants and planters signed agreements promising to stop importing goods taxed by the Townshend Acts. The colonists hoped that the new boycott would win repeal of the Townshend Acts.

The colonists began to view Britain's treatment of them as increasingly oppressive, or severe. To protest British policies, some angry colonists formed the Sons of Liberty. From Boston to Charleston, Sons of Liberty staged mock hangings of cloth or straw effigies, or likenesses, dressed as British officials. The hangings were meant to show tax collectors what might happen to them if they collected the unpopular taxes.

Some women joined the Daughters of Liberty. They paraded, signed petitions, and organized a boycott of fine British cloth. They urged colonial women to raise more sheep, prepare more wool, and spin and weave their own cloth. A slogan of the Daughters of Liberty declared, "It is better to wear a Homespun coat than to lose our Liberty."

Some Sons and Daughters of Liberty also used other methods to support their cause. They visited merchants and urged them to boycott British imports. A few even threatened people who continued to buy British goods.

☑ READING CHECK **Summarize** How did many colonists respond to the Townshend Acts?

Leaders Emerge in the Struggle with Britain

As the struggle over taxes continued, new leaders emerged in all the colonies. Men and women in New England and Virginia were especially active and **influential** in the colonial cause.

Massachusetts Citizens Fight for Their Beliefs Samuel Adams of Boston stood firmly against Britain. Adams seemed an unlikely leader. He was a failure in business and a poor public speaker. Often, he wore a red suit and a cheap gray wig for which people poked fun at him. Still, Adams loved politics. He always attended Boston town meetings and Sons of Liberty rallies. Adams's real talent was organizing people. He worked behind the scenes, arranging protests and stirring public support.

Sam's cousin John was another important Massachusetts leader. John Adams had been a schoolteacher before becoming a skilled lawyer. Adams longed for fame and could often be difficult. Still, he was more cautious than his cousin Sam. He weighed evidence carefully before taking any actions. His knowledge of British law earned him much respect.

Mercy Otis Warren also aided the colonial cause. Warren wrote plays that made fun of British officials. The plays were published in newspapers and widely read in the colonies. Warren formed a close friendship with Abigail Adams, the wife of John Adams. The two women used their pens to spur the colonists to action. They also called for greater rights for women in the colonies.

▲ Mercy Otis Warren's popular plays making fun of British officials motivated colonists to take action against Britain.

Academic Vocabulary
influential • *adj.,* having great influence or power; effective

INTERACTIVE

Important People of the American Revolution

Virginians Join the Cause Virginia contributed many leaders to the struggle against taxes. In the House of Burgesses, George Washington joined other Virginians to protest the Townshend Acts.

A young lawyer, Patrick Henry, became well known as a vocal critic of British policies. His speeches in the House of Burgesses moved listeners to both tears and anger. Once, Henry attacked Britain with such fury that some listeners cried out, "Treason!" Henry boldly replied, "If this be treason, make the most of it!" Henry's words moved a young listener, Thomas Jefferson. At the time, Jefferson was a 22-year-old law student.

✓ READING CHECK **Use Evidence** How did some colonists show their strengths as leaders?

The Boston Massacre

Port cities such as Boston and New York were centers of protest. In New York, a dispute arose over the Quartering Act. Under that law, colonists had to provide housing, candles, bedding, and beverages to soldiers stationed in the colonies. The colonists did not want to house the soldiers. Many, including Sam Adams, did not think the soldiers should be stationed in the colonies at all during peacetime. When the New York Assembly refused to obey the Quartering Act, Britain dismissed the assembly in 1767.

Britain also sent two regiments to Boston to protect customs officers from local citizens. To many Bostonians, the soldiers were a daily reminder that Britain was trying to bully them into paying unjust taxes. When British soldiers walked along the streets of Boston, they risked insults or even beatings. A serious clash was not long in coming.

A Crowd Challenges British Soldiers On March 5, 1770, a crowd gathered outside the Boston customs house. Colonists shouted insults at the "lobsterbacks," as they called the red-coated soldiers.

Analyze Images This engraving of the Boston Massacre by Paul Revere helped spread anti-British feeling among the colonists. **Synthesize Visual Information** In what way could you say the image is inflammatory, or able to arouse anger in those who saw it?

BIOGRAPHY
5 Things to Know About > PATRICK HENRY
Patriot Leader (1736–1799)

- Favored independence from Britain
- Known for the famous words, "Give me liberty or give me death!"
- Known for his wit and oratorical skills
- Was first governor of Virginia after independence was declared
- Succeeded as a criminal lawyer before the Revolutionary War

Critical Thinking Why would speaking skills be an advantage to a colonial leader?

Then the Boston crowd began to throw snowballs, oyster shells, and chunks of ice at the soldiers.

The crowd grew larger and rowdier. Suddenly, the soldiers panicked. They fired into the crowd. When the smoke from the musket volley cleared, five people lay dead or dying. Among the first to die were Samuel Maverick, a 17-year-old white youth, and Crispus Attucks, a free black sailor.

Colonists React to the Massacre Colonists were quick to protest the incident, which they called the Boston Massacre. A Boston silversmith named Paul Revere fanned anti-British feeling with an engraving that showed British soldiers firing on unarmed colonists. Sam Adams wrote letters to other colonists to build outrage about the shooting.

The soldiers were arrested and tried in court. John Adams agreed to defend them, saying that they deserved a fair trial. He wanted to show the world that the colonists believed in justice, even if the British government did not. At the trial, Adams argued that the crowd had provoked the soldiers. His arguments convinced the jury. In the end, the heaviest punishment any soldier received was a branding on the hand.

Samuel Adams later expanded on the idea of a letter-writing campaign by forming a **committee of correspondence**. Members of the committee regularly wrote letters and pamphlets reporting to other colonies on events in Massachusetts. Within three months, there were 80 committees organized in Massachusetts. Before long, committees of correspondence became a major tool of protest in every colony.

The King Repeals Most Colonial Taxes By chance, on the very day of the Boston Massacre, a bill was introduced into Parliament to repeal most of the Townshend Acts. British merchants, harmed by the American boycott of British goods, had again pressured Parliament to end the taxes. The Quartering Act was repealed and most of the taxes that had angered the Americans were ended. However, King George III asked Parliament to retain the tax on tea.

▼ Crispus Attucks was one of five colonists killed at the Boston Massacre.

Growth of Colonial Cities

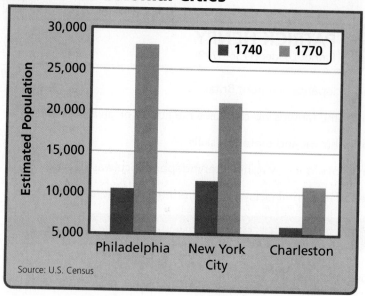

Source: U.S. Census

News of the repeal delighted the colonists. Most people dismissed the remaining tax on tea as unimportant and ended their boycott of British goods. For a few years, calm returned. Yet the angry debate over taxes had forced the colonists to begin thinking more carefully about their political rights.

☑ READING CHECK **Identify Supporting Details** Why did John Adams choose to defend the British soldiers after the Boston Massacre?

Analyze Charts Colonial cities grew both in size and density. **Use Visual Information** Which city was the largest in 1740? In 1770?

An American Identity Develops

Before the French and Indian War, the colonists had lived mostly apart from British troops and were mainly content to be British subjects. After the war and with the debate over taxes, they grew to resent the British presence. The colonists had begun to see themselves as Americans, and the troops represented the British crown in their homeland.

The committees of correspondence and newspapers in New York, Boston, and Philadelphia kept people connected to what was happening in their cities and the British reactions to colonial unrest. Colonists felt more economically, politically, and socially tied to each other than to Britain.

☑ READING CHECK **Recognize Multiple Causes** What caused the colonists to develop an identity as Americans?

☑ Lesson Check

Practice Vocabulary

1. How did the colonists **boycott** and use **petitions** to get British tax laws **repealed**?

2. What role did the **committees of correspondence** play?

Critical Thinking and Writing

3. **Identify Supporting Details** What details about the colonists' response to the Stamp Act tell you that it was one cause of the American Revolution?

4. **Infer** Based on James Otis's response to British writs of assistance, what concerns did the colonists have about British searches?

5. **Understand Effects** How did the Boston Massacre influence the colonists' feelings toward Britain?

6. **Writing Workshop: Develop a Clear Thesis** Write a sentence in your 📓 Active Journal that explains why there was an American Revolution. This sentence will become the thesis statement for the essay you will write at the end of the Topic.

John and Abigail Adams, Letters

Husband and wife John and Abigail Adams were key figures in the American Revolution and did much to further the Patriot cause. Below are excerpts from two of their letters to each other about the Declaration of Independence.

▶ Abigail Adams was an educated woman for her time. Her letters say much about her ideas about independence.

"Time has been given for the whole People, maturely to consider the great Question of Independence, and to ripen their judgment, ① dissipate their Fears, and allure their Hopes, by discussing it in Newspapers and Pamphlets, by debating it in Assemblies, Conventions, Committees of Safety and Inspection, in Town and County Meetings, as well as in private Conversations, ② so that the whole People, in every Colony of the thirteen, have now adopted it as their own Act. This will cement the Union . . . ."

—John Adams, Philadelphia, 3 July 1776

"I long to hear that you have declared an independency—and by the way in the new Code of Laws which I suppose it will be necessary for you to make I desire you would Remember the Ladies, and be more generous and ③ favourable to them than your ancestors. Do not put such unlimited power into the hands of the Husbands. Remember all Men would be tyrants if they could. If [particular] care and attention is not paid to the [Ladies] we are determined to foment a [Rebellion], and ④ will not hold ourselves bound by any Laws in which we have no voice, or Representation."

—Abigail Adams, Braintree, 31 March, 1776

Analyzing Primary Sources

Cite specific evidence from the letters to support your answers.

1. **Determine Author's Point of View** How does John Adams think that the colonists can form a unified opinion on the question of declaring independence from Britain?

2. **Determine Author's Purpose** What was Abigail's purpose in writing to her husband while he was a member of the Continental Congress?

3. **Draw Conclusions** What happened in 1776 that may have sparked Abigail's interest in women's rights?

Reading and Vocabulary Support

① *Dissipate* means "to make disappear."

② Who is John Adams including in his opinion that independence should be considered and accepted?

③ Some spellings in Abigail's letter are British spellings, and others may be spellings used at the time.

④ What phrase in Abigail's letter compares women's views on laws to the colonists' view on British laws?

LESSON 3
Taking Up Arms

BOUNCE TO ACTIVATE ▶ VIDEO

GET READY TO READ

START UP

Examine the illustration. Write a sentence contrasting the colonists with the British troops at Lexington.

GUIDING QUESTIONS

- What was the Boston Tea Party, and how did later British actions heighten tensions among the colonists?
- What actions were taken at the First and Second Continental Congresses?
- What advantages and disadvantages did each side have as the Revolutionary War began?

TAKE NOTES

Literacy Skills: Summarize
Use the graphic organizer in your 📕 Active Journal to take notes as you read the lesson.

PRACTICE VOCABULARY

Use the graphic organizer in your 📕 Active Journal to practice the vocabulary words.

Vocabulary

civil disobedience   Patriot
militia   Loyalist
minutemen

Academic Vocabulary

consequently
approach

The calm between the colonies and England did not last long. Economic and political disputes continued, this time over a simple drink. Tea was tremendously popular in the colonies. By 1770, at least one million Americans brewed tea twice a day. People "would rather go without their dinners than without a dish of tea," a visitor to the colonies noted.

The Boston Tea Party

Since the 1720s, Parliament had given the British East India Company exclusive rights to sell tea to the American colonies. Parliament protected this by mandating that tea sold to the colonies had to be shipped to England first so taxes could be paid. Then the tea was shipped to colonial tea merchants for sale in the American colonies.

Mercantilist System This system met resistance due to the taxation of tea in the American colonies. Remember, to maintain its authority over the colonies, Parliament had kept a tax on tea when repealing the Townshend Acts. The tax was a small one, but colonists resented it.

As a result, many colonists refused to buy British tea. Also, the colonists were able to get cheaper tea directly from Dutch and French traders who smuggled it to American merchants.

Mercantilist Policies Lead to the Tea Act In the 1770s, the British East India Company found itself in deep financial trouble, due in part to dwindling tea sales in the American colonies. As a result, more than 15 million pounds of tea sat unsold in British warehouses.

Parliament tried to help the British East India Company by passing the Tea Act of 1773. The act let the company bypass colonial tea merchants and sell directly to colonists.

The Tea Act also gave the British East India Company a rebate on tea taxes. Although colonists would still have to pay the tea tax, they would not have to pay the higher price charged by colonial tea merchants. As a result, the tea itself would cost less than ever before. Parliament hoped this would encourage Americans to buy more British tea.

To the surprise of Parliament, colonists protested the Tea Act. Many colonists were opposed to British mercantilist policies that were supposed to generate wealth for England by taxing the colonies. However, American tea merchants were especially angry because they had been cut out of the tea trade. They believed that allowing the government-sponsored British East India Company to sell tea to Americans violated their right to conduct free enterprise.

Even tea drinkers, who would have benefited from the law, scorned the Tea Act. They believed that it was a British trick to make them accept Parliament's right to tax the colonies.

A Boycott Against Tea Once again, colonists responded to the new law with a boycott. A Philadelphia poet, Hannah Griffitts, urged American women to:

Primary Source

"Stand firmly resolved and bid Grenville to see That rather than freedom we part with our tea, And well as we love the dear drink when a-dry, As American patriots our taste we deny."

—Hannah Griffitts in Milcah Martha Moore's *Commonplace Book*, 1773

Daughters of Liberty and women like Griffitts led the boycott. They served coffee or made "liberty tea" from raspberry leaves. At some ports, Sons of Liberty enforced the boycott by keeping the British East India Company from unloading cargoes of tea.

An Act of Civil Disobedience Three ships loaded with tea reached Boston Harbor in late November 1773. The colonial governor of Massachusetts, Thomas Hutchinson, insisted that they unload their cargo as usual.

Did you know?

The tea that the East India Company ships delivered to Boston Harbor came from China. There were five varieties and 340 chests of tea on board the ships *Beaver* and *Dartmouth*.

Analyze Images The colonists loved tea but were prepared to give it up rather than pay British taxes on it. **Use Visual Information** What details about this tea cup from the 1700s lead you to believe that tea was important to the colonists?

Analyze Images On December 16, 1773, a group of colonists emptied hundreds of tea chests into Boston Harbor to protest British taxation. **Infer** Why might this act of civil disobedience mark a turning point?

Sam Adams and the Sons of Liberty had other plans. On the night of December 16, they met in Old South Meeting House. They sent a message to the governor, demanding that the ships leave the harbor. When the governor rejected the demand, Adams stood up and declared, "This meeting can do nothing further to save the country."

Adams's words seemed to be a signal. As if on cue, a group of men in American Indian disguises burst into the meetinghouse. From the gallery above, voices cried, "Boston harbor a teapot tonight! The Mohawks are come!"

The disguised colonists left the meetinghouse and headed for the harbor. Others joined them along the way. Under a nearly full moon, the men boarded the ships, split open the tea chests, and dumped the tea into the harbor.

By 10 P.M., the Boston Tea Party, as it was later called, was over. The contents of 342 chests of tea floated in Boston Harbor. The next day, John Adams wrote about the event in his diary.

Primary Source

"This destruction of the tea is so bold, so daring, so firm . . . it must have such important and lasting results that I can't help considering it a turning point in history."

—Diary of John Adams, December 17, 1773

The Boston Tea Party was an important act of **civil disobedience**. Civil disobedience is the nonviolent refusal to obey laws that one considers unjust. The colonists had many reasons for this act of civil disobedience. They wanted to voice their discontent to the British without hurting anyone. They also wanted to stop the tea from entering Boston. The impact of their civil disobedience was perhaps greater than they had expected. Harsh punishment would come from Britain.

READING CHECK Identify Supporting Details Why were many colonists dissatisfied with the Tea Act?

How Did King George III Strike Back at Boston?

Colonists had mixed reactions to the Boston Tea Party. Some cheered it as a firm protest against unfair British laws. Others worried that it would encourage lawlessness in the colonies. Even those who condemned the Boston Tea Party, though, were shocked at Britain's harsh response to it. The unrest in Boston and the British reaction to the Tea Party would be yet another cause of the Revolution.

The Intolerable Acts Anger Massachusetts The British were outraged by what they saw as Boston's lawless behavior. In 1774, Parliament, encouraged by King George III, acted to punish Massachusetts.

Colonists called the four laws they passed the Intolerable Acts because they were so harsh. These Acts pushed the colonists closer to revolution.

First, Parliament shut down the port of Boston. No ship could enter or leave the harbor—not even a small boat. The harbor would remain closed until the colonists paid for the tea they had destroyed in the Boston Tea Party and repaid British officials, such as Thomas Hutchinson, for damage to personal property. Boston's harbor was central to the life of the city. With the closing of the port, merchants could not sell their goods, and **consequently**, the colony's economy suffered.

Second, Parliament forbade Massachusetts colonists to hold town meetings more than once a year without the governor's permission. In the past, colonists had called town meetings whenever they wished. Public officials would now be selected by the king's governor rather than be elected by citizens.

Third, Parliament allowed customs officers and other officials who might be charged with major crimes to be tried in Britain or Canada instead of in Massachusetts. Colonists protested. They argued that a dishonest official could break the law in the colonies and avoid punishment by being tried before a sympathetic jury.

Fourth, Parliament passed a new Quartering Act. No longer would redcoats camp in tents on Boston Common. Instead, colonists would have to house British soldiers in their homes when no other housing was available. Colonists viewed this act as yet another tax, because they had to house and feed the soldiers. Many objected to having the British army stationed in the colonies at all.

Academic Vocabulary
consequently • *adv.*, as a result

▼ Following the Boston Tea Party, British warships closed the port of Boston. Parliament demanded that colonists repay the damages from the loss of tea before they would reopen the port.

VIEW OF PART OF THE TOWN OF BOSTON IN NEW ENGLAND AND BRITTISH SHIPS OF WAR LANDING THEIR TROOPS

▲ The First Continental Congress met in September 1774, at Carpenters' Hall in Philadelphia. The delegates resolved to suspend trade with Britain and encouraged the colonies to form small armies of citizens called militias.

Benjamin Franklin's sister, Jane Mecum, wrote to her brother complaining of the British troops and their behavior in Boston:

Primary Source

". . . But at present we have a m[e]lancholy Prospect for this winter at Least the towns being so full of Profl[i]gate [soldiers] and many such officers there is hardly four and twenty hours Pas[s]es without some fray amongst them and [one] can walk but a lit[t]le way in the street without hearing th[eir] Profane language."

—Letter from Jane Franklin Mecum to Benjamin Franklin, November 21, 1774

The Quebec Act Redraws Borders Parliament also passed the Quebec Act. It set up a government for Canada and gave complete religious freedom to French Catholics. The Quebec Act also extended the borders of Quebec to include the land between the Ohio and Missouri rivers. The act pleased French Canadians. American colonists were angry, however, because some of the colonies claimed these lands.

The Intolerable Acts Draw Other Colonies Into the Struggle The committees of correspondence spread news of the Intolerable Acts to other colonies. They warned that the people of Boston faced hunger while their port was closed. People from other colonies responded by sending rice from South Carolina, corn from Virginia, and flour from Pennsylvania.

In the Virginia Assembly, Thomas Jefferson suggested that a day be set aside to mark the shame of the Intolerable Acts. The royal governor of Virginia rejected the idea. However, on June 1, 1774, church bells tolled slowly. Merchants closed their shops. Many colonists prayed and fasted all day.

In September 1774, colonial leaders called a meeting in Philadelphia. Delegates from 12 colonies gathered in what became known as the First Continental Congress. Only Georgia did not send delegates.

After much debate, the delegates passed a resolution backing Massachusetts in its struggle. They agreed to boycott all British goods and to stop exporting goods to Britain until the Intolerable Acts were repealed. The delegates also urged each colony to set up and train its own militia (mih LISH uh). A **militia** is an army of citizens who serve as soldiers during an emergency.

Before leaving Philadelphia, the delegates agreed to meet again in May 1775. Little did they suspect that before then, an incident in Massachusetts would change the fate of the colonies forever.

☑ **READING CHECK** Identify Main Ideas How did other colonies respond to the Intolerable Acts?

The Battles of Lexington and Concord

In Massachusetts, colonists were already preparing to resist. Newspapers called on citizens to prevent what they called "the Massacre of American Liberty." Volunteers known as **minutemen** trained regularly. Minutemen got their name because they kept their muskets at hand and were prepared to fight at a minute's notice. In towns near Boston, minutemen collected weapons and gunpowder. Meanwhile, Britain built up its forces. More troops arrived in Boston, bringing the total number of British soldiers in that city to 4,000.

Early in 1775, General Thomas Gage, the British commander, sent scouts to towns near Boston. They reported that minutemen had a large store of arms in Concord, a village about 18 miles from Boston. Gage planned a surprise march to Concord to seize the arms.

The Redcoats Cross the Charles River On April 18, about 700 British troops quietly left Boston in the darkness. Their goal was to seize the colonial arms. The Sons of Liberty were watching. As soon as the British set out, the Americans hung two lamps from the Old North Church in Boston. This signal meant that the redcoats were crossing the Charles River. The British had decided to cross the river rather than take a much longer route toward Concord by land.

▼ This statue honors Paul Revere and his ride to warn the colonists.

Colonists who were waiting across the Charles River saw the signal. Messengers mounted their horses and galloped through the night toward Concord. One midnight rider was Paul Revere. "The redcoats are coming! The redcoats are coming!" shouted Revere as he passed through each sleepy village along the way.

Fighting in Lexington and Concord
At daybreak on April 19, the redcoats reached Lexington, a town near Concord. On the village green, some 70 minutemen were waiting, commanded by Captain John Parker. The British ordered the minutemen to go home. Outnumbered, the colonists began to leave the village green.

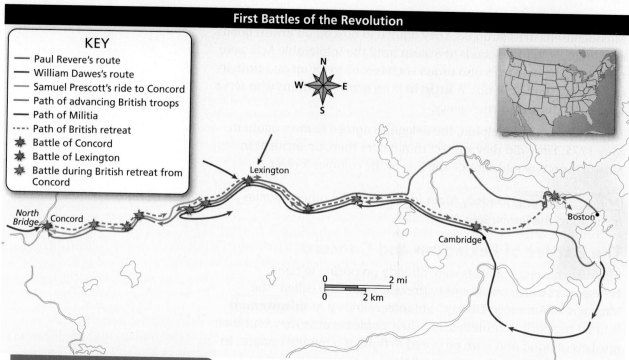

KEY
— Paul Revere's route
— William Dawes's route
— Samuel Prescott's ride to Concord
— Path of advancing British troops
— Path of Militia
---- Path of British retreat
✴ Battle of Concord
✴ Battle of Lexington
✴ Battle during British retreat from Concord

North Bridge • Concord
Lexington
Cambridge
Boston

0   2 mi
0   2 km

GEOGRAPHY SKILLS

The first battles the colonists fought were in Lexington and Concord, Massachusetts.

1. **Place** What geographic feature did the British encounter on their advance route but not on their retreat?

2. **Summarize** Why were the minutemen so prepared for the arrival of the British troops in Concord?

Suddenly, a shot rang out. No one knows who fired it. In the brief struggle that followed, eight colonists were killed.

The British pushed on to Concord. Finding no arms in the village, they turned back to Boston. On a bridge outside Concord, they met approximately 300 minutemen. Again, fighting broke out. This time, the British were forced to retreat because the minutemen used the geography of the region to their advantage. As the redcoats withdrew, colonial sharpshooters took deadly aim at them from the woods, making it difficult for the British soldiers to fire back. Local women also fired at the British from the windows of their homes. By the time they reached Boston, the redcoats had lost 73 men. Another 200 British soldiers were wounded or missing.

News of the battles of Lexington and Concord spread swiftly. To many colonists, the fighting ended all hope of a peaceful settlement. Only war would decide the future of the 13 colonies.

More than 60 years after the battles of Lexington and Concord, a well-known New England writer, Ralph Waldo Emerson, wrote a poem honoring the minutemen. Emerson's "Concord Hymn" created a vivid picture of the clash at Concord. It begins:

Primary Source

"By the rude bridge that arched the flood,
Their flag to April's breeze unfurled,
Here once the embattled farmers stood,
And fired the shot heard round the world."

—Ralph Waldo Emerson, "Concord Hymn," 1837

The "embattled farmers" would have years of difficult fighting in front of them. Lexington and Concord marked the beginning of the Revolutionary War.

The war and disagreements between the American colonists and the British prior to the war represent the era called the American Revolution. This period of struggle led to independence from Britain.

✓ READING CHECK Identify Cause and Effect How were the minutemen able to defeat the British at Concord?

The Fighting Continues

Just a few weeks after the battles at Lexington and Concord, on May 10, 1775, colonial delegates met at the Second Continental Congress in Philadelphia. The delegates represented the 13 British colonies from New Hampshire to Georgia. Most of the delegates still hoped to avoid a final break with Britain. However, while the delegates were meeting, the fighting spread.

King George III Rejects Peace After much debate, the delegates sent a petition to King George. In the Olive Branch Petition, they declared their loyalty to the king and asked him to repeal the Intolerable Acts.

George III was furious when he heard about the petition. The colonists, he raged, were trying to begin a war "for the purpose of establishing an independent empire!" The king vowed to bring the rebels to justice. He ordered 20,000 more troops to the colonies to crush the revolt.

Congress did not learn of the king's response until months later. But even before the petition was sent, leaders like John and Sam Adams were convinced that war could not be avoided.

Vermont Rebels Gain a Route to Canada Ethan Allen, a Vermont blacksmith, did not wait for Congress to act. Allen decided to lead a band of Vermonters, known as the Green Mountain Boys, in a surprise attack on Fort Ticonderoga, located at the southern tip of Lake Champlain. Allen knew that the fort held cannons that the colonists could use, and its strategic location would help colonists control the region.

In early May, the Green Mountain Boys crept quietly through the morning mists to Fort Ticonderoga. They quickly overpowered the guard on duty and entered the fort. Allen rushed to the room where the British commander slept. "Come out, you old rat!" he shouted. The commander demanded to know by whose authority Allen acted. "In the name of the Great Jehovah and the Continental Congress!" Allen replied.

The British commander surrendered Ticonderoga. By capturing the fort, the Green Mountain Boys won a valuable supply of cannons and gunpowder. Allen's success also gave Americans control of a key route into Canada.

Quest CONNECTIONS

An olive branch is a symbol of peace. How might the colonists react to George III's response to their petition? Record your findings in your 📖 Active Journal.

Analyze Images When King George III, seen here, read the Olive Branch Petition from the colonists, he was so angered by the colonists' actions that he sent even more troops to North America. **Infer** How do you think the colonists will react to more troops coming to their cities and towns?

George Washington Takes Command In the meantime, the Second Continental Congress had to decide what to do about the makeshift army gathering around Boston. In June, delegates took the bold step of setting up the Continental Army. They appointed George Washington of Virginia as commander.

☑ READING CHECK **Identify Supporting Details** Why was Fort Ticonderoga important to the colonists?

Opposing Sides at War

The colonists who favored war against Britain called themselves **Patriots**. They thought British rule was harsh and unjust. About one third of the colonists were Patriots, one third sided with the British, and one third did not take sides.

Academic Vocabulary
approach • *v.*, to come near

Washington Leads the Patriots The Patriots entered the war with many disadvantages. Colonial forces were poorly organized and untrained. They had few cannons, little gunpowder, and no navy. Also, few colonists wanted to enlist in the Continental Army for long terms of service. They preferred to fight near home with a local militia.

Yet, the Patriots also had advantages. Many Patriots owned rifles and were good shots. Their leader, George Washington, had experience and developed into an able commander. Furthermore, Patriots were determined to fight to defend their homes and property. Reuben Stebbins of Massachusetts was typical of many patriotic farmers. When the British **approached**, he rode off to battle. "We'll see who's going t'own this farm!" he cried.

Analyze Charts The Revolutionary War was largely a fight between the colonists and the British. **Draw Conclusions** Why was it also a fight between the colonists themselves?

★ AMERICANS IN CONFLICT ★

The **Revolutionary War** was also a conflict between groups living in the colonies. During the Revolution, families fought each other. Communities were split apart.

1775-1783
80,000 to 100,000 **Loyalists** left the colonies during the war.

1760
Everyone is a Tory and supports the King.

1775
The War begins . . . relatives, friends, and neighbors take sides.

1776
Population of the United States is 2.5 million.

Source: United States Census Bureau

★ ★ ★ ★ ★ **PATRIOTS** ★ ★ ★ ★ ★
• Called **Rebels** by the Loyalists
• Felt oppressed by British rule and taxation
• Led by well-educated and wealthy individuals
• Supported Declaration of Independence and freedom from British rule

★ ★ ★ ★ ★ **LOYALISTS** ★ ★ ★ ★ ★
• Called **Tories** by the Patriots
• Mostly government officials, merchants, bankers, and tradesmen who had financial interests in maintaining British rule
• Felt it was morally wrong to oppose the King
• Started their own fighting regiments that were not part of the British Army

British Advantages and Disadvantages The British were a powerful foe. They had highly trained, experienced troops. Their navy was the best in the world. Also, many colonists supported them.

Still, Britain faced problems. Its armies were 3,000 miles from home. News and supplies took months to travel from Britain to North America. Also, British soldiers risked attacks by colonial militias once they marched out of the cities into the countryside.

Loyalists Favor the King American colonists who remained loyal to Britain were known as **Loyalists**. They included wealthy merchants and former officials of the royal government. However, some farmers and craftsworkers were also Loyalists. There were more Loyalists in the Middle Colonies and the South than in New England.

Loyalists faced hard times during the war. Patriots tarred and feathered people known to favor the British. Many Loyalists fled to England or Canada. Others found shelter in cities controlled by the British. Those who fled lost their homes, stores, and farms.

☑ **READING CHECK** **Identify Main Ideas** What positions did colonists take in regard to the war as it began?

▲ As commander of the Continental Army, Washington knew that he would be fighting against one of the world's toughest armies. He set off at once to take charge of the forces around Boston.

☑ Lesson Check

Practice Vocabulary

1. Contrast the **Patriots** and the **Loyalists**.

2. Explain how **militia** and **minutemen** played a role in the fighting between colonists and the British.

Critical Thinking and Writing

3. **Recognize Multiple Causes** Why did the colonists choose to throw British tea into Boston Harbor?

4. **Infer** Why did Ralph Waldo Emerson call the first shot fired in Lexington "the shot heard round the world"?

5. **Summarize** How did King George react to the Olive Branch Petition?

6. **Writing Workshop: Support Thesis with Details** Think of details—facts, events, ideas—that support the thesis statement you wrote about why there was an American Revolution. Write down as many solid details as you can in your 📕 Active Journal.

Compare Different Points of View

Follow these steps to compare different points of view.

INTERACTIVE

Compare Viewpoints

1 **Identify the event and the different points of view.** What is the issue that these points of view are addressing? Use what you know about Thomas Paine to assess his motivation for writing *Common Sense*.

2 **Identify the facts in each point of view.** Facts are statements that can be proved to be true. When both points of view agree about something, it is probably a fact. Does either point of view contain a fact or facts? If so, what are they?

3 **Identify the opinions in each point of view.** What is Inglis's opinion? Paine's? What words does Paine use to persuade the reader to adopt Paine's point of view?

4 **Develop your own opinion about the event.** Your opinion should be based on the facts and what you know about the people giving the opinions.

Primary Source

By a declaration for independency, every avenue to an accommodation with Great Britain would be closed. The sword only could then decide the quarrel, and the sword would not be sheathed till one had conquered the other. Besides the unsuitableness of the republican form to the genius of the people, America is too extensive for it. That form may do well enough for a single city, or small territory; but would be utterly improper for such a continent as this. America is too unwieldy for the feeble, dilatory [unhurried] administration of democracy.

—Charles Inglis, *The Deceiver Unmasked*, 1776

Primary Source

I challenge the warmest advocate for reconciliation to show a single advantage that this continent can reap by being connected with Great Britain. I repeat the challenge; not a single advantage is derived. ... Everything that is right or reasonable pleads for separation. The blood of the slain, the weeping voice of nature cries: 'TIS TIME TO PART.

—Thomas Paine, *Common Sense*, 1776

LESSON 4
The Move Toward Independence

BOUNCE TO ACTIVATE   ▶ VIDEO

GET READY TO READ

START UP
Examine the illustration of crowds celebrating the reading of the Declaration of Independence. Write a question you have about the Declaration.

GUIDING QUESTIONS
- What are the main ideas of the Declaration of Independence?
- What challenges faced the Continental Army at the beginning of the war?
- What helped turn the tide of the war?

TAKE NOTES
Literacy Skills: Use Evidence
Use the graphic organizer in your 📖 Active Journal to take notes as you read the lesson.

PRACTICE VOCABULARY
Use the vocabulary activity in your 📖 Active Journal to practice the vocabulary words.

Vocabulary

blockade   natural rights
mercenary   unalienable rights
traitor
preamble

Academic Vocabulary

evident
ensure

Lexington and Concord marked the start of armed conflict between colonists and the British—the beginning of the American Revolution. As the fighting spread, many colonists came to believe that Parliament did not have the right to make any laws for the 13 colonies. After all, they argued, the colonies had their own elected legislatures. Many felt it was time for the colonies to become completely independent from Britain.

The War Comes to Boston
During the first year of conflict, much of the fighting centered around Boston. About 6,000 British troops were stationed there. Colonial militia surrounded the city and prevented the British from marching out.

War Breaks Out Near Boston Harbor
Even before Washington reached Boston, the Patriots took action. On June 16, 1775, Colonel William Prescott led 1,200 minutemen up Bunker Hill, across the Charles River from Boston. From there, they could fire on British ships in Boston Harbor. Prescott, however, noticed that nearby Breed's Hill was an even better place.

Analyze Images In this illustration, British military forces clash with colonial militia atop Breed's Hill during the Battle of Bunker Hill on June 17, 1775.
Synthesize Visual Information Which forces did the artist want the viewer to believe were winning this battle? State visual clues that support your answer.

INTERACTIVE

Thomas Paine's
Common Sense

He could use the local geography to his advantage. A hilltop would be easier to defend, so he ordered his men to move there.

At sunrise, the British general, William Howe, spotted the Americans. He ferried about 2,400 redcoats across the river to attack the rebels' position. As the British approached, the Patriots held their fire.

When the Americans finally fired, the British were forced to retreat. A second British attack was also turned back. On the third try, the British pushed over the top. They took both Bunker Hill and Breed's Hill, but they paid a high price for their victory. More than 1,000 redcoats lay dead or wounded. American losses numbered only about 400.

The Battle of Bunker Hill was the first major battle of the Revolution. It proved that the Americans could fight bravely. It also showed that the British would not be easy to defeat. Furthermore, it hinted that one effect of the Revolution would be continued bloodshed from a long and bitter war.

Washington Forces the British out of Boston When Washington reached Boston a few weeks after the Battle of Bunker Hill, he found about 16,000 troops camped in huts and tents around the city.

General Washington quickly began to turn raw recruits into a trained army. His job was especially difficult because soldiers from different colonies mistrusted one another. He wrote about their behavior.

"Connecticut wants no Massachusetts men in her corps." And "Massachusetts thinks there is no necessity for a Rhode Islander to be introduced into her [ranks]." However, Washington won the loyalty of his troops. They, in turn, learned to take orders and work together.

In January 1776, Washington had a stroke of good fortune. The cannons that the Green Mountain Boys had captured at Fort Ticonderoga arrived in Boston. Soldiers had dragged them across the mountains from Fort Ticonderoga. Washington had the cannons placed in a strategic location on Dorchester Heights, overlooking the harbor.

Once General Howe saw the American cannons in place, he knew that he could not hold Boston. In March 1776, he and his troops sailed from Boston to Halifax, Canada. About 1,000 American Loyalists went with them.

Although the British left New England, they did not give up. King George III ordered a blockade of all colonial ports. A **blockade** is the shutting of a port to keep people or supplies from moving in or out. The king also used **mercenaries**, or troops for hire, from Germany to help fight the colonists.

☑ READING CHECK Identify Supporting Details How did the colonists use the physical geography of Boston to their advantage?

What Did Thomas Paine Say in *Common Sense*?

Thomas Paine was a British writer and editor who moved to Philadelphia in 1774. After Lexington and Concord, Paine wrote the pamphlet *Common Sense*, in which he set out to change the colonists' attitudes toward Britain and the king. Colonists, he said, did not owe loyalty to George III or any other monarch. The very idea of having kings and queens was wrong, he said.

Primary Source

"In England a King hath little more to do than to make war and give away [jobs]; which in plain terms, is to impoverish the nation.
. . . Of more worth is one honest man to society and in the sight of God, than all the crowned ruffians that ever lived."

—Thomas Paine, *Common Sense*, 1776

▼ Thomas Paine's criticism of British rule in *Common Sense* prompted many colonists to consider the option of declaring full independence from Britain.

The colonists did not owe anything to Britain, either, Paine went on. If the British had helped the colonists, they had done so for their own profit. It could only hurt the colonists to remain under British rule. "Everything that is right or reasonable pleads for separation," he concluded. " 'Tis time to part." *Common Sense* was a great success, selling over 500,000 copies in six months. Paine's writing played an important role in moving toward revolution.

✓ **READING CHECK** Identify Main Ideas What was the main idea of *Common Sense*?

What Steps Did Colonial Leaders Take Toward Independence?

Common Sense caused many colonial leaders to move toward declaring independence from Britain. It also deeply impressed many members of the Continental Congress. Richard Henry Lee of Virginia wrote to Washington, "I am now convinced . . . of the necessity for separation." In June 1776, Lee rose to his feet in Congress to introduce a resolution in favor of independence:

Primary Source

"*Resolved*, That these United Colonies are and of right ought to be, free and independent States, that they are absolved from all allegiance to the British Crown, and that all political connection between them and the State of Great Britain is, and ought to be, totally dissolved."

—Richard Henry Lee, Resolution at the Second Continental Congress, June 7, 1776

Analyze Images Thomas Jefferson labored several days writing the Declaration of Independence. In this painting, Jefferson and other committee members present the Declaration to the Continental Congress. **Infer** Why do you think a painting was made of this particular event?

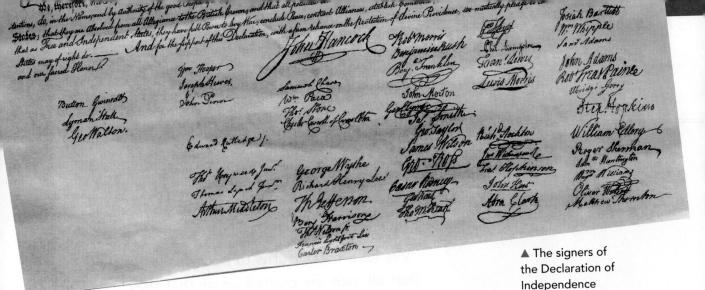

▲ The signers of the Declaration of Independence

Drafting the Declaration of Independence The delegates faced a difficult decision. There could be no turning back once they declared independence. If they fell into British hands, they would be hanged as traitors. A **traitor** is a person who betrays his or her country.

After long debate, the Congress took a fateful step. It appointed a committee to draft a formal declaration of independence. The committee included John Adams, Benjamin Franklin, Thomas Jefferson, Robert Livingston, and Roger Sherman. Their job was to tell the world why the colonies were breaking away from Britain.

The committee asked Thomas Jefferson to write the document. Jefferson was one of the youngest delegates. He was a quiet man who spoke little at formal meetings.

Among friends, however, he liked to sprawl in a chair with his long legs stretched out and talk for hours. His ability to write clearly and gracefully had earned him great respect.

Adopting the Declaration of Independence In late June, Jefferson completed the Declaration, and it was read to the Congress. On July 2, the Continental Congress voted that the 13 colonies were "free and independent States." After polishing Jefferson's language, the delegates adopted the document on the night of July 4, 1776. They then ordered the Declaration of Independence to be printed.

John Hancock, president of the Continental Congress, signed the Declaration first. He penned his signature boldly, in large, clear letters. "There," he said, "I guess King George will be able to read that."

Copies of the Declaration were distributed throughout the colonies. Patriots greeted the news of independence with joyous—and sometimes rowdy—celebrations.

In New York, colonists tore down a statue of King George III. In Boston, the sound of cannons could be heard for hours.

 READING CHECK **Understand Effects** What were the potential consequences for the delegates who chose to declare independence?

Quick Activity

See how the delegates edited Jefferson's language to the preamble in your 📕 Active Journal.

⬤ **INTERACTIVE**

Interactive Declaration of Independence

Did you know?

The Declaration of Independence was not actually signed on July 4, but on August 2.

The Declaration of Independence

The Declaration of Independence consists of a **preamble**, or introduction, followed by three main parts.

Unalienable Human Rights The first section of the Declaration stresses the idea of **natural rights**, or rights that belong to all people from birth. In bold, ringing words, Jefferson wrote:

Primary Source

"We hold these truths to be self-evident, that all men are created equal; that they are endowed by their Creator with certain unalienable rights; that among these are life, liberty, and the pursuit of happiness."

—The Declaration of Independence

▲ Bells such as these were rung at the reading of the Declaration of Independence.

According to the Declaration of Independence, people form governments in order to protect their natural rights and liberties. Some of these principles were also part of the Magna Carta, a document that challenged the power of King John of England 500 years before the writing of the Declaration.

These **unalienable rights**—including the rights to be free and to choose how to live—cannot be taken away by governments, for governments can exist only if they have the "consent of the governed." If a government fails to protect the rights of its citizens, then it is the people's "right [and] duty, to throw off such government, and to provide new guards for their future security." Ideas such as unalienable rights, adopted by the Founding Fathers (men such as George Washington, John Adams, Benjamin Franklin, and Thomas Jefferson), are good examples of the civic virtues that have since become the cornerstone of American government. These values continue to **ensure** that human rights are protected and human needs are met in our nation.

Colonial Grievances The second part of the Declaration lists the wrongs, or grievances, that led the Americans to break away from Britain. Jefferson condemned King George III for disbanding colonial legislatures and for sending troops to the colonies in peacetime. He complained about limits on trade and about taxes imposed without the consent of the people.

Jefferson listed many other grievances to show why the colonists had the right to rebel. He also pointed out that the colonies had petitioned the king to correct these injustices. Yet, the injustices remained. A ruler who treated his subjects in this manner, he boldly concluded, is a tyrant and not fit to rule:

Academic Vocabulary

evident • *adj.*, obvious, apparent

ensure • *v.*, to make certain, to secure

Primary Source

"In every state of these oppressions, we have petitioned for redress [remedy] in the most humble terms; our repeated petitions have been answered only by repeated injury. A prince whose character is thus marked by every act which may define a tyrant is unfit to be the ruler of a free people."

—The Declaration of Independence

Independence The last part of the Declaration announces that the colonies are the United States of America. All political ties with Britain have been cut.

As a free and independent nation, the United States has the full power to "levy war, conclude peace, contract alliances, establish commerce, and to do all other acts and things which independent states may of right do."

The signers closed the declaration with a solemn pledge: "And, for the support of this declaration, with a firm reliance on the protection of Divine Providence, we mutually pledge to each other our lives, our fortunes, and our sacred honor."

✓ **READING CHECK** **Identify Main Ideas** What are some of the grievances Jefferson included in the Declaration?

Analyze Images Benjamin Franklin created this illustration encouraging colonists to band together in 1754 during the French and Indian War. It was later used for the same purpose during the American Revolution. **Draw Conclusions** What about this image made it appropriate and popular during the Revolutionary War era?

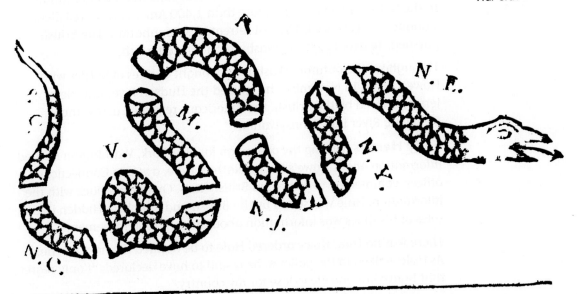

JOIN, or DIE.

Analyze Images The British hired Hessian mercenaries to compensate for a shortage of British troops. At the time, British troops were fighting in other wars. **Identify Cause and Effect** What would be the effect of Britain hiring mercenaries to fight in North America?

What Challenges Faced the Continental Army?

Through an odd coincidence, the British began landing troops in New York in the same month that the Continental Congress voted for independence, July 1776. General George Washington, expecting the attack, had led his forces south from Boston to New York City. His army, however, was no match for the British under the command of General Howe. Howe had about 34,000 troops and 10,000 sailors. He also had ships to ferry them ashore. Washington had fewer than 20,000 poorly trained troops, which he spread in various locations to defend New York. Worse, he had no navy.

An Early Defeat In August, Howe's army landed on Long Island. In the Battle of Long Island, more than 1,400 Americans were killed, wounded, or captured. The rest retreated to Manhattan. The British pursued. To avoid capture, Washington hurried north.

Throughout the autumn, Washington fought a series of battles with Howe's army. In November, he crossed the Hudson River into New Jersey. Chased by the British, the Americans retreated across the Delaware River into Pennsylvania.

Early Heroes During the campaign for New York, Washington needed information about Howe's forces. Nathan Hale, a young Connecticut officer, volunteered to go behind British lines. On his way back with the information, Hale was seized by the British and searched. Hidden in the soles of his shoes was information about British troop movements.

There was no trial. Howe ordered Hale to be hanged the next morning. As Hale walked to the gallows, he is said to have declared: "I only regret that I have but one life to lose for my country."

Even as Washington's army retreated and the British took New York City, many people there remained as loyal to the American cause as Hale. Haym Salomon (HY um SAL uh mun), was a Jewish immigrant.

He came from Poland, was arrested by the British in September 1776 and thrown into prison. Salomon had supported the American cause from the start, helping the new government get loans. Salomon even gave his own money to soldiers for equipment. He managed to escape to Philadelphia and continued to aid the fight.

▲ Haym Salomon helped the Patriots' cause and was imprisoned by the British for it.

✅ **READING CHECK** **Identify Main Ideas** What advantage did the British have in the Battle of Long Island?

A Surprise Attack Leads to Victory

Months of hard campaigning took a toll on the Continental Army. In December 1776, Washington described his troops as sick, dirty, and "so thinly clad as to be unfit for service." Every day, soldiers deserted. Washington wrote to his brother: "I am wearied to death."

Washington then decided on a bold move: a surprise attack on Trenton, New Jersey. The Delaware River separated the British in Trenton and the Americans, and the soldiers guarding Trenton would not expect American troops to cross it. On Christmas night, Washington secretly led his troops across the icy river. Soldiers shivered as spray from the river froze on their faces. Once ashore, they marched through swirling snow. Some had no shoes. They tied rags around their feet. "Soldiers, keep by your officers," Washington urged.

Early on December 26, the Americans surprised the Hessian troops guarding Trenton and took most of them prisoner. The Hessians were soldiers from Germany. An American summed up the Battle of Trenton: "Hessian population of Trenton at 8 A.M.—1,408 men and 39 officers; Hessian population at 9 A.M.—0."

Continental vs. British Forces

	CONTINENTAL	BRITISH
TOTAL FORCES	about 90,000 as a peak estimate	more than 70,000
COMPOSITION OF FORCES	Continental Army, State Militias	Army, Navy, hired mercenaries
ALLIES	France, Spain	Native Americans, Loyalists
QUALITY OF FORCES	untrained, unconventional	trained, disciplined
MOTIVATION	freedom from British control	regain British control
SUPPLIES	very limited weapons, food, and clothing	better availability of weapons, food, and clothing, but moving supplies was difficult

Analyze Charts Study the chart. **Summarize** Which forces, the Continental or the British, appear to be better prepared for battle? Why?

▲ At the Battle of Bennington in August 1777, the Continental Army defeated part of John Burgoyne's army.

British General Charles Cornwallis set out at once to retake Trenton and to capture Washington. Late on January 2, 1777, he saw the lights of Washington's campfires. "At last we have run down the old fox," he said, "and we will bag him in the morning."

Washington fooled Cornwallis. He left the fires burning and slipped behind British lines to attack a British force that was marching toward Princeton. There, the Continental Army won another victory. From Princeton, Washington moved to Morristown, where the army would spend the winter. The victories at Trenton and Princeton gave the Americans new hope.

✓ READING CHECK Identify Supporting Details What advantages did Washington have in the Battle of Trenton?

How Did the Tide Turn for the Americans?

In London, British officials were dismayed by the army's failure to crush the rebels. Early in 1777, General John Burgoyne (bur GOIN) presented a new plan for victory. If British troops cut off New England from the other colonies, he argued, the war would soon be over.

▼ General John Burgoyne surrenders to General Horatio Gates after the British defeat at Saratoga.

The New England Strategy Burgoyne wanted three British armies to march on Albany, New York, from different directions to crush American forces there. Once they controlled the Hudson River, the British could stop the flow of soldiers and supplies from New England to Washington's army.

Burgoyne's plan called for General Howe to march on Albany from New York City. George III, however, wanted Howe to capture Philadelphia first.

In July 1777, Howe sailed from New York to the Chesapeake Bay, where he began his march on Philadelphia. Howe captured Philadelphia, defeating the Americans at the battles of Brandywine and Germantown. But instead of moving toward Albany to meet Burgoyne as planned, he retired to comfortable quarters in Philadelphia for the winter. For his part, Washington retreated to Valley Forge, Pennsylvania.

Meanwhile, British armies under Burgoyne and Barry St. Leger (lay ZHAIR) marched from Canada toward Albany. St. Leger tried to take Fort Stanwix. However, a strong American army, led by Benedict Arnold, drove him back.

American Troops Prevail at Saratoga Only Burgoyne was left to march on Albany. His army moved slowly because it had many heavy baggage carts to drag through the woods. To slow Burgoyne further, Patriots cut down trees and dammed up streams to block the route.

Despite these obstacles, Burgoyne recaptured Fort Ticonderoga, shocking Americans. However, he delayed at the fort, giving American forces time to regroup. He also sent troops into Vermont to find food and horses. There, Patriots attacked the redcoats. At the Battle of Bennington, they wounded or captured nearly 1,000 British.

GEOGRAPHY SKILLS

The battles of the American Revolution took place in every region of the 13 colonies.

1. **Region** During the early years of the war, in what region did the fighting mostly take place?

2. **Summarize** What were the results of the battles of 1777 that were part of General Burgoyne's plan?

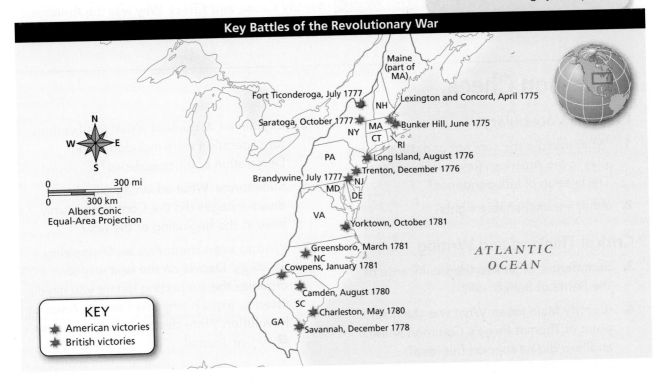

Key Battles of the Revolutionary War

Maine (part of MA)

Fort Ticonderoga, July 1777
Lexington and Concord, April 1775
NH
Saratoga, October 1777
MA
Bunker Hill, June 1775
NY
CT
RI
PA
Long Island, August 1776
Trenton, December 1776
Brandywine, July 1777
NJ
MD
DE
VA
Yorktown, October 1781

ATLANTIC OCEAN

Greensboro, March 1781
NC
Cowpens, January 1781
Camden, August 1780
SC
Charleston, May 1780
GA
Savannah, December 1778

N
W   E
S

0   300 mi
0   300 km
Albers Conic
Equal-Area Projection

KEY
★ American victories
★ British victories

▲ King Louis XVI of France aided the American Revolution, but he would later face revolution in his own country.

Burgoyne's troubles grew. The Green Mountain Boys hurried into New York to help American forces there. At the village of Saratoga, the Americans surrounded the British. When Burgoyne tried to break free, the Americans beat him back. Realizing that he was trapped, Burgoyne surrendered his entire army to the Americans on October 17, 1777.

The American victory at the Battle of Saratoga was a major turning point in the war. It ended the British threat to New England. It boosted American spirits at a time when Washington's army was suffering defeats. Most importantly, it convinced France to become an ally of the United States. Nations that are allies work together to achieve a common goal.

France Aids the American Cause The Continental Congress had long hoped for French aid. In 1776, the Congress had sent Benjamin Franklin to Paris to persuade Louis XVI, the French king, to give the Americans weapons and other badly needed supplies. In addition, the Congress wanted France to declare war on Britain.

The French were eager to defeat Britain, but they were also cautious. Louis XVI did not want to help the Americans openly unless he was sure that they could win. The American victory at Saratoga convinced France that the United States could stand up to Britain. In February 1778, France became the first nation to sign a treaty with the United States. It recognized the new nation and agreed to provide military aid.

☑ **READING CHECK** **Identify Cause and Effect** Why was the American victory at Saratoga significant to the Patriots?

☑ Lesson Check

Practice Vocabulary

1. What role did the concept of **natural rights** play in the American Revolution and the Declaration of Independence?

2. What are **unalienable rights**?

Critical Thinking and Writing

3. **Summarize** What was the significance of the Battle of Bunker Hill?

4. **Identify Main Ideas** What was the main point of Thomas Paine's *Common Sense*, and how did he support this idea?

5. **Explain an Argument** What justifications for separation were included in the Declaration of Independence?

6. **Summarize** What advantages and disadvantages did the Continental Army have at the beginning of the war?

7. **Writing Workshop: Pick an Organizing Strategy** Decide on the best way to organize the supporting details you have listed to explain why there was an American Revolution. Note this organization in your 📓 Active Journal.

Thomas Paine, *Common Sense*

Thomas Paine's pamphlet *Common Sense* stirred the emotions of colonists and rallied many to the Patriot cause.

▶ Thomas Paine is called one of the Founding Fathers of the United States.

I have heard it asserted by some, that as America hath flourished under her former connection with Great Britain, that the same connection is necessary towards her future happiness, and will always have the same effect. Nothing can be more ① <u>fallacious</u> than this kind of argument. ② We may as well assert <u>that because a child has thrived</u> upon milk, that it is never to have meat, or that the first twenty years of our lives is to become a precedent for the next twenty. But even this is admitting more than is true; for I answer roundly, that America would have flourished as much, and probably much more, had no European power had any thing to do with her. ③ The commerce, by which she hath enriched herself, are the necessaries of life, and will always have a market while eating is the custom of Europe.

But she has protected us, say some. That she has engrossed us is true, and defended the continent at our expense as well as her own, is admitted; and she would have defended Turkey from the same motive, ④ <u>viz.</u> the sake of trade and dominion. ⑤

Alas! we have been long led away by ancient prejudices, and made large sacrifices to superstition. We have boasted the protection of Great Britain, without considering, that her motive was INTEREST not ATTACHMENT; that she did not protect us from OUR ENEMIES on OUR ACCOUNT, but from HER ENEMIES on HER OWN ACCOUNT, from those who had no quarrel with us on any OTHER ACCOUNT, and who will always be our enemies on the SAME ACCOUNT. Let Britain wave her pretensions to the Continent, or the Continent throw off the dependence, and we should be at peace with France and Spain, were they at war with Britain.

Analyzing Primary Sources

Cite specific evidence from the document to support your answers.

1. **Analyze Style and Rhetoric** In the first paragraph, how does Paine paint a picture that everyday people could understand?

2. **Analyze Style and Rhetoric** Why does Paine capitalize words in the last paragraph?

Reading and Vocabulary Support

① *Fallacious* means "false."

② To what is Paine comparing the colonies?

③ What argument against independence does Paine refute in the first paragraph?

④ *Viz.* means "namely."

⑤ What argument against independence does Paine refute in the second paragraph?

Quest CONNECTIONS

Thomas Paine makes an argument for separating from Britain. Which argument might convince you to join the Patriot cause? Record your findings in your 📕 Active Journal.

LESSON 5

Winning Independence

BOUNCE TO ACTIVATE

▶ VIDEO

GET READY TO READ

Once France had agreed to support the Americans, the Netherlands and Spain also joined in the war against Britain. France, the Netherlands, and Spain all provided loans to the United States.

Europeans Aid the Colonies

On the southwestern frontier, Americans received help from New Spain. In the early years of the war, Bernardo de Gálvez (bayr NARDO day GOLL vess), governor of Spanish Louisiana, favored the Patriots. He secretly supplied medicine, cloth, muskets, and gunpowder to the Americans.

When Spain entered the war against Britain in 1779, Gálvez took a more active role. He seized British forts along the Mississippi River and the Gulf of Mexico. He also drove the British out of West Florida. Galveston, Texas, is named after this leader.

Foreign Individuals Contribute After France began to aid the United States, even before other European nations agreed to help the United States, individual volunteers had been coming from Europe.

They wanted to join the American cause. Some became leading officers in the American army.

INTERACTIVE

Foreign Aid Plays a Role

The Marquis de Lafayette (mar KEE dah lah fay ET), a young French noble, convinced France to send several thousand trained soldiers to help the Patriot cause. Lafayette, who fought at Brandywine, became one of Washington's most trusted friends.

From the German state of Prussia came Friedrich von Steuben (STOO bun), who helped train Washington's troops to march and drill. Von Steuben had served in the Prussian army, which was considered the best in Europe.

Two Polish officers also joined the Americans. Thaddeus Kosciuszko (kosh CHUSH ko), an engineer, helped build forts and other defenses. Casimir Pulaski trained **cavalry**, or troops on horseback.

✅ READING CHECK Identify Main Ideas In what ways did Europeans help the American war effort?

Winter at Valley Forge

The victory at Saratoga and the promise of help from Europe boosted American morale. Washington's Continental Army began preparing for the winter of 1777–1778 by building a makeshift camp at Valley Forge.

Conditions at Valley Forge were difficult, but the soldiers endured. About 2,000 huts were built as shelter. Several soldiers were improperly dressed, although many did have proper uniforms. As the winter wore on, soldiers also suffered from disease, a common problem in military camps. An army surgeon from Connecticut wrote about his hardships:

Analyze Images The winter at Valley Forge was hard on Washington's soldiers. **Classify and Categorize** Which details in the illustration show the cause of hardships soldiers suffered?

Primary Source

"I am sick—discontented—and out of humor. Poor food—hard lodging— cold weather—fatigue—nasty clothes—nasty cookery. . . . There comes a bowl of beef soup, full of burnt leaves and dirt. . . . "

—Albigence Waldo, *Diary*, December 14, 1777

As news of the hardships at Valley Forge spread, Patriots from around the nation sent help. Women collected food, medicine, warm clothes, and ammunition for the army. Some women, like Martha Washington, wife of the commander, went to Valley Forge to help the sick and wounded.

Analyze Images The Marquis de Lafayette, George Washington, and their troops spent the winter at Valley Forge training for upcoming battles. **Draw Conclusions** Do you think the winter experienced by the Continental Army at Valley Forge weakened or strengthened it? Why?

 **INTERACTIVE**

Notable People of the American Revolution

The arrival of desperately needed supplies was soon followed by warmer weather. The drills of Friedrich von Steuben helped the Continentals to march and fight with new skill. By the spring of 1778, the army at Valley Forge was more hopeful. Washington could not know it at the time, but the Patriots' bleakest hour had passed.

☑ **READING CHECK** **Identify Supporting Details** How did people help the soldiers at Valley Forge?

How Did Women Contribute to the War Effort?

When men went off to fight in the Revolution, women took on added work at home. Some planted and harvested the crops. Others made shoes and wove cloth for blankets and uniforms. One woman, Betsy Hagar, worked with blacksmith Samuel Leverett repairing cannons and guns for Patriot soldiers after the Battle of Concord.

Supporting the Army Many women joined their husbands at the front. They cared for the wounded, washed clothes, and cooked. Martha Washington joined her husband whenever she could. Some women achieved lasting fame for their wartime service.

Betsy Ross of Philadelphia sewed flags for Washington's army. Legend claims that she made the first American flag of stars and stripes.

A few women even took part in battle. During the Battle of Monmouth in 1778, Mary Ludwig Hays carried water to her husband and other soldiers. The soldiers called her Molly Pitcher. When her husband was wounded, she took his place, loading and firing the cannon.

Women's Rights and the Revolution As women participated in the war, they began to think differently about their rights. Those women who had taken charge of farms or their husbands' businesses became more confident and willing to speak out. The Revolution established important ideals of liberty and equality. In later years, these ideals would help encourage women to campaign for equal treatment—and eventually to win it.

✓ READING CHECK **Identify Supporting Details** How did many women assist the Revolutionary War effort?

▲ Mary Ludwig Hays, known as Molly Pitcher for carrying water to soldiers during battle, helped fight for independence.

How Did African Americans Serve in the War?

By 1776, more than a half million African Americans lived in the colonies. This large racial group was quickly emerging as part of the American identity due to African American contributions during the Revolution. At first, the Continental Congress refused to let African Americans, whether free or enslaved, join the army. Some members doubted the loyalty of armed African Americans. The British, however, offered freedom to some enslaved men who would serve the king. Washington feared that this would greatly increase the ranks of the British army. In response, Washington changed his policy and asked Congress to allow free African Americans to enlist.

Deciding to Fight About 5,000 African Americans, from all the colonies except South Carolina, served in the army. Another 2,000 served in the navy which, from the start, allowed African Americans to join. At least nine African-American minutemen saw action at Lexington and Concord.

Some African Americans formed special regiments. Others served in white regiments as drummers, fifers, spies, and guides.

5 BIOGRAPHY **Things to Know About** ▶ **PHILLIS WHEATLEY**
Poet 1753–1784

- Was first published African American female poet
- Born in West Africa; kidnapped and sold into slavery in Boston at age 7
- Mastered English, Greek, and Latin
- Wrote famous poem, "To His Excellency General Washington"
- Became a social success on London trip and later was freed

Critical Thinking What events during the war may have moved Wheatley to write a poem to General George Washington?

African Americans and the Revolution

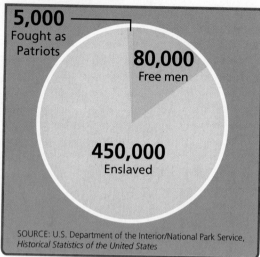

5,000
Fought as Patriots

80,000
Free men

450,000
Enslaved

SOURCE: U.S. Department of the Interior/National Park Service, *Historical Statistics of the United States*

Analyze Graphs This circle graph shows the African American population engaged in the Patriot cause. **Draw Conclusions** What does this data tell you about the status of African Americans during the Revolution?

African Americans like Wentworth Cheswell served the Patriot cause from the start. A New Hampshire schoolmaster, Cheswell was a free African-American man who, like Paul Revere, rode all night from Boston to warn his community that the British were on the march. He later enlisted in the army to help fight at Saratoga.

Enslaved African Americans faced more difficult choices. If they joined the American army or continued to work on Patriot plantations, the British might capture and sell them. If they tried to flee to the British army to gain freedom, they risked being hanged by angry Patriots.

Belief in Freedom Yet, many slaves did flee their masters, especially those who lived near the coast. The British navy patrolled the coast. One British captain reported that "near 500" runaway slaves offered their services to him. Toward the end of the war, several thousand enslaved people sought freedom by following British troops through the Carolinas.

African-American Patriots hoped that the Revolution would bring an end to slavery. After all, the Declaration of Independence proclaimed that "all men are created equal." The promise of the natural rights professed in the Declaration motivated African Americans to try to secure these rights.

▲ At the Battle of Wyoming in 1778, Loyalists and American Indians, allied with the British, killed 360 colonial settlers in the Wyoming Valley of Pennsylvania.

Some white leaders also hoped the war would end slavery. James Otis wrote that "the colonists are by the law of nature free born, as indeed all men are, white or black." Quakers in particular spoke out strongly against slavery.

During the American Revolution, several states moved to make slavery illegal, including Massachusetts, New Hampshire, and Pennsylvania. Other states also began to debate the slavery issue.

✓ READING CHECK Identify Main Ideas What difficult consequences did many enslaved African Americans face when choosing sides in the American Revolution?

American Indians Choose Sides

At first, both sides tried to persuade American Indians to stay out of the conflict. However, as the war spread to American Indian lands in the West, the Americans and British both tried to win the support of American Indian groups. In the end, the British were more successful in creating alliances. They convinced many American Indians that a Patriot victory would mean more white settlers crossing the Appalachians and taking their lands.

In the South, the Cherokee, Creek, Choctaw, and Chickasaw supported the British. The British encouraged the Cherokee to attack dozens of settlements. Only after hard fighting were Patriot militia able to drive the Cherokee back into the mountains.

Fighting was equally fierce on the northern frontier. In 1778, Iroquois forces led by the Mohawk leader Joseph Brant joined with Loyalists in raiding settlements in Pennsylvania and New York. The next year, Patriots struck back by destroying dozens of Iroquois villages.

Farther west, in 1778, George Rogers Clark led Virginia frontier fighters against the British in the Ohio Valley. With help from Miami Indians, Clark captured the British forts at Kaskaskia and Cahokia near the Mississippi River.

He then plotted a surprise attack on the British fort at Vincennes. Clark's small force spread out through the woods to make their numbers appear greater than they really were. The British commander surrendered Vincennes in February 1779.

✓ READING CHECK Identify Main Ideas Why were the British generally more successful at becoming allies with American Indian groups?

Fighting for Independence at Sea and in the South

At sea, the Americans could do little against the powerful British navy. British ships blockaded American ports, which were oftentimes important supply routes for Patriot troops and towns. From time to time, however, a bold American captain captured a British ship.

Analyze Images Captain John Paul Jones shouts orders to his crew during battle aboard his ship *Bonhomme Richard*. Jones and his crew captured the British warship *Serapis*. **Infer** What can you infer about the character of John Paul Jones from the caption and the illustration?

Analyze Images Benedict Arnold, although a traitor, was an able general for the Continental Army. **Identify Cause and Effect** What effect did Arnold's treason have on the British army that welcomed him?

The greatest American sea victory took place in September 1779 in Britain's backyard, on the North Sea. After a hard-fought battle, Captain John Paul Jones captured the powerful British warship *Serapis*. Jones was one of many important military leaders who contributed to the American cause during the war.

Battles in the South The South became the main battleground of the war in 1778. Sir Henry Clinton, the new British commander-in-chief, knew that many Loyalists lived in the southern backcountry. He hoped that Loyalists would join the British troops.

At first, Clinton's plan seemed to work. In short order, beginning in December 1778, the British seized Savannah in Georgia and Charleston and Camden in South Carolina. "I have almost **ceased** to hope," wrote Washington when he learned of the defeats.

Patriots and Loyalists Clash In the Carolina backcountry, Patriots and Loyalists launched violent raids against one another. Both sides burned farms and killed civilians.

After 1780, attacks by British troops and Loyalist militia became especially cruel. As a result, more settlers began to side with the Patriots. As one Loyalist admitted, "Great Britain has now a hundred enemies, where it had one before."

Momentum Shifts Toward the Patriots Two able American generals helped turn the tide against the redcoats. The main British army was led by General Charles Cornwallis.

In 1780, General Nathanael Greene took command of the Continental Army in the South. Using his knowledge of local geography, Greene engaged the British only on ground that put them at a disadvantage.

In January 1781, General Daniel Morgan won an important victory at Cowpens, South Carolina. Morgan divided his soldiers into a front line and a rear line. He ordered the front line to retreat after firing just two volleys. The British, thinking the Americans were retreating, charged. They moved into the fire of Morgan's second rank. In this way, the Americans won the Battle of Cowpens.

Greene and Morgan combined their armies when they fought Cornwallis at Guilford Courthouse, near present-day Greensboro, North Carolina. The battle was one of the bloodiest of the war. Although the Americans retreated, the British **sustained** great losses.

Adapting Tactics to Geography Known as the Swamp Fox, Francis Marion of South Carolina led a small band of militia that used **guerrilla**, or hit-and-run, tactics to harass the British. Marion's band took advantage of the region's environment, appearing suddenly out of the swamps, attacking quickly, and retreating swiftly back into the swamps.

Academic Vocabulary
cease • *v.*, to stop or end
sustain • *v.*, to undergo

✓ READING CHECK **Identify Supporting Details** What did a superior navy allow the British to do?

A Decisive Win Brings the War to a Close

Cornwallis abandoned his plan to take the Carolinas. In the spring of 1781, he moved his troops north into Virginia. He planned to conquer Virginia and cut off the Americans' supply routes to the South.

Benedict Arnold's Betrayal The British had achieved some success in Virginia, even before the arrival of Cornwallis. Benedict Arnold was now leading British troops. Arnold captured and burned the capital city of Richmond and other towns.

Arnold had turned traitor to the American cause in September 1780, while commanding West Point, a key fort in New York. The ambitious general was angry because he felt that he had not received enough credit for his victories. He also needed money. Arnold secretly agreed to turn over West Point to the British. The plot was uncovered by a Patriot patrol, but Arnold escaped to join the British.

Arnold's treason and his raids on towns in Connecticut and Virginia enraged the Patriots. Washington ordered Arnold to be hanged. However, he was never captured.

The British Are Trapped at Yorktown Cornwallis hoped to meet with the same kind of success in Virginia that Arnold had achieved. At first, things went well. Cornwallis sent Loyalist troops to attack Charlottesville, where the Virginia legislature was meeting. Governor Thomas Jefferson and other officials had to flee.

American troops under Lafayette fought back by staging raids against the British. Lafayette did not have enough troops to fight a major battle. Still, his strategy kept Cornwallis at bay.

GEOGRAPHY SKILLS

The last battle of the war was fought in the Chesapeake Bay region.

1. **Location** Why was Cornwallis's position a problem for his troops?

2. **Summarize** What role did the French and American navies play in the Battle of Yorktown?

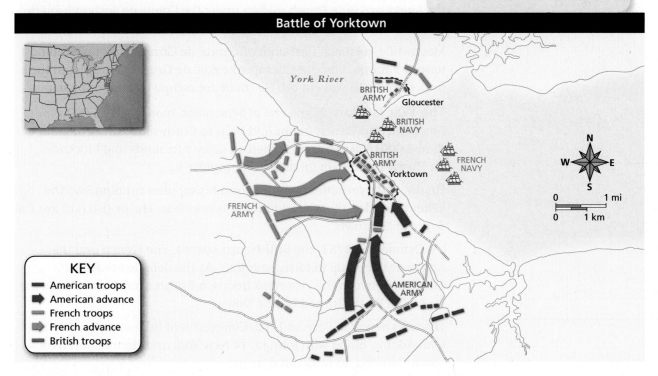

Battle of Yorktown

York River

BRITISH ARMY

Gloucester

BRITISH NAVY

BRITISH ARMY

Yorktown

FRENCH NAVY

FRENCH ARMY

AMERICAN ARMY

N
W E
S

0   1 mi
0   1 km

KEY
- American troops
- American advance
- French troops
- French advance
- British troops

▲ Yorktown was a stunning victory for the American and French armies. As troops gathered to accept the formal British surrender, Cornwallis, claiming illness, did not attend the ceremony.

Then, Cornwallis made a mistake. He disregarded an order from Sir Henry Clinton to send part of his army to New York. Instead, he retreated to Yorktown peninsula, a strip of land jutting into the Chesapeake Bay. He felt confident that British ships could supply his army from the sea.

Washington saw an opportunity to trap Cornwallis on the Yorktown peninsula. He marched his Continental troops south from New York. With the Americans were French soldiers under the Comte de Rochambeau (roh shahm BOH). The combined army rushed to join Lafayette in Virginia.

Meanwhile, a French fleet under Admiral de Grasse was also heading toward Virginia. Once in Chesapeake Bay, de Grasse's fleet closed the trap. Cornwallis was cut off. He could not escape by land or by sea.

The War Is Won By the end of September, more than 16,000 American and French troops laid siege to Cornwallis's army of fewer than 8,000. A **siege** occurs when an army surrounds and blockades an enemy position in an attempt to capture it.

Finally, with casualties mounting and his supplies running low, the general decided that the situation was hopeless. The British had lost the Battle of Yorktown.

On October 19, 1781, the British surrendered. The French and the Americans lined up in facing columns. As the defeated redcoats marched between the victorious troops, a British army band played the tune "The World Turned Upside Down."

The talks began in Paris in 1782. Congress sent Benjamin Franklin and John Adams, along with John Jay of New York and Henry Laurens of South Carolina, to work out a treaty.

Because Britain was eager to end the war, the Americans got most of what they wanted.

Under the Treaty of Paris, the British recognized the United States as an independent nation. It extended from the Atlantic Ocean to the Mississippi River. The northern border of the United States stopped at the Great Lakes. The southern border stopped at Florida, which was returned to Spain.

For their part, the Americans agreed to ask the state legislatures to pay Loyalists for property they had lost in the war. In the end, most states ignored Loyalist claims.

On April 15, 1783, Congress **ratified**, or approved, the Treaty of Paris. It was almost eight years to the day since the battles of Lexington and Concord.

✓ READING CHECK Identify Cause and Effect What were the results of the Treaty of Paris?

Explaining the American Victory

Geography played an important role in the American victory. The British had to send soldiers and supplies several thousand miles from home. They also had to fight an enemy that was spread over a wide area. The Americans also were familiar with the local geography.

Help from other nations was crucial to the American cause. Spanish forces attacked the British along the Gulf of Mexico and in the Mississippi Valley. French money helped pay for supplies, and French military aid supported American troops.

GEOGRAPHY **SKILLS**

After the Treaty of Paris in 1783, the new United States gained some territory.

1. **Movement** In what direction do you think new U.S. immigrants would move when they looked for land to farm?

2. **Cite Evidence** How did the Treaty of Paris of 1783 change the balance of power in North America?

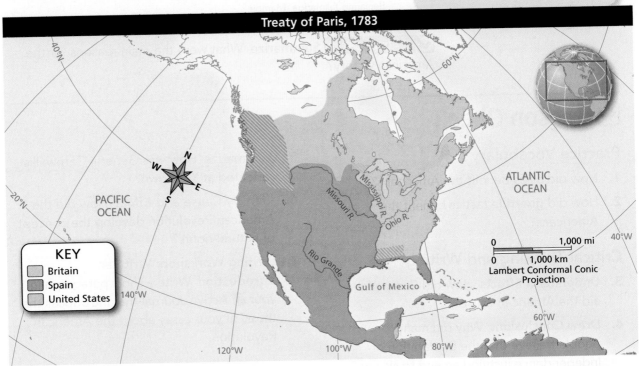

Treaty of Paris, 1783

KEY
- Britain
- Spain
- United States

PACIFIC OCEAN

ATLANTIC OCEAN

Missouri R.
Mississippi R.
Ohio R.
Rio Grande
Gulf of Mexico

0   1,000 mi
0   1,000 km
Lambert Conformal Conic Projection

Analyze Images Here, Washington rides in triumph through the streets of New York City. **Identify Supporting Details** What details in the image help to show George Washington as an important military figure?

Throughout the war the colonists benefited from their ability to unify for a shared American cause. The American Revolution inspired people of many different racial and minority groups as well as social classes to fight for the same American ideals of freedom and rights. Ideals from the Revolution would help define the American identity. Patriotism was another important factor in the American victory. Soldiers were fighting for their homes and their beliefs.

Gradually, Washington's inexperienced troops learned how to drill, how to march, and how to fight the British. Perhaps most important was Washington himself. By the end of the war, the general's leadership and military skills were respected by Americans and British alike. In December 1783, General Washington, before resigning, bid farewell to his officers at Fraunces Tavern in New York City. Colonel Benjamin Tallmadge recalled the event:

Primary Source

"Such a scene of sorrow and weeping I had never before witnessed. . . . We were then about to part from the man who had conducted us through a long and bloody war . . ."

—Benjamin Tallmadge, Memoir

✓ READING CHECK **Summarize** What were the main reasons for the American victory?

✓ Lesson Check

Practice Vocabulary

1. How did allies benefit the Americans?

2. How did **guerrilla** tactics benefit the Americans?

Critical Thinking and Writing

3. **Understand Effects** How did Europeans aid the American cause?

4. **Draw Conclusions** Why did many people believe that the Declaration of Independence justified an end to slavery?

5. **Summarize** How was General Cornwallis defeated at Yorktown?

6. **Identify Cause and Effect** How did the American Revolution develop the concept of natural rights?

7. **Writing Workshop: Write an Introduction** Write a short paragraph in your 📔 Active Journal that introduces the thesis of your essay about the American Revolution.

Relate Events in Time

Follow these steps to relate events in time.

INTERACTIVE

Sequence

1 Identify key events and topics Note the time period, people, and events you are focusing on. For example, where were Revolutionary battles fought? Who were some of the leaders in those battles?

2 Look for clues about time Important clues include information about dates and times of key events. For example, which battles took place in 1776? Is there action in two different regions in the same year? What can you infer about the war by relating the dates of battles in the different regions?

3 Look for clues about relationships Besides dates, a variety of words can signal how key events are related in time. Examples include words such as *before* and *after*, *meanwhile*, *several months ago*, and *in the winter* or other season. For example, what battle happened directly after Lexington and Concord? When did Washington retreat from New York?

REVOLUTIONARY BATTLES BY REGION

North	West	South
• **June 17, 1775** After the skirmish at Lexington and Concord, the British and Americans fight again at Bunker Hill in Massachusetts. • **August 27, 1776** General George Washington retreats from New York after losing the Battle of Long Island. • **December 26, 1776** After crossing the Delaware River, Washington surprises the British and wins the Battle of Trenton, New Jersey.	• **July 3, 1778** Loyalist officer Colonel John Butler leads British and American Indian militia against a Patriot militia at Battle of Wyoming in Pennsylvania. • **February 1779** George Rogers Clark and a small Patriot force take British fort in surprise attack in Battle of Vincennes.	• **December 1778** The British seize Savannah, Georgia. • **January 17, 1781** General Daniel Morgan leads continental soldiers and backwoodsmen against British officer Banastre Tarleton in Battle of Cowpens, South Carolina. • **October 19, 1781** British General Lord Cornwallis surrenders to American General George Washington at Yorktown, Virginia.

VISUAL REVIEW

Major Events Leading to the Declaration of Independence

British Action	Mercantilism and Taxation Without Representation	British Actions
• Proclamation of 1763: restricted colonists' movement west	• Sugar Act 1764: taxed molasses • Stamp Act 1765: taxed documents and other papers	• Quartering Act 1765: required colonists to house British troops • Townshend Acts 1767: assessed more taxes

Events	British Action	Battles
• Boston Massacre 1770 • Tea Act 1773 • Boston Tea Party 1773	• Intolerable Acts 1774	• Lexington and Concord 1775 • Battle of Bunker Hill 1775

MAJOR FIGURES OF THE REVOLUTIONARY ERA

Soldiers	Political Leaders	Patriots
• George Washington • John Paul Jones • Green Mountain Boys and Ethan Allen	• King George III • Thomas Jefferson • Benjamin Franklin • John Adams • Patrick Henry • John Hancock	• Abigail Adams • Samuel Adams • Nathan Hale • Thomas Paine

READING REVIEW

Use the Take Notes and Practice Vocabulary activities in your
📓 Active Journal to help you review the topic.

👆 INTERACTIVE

Practice Vocabulary using Topic Mini-Games.

Quest FINDINGS

Write your blog

Get help for writing your blog in your 📓 Active Journal.

ASSESSMENT

Vocabulary and Key Ideas

1. **Describe** What is the difference between **natural rights** and **unalienable rights**?

2. **Identify** Name two allies of the United States during the American Revolution. Why were they considered allies?

3. **Check Understanding** Why was the Boston Tea Party considered an example of **civil disobedience**?

4. **Recall** How did **Patriots** and **Loyalists** differ?

5. **Identify** After the **preamble**, what are the three parts of the Declaration of Independence, and what is the purpose of each?

6. **Check Understanding** Why was the Battle of Saratoga important?

7. **Identify Main Ideas** How did the Stamp Act help fuel the Boston Massacre?

Critical Thinking and Writing

8. **Summarize** List three factors that contributed to the colonies winning the American Revolution.

9. **Identify Cause and Effect** What motivated African American soldiers to fight with the Patriots during the Revolution?

10. **Compare and Contrast** Compare and contrast the Treaty of Paris signed in 1763 and the Treaty of Paris signed in 1783.

11. **Summarize** What was the relationship of American Indians to Europeans and to the colonists during the Revolutionary Era?

12. **Revisit the Essential Question** Was the American Revolution justified? Explain your answer in one or two paragraphs.

13. **Writing Workshop: Write an Explanatory Essay** Using the notes you created in your 📖 Active Journal, answer the following question in a three-paragraph essay: Why was there an American Revolution?

Analyze Primary Sources

14. Who is most likely to have made the following statement?
    A. a Patriot
    B. a Loyalist
    C. a British citizen
    D. a mercenary

"Our Colonies must be the biggest Beggars in the World, if such small Duties appear to be intolerable in their Eyes."

Analyze Maps

Use the map to answer the following questions.

15. Which letters represent Lexington, Concord, and Saratoga? In which region of the colonies did these battles take place?

16. Which letter represents the Battle of Trenton? From which colony did Washington cross over the Delaware River to fight this battle?

17. Which letter represents the Battle of Yorktown? How did the geography of this location help lead to Cornwallis's defeat?

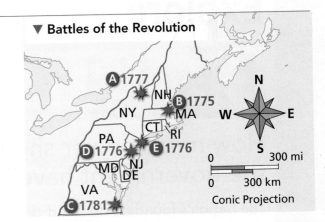

▼ **Battles of the Revolution**

A Constitution for the United States

(1776–Present)

GO ONLINE
to access your
digital course

- ▶ VIDEO
- ◀)) AUDIO
- 📖 ETEXT
- 👆 INTERACTIVE
- ✏️ WRITING
- 🎮 GAMES
- 📄 WORKSHEET
- ☑️ ASSESSMENT

Go back to the late 1700s,

when the **NATION'S FOUNDERS PRODUCED A CONSTITUTION FOR THE UNITED STATES.** See how these leaders applied the ideals of the Declaration of Independence to create a government that has served Americans well for more than 200 years.

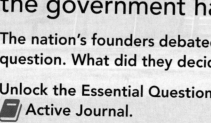

Explore

The Essential Question

How much power should the government have?

The nation's founders debated this question. What did they decide?

Unlock the Essential Question in your 📓 Active Journal.

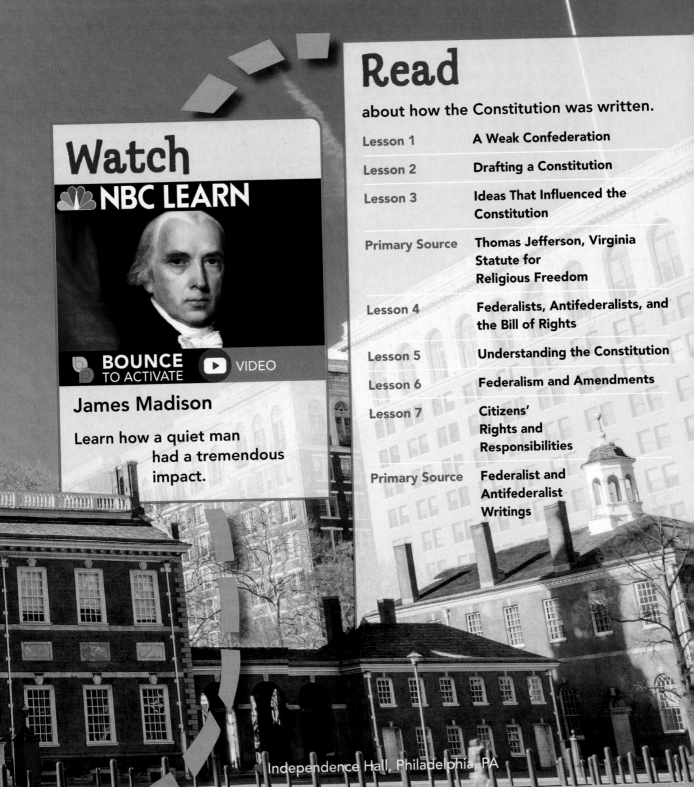

Watch

NBC LEARN

BOUNCE TO ACTIVATE ▶ VIDEO

James Madison

Learn how a quiet man had a tremendous impact.

Read

about how the Constitution was written.

Independence Hall, Philadelphia, PA

A Constitution for the United States (1776–Present)

Learn more about the early United States by making your own map and timeline in your 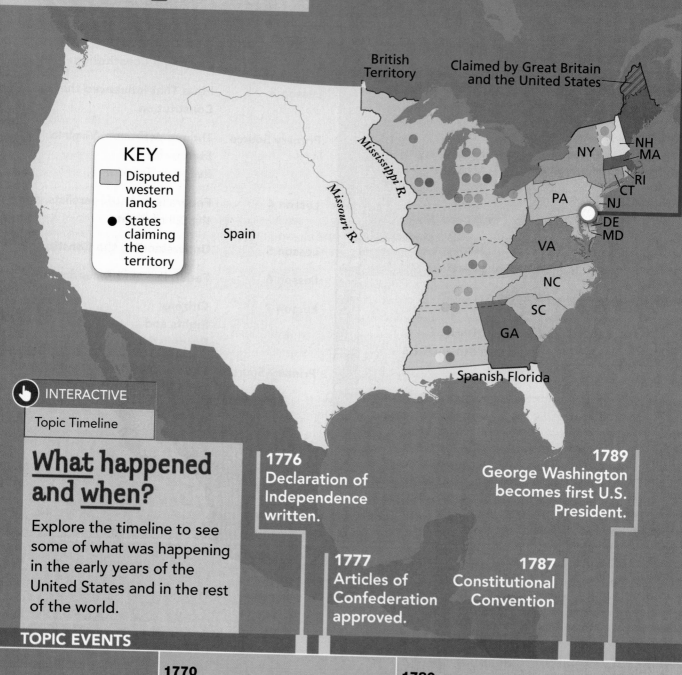 Active Journal.

British Territory

Claimed by Great Britain and the United States

KEY
- Disputed western lands
- • States claiming the territory

Mississippi R.

Missouri R.

Spain

NH
MA
NY
RI
CT
PA
NJ
DE
MD
VA
NC
SC
GA

Spanish Florida

🖐 INTERACTIVE

Topic Timeline

What happened and when?

Explore the timeline to see some of what was happening in the early years of the United States and in the rest of the world.

1776
Declaration of Independence written.

1789
George Washington becomes first U.S. President.

1777
Articles of Confederation approved.

1787
Constitutional Convention

TOPIC EVENTS

1770

1780

WORLD EVENTS

1789
French Revolution begins.

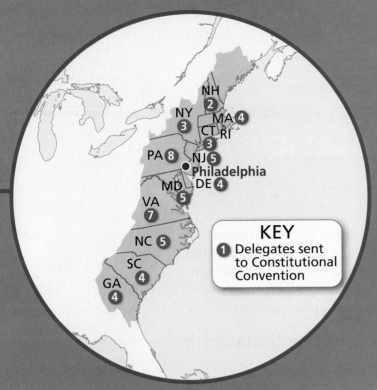

NH **2**
NY **3**
MA **4**
CT **3**
RI
PA **8**
NJ **5**
● Philadelphia
MD
DE **4**
VA **7**
5
NC **5**
SC **4**
GA **4**

KEY
1 Delegates sent to Constitutional Convention

INTERACTIVE

Topic Map

Why did leaders from throughout the United States travel to Philadelphia in 1787?

These leaders were determined to make the existing constitution—and the government—stronger.

1800
Federal government moves to Washington, D.C.

1791
Bill of Rights ratified.

1803
Louisiana Purchase completed.

1790

1800

1810

1799
Rosetta Stone discovered.

1806
Holy Roman Empire ends.

Who will you meet?

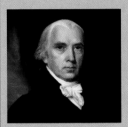

James Madison, the "Father of the Constitution"

Roger Sherman, who masterminded the Great Compromise

Alexander Hamilton, who pushed for a stronger national government

Quest
Civic Dicsussion Inquiry

Senate Representation

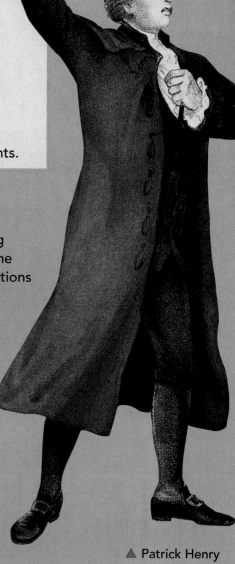

Quest KICK OFF

You are a member of the U.S. House of Representatives. Another representative has proposed an amendment to the Constitution. It would change the number of senators from each state so that the number is based on each state's population. Help decide the answer to this question:

Should representation in the Senate be based on population?

Be ready! Other representatives will challenge your arguments.

1 Ask Questions

You are determined to know the best answer to the Guiding Question. Get started by making a list of questions about the major debates in the Constitutional Convention. Write questions in your 📘 Active Journal.

2 Investigate

As you read the lessons in this Topic, look for **Quest CONNECTIONS** that provide information about the structure of the U.S. Congress. Collect examples in your 📘 Active Journal.

3 Examine Sources

Next, explore sources that support differing viewpoints about Senate representation based on population. Collect examples in your 📘 Active Journal.

▲ Patrick Henry

Quest FINDINGS

4 Discuss!

After you collect clues and examine sources, prepare to discuss this question: Should representation in the Senate be based on population? Use your knowledge of the Constitutional Convention and your sources to answer YES or NO to the question.

LESSON 1
A Weak Confederation

BOUNCE TO ACTIVATE   ▶ VIDEO

GET READY TO READ

START UP
Look at the image of the Second Continental Congress. What principles did these men support?

GUIDING QUESTIONS
- What were the strengths and weaknesses of the Articles of Confederation?
- How did Congress plan for governing the Northwest Territory and opening it to settlers?
- How did Shays' Rebellion influence leaders to revise the Articles of Confederation?

TAKE NOTES
Literacy Skills Summarize
Use the graphic organizer in your 📙 Active Journal to take notes as you read the lesson.

PRACTICE VOCABULARY
Use the vocabulary activity in your 📙 Active Journal to practice the vocabulary words.

Vocabulary		Academic Vocabulary
constitution	cede	privatize
bill of rights	currency	depression
Articles of Confederation	Northwest Ordinance	
	Shays' Rebellion	

When Americans declared their independence in 1776, they also assumed the right to govern themselves. The next year, the Continental Congress drew up plans for a national government. By that time, several states had already begun to create their own governments.

How Were State Constitutions Similar?

Americans fought the Revolution to uphold the principles and ideas set forth in the Declaration of Independence. These include freedom, liberty, equality, democracy, and the concept that people have natural rights. States sought to reflect those principles in their **constitutions**, the documents that set out the basic laws, principles, organization, and processes of a government. They wanted to spell out the rights of all citizens and limit the power of government.

People valued the rights that state governments protected. Virginia's constitution included a **bill of rights**, or list of freedoms that the government promises to protect.

▲ The constitution of the state of Massachusetts declared that the primary purpose of the Massachusetts state government is to protect the natural rights of its inhabitants.

Virginia's bill of rights guaranteed trial by jury, freedom of religion, and freedom of the press. Several other states followed Virginia's lead. For example, the Massachusetts state constitution guaranteed people:

Primary Source

". . . the right of enjoying and defending their lives and liberties; that of acquiring, possessing, and protecting property; in [short], that of seeking and obtaining their safety and happiness."

—Massachusetts Constitution of 1780

The new state governments were structured somewhat like the colonial governments had been. The states divided power between an executive and a legislature. Voters elected members of the legislature, who passed laws. Every state but Pennsylvania had a governor to execute, or carry out, the laws.

Under the state constitutions, more people had the right to vote than in colonial times. To vote, a citizen had to be white, male, and over age 21. He had to own a certain amount of property or pay a certain amount of taxes. For a time, some women in New Jersey could vote. In a few states, free African American men who owned property could vote.

✓READING CHECK Identify Main Ideas What freedoms did many states agree to protect?

The Articles of Confederation

As citizens formed state governments, the Continental Congress was drafting a plan for the nation as a whole. The delegates agreed on the principles for which the Revolution was being fought. But incorporating those principles into a plan of government was a struggle. Although they used state constitutions as guides, the delegates found it hard to write a constitution that all states would approve.

States did not want to give up power to a central government. Few Americans saw themselves as citizens of one nation. Instead, they felt loyal to their own states. Also, people feared replacing the "tyranny" of British rule with another strong government. After much debate, the Continental Congress approved the first American constitution in 1777. The **Articles of Confederation** created a loose alliance of 13 independent states.

Strengths and Weaknesses Under the Articles of Confederation, the United States became a union of states that were linked by a weak central government.

In a sense, the Articles simply put into law the existing reality of government in the colonies—a Congress with delegates acting on behalf of states that retained most of the power.

The new nation was still at war, its revolution not yet won. It was not the time to discuss the political relationship between the states and Congress. The Articles of Confederation represented an effective compromise during a difficult time.

As a plan of government, the Articles of Confederation had strengths. It left states free to make decisions for themselves. It prevented the federal government from gaining too much power.

Under the Articles, each state sent one delegate to Congress. Thus each state, no matter its size or population, had one vote. Congress did have the power to declare war. It could appoint military officers, coin money, and operate post offices. It also could conduct foreign affairs and sign treaties.

However, the Articles of Confederation had weaknesses as well. Compared to the states, Congress had very limited powers. Congress could pass laws, but nine states had to approve a law before it could go into effect. Even then it was up to the states to enforce the laws passed by Congress. The Articles included no president to execute laws.

Congress could not regulate trade between states or between states and foreign countries. Nor did it have the power to tax. To raise money, Congress had to ask the states for funds or borrow them. No state could be forced to contribute funds to the national treasury. There was also no system of courts to settle conflicts between states.

Dispute Over Western Lands One major dispute arose before the Articles of Confederation went into effect. Maryland refused to ratify the Articles unless Virginia and other states **ceded**, or gave up, their claims to lands west of the Appalachians.

GEOGRAPHY **SKILLS**

This map shows the states that disputed western areas, and the dates each state ceded its claim to the federal government.

1. **Interaction** What impact would disputed claims have had on the relationships among the states?

2. **Infer** What factors would have caused states to cede their claims?

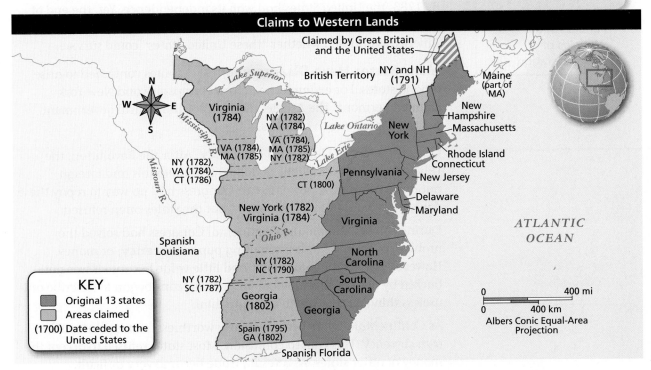

Claims to Western Lands

KEY
- Original 13 states
- Areas claimed
- (1700) Date ceded to the United States

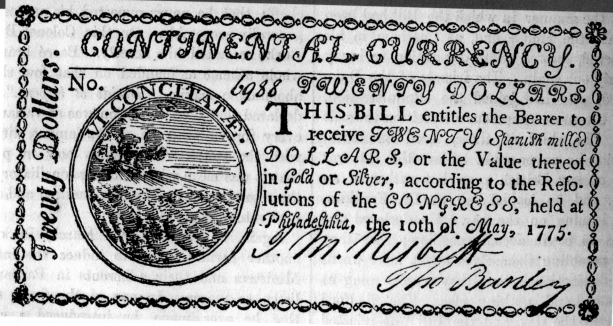

CONTINENTAL CURRENCY.

No.

6988 TWENTY DOLLARS.

THIS BILL entitles the Bearer to receive TWENTY Spanish milled DOLLARS, or the Value thereof in Gold or Silver, according to the Refolutions of the CONGRESS, held at Philadelphia, the 10th of May, 1775.

Twenty Dollars.

Analyze Images This $20 Continental bill was worth little in the eyes of the states. **Infer** If Congress had no power to raise money, how did that affect the value of the currency it issued?

INTERACTIVE

Problems and Effects of the Articles of Confederation

Like other small states, Maryland feared that "landed" states would become too powerful. One by one, the states agreed to cede their western claims to Congress. Finally, only Virginia held out. However, Thomas Jefferson and other leading Virginians recognized the great need to form a central government. They persuaded state lawmakers to give up Virginia's claims in the West.

With its demands met, Maryland ratified the Articles of Confederation in 1781. The new American government could at last go into effect.

READING CHECK **Identify Supporting Details** What were the functions of Congress under the Articles of Confederation?

Weaknesses of the Confederation

By 1783, the United States had won its independence. Yet, the end of the American Revolution did not solve the confederation's troubles. Americans doubted whether "these United States" could survive.

Many States Have Disagreements Disputes continued to arise among states. For example, both New Hampshire and New York claimed Vermont. The Articles did not give the central government power to resolve such conflicts.

Concerns Over Debt and Currency After the Revolution, the United States owed millions of dollars to individuals and foreign nations. Without the power to tax, Congress had no way to repay these debts. It asked the states for money, but the states often refused.

During the Revolution, the Continental Congress had solved the problem of raising funds by printing paper **currency**, or money. However, the Continental dollar had little value because it was not backed by gold or silver. Before long, Americans began to describe any useless thing as "not worth a Continental."

As Continental dollars became nearly worthless, states printed their own currency. This caused confusion. Most states refused to accept the money of other states. As a result, trade became very difficult.

Foreign Countries Promote Their Own Interests Foreign countries took advantage of the confederation's weakness. Ignoring the Treaty of Paris, Britain refused to withdraw its troops from American territory on the Great Lakes. Spain closed its port in New Orleans to American shipping. This was a serious blow to western farmers, who depended on the port to ship their products to the East.

✓READING CHECK **Understand Effects** Why did trade between states become increasingly difficult?

An Orderly Expansion

Despite its troubles, Congress did pass important laws about how to govern the Northwest Territory. This was the U.S. territory west of Pennsylvania, north of the Ohio River, south of the Great Lakes, and east of the Mississippi. The laws established how territories would be governed and how they could become states.

The Land Ordinance of 1785 set up a system for settling the Northwest Territory. The ordinance called for the territory to be surveyed and divided into townships. Each township would then be further divided into 36 sections of one square mile each (640 acres).

Congress planned to sell sections to settlers for a minimum of $640 apiece. In this way, much of this federally owned land was **privatized**, or moved from public to private ownership. One section in every township was set aside for public schools. Selling the land provided income for the government.

In 1787, Congress passed the **Northwest Ordinance**. The law set up a government for the Northwest Territory, guaranteed basic rights to settlers, and outlawed slavery there.

Academic Vocabulary

privatize • *v.*, to put private individuals or companies in charge of something

Analyze Images This infographic summarizes the changes that occurred after the Northwest Ordinance passed. **Infer** How did the ordinance reduce conflict among the states?

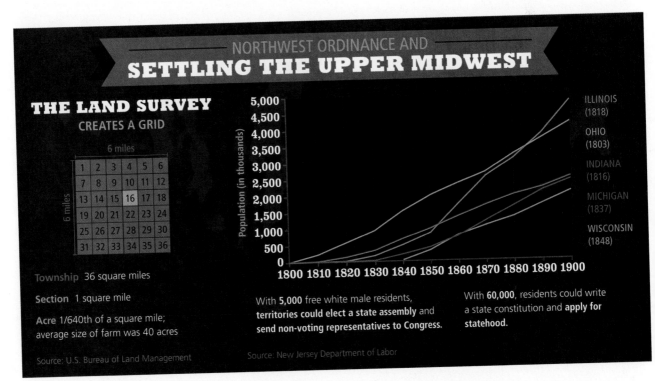

NORTHWEST ORDINANCE AND
SETTLING THE UPPER MIDWEST

THE LAND SURVEY
CREATES A GRID

6 miles

1	2	3	4	5	6
7	8	9	10	11	12
13	14	15	16	17	18
19	20	21	22	23	24
25	26	27	28	29	30
31	32	33	34	35	36

6 miles

Township 36 square miles

Section 1 square mile

Acre 1/640th of a square mile; average size of farm was 40 acres

Source: U.S. Bureau of Land Management

ILLINOIS (1818)
OHIO (1803)
INDIANA (1816)
MICHIGAN (1837)
WISCONSIN (1848)

Population (in thousands): 5,000 / 4,500 / 4,000 / 3,500 / 3,000 / 2,500 / 2,000 / 1,500 / 1,000 / 500 / 0

1800 1810 1820 1830 1840 1850 1860 1870 1880 1890 1900

With **5,000** free white male residents, territories could elect a state assembly and send non-voting representatives to Congress.

With **60,000**, residents could write a state constitution and **apply for statehood**.

Source: New Jersey Department of Labor

Academic Vocabulary

depression • *n.*, a period when business activity slows, prices and wages fall, and unemployment rises

It encouraged public education and said the vast region could be divided into separate territories in the future.

The Northwest Ordinance stated that new territories should be admitted as new states, rather than become part of existing ones. It provided a process, to admit new states to the nation. Once a territory had a population of 60,000 free settlers, it could ask Congress to be admitted as a new state. Ohio, Indiana, Illinois, Michigan, and Wisconsin were created from the Northwest Territory.

However, the lands in this area were already home to American Indian nations. Although the Ordinance stated "the utmost good shall always be observed" toward these nations, conflict would arise and continue for many years.

Despite the drawbacks of the Articles of Confederation, the laws Congress created relating to the Northwest Territory proved to be a major success. These laws defined the basic rights of settlers and established federal support for education.

✓ READING CHECK Identify Main Ideas What was the purpose of the Northwest Ordinance?

How Did Economic Problems Lead to Change?

The Northwest Ordinance was the finest achievement of the national government under the Articles. Still, the government was unable to solve its economic problems. After the Revolution, the nation suffered an economic depression. A **depression** is a period when business activity slows, prices and wages fall, and unemployment rises.

Analyze Images Some Americans moved west after the Revolution, seeking new opportunities. **Infer** What do you think people were seeking?

Farmers Demand Fair Treatment The depression hit farmers hard. The war had created a high demand for farm products. Farmers borrowed money for land, seed, animals, and tools. However, when the Revolution ended, demand for farm goods went down. As prices fell, many farmers could not repay their loans.

In Massachusetts, matters worsened when the state raised taxes. The courts seized the farms of those who could not pay their taxes or loans. Angry farmers felt they were being treated unfairly.

Daniel Shays, a Massachusetts farmer who had fought at Bunker Hill and Saratoga, organized an uprising in 1786. More than 1,000 farmers took part in **Shays' Rebellion**. They attacked courthouses and prevented the state from seizing farms when farmers could not pay their debts. Finally, the Massachusetts legislature sent the militia to drive them off.

A Call For Revision Many Americans saw Shays' Rebellion as a sign that the Articles of Confederation did not work.

To avert a crisis, leaders from several states called for a convention to revise the Articles of Confederation. They met in Philadelphia in May 1787. In the end, this convention would create an entirely new framework of government.

☑ READING CHECK **Identify Implied Main Ideas** What did Shays' Rebellion show to many people?

Analyze Images Shays' Rebellion resulted in bloodshed when state militia attacked angry rioters led by Daniel Shays. **Draw Conclusions** How did Shays' Rebellion test the strength of the new federal government?

☑ Lesson Check

Practice Vocabulary

1. How did the Land Ordinance of 1785 and the **Northwest Ordinance** of 1787 **privatize** national resources?

2. Why did **currency** issues and **Shays' Rebellion** cause some leaders to decide that the **Articles of Confederation** should be revised?

Critical Thinking and Writing

3. **Identify Supporting Details** What were three weaknesses of the central government under the Articles of Confederation?

4. **Draw Conclusions** Why do you think slavery was outlawed in the Northwest Territory?

5. **Evaluate Explanations** Many American leaders, pointed to Shays' Rebellion as proof that the Articles of Confederation. were weak. Does this explanation for revising the Articles make sense to you? Why or why not?

6. **Revisit the Essential Question** How much power should the government have? Restrict your answer to what you have learned in this lesson.

7. **Writing Workshop: Introduce Claims** Write a brief paragraph in your 📓 Active Journal introducing two sides of the argument about how much power the government should have. This paragraph will get you started on an essay you will write at the end of the Topic.

Drafting a Constitution

BOUNCE TO ACTIVATE ▶ VIDEO

GET READY TO READ

START UP

Look at the image of the delegates. What issues are these men going to face?

GUIDING QUESTIONS

- What was the Revolution's legacy?
- Who led the Constitutional Convention?
- What were the main differences between the two rival plans for the new Constitution?
- How much power should the federal government have, and what should it do?

TAKE NOTES

Literacy Skills Compare and Contrast
Use the graphic organizer in your 📓 Active Journal to take notes as you read the lesson.

PRACTICE VOCABULARY

Use the vocabulary activity in your 📓 Active Journal to practice the vocabulary words.

Vocabulary		Academic Vocabulary
Constitutional Convention	compromise	legacy
Virginia Plan	Great Compromise	ethical
New Jersey Plan	Three-Fifths Compromise	

The **Constitutional Convention** opened on May 25, 1787, in Philadelphia, Pennsylvania. Its purpose was to revise the Articles of Confederation. Every state except Rhode Island sent representatives. All of them wanted to honor the **legacy** of the Revolution and the principles for which they had fought. Yet not all delegates would agree on how to achieve that goal.

Who Led the Convention?

The convention would prove historic because it did not revise the Articles of Confederation. Instead, its delegates produced a new United States Constitution. That document established a government that has survived more than 200 years.

A Remarkable Group The convention's 55 delegates were a remarkable group. Eight of them had signed the Declaration of Independence, including the oldest, Benjamin Franklin. At age 81, Franklin was wise in the ways of government and human nature.

George Washington, age 55, represented Virginia. He was so well respected that the delegates at once elected him president of the Convention. Washington had long called for a stronger central government. Yet his role in the debates would be limited. It was his presence at the Convention that was important.

Most of the delegates belonged to a new generation of American leaders. Nearly half were young men in their thirties, including Alexander Hamilton of New York. During the Revolution, Hamilton had served for a time as Washington's private secretary. Hamilton despised the Articles of Confederation. "The nation," he wrote, "is sick and wants powerful remedies." The powerful remedy he prescribed was a strong central government.

Another of the younger delegates was Gouverneur Morris of Pennsylvania. Like Hamilton, he favored a strong central government. He would make his opinion known through many speeches at the Convention. Morris would also polish the final draft of the Constitution.

James Wilson, too, represented Pennsylvania at the Convention. Other delegates admired Wilson's political knowledge, which he would use to help clarify the issues facing the Convention.

A Student of History and Politics
Perhaps the best-prepared delegate was 36-year-old James Madison of Virginia. For months, the quiet, shy Madison had been reading books on history, politics, and commerce.

His intelligence and his ideas about how to structure a democratic government strongly influenced the other delegates. Today, Madison is often called the "Father of the Constitution."

Keeping Conversations Among Themselves
When the Convention began, the delegates decided to keep their talks private. They wanted to speak their minds freely in front of other delegates and be able to explore issues without pressures from outside.

Most of them thought the Articles of Confederation had made the central government too weak. They agreed that the government must be stronger, but not too strong. They did not want anything resembling the British monarchy.

✓ READING CHECK **Compare and Contrast** How were the delegates to the Convention alike and different?

Academic Vocabulary

legacy • *n.*, something received by a predecessor or from the past

INTERACTIVE

Delegates to the Constitutional Convention

Analyze Images George Washington (in black, at right) was chosen by his fellow delegates to lead the Constitutional Convention in 1787. **Infer** Why do you think the delegates chose Washington to lead the proceedings?

Disagreements Over a New Government

Soon after the meeting began, the delegates realized they would have to do more than simply revise the Articles of Confederation. They chose instead to write an entirely new constitution for the nation. They disagreed, however, about the form the new national government should take.

Virginia Proposes a Plan Edmund Randolph and James Madison, both from Virginia, proposed a plan for the new government. This **Virginia Plan** called for a strong national government with three branches that would be responsible for different tasks. Each would keep the others from growing too powerful.

Under the Virginia Plan, the legislature would consist of two houses. The number of representatives would be based on population. Thus, in both houses, larger states would have more representatives than smaller ones. Small states opposed the Virginia Plan. They feared that the large states could easily outvote them in Congress. Supporters of the Virginia Plan replied that it was only fair for a state with more people to have more representatives.

New Jersey's Proposal After two weeks of debate, William Paterson of New Jersey presented a plan that had the support of the small states. Like the Virginia Plan, the **New Jersey Plan** called for three branches of government. However, it provided for a legislature that had only one house. Each state, regardless of its population, would have one vote in the legislature, just as it had under the Articles of Confederation.

READING CHECK Identify Main Ideas What was the essential difference between the Virginia Plan and the New Jersey Plan?

Quest CONNECTIONS

How did states respond to these plans? Record your findings in your 📔 Active Journal.

Analyze Images Oliver Ellsworth and Roger Sherman, delegates from Connecticut, devised a solution to the problem of representation. **Summarize** Explain what their solution was.

The Great Compromise

For a while, no agreement could be reached. Tempers flared. The Convention seemed ready to fall apart. Finally, Roger Sherman of Connecticut worked out a **compromise**. A compromise, a solution in which each side gives up some of its demands to reach an agreement.

Sherman's compromise called for the creation of a two-house legislature. Members of the lower house, the House of Representatives, would be elected by popular vote. As the larger states wished, seats would be awarded to each state based on population. Members of the upper house, called the Senate, would be chosen by state legislatures. Each state, no matter what its size, would have two senators. Small states particularly liked this part of Sherman's compromise.

Virginia and New Jersey Plans

VIRGINIA PLAN
- Population as basis for house representation
- Two houses with seats based on population
- One house is elected by the people, the other house by state legislators
- Chief executive is chosen by the legislature
- Judicial branch is chosen by the legislature

- Three branches of government to prevent abuse of power
- Legislative branch consists of elected representatives

NEW JERSEY PLAN
- Drafted in response to Virginia Plan
- One house with one seat and one vote regardless of population as in the Articles of Confederation
- Executive branch consists of several executives
- Judicial branch is chosen by the executive branch

Analyze Images This diagram summarizes the two plans presented for the new federal government. **Use Visual Information** How did the New Jersey Plan and Virginia Plan differ in their approach to the executive branch of government?

On July 16, the delegates narrowly approved Sherman's plan. It became known as the **Great Compromise**. Each side, in an admirable show of civic virtue, gave up some demands to achieve unity. With a margin of just one vote, the delegates had found a peaceful solution to a problem that had threatened to bring the convention to a halt.

☑ READING CHECK **Identify Supporting Details** How did the Great Compromise address the concerns of small and large states?

The Three-Fifths Compromise

Just as there were disagreements between large states and small states, there were also disagreements between northern states and southern states. The most serious disagreements concerned slavery. Would enslaved people be counted as part of a state's population? Would the slave trade continue to bring enslaved Africans into the United States?

The States Reach an Agreement Southerners wanted to include enslaved people in their states' population counts because that would give southern states more representatives in the House of Representatives. Southern states stood to gain greatly if enslaved people were counted. Extra representatives meant additional influence.

Northerners objected. They argued that since enslaved people could not vote, they should not be counted when assigning representatives.

Once again, the delegates compromised. They agreed that three-fifths of the enslaved people in any state would be counted.

In other words, if a state had 5,000 enslaved residents, 3,000 of them would be included in the state's population count. This agreement became known as the **Three-Fifths Compromise**.

Quick Activity

Study the biographies and writings of delegates and draw conclusions about the relationships between their backgrounds and points of view.

THE THREE-FIFTHS COMPROMISE

ISSUE AND COMPROMISE

THE NORTHERN VIEW
We'll be outvoted if we let them count slaves, and slaves are unable to vote.

THE COMPROMISE
Each slave counts as $\frac{3}{5}$ of a person.

THE SOUTHERN VIEW
Our slaves should be counted as part of our population and representation.

ESTIMATING THE EFFECT OF COMPROMISE

REPRESENTATION FOR VIRGINIA 1790

POPULATION
442,177 FREE WHITES
292,627 ENSLAVED

STEP 1
$\frac{3}{5}$ OF 292,627 ENSLAVED POPULATION
= 175,576

STEP 2
175,576 ENSLAVED + 442,177 FREE
= 617,753 TOTAL

STEP 3
Counting only the free population, Virginia would have **15 representatives.**

Counting the free + enslaved populations, Virginia would have **25 representatives.**

Counting free + $\frac{3}{5}$ enslaved populations, Virginia would have **20 representatives.**

Source: University of Delaware

EFFECT ON SOUTHERN REPRESENTATION

SOUTHERN REPRESENTATION IN THE HOUSE 1790

31%
NOT COUNTING THREE-FIFTHS OF SLAVES

43%
COUNTING THREE-FIFTHS OF SLAVES

Analyze Images The Three-Fifths Compromise balanced regional concerns. **Use Visual Information** How did southern states benefit from the Three-Fifths Compromise?

The fraction in the Three-Fifths Compromise had come from a rule about taxes in the Articles of Confederation. The new compromise balanced the concerns of northerners and southerners.

Further Disagreement Over Slavery By 1787, some northern states had banned the slave trade within their borders. Delegates from these states urged that the importation of slaves be banned in the entire nation. Southerners argued that such a ban would ruin their economy.

In the end, northern and southern states compromised once more. Northerners agreed that Congress could not outlaw the slave trade for at least 20 years. After that, Congress could regulate the slave trade if it wished. Northerners also agreed that no state could stop a person fleeing slavery from being returned to an owner. This clause in the Constitution became known as the fugitive slave clause.

Academic Vocabulary
ethical • *adj.,* following accepted standards for conduct or behavior

The compromises, however, also brought up an **ethical** question. How could the nation's ideals of freedom, liberty, and democracy be adopted alongside slavery?

READING CHECK Identify Main Ideas Why did many of the northern states object to including enslaved people in population counts?

The Convention Comes to a Conclusion

After a long summer full of struggle and argument, the Constitution was ready to be signed on September 17, 1787. Its opening lines, or Preamble, expressed the goals of the Framers: "We the People of the United States, in order to form a more perfect union . . . " Had they succeeded in carrying out the ideals of the Declaration of Independence? History's judgment has largely agreed that they did.

As the delegates gathered for the last time, Benjamin Franklin rose and said:

Primary Source

"I cannot help expressing a wish, that every member of the Convention who may still have objections to it, would with me, on this occasion, doubt a little of his own infallibility, and . . . put his name to this instrument."

—Benjamin Franklin, *Records of the Federal Convention of 1787*

Three delegates refused to sign. Edmund Randolph and George Mason of Virginia, along with Elbridge Gerry of Massachusetts, feared that the new Constitution handed over too much power to the national government.

The Constitution's creation began a process in which states had to decide whether to approve the Constitution. Each state would hold a convention to approve or reject the plan for the new government. Once nine states endorsed it, the Constitution would become law.

☑ READING CHECK Identify Supporting Details Why did some delegates choose not to sign the Constitution?

Analyze Images Although some northern states wanted to ban slavery, the Constitutional Convention did not end slavery or the slave trade. **Summarize** Explain why the delegates decided to compromise on this issue.

☑ Lesson Check

Practice Vocabulary

1. How did the legislative branch of government differ under the **Virginia Plan** and the **New Jersey Plan**?

2. What role did **compromise** play at the **Constitutional Convention**?

Critical Thinking and Writing

3. Draw Conclusions Could the Constitution have been produced if George Washington had not attended the Convention? Explain.

4. Infer What is so significant about the Preamble's opening words, "We the People of the United States . . ."?

5. Writing Workshop: Support Claims Write a few sentences in your 📓 Active Journal that support claims concerning how much power the government should have. These sentences will help you develop the essay that you will write at the end of the Topic.

LESSON 3

Ideas That Influenced the Constitution

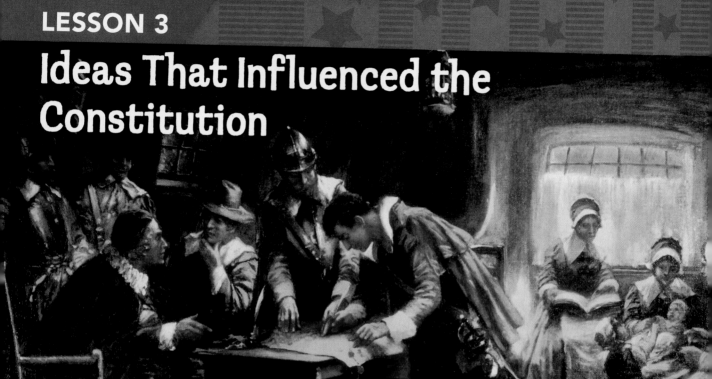

BOUNCE TO ACTIVATE   ▶ VIDEO

GET READY TO READ

START UP
Look at the image of the signing of the Mayflower Compact. How did that document influence the Constitution?

GUIDING QUESTIONS
• What did American leaders learn about government from studying ancient Rome?
• How did ideas and traditions from Europe and the colonial past shape the Constitution?

TAKE NOTES
Literacy Skills Classify and Categorize
Use the graphic organizer in your 📓 Active Journal to take notes as you read the lesson.

PRACTICE VOCABULARY
Use the vocabulary activity in your 📓 Active Journal to practice the vocabulary words.

Vocabulary	Academic Vocabulary
republic	civic
dictatorship	free enterprise
Magna Carta	
English Bill of Rights	
separation of powers	

Long before the Revolution, John Adams called on Americans to investigate how governments worked. He urged them to "search into the spirit of the British constitution" and study the great examples of ancient Greece and Rome. Adams knew the new nation could learn much from the past.

The delegates to the Constitutional Convention followed his advice.

What Did Americans Learn from the Roman Republic?
The delegates wanted to create a **republic**, a government in which citizens rule themselves through elected representatives. Few republics in the history of the world survived very long. To create one that would last, American leaders looked to the ancient examples of Greece and Rome.

What Was Civic Republicanism?
Americans greatly admired the Roman Republic. Independence and public service were virtues that the founders saw in the citizens of Rome.

Roman citizens were willing to serve in public office because they were devoted to their republic. The tradition of encouraging citizen participation to promote the common good, or the well-being of the community, became known as **civic** republicanism. The founders kept this in mind as they worked.

Academic Vocabulary
civic • *adj.,* having to do with being a citizen

A Belief in Independent Citizens At the same time, the Founding Fathers saw the collapse of Rome's republic as a warning to the United States. No republic could survive unless its citizens remained independent and devoted to public service without the desire for personal or financial gains. Under the ruler Caesar Augustus, Rome eventually became a **dictatorship**, a government in which one person or a small group holds complete authority. The leaders of the American Revolution believed that Romans stumbled once they allowed corruption to take over.

Historians today admit that the Founding Fathers somewhat exaggerated the virtues of Rome's republic. Yet the lessons they learned still have force. Republics do not always die because they are invaded from outside. They can decay from within unless their citizens put the nation's needs above their own. Achieving this republican ideal takes dedication and also education, as American leaders knew. They had encouraged education in the Northwest Ordinance. Thomas Jefferson later wrote, "If a nation expects to be ignorant and free, in a state of civilization, it expects what never was and never will be."

☑ READING CHECK **Identify Supporting Details** What qualities of citizens in the Roman Republic did many of the founders admire?

Analyze Images
The Roman Republic inspired the founders because it was a long-lasting representative government. **Infer** Based on the image, who among the Roman population were citizens?

ROME ANTIQUE.

INTERACTIVE

Influences on the
Constitution

How Did English Documents Influence the Framers?

Greece and Rome were not the only examples of democratic government. Despite their quarrel with Britain, leaders of the Revolution valued British traditions of freedom.

The Magna Carta King John of England signed the **Magna Carta** in 1215. The Magna Carta contained two basic ideas that helped to shape both British and American government. First, it made it clear that English monarchs themselves had to obey the law.

King John agreed not to raise taxes without first consulting the Great Council of nobles and church officials. Eventually, the Great Council grew into the British Parliament.

Just as important, the Magna Carta stated that English nobles had certain rights—rights that were later extended to other classes of people as well. These included rights to trial by jury and the right to private property. The idea of private property rights strongly influenced the beliefs of early Americans, which partly explains the development of a **free enterprise** system throughout the nation.

The English Bill of Rights In 1689, the **English Bill of Rights** went further in protecting the rights of citizens. The document said that parliamentary elections should be held regularly.

It upheld the right to trial by jury and allowed some citizens to bear arms. It also affirmed the right of habeas corpus, the idea that no one could be held in prison without first being charged with a specific crime.

READING CHECK **Identify Central Issues** What are some of the significant ideas found in the Magna Carta?

Academic Vocabulary

free enterprise • *n.,* an economic system in which businesses compete freely with little government control

Analyze Images This illustration shows King John of England signing the Magna Carta in 1215. **Identify Main Ideas** How might the Magna Carta have influenced the ideas of the Framers of the United States Constitution?

What American Traditions Did the Framers Draw On?

Americans enjoyed a long tradition of representative government. The Virginia colonists set up the House of Burgesses. Eventually, each colony elected its own legislature.

Self-Government Americans were used to governing themselves, sometimes without representatives. In New England, the residents of the town took a direct and active role in making their town's laws at an annual Town Meeting.

Americans were also used to relying on written documents that clearly identified the powers and limits of government. The Mayflower Compact, written in 1620, was the first document of self-government in North America. Each of the colonies had a written charter granted by the monarch or by Parliament.

Answerable to the People The Framers of the Constitution also drew on their own experiences. They bitterly remembered their grievances against the English king. In writing the Constitution, they sought to prevent such abuses.

Analyze Images In this engraving, William and Mary receive the English Bill of Rights. **Cite Evidence** How did the English Bill of Rights expand the rights given to citizens in the Magna Carta?

For example, the Declaration of Independence accused the king of placing military power above civilian authority. The Constitution made the elected President "Commander in Chief of the Army and Navy . . . and of the militia of the several states." The Declaration protested that the king had made judges "dependent on his will alone." The Constitution set up a court system independent of the President and legislature.

The Framers were very familiar with the workings of the Second Continental Congress, the Articles of Confederation, and their own state governments. Much that went into the Constitution came either from the Articles or from the state constitutions.

Limits to Democratic Rights Not all Americans enjoyed the same democratic rights during this period. State voting laws generally reflected colonial ideas about race, gender, and wealth. Only white male adults who owned property could vote or hold office in much of the country.

This left out the vast majority of women, African Americans, and Native Americans. A few states, mostly in New England, did allow free black men to vote if they met property qualifications, but the number who met those qualifications was very small. Unmarried women were allowed to own property and live independently and even enter into contracts. Married women were not so fortunate. Everything they owned before marriage or earned during it became their husbands' property. In either case, women had no political rights.

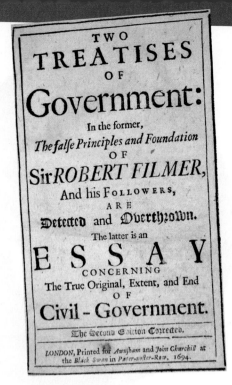

▲ John Locke's writings suggested the idea that governments exist to secure and protect the rights of their citizens.

INTERACTIVE

Two Treatises of Government

The Influence of the Enlightenment

The Constitution was also based on the ideas of the European Enlightenment. Enlightenment thinkers believed that people could improve society through the use of reason. Many of the Constitution's Framers had read the works of Enlightenment thinkers.

John Locke The English writer John Locke published *Two Treatises of Government* in 1690. In it, he stated two important ideas. First, Locke declared that all people had natural rights to life, liberty, and property.

Second, he suggested that government is an agreement between the ruler and the ruled. The ruler must enforce the laws and protect the people. If a ruler violates the people's natural rights, the people have a right to rebel.

Locke's ideas were popular among Americans. The Framers of the Constitution wanted to protect people's natural rights and limit the power of government. They saw the Constitution as a contract between the people and their government.

Locke's principle of a natural right to property was established in the Constitution. Certain guarantees in the Constitution protect the rights of people to own private property, enforce contracts, and engage freely in business activities. These freedoms are essential to a free enterprise system. Article I of the Constitution also gave Congress the power to regulate commerce and encourage the free flow of goods between states. This created an environment in which business could thrive.

Some Grievances Against the King

GRIEVANCE IN DECLARATION OF INDEPENDENCE	MODERN INTERPRETATION
He has forbidden his governors to pass laws of immediate and pressing importance, unless suspended in their operation till his assent should be obtained; and, when so suspended, he has utterly neglected to attend to them.	Colonial government in the colonies cannot function with the king's interference.
He has dissolved representative houses, repeatedly, for opposing, with manly firmness, his invasions on the rights of the people.	Colonial governments are not free to speak out against royal policies without fear of retribution.
He has kept among us, in time of peace, standing armies, without the consent of our legislatures.	The colonies have no representation in the British Parliament.
He has excited domestic insurrections amongst us and has endeavored to bring on the inhabitants of our frontiers, the merciless Indian savages, whose known rule of warfare is an undistinguished destruction of all ages, sexes, and conditions.	The king's actions are causing conflicts between Loyalists and Patriots. He is also attempting to pit the Native Americans against the colonists by appearing as if he is protecting Native American lands from further western settlement.

Analyze Images This lists some of the colonists' complaints. **Summarize** What role did American Indians play in the colonists' grievances?

Charles-Louis Montesquieu The French Enlightenment thinker Charles-Louis Baron de Montesquieu (MAHN tus kyoo) influenced American ideas of how a government should be constructed.

In his 1748 book *The Spirit of the Laws,* Montesquieu stressed the importance of the rule of law. The powers of government, he said, should be clearly defined and divided up.

He suggested that three separate branches be created. The legislative branch would pass the laws. The executive branch would carry out the laws. The judicial branch, or system of courts, would decide whether laws or the Constitution were violated. This idea, known as the **separation of powers**, was designed to keep any person or group from gaining too much power.

A New Tradition Emerges The founders drew on many traditions. In the end, though, the new system of government was not quite like anything that came before it.

When John Adams received the news from Philadelphia while serving as an ambassador to Great Britain, he wrote, "As we say at sea, huzza for the new world and farewell to the old one!" He called the Constitution "the greatest single effort of national deliberation that the world has ever seen."

Analyze Images Baron de Montesquieu was a French Enlightenment thinker. **Summarize** How did Montesquieu's idea of the separation of powers affect the structure of the United States Constitution?

✓ READING CHECK **Identify Supporting Details** What idea from Baron de Montesquieu influenced American government?

✓ Lesson Check

Practice Vocabulary

1. How did the **Magna Carta** and **the English Bill of Rights** influence the Framers' ideas about the structure of the United States government?

2. Why do you think the founders were drawn to Montesquieu's ideas about rule of law and **separation of powers**?

Critical Thinking and Writing

3. **Draw Conclusions** The British constitution is unwritten. Why do you think the Framers insisted on a written Constitution?

4. **Understand Effects** Why do you think English political traditions had such a strong influence on the founders?

5. **Writing Workshop: Distinguish Claims from Opposing Claims** Think about the claims that you have introduced and supported concerning how much power the government should have. For each claim, write an opposing claim in your 📓 Active Journal. This will help you write the essay at the end of the Topic.

Thomas Jefferson, Virginia Statute for Religious Freedom

The Virginia Statute for Religious Freedom, drafted by Thomas Jefferson, was a forerunner of the First Amendment, which guarantees the free exercise of religion.

◀ Jefferson first drafted this document in 1777, and the Virginia legislature passed it in 1786.

Reading and Vocabulary Support

① Something that is temporal has to do with earthly life.

② Civil incapacitations are disadvantages a citizen might face.

③ To be compelled is to be forced.

④ Civil capacities refer to the ability of a citizen to participate in the political process. See the related phrase in Item 2, *civil incapacitations.*

Whereas, Almighty God hath created the mind free; that all attempts to influence it by temporal ① punishments or burthens [burdens], or by civil incapacitations ② tend only to beget habits of hypocrisy and meanness, and are a departure from the plan of the holy author of our religion, . . . Be it enacted by General Assembly that no man shall be compelled ③ to frequent or support any religious worship, place, or ministry whatsoever, nor shall be enforced, restrained, molested, or burthened in his body or goods, nor shall otherwise suffer on account of his religious opinions or belief, but that all men shall be free to profess, and by argument to maintain, their opinions in matters of Religion, and that the same shall in no wise diminish, enlarge or affect their civil capacities. ④ And though we well know that this Assembly elected by the people for the ordinary purposes of Legislation only, have no power to restrain the acts of succeeding Assemblies constituted with powers equal to our own, and that therefore to declare this act irrevocable would be of no effect in law; yet we are free to declare, and do declare that the rights hereby asserted, are of the natural rights of mankind, and that if any act shall be hereafter passed to repeal the present or to narrow its operation, such act will be an infringement of natural right.

Analyzing Primary Sources

Cite specific evidence from the document to support your answers.

1. **Vocabulary: Determine Meaning** What phrase in this document means that no one should be forced to attend a church?

2. **Compare and Contrast** Jefferson also drafted the Declaration of Independence. What principle, or "truth," that appears in the Declaration can also be found in this Statute of Religious Freedom?

Federalists, Antifederalists, and the Bill of Rights

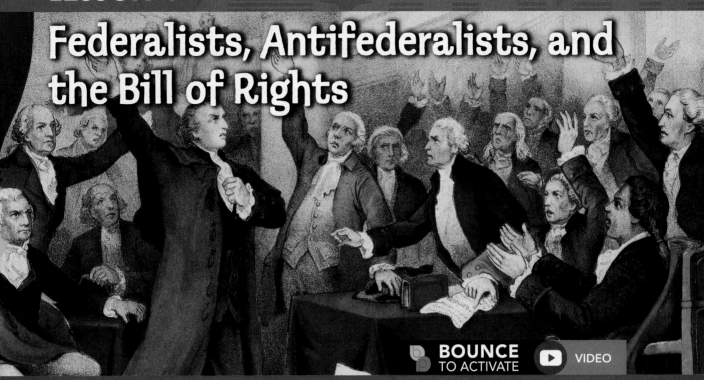

GET READY TO READ

START UP
Study the image of Patrick Henry. Write a sentence about something you feel strongly about.

GUIDING QUESTIONS
- What were the main arguments for and against ratifying the Constitution?
- Why did Antifederalists insist on adding a bill of rights to the Constitution?
- What difficulties were encountered during the process of ratification?

TAKE NOTES

Literacy Skills Sequence
Use the graphic organizer in your 🗐 Active Journal to take notes as you read the lesson.

PRACTICE VOCABULARY
Use the vocabulary activity in your 🗐 Active Journal to practice the vocabulary words.

Vocabulary	Academic Vocabulary
ratify	statute
Federalist	compel
Antifederalist	
Federalist Papers	
amend	

The Framers of the Constitution sent the document to Congress, along with a letter from George Washington. Washington warmly approved the document. He predicted that the Constitution would "promote the lasting welfare of that country so dear to us all."

The Federalists and the Antifederalists Debate

The Framers had set up a process for the states to approve, or **ratify**, the new government. The Constitution would go into effect when at least 9 of the 13 states had ratified it. In 1787 and 1788, voters in each state elected delegates to special state conventions. These delegates would decide whether to ratify the Constitution.

For Ratification: The Arguments of the Federalists In every state, heated debates took place. Supporters of the Constitution called themselves **Federalists** because they favored a strong federal, or national, government. They called people who opposed the Constitution **Antifederalists**.

When he was just 14, Alexander Hamilton was helping run a business on St. Croix, managing men much older than himself.

Federalists argued that the Articles of Confederation left too much power with the individual states. This imbalance produced a dangerously weak central government. Disputes among the states, Federalists said, made it too difficult for the government to function.

Federalists believed that the Constitution gave the national government the authority it needed to function effectively. At the same time, they said, the Constitution still protected the rights and powers of the individual states.

Federalists James Madison, Alexander Hamilton, and John Jay wrote a series of essays, known today as the **Federalist Papers**. Their purpose was to explain and defend the Constitution. They used pen names, but most people knew who they were. Today, the Federalist Papers remain among the best discussions of the political theory behind the American system of government.

Courts still refer to the *Federalist Papers* in making decisions about the principles and role of government. In this way, they have had a lasting influence on the U.S. system of government.

Against Ratification: The Arguments of the Antifederalists

Antifederalists felt that the Constitution made the national government too strong and left the states too weak. They also thought that the Constitution gave the President too much power. Patrick Henry of Virginia protested:

Primary Source

"This Constitution is said to have beautiful features, but . . . they appear to me horribly frightful. . . . Your President may become king."

—Patrick Henry, Speech to the Virginia Convention, June 1788

BIOGRAPHY
5 Things to Know About

ALEXANDER HAMILTON
First U.S. secretary of the treasury 1755–1804

- Hamilton was born on the British island of Nevis in the West Indies.

- He represented New York State at the Constitutional Convention.

- He wrote more than 50 of the 85 Federalist Papers, in which he argued forcefully for a strong central government.

- He was killed in a duel with rival Aaron Burr.

- He was the subject of an award-winning musical that opened on Broadway in 2015.

Critical Thinking If he had not been killed in a duel, do you think Hamilton would have become President? Why or why not?

Most people expected George Washington to be elected President. Antifederalists admired Washington, but they warned that future Presidents might lack Washington's honor and skill. For this reason, they said, the office should not be too powerful.

☑ **READING CHECK** **Identify Main Ideas** What issues of power led Antifederalists to oppose the Constitution?

Why Did Antifederalists Demand a Bill of Rights?

The chief objection of Antifederalists was that the Constitution did not have a specific bill, or list, of guaranteed protections of individual rights. Federalists held that it was impossible to list all the natural rights of people. Besides, they said, the Constitution protected citizens well enough as it was.

Antifederalists responded that a bill of rights was needed to protect such basic liberties as freedom of speech and religion. Unless these rights were spelled out, they could be too easily ignored or denied by the government. Americans, after all, had just fought a revolution to protect their freedoms against a too-powerful government. Violations of those freedoms were the main grievances cited in the Declaration of Independence. Antifederalists argued that a bill of rights was needed to address those grievances.

Under the new Constitution, the President would have veto power over Congress—the people's representatives. Surely placing so much power in one man's hands, the Antifederalists argued, likewise demanded the protection of a bill of rights.

One of the strongest supporters of a bill of rights was George Mason of Virginia. In 1776, Mason had written the bill of rights for Virginia's constitution. After the Constitutional Convention refused to include a bill of rights, Mason joined the Antifederalists. He wrote a pamphlet opposing the ratification of the Constitution. The pamphlet was titled, simply, "Objections to This Constitution of Government." Its opening words were equally direct: "There is no Declaration of Rights."

☑ **READING CHECK** **Identify Supporting Details** What was the purpose of George Mason's pamphlet?

The Ratification Process

One by one, the states voted. Delaware led the way, ratifying on December 7, 1787. Five days later, with the strong support of James Wilson, Pennsylvania ratified the Constitution. New Jersey soon followed. In these states, as in the states that ratified later, the main cause behind ratification was that Federalists were able to convince a majority of delegates that the Constitution would bring an improved system of government.

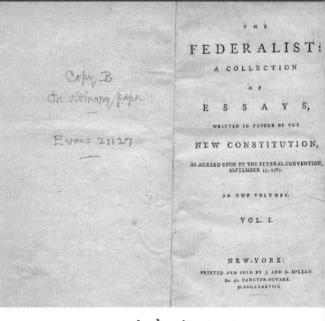

Analyze Images The *Federalist essays* presented the argument for a strong central government. **Infer** What might have happened if *these essays* had not been written?

INTERACTIVE

Federalists versus Antifederalists

INTERACTIVE

Ratification of the
Constitution

The Debate in New England Massachusetts was the first key battleground. There, the old patriots Sam Adams and John Hancock held back their support. The delay seemed "very ominous," wrote Madison. Finally, Adams and Hancock convinced the state convention to recommend adding a bill of rights to the Constitution.

Still the debate continued. "Some gentlemen say, don't be in a hurry . . . don't take a leap in the dark," a Federalist farmer told his fellow delegates. "I say . . . gather fruit when it is ripe." In February 1788, Massachusetts became the sixth state to ratify.

In June, New Hampshire joined ranks as the ninth state. The new government could now go into effect. Still, the nation's unity remained in doubt. New York and Virginia, two of the largest states, had not yet ratified the plan. In both states, Federalists and Antifederalists were closely matched.

A Vote to Ratify After Long Debates In Virginia, Patrick Henry, George Mason, and Governor Edmund Randolph led the opposition. Still a spellbinding speaker, Henry at one point spoke for seven hours. Soft-spoken James Madison could not match Henry's dramatic style. Yet his arguments in favor of the Constitution were always clear, patient, and to the point.

The tide finally turned when Governor Randolph changed his mind. He gave his support only when the Federalists promised to support a bill of rights. Virginia voted to ratify in late June.

Analyze Timelines

Ratifying the Constitution was a long process, taking a year and a half. **Sequence** Which was the first state to vote for ratification? Which was the last?

In New York, the struggle went on for another month. In July 1788, the state convention voted to ratify. North Carolina followed in November 1789. Only Rhode Island, which had refused to send delegates to the Constitutional Convention, remained. On May 29, 1790, Rhode Island

Voting for Ratification

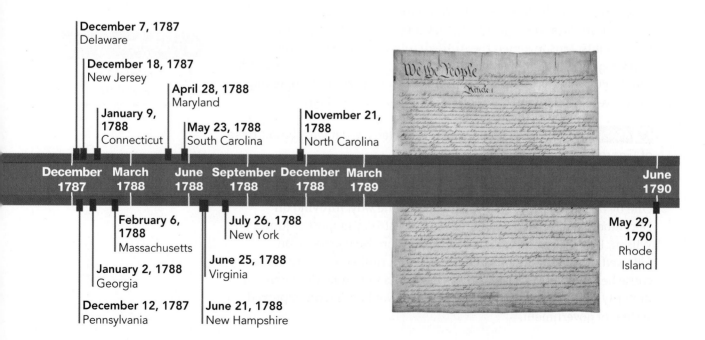

December 7, 1787
Delaware

December 18, 1787
New Jersey

April 28, 1788
Maryland

January 9, 1788
Connecticut

May 23, 1788
South Carolina

November 21, 1788
North Carolina

December 1787 | March 1788 | June 1788 | September 1788 | December 1788 | March 1789 | June 1790

February 6, 1788
Massachusetts

July 26, 1788
New York

January 2, 1788
Georgia

June 25, 1788
Virginia

May 29, 1790
Rhode Island

December 12, 1787
Pennsylvania

June 21, 1788
New Hampshire

became the last state to ratify the Constitution. The effect of ratification was to create a new system of government for the United States, the same basic system that remains in effect today.

Celebration of a New Constitution Throughout the land, Americans celebrated the news that the Constitution was ratified. The city of Philadelphia set its festival for July 4, 1788.

A festive parade filed along Market Street, led by soldiers who had fought in the Revolution. Thousands cheered as six colorfully outfitted horses pulled a blue carriage shaped like an eagle. Thirteen stars and stripes were painted on the front, and the Constitution was raised proudly above it. Benjamin Rush, a Philadelphia doctor and strong supporter of the Constitution, wrote to a friend, "Tis done. We have become a nation."

☑ READING CHECK Identify Cause and Effect What factor encouraged many states to vote for ratification?

Analyze Images A parade in New York celebrates the Constitution's ratification. **Infer** Why do you think people dedicated a float to Alexander Hamilton?

New Amendments

Americans voted in the first election under the Constitution in January 1789. As expected, George Washington was elected President, while John Adams was elected Vice President.

After the election the Congress met in New York City, which was chosen as the nation's capital. Congress quickly turned its attention to adding a bill of rights to the Constitution. Several states had agreed to ratify the Constitution only on the condition that a bill of rights be added.

Amending the Constitution The Framers had established a way to **amend**, or change, the Constitution to modify the rules for the national government. They did not want people to make changes lightly, however. Thus, they made the process of amending the Constitution fairly difficult. In 1789, the first Congress proposed a set of 12 amendments, written by James Madison. As required by the Constitution, the amendments then went for ratification by the states, three fourths of which had to ratify an amendment for it to take effect. By December 1791, three fourths of the states had ratified 10 of the 12 amendments. Together, these 10 amendments became known as the Bill of Rights.

The Bill of Rights James Madison insisted that the Bill of Rights does not *give* Americans any rights. The rights listed, he said, are natural rights that belong to all human beings. The Bill of Rights simply prevents the government from taking these rights away.

Some of the first 10 amendments were intended to prevent the kind of abuse Americans had suffered under British rule.

For example, the Declaration of Independence had condemned the king for forcing colonists to quarter, or house, troops in their homes and for suspending trial by jury. The Third Amendment forbids the government to quarter troops in citizens' homes without their consent. The Sixth and Seventh Amendments guarantee the right to trial by jury.

Religious Freedom Other amendments protected individual rights, as many states had already done. A forerunner of the First Amendment was the Virginia Statute for Religious Freedom, written by Thomas Jefferson and made a state law in 1786. The **statute** said that "No man shall be **compelled** to frequent or support any religious worship . . . or otherwise suffer, on account of his religious opinions or belief."

Religious freedom became the very first right listed in the First Amendment. Jefferson later wrote that the First Amendment built "a wall of separation between Church & State." James Madison supported Jefferson's belief that the state, or government, should not promote religion. But not all founders agreed. Patrick Henry wanted Virginia to establish Christianity as the state religion. Others insisted that only Christians should be allowed to hold office. Still, the First Amendment made it clear that "Congress shall make no law respecting an establishment of religion." The First Amendment also emphasized a key element of the republic: freedom of speech, or people's right to express their point of view without fear of government punishment.

With the Bill of Rights in place, the new framework of government was complete. Over time, the Constitution would grow and change along with the nation.

Analyze Images James Madison supported the separation of church and state. **Compare and Contrast** How did Madison's stance differ from Patrick Henry's?

Academic Vocabulary

statute • *n.*, a law or rule

compel • *v.*, to force

✓ READING CHECK **Identify Supporting Details** What amendments make up the Bill of Rights in the Constitution?

✓ Lesson Check

Practice Vocabulary

1. What was the key argument that the **Federalists** made to persuade states to **ratify** the Constitution?

2. Why did **Antifederalists** insist on a **bill of rights**?

Critical Thinking and Writing

3. **Summarize** the procedure for ratifying the Constitution.

4. **Express Problems Clearly** In June 1788, when nine states had approved the Constitution, it was officially ratified. Why did the issue of ratification still seem unsettled?

5. **Writing Workshop: Use Credible Sources** In your 📓 Active Journal, make a list of sources you might use to support or oppose claims regarding this question: How much power should the federal government have, and what should its responsibilities include?

Federalist and Antifederalist Writings

Federalists John Jay, James Madison, and Alexander Hamilton wrote anonymous essays arguing that states should ratify the Constitution. Antifederalists responded with their own writings identifying problems with the Constitution.

▶ Title page from *The Federalist: A Collection of Essays*.

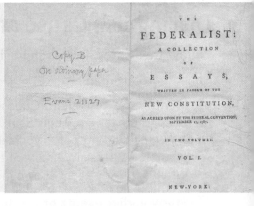

"The proposed Constitution, so far from implying an abolition of the State governments, makes them <u>constituent</u> ① parts of the national sovereignty, by allowing them a direct representation in the Senate, and leaves in their possession certain exclusive and very important portions of sovereign power. This fully corresponds, in every rational import of the terms, with the idea of a federal government."

—Alexander Hamilton, *Federalist* No. 9

"There is no Declaration of Rights, and the laws of the general government being <u>paramount</u> ② to the laws and constitution of the several States, the Declarations of Rights in the separate States are no security ③. . . . There is no declaration of any kind, for preserving the liberty of the press, or the trial by jury in civil causes; nor against the danger of standing armies in times of peace."

—George Mason, "Objections to the Constitution"

Analyzing Primary Sources

Cite specific evidence from these documents to support your answers.

1. **Compare Authors' Treatment of Similar Topics** Which of these statements most directly tries to address people's concerns about federalism? Explain your answer.

2. **Cite Evidence** How were George Mason's main objections to the Constitution later resolved?

3. **Write a Summary** Provide a brief summary of both excerpts. Take care to be objective, not introducing your own opinion into the summaries.

Reading and Vocabulary Support

① *Constituent* parts together make up the whole. In this case, what is the whole and what are the constituent parts?

② *Paramount* means "dominant" or "supreme."

③ Summarize how Hamilton's statement answers this antifederalist objection to the Constitution.

Distinguish Cause and Effect

Follow these steps to distinguish cause and effect.

INTERACTIVE

Analyze Cause and Effect

1 **Identify the key event.** Choose one event or condition as a starting point. Once you know the starting point, you can look for possible causes and effects of that event. What is the key event shown in the chart?

2 **Study earlier events or conditions as possible causes.** A cause of the key event must happen before the key event. Look for earlier events by asking, "Why did the key event happen?" or "What led to the key event?" You may also find such clue words as *because* and *reason* that suggest that one thing caused another. Look at the causes listed in the chart. How did each event or action help lead to the later creation of the Bill of Rights?

3 **Study later events or conditions as possible effects.** Effects must follow the key event. They may include short-term effects or longer-lasting ones. To find later events, ask, "What did the key event lead to?" or "What was a result of the key event?" You may also find clue words or phrases, such as *brought about, led to, as a result,* or *therefore.* Why might we call each of the effects in the chart both a short-term and a long-term effect of adding the Bill of Rights to the Constitution?

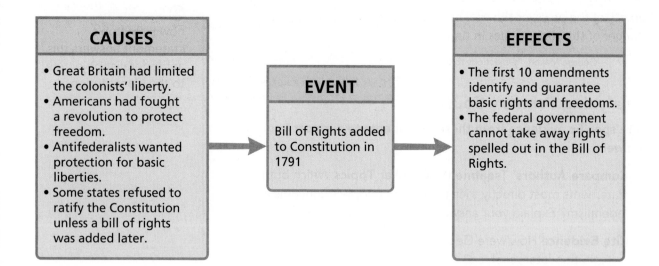

CAUSES

- Great Britain had limited the colonists' liberty.
- Americans had fought a revolution to protect freedom.
- Antifederalists wanted protection for basic liberties.
- Some states refused to ratify the Constitution unless a bill of rights was added later.

EVENT

Bill of Rights added to Constitution in 1791

EFFECTS

- The first 10 amendments identify and guarantee basic rights and freedoms.
- The federal government cannot take away rights spelled out in the Bill of Rights.

Understanding the Constitution

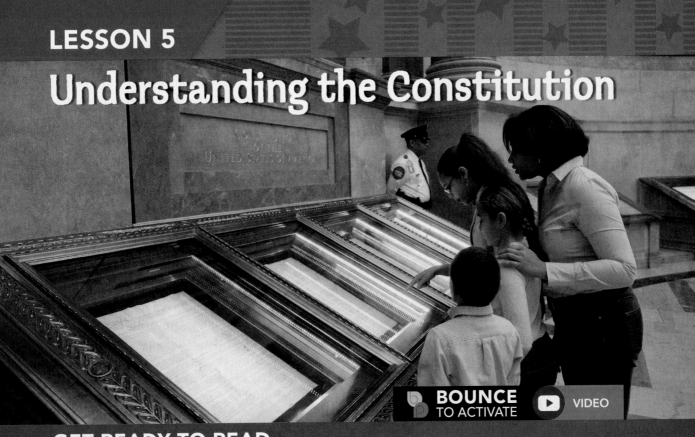

GET READY TO READ

START UP

Look at the photograph of people examining an original copy of the Constitution. Has the Constitution changed?

GUIDING QUESTIONS

- What are the basic goals of the Constitution, as defined in its Preamble?
- What are the powers and duties of each branch of government, as set forth by the Constitution?

TAKE NOTES

Literacy Skills Classify and Categorize

Use the graphic organizer in your 🗐 Active Journal to take notes as you read the lesson.

PRACTICE VOCABULARY

Use the vocabulary activity in your 🗐 Active Journal to practice the vocabulary words.

Vocabulary	Academic Vocabulary
popular sovereignty	civilian
bill	liberty
veto	
override	
impeach	

By December 1791, the Constitution had been ratified and the Bill of Rights added. Americans could now familiarize themselves with the new structure of their government.

First Comes the Preamble

The Constitution consists of the Preamble, articles, and amendments. The Preamble states the Constitution's six goals. They are:

To Form a More Perfect Union When the Constitution was written, the states saw themselves almost as separate nations. The Framers wanted to work together as a unified nation. Fortunately for us, they achieved this goal. Think of what it would be like if you had to exchange your money every time you visited another state!

To Establish Justice The Framers knew the nation needed a uniform system to settle legal disputes. Today, the American justice system requires that the law be applied fairly to every American, regardless of his or her race, religion, gender, or country of origin.

Analyze Images A National Guardsman helps a family. **Use Evidence** How does helping the public during times of emergency ensure domestic tranquillity?

To Ensure Domestic Tranquillity
Under the Constitution, the national government has the power to ensure domestic tranquillity, or peace and order within our nation's borders. Have you seen reports of the National Guard providing assistance in a disaster area? That is one way that the government works to ensure domestic tranquillity.

To Provide for the Common Defense
Every country has a duty to protect its citizens against foreign attack. The Framers of the Constitution gave the national government the power to raise armies and navies. At the same time, they placed the military under **civilian**, or nonmilitary, control.

To Promote the General Welfare
The Constitution set out to give the national government the means to promote the general welfare, or the well-being of all its citizens. For example, today the National Institutes of Health leads the fight against many diseases.

To Secure the Blessings of Liberty
During the Revolution, the colonists fought and died for **liberty**, or freedom. It is no surprise that the Framers made liberty a major goal of the Constitution. Over the years, amendments to the Constitution have extended the "blessings of liberty" to all Americans.

The Articles and the Amendments
The main body of the Constitution is a short document, divided into seven parts called articles. Together, they establish the framework for our government.

Seven Articles
The first three articles describe the three branches of the national government: legislative, executive, and judicial. Article 1 establishes the powers of and limits on Congress. Articles 2 and 3 do the same for the President and the courts.

Article 4 deals with relations among the states. It requires states to honor one another's laws and legal decisions. It also sets out a system for admitting new states. Article 5 provides a process to amend the Constitution.

Article 6 states that the Constitution is the "supreme law of the land." This means that states may not make laws that violate the Constitution. If a state law conflicts with a federal law, the federal law prevails.

Academic Vocabulary

civilian • *adj.*, nonmilitary

liberty • *n.*, freedom

The final article, Article 7, sets up a procedure for the states to ratify the Constitution.

Twenty-Seven Amendments In more than 200 years, only 27 formal changes have been made to the Constitution. The first 10 amendments, known as the Bill of Rights, were added in 1791.

☑ READING CHECK **Identify Supporting Details** What is each of the seven main parts of the Constitution called?

Seven Basic Principles

The Constitution reflects seven basic principles. They are popular sovereignty, limited government, separation of powers, checks and balances, federalism, republicanism, and individual rights.

Popular Sovereignty The Framers of the Constitution lived at a time when monarchs claimed that their power came from God. The Preamble, with its phrase "We the people," reflects a revolutionary new idea: that a government gets its authority from the people. This principle, known as **popular sovereignty**, states that the people have the right to alter or abolish their government. Why? Because the people have supreme power, or sovereignty, over the government. No one rules because of divine right.

Analyze Images The first woman elected to Congress was Jeannette Rankin of Montana in 1916. **Infer** Why is it important for Congress to include men and women?

INTERACTIVE

The Federal System

Limited Government The colonists had lived under a British government with nearly unlimited powers. To avoid giving too much power to their new government, the Framers made limited government a principle of the Constitution. In a limited government, the government has only the powers that the Constitution gives it. Just as important, everyone from you to the President must obey the law.

Separation of Powers To further limit government power, the Framers provided for separation of powers. The Constitution separates the government into three branches. The legislative branch, or Congress, makes the laws. The executive branch, headed by the President, carries out the laws. The judicial branch, or courts, determines whether actions violate laws and whether laws violate the Constitution.

Checks and Balances A system of checks and balances safeguards against abuse of power. Each branch of government has the power to check, or limit, the actions of the other two. The separation of powers allows for this system of checks and balances. One reason the government has survived for more than 200 years is because of this system.

Analyze Charts The graphic explains the separation of powers. **Use Visual Information** How is the power to make and enforce laws divided among the three branches of government?

Federalism The Constitution also reflects the principle of federalism, or the division of power between the federal government and the states. Among the powers the Constitution gives the federal government are the power to coin money, declare war, and regulate trade between the states. States regulate trade within their own borders, make rules for state elections, and establish schools. Powers not clearly given to the federal government belong to the states.

Separation of Powers

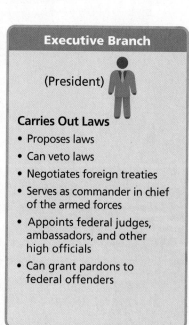
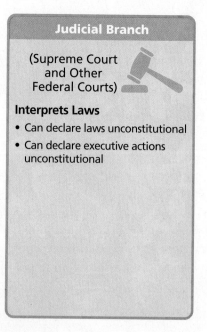

Legislative Branch

(Congress)

Passes Laws
- Can override President's veto
- Approves treaties and presidential appointments
- Can impeach and remove President and other high officials
- Creates lower federal courts
- Appropriates money
- Prints and coins money
- Raises and supports armed forces
- Can declare war
- Regulates foreign and interstate trade

Executive Branch

(President)

Carries Out Laws
- Proposes laws
- Can veto laws
- Negotiates foreign treaties
- Serves as commander in chief of the armed forces
- Appoints federal judges, ambassadors, and other high officials
- Can grant pardons to federal offenders

Judicial Branch

(Supreme Court and Other Federal Courts)

Interprets Laws
- Can declare laws unconstitutional
- Can declare executive actions unconstitutional

Some powers are shared between the federal government and the states. Thus, federalism results in dual sovereignty. That is, the federal government and the states both exercise authority over the same territory and people.

Republicanism The Constitution provides for a republican form of government. The United States is a constitutional republic. This means that the Constitution provides the basis for its republican form of government. Instead of taking part directly in government, citizens elect representatives to carry out their will. Once in office, representatives vote according to their own judgment. However, they must remain open to the opinions of the people they represent. For that reason, members of Congress maintain Web sites and offices in their home districts.

Individual Rights The final principle the U.S. Constitution reflects is individual rights, such as freedom of speech, freedom of religion, and the right to trial by jury. You will read more about the rights protected by the Constitution later.

☑ READING CHECK **Identify Supporting Details** Which of these principles restrict government power?

The Legislative Branch—Congress

The first and longest article of the Constitution deals with the legislative, or lawmaking, branch. Article I sets up Congress to make the nation's laws. Congress is made up of two bodies: the House of Representatives and the Senate.

The House of Representatives The larger of the two bodies is the House of Representatives, which currently has 435 members. Representation in the House is based on population, with larger states having more representatives than smaller states. Every state has at least one representative.

Representatives are elected by the people of their district for two-year terms. As a result, the entire House is up for election every other year. Representatives may run for reelection as many times as they want.

The leader of the House is called the Speaker. The Speaker of the House is one of the most powerful people in the federal government. The Speaker regulates debates and controls the agenda. If the President dies or leaves office, the Speaker of the House is next in line after the Vice President to become President.

The Senate Unlike the House, the Senate is based on equal representation of the states, with two senators for each state. Senators are elected to six-year terms. Their terms overlap, however, so that one third of the members come up for election every two years.

Analyze Images The U.S. Capitol building is home to the House and Senate, as well as many offices. **Infer** Why does Congress have such an impressive building?

▶ INTERACTIVE

The U.S. Congress

Quest CONNECTIONS

Which states have the largest and smallest numbers of representatives? Record your findings in your 📓 Active Journal.

This way, there is always a majority of experienced senators.

Not all of the founders trusted the judgment of the common people. As a result, they called for senators to be chosen by state legislatures. Over the years, the nation slowly became more democratic. The Seventeenth Amendment, ratified in 1913, provided that senators be directly elected by the people of each state, like members of the House.

The Vice President of the United States is president of the Senate. The Vice President presides over the Senate and casts a vote when there is a tie. The Vice President cannot, however, take part in Senate debates. When the Vice President is absent, the Senate's president pro tempore, or temporary president, presides over the proceedings.

Analyze Images Sixty members of the House of Representatives, including John Lewis of Georgia, Nancy Pelosi of California, and Charles Rangel of New York, held a sit-in during a Congressional session to demand action on gun safety in June 2016. **Infer** Why do you think these representatives took such an extreme action?

Powers of Congress The most important power of Congress is the power to make the nation's laws. All laws start as proposals called **bills**. A new bill may be introduced in either the House or the Senate. However, an appropriations bill, which is a bill that sets aside money for government programs or operations, must be introduced in the House. After a bill is introduced, it is debated. If both houses vote to approve the bill, it is then sent to the President. If the President signs the bill, it becomes a law.

The Constitution gives Congress many other powers besides lawmaking. Article I, Section 8, lists most of the powers of Congress. They include the power to borrow money and the power to levy, or require people to pay, taxes. Congress also has the power to coin money, to establish post offices, to fix standard weights and measures, and to declare war.

A clause in Article I, Section 8, also gives Congress the power to regulate commerce between states, with foreign nations, "and with the Indian tribes." When the Constitution was written, Native American nations were considered fully independent. Over time, Congress has used this commerce clause to assume complete authority over the affairs of those nations.

The Elastic Clause Not all the powers of Congress are specifically listed. Article I, Section 8, Clause 18, states that Congress can "make all laws which shall be necessary and proper" for carrying out its specific duties. This clause is known as the elastic clause because it enables Congress to stretch its powers to deal with the changing needs of the nation.

Americans have long debated the true meaning of the elastic clause. What did the Framers mean by the words *necessary* and *proper*? For example, early leaders debated whether the elastic clause gave Congress the right to set up a national bank, even though the Constitution does not specifically give Congress that power.

Today, political parties still have different points of view on how the elastic clause should be used. Some Americans continue to worry that Congress might use the elastic clause to abuse its powers. Sometimes, the terms *strict constructionists* and *loose constructionists* are used to refer to people with different views of the clause.

Strict constructionists think that Congress (and the courts that interpret laws) should strictly construe, or narrowly interpret, the elastic clause. They believe the elastic clause should be used to stretch the powers of government rarely, and only to a small degree. Partly because many members of the Republican Party today are strict constructionists, that party particularly believes in reducing or eliminating some government programs.

In contrast, loose constructionists think that Congress (and the courts that interpret laws) should loosely construe, or broadly interpret, the elastic clause. They think the elastic clause should be used to stretch the powers of government as often as needed, and to a greater degree. Many members of the Democratic Party today are loose constructionists. Because they believe that the role of the federal government can and should expand as needed, they may support government programs opposed by members of the Republican Party.

The Committee System

The First Congress, meeting from 1789 to 1791, considered a total of 31 new bills. Today, more than 10,000 bills are introduced in Congress each year. Clearly, it would be impossible for every member of Congress to give each new bill careful study. To deal with this problem, Congress relies on committees.

Both the House and the Senate have permanent, or standing, committees. Each committee deals with a specific topic, such as agriculture, banking, business, defense, education, science, or transportation. Members who have served longest are usually appointed to the most important committees.

Did you know?

Besides formal committees, members of Congress who have common interests and concerns can form unofficial groups called caucuses.

Analyze Images When a member of the federal government speaks up, is that person expressing an opinion or trying to exert influence? **Analyze Political Cartoons** How do you think the cartoonist would answer that question?

"Ruth Bader Ginsburg was just plain wrong trying to influence the Presidential election. That'd be just like if the Senate tried to influence the Supreme Court by refusing to vote on a President's nominee."

Analyze Images Although Republican candidate Donald J. Trump lost the popular vote to Democrat Hillary Clinton, he won the electoral college vote and so became President in 2017. **Cite Evidence** Should the Electoral College still be used to elect the President? Support your opinion with evidence.

Congress may sometimes create joint committees made up of both Senate and House members. One of the most important kinds of joint committees is the conference committee. Its task is to settle differences between House and Senate versions of the same bill.

☑ READING CHECK **Identify Supporting Details** How does a bill become a law?

The Executive Branch—The President

Article II of the Constitution sets up an executive branch to carry out the laws and run the affairs of the national government. The President is the head of the executive branch. Other members include the Vice President and the executive departments. The heads of the executive departments, who advise the President, are called the Cabinet.

The Many Roles of the President You are probably more familiar with the President than with any other government leader. You see him on television climbing in and out of airplanes, greeting foreign leaders, or making speeches. Yet, many Americans do not know exactly what the President does.

The Framers thought that Congress would be the most important branch of government. Thus, while the Constitution is very specific about the role of the legislature, it offers fewer details about the powers of the President. Beginning with George Washington, Presidents have often taken those actions they thought necessary to carry out the job. In this way, they have shaped the job of President to meet the nation's changing needs.

The President is our highest elected official and, along with the Vice President, the only one who represents all Americans. As head of the executive branch, the President has the duty to carry out the nation's laws. The President directs foreign policy and has the power to make treaties with other nations and to appoint ambassadors.

The President is commander in chief of the armed forces. (Only Congress, however, has the power to declare war.) As the nation's chief legislator, the President suggests new laws and works for their passage.

The President can grant pardons and call special sessions of Congress. The President is also the living symbol of the nation. Presidents welcome foreign leaders, make speeches to commemorate national holidays, and give medals to national heroes.

The Electoral College The President is elected for a four-year term. As a result of the Twenty-second Amendment, adopted in 1951, no President may be elected to more than two complete terms.

The Framers set up a complex system for electing the President, known as the electoral college. When Americans vote for President, they do not vote directly for the candidate of their choice. Rather, they vote for a group of electors who are pledged to the candidate. The number of a state's electors equals the number of its Senators and representatives. No state has fewer than three electors.

A few weeks after Election Day, the electors meet in each state to cast their votes for President. In most states, the candidate with the majority of the popular vote in that state receives all that state's electoral votes. The candidate who receives a majority of the electoral votes nationwide becomes President. This is part of another key principle in the United States: majority rule. Whether passing a bill in a legislature or electing an official, a majority of the votes—more than 50 percent—is usually needed.

Because of the "winner-take-all" nature of the electoral college, a candidate can lose the popular vote nationwide but still be elected President. This has happened five times. Today, some people favor replacing the electoral college with a system that directly elects the President by popular vote. Others oppose any change, pointing out that the electoral college has served the nation well for more than 200 years.

READING CHECK Draw Conclusions Why is it said that the President represents all Americans?

The Judicial Branch—The Supreme Court

Article III of the Constitution establishes a Supreme Court and authorizes Congress to establish any other courts that are needed. Under the Judiciary Act of 1789, Congress set up the system of federal courts that is still in place today.

GEOGRAPHY **SKILLS**

A state's number of electors is based on the combined total of its Senators and representatives.

1. **Movement** As the population shifts, how would the number of electors change?

2. **Infer** What can you infer about a state's population from the number of electors it has?

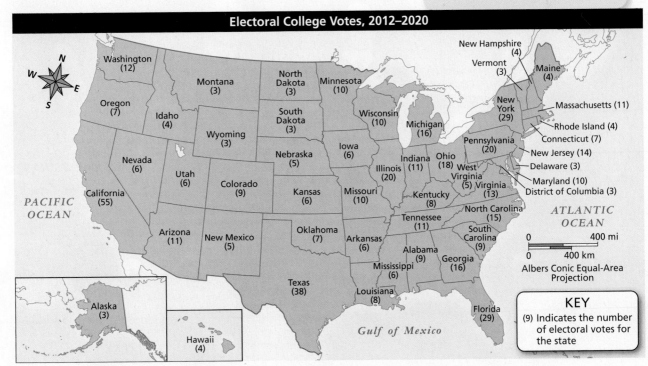

Electoral College Votes, 2012–2020

New Hampshire (4)
Washington (12)
Montana (3)
North Dakota (3)
Minnesota (10)
Vermont (3)
Maine (4)
Oregon (7)
Idaho (4)
South Dakota (3)
Wisconsin (10)
New York (29)
Massachusetts (11)
Michigan (16)
Rhode Island (4)
Wyoming (3)
Pennsylvania (20)
Connecticut (7)
Nevada (6)
Nebraska (5)
Iowa (6)
Indiana (11)
Ohio (18)
New Jersey (14)
Illinois (20)
West Virginia (5)
Delaware (3)
Utah (6)
Colorado (9)
Kansas (6)
Missouri (10)
Kentucky (8)
Virginia (13)
Maryland (10)
District of Columbia (3)
California (55)
North Carolina (15)
PACIFIC OCEAN
Tennessee (11)
South Carolina (9)
ATLANTIC OCEAN
Arizona (11)
New Mexico (5)
Oklahoma (7)
Arkansas (6)
Alabama (9)
Georgia (16)
Mississippi (6)
Texas (38)
Louisiana (8)
Florida (29)
Gulf of Mexico
Alaska (3)
Hawaii (4)

0   400 mi
0   400 km
Albers Conic Equal-Area Projection

KEY
(9) Indicates the number of electoral votes for the state

Lower Courts Most federal cases begin in district courts. Evidence is presented during trials, and a jury or a judge decides the facts of the case. A party that disagrees with the decision of the judge or jury may appeal it, that is, ask that the decision be reviewed by a higher court. The next level of courts is the appellate courts, or courts of appeal.

Appellate court judges review decisions of district courts to decide whether the lower court judges interpreted and applied the law correctly.

Supreme Court At the top of the American judicial system is the Supreme Court. The Court is made up of a Chief Justice and eight Associate Justices. The President appoints the Justices, but Congress must approve the appointments. Justices serve for life.

The main job of the Supreme Court is to serve as the nation's final court of appeals. It hears cases that have been tried and appealed in lower courts. Because its decisions are final, the Supreme Court is called "the court of last resort."

The Supreme Court hears and decides fewer than 100 cases each year. Most of the cases are appeals from lower courts that involve federal laws. After hearing oral arguments, the Justices vote. Decisions require a majority vote of at least five Justices.

Early on, the Court asserted the right to declare whether acts of the President or laws passed by Congress are unconstitutional, that is, not allowed under the Constitution. This power is called judicial review. The need for judicial review was first discussed in the *Federalist Papers*,

Analyze Images Members of the Supreme Court hear cases from lower courts and address the constitutionality of laws. **Identify Main Ideas** How does the work of the Supreme Court support the system of checks and balances?

UNITED STATES SUPREME COURT

Reviews more than 7,000 petitions a year and selects 100–150 cases based on:	• National importance of the case • Need to eliminate conflicting court opinions related to a case	• Opportunity to set a precedent • Agreement among 4 of 9 Justices to accept a case

Original Jurisdiction

- Disputes between states or between a state and citizens of another state
- Actions involving ambassadors or vice consuls of foreign nations
- Actions between the U.S. and a state

State Route

State Supreme Court
- Appeals of appellate court cases

Appellate Court
- Appeals of trial court cases

Trial Court
- Civil and criminal cases
- Juries render verdicts
- Judges enforce procedures

Federal Route

Court of Appeals
- Appeals of cases originating in U.S. district courts
- Reviews decisions by federal agencies

District Court
- Civil and criminal cases
- Juries render verdicts
- Judges ensure fair trial

Analyze Images A case can reach the Supreme Court through several paths. **Draw Conclusions** Why do you think so few cases reach the Supreme Court?

and the Supreme Court has argued that the power is implicit in the Constitution, but it was not established until the 1803 case *Marbury* v. *Madison,* which gave the Supreme Court the power of judicial review.

Although powerful, the Supreme Court is limited by the system of checks and balances. One check on its power is that Congress can, in certain circumstances, remove Supreme Court Justices from office. Also, the Supreme Court does not have the power to pass or enforce laws. It can only provide judicial review of laws.

✓ READING CHECK **Check Understanding** What was significant about the Supreme Court decision in the case *Marbury* v. *Madison* (1803)?

What System Exists to Prevent the Abuse of Power?

The Framers hoped that the separation of powers among three branches would prevent the rise of an all-powerful leader who would rob the people of their liberty. But how could they prevent one of the branches from abusing its power? To answer this problem, they set up a system of checks and balances.

The system of checks and balances allows each of the three branches of government to check, or limit, the power of the other two. The President, for example, can check the actions of Congress by **vetoing**, or rejecting, bills that Congress has passed. Congress can check the President by **overriding**, or overruling, the veto, with a two-thirds vote in both houses. Congress must also approve presidential appointments and ratify treaties made by the President. The Supreme Court can check both the President and Congress by declaring laws unconstitutional through its power of judicial review.

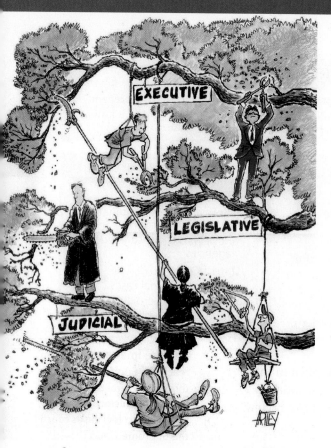

Congress's most extreme check on the President is its power to remove the President from office. To do this, the House of Representatives must **impeach**, or bring charges of serious wrongdoing against, the President. The Senate then conducts a trial. If two thirds of the senators vote to convict, the President must leave office. Throughout our history, only two Presidents—Andrew Johnson and Bill Clinton— have been impeached by the House. Neither was convicted by the Senate.

The principle of checks and balances is based on the principle of separation of powers. Because the powers of government are separated into three branches, each branch can check the power of the other two. Like many principles in the Constitution, separation of powers and the system of checks and balances came from European philosophers of the Enlightenment.

READING CHECK Identify Supporting Details What checks does Congress have over the President?

Analyze Images Here, each tree branch represents a branch of government—executive, legislative, and judicial. **Analyze Political Cartoons** How does the cartoon show that each branch can limit the power of the other two?

☑ Lesson Check

Practice Vocabulary

1. What words in the Preamble to the Constitution reflect the principle of **popular sovereignty**?

2. What roles do **vetoing** and **overriding** play in the process of turning a **bill** into a law?

Critical Thinking and Writing

3. Draw Conclusions Why is Article 6, which declares that the Constitution is the "supreme law of the land," so important?

4. Draw Conclusions Why do you think the Constitution deals with the legislative branch in its very first—and longest—article?

5. Writing Workshop: Clarify Relationships with Transition Words In your argument concerning how much power the federal government should have and what it should do, you can clarify relationships between ideas by using transition words and phrases. They can help compare ideas (*similarly*) or contrast them (*but, on the contrary*). They can also simply make an idea clearer (*to put it another way*). Think of more possible transition words and phrases and write them in your ▰ Active Journal.

LESSON 6
Federalism and Amendments

BOUNCE TO ACTIVATE   ▶ VIDEO

GET READY TO READ

The Constitution of the United States spells out the powers of government. Its first 10 Amendments, or Bill of Rights, ensure the fundamental liberties of the American people. Although created more than 200 years ago, the Constitution is a living document that can be changed as the world changes.

Constitutional Amendment

The Framers foresaw that Americans might need to change the Constitution to address flaws or changed circumstances. However, they did not want to make it too easy to change the Constitution. As a result, they created a complex amendment process. The process may take months, or even years, to complete.

Article 5 outlines two ways to propose an amendment. An amendment may be proposed by two thirds of both the House and the Senate, or by a national convention called by Congress at the request of two thirds of the state legislatures. The second method has never been used.

An amendment may also be ratified in one of two ways. An amendment may be approved by the legislatures of three fourths of the states. Every amendment but the Twenty-first was ratified using this method. In the second method, an amendment may be approved by special conventions in three fourths of the states.

Not all amendments proposed by Congress have been ratified. In fact, Congress has proposed six amendments that the states refused to ratify.

☑ READING CHECK **Identify** Which article of the Constitution outlines the amendment process?

INTERACTIVE

The First Amendment

What Fundamental Liberties Does the Bill of Rights Ensure?

As one of its first acts, the new Congress drafted a series of amendments in 1789 and sent them to the states for approval. In 1791, the **Bill of Rights**, the first ten amendments, became part of the Constitution.

Free Speech, Press, and Religious Freedom The First Amendment safeguards basic individual liberties. It protects freedom of religion, speech, and the press. It also guarantees the right to assemble peacefully and to petition the government to change its policies.

The First Amendment's guarantee of freedom of religion allows Americans to practice religion as they please, or not at all, without fear of government interference. This guarantee has encouraged the religious diversity that is part of the American way of life.

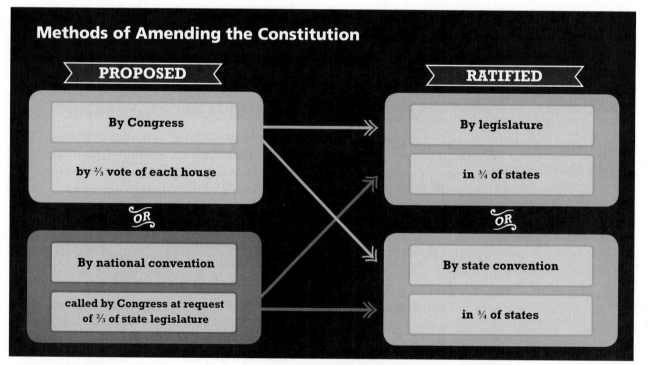

Methods of Amending the Constitution

PROPOSED	RATIFIED
By Congress — by ⅔ vote of each house	By legislature — in ¾ of states
OR	OR
By national convention — called by Congress at request of ⅔ of state legislature	By state convention — in ¾ of states

Analyze Images This graphic shows the process for amending the Constitution. **Use Visual Information** After an amendment to the Constitution has been proposed by both the Senate and the House of Representatives, what two options exist for the states to ratify the amendment?

Analyze Images
Minutemen armed themselves before leaving for the Battle of Concord. **Draw Conclusions** In what ways did the Framers' recent experience with revolution affect what they included in the Constitution and Bill of Rights?

Because of the First Amendment's guarantee of free speech, you cannot be arrested for criticizing a government official. Still, there are limits on the First Amendment. For example, the government can limit free speech if there is "a clear and present danger," such as in time of war.

Freedom of the press means that you can read newspapers that do not support the views of the government. A free press is independent and is responsible only to its readers. It functions as a "watchdog," keeping an eye on the government.

These freedoms are important in a constitutional republic. They allow citizens to make informed decisions and participate freely in the political process.

Protection Against Abuse of Power The Second Amendment states, "A well-regulated militia being necessary to the security of a free state, the right of the people to keep and bear arms shall not be **infringed**." This and other amendments reflect the colonists' experiences under British rule. The Third Amendment says that Congress may not force citizens to put up troops in their homes. The Fourth Amendment protects Americans from unlawful searches of home or property.

Academic Vocabulary
infringe • *v.*, to restrict or put limits on

INTERACTIVE

Methods of Amending the Constitution

Quick Activity

Discuss with a small group if there are ever times when speech should not be protected.

Academic Vocabulary
incriminate • *v.*, to give evidence against

Since early times, Americans have debated the exact meaning of the Second Amendment. Some believe that it guarantees individuals a basic right to bear arms. Others argue that it simply guarantees the individual states the right to maintain militias. The question of limits to gun ownership is one of the most complex and controversial constitutional issues facing Americans today.

Protecting the Rights of the Accused The Fifth through Eighth amendments deal with the rights of people accused of crimes. The Fifth Amendment states that people cannot be forced to **incriminate**, or give evidence against, themselves. The Sixth Amendment guarantees the right to a speedy and public trial by an impartial, or fair, jury. It also states that people accused of crimes have the right to know the charges against them, as well as the right to confront the person making the charges. The Seventh Amendment provides for juries for **civil** trials. The Eighth Amendment forbids excessive bail or fines or "cruel and unusual punishments."

Upholding Individual Rights Some Americans had opposed adding a Bill of Rights. They argued that if specific rights were listed in the Constitution, Americans might lose other rights that were not listed. The Ninth Amendment makes clear that a citizen's individual rights are not limited to those listed in the Constitution.

The Tenth Amendment reaffirmed the Framers' plan to create a limited federal government. It states that all powers not given to the national government or denied to the states belong to, or are reserved for, for the states or the people.

✔ **READING CHECK** **Draw Conclusions** Why do you think the Framers devoted four amendments to protecting the rights of the accused?

Analyze Diagrams
Many amendments were suggested when the Constitution was being considered. **Use Visual Information** Approximately what percentage of the more than 200 amendments proposed by the states' ratifying conventions finally made it into the Bill of Rights?

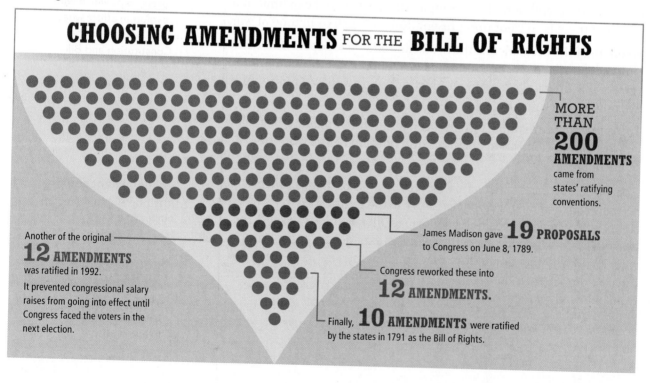

CHOOSING AMENDMENTS FOR THE BILL OF RIGHTS

MORE THAN 200 AMENDMENTS came from states' ratifying conventions.

James Madison gave **19 PROPOSALS** to Congress on June 8, 1789.

Congress reworked these into **12 AMENDMENTS.**

Finally, **10 AMENDMENTS** were ratified by the states in 1791 as the Bill of Rights.

Another of the original **12 AMENDMENTS** was ratified in 1992. It prevented congressional salary raises from going into effect until Congress faced the voters in the next election.

Analyze Images The members of both houses of the California legislature, as well as the governor, carry out their duties at the state capitol in Sacramento. **Infer** Do you think having the legislative and executive branches in one building fosters cooperation? Why or why not?

Why Have Additional Amendments Been Created?

Since the addition of the Bill of Rights, the Constitution has been amended only 17 times. Additional amendments have adapted the Constitution to the needs of a changing society. Many later amendments reflect evolving attitudes about equality and the expansion of democracy.

The Thirteenth, Fourteenth, and Fifteenth amendments are known as the Civil War Amendments. The Thirteenth Amendment abolished slavery. The Fourteenth Amendment guaranteed citizenship to former slaves. The Fifteenth Amendment declared that states may not deny the vote to any citizen on the basis of "race, color, or previous condition of servitude." This guaranteed African American men the right to vote.

Other amendments further expanded voting rights. The Nineteenth Amendment, ratified in 1920, gave women the right to vote.

Women achieved this victory after more than 70 years of struggle. In 1971, changing attitudes toward the rights and responsibilities of young people led to the Twenty-sixth Amendment. It lowered the minimum voting age from 21 to 18.

READING CHECK **Understand Effects** How did the Fifteenth and Nineteenth amendments reflect changing attitudes about equality?

State Government

One principle of the Constitution is federalism, or the division of powers between the federal and state governments. The federal government deals with national issues. The states have the power to meet more local needs. There are also some powers that are shared. State governments provide many basic services that Americans use each day.

The Question of States' Rights Many Americans originally opposed the Constitution because they thought it gave too much power to the federal government at the expense of the state governments. The Tenth Amendment was written to help ensure that the states keep powers not granted the federal government:

Primary Source

"The powers not delegated to the United States by the Constitution, nor prohibited by it to the states, are reserved to the states respectively, or to the people."

—Tenth Amendment to the Constitution

Some Americans point to the Tenth Amendment as support for what is often called states' rights, or the idea that the federal government should not infringe on states' powers. A similar idea is that of state sovereignty, or the idea that, within a state, the state government is supreme.

Analyze Images In 2016, members of the Standing Rock Sioux protested plans to build an oil pipeline that would cross the river that provides their water. Thousands of other people joined their protest, and the planned route was denied. **Draw Conclusions** What role might social media have played in the success of the protest?

Analyze Images State and local governments provide infrastructure, such as this bridge in California. **Infer** If a city gets most of its revenue from property taxes and property values decline sharply, will there be enough money for large projects? Why or why not?

The federal government has used the elastic clause to assume powers that some believe belong to the states. The debate over how power should be shared between the federal and state governments has been a matter of controversy through most of American history.

State Constitutions Each of the 50 states has a constitution that sets forth the principles and framework of its government. Although constitutions vary from state to state, they must all conform to the Constitution of the United States. If a conflict arises, the national Constitution—the "supreme law of the land"—prevails.

Most state constitutions resemble the national Constitution in form. They start with a preamble stating their goals and include a bill of rights guaranteeing individual liberties. State constitutions tend to be longer and more detailed than the national Constitution. Many include provisions on finance, education, and other matters.

State constitutions set up a government with three branches. The powers of the legislative, executive, and judicial branches on the state level are similar to those of the national government.

Changing State Constitutions State constitutions can be changed in several ways. In the most common method, amendments are proposed by the state legislature and approved by the people in an election.

In almost one half of the states, citizens can act directly to change the constitution. In a process known as the **constitutional initiative**, sponsors of an amendment gather signatures on a petition. When the required number of signatures is attained, the petition goes to the legislature or to the voters for approval.

Finally, a state can rewrite its constitution. With the approval of the legislature or the people, the state may call a constitutional convention. The new constitution is then submitted to the people for approval.

The States' Obligations to Citizens

State governments provide a wide range of services. They maintain law and order, enforce criminal law, protect property, and regulate business. They also supervise public education, provide public health and welfare programs, build and maintain highways, operate state parks and forests, and regulate use of state-owned land.

The states, not the federal government, have the main responsibility for public education in the United States. Most students attend schools paid for and managed by the state. The state sets general standards for schools and establishes a recommended course of study. It also sets requirements for promotion and graduation.

Each state must build and maintain its own **infrastructure**, or system of transit lines, roads, bridges, and tunnels. State departments or agencies manage more than 6,000 state parks and recreation areas. To help maintain high standards, state governments license professionals, such as doctors, lawyers, and teachers.

Analyze Images Locally supported public education is important not only to the states but also to the nation. **Cite Evidence** How are a community's property values related to the quality of education its children receive?

When you are old enough to drive, the state will test you and, if you pass, give you a license. State police keep highways safe and protect us against criminal acts.

✓ READING CHECK Classify and Categorize What are some examples of services that states provide to their citizens?

What Responsibilities Do Local Governments Have?

The Constitution defines the powers of the federal and state governments. But it does not mention **local government**.

Local governments have perhaps the greatest impact on our daily lives. At the same time, it is on the local level that citizens have the greatest opportunity to influence government.

Public Education The service that local governments spend the most money on is education. While state governments set standards for schools, it is the cities, towns, or school districts that actually run them. Local school boards build schools and hire teachers and staff. They also have a strong say in which courses will be taught. However, school officials must make all decisions within the guidelines set by state law.

Education is one area of local government where citizens exert a great deal of control. Local residents may give up part of their time to serve on local school boards. In most communities, voters have the right to approve or turn down the annual school budget.

Many Other Services Local governments provide a variety of other services, including public safety, trash collection, public works, and library services. Many towns and cities also provide recreational facilities, such as parks.

✓ READING CHECK Identify Supporting Details On what service for citizens do local governments spend the most money?

Analyze Images Local governments take responsibility for providing citizens with public services, such as firefighters and police as well as trash and snow removal. **Infer** Describe how a winter where there is more snowfall than normal would affect a city's budget.

✓ Lesson Check

Practice Vocabulary

1. Which amendment in the **Bill of Rights** do you think meant more to Antifederalists, the First Amendment or the Second Amendment? Explain.

2. What is **constitutional initiative**?

Critical Thinking and Writing

3. Why do you think the Framers thought it was important to be able to amend the Constitution, but then made it difficult to do so?

4. **Use Evidence** How would you use the Tenth Amendment of the Constitution to support the idea that the federal government should not assume more power than it already has?

5. **Writing Workshop: Shape Tone** Think about the tone you want to take in your essay. To help shape your tone, write a few sentences in your 📒 Active Journal that reflect your personality and your feelings about the subject matter, while maintaining the formal style and informative approach required in presenting an argument.

Identify Sources of Continuity

Follow these steps to learn to identify sources of continuity in American society.

INTERACTIVE

Identify Trends

1 Gather information about the society. Look at a variety of resources to learn about life in the society that you are studying. What resources might help you learn about life in early America?

2 Identify possible sources of continuity in the society. Look for information about the society's government, values, economy, history, language, and culture. Imagine you are looking for information about these aspects of U.S. society. Would the source give you a complete picture? Which aspects would it help you with?

3 Choose the important sources of continuity. You may want to list the sources of continuity and take notes about each one. Why are legal documents so important to establishing continuity in a society?

4 Summarize what you discover. Use the information you have learned to make a general statement. Study the information in the source. What does it reveal about continuity in the political history of the United States?

Secondary Sources

Magna Carta: In 1215, King John of England signed the Magna Carta. This document limited the king's power, ensuring that even the king had to obey the law. It protected certain individual rights, including the right to trial and the right to private property. It also forced the king to consult with his nobles. Over time, this led to the establishment of a two-house Parliament.

English Bill of Rights: A revolution in 1689 increased Parliament's power and decreased the power of the king. The resulting English Bill of Rights restated many of the rights listed in the Magna Carta. It added the right of habeas corpus, the idea that no person could be held in prison without first being charged with a specific crime. It gave citizens the right to bear arms and also called for regular parliamentary elections.

State Constitutions: Colonies established representative governments, based in part on ideas developed in England. Eventually, each colony elected its own legislature.

U.S. Constitution and Bill of Rights: In 1787, the Framers of the Constitution called upon their knowledge of English political history and existing state constitutions to establish a new national government. They sought to prevent abuse of power by dividing the government into a legislative branch with two houses, an executive branch and a judicial branch. The Constitution called for regular elections of members of Congress and the President. A Bill of Rights, aimed at protecting individual rights, followed.

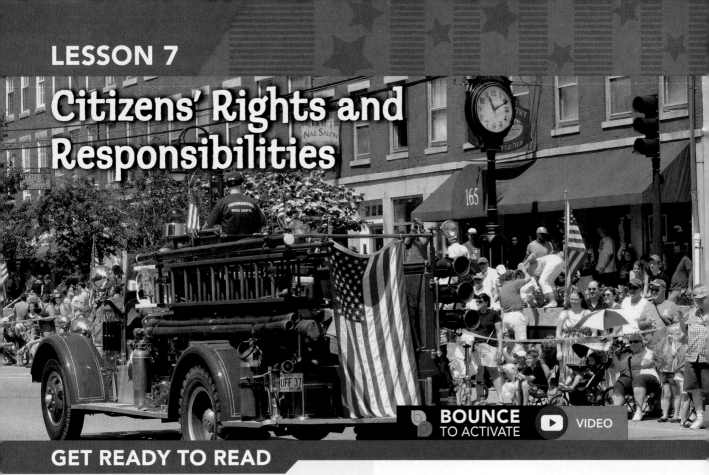

Citizens' Rights and Responsibilities

BOUNCE TO ACTIVATE ▶ VIDEO

GET READY TO READ

START UP

Look at the photograph of people enjoying a Fourth of July parade. What does it mean to be an American citizen?

GUIDING QUESTIONS

- What makes a person a citizen of the United States?
- How can Americans develop democratic values?
- What responsibilities do citizens have?

TAKE NOTES

Literacy Skills Use Evidence

Use the graphic organizer in your 📓 Active Journal to take notes as you read the lesson.

PRACTICE VOCABULARY

Use the vocabulary activity in your 📓 Active Journal to practice the vocabulary words.

Vocabulary

citizen   jury duty
naturalized
immigrant
resident alien
civic virtue
patriotism

Academic Vocabulary

responsibility
respect

The nation provides its people with many rights, including freedom to speak our minds and the knowledge that we are being protected. However, citizens also owe a debt to the nation.

American Citizenship

A **citizen** is a person who owes loyalty to a particular nation and is entitled to all its rights and protections.

To be a citizen of the United States, you must have fulfilled one of three requirements:

- You were born in the United States, or at least one parent is a citizen of the United States.
- You were **naturalized**, that is, you have completed the official legal process for becoming a citizen if you were born outside the United States.
- You were 18 or younger when your parents were naturalized.

Becoming a Citizen Many millions of immigrants have become naturalized citizens of the United States.

Analyze Images A group of immigrants celebrate after being sworn in as new United States citizens. **Use Visual Information** Are there any generalizations you can make about immigrants?

An **immigrant** is a person who enters another country in order to settle there. To illustrate the naturalization process, we will look at one immigrant's story.

At age 15, Carla Rojas came to the United States from Argentina. Her mother returned home two years later, but Rojas decided to remain. After submitting numerous documents and photographs and attending several interviews, she received permission to remain in the country as a **resident alien**, or noncitizen living in the country.

After a required five-year waiting period, Rojas submitted an application for citizenship. She had to take a test to show that she was comfortable with the English language and that she was familiar with American history and government. She also had to show that she was of "good moral character." Then, a naturalization examiner interviewed her about her reasons for becoming a citizen.

At last, Rojas stood before a judge and took the oath that confirmed her as an American citizen:

Primary Source

INTERACTIVE

Civic Responsibility

"I hereby declare, on oath, that . . . I will support and defend the Constitution and laws of the United States against all enemies . . . that I will bear true faith and allegiance to the same . . . so help me God."

—Oath of Allegiance to the United States

A naturalized citizen enjoys every right of a natural-born citizen except one. Only natural-born American citizens may serve as President or Vice President.

The Rights and Responsibilities of Citizens All American citizens have equal rights under the law. Americans have the right to speak freely, to worship as they choose, to vote, and to serve on juries. These rights are not based on inherited wealth or family connections. They are the rights of American citizens.

Still, nothing is free. As you will see, if we want to enjoy the rights of citizenship, we must also accept its **responsibilities**.

These rights and responsibilities reflect America's national identity—the common set of values that unite Americans. For example, citizens have both the right and the responsibility to vote. This reflects the principles of independence, liberty, and self-governance upheld in the Constitution and valued by the American people.

> **Academic Vocabulary**
> **responsibility** • *n.,* a duty or task one is expected to carry out
> **respect** • *n.,* understanding when something is serious and acting appropriately

✔ READING CHECK **Define** What is a citizen?

Civic Virtue, Citizenship, and Democratic Values

The founders of our country admired **civic virtue**, that is, the willingness to work for the good of the nation or community even at great sacrifice. They looked to Roman models such as Cincinnatus, who, it was said, gave up a peaceful life on his farm when called upon to lead Rome. Again and again, leaders such as George Washington, Thomas Jefferson, and John Adams put the common good ahead of their own wishes. These three presidents maintained that democracy requires virtuous behavior by citizens. Citizens must put the greater good ahead of their own desires when they follow the law, serve on juries, and make informed decisions about voting.

The leaders feared that without this responsible behavior, American liberty would be at risk. How can a democracy run if individuals do not think about what is best for society and not just for themselves?

You do not have to go to great lengths to be a good citizen. At home, at school, and in the community, you can work to develop the values that are the foundation of our democratic system. Among these basic values are honesty and compassion. Others include patriotism, **respect**, responsibility, and courage.

▼ One way students can express their civic virtue is by reciting the Pledge of Allegiance at school.

A key democratic value is **patriotism**, or a feeling of love and devotion toward one's country. A sense of patriotism inspires Americans to serve their nation. It also encourages us to fulfill the ideals set forth in the Declaration of Independence, the Constitution, and the Bill of Rights.

As citizens, we must respect ourselves, our families, our neighbors, and the other members of our community. Respect may also involve objects or ideas. For example, a good citizen respects the property of others.

Responsibility may be both personal and public. We must accept responsibility for ourselves and the consequences of our actions and behaviors. In a democracy, individuals are expected to look out for themselves and for one another. For example, parents have a duty to support their families and teach their children. This is important because children depend on parents and families depend on one another. As a student, you have a responsibility to learn.

Courage may be either physical or moral. Soldiers, police, or firefighters display physical courage when they risk their lives for the good of others. Moral courage enables us to do the right thing even when it is unpopular, difficult, or dangerous. Americans such as Abraham Lincoln, Susan B. Anthony, and Martin Luther King, Jr., showed their courage when they faced risks to defend democratic values.

Analyze Images Taking part in beach and park clean-ups is a common way for students to get involved. **Infer** In what ways does a beach clean-up show responsible citizenship?

✓READING CHECK **Define** What is civic virtue?

Voter Turnout, 1900–2000

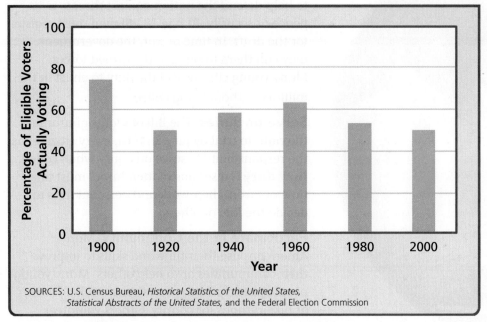

SOURCES: U.S. Census Bureau, *Historical Statistics of the United States,*
Statistical Abstracts of the United States, and the Federal Election Commission

Analyze Data The chart shows how many people voted in elections between
1900 and 2000. **Infer** Based on the information in the chart, what trend can you
identify in the percentage of the population actually voting from 1960 to 2000?

Responsible Citizenship

As citizens, we must accept our own civic responsibilities. Only if
government and citizens work together can we meet our needs as a
democratic society. Here are some important responsibilities.

Vote As citizens of a republic, we have the right to select the people
who will represent us in government. But if that right is to have any
meaning, then we must fulfill our responsibility to vote. A good citizen
studies the candidates and the issues before casting a vote in order to
make responsible choices.

INTERACTIVE

Voting Responsibly

Obey Laws and Rules In the Constitution, "we the people" give the
government the power to make laws for us. Thus, we have a duty to
obey the nation's laws. We have thousands of laws that keep us from
hurting one another, regulate contracts, and protect citizens' rights.
No one can know them all, but you must know and obey the laws that
affect your life and actions.

You also have a responsibility to obey rules. You already have rules at
home and rules at school—even rules to games you play. These rules are
not enforced by the government as laws are. Like laws, however, they
keep us safe, help us live together, and teach us to be accountable for
our behavior. By learning to obey rules such as not to hit or cheat when
we are young, we learn about responsible citizenship.

Defend the Nation Americans have the duty to help defend the nation against threats to its peace or security. At age 18, all men must register for the draft. In time of war, the government may call them to serve in the armed forces. Many young citizens feel the duty to enlist in the military without being called.

Serve on Juries The Bill of Rights guarantees the right to trial by jury. In turn, every citizen has the responsibility to serve on a jury when called. **Jury duty** is a serious matter. Jurors must take time out from their work and personal lives to decide the fate of others.

Participate in the Community Many Americans use their time and skills to improve their communities or to help others. Many young people participate in marathons, walk-a-thons, or bike-a-thons for charity. Others volunteer in hospitals or fire departments. When serious natural disasters damage cities and regions, millions of citizens aid in rescue efforts, donate blood, or contribute money and supplies.

Analyze Images
As citizens, it is our responsibility to stay informed on current events. **Use Evidence** Share examples of how citizens have used knowledge to be free and exercise their rights.

Stay Informed on Public Issues Thomas Jefferson observed, "If a nation expects to be ignorant and free . . . it expects what never was and never will be." You cannot protect your rights as a citizen unless you know what they are. You cannot choose elected officials who will make good decisions unless you know where they stand on the issues. It is your responsibility to be informed. You can watch television news programs and read newspapers, magazines, or government pamphlets. Your work in school will help you become educated about our history, our government, and the workings of our society.

☑ **READING CHECK** **Identify Supporting Details** What are some ways a citizen can stay informed about public issues?

☑ Lesson Check

Practice Vocabulary

1. Explain how an **immigrant** can become a **naturalized citizen**.

2. Does a **resident alien** have the right to vote?

Critical Thinking and Writing

3. **Summarize** What are the main responsibilities of United States citizens?

4. **Infer** What might be the reason behind the declining number of citizens who vote?

5. **Writing Workshop: Write a Conclusion** Think about the argument that you have been working on about how much power the government should have. Now, write a conclusion for your argument in your 📖 Active Journal.

Hamilton and Madison Disagree

Alexander Hamilton and James Madison were both federalists, but they had differing views about government "by the people." Read the excerpts from the writings of each man.

▶ Alexander Hamilton believed that the people were the power behind government.

1) Alexander Hamilton expressed his faith in the people when he wrote the following:

"The fabric of American empire ① ought to rest on the solid basis of THE CONSENT OF THE PEOPLE. The streams of national power ought to flow from that pure, original fountain of all legitimate authority." ②

—Alexander Hamilton, *Federalist* No. 22

2) Madison expressed his fear of majority tyranny in an October 17, 1788, letter to Thomas Jefferson:

"Wherever the real power in a Government lies, there is the danger of oppression. In our Governments, the real power lies in the majority of the Community, and the invasion of private rights is chiefly to be apprehended, not from acts of Government contrary to the sense of its constituents, but from acts in which the Government is the mere instrument of the major number of the constituents. ③ This is a truth of great importance, but not yet sufficiently attended to. ... Whenever there is an interest and power to do wrong, wrong will generally be done, and not less readily by [a majority of the people] than by a ... prince."

—James Madison, Letter to Thomas Jefferson (1788), *Letters and Other Writings of James Madison,* Volume 3

Analyzing Primary Sources

Cite specific evidence from the documents to support your answers.

1. What common ground did Hamilton and Madison share in their points of view?

2. Do you think Madison had faith in people? Why or why not?

Reading and Vocabulary Support

① Hamilton did not literally mean an empire.

② The consent of the governed was one of the ideas the founders took from the work of John Locke.

③ What do you think Madison means by this statement?

☑ Review and Assessment

VISUAL REVIEW

Comparing the Articles of Confederation and the Constitution

THE ARTICLES OF CONFEDERATION

- Weak central government
- No President
- No court system
- One-part Congress
- One Congressional delegate per state
- States free to make decisions for themselves
- Congress cannot enforce laws, regulate trade, levy taxes, resolve conflicts between states

BOTH

- A union of states
- A national legislature
- Congress can declare war, enter into treaties, coin money, operate post offices

THE CONSTITUTION

- Strong central government
- Separation of powers among legislative, executive, and judicial branches
- President leads the executive branch
- Two-part Congress
- In Senate, two senators per state
- In House, a number of representatives based on population
- Congress can levy taxes, regulate trade
- Federal laws supreme over state laws

Federalism

Federal Government	State Governments
• Administers delegated powers—those assigned to it in the Constitution • Deals with national issues • Makes and enforces laws for the country • Coins money • Declares war • Regulates trade between the states	• Administer reserved powers—those not given to the federal government • Deal with state and local issues • Make and enforce laws for the state • Maintain law and order • Protect property • Regulate business and trade within their borders • Make rules for state elections • Supervise public education • Provide public health and welfare programs • Build and maintain infrastructure

READING REVIEW

Use the Take Notes and Practice Vocabulary activities in your 📘 Active Journal to review the topic.

INTERACTIVE

Practice Vocabulary Using the Topic Mini-Games

Quest FINDINGS

Write Your Opinion

Get help for writing your response in your 📘 Active Journal.

ASSESSMENT

Vocabulary and Key Ideas

1. **Recall** How did the **Northwest Ordinance** address the slavery issue?

2. **Identify Main Ideas** What role did **compromise** play at the **Constitutional Convention** in 1787?

3. **Define** What is **popular sovereignty**?

4. **Identify Main Ideas** What protections in the **English Bill of Rights** can be found in the Constitution?

5. **Identify** What key ideals from the Declaration of Independence did the Framers include in the Constitution?

6. **Check Understanding** How does the power of the veto reflect the system of checks and balances?

7. **Identify Main Ideas** Why is jury duty considered an important responsibility of citizenship?

Critical Thinking and Writing

8. **Draw Conclusions** Why do you think the central government did not respond to Shays' Rebellion by sending in troops?

9. **Infer** Why was it important for the Framers to include, in the Constitution, key ideals from the Declaration of Independence?

10. **Identify Cause and Effect** What prevented many state convention delegates from voting to ratify the Constitution?

11. **Classify and Categorize** What branch of government is a Supreme Court justice part of? The President? A senator?

12. **Revisit the Essential Question** Does the federal government have enough power to carry out its constitutional responsibilities? Explain.

13. **Writing Workshop: Write an Argumentative Essay** Using the outline you created in your 📕 Active Journal, answer the following question in a three-paragraph argumentative essay: How much power should the federal government have, and what should its responsibilities be?

Analyze Primary Sources

14. Who most likely wrote this source?
    - A. George Washington
    - B. James Madison
    - C. Benjamin Franklin
    - D. Thomas Jefferson

"In the compound republic of America, the power surrendered by the people is first divided between two distinct governments, and then the portion allotted to each subdivided among distinct and separate departments. Hence a double security arises to the rights of the people. The different governments will control each other, at the same time that each will be controlled by itself."

—*from Federalist No. 51*

Analyze Maps

Use the map at right to answer the following questions:

15. Which state did not send a delegate?

16. How many states sent four delegates?

17. How many delegates did Georgia send?

18. Which state sent the most delegates?

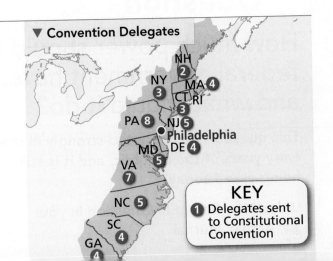

▼ **Convention Delegates**

KEY
❶ Delegates sent to Constitutional Convention

The Early Republic, 1789–1825

GO ONLINE
to access your
digital course

 VIDEO

 AUDIO

 ETEXT

 INTERACTIVE

 WRITING

 GAMES

 WORKSHEET

ASSESSMENT

Go back in time

to **WHEN THE NATION WAS YOUNG.** You'll meet our first five Presidents, as well as explorers and leaders who shaped the country. You'll also find out how "everyday" people lived in the early republic.

▲ Meriwether Lewis and William Clark greet a group of American Indians known to their guide, Sacajawea.

Explore
The Essential Question

How much power should the federal government have, and what should it do?

This question was debated strongly in the early years of the republic, and it is still being asked today.

Unlock the Essential Question in your Active Journal.

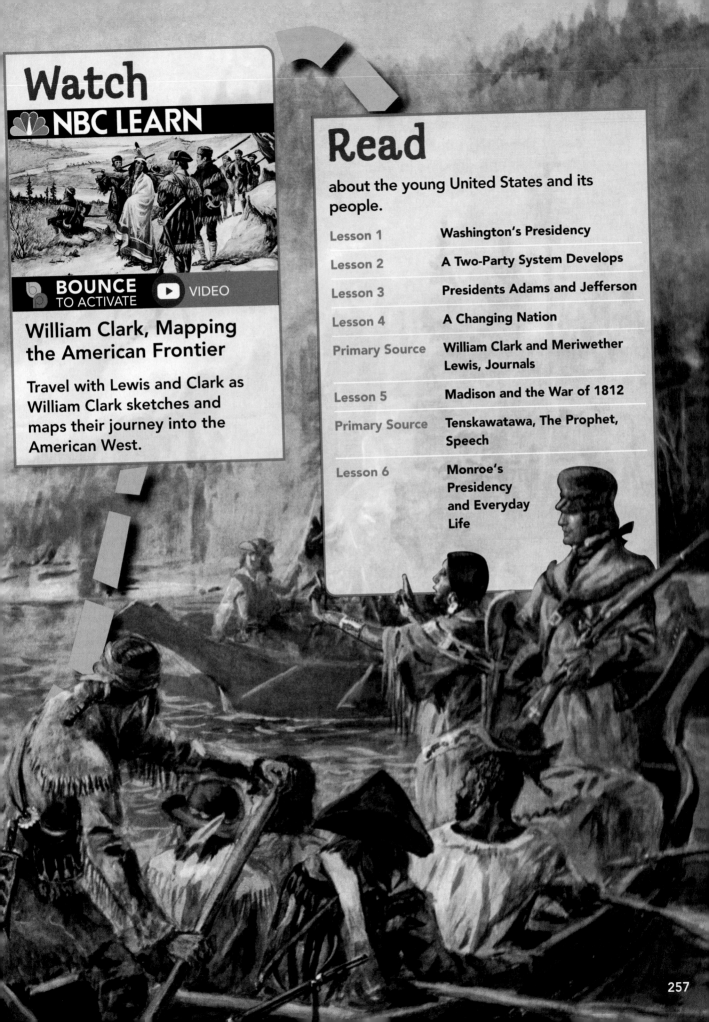

Watch

NBC LEARN

BOUNCE TO ACTIVATE ▶ VIDEO

William Clark, Mapping the American Frontier

Travel with Lewis and Clark as William Clark sketches and maps their journey into the American West.

Read

about the young United States and its people.

Learn more about the early republic by making your own map and timeline in your Active Journal.

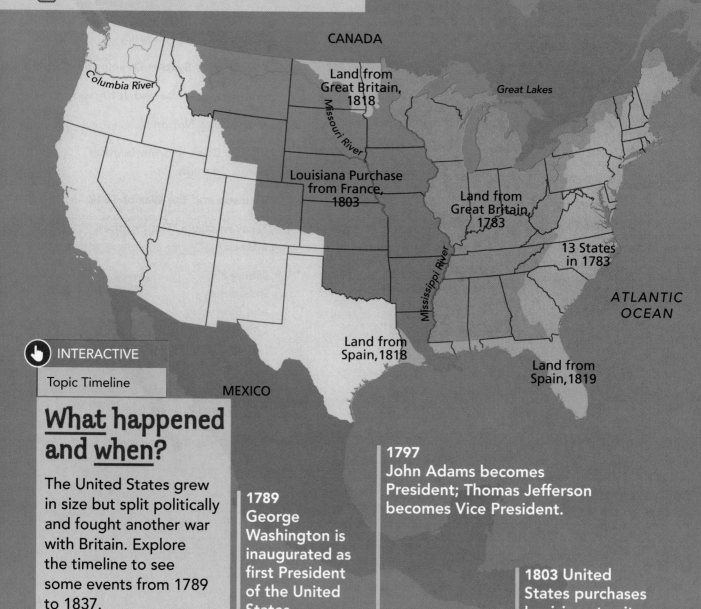

CANADA

Columbia River

Land from Great Britain, 1818

Great Lakes

Missouri River

Louisiana Purchase from France, 1803

Land from Great Britain 1783

13 States in 1783

Mississippi River

ATLANTIC OCEAN

Land from Spain, 1818

Land from Spain, 1819

MEXICO

INTERACTIVE

Topic Timeline

What happened and when?

The United States grew in size but split politically and fought another war with Britain. Explore the timeline to see some events from 1789 to 1837.

1789 George Washington is inaugurated as first President of the United States.

1797 John Adams becomes President; Thomas Jefferson becomes Vice President.

1803 United States purchases Louisiana territory.

TOPIC EVENTS

| 1780 | 1790 | 1800 |

WORLD EVENTS

1792 Mary Wollstonecraft publishes *Vindication of the Rights of Women*.

1804 Haiti declares independence from France.

INTERACTIVE

Topic Map

Where did the nation expand?

From 13 states hugging the Atlantic coast, the nation expanded westward. On the map, locate the acquisitions of land that made this expansion possible.

1812
War of 1812 begins.

1819
Supreme Court rules in *McCulloch* v. *Maryland.*

1823
President Monroe creates Monroe Doctrine.

| 1810 | 1820 | 1830 | 1840 |

1810
Argentina declares its independence from Spanish royalist leaders.

1837
Louis Daguerre experiments with photography.

Who will you meet?

Alexander Hamilton, the man who stabilized the economy but lost a duel

James Monroe, the fifth President, who told Europe to stay out of America's business

John Marshall, Supreme Court Justice who expanded the powers of the Court

259

Quest
Project-Based Learning Inquiry

Stay Out? Or Get Involved?

Quest KICK OFF

You are working for a member of President Jefferson's Cabinet and must decide how to respond to war between Britain and France. Consider this question:

How do we determine which actions are in the best interest of the United States when other nations go to war?

What events will help you decide on the best course of action? Explore the Essential Question "How much power should the federal government have, and what should it do?" in this Quest.

▲ This photograph shows a modern Cabinet meeting with President Obama presiding.

1 Ask Questions

Think of questions you would ask about factors such as events and their outcomes that would help you decide on the best course of action when other nations go to war. Write your questions in your 📙 Active Journal.

2 Investigate

As you read the lessons in this Topic, look for **Quest CONNECTIONS** that provide information on events and issues that affected the U.S. response to war between other nations. Take notes in your 📙 Active Journal.

3 Conduct Research

Next explore primary sources from the period of the early republic. They'll help you decide on the best course of action to take. Record notes in your 📙 Active Journal.

Quest FINDINGS

4 Write a Position Paper

Hold a mock Cabinet meeting to review your notes, decide on the best course of action, and document this problem-solving process. In a small group, write a position paper summarizing the chosen solution. Get help for writing the paper in your 📙 Active Journal.

LESSON 1
Washington's Presidency

BOUNCE TO ACTIVATE ▶ VIDEO

GET READY TO READ

START UP
President Washington reviews his troops before the Whiskey Rebellion. Write a prediction about events during Washington's presidency.

GUIDING QUESTIONS
- What steps did President Washington take to set up the government of the new republic?
- What were the causes and effects of the Whiskey Rebellion?
- What was the impact of Washington's foreign policy outlined in his Farewell Address?

TAKE NOTES
Literacy Skills: Summarize
Use the graphic organizer in your 📙 Active Journal to take notes as you read the lesson.

PRACTICE VOCABULARY
Use the vocabulary activity in your 📙 Active Journal to practice the vocabulary words.

Vocabulary		Academic Vocabulary
inauguration	tariff	accordingly
precedent	speculator	invoke
Cabinet	neutral	
bond		

George Washington was inaugurated in New York City on April 30, 1789. A presidential **inauguration** is the ceremony in which the President officially takes the oath of office. A witness reported that the new President looked "grave, almost to sadness." Washington, no doubt, felt a great burden. He knew that Americans were looking to him to make the new government work.

How Did Washington Shape the American Presidency?

Washington's presidency marked the beginning of what historians call the early republic. This period, between 1789 and about 1825, began when the first U.S. government was formed under the Constitution. Decisions made during the early republic had a lasting impact on the institutions and culture of the United States. As the first President, Washington showed his strong leadership and set an example for future generations.

The Constitution provided a framework for the new government of the United States.

It did not explain how the President should govern from day to day. "There is scarcely any part of my conduct," he said, "which may not hereafter be drawn into precedent." A **precedent** (PRES uh dent) is an act or a decision that sets an example for others to follow.

Washington set an important precedent at the end of his second term. In 1796, he decided not to run for a third term. Not until 1940 did any President seek a third term.

The First Cabinet
The Constitution says little about how the executive branch should be organized. It was clear, however, that the President needed talented people to help him carry out his duties.

In 1789, the first Congress created five executive departments. They were the departments of State, Treasury, and War and the offices of Attorney General and Postmaster General. The heads of these departments made up the President's **Cabinet**. Members of the Cabinet gave Washington advice and were responsible for directing their departments.

Analyze Images John Jay led the new nation's judicial branch when he became the first Chief Justice of the United States Supreme Court in 1789. **Use Visual Information** On what kind of a book do you think the Chief Justice lays his hand? Hint: The Supreme Court is the highest court, making decisions about U.S. laws.

As a proven leader himself, Washington knew he needed to appoint others with similar qualities to his Cabinet. He needed effective leaders who had the ability to persuade others to adopt new proposals and implement his ideas.

Washington set a precedent by choosing well-known leaders to serve in his Cabinet. The two most influential Cabinet members were the Secretary of State, Thomas Jefferson, and the Secretary of the Treasury, Alexander Hamilton.

Establishing a Court System
The Constitution calls for a Supreme Court. Congress, however, had to set up the federal court system. As one of its first actions, Congress passed the Judiciary Act of 1789. It called for the Supreme Court to consist of one Chief Justice and five Associate Justices. Today, the Supreme Court has eight Associate Justices because Congress later amended the Judiciary Act. Washington named John Jay the first Chief Justice of the United States.

The Judiciary Act also set up a system of district courts and circuit courts across the nation. Decisions made in these lower courts could be appealed to the Supreme Court, the highest court in the land.

✓ **READING CHECK** **Identify Main Ideas** Why was the Cabinet created?

How Did Alexander Hamilton Deal with the National Debt?

As Secretary of the Treasury, Alexander Hamilton faced many problems. Among the most pressing was the large national debt. This is the total amount of money that a government owes to others.

During the Revolution, both the national government and individual states had desperately needed money. They had borrowed heavily from foreign countries and ordinary citizens to pay soldiers and buy supplies. Then, as now, governments borrowed money by issuing bonds. A **bond** is a certificate that promises to repay the money loaned, plus interest, on a certain date. For example, if a person pays $100 for a bond, the government agrees to pay back $100 plus interest (an additional sum of money) by a certain time.

A Plan to Reduce the Debt Hamilton wanted to pay off the government's debts and create a stable economic system for the United States. The plan he proposed showed that Cabinet members could provide strong leadership.

Hamilton called for the government to repay both federal and state debts. His first act in government was to ask Congress to pass a **tariff**, or tax on imports, to pay for the government. Congress passed this tariff in 1789. Hamilton wanted the government to buy up all the bonds issued by both the national and state governments before 1789. He then planned to issue new bonds to pay off the old debts. As the economy improved and income from the tariff increased, the government would then be able to pay off the new bonds. Many people, including bankers and investors, welcomed Hamilton's plan. Others attacked it.

Analyze Graphs This graph shows U.S. financial problems after the Revolutionary War. **Infer** Based on the information in the graph, what can you conclude about the economic situation of the federal government when Washington took office?

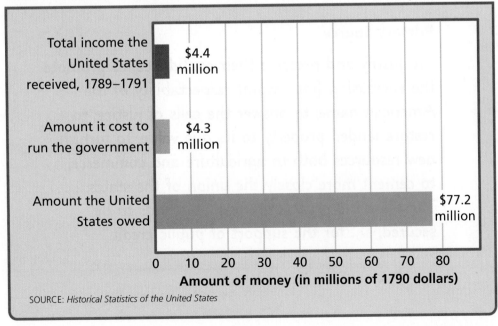

U.S. Financial Problems, 1789–1791

Total income the United States received, 1789–1791: $4.4 million

Amount it cost to run the government: $4.3 million

Amount the United States owed: $77.2 million

Amount of money (in millions of 1790 dollars)

SOURCE: *Historical Statistics of the United States*

State Debt Assumed by the New Federal Government, 1790

STATE	ASSUMED DEBT (IN DOLLARS)	STATE	ASSUMED DEBT (IN DOLLARS)
New Hampshire	300,000	Delaware	200,000
Massachusetts	4,000,000	Maryland	800,000
Rhode Island	200,000	Virginia	3,500,000
Connecticut	1,600,000	North Carolina	2,400,000
New York	1,200,000	South Carolina	4,000,000
New Jersey	800,000	Georgia	300,000
Pennsylvania	2,200,000		

SOURCE: Library of Congress

Analyze Graphs Hamilton agreed to pay off state debts as well as federal debts. **Draw Conclusions** Considering the differences among the states' debt levels, why might some states have objected to the federal government taking over every state's debts?

Hamilton's Plan James Madison led the opposition. Madison argued that Hamilton's plan rewarded speculators. A **speculator** is someone who invests in a risky venture in the hope of making a large profit.

During the Revolution, the government had issued bonds to soldiers and citizens who supplied goods. Many of these bondholders needed cash to survive and sold their bonds to speculators. Speculators bought bonds worth one dollar for only 10 or 15 cents. If the government paid off the old bonds in full, speculators stood to make fortunes. Madison thought that speculators did not deserve to profit.

Hamilton replied that the United States must repay its debts in full. The support of investors, he argued, was crucial to building the new nation's economy:

Primary Source

"To justify and preserve their confidence; to promote the encreasing [increasing] respectability of the American name; to answer the calls of justice; to restore landed property to its due value; to furnish new resources both to agriculture and commerce; to cement more closely the union of the states; . . . These are the great and invaluable ends to be secured, . . . for the support of public credit."

—Alexander Hamilton, "Report on Public Credit," January 9, 1790

After much debate, Congress approved full repayment of the national debt.

As a southerner, Madison also led the fight against the other part of Hamilton's plan, the repaying of state debts. By 1789, most southern states had paid off their debts from the Revolution. They thought that other states should do the same. The New England states, for example, still owed a lot. Thus, some northern states stood to gain more than others from the plan. As a result, the southern states bitterly opposed Hamilton's plan.

This fight over how to use scarce resources was only one of many in the early republic. To make government work, there were compromises.

Reaching a Compromise In the end, Hamilton proposed a compromise. Many southerners wanted the nation's capital to be located in the South. Hamilton offered to support that goal if southerners agreed to his plan to repay state debts.

Madison and others accepted the compromise. In July 1790, Congress voted to repay state debts and to build a new capital city. The new capital would not be part of any state. Instead, it would be built along the Potomac River on land given up by two southern states, Virginia and Maryland. Congress called the area the District of Columbia. Washington, the new capital, would be located in the District. Today, it is known as Washington, D.C., with *D.C.* standing for *District of Columbia.* Plans called for the new capital to be ready by 1800. Meanwhile, the nation's capital was moved from New York to Philadelphia.

✔ **READING CHECK** **Identify Cause and Effect** Why were federal and state debts so high?

Analyze Images
Locating the nation's capital in what is now Washington, D.C., was the result of a compromise in which southern states agreed that the federal government would take over state debts, mainly helping northern states. **Infer** What about Washington's location helped southern states accept the compromise?

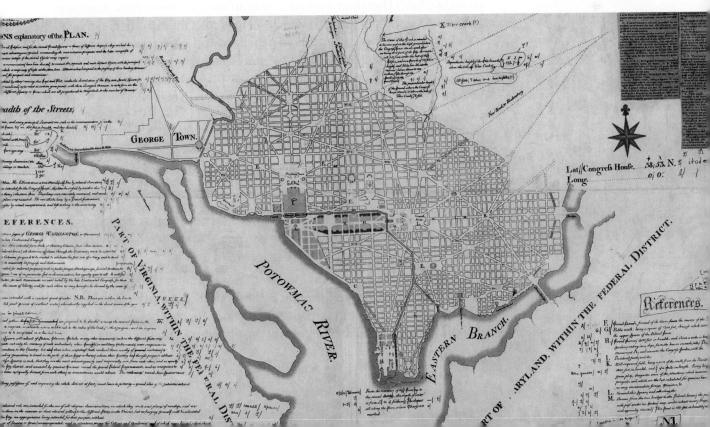

How Did Hamilton Create a Stable Economy?

Hamilton's next challenge was to strengthen the faltering national economy. **Accordingly**, his economic plan was designed to help both agriculture and industry.

Hamilton called on Congress to set up a national bank. In 1791, Congress created the first Bank of the United States. The government deposited money from taxes in the Bank. In turn, the Bank issued paper money to pay the government's bills and to make loans to farmers and businesses. Through these loans, the Bank encouraged economic growth and the development of a free-enterprise economic system.

To help American manufacturers, Hamilton asked Congress to pass a new tariff on foreign goods brought into the country. He wanted a high tariff to make imported goods more expensive than American-made goods. A tariff meant to protect local industry from foreign competition is called a protective tariff.

Analyze Images This building in Philadelphia was the headquarters of the first Bank of the United States. The Bank was founded in 1791. **Sequence** Why do you think the founding of the first bank came after the Revolution?

Hamilton's plan sparked arguments over taxation. In the North, where there were more and more factories, many people supported Hamilton's plan. Southern farmers, however, bought many imported goods. They opposed a protective tariff that would make imports more expensive.

In the end, Congress did pass a tariff, but it was much lower than the protective tariff Hamilton wanted. The tariff was also lower than American manufacturers would have liked in order to protect them from foreign competition. However, the tariff did help to pay off government debt, a central point in Hamilton's economic plan. The government needed to find a form of taxation that allowed it to pay off lenders because attracting lenders is key to financing government in a free market economy.

✅ **READING CHECK** **Identify Supporting Details** What is the purpose of a protective tariff?

A New Tax Leads to Rebellion

To help reduce the national debt, Congress approved a tax on all liquor made and sold in the United States. Hamilton wanted this tax to raise money for the treasury. Instead, the new tax sparked a rebellion that tested the strength of the new government.

This tax was the first implemented by Congress under its new constitutional authority. Hamilton believed that reasonable taxes on alcohol would help to moderate consumption. He also hoped to gain a rich source of revenue for the federal government to pay its debts.

Academic Vocabulary

accordingly • *adv.*, in a fitting or appropriate way

However, the new law varied the tax rate and often left smaller liquor manufacturers paying more than larger ones. Furthermore, the tax had to be paid in cash. This was often difficult for small distilleries. Large liquor enterprises in the East had less trouble with the tax than those on the frontier or in small towns.

Hamilton, though himself a man of humble origins, did not fully appreciate the economic concerns of Americans who lived on farms or in small towns. A large number of them opposed the new tax.

The Whiskey Rebellion Like many Americans, backcountry farmers grew corn. However, corn was bulky and expensive to haul long distances over rough roads. The cost of transport made western corn too expensive to sell in the East. Instead, farmers converted their corn into whiskey. Barrels of whiskey were worth much more and could be sold for a profit in the East, despite the cost of transport.

Back country farmers hated the tax on whiskey because it sharply reduced their income. Many refused to pay it. They compared it to the taxes Britain had forced on the colonies.

In 1794, when officials in western Pennsylvania tried to collect the tax, farmers rebelled. During the Whiskey Rebellion thousands marched in protest through the streets of Pittsburgh. They sang revolutionary songs and tarred and feathered the tax collectors.

Washington Shows Leadership President Washington responded quickly. He showed his abilities as a military leader once again.

INTERACTIVE

A Controversial Tax

Analyze Images
Frontiersmen tar and feather a government tax collector during the Whiskey Rebellion to protest a tax on liquor. **Classify and Categorize** How would you describe the behavior of the crowd in the picture?

Analyze Images In this image showing the French Revolution, a mob in Paris burns symbols of the monarchy. **Understand Effects** What do you think some Americans thought about the increasing violence of the French Revolution?

He called up the militia and dispatched them to Pennsylvania. When the rebels heard that thousands of troops were marching against them, they fled back to their farms. Hamilton wanted the leaders of the rebellion executed, but Washington disagreed and pardoned them. He believed that the government had shown its strength to all. Now, it was time to show mercy.

The Whiskey Rebellion tested the will of the new government. Washington's quick response proved to Americans that their new government would act firmly in times of crisis. The President also showed those who disagreed with the government that violence would not be tolerated.

☑ **READING CHECK** **Identify Cause and Effect** What was the main cause of the Whiskey Rebellion?

How Did Americans React to the French Revolution?

Late in 1789, French ships arrived in American ports with startling news. On July 14, an angry mob in Paris, France, had destroyed the Bastille (bahs TEEL), an ancient fort that was used as a prison. The attack on the Bastille was an early event in the French Revolution. Before long, the revolution would topple the monarch and lead to the execution of thousands of ordinary French citizens.

The French Revolution broke out a few years after Americans had won their independence. Like Americans, the French fought for liberty and equality. As the French Revolution grew more violent, however, it deepened political divisions within the United States.

The French had many reasons to rebel against their king, Louis XVI. The peasants and the middle class paid heavy taxes, while nobles paid none. Reformers wanted a constitution to limit the king's power and protect basic rights, as the American Constitution did.

Supporting Liberty in France At first, most Americans supported the French Revolution. Americans knew what it meant to struggle for liberty. Also, during the American Revolution, France had been an ally. Many Americans admired the Marquis de Lafayette, a leading French reformer who had fought with them in the American Revolution.

However, the French Revolution frightened most European rulers and nobles. They wanted to prevent revolutionary ideas from spreading to their lands. When two European countries, Austria and Prussia, **invoked** other rulers to help the French king regain his throne in 1792, France declared war.

By 1793, the French Revolution was turning more and more violent. Radical reformers gained power. They beheaded the king and later the queen. During the Reign of Terror, tens of thousands of ordinary French citizens were executed.

Differing Opinions Violence in France divided Americans. Some, like Thomas Jefferson, continued to support the French revolutionaries. He felt that the French had the right to use violence to win freedom, although he condemned the executions of the king and queen.

INTERACTIVE

Foreign Affairs
Under Washington

Academic Vocabulary
invoke • *v.*, to call on; to appeal to

Analyze Diagrams The information in the chart reflects Washington's foreign policy. **Identify Main Ideas** Based on the chart, how did Washington deal with European powers? How did his actions reflect his foreign policy preferences?

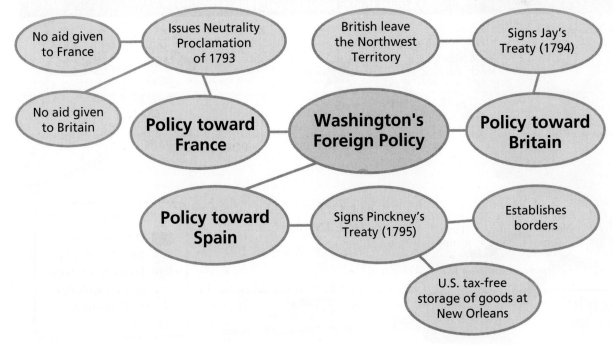

No aid given to France

Issues Neutrality Proclamation of 1793

British leave the Northwest Territory

Signs Jay's Treaty (1794)

No aid given to Britain

Policy toward France

Washington's Foreign Policy

Policy toward Britain

Policy toward Spain

Signs Pinckney's Treaty (1795)

Establishes borders

U.S. tax-free storage of goods at New Orleans

Quest CONNECTIONS

What was Washington's foreign policy? Why did he form this policy? Record your findings in your 📓 Active Journal.

Alexander Hamilton, John Adams, and others strongly disagreed about the use of violence. One could no more create democracy through widespread violence, claimed Adams, "than a snowball can exist in the streets of Philadelphia under a burning sun."

President Washington's Foreign Policy The French armies' attack on Austria led Britain to declare war on France. Europe was soon plunged into a string of wars that lasted on and off for more than 20 years. The fight between France and Britain, Europe's two leading powers, threatened the economy of the United States. These countries were America's main trading partners.

GEOGRAPHY SKILLS

Paris was the site of the violent French Revolution. The map also identifies places where the United States faced British hostility or outright aggression.

1. **Location** Near what bodies of water did the United States face British aggression in America?

2. **Draw Conclusions** Which nation—Britain or France—appeared to pose a more serious threat to the United States? Why?

Faced with war in Europe, President Washington had to decide on a foreign policy. Foreign policy is a nation's plan of action toward other nations. During the American Revolution, the United States and France had signed a treaty that made the two countries allies. Now, France wanted to use American ports to supply its ships and launch attacks on British ships. Allowing France to use American ports would expose the United States, still recovering from the Revolutionary War, to new British attacks. Washington worried that the United States could not honor its treaty with France and still remain neutral in the European conflict. Remaining **neutral** means not taking sides in a conflict.

Washington also hoped to protect the American economy from the conflict between Britain and France. Merchants and farmers in the United States depended on American ports to maintain overseas trade with Britain and other countries. The British navy ensured the safety of American trading ships.

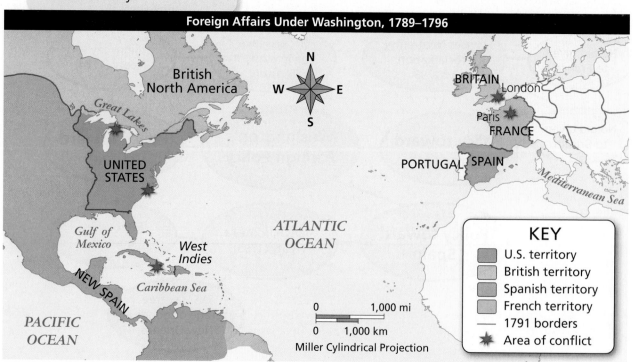

Foreign Affairs Under Washington, 1789–1796

KEY
- U.S. territory
- British territory
- Spanish territory
- French territory
- 1791 borders
- ✳ Area of conflict

Still, many Americans favored France. Staying neutral appeared to be Washington's best option.

Protecting American Interests The issue of the treaty deepened the divisions within Washington's Cabinet. Hamilton pointed out that the United States had signed the treaty with Louis XVI. With the king dead, he argued, the treaty was no longer valid. Jefferson, a supporter of France, urged strict acceptance of the treaty.

After much debate, Washington issued the Neutrality Proclamation in April 1793. It stated that the United States would not support either side in the war. Further, it forbade Americans from aiding either Britain or France. The Neutrality Proclamation was a defeat for Jefferson. This and other defeats eventually led Jefferson to leave the Cabinet.

☑ READING CHECK **Identify Main Ideas** Why did Washington decide on neutrality as his foreign policy?

Washington Defends Neutrality

Declaring neutrality was easier than enforcing it. Americans wanted to trade with both Britain and France. However, those warring nations seized American cargoes headed for each other's ports.

Jay's Treaty In 1793, the British captured more than 250 American ships trading in the French West Indies. Some Americans called for war. Washington, however, knew that the United States was too weak to fight. He sent Chief Justice John Jay to Britain for talks.

Jay negotiated an agreement that called for Britain to pay damages for the seized American ships. Britain also agreed to give up the forts it still held in the West. Meanwhile, Americans had to pay debts long owed to British merchants.

Jay's Treaty sparked loud protests because it did nothing to protect the rights of neutral American ships. After furious debate, the Senate finally approved the treaty in 1795.

The Impact of Washington's Farewell Address After serving two terms as President, George Washington refused to serve a third.

Analyze Political Cartoons In this political cartoon, citizens burn an effigy of John Jay to protest Jay's Treaty, which they believed favored Britain. **Use Visual Information** How does the burning of the stuffed figure of John Jay make the image more powerful than if the mob did not burn the figure?

Friends, & Fellow-citizens.

The period for a new election of a citizen, to administer the Executive government of the United States, being far distant, and the time actually arrived, when your thoughts must be employed in designating the person, who is to be cloathed with that important trust, it appears to me proper, especially as it may conduce to a more distinct expression of the public voice, that I should now apprise you of the resolution I have formed, to decline being considered among the number of those, out of whom a choice is to be made. —

I beg you, at the same time to do me the justice to be assured that this resolution has not been taken, without a strict regard to all the considerations app...

Analyze Images In his Farewell Address, Washington gave clear warnings about the dangers of political entanglement with other nations. **Identify Main Ideas** Why did Washington fear such entanglements?

Before retiring in 1796, Washington published his Farewell Address. In it, he advised Americans against becoming involved in European affairs:

Primary Source

"Tis our true policy to steer clear of permanent Alliances, with any portion of the foreign World. . . . The great rule of conduct for us, in regard to foreign nations is . . . to have with them as little political connection as possible."

—George Washington, Farewell Address, 1796

Washington did not oppose foreign trade, but he did reject alliances that could drag the country into war. His advice guided American foreign policy for many years.

✓ READING CHECK **Identify Main Ideas** What advice did Washington give in his final address?

✓ Lesson Check

Practice Vocabulary

1. Why were many of President George Washington's actions considered **precedents**?

2. How were **bonds** and **speculators** related in the early republic?

Critical Thinking and Writing

3. **Identify Main Ideas** Explain Hamilton's argument in favor of paying the nation's debts in full.

4. **Identify Cause and Effect** Why was the nation's capital built as a new city in the South?

5. **Summarize** What was George Washington's response to the Whiskey Rebellion, and what effect did his response have on the nation?

6. **Writing Workshop: Generate Questions to Focus Research** In your 🗒 Active Journal, write at least three questions about the country's physical landscapes, political divisions, and territorial expansion during the early republic. These questions will help focus your research and help you to write a research paper at the end of the Topic.

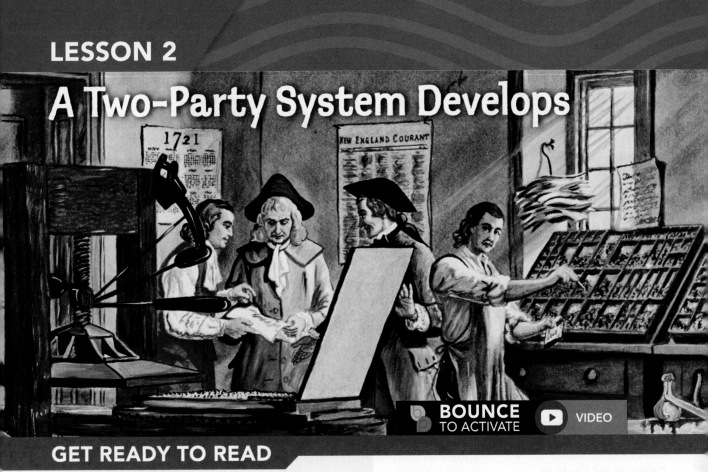

LESSON 2

A Two-Party System Develops

BOUNCE TO ACTIVATE   VIDEO

GET READY TO READ

START UP

Study the illustration. What do you think people were reading about in newspapers in the 1790s? Write your thoughts in your 📘 Active Journal.

GUIDING QUESTIONS

- How did the government change during the early republic?
- In what ways did Hamilton's and Jefferson's views of government differ?
- How did political parties develop?
- What political tensions appeared during the election of 1796?

TAKE NOTES

Literacy Skills: Compare and Contrast

Use the graphic organizer in your 📘 Active Journal to take notes as you read the lesson.

PRACTICE VOCABULARY

Use the vocabulary activity in your 📘 Active Journal to practice the vocabulary words.

Vocabulary

faction
unconstitutional

Democratic
Republicans
Federalists

Academic Vocabulary

unify
subsidize

Political disagreements divided Americans early on. "Men who have been [friends] all their lives," noted Jefferson, "cross streets to avoid meeting, and turn their heads another way, lest they should be obliged to touch their hats." Washington was able to **unify** Americans with different political beliefs. He opposed political parties. Before he left office in 1797, however, two rival parties had emerged.

How Did Politics Divide Americans?

Americans saw political parties as a threat to national unity. They agreed with George Washington, who warned that parties would lead to "jealousies and false alarms."

Opposing Factions Grow in the Cabinet Despite the President's warning, **factions**, or opposing groups, grew up around two members of his Cabinet, Alexander Hamilton and Thomas Jefferson. The two men differed in both background and politics. Born in the West Indies, Hamilton had worked his way up from

Differing Views: Jefferson vs. Hamilton

JEFFERSON	HAMILTON
• Wanted strong state governments	• Wanted a strong central government
• Sympathetic to France	• Sympathetic to England
• Opposed a national bank	• Favored a national bank
• Thought the government should be controlled by ordinary Americans	• Thought the government should be controlled by the elite of society
• Wanted liberties to be protected by law	• Opposed to protecting individual liberties by law
• Believed the American government should not be modeled on the English government	• Wanted to model the American government after the English government

Analyze Charts Thomas Jefferson and Alexander Hamilton held opposing views on many issues. **Compare and Contrast** How did Jefferson's views on civil liberties differ from Hamilton's?

poverty. Hamilton believed that the wealthy and educated should control the government. He thought that supporting business and trade was the best way to improve the nation's economy. Hamilton also favored Britain over France.

Unlike Hamilton, Jefferson came from a wealthy family of Virginia planters. He owned large plantations and enslaved African Americans. Despite his wealth, Jefferson believed that the government should represent ordinary white people, not just the wealthy and educated. Jefferson strongly believed that public education was necessary for a free republican society. Jefferson supported policies that favored small farmers rather than businessmen. He also favored France over Britain.

✓ READING CHECK **Identify Main Ideas** Why did many Americans distrust political parties?

What Issues Divided Hamilton and Jefferson?

The disagreements between Hamilton and Jefferson were not just differences of opinion. Their quarrels were rooted in their different views about what was best for the new nation.

Foundations of the American Economy The two leaders differed on economic policy. Hamilton wanted the United States to model itself on Britain. The government, he thought, should encourage manufacturing and trade. He believed the government should **subsidize** the building of roads and canals to encourage commerce. He also favored the growth of cities and the merchant class.

Jefferson thought that farmers were the backbone of the new nation. "Cultivators of the earth," he wrote, "are the most valuable citizens."

Academic Vocabulary

unify • v., to bring together as one; to unite; to combine

subsidize • v., to help pay for the cost of something

He feared that a manufacturing economy would corrupt the United States by concentrating power in the hands of wealthy Americans.

Federalism Hamilton and Jefferson also disagreed about the power of the federal government. Hamilton wanted the federal government to have greater power than state governments. A strong federal government, he argued, was needed to increase commerce. It would also be able to restrain mob violence like that of the Whiskey Rebellion. Earlier, he had written in his notes for a speech:

INTERACTIVE

Early American Leaders

Primary Source

"The general government must, in this case, not only have a strong soul, but strong organs by which that soul is to operate."

—Alexander Hamilton, Notes, June 18, 1787

In contrast, Jefferson wanted as small a federal government as possible, in order to protect individual freedom. He feared that a strong federal government might take over powers that the Constitution gave to the states.

Interpreting the Constitution Jefferson and Hamilton also clashed over the Bank of the United States. Jefferson worried that a national bank would give too much power to the government and to wealthy investors who would help run the bank.

Jefferson opposed the law setting up the bank. He claimed that it was **unconstitutional**, or not permitted by the Constitution. Nowhere did the Constitution give Congress the power to create a Bank, he argued. For Jefferson, any power not specifically given to the federal government belonged to the states.

Analyze Images Jefferson believed that farmers were the backbone of the nation. Hamilton believed in supporting manufacturing and trade in cities such as Boston and New York. **Recognize Multiple Causes** How do you think these two views resulted in these men having different points of view on how to run the U.S. government?

Hamilton did not agree with Jefferson's strict interpretation of the Constitution. He preferred a loose interpretation of the Constitution. The Constitution gave Congress the power to make all laws "necessary and proper" to carry out its duties. Hamilton argued that the Bank was necessary for the government to collect taxes and pay its bills.

Britain or France? Finally, the two leaders disagreed over foreign policy. Hamilton wanted close ties with Britain, because it was a major trading partner. Jefferson favored France, the first ally of the United States.

✓ READING CHECK **Identify Supporting Details** How did Hamilton feel about division of power between the U.S. government and the states?

Political Parties Take Shape

At first, Hamilton and Jefferson clashed in private. Then Congress began to pass many of Hamilton's programs. James Madison shared many of Jefferson's views, and the two men decided to organize supporters of their views.

Analyze Political Cartoons In this cartoon, Congressman Matthew Lyon, a Democratic Republican, defends himself from Roger Griswold, a Federalist. **Infer** What does this cartoon suggest about the conflict between the parties?

Functions and Responsibilities of a Free Press

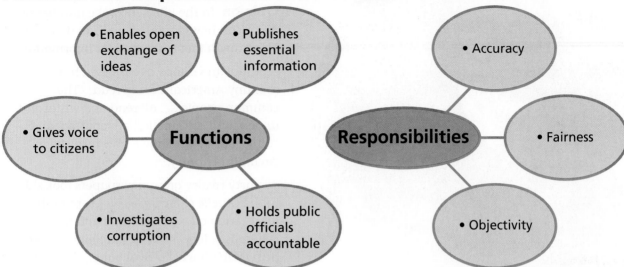

Functions
- Enables open exchange of ideas
- Publishes essential information
- Gives voice to citizens
- Investigates corruption
- Holds public officials accountable

Responsibilities
- Accuracy
- Fairness
- Objectivity

Jefferson and Madison moved cautiously at first. In 1791, they went to New York, telling people that they wanted to study its wildlife. In fact, Jefferson was interested in nature. Their main goal, though, was to meet with leading New York politicians such as Governor George Clinton and Aaron Burr, a fierce critic of Hamilton. Jefferson asked them to help defeat Hamilton's program by convincing New Yorkers to vote for Jefferson's supporters.

Republicans and Federalists Soon, leaders in other states were organizing to support either Hamilton or Jefferson. Jefferson's supporters called themselves **Democratic Republicans**, often shortened to Republicans. Today's Republican Party is not related to Jefferson's party. The Jeffersonian Republicans included small farmers, artisans, and some wealthy planters in the South.

Hamilton and his supporters were called **Federalists** because they wanted a strong federal government. In fact, Jefferson wrote a letter to President Washington calling Hamilton and his supporters a "corrupt squadron" whose

Primary Source

"ultimate object . . . is to prepare the way for a change, from the present republican form of government, to that of a monarchy, of which the English constitution is to be the model."

—Thomas Jefferson to George Washington, May 23, 1792

Federalists drew support mainly from merchants and manufacturers in such cities as Boston and New York. They also had the backing of some southern planters.

Analyze Charts A free press is essential to people living under a democratic form of government. **Identify Cause and Effect** What would be the effect if any of the functions or responsibilities of a free press were abandoned? Explain the consequences.

Quick Activity

Take sides. Tell whether you would support Hamilton's or Jefferson's views on the role of government. Write your ideas in your Active Journal.

▲ Philip Freneau's newspaper *the National Gazette* presented a counterpart to John Fenno's Federalist newspaper.

Newspapers Influence Public Opinion In the late 1700s, the number of American newspapers more than doubled. This growth met a demand for information.

A European visitor was surprised that so many Americans could read. "The common people . . . all read and write, and understand arithmetic," he reported, and "almost every little town now furnishes a circulating library."

As party rivalry grew, newspapers took sides. In the *Gazette of the United States,* publisher John Fenno backed Hamilton and the Federalists. Jefferson's friend Philip Freneau (frih NOH) started a rival paper, the *National Gazette,* which supported Republicans.

Newspapers had great influence on public opinion. In stinging language, they raged against political opponents. Often, articles mixed rumor and opinion with facts. Emotional attacks and counterattacks fanned the flames of party rivalry.

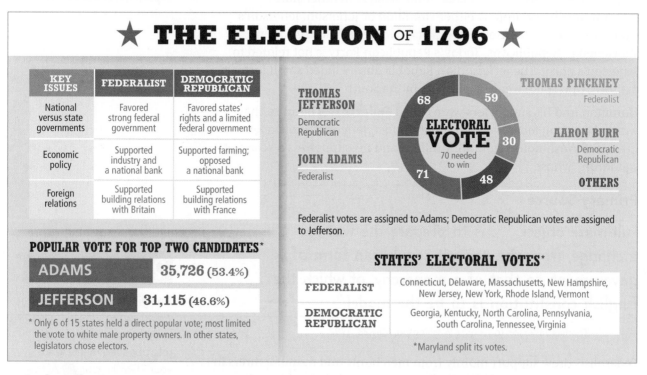

★ THE ELECTION OF 1796 ★

KEY ISSUES	FEDERALIST	DEMOCRATIC REPUBLICAN
National versus state governments	Favored strong federal government	Favored states' rights and a limited federal government
Economic policy	Supported industry and a national bank	Supported farming; opposed a national bank
Foreign relations	Supported building relations with Britain	Supported building relations with France

THOMAS JEFFERSON
Democratic Republican

JOHN ADAMS
Federalist

ELECTORAL VOTE
70 needed to win
68 59
71 48
30

THOMAS PINCKNEY
Federalist

AARON BURR
Democratic Republican

OTHERS

Federalist votes are assigned to Adams; Democratic Republican votes are assigned to Jefferson.

POPULAR VOTE FOR TOP TWO CANDIDATES*

ADAMS	35,726 (53.4%)
JEFFERSON	31,115 (46.6%)

* Only 6 of 15 states held a direct popular vote; most limited the vote to white male property owners. In other states, legislators chose electors.

STATES' ELECTORAL VOTES*

FEDERALIST	Connecticut, Delaware, Massachusetts, New Hampshire, New Jersey, New York, Rhode Island, Vermont
DEMOCRATIC REPUBLICAN	Georgia, Kentucky, North Carolina, Pennsylvania, South Carolina, Tennessee, Virginia

*Maryland split its votes.

Analyze Charts Study the chart. **Identify Main Ideas** Which political party championed agriculture and campaigned against the establishment of a national bank? Which candidate finished third in the electoral vote tally?

Choosing Washington's Successor Political parties played a large role in the election of George Washington's successor. In 1796, Democratic Republicans backed Thomas Jefferson for President and Aaron Burr for Vice President. Federalists supported John Adams for President and Thomas Pinckney for Vice President. The election had an unexpected outcome.

Under the Constitution, the person with the most electoral votes becomes President. At that time, the candidate with the next highest total was made Vice President. John Adams, a Federalist, won office as President. The leader of the Democratic Republicans, Thomas Jefferson, became Vice President.

Having the President and Vice President from opposing parties further increased political tensions. John Adams took office in March 1797 as the nation's second President. Events soon deepened the distrust between him and Jefferson.

☑ READING CHECK Summarize How did political parties begin in the United States?

▲ John Adams succeeded George Washington and became the second President of the United States in the election of 1796.

☑ Lesson Check

Practice Vocabulary

1. What **factions** developed despite Washington's warnings?

2. What makes a law **unconstitutional**?

Critical Thinking and Writing

3. **Compare and Contrast** What were Hamilton's and Jefferson's views on the power of the federal government?

4. **Draw Conclusions** Why did Thomas Jefferson, who claimed to dislike political parties, lead the way in founding a party?

5. **Summarize** In the late 1700s, the number of newspapers in the United States increased greatly. What are the functions and responsibilities of a free press in a democracy?

6. **Writing Workshop: Find and Use Credible Sources** Choose reliable print and Internet sources that you will use for your research paper at the end of this Topic. List them in your 📓 Active Journal. Take careful notes from your sources.

Distinguish Fact From Opinion

Follow these steps to distinguish fact from opinion.

INTERACTIVE

Distinguish Between
Fact and Opinion

1 **Decide which statements are facts.** Facts are based on evidence and can be proved true. Find two facts in the diary entry. How could you prove each statement is a fact? What questions will you ask as you examine each bit of information?

2 **Decide which statements are opinions.** An opinion is a personal interpretation of an event. It reflects feelings, judgments, or beliefs. Find two opinions in the diary entry. How can you tell that each is an opinion? What questions will you ask as you examine whether a piece of information is an opinion?

3 **Recognize how the author mixes fact and opinion.** Find a sentence that includes both a fact and an opinion. What is the fact? What is the opinion? Why do you think the author mixed facts and opinions? Who do you think the writer is addressing, and does that make a difference in the way the writer expresses his or her ideas?

Diary Entry

February 28

After dinner tonight, I finished reading today's edition of the *Gazette of the United States*. The publisher of the newspaper is John Fenno. In my opinion, he is right to favor the Federalist leader, Alexander Hamilton. Of course, I am a merchant, and I agree with Hamilton's support of trade and manufacturing. To me, it is a more worthwhile policy than Mr. Jefferson's support of farmers.

I believe that I have Hamilton alone to thank for the National Bank. This Bank, established by Congress in 1791, has the power to make loans to businesses, such as my dry goods store. Of course, the federal bank is opposed by that friend of the states, Thomas Jefferson, who isn't thinking of our country's future. I only hope that Mr. Hamilton's party wins the next election. Isaac Smith

— A fictional diary entry of a merchant living in colonial Philadelphia in the 1790s

LESSON 3

Presidents Adams and Jefferson

▶ VIDEO

GET READY TO READ

START UP

Examine this picture of the new capital of Washington, D.C. Make a prediction about events in the new capital in your 📓 Active Journal.

GUIDING QUESTIONS

- How did John Adams's foreign policy compare with Washington's foreign policy?
- What was the controversy over the Alien and Sedition Acts?
- What is the significance of the Supreme Court case *Marbury* v. *Madison*?

TAKE NOTES

Literacy Skills: Identify Main Ideas

Use the graphic organizer in your 📓 Active Journal to take notes as you read this lesson.

PRACTICE VOCABULARY

Use the vocabulary activity in your 📓 Active Journal to practice the vocabulary words.

Vocabulary		Academic Vocabulary
tribute	laissez faire	expel
sedition	judicial	constitute
nullify	review	
states' rights		

No sooner had John Adams taken office than he faced a crisis with France. The French objected to Jay's Treaty because they felt that it put the United States on the side of Britain. In 1797, French ships began to seize American ships in the West Indies, as the British had done.

Conflict With France

As the conflict between the two nations escalated, Americans once again called for war, this time against France. To avoid war, Adams sent diplomats to Paris to discuss the rights of neutral nations.

The XYZ Affair The French foreign minister, Charles Maurice de Talleyrand, did not deal directly with the Americans. Instead, he sent three agents to offer the Americans a deal. Before Talleyrand would even begin talks, the agents said, he wanted $250,000 for himself and a $10 million loan to France. "Not a sixpence!" replied one of the Americans, angrily. (A sixpence was a British coin worth six pennies.)

Lesson 5.3 • Presidents Adams and Jefferson **281**

Quest CONNECTIONS

Think about the XYZ Affair and Adams's response to French attacks on ships. What do these events suggest about dealing with conflicts? Record your ideas in your 📓 Active Journal.

The diplomats informed Adams about the offer. He then told Congress. Adams referred to the agents only as X, Y, and Z.

Many Americans were outraged when news reached them about the XYZ Affair in 1798. (The affair had taken place in 1797, but it took time for news to cross the ocean by ship.) They took up the slogan, "Millions for defense, but not one cent for **tribute**!" They were willing to spend money to defend their country, but they would not pay a bribe to another nation.

The XYZ Affair ignited war fever in the United States. Despite strong pressure, Adams refused to ask Congress to declare war on France. Like Washington, he wanted to keep the country out of European affairs. However, he could not ignore French attacks on American ships, so he strengthened the navy by building frigates, fast-sailing ships with many guns. That move convinced France to stop attacking American ships.

Adams's Foreign Policy Divides the Federalists

Led by Hamilton, many Federalists criticized Adams. They hoped a war would weaken the Democratic Republicans, who supported France. War would also force the nation to build its military forces.

A strong military would increase federal power, a key Federalist goal. Many Federalists also favored Britain in its war against France.

Although Adams was a Federalist, he resisted Hamilton's pressure for war. Their disagreement created a split in the Federalist party.

Analyze Political Cartoons In this cartoon depicting the XYZ Affair, a five-headed monster demands a bribe from three Americans. **Use Evidence** What details in the cartoon reflect the cartoonist's attitude toward the French?

Over Hamilton's opposition, Adams again sent diplomats to France. When they arrived, they found an ambitious young army officer, Napoleon Bonaparte, in charge. Napoleon was planning for war against several European powers. Thus, he had no time for a war with the United States. He signed an agreement to stop seizing American ships.

Like Washington, Adams kept the nation out of war. His actions showed his qualities of leadership and courage. His success, however, cost him the support of many Federalists and weakened the party for the election of 1800.

☑ READING CHECK **Summarize** Why did many Federalists support a war with France?

What Were the Alien and Sedition Acts?

In 1798, during the crisis with France, Federalists pushed several laws through Congress. These laws were known as the Alien and Sedition Acts.

Under the Alien Act, the President could **expel** any alien, or foreigner, thought to be dangerous to the country. Another law made it harder for immigrants to become citizens. Before 1798, white immigrants could become citizens after living in the United States for five years. The new law made immigrants wait 14 years. The Federalists passed this act because many recent immigrants supported Jefferson and the Democratic Republicans. The act would keep these immigrants from voting for years.

The Democratic Republicans grew even angrier when Congress passed the Sedition Act. **Sedition** means stirring up rebellion against a government. Under this law, citizens could be fined or jailed if they criticized the government or its officials. In fact, several Democratic Republican newspaper editors, and even members of Congress, were fined and jailed for expressing their opinions.

Democratic Republicans protested that the Sedition Act violated the Constitution. The First Amendment, they argued, protected freedom of speech and of the press. Jefferson warned that the new laws threatened American liberties:

Primary Source

"They have brought into the lower house a sedition bill, which . . . undertakes to make printing certain matters criminal . . . Indeed this bill & the alien bill both are so [against] the Constitution as to show they mean to pay no respect to it."

—Thomas Jefferson, *The Writings of Thomas Jefferson*, 1798

▲ Representative Albert Gallatin opposed Federalists in their attempts to fund the fighting with France. Some believed that the Alien and Sedition Acts were written to remove Gallatin from power.

 INTERACTIVE

Relations With France

Academic Vocabulary
expel • *v.*, to push or force out

KENTUCKY LEGISLATURE.

In the House of Representatives,
NOVEMBER 10th, 1798.

THE HOUSE according to the standing Order of the Day, resolved itself into a Committee of the Whole on the state of the Commonwealth,

Mr. CALDWELL in the Chair,

And after sometime spent therein the Speaker resumed the Chair, and Mr. Caldwell reported, that the Committee had according to order had under consideration the Governor's Address, and had come to the following Resolutions thereupon, which he delivered in at the Clerk's table, where they were twice read and agreed to by the House.

I. RESOLVED, that the several states composing the United States of America, are not united on the principle of unlimited submission to their General Government; but that by compact under the style and title of a Constitution for the United States and of amendments thereto, they constituted a General Government for special purposes, delegated to that Government certain definite powers, referring each state to itself, the residuary mass of right to their own self Government; and that whensoever the General Government assumes undelegated powers, its acts are unauthoritative, void, and of no force: That to this compact each state acceded as a state, and is an integral party, its co-states forming as to itself, the other party: That the Government created by this compact was not made the exclusive or final *judge* of the extent of the powers delegated to itself; since that would have made its discretion, and not the constitution, the measure of its powers; but that as in all other cases of compact among parties having no common Judge, each party has an equal right to judge for itself, as well of infractions as of the mode and measure of redress.

II. Resolved, that the Constitution of the United States having delegated to Congress a power to punish treason, counterfeiting the securities and current coin of the United States, piracies and felonies committed on the High Seas, and offences against the laws of nations, and no other crimes whatever, and it being true as a general principle, and one of the amendments to the Constitution having also declared, " that the powers not delegated to the United States by the Constitution, nor prohibited by it to the states, are reserved to the states respectively, or to the people," therefore also the same act of Congress passed on the 14th day of July, 1798, and entitled " An act in addition to the act entitled an act for the punishment of certain crimes against the United States;" as also the act passed by them on the 27th day of June, 1798, entitled " An act to punish frauds committed on the Bank of the United States" (and all other their acts which assume to create, define, or punish crimes other than those enumerated in the constitution) are altogether void and of no force, and that the power to create, define, and punish such other crimes is reserved, and of right appertains solely and exclusively to the respective states, each within its own Territory.

III. Resolved, that it is true as a general principle, and is also expressly declared by one of the amendments to the Constitution that " the powers not delegated to the United States by the Constitution, nor prohibited by it to the states, are reserved to the states respectively or to the people;" and that no power over the freedom of religion, freedom of speech, or freedom of the press being delegated to the United States by the Constitution, nor prohibited by it to the states, all lawful powers respecting the same did of right remain, and were reserved to the states, or to the people: That thus was manifested their determination to retain to themselves the right of judging how far the licentiousness of speech and of the press may be abridged without lessening their useful freedom, and how far those abuses which cannot be separated from

Analyze Images
The Kentucky Resolution declared that a state could nullify federal laws it deemed unconstitutional. **Identify Cause and Effect** Why did Jefferson and Madison urge states to pass such resolutions?

Academic Vocabulary
constitute • *v.*, to set up; to establish

States Challenge the Federal Government
Vice President Jefferson bitterly opposed the Alien and Sedition Acts. He could not ask the courts for help because the Federalists controlled them. So, he urged the states to take strong action against the acts. He argued that the states had the right to **nullify**, or cancel, a law passed by the federal government. In this way, states could resist the power of the federal government.

With help from Jefferson and Madison, Kentucky and Virginia passed resolutions in 1798 and 1799. The Kentucky and Virginia resolutions claimed that each state "has an equal right to judge for itself" whether a law is constitutional. If a state decides a law is unconstitutional, said the resolutions, it has the power to nullify that law within its borders. Jefferson wrote:

Primary Source

"Resolved, that the several states composing the United States of America, are not united on the principle of unlimited submission to their General Government; but that by compact under the style and title of a Constitution for the United States and of amendments thereto, they constituted a General Government for special purposes, delegated to that Government certain definite powers, reserving each state to itself, the residuary [remaining] mass of right to their own self Government; and that whensoever the General Government assumes undelegated powers, its acts are unauthoritative, void, and of no force. . . ."

—Thomas Jefferson, November 10, 1798

The Kentucky and Virginia resolutions raised the issue of **states' rights**. Did the federal government have only those powers that were listed in the Constitution? If so, did the states possess all other powers?

For example, could a state declare a federal law unconstitutional? Soon the Alien and Sedition Acts were changed or dropped.

☑ READING CHECK **Identify Main Ideas** What did some states argue after the Alien and Sedition Acts became law?

Why Was the Presidential Election of 1800 Important?

By 1800, the war cry against France was fading. As the election neared, Democratic Republicans focused on two issues. First, they attacked the Federalists for raising taxes to prepare for war. Second, they opposed the unpopular Alien and Sedition Acts.

Democratic Republicans backed Thomas Jefferson for President and Aaron Burr for Vice President. Despite the bitter split in the Federalist party, John Adams was again named its candidate.

Political Power Goes to a Different Party In the race for the presidency, Democratic Republicans won the popular vote. The electoral college was also dominated by Democratic Republicans. When the electoral college voted, Jefferson and Burr each received 73 votes. At the time, the electoral college did not vote separately for President and Vice President. Instead, the college voted for two candidates. The candidate winning the most votes became President, and the runner-up became Vice President. Because each Democratic Republican elector cast one vote for Jefferson and one vote for Burr, there was no clear winner.

Under the Constitution, if no candidate wins the electoral vote, the House of Representatives decides the election. After four days and 36 votes, the tie was broken. The House chose Jefferson as President.

Analyze Graphs Study the data shown. **Draw Conclusions** What explains the controversy over the electoral system that erupted after the 1800 presidential election?

★ THE ELECTION OF 1800 ★

KEY ISSUES	FEDERALIST	DEMOCRATIC REPUBLICAN
Standing army	Supported it	Opposed it
Alien and Sedition Acts	Supported them to limit power of the Democratic Republicans	Opposed them as a threat to individual liberty
Attitude toward government	Believed common people needed guidance	Believed people should govern themselves

THOMAS JEFFERSON
Democratic Republican

AARON BURR
Democratic Republican

ELECTORAL VOTE
70 needed to win

73   64

73   65

CHARLES PINCKNEY
Federalist

JOHN ADAMS
Federalist

The House of Representatives resolved the tie after 6 days and 36 ballots, and Thomas Jefferson became president. The Twelfth Amendment (ratified 1804) gave each Electoral College member one vote for president and one for vice president, reducing the likelihood of ties.

POPULAR VOTE FOR TOP TWO CANDIDATES*

JEFFERSON	41,330 (61.4%)
ADAMS	25,952 (28.6%)

* Only 6 of 15 states held a direct popular vote; most limited the vote to white male property owners. In other states, legislators chose electors.

STATES' ELECTORAL VOTES*

FEDERALIST	Connecticut, Delaware, Massachusetts, New Hampshire, New Jersey, Rhode Island, Vermont
DEMOCRATIC REPUBLICAN	Georgia, Kentucky, New York, South Carolina, Tennessee, Virginia

*Maryland, Pennsylvania, and North Carolina split their votes.

Burr became Vice President. The election of 1800 set an important precedent. From then until today, power has passed peacefully from one party to another.

Soon after, Congress passed the Twelfth Amendment. It required electors to hold separate votes for President and Vice President. The states ratified the amendment in 1804.

The Federalist Era Comes to a Close After 1800, the Federalist party slowly declined. Federalists won fewer seats in Congress. In 1804, the party was greatly weakened after its leader, Alexander Hamilton, was killed in a duel with Aaron Burr. Despite its early decline, the Federalist party did help shape the new nation. Even Democratic Republican Presidents kept most of Hamilton's economic programs.

✅ **READING CHECK** **Identify Supporting Details** Why did the House of Representatives have to decide the 1800 election?

How Did President Jefferson Redefine Government?

When Thomas Jefferson took office as the third President, some Federalists were worried about his political beliefs. They knew that he supported the French Revolution, and they feared that he might bring revolutionary change to the United States. They were also afraid that he might punish Federalists who had used the Alien and Sedition Acts to jail Democratic Republicans.

In his inaugural address, Jefferson tried to calm Federalists' fears. He promised that, although the Democratic Republicans were in the majority, he would not treat the Federalists harshly. "The minority possess their equal rights, which equal laws must protect," he said.

Analyze Images This painting shows Alexander Hamilton, at the right, about to lose his life in a duel with Aaron Burr in 1804. **Infer** What can you infer about the custom of dueling at this time, and why do you think it is an illegal act today?

He called for an end to the political disputes of the past few years. "We are all Republicans, we are all Federalists," the President stated conclusively.

Jefferson had no plan to punish Federalists. He did, however, want to change their policies. In his view, the Federalists had made the national government too large and too powerful.

Promoting a Free Market Economy One way Jefferson wanted to lessen government power was by reducing the federal budget. Such budget cuts would also keep the federal debt low. His Secretary of the Treasury, Albert Gallatin (GAL uh tin), helped him achieve this goal. A financial wizard, Gallatin reduced government spending through careful management.

Jefferson believed in an economic idea known as **laissez faire** (les ay FAYR), a French term for "let do," meaning letting people do as they please. The idea of laissez faire was promoted by the Scottish economist Adam Smith.

In his book *The Wealth of Nations,* Smith argued in favor of a system of free markets, where goods and services are exchanged between buyers and sellers with as little government interference as possible. Free competition, Smith said, would benefit everyone, not just the wealthy.

Laissez-faire economists believed that government should play as small a role as possible in economic affairs. Laissez faire was very different from the Federalist idea of government. Alexander Hamilton, you recall, wanted government to promote trade and manufacturing.

Jefferson Scales Back Government Jefferson believed that the government should protect citizens' rights. Beyond that, he wanted the federal government to take a less active role. He cut the federal budget and decreased the size of government departments.

▲ Adam Smith, in his 1776 book, *The Wealth of Nations*, described details of a free enterprise economy.

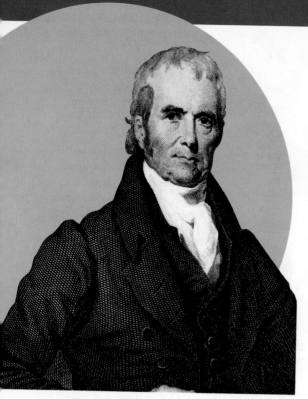

▲ Chief Justice John Marshall, a Federalist, helped to strengthen the U.S. Supreme Court by establishing its power to declare laws unconstitutional.

With the approval of Congress, he reduced the size of the army and navy. He also asked Congress to repeal the unpopular whiskey tax.

The Sedition Act expired the day before Jefferson took office. Jefferson hated the law, and he pardoned those who were in jail because of it. He also asked Congress to restore the law allowing foreign-born white people to become citizens after only a five-year waiting period.

Some Federalist Economic Policies Remain Jefferson did not discard all Federalist programs. On the advice of Albert Gallatin, he kept the Bank of the United States. The federal government also continued to pay off state debts, which it had taken over while Washington was President. In addition, Jefferson let many Federalists keep their government jobs.

☑ READING CHECK **Summarize** How would you define Jefferson's idea of government?

Landmark Supreme Court Cases

The election of 1800 gave Democratic Republicans control of Congress. Federalists, however, remained powerful in the courts.

Several months passed between Jefferson's election and his inauguration. In that time, Federalists in the old Congress passed the Judiciary Act of 1801, increasing the number of federal judges. President Adams then appointed Federalists to fill these new judicial positions. When Jefferson took office, Jeffersonians repealed this part of the act, firing 16 Federalist judges.

One of the judges that Adams appointed was John Marshall, the Chief Justice of the United States. Like Jefferson, Marshall was a rich Virginia planter with a brilliant mind. Unlike Jefferson, however, Marshall was a staunch Federalist. He wanted to make the federal government stronger.

The framers of the Constitution expected the courts to balance the powers of the President and Congress. However, John Marshall found the courts to be much weaker than the other branches of government. In his view, it was not clear what powers the federal courts had.

The Issues Behind *Marbury* v. *Madison*

In 1803, John Marshall showed courage and leadership by deciding a case that increased the power of the Supreme Court. The case involved William Marbury, one of the judges appointed by Adams. Adams made the appointment on his last night as President. The Republicans refused to accept this "midnight judge." They accused Federalists of using unfair tactics to keep control of the courts. Jefferson ordered Secretary of State James Madison not to deliver the official papers confirming Marbury's appointment.

👆 **INTERACTIVE**

Jefferson's Goals and Policies

Marbury sued Madison. According to the Judiciary Act of 1789, only the Supreme Court could decide a case that was brought against a federal official. Therefore, the case of *Marbury* v. *Madison* was tried before the Supreme Court.

The Significance of the *Marbury* v. *Madison* Decision The Supreme Court ruled against Marbury. Chief Justice Marshall wrote the decision, stating that the Judiciary Act was unconstitutional. The Constitution, Marshall argued, did not give the Supreme Court the right to decide cases brought against federal officials. Therefore, Congress could not give the Court that power simply by passing the Judiciary Act.

As a result of *Marbury* v. *Madison*, Congress had to amend, or change, the Judiciary Act to respond to the Supreme Court's objections. The part of the Judiciary Act of 1789 that the Supreme Court rejected could no longer be law.

The Supreme Court's decision in *Marbury* v. *Madison* set an important precedent. It gave the Supreme Court the power to decide whether laws passed by Congress were constitutional and to reject laws that it considered to be unconstitutional. This power of the Court is called **judicial review**.

The Reactions of Jefferson and Congress Jefferson was displeased with the decision. True, Marshall had ruled against Marbury, the Federalist judge.

But Marshall's decision gave more power to the Supreme Court, where Federalists were still strong. Jefferson also argued that the decision upset the balance of power among the three branches of government.

Primary Source

"The opinion which gives to the judges the right to decide what laws are constitutional and what not, not only for themselves . . . but for the Legislature and Executive also . . . would make the Judiciary a [tyrannical] branch."

—Thomas Jefferson, letter to Abigail Adams, 1804

Analyze Images These bronze doors lead into the Supreme Court chambers. The carved panels show important moments in legal history—including John Marshall discussing *Marbury* v. *Madison*. **Draw Conclusions** In what way do you think these bronze doors could be a symbol of rule of law in the United States?

▲ This is the original Supreme Court chambers where Supreme Court cases were heard between 1810 and 1860.

Jefferson did not want the judiciary to gain power over the executive branch. He refused the Court's order to testify at an important trial, saying it would upset the equality of the branches. He also used executive privilege to decide which government papers to show the Court and which to withhold.

In 1810, a year after Jefferson left office, Marshall's Supreme Court decided another landmark case involving judicial review. In *Fletcher* v. *Peck*, the Court ruled that the state of Georgia could not revoke a corrupt land sale. It was the first time the Court ruled a state law unconstitutional. By doing so, the Court also reinforced the idea that contracts cannot be broken.

In the end, the President and Congress accepted the right of the Court to overturn laws. Today, judicial review remains one of the most important powers of the Supreme Court.

✓ READING CHECK **Identify Main Ideas** Why is the Supreme Court case *Marbury* v. *Madison* significant?

✓ Lesson Check

Practice Vocabulary

1. What is a **laissez-faire** economy?

2. How did **judicial review** increase the power of the Supreme Court?

Critical Thinking and Writing

3. **Understand Effects** How did the Federalists contribute to shaping the United States as we know it today?

4. **Identify Cause and Effect** What was the important change in the Constitution that was prompted by the results of the election of 1800?

5. **Summarize** What were President Jefferson's economic policies?

6. **Writing Workshop: Pick an Organizing Strategy** Decide on an effective method of organizing the information you have gathered. Note this strategy in your 📕 Active Journal.

Detect Historical Points of View

Follow these steps to detect historical points of view.

INTERACTIVE

Compare Viewpoints

1 Identify the context. If you know the history of the period when a document was written, you can better understand the writer's point of view.

   a. Why was this letter written?

   b. How did the Bill of Rights settle the issue of an American national church?

2 Identify the author's main idea. Ask yourself what main point the author is making. What is the main idea of Jefferson's letter?

3 Look for key words and phrases. The writer may use words or phrases that strongly indicate the point of view being expressed. What is an example of a key word or phrase that sums up Jefferson's point of view?

4 Identify the author's point of view. Ask how the writer feels about the subject. How does Jefferson feel about establishing a national day of fasting and thanksgiving?

5 Relate the point of view to the context. Ask how the point of view was affected by historical context.

   a. Jefferson's presidency began in 1801. What actions did he take that give clues to his point of view about the government's role?

   b. How was Jefferson's point of view influenced by the events of the time?

Primary Source

The Danbury Baptist Association wrote to President Jefferson, asking why he would not establish national days of fasting and thanksgiving, as previous presidents had done. Jefferson answered the letter in 1802. His carefully worded reply reflects his opinion about the separation of government and religion in the new nation.

"Believing with you that religion is a matter which lies solely between man & his god, that he owes account to none other for his faith or his worship, that the legitimate powers of government reach actions only, and not opinions, I contemplate with sovereign reverence that act of the whole American people which declared that their legislature should make no law respecting an establishment of religion, or prohibiting the free exercise thereof, thus building a wall of separation between church and state."

— Thomas Jefferson, Jan. 1, 1802

LESSON 4

A Changing Nation

BOUNCE TO ACTIVATE · VIDEO

GET READY TO READ

START UP

Study the illustration of the Lewis and Clark expedition. Predict the significance of the expedition to the country in your 📄 Active Journal.

GUIDING QUESTIONS

- What was the reason for the Louisiana Purchase, and what were the results of it?
- Was the Louisiana Purchase constitutional?
- How did major western rivers play a role in the discoveries made by Lewis and Clark and Pike?

TAKE NOTES

Literacy Skills: Analyze Text Structure
Use the graphic organizer in your 📄 Active Journal to take notes as you read the lesson.

PRACTICE VOCABULARY

Use the vocabulary activity in your 📄 Active Journal to practice the vocabulary words.

Vocabulary	Academic Vocabulary
expedition	vital
continental divide	exceed
impressment	
embargo	
smuggling	

The United States overcame a number of challenges in its early years, including creating a stable economic system, setting up the courts, and defining the authority of the central government. As the economy continued to grow, Americans needed to protect their economic interests. The Louisiana Territory became a key part of this effort to expand the physical reach of the nation.

The Louisiana Purchase

The town of New Orleans was founded by the French. It lies at the mouth of the Mississippi River, where it empties into the Gulf of Mexico. By the early 1800s, it was the largest port in the South. President Jefferson feared that France would limit American access to New Orleans and the Mississippi River. To gain control of this important area, he decided to purchase it from the French.

Geography Shapes Domestic and Foreign Policy By 1800, almost one million Americans lived between the Appalachian Mountains and the Mississippi River. Most were farmers.

With few roads west of the Appalachians, western farmers relied on the Mississippi River to ship their wheat and corn. First, they sent their produce down the river to the city of New Orleans. From there, oceangoing ships carried the produce across the Gulf of Mexico, around Florida, and up to ports along the Atlantic coast.

Spain, which controlled New Orleans, sometimes threatened to close the port to Americans. In 1795, President Washington sent Thomas Pinckney to find a way to keep the **vital** port open. In the Pinckney Treaty Spain agreed to let Americans ship their goods down the Mississippi and store them in New Orleans.

For a time, Americans shipped their goods through New Orleans peacefully. In 1800, however, Spain signed a new treaty giving Louisiana back to the French. President Jefferson was alarmed. He knew that the French ruler, Napoleon Bonaparte, had already set out to conquer Europe. Would he now try to build an empire in North America?

Jefferson had reason to worry. Napoleon wanted to grow food in Louisiana and ship it to French islands in the West Indies. However, events in Haiti, a French colony in the Caribbean, soon ruined Napoleon's plan. Inspired by the French Revolution, which in turn had been inspired by the American Revolution, enslaved Africans in Haiti decided to fight for their liberty. Toussaint L'Ouverture (too SAN loo vehr TYOOR) led the revolt. By 1801, Toussaint and his followers had nearly forced the French out of Haiti.

Napoleon sent troops to retake Haiti. Although the French captured Toussaint, they did not regain control of the island. In 1804, Haitians declared their independence.

Negotiations for Louisiana Jefferson sent Robert Livingston and James Monroe to buy New Orleans and West Florida from Napoleon. Jefferson said they could offer as much as $10 million. Livingston and Monroe negotiated with Charles Maurice de Talleyrand, the French foreign minister. At first, Talleyrand showed little interest in their offer. However, losing Haiti caused Napoleon to give up his plan for an empire in the Americas. He also needed money to pay for his costly wars in Europe. Suddenly, Talleyrand asked Livingston if the United States wanted to buy all of Louisiana, not just New Orleans.

The question surprised Livingston. He offered $4 million. "Too low," replied Talleyrand. "Reflect and see me tomorrow."

Livingston and Monroe carefully debated the matter. They had no authority to buy all of Louisiana or to **exceed** $10 million. However, they knew that Jefferson wanted control of the Mississippi.

They agreed to pay the French $15 million for Louisiana. "This is the noblest work of our whole lives," declared Livingston when he signed the treaty. "From this day the United States take their place among the powers of the first rank."

Academic Vocabulary

vital • *adj.*, extremely important

exceed • *v.*, to go above and beyond

▼ Toussaint L'Ouverture led a revolt by enslaved Africans to win independence from France for Haiti.

UNDER MY WINGS EVERY THING PROSPERS

Analyze Images This painting of New Orleans was made to celebrate the Louisiana Purchase in 1803. Read the banner. **Identify Supporting Details** Why do you think the city of New Orleans was hopeful it would prosper under the U.S. government?

Does the President Have the Power to Buy Land? Jefferson hailed the news from France. Still, he was not sure whether the President of the United States had the power to purchase Louisiana. He had always insisted that the federal government had only those powers spelled out in the Constitution. The document said nothing about a President having the power to buy land. Jefferson wrote:

Primary Source

"The General Government has no powers but such as the Constitution has given it; and it has not given it a power of holding foreign territory, & still less of incorporating it into the Union. An amendment of the Constitution seems necessary for this."

—Thomas Jefferson to John Dickinson, August 9, 1803

In the end, Jefferson decided that he did have the authority to buy Louisiana. The Constitution, he reasoned, allowed the President to make treaties, and buying the Louisiana territory was part of a treaty. Federalists opposed the purchase as unconstitutional and feared it would weaken the other states. But the Democratic Republicans supported it, and the Senate approved the treaty. The Louisiana Purchase went into effect. In 1803, the United States took control of the vast lands west of the Mississippi. With one stroke, the size of the nation had almost doubled.

> **Quick Activity**
>
> Explore the importance of the western rivers in your 📓 *Active Journal*.

✅ **READING CHECK** **Identify Cause and Effect** Why did Jefferson want to gain control of New Orleans?

How Did Americans Explore These New Lands?

Few Americans knew anything about the Louisiana territory. In 1803, Congress provided money for a team of explorers to study the new lands. Jefferson chose Meriwether Lewis, his private secretary, to head the **expedition**, or long voyage of exploration. Lewis asked William Clark to go with him. Jefferson asked Lewis and Clark to map a route to the Pacific Ocean. He also told them to study the geography of the territory, including the rivers:

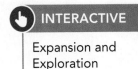

INTERACTIVE

Expansion and Exploration

Primary Source

"The object of your mission is to explore the Missouri river, & such principal stream of it as by [its] course and communication with the waters of the Pacific ocean whether the Columbia, Oregon, Colorado or any other river may offer the most direct & practicable water communication across this continent for the purposes of commerce."

—Thomas Jefferson, letter to Meriwether Lewis, 1803

Jefferson also instructed Lewis and Clark to learn about the American Indian nations who lived in the Louisiana Purchase. These American Indians carried on a busy trade with English, French, and Spanish merchants. Jefferson hoped that the Indians might trade with American merchants instead. He urged Lewis and Clark to tell the Indians of "our wish to be neighborly, friendly, and useful to them."

GEOGRAPHY SKILLS

For $15 million, Jefferson added the Louisiana Purchase to land owned by the United States.

1. **Location** What foreign territories bordered the Louisiana Purchase?

2. **Synthesize Visual Information** How did the Louisiana Purchase change the territory of the United States?

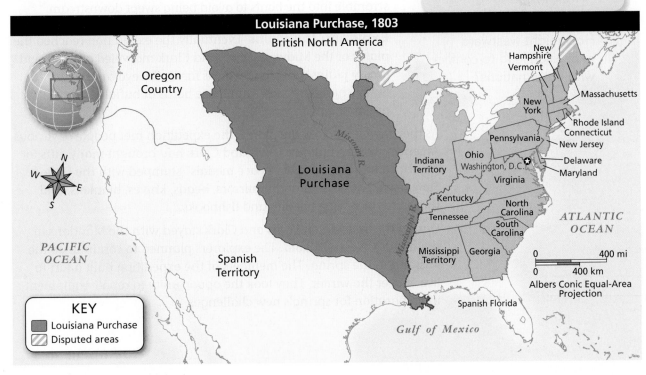

Louisiana Purchase, 1803

British North America

New Hampshire
Vermont

Oregon Country

Massachusetts

New York

Rhode Island
Connecticut
New Jersey

Pennsylvania

Missouri R.

Indiana Territory

Ohio

Washington, D.C.

Delaware
Maryland

Louisiana Purchase

Virginia

Kentucky

Tennessee

North Carolina

South Carolina

ATLANTIC OCEAN

PACIFIC OCEAN

Spanish Territory

Mississippi Territory

Georgia

Mississippi R.

0   400 mi
0   400 km

Albers Conic Equal-Area Projection

Spanish Florida

Gulf of Mexico

KEY
Louisiana Purchase
Disputed areas

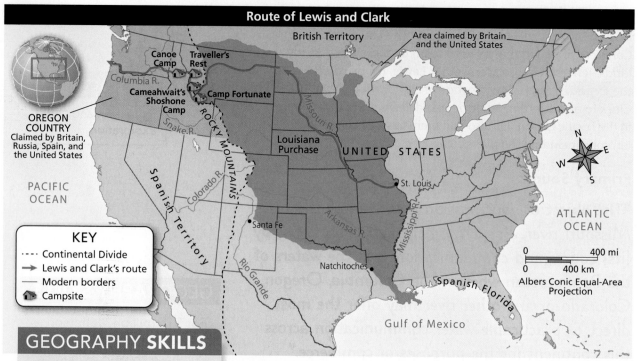

Route of Lewis and Clark

British Territory

Area claimed by Britain and the United States

Canoe Camp

Traveller's Rest

Columbia R.

Cameahwait's Shoshone Camp

Camp Fortunate

Missouri R.

OREGON COUNTRY
Claimed by Britain, Russia, Spain, and the United States

Snake R.

ROCKY MOUNTAINS

Louisiana Purchase

UNITED STATES

PACIFIC OCEAN

Colorado R.

Spanish Territory

St. Louis

Santa Fe

ATLANTIC OCEAN

KEY
- - - - Continental Divide
→ Lewis and Clark's route
— Modern borders
🏠 Campsite

Arkansas R.

Mississippi R.

Rio Grande

Natchitoches

Spanish Florida

Gulf of Mexico

0   400 mi
0   400 km
Albers Conic Equal-Area Projection

GEOGRAPHY SKILLS

The Lewis and Clark expedition helped Americans learn more about western lands.

1. **Interaction** What natural feature did Lewis and Clark use to help them travel through the Louisiana Purchase and Oregon Country?

2. **Draw Conclusions** How might westward expansion lead to conflict with other nations?

The Expedition Begins Dozens of adventurous young men eagerly competed to join the expedition. Lewis and Clark judged volunteers on the basis of their character, strength, hunting skills, and ability to survive in the wilderness. In the end, about 50 men made up the "Corps of Discovery."

In May 1804, Lewis and Clark started up the Missouri River from St. Louis. At first, the expedition's boats made slow progress against the Missouri's swift current. One night, the current tore away the riverbank where they were camping. The party had to scramble into the boats to avoid being swept downstream.

Exploring the Plains Eventually the expedition reached the plains of the Midwest. Lewis and Clark marveled at the broad, grassy plains that stretched "as far as the eye can reach." Everywhere, they saw "immense herds of buffalo, deer, elk, and antelope."

As they traveled across the plains, the expedition met people of various American Indian nations. Lewis and Clark had brought many gifts for American Indians, such as "peace medals" stamped with the United States seal. They also brought mirrors, beads, knives, blankets, and thousands of sewing needles and fishhooks.

During the first winter, Lewis and Clark stayed with the Mandans in present-day North Dakota. The explorers planned to continue up the Missouri in the spring. The members of the expedition built a fort to live in over the winter. They took the opportunity to repair equipment in preparation for spring's new challenges.

The Mandans lived along the upper Missouri River. They grew corn, beans, and squash, and hunted buffalo. During the winter, they helped the explorers find food and hunt buffalo. They also traded with the expedition members.

Staying with the Mandans was a woman named Sacajawea (sak uh juh WEE uh). Sacajawea belonged to the Shoshone (shoh SHOH nee) people, who lived in the Rockies. She and her French Canadian husband agreed to accompany Lewis and Clark as translators. Sacajawea carried her baby with her on the journey.

Crossing the Rocky Mountains In early spring, the party set out again. In the foothills of the Rockies, the landscape and wildlife changed. Bighorn sheep ran along the high hills. The thorns of prickly pear cactus jabbed the explorers' moccasins. Once, a grizzly bear chased Lewis while he was exploring alone.

Crossing the Rocky Mountains meant crossing the Continental Divide. A **continental divide** is a ridge that separates river systems flowing toward opposite sides of a continent. In North America, some rivers flow east from the crest of the Rockies into the Mississippi, which drains into the Gulf of Mexico. Other rivers flow west from the Rockies and empty into the Pacific Ocean.

Past the Rockies, Lewis and Clark would be able to travel by river toward the Pacific. But to cross the Continental Divide, they needed horses. They began looking for the Shoshone, who had been using horses since Europeans had brought them to the Americas.

Finally, Lewis and Clark met some Shoshones. One of them was Sacajawea's brother, whom she had not seen for many years. Upon seeing her own people, wrote Clark, she began to "dance and show every mark of the most extravagant joy." The Shoshones supplied the expedition with the food and horses Lewis and Clark needed. They also advised the explorers about the best route to take over the Rockies.

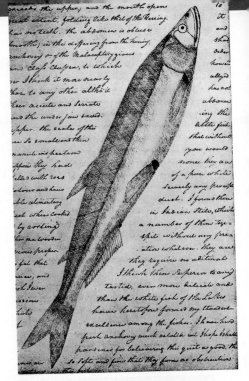

▲ On his expedition, William Clark encountered new people, animals, and land features. He drew this illustration of a trout.

5 BIOGRAPHY Things to Know About

SACAJAWEA
Shoshone Guide (1786?–1812)

- She was a teenager when she guided Lewis and Clark.
- Finding edible plants, Sacajawea helped feed the members of the expedition.
- Through quick action, she saved valuable supplies from floating downstream when a boat capsized.
- After the expedition, she moved to St. Louis, but then returned to live in the West.
- Her children were adopted by William Clark when she died.

Critical Thinking What words describe the help Sacajawea gave to the Lewis and Clark expedition?

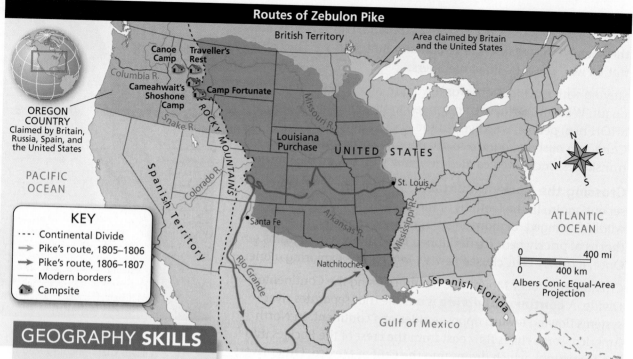

Routes of Zebulon Pike

British Territory

Area claimed by Britain and the United States

Canoe Camp

Traveller's Rest

Columbia R.

Cameahwait's Shoshone Camp

Camp Fortunate

OREGON COUNTRY
Claimed by Britain, Russia, Spain, and the United States

Snake R.

ROCKY MOUNTAINS

Missouri R.

Louisiana Purchase

UNITED STATES

St. Louis

PACIFIC OCEAN

Colorado R.

Spanish Territory

Santa Fe

Arkansas R.

Mississippi R.

ATLANTIC OCEAN

KEY
- - - - Continental Divide
➡ Pike's route, 1805–1806
➡ Pike's route, 1806–1807
— Modern borders
🏚 Campsite

Rio Grande

Natchitoches

Spanish Florida

0   400 mi
0   400 km
Albers Conic Equal-Area Projection

Gulf of Mexico

GEOGRAPHY SKILLS

Lewis and Clark's expedition took them into the northwest, where they established campsites. Zebulon Pike also explored the Louisiana Purchase, as well as Spanish territory.

1. **Interaction** What prominent geographic feature may have influenced Pike's route?

2. **Summarize** Summarize Pike's expeditions.

Reaching the Pacific After building canoes, Lewis and Clark's party floated toward the Columbia River into the Pacific Northwest. Finally, on November 7, 1805, Clark wrote in his journal, "Great joy in camp. We are in view of the ocean, this great Pacific Ocean which we have been so long anxious to see." Lewis and Clark had reached their goal. Viewing the Pacific from present-day Oregon, Lewis and Clark claimed the region for the United States by right of discovery.

The return trip to St. Louis took another year. In 1806, Americans celebrated the return of Lewis and Clark. The explorers brought back much useful information about the land and major rivers now part of the United States. The Mississippi, Missouri, Columbia, and Rio Grande rivers would provide settlers routes and a great natural resource as they moved west in later years.

Pike's Expedition Before Lewis and Clark returned, Jefferson sent another explorer, Zebulon Pike, to explore the southwestern part of the Louisiana Purchase. Pike set out from St. Louis. From 1805 to 1807, he explored the upper Mississippi River, the Arkansas River, and parts of present-day Colorado and New Mexico. In November 1806, Pike viewed a mountain peak rising above the Colorado plains. Today, this mountain is known as Pikes Peak.

Continuing southward, Pike entered Spanish territory. Spanish troops soon arrested Pike and his men and took them into present-day Mexico. The Americans were later escorted through Texas back into the United States. The Spanish took Pike's maps and journals, but he was able to hide one map in the barrel of his gun. His report on the expedition greatly expanded Americans' knowledge about the Southwest.

The journeys of Pike and Lewis and Clark excited Americans. However, settlers did not move into the rugged western lands for a number of years. As you will read, they first settled the region closest to the Mississippi River. Soon, the territory around New Orleans had a large enough population of American citizens for the settlers to apply for statehood. In 1812, this territory entered the Union as the state of Louisiana.

✓ **READING CHECK** **Identify Supporting Details** Why did President Jefferson want Lewis and Clark to treat American Indians fairly on their journey?

Challenges to American Shipping

After the Revolution, American overseas trade grew rapidly. Ships sailed from New England on voyages that sometimes lasted three years. President Jefferson's foreign policy during this time centered around protecting American shipping.

An Era of Trade Wherever they went, Yankee captains kept a sharp lookout for new goods and new markets. Clever traders sawed winter ice from New England ponds into blocks, packed it in sawdust, and carried it to India. There, they traded the ice for silk and spices. In 1784, the *Empress of China* became the first American ship to trade with China. New England merchants quickly built up a profitable China trade.

More than ten years before Lewis and Clark, Yankee merchants sailed up the Pacific coast of North America. So many traders from Boston visited the Pacific Northwest that American Indians there called every white man "Boston." Traders bought furs from American Indians and sold them for large profits in China.

Analyze Images
American trading ships in the late 1700s and early 1800s began trading with China. One route took them around the tip of South America. Another took them around Africa. **Synthesize Visual Information** What details in the picture indicate that China traded with more than one country?

Jefferson Protects U.S. Ships Traders ran great risks, especially in the Mediterranean Sea. Pirates from the Barbary States, countries along the coast of North Africa, attacked passing vessels. To protect American ships, the United States paid a yearly tribute to rulers of the Barbary States such as Tripoli.

In 1801, Tripoli increased its demands for tribute. When Jefferson refused to pay, Tripoli declared war on the United States. Jefferson then ordered the navy to blockade the port of Tripoli, a city in northern Africa.

During the blockade, the American ship *Philadelphia* ran aground near Tripoli. Pirates boarded the ship and hauled the crew off to prison. The pirates planned to use the *Philadelphia* to attack other ships.

To prevent this, American naval officer Stephen Decatur and his crew quietly sailed into Tripoli harbor by night. They then set the captured American ship on fire.

In the meantime, American marines landed on the coast of North Africa, marched 500 miles, and, with the help of allies, successfully captured, the port of Derna. However, during the fight, the ruler of Tripoli signed a treaty promising not to interfere with American ships.

Analyze Images This illustration shows American sailors being impressed, or taken by force, into the British navy. **Use Evidence** How do you think American sailors who were impressed on British ships were treated?

Caught Between France and Britain American ships faced another problem. Britain and France went to war again in 1803. At first, Americans profited from the conflict. British and French ships were too busy fighting to engage in trade. American merchants eagerly traded with both sides. As profits increased, Americans hurried to build new ships.

Neither Britain nor France wanted the United States to sell supplies to its enemy. As in the 1790s, they ignored American claims of neutrality. Napoleon seized American ships bound for England. At the same time, the British stopped Yankee traders on their way to France. Between 1805 and 1807, hundreds of American ships were captured.

Needing more sailors, the British navy stepped up **impressment**, the practice of forcing people into service. In Britain, impressment gangs raided English villages and took young men to serve in the navy. On the seas, British ships stopped American vessels, seizing any British sailors serving on American ships. Many American-born sailors were also impressed. Furious Americans clamored for war.

☑ **READING CHECK** **Identify Cause and Effect** Why were Britain and France seizing American ships?

A Ban on Trade

Jefferson knew that the small American fleet was no match for the powerful British navy. Like Washington and Adams, he sought a foreign policy that would avoid war.

An Embargo on Foreign Trade Jefferson hoped that an American **embargo**, or ban on trade, would hurt France and Britain by cutting off needed supplies. "Our trade is the most powerful weapon we can use in our defense," one Democratic-Republican newspaper wrote. In 1807, Jefferson persuaded Congress to impose a total embargo on foreign trade. This meant that American traders could not receive goods from European traders, and American traders could not ship their goods to Europe.

The Embargo Act did hurt Britain and France. But it hurt Americans even more. Supplies of imports such as sugar, tea, and molasses were cut off. Exports dropped by more than $80 million in one year. Docks in the South were piled high with cotton and tobacco. The Embargo Act hurt New England merchants most of all.

Merchants protested loudly against the embargo. Some turned to **smuggling**, importing or exporting goods in violation of trade laws. Jefferson began using the navy and federal troops to enforce the embargo. On the border between New York and Canada, some smugglers engaged in skirmishes with federal troops.

The two political parties had different points of view on the embargo. Democratic Republicans mostly supported the embargo as a way to protect the country and punish France and Britain. Most Federalists opposed the embargo as damaging to the economy.

Quest CONNECTIONS

Think about the pros and cons of Jefferson's decision to place an embargo on French and British goods. Then write in your 📓 Active Journal whether his actions could start a war.

Analyze Graphs Study the data in the chart. **Identify Cause and Effect** Which data explain why Congress canceled Jefferson's Embargo Act in 1809?

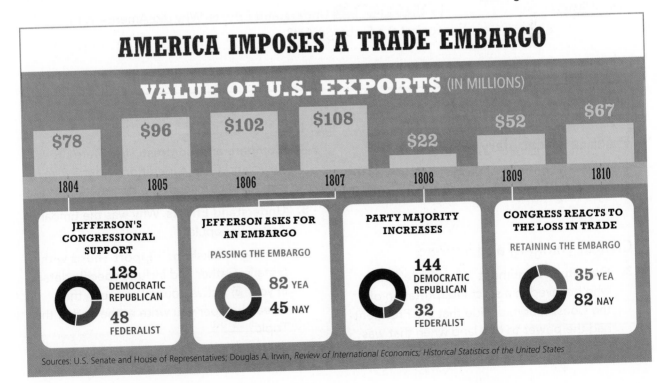

AMERICA IMPOSES A TRADE EMBARGO

VALUE OF U.S. EXPORTS (IN MILLIONS)

Year	Value
1804	$78
1805	$96
1806	$102
1807	$108
1808	$22
1809	$52
1810	$67

JEFFERSON'S CONGRESSIONAL SUPPORT
128 DEMOCRATIC REPUBLICAN
48 FEDERALIST

JEFFERSON ASKS FOR AN EMBARGO
PASSING THE EMBARGO
82 YEA
45 NAY

PARTY MAJORITY INCREASES
144 DEMOCRATIC REPUBLICAN
32 FEDERALIST

CONGRESS REACTS TO THE LOSS IN TRADE
RETAINING THE EMBARGO
35 YEA
82 NAY

Sources: U.S. Senate and House of Representatives; Douglas A. Irwin, *Review of International Economics; Historical Statistics of the United States*

Analyze Images Trade with China introduced Americans to fine porcelain, silks, and silver made by Chinese craftspeople for the Western market. **Draw Conclusions** What effect do you think the China trade had on people living in the United States?

Congress Replaces the Embargo In 1809, Jefferson admitted that the Embargo Act had failed. Congress replaced it with the milder Nonintercourse Act. It allowed Americans to carry on trade with all nations except Britain and France. The Embargo Act had decreased support for the Democratic Republican party, as Americans hurt by the policy turned to the Federalists instead. Federalists favored maintaining closer relations with Britain.

They wanted to build ties with Britain because Britain was the main trading partner of the United States, and the powerful British navy could protect American merchants.

Although the embargo was the most unpopular measure of Jefferson's presidency, the Democratic Republicans still remained strong. Following President Washington's precedent, Jefferson refused to run for a third term. Democratic Republican James Madison easily won the 1808 presidential election. Madison hoped that Britain and France would soon agree to respect American neutrality.

☑ **READING CHECK Understand Effects** Why did Americans turn against the Embargo Act?

☑ Lesson Check

Practice Vocabulary

1. How is a **continental divide** related to rivers?

2. Why did **impressment** make Americans angry?

Critical Thinking and Writing

3. **Explain an Argument** Why did Jefferson, who believed in a strict interpretation of the Constitution, decide that the President had the power to buy land when that was not mentioned in the Constitution?

4. **Compare and Contrast** How were the Lewis and Clark expedition and the Pike expedition similar and different?

5. **Understand Effects** Why was the Embargo Act so unpopular?

6. **Writing Workshop: Support Thesis with Details** Gather and include specific details in your ▤ Active Journal to use in the research paper you write at the end of this Topic.

William Clark and Meriwether Lewis, Journals

As Lewis and Clark traveled through the American West on their expedition, each took notes about what they observed and explored.

▶ William Clark drew this bird and many other animals and plants in the expedition diary.

William Clark, August the 1st 1804

a fair morning Despatched [Dispatched] two men after the horses lost yesterday, . . . The Prarie [prairie] which is Situated below our Camp is above the ① high water leavel [level] and rich Covered with Grass from 5 to 8 feet high intersperced [interspersed] with Copse of Hazel, Plumbs, Currents [currants] (like those of the U.S.) Rasberries [raspberries] & Grapes of Dift.[different] Kinds. also produceing [producing] a Variety of Plants and flowers not Common in the United States ②

Meriwether Lewis, May 1st 1806

the courses and distances of this day are ③ N. 45 E. 9 M. and N. 75 E. 17 M. along the Northern side of this creek to our encampment. some time after we had encamped three young men arrived from the ④ Wallahwollah village bringing with them a steel trap belonging to one of our party which had been negligently left behind; . . . during our stay with them they several times found the knives of the men which had been carelessly lossed [lost] by them and returned them. ⑤ I think we can justly affirm to the honor of these people that they are the most hospitable, honest, and sincere people that we have met with in our voyage.

Analyzing Primary Sources

Cite specific evidence from the documents to support your answers.

1. **Cite Evidence** Recall what Jefferson asked Lewis and Clark to do regarding the American Indians they met. Did they fulfill that request? Support your answer.

2. **Analyze Style and Rhetoric** What words does Lewis use to describe the behavior of the members of the expedition?

Reading and Vocabulary Support

① What does "high water level" tell you about where Lewis and Clark are traveling?

② How might the information in Clark's journal interest possible settlers?

③ Lewis is giving the geographic coordinates that tell where they are and how far they have traveled.

④ The Wallahwollahs were an American Indian group.

⑤ What is Lewis complimenting the Wallahwollahs for?

LESSON 5

Madison and the War of 1812

BOUNCE TO ACTIVATE ▶ VIDEO

GET READY TO READ

START UP

Study the illustration of the British burning Washington, D.C., during the War of 1812. Scan the lesson images and captions, then write in your 📓 Active Journal a reason why the United States went to war.

GUIDING QUESTIONS

- Why was there conflict between white settlers and American Indians during the early 1800s?
- What were the causes of the War of 1812?
- What were the key events and consequences of the War of 1812?

TAKE NOTES

Literacy Skills: Sequence

Use the graphic organizer in your 📓 Active Journal to take notes as you read the lesson.

PRACTICE VOCABULARY

Use the vocabulary activity in your 📓 Active Journal to practice the vocabulary words.

Vocabulary

confederation

War Hawks

nationalism

Academic Vocabulary

decisive

commence

About 900,000 white settlers moved west of the Appalachians between 1790 and 1810. Some American Indian groups resented these newcomers, who built farms on their lands and hunted the animals they needed for food. The settlers ignored treaties that the United States had signed with American Indian nations of the region.

What Caused Conflict in Ohio?

Fighting often broke out between these American Indian groups and the settlers. Isolated acts of violence led to larger acts of revenge. As both sides killed innocent people, warfare spread. In Ohio, Little Turtle of the Miamis and Blue Jacket of the Shawnees organized a resistance movement in 1791. Armed with British muskets and gunpowder, the Miamis and Shawnees drove white settlers from the area.

President Washington had sent General Anthony Wayne into Ohio in 1794. Forces from the Delaware, Miami, Iroquois, Wabash, and others gathered at a place called Fallen Timbers.

They thought that Wayne would have trouble fighting there because fallen trees covered the land. But Wayne's well-trained army pushed through the tangle of logs and defeated the American Indians.

Treaties Are Made In 1795, leaders of the Miami and other American Indian nations signed the Treaty of Greenville. They gave up land that would later become part of Ohio. In return, they received $20,000 and the promise of more money if they kept the peace.

The Treaty of Greenville was one of more than 300 treaties made between the U.S. government and American Indians during the early republic. Often, a series of treaties were made between an American Indian nation and the U.S. government. In return for American Indian acceptance of the treaty's terms, the government gave American Indian nations a sum of money and, in some instances, equipment. For example, in the Treaty of Fort Wilkinson, the United States gave the Creek nation $3,000 at the signing, and $1,000 every year for 10 years, "$10,000 in goods and merchandise," and "two sets of blacksmiths tools and men to work them, for the term of three years."

Tecumseh's Confederation Confronts the New Republic Ohio joined the Union in 1803. By then, white settlers were pushing beyond Ohio into the Indiana Territory. Angry Shawnees, Kickapoos, and Ottawas vowed to keep settlers from taking more American Indian land. They included two Shawnee leaders: Tecumseh and his brother Tenskwatawa (ten SKWAH tuh wuh), a religious leader also called the Prophet. The Kickapoo, Ottawa, Chippewa, and Piankashaw joined with the Shawnee leaders. The Miami initially remained neutral.

The Wyandot, Seneca, and Delaware stayed allied with the United States. So did the Choctaw, Cherokee, Chickasaw, and some groups of Creek.

The U.S. government had treaties with several of these American Indian groups that said both sides would cease fighting. The treaties kept these groups from rallying together against the United States.

A New Settlement in Indiana Territory The Prophet and Tecumseh taught that white customs corrupted the American Indian way of life. They said that many American Indians depended too much on white trade goods.

GEOGRAPHY SKILLS

American Indians lost their lands through "sales," treaties, and force.

1. **Movement** In which direction were American Indians pushed because of the loss of their land?

2. **Infer** Why do you think American Indians gave up these lands?

American Indian Lands

KEY
- Land lost before 1750
- Land lost 1750–1784
- Land lost 1784–1810
- Present-day borders

These included muskets, cloth, cooking pots, and whiskey. They believed that by returning to their old ways, American Indians could gain the power to resist the white invaders.

In 1808, the Prophet built a village for his followers along Tippecanoe Creek in Indiana Territory. American Indians from lands as far away as present-day Missouri, Iowa, and Minnesota traveled to Prophetstown to hear his message.

Tecumseh worked to organize the groups of the Northwest into a **confederation**, or alliance with a shared military command. He called for unity against settlers:

Primary Source

"The whites have driven us from the great salt water, forced us over the mountains. . . . The way, the only way, to check and stop this evil is for all red men to unite in claiming a common equal right in the land."

—Tecumseh, quoted in *Tecumseh: Vision of Glory* (Tucker)

Tecumseh impressed white leaders. Governor William Henry Harrison grudgingly admitted, "He is one of those uncommon geniuses which spring up occasionally to produce revolutions and overturn the established order of things."

A Major Battle at Tippecanoe Rivalries among American Indian nations kept Tecumseh from uniting all Indians east of the Mississippi River. Still, white settlers were alarmed at his success.

BIOGRAPHY
5 Things to Know About

TECUMSEH
Shawnee Leader and Orator (1768–1813)

- He led American Indian resistance to white settlement in the Ohio River Valley.

- At age 14, he fought with the British against colonists in the American Revolution.

- By supporting a confederation of American Indian groups, he strengthened their forces to fight the U.S. military.

- His outstanding speaking skills were admired by American Indians and whites.

- He spoke out against cruelty on both sides of conflicts between American Indians and the U.S. government.

Critical Thinking Of people living today or in the recent past, who could you say has leadership skills similar to those of Tecumseh? Explain your reasoning.

Analyze Images Both sides suffered heavy losses, but General Henry Harrison's troops were able to destroy Prophetstown during the Battle of Tippecanoe in 1811. **Summarize** How does the image confirm or refute that there were heavy losses on both sides in this battle?

In 1811, Harrison marched 1,000 soldiers against Prophetstown on the Tippecanoe Creek. The Prophet was in charge. Tecumseh was away trying to organize Indians in the South. The Prophet led a surprise night attack on Harrison's troops. Both sides suffered heavy losses in the Battle of Tippecanoe.

In the end, Harrison's troops defeated the Prophet's forces and destroyed Prophetstown. Whites celebrated the battle as a major victory. Still, Tecumseh and his followers continued to resist white settlement.

☑ READING CHECK **Identify Supporting Details** Why did Tecumseh advise many American Indians to stop trading with the settlers?

What Were the Causes of the War of 1812?

Fighting with American Indians hurt relations between the United States and Britain. The British were supplying guns and ammunition to the American Indians on the frontier. They also encouraged Indians to attack U.S. settlements.

Meanwhile, the ban on trade with Britain and France expired. Congress then authorized President Madison to make a tantalizing offer. If either the British or French stopped seizing American ships, the United States would reopen trade with that nation. Napoleon quickly announced that France would respect American neutrality. Britain did not respond to the offer. As promised, the United States resumed trade with France, but continued to ban all shipments to or from Britain.

A Push for War While Madison did not want war, other Americans were not as cautious. In New England, antiwar feelings ran strong. However, members of Congress from the South and the West called for war. They were known as **War Hawks**.

 INTERACTIVE

Indian Lands Lost by 1810

War Hawks were stirred by a strong sense of **nationalism**, or devotion to one's country. War Hawks felt that Britain was treating the United States as if it were still a British colony. They were willing to fight a war to defend American rights.

The most outspoken War Hawk was Henry Clay of Kentucky. Clay wanted to punish Britain for seizing American ships. He also hoped to conquer Canada. "The militia of Kentucky are alone [able] to place Montreal and Upper Canada at your feet," Clay boasted to Congress.

War Hawks saw other advantages of war with Britain. If Americans went to war with Britain, War Hawks said, the United States could seize Florida from Britain's ally, Spain. They also pointed out that Britain was arming American Indians on the frontier and encouraging them to attack settlers. The War Hawks felt that winning a war against Britain would bring lasting safety to settlers on the frontier.

War Is Declared The United States and Britain drifted closer to war as the security of American ships remained an issue. The British continued to board American ships and impress American seamen. To cut off American trade with France, British warships blockaded some American ports. In May 1811, near New York Harbor, a battle broke out between an American frigate and a British ship. The Americans crippled the British ship and left 32 British sailors dead or wounded.

War Hawks urged Congress to prepare for war. Other members of Congress disagreed. John Randolph of Virginia warned that the people of the United States would "not submit to be taxed for this war of conquest and dominion." Representatives of New England were especially concerned. They feared that the British navy would attack New England seaports.

At last, President Madison gave in to war fever. In June 1812, he asked Congress to declare war on Britain. The House and Senate both voted in favor of war. Americans would soon learn, though, that declaring war was easier than winning.

☑ READING CHECK Identify Supporting Details Who were the War Hawks?

Early Events in the War of 1812

The American declaration of war took the British by surprise. They were locked in a bitter struggle with Napoleon and could not spare troops to fight the United States. As the war **commenced**, however, the United States faced difficulties of its own.

The Difficulties of Building a Military The United States was not ready for war. Because Jefferson had reduced spending on defense, the navy had only 17 ships to meet the huge British fleet. The army was small and ill equipped, and many of the officers knew little about warfare. "The state of the army," said a member of Congress, "is enough to make any man who has the smallest love of country wish to get rid of it." These problems made it difficult to maintain national security.

Since there were few regular troops, the government relied on volunteers. Congress voted to give them a bounty of cash and land.

▲ As a War Hawk, Henry Clay seized the conflict with Britain as an opportunity to push his plan to conquer Canada from the British.

Academic Vocabulary
commence • v., to begin

THE WAR OF 1812

CAUSES

★ British interfere with American shipping.

★ British kidnap American sailors.

★ Americans believe British are persuading American Indians to fight settlers.

★ Some members of Congress (War Hawks) want U.S. expansion into Canada.

CONGRESS IS DIVIDED OVER THE FIRST DECLARATION OF WAR

HOUSE
62% IN FAVOR — 38% OPPOSED

SENATE
59% — 41%

Source: Library of Congress

PREPAREDNESS FOR WAR

	UNITED STATES	BRITAIN
TROOPS	12,000	10,000 BRITISH & CANADIAN TROOPS
WARSHIPS	17	584
SAILORS	4,000	140,000 (WORLDWIDE)
MARINES	1,800	31,000

Sources: Donald R. Hickey, *War of 1812*; U.S. Naval Institute

Analyze Charts The United States faced the world's greatest power in the War of 1812. **Infer** What information above helps explain the percentage of people opposed to war in Congress?

The money was equal to about a year's salary for most workers. Attracted by the high pay and the chance to own their own farms, young men eagerly enlisted. They were poorly trained, however, with little experience in battle. Many deserted after a few months.

Surprising Victories at Sea The British navy blockaded American ports to stop American trade. Though unable to break the blockade, several American sea captains won stunning victories.

One famous battle took place early in the war, in August 1812. As he was sailing near Newfoundland, Isaac Hull, captain of the U.S.S. *Constitution,* spotted the British ship HMS *Guerrière* (geh ree AIR). For nearly an hour, the two ships jockeyed for position. At last, the guns of the *Constitution* roared into action. They tore holes in the sides of the *Guerrière* and shot off both masts. Stunned, the British captain had no choice but to surrender.

American sea captains won other victories at sea. These victories cheered Americans but did little to win the war.

READING CHECK Identify Supporting Details What problems did the U.S. military face?

How Did the War Affect Canada?

One goal of the War Hawks was to conquer Canada. They were convinced that Canadians would welcome the chance to throw off British rule and join the United States.

An Untested Force General William Hull moved American troops into Canada from Detroit. The Canadians had only a few untrained troops to ward off the invasion. However, they were led by a clever British general, Isaac Brock.

Brock paraded his soldiers in red coats to make it appear that experienced British troops were helping the Canadians. He also led Americans to think that a large number of American Indians were fighting alongside the Canadians. Brock's scare tactics worked. Hull retreated from Canada. Other attempts to invade Canada also failed.

However, on April 27, 1813, U.S. soldiers crossed Lake Ontario and successfully captured York, present-day Toronto. The Americans seized British guns and supplies, and they set fire to public buildings.

Analyze Images The U.S. Navy surprised British naval forces early in the war when the U.S.S. *Constitution* defeated Britain's HMS *Guerriere* near Newfoundland. **Identify Supporting Details** What details in the image give strength to the U.S.S. *Constitution's* nickname, "Old Ironsides"?

American Victory on Lake Erie In 1813, the Americans, armed with the guns and supplies they had seized at York, set out to win control of Lake Erie. Captain Oliver Hazard Perry had no fleet, so he designed and built his own ships. In September 1813, he sailed his tiny fleet against the British.

During the Battle of Lake Erie, the British battered Perry's own ship and left it helpless. Perry rowed over to another American ship and continued to fight. Finally, the Americans won the battle. Captain Perry wrote his message of victory on the back of an envelope: "We have met the enemy and they are ours."

American Indian Losses After losing control of Lake Erie, the British and their ally Tecumseh retreated from Detroit into Canada. General William Henry Harrison, veteran of Tippecanoe, pursued them. The Americans won a **decisive** victory at the Battle of the Thames (temz). Tecumseh died in the fighting. Without Tecumseh's leadership, the Indian confederation soon fell apart.

Analyze Images After the British destroyed his flagship, the *Lawrence*, Captain Oliver Perry escaped to another American ship. Perry's fleet would regroup and eventually win the Battle of Lake Erie. **Classify and Categorize** How would you compare and contrast the actions of Perry to those of revolutionary naval hero John Paul Jones?

✔ READING CHECK **Summarize** What became of the War Hawks' plan to conquer Canada?

The End of the War

While Tecumseh was defeated in Canada, some sections of the Creek continued their fight against U.S. settlers in the South. Andrew Jackson, a Tennessee officer, took command of American troops in the Creek War. In March 1814, with the help of Cherokee, Choctaw, and friendly Creek, Jackson won a crushing victory at the Battle of Horseshoe Bend. The leader of the enemy Creek walked alone into Jackson's camp to surrender. "Your people have destroyed my nation," he said.

Washington, D.C., Burns In the spring of 1814, Britain and its allies defeated France. With the war in Europe over, Britain could send more troops and ships to fight the United States.

In August 1814, British ships sailed into Chesapeake Bay and landed an invasion force about 30 miles from Washington, D.C. American troops met the British at Bladensburg, Maryland. As President Madison watched, the British quickly scattered the untrained Americans. The British met little further resistance on their march to the capital.

In the White House, First Lady Dolley Madison waited for her husband to return. Hastily, she scrawled a note to her sister about the attack.

Academic Vocabulary
decisive • *adj.* clearly settling a dispute or question

Analyze Images This painting shows the American artillery aimed at the British fleet at Fort McHenry in Baltimore Harbor. **Use Visual Information** Why do you think the painter has placed the American flag flying above the action of the soldiers?

Primary Source

"Will you believe it, my sister? We have had a battle or skirmish near Bladensburg and here I am still within sound of the cannon! Mr. Madison comes not. May God protect us. Two messengers covered with dust come bid me fly. But here I mean to wait for him."

—Dolley Madison, *Memoirs and Letters of Dolley Madison*

Soon after, British troops marched into the capital. Dolley Madison gathered up important papers of the President and a portrait of George Washington. Then, she fled south. She was not there to see the British set fire to the White House and other buildings. The British considered this an act of revenge for the burning of York.

From Washington, the British marched north toward the city of Baltimore. The key to Baltimore's defense was Fort McHenry on Baltimore Harbor. From the evening of September 13 until dawn on September 14 during the Battle of Baltimore, British rockets bombarded the harbor.

When the early morning fog lifted, the "broad stripes and bright stars" of the American flag still waved over Fort McHenry. American forces had won the Battle of Baltimore. The British withdrew, and the threat to the nation's capital ended. Francis Scott Key, a young American lawyer who witnessed the battle, wrote a poem about it. Soon, his poem, "The Star-Spangled Banner," was published and set to music. Today, it is the national anthem of the United States.

Jackson Becomes a Hero in the Battle of New Orleans In late 1814, the British prepared to attack New Orleans. From there, they hoped to sail up the Mississippi. However, Andrew Jackson was waiting. Jackson had turned his frontier fighters into a strong army.

Did you know?

When Dolley Madison fled the White House, she left dinner on the table for her husband and his aides. The British ate the meal before burning the building down.

He took Pensacola in Spanish Florida to keep the British from using it as a base. He then marched through Mobile and set up camp in New Orleans.

Jackson's force included thousands of frontiersmen and Choctaw. The Choctaw were longtime rivals of the Indian nations who had been allied with the British. Many of Jackson's troops were expert riflemen. Citizens of New Orleans also joined the army to defend their city from the British. Among the volunteers were hundreds of African Americans.

The American soldiers dug trenches to defend themselves. On January 8, 1815, the British attacked. Again and again, British soldiers marched toward the American trenches. More than 2,000 British fell under the deadly fire of American sharpshooters and, especially, American cannons. Only seven Americans died.

Americans cheered the victory at the Battle of New Orleans. Overnight, Andrew Jackson became a national hero. His fame did not dim even when Americans learned that the battle had taken place two weeks after the war had ended. The United States and Britain had already signed a treaty in Europe, but news took two months to cross the ocean by sailing ship.

African Americans in the War The Battle of New Orleans was not the only place where black and white soldiers fought together. Throughout the War of 1812, African Americans joined in defending the nation against the British.

After the British attacks on Washington and Baltimore, African American volunteers helped defend Philadelphia against a possible attack. Bishop Richard Allen and the Reverend Absalom Jones recruited some 2,000 men to build Philadelphia's fortifications.

GEOGRAPHY SKILLS

Both sides won battles in the War of 1812, with no clear overall winner. The inset map shows the movement of Andrew Jackson's forces.

1. **Movement** From where and which direction did American forces move to fight the British in Frenchtown?

2. **Use Visual Information** How is the role of the British navy reflected on the map?

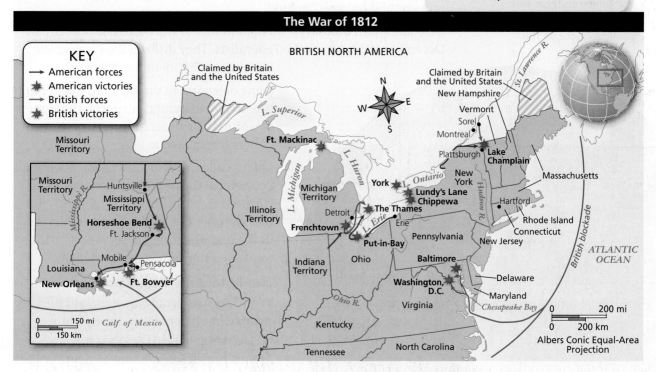

The War of 1812

KEY
→ American forces
⁕ American victories
→ British forces
⁕ British victories

The state of New York organized two regiments of black volunteers to serve in the army.

African Americans also served with distinction in the U.S. Navy. They helped win the Battle of Lake Erie as well as other naval battles. Commander Nathaniel Shaler praised one particular black sailor who was wounded in battle:

Primary Source

"He fell near me, and several times requested to be thrown overboard, saying he was only in the way of others. When America has such [sailors], she has little to fear from the tyrants of the ocean."

—Nathaniel Shaler, letter to his agent, January 1, 1813

✓READING CHECK **Identify Main Ideas** What achievement made Andrew Jackson well known throughout the country?

What Were the Consequences of the War of 1812?

By late 1814, Americans knew that peace talks had commenced, but they did not know if they would succeed or how long they would last. As Jackson was preparing to fight the British at New Orleans, New Englanders were meeting to protest "Mr. Madison's War."

New Englanders Protest the War The British blockade had hurt New England's sea trade. Also, many New Englanders feared that the United States might win land in Florida and Canada. If new states were carved out of these lands, the South and the West would become more influential than New England.

Delegates from around New England met in Hartford, Connecticut, in December 1814. Most were Federalists. They disliked the Democratic Republican President and the war.

Some delegates to the Hartford Convention threatened to nullify, or cancel, the state of war in their states if the war continued. Others threatened to leave the Union.

Then, while the delegates debated what to do, news of the peace treaty arrived. The Hartford Convention ended quickly. With the war over, the protest was meaningless. In the end, the threat of secession further weakened the dying Federalist party.

The Indecisive Results of the War A peace treaty was signed in the city of Ghent, in present-day Belgium, on December 24, 1814. John Quincy Adams, son of John Adams and one of the

Analyze Images Cyrus Tiffany, an African American sailor shown here with his hand on the coat of Captain Oliver H. Perry, helped save the captain's life at the Battle of Lake Erie. **Compare and Contrast** How are the actions of Tiffany and the man described in the Primary Source quote on this page similar?

American delegates, summed up the Treaty of Ghent in one sentence: "Nothing was adjusted, nothing was settled."

Britain and the United States agreed to restore prewar conditions. The treaty said nothing about impressment or neutrality. These issues had faded due to the end of the wars in Europe. Other issues were settled later. In 1818, for example, the two nations settled a dispute over the border between Canada and the United States.

Looking back, some Americans felt that the War of 1812 had been a mistake. Others argued that Europe would now treat the young republic with more respect. The victories of heroes like Oliver Hazard Perry, William Henry Harrison, and Andrew Jackson gave Americans new pride in their country. As one Democratic Republican leader remarked, "The people are now more American. They feel and act more as a nation."

▲ As the commander who won a victory at the Battle of New Orleans, shown here, General Andrew Jackson became a military hero. His fame would later help him become President.

☑ READING CHECK **Identify Supporting Details** What was the purpose of the Hartford Convention?

☑ Lesson Check

Practice Vocabulary

1. What was the relationship between **War Hawks** and **nationalism**?

2. Why would Tecumseh work for a **confederation**?

Critical Thinking and Writing

3. **Draw Conclusions** Why were American Indian groups resistant to white settlement west of the Appalachians?

4. **Summarize** What did Andrew Jackson do that made him a national hero?

5. **Compare and Contrast** U.S. military strength before and after the War of 1812.

6. **Writing Workshop: Clarify Relationships with Transition Words** Be sure to consider transition words that you can use to show the relationships between facts in your research paper. List some in your 📓 Active Journal.

Tenskwatawa, The Prophet, Speech

Tenskwatawa, a Shawnee religious leader called The Prophet, spoke out about the harm white settlers brought as they moved westward and imposed changes on the American Indian way of life.

◀ Tenskwatawa, a Shawnee religious leader, was the brother of Tecumseh.

Reading and Vocabulary Support

① An *awl* is a small metal tool used to punch holes into leather or heavy cloth.

② What does Tenskwatawa mean when he says, "We shut our ears to The Great Good Spirit"?

③ Why do you think people do not want to hear that they have been foolish?

④ One meaning of the word *corrupt* is to bribe. Why does The Prophet use the word *corrupted*?

⑤ What does Tenskwatawa say has caused his people to "beg for everything"?

For many years we traded furs to the English or the French, for wool blankets and guns and iron things, for steel ① awls and needles and axes, for mirrors, for pretty things made of beads and silver. And for liquor. This was foolish, but we did not know it. ② We shut our ears to the Great Good Spirit. We did not want to hear that we were being ③ foolish.

But now those things of the white men have ④ corrupted us, and made us weak and needful. Our men forgot how to hunt without noisy guns. Our women dont want to make fire without steel, or cook without iron, or sew without metal awls and needles, or fish without steel hooks. Some look in those mirrors all the time, and no longer teach their daughters to make leather or render bear oil. ⑤ We learned to need the white men's goods, and so now a People who never had to beg for anything must beg for everything!

— Tenskwatawa, The Prophet, ca. 1804

Analyzing Primary Sources

Cite specific evidence from the document to support your answers.

1. **Cite Evidence** How does Tenskwatawa say that white settlers "corrupted" American Indians?

2. **Analyze Style and Rhetoric** Which words does Tenskwatawa use that may have raised the emotions of his American Indian audience?

Monroe's Presidency and Everyday Life

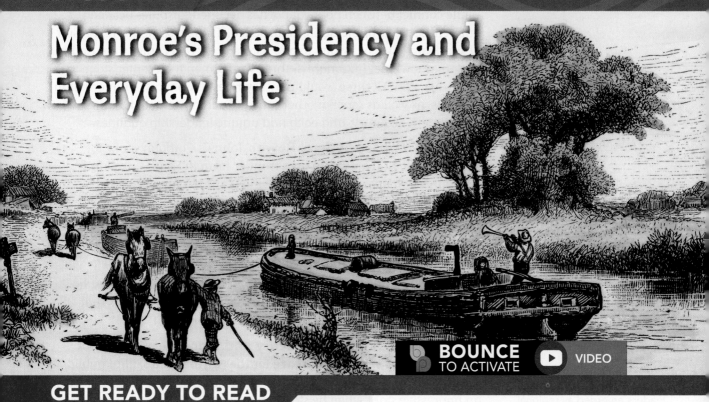

BOUNCE TO ACTIVATE ▶ VIDEO

GET READY TO READ

START UP

Study the illustration of the Erie Canal, which was built between 1817 and 1825 to connect the Hudson River with Lake Erie. In your 📓 Active Journal write about what you think daily life was like in the early 1800s.

GUIDING QUESTIONS

- What role did regional differences begin to play in the early republic?
- How did John Marshall's Supreme Court expand the power of the federal government?
- What was President Monroe's foreign policy?
- What was life like in the early republic?

TAKE NOTES

Literacy Skills: Draw Conclusions
Use the graphic organizer in your 📓 Active Journal to take notes as you read the lesson.

PRACTICE VOCABULARY

Use the vocabulary activity in your 📓 Active Journal to practice the vocabulary words.

Vocabulary

sectionalism   interstate commerce

American   Monroe Doctrine
  System   intervention

Academic Vocabulary

advocate
regulate

In 1816, the Democratic Republican candidate for President, James Monroe, easily defeated Federalist Senator Rufus King of New York. The election showed how seriously the Federalists had declined in popularity. Many had voted for Monroe.

How Did Sectionalism Affect the Early Republic?

Monroe was the last Revolutionary War officer to become President. He was almost 60 years old when he took office. Americans were fond of his old-fashioned ways. In 1817, he made a goodwill tour of the country. In Boston, crowds cheered. Boston newspapers expressed surprise at this warm welcome for a Democratic Republican from Virginia. Boston had long been a Federalist stronghold.

An Era of Good Feelings Monroe hoped to create a new sense of national unity. One newspaper wrote that the United States was entering an "era of good feelings." By the time Monroe ran for a second term in 1820, no candidate opposed him. The Federalist Party had disappeared.

While conflict between political parties declined, disputes between different sections of the nation sharpened. These disputes were a result of **sectionalism**, or loyalty to one's state or section rather than to the nation as a whole. In Congress, three young men took center stage in these disputes. All three would play key roles in Congress for more than 30 years, as well as serve in other offices. Each represented a different section of the country, and each had unique leadership qualities.

Calhoun Opposes Federal Power John C. Calhoun spoke for the South. He had grown up on a frontier farm in South Carolina. Calhoun's immense energy and striking features earned him the nickname "young Hercules."

He was slim and handsome, with deep-set eyes and a high forehead. His way of speaking was so intense that it sometimes made people uncomfortable to be in his presence.

Calhoun had supported the War of 1812. Like many southerners, he was a firm defender of slavery. In general, he opposed policies that would strengthen the power of the federal government.

Webster Stands Against Slavery and War Daniel Webster of New Hampshire was an **advocate** for the North and a skillful public speaker. With eyes flashing and shoulders thrown back, Webster was an impressive sight when he stood up to speak in Congress. An observer described him as a "great cannon loaded to the lips."

Analyze Charts Three leaders emerged as regional differences developed in the early republic. **Compare and Contrast** Who supported the War of 1812 and the idea of a strong federal government?

Like many New Englanders, Webster had opposed the War of 1812. He even refused to vote for taxes to pay for the war effort. After the war, he wanted the federal government to take a larger role in building the economy. Unlike Calhoun, Webster thought that slavery was evil.

Sectional Leaders: Calhoun, Webster, and Clay

JOHN C. CALHOUN	DANIEL WEBSTER	HENRY CLAY
• From South Carolina	• From New Hampshire	• From Kentucky
• Skilled orator, lawyer, and senator	• Skilled orator, lawyer, and senator	• Skilled orator, lawyer, and senator
• Sectional leader and spokesman for his region (South)	• Sectional leader and spokesman for his region (North)	• Sectional leader and spokesman for his region (West)
• Supported the War of 1812	• Against the War of 1812	• Supported the War of 1812
• Opposed the idea of a strong federal government	• Supported the idea of a strong federal government	• Supported the idea of a strong federal government
• Strong supporter of slavery	• Wanted slavery abolished	• Supported compromise over slavery
• Showed a concern for the country's economy	• Showed a concern for the country's economy	• Showed a concern for the country's economy
• Opposed the Compromise of 1850	• Defended the Compromise of 1850	• Defended the Compromise of 1850

Clay Supports Active Government Henry Clay spoke for the West. You have already met Clay as a leader of the War Hawks, who pushed for war against Britain in 1812.

Clay was born in Virginia but moved to Kentucky when he was 20. As a young lawyer, he was once fined for brawling with an opponent. Usually, however, he charmed both friends and rivals. Supporters called him "Gallant Harry of the West." Like Webster, Clay strongly favored a more active role for the central government in promoting the country's growth.

☑ READING CHECK **Compare and Contrast** Which position did Webster share with Clay?

How Was a Stable Economy Created After the War?

After the War of 1812, leaders such as Calhoun, Webster, and Clay had to deal with serious economic issues. Despite the nation's great physical growth and the soaring spirits of its people, the economy faced severe problems. This was due in part to the lack of a national bank.

The charter that had set up the first Bank of the United States ran out in 1811. Without the Bank to lend money and **regulate** the nation's money supply, the economy suffered. State banks made loans and issued money. However, they often put too much money into circulation. With so much money available to spend, prices rose rapidly.

In the nation's early years, Democratic Republicans such as Jefferson and Madison had opposed a national bank because they saw it as unconstitutional. They thought that the Constitution did not give the federal government the right to charter corporations. By 1816, however, many Democratic Republicans believed that a bank was needed. They supported a law to charter the second Bank of the United States. By lending money and restoring order to the nation's money supply, the Bank helped American businesses grow.

Protection Against Foreign Competition Another economic problem was foreign competition from Britain. In the early 1800s, the Embargo Act and then the War of 1812 kept most British goods out of the United States. In response, American business leaders such as Francis Cabot Lowell established their own mills and factories. As a result, American industry grew quickly until 1815.

Foreign Goods Cause Domestic Problems With the end of the War of 1812, British goods again poured into the United States. Because the British had a head start in industrializing, they could make and sell goods more cheaply than Americans could. Most British factory buildings and machines were older and had already been paid for. In contrast, Americans still had to pay for their new factory buildings.

Sometimes, British manufacturers sold cloth in the United States for less than it cost to make so that they could capture the market.

Analyze Images When the charter for the first Bank of the United States expired, state banks like this one in North Carolina began to make loans and print too much money, which caused prices to rise rapidly. **Infer** How do people usually react to higher prices?

Academic Vocabulary
regulate • *v.*, to make or use laws that control something

Analyze Images

Inventions, such as the power loom shown here, helped propel American industry forward. **Identify Supporting Details** Who are the workers in the mill, and how do you think the work affected their lives?

British manufacturers hoped to put American rivals out of business. Then, the British planned to raise prices.

The Regional Impacts of Tariffs This British strategy caused dozens of New England businesses to fail. Angry owners asked Congress to place a protective tariff on all goods imported from Europe. As you have read, the purpose of a protective tariff is to protect a country's industries from foreign competition.

Congress responded by passing the Tariff of 1816. It greatly raised tariffs on imports. This increase made imported goods far more expensive than similar American-made goods.

The Tariff of 1816 impacted the North, West, and South differently because each region had a different economy. The North was the base of America's manufacturing. It therefore benefited the most. Higher prices on foreign goods made American goods more competitive. American factories sold more products, and businesses grew.

The economies of the South and West relied heavily on farming. They were not as financially invested in manufacturing and therefore did not experience the same benefits as the North. Goods like cloth and iron became more expensive to southern and western consumers. Northerners gained income as a result.

Higher tariffs led to angry protests. Lacking factories, southerners did not benefit from the tariff. Also, southerners bought many British goods. The new tariff drove up the price of British-made goods. Southerners complained that the tariff made northern manufacturers rich at the expense of the South.

Henry Clay Fights Sectionalism The bitter dispute over tariffs contributed to the growth of sectionalism. Americans identified themselves as southerners, northerners, or westerners. In Congress, representatives from different sections often clashed.

Henry Clay wanted to promote economic growth for all sections. His program, known as the **American System**, called for high tariffs on imports, which would help northern factories. With wealth from industry, Clay believed, northerners would have the money to buy farm products from the West and the South.

This exchange would strengthen a common market among the states, which the Constitution supported and protected in the clause on interstate commerce. High tariffs would also reduce American dependence on foreign goods.

Clay also urged Congress to use money from tariffs to build roads, bridges, and canals. A better transportation system, he believed, would make it easier and cheaper for farmers in the West and the South to ship goods to city markets.

Clay's American System never fully went into effect. While tariffs remained high, Congress spent little on internal improvements such as new roads, bridges, and canals. Southerners in particular disliked Clay's plan. The South had many fine rivers on which to transport goods. Many southerners opposed paying for roads and canals that brought them no direct benefits.

Some Americans also thought Clay's plan for developing transportation with federal support was unconstitutional. They did not believe the federal government had the authority to build such projects. They believed that by regulating industry and building roads and canals, the federal government would gain too much power.

✓ READING CHECK Identify Main Ideas Why did many states in the South and West oppose the Tariff of 1816?

How Did Supreme Court Decisions Expand Federal Power?

Under Chief Justice John Marshall, the Supreme Court strengthened the power of the federal government. The Court gave the federal government the power to regulate the economy.

Analyze Graphs Cotton played a key role in the early U.S. economy, especially in the South. **Identify Cause and Effect** As cotton production soared, what other features of the American economy also grew?

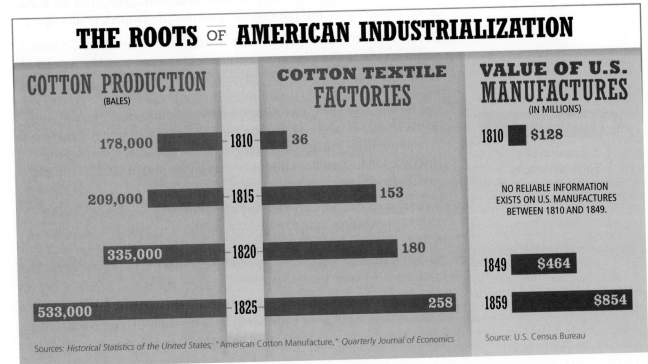

THE ROOTS OF AMERICAN INDUSTRIALIZATION

COTTON PRODUCTION (BALES)		COTTON TEXTILE FACTORIES	VALUE OF U.S. MANUFACTURES (IN MILLIONS)
178,000	1810	36	1810 $128
209,000	1815	153	NO RELIABLE INFORMATION EXISTS ON U.S. MANUFACTURES BETWEEN 1810 AND 1849.
335,000	1820	180	
533,000	1825	258	1849 $464
			1859 $854

Sources: *Historical Statistics of the United States;* "American Cotton Manufacture," *Quarterly Journal of Economics*

Source: U.S. Census Bureau

Analyze Images Robert Fulton built the first successful steamboats, shown here, and ran them as ferries from New York to New Jersey. **Synthesize Visual Information** What details in this image show how technology was changing American society?

INTERACTIVE

Expansion of Federal Powers

A Broad Definition of "Necessary and Proper" After Congress chartered the second Bank of the United States, Maryland tried to tax the Bank in order to drive it out of the state. James McCulloch, the Bank cashier, refused to pay the tax.

In the case of *McCulloch v. Maryland* (1819), the Court ruled that states had no right to interfere with federal institutions within their borders. The ruling strengthened federal power. It also allowed the Bank of the United States to continue, which helped the U.S. economy expand.

The Court decision addressed the issue of the meaning of the "necessary and proper" clause of the U.S. Constitution. It ruled that the federal government had the power to charter the Bank of the United States under the clause. This clause states that "The Congress shall have Power . . . To make all Laws which shall be necessary and proper" for carrying out functions outlined elsewhere in the Constitution. Since the Constitution gave the federal government the power to tax and borrow money and to regulate business, the Court stated that creating a bank could be considered "necessary and proper" to carrying out these powers.

The Supreme Court took a "loose constructionist" view of the Constitution, believing that the "necessary and proper" clause should be interpreted loosely as circumstances changed. Many Americans disagreed with the Court. Those who disagreed took a "strict constructionist" view that the "necessary and proper" clause permitted only actions absolutely necessary for performing the government's constitutional duties. Strict constructionists mostly agreed that the Bank of the United States was not necessary for the government to function.

Broad Powers Over Interstate Trade In another case, *Gibbons v. Ogden* (1824), the Supreme Court upheld the power of the federal government to regulate trade between states. The Court struck down a New York law that tried to control steamboat travel between New York and New Jersey. The Court ruled that a state could regulate trade only within its own borders. Only the federal government had the power to regulate **interstate commerce**, or trade between different states. This decision helped the national economy by making it easier for the government to regulate trade.

These rulings not only affected the government. They also changed daily life for people in the United States. The New York law had given a monopoly, or exclusive rights, to Robert Fulton's steamboat company to run ferries to New Jersey. Fulton's company was the only one allowed to run ferries between the two states.

When the Supreme Court struck down this New York law, Fulton's monopoly on steamboat traffic ended. As a result, his company could not compete with companies that charged a lower fare.

People working for Fulton lost their jobs. However, the increased competition was good for consumers because it led to lower fares.

This ruling helped create a single common market among the states for goods and services, regulated by the federal government. Having clear national laws to follow made it easier for people to do business nationwide. The Constitution's clauses on common coinage and full faith and credit also protect a common market. In these clauses, the Constitution gives only the federal government the power to coin money, and it requires that states recognize the laws and court decisions of other states.

Decisions About Contracts and Corporations

Remember that in 1810, the Supreme Court ruled in a case where the state of Georgia tried to revoke a land sale. Its decision in *Fletcher* v. *Peck* upheld the idea that a contract cannot be broken.

In 1819 *Trustees of Dartmouth College* v. *Woodward*, another Supreme Court case, encouraged the growth of private businesses. When the president of private Dartmouth College was removed by its board of trustees, the state of New Hampshire tried to force the college to become a public state school. This would allow the governor to appoint the trustees.

The Supreme Court ruled that the contract clause of the Constitution applied to private corporations like Dartmouth. This landmark decision helped to encourage the growth of American businesses because it kept states from interfering with private corporations.

In the Supreme Court case, *Fletcher* v. *Peck*, the court declared as unconstitutional Georgia's repeal of a law that had allowed the state to purchase a land grant and sell off properties to speculators. The Supreme Court ruled that the state could not violate contracts made during the sale of properties, even if the contracts were illegal. This case further reinforced the idea that contracts need to be protected.

✔ **READING CHECK** **Identify Cause and Effect** How did the decision in *McCulloch* v. *Maryland* increase federal power?

Independence in Latin America

By 1810, many people in Spain's colonies in the Americas were eager for independence. They had many reasons to be unhappy. Most people, even wealthy creoles, had little or no say in government. In Latin America, the term *creole* described people born to Spanish parents there. They demanded a role in government. Opposition to Spain was also growing among American Indians. Harsh rules kept American Indians forever in debt. All over Latin America, people were eager to be free of the Spanish.

Independence

A Mexican priest named Miguel Hidalgo (mee GEL ee DAHL goh) called on Mexicans to fight for independence from Spain in 1810.

▼ Mexican freedom fighter Miguel Hidalgo declares Mexico's independence from Spain.

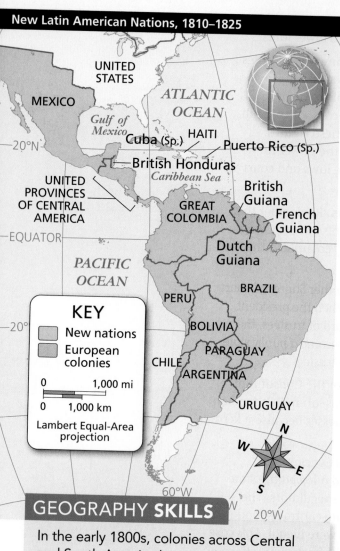

KEY

New nations

European colonies

0   1,000 mi

0   1,000 km

Lambert Equal-Area projection

GEOGRAPHY SKILLS

In the early 1800s, colonies across Central and South America became free from Spanish rule as a result of revolution.

1. **Location** Which European countries continued to exercise control in South America?

2. **Use Visual Information** Which colonies remained under the control of Spain?

Many Mexicans answered his call. Rebel forces won control of several provinces before Father Hidalgo was captured. In 1811, Hidalgo was executed.

Another priest, José Morelos (hoh SAY moh RAY lohs), took up the fight. Because he called for a program to give land to peasants, wealthy creoles opposed him. Before long, Morelos, too, was captured and killed by the Spanish.

Slowly, though, creoles began to join the revolutionary movement. In 1821, revolutionary forces led by creoles won control of Mexico. A few years later, Mexico became a republic with its own constitution.

South America Frees Itself From Spanish Rule In South America, too, a series of revolutions freed colonies from Spanish rule. The best-known revolutionary leader was Simón Bolívar (see MOHN boh LEE vahr). He became known as the Liberator for his role in the Latin American wars of independence.

In a bold move, Bolívar led an army of rebel forces from Venezuela over the high Andes Mountains into Colombia. There, Bolívar defeated Spanish forces in 1819.

Soon after, Bolívar became President of the independent Republic of Great Colombia. It included the present-day nations of Venezuela, Colombia, Ecuador, and Panama.

Independence Movements Spread Other independent nations emerged in Latin America. José de San Martín (sahn mahr TEEN) led Argentina to freedom in 1816. He then helped the people of Chile and Peru win independence.

In 1821, the peoples of Central America declared independence from Spain. By 1825, Spain had lost all its colonies in Latin America except Puerto Rico and Cuba.

The New Republics Spain's former colonies formed several separate republics and modeled their constitutions on that of the United States. However, the new republics had a hard time setting up stable governments.

Under Spanish rule, the colonists had gained little or no experience in self-government. Powerful leaders took advantage of the turmoil to seize control. As a result, the new nations were often unable to achieve democratic rule.

☑ READING CHECK **Compare and Contrast** In what ways was the achievement of independence for the Spanish colonies and the establishment of republics in Latin America similar to that which occurred in the British colonies that became the United States?

How Did the United States Gain Florida?

Spain lost another one of its colonies, Florida—not to independence, but to the United States. Many Americans wanted to gain possession of Florida. White southerners were especially worried about disturbances across the border. Creek and Seminole Indians in Florida sometimes raided settlements in Georgia. Also, Florida was a refuge for many Africans and African Americans who escaped slavery.

Jackson Invades Spanish Florida Since the 1700s, Spanish officials had protected enslaved Africans who had fled from plantations in Georgia and South Carolina. The Seminole allowed Africans to live near their villages. In return, these "black Seminole" gave the Seminole a share of the crops they raised. The black Seminoles adopted many Seminole customs.

One settlement on the Apalachicola River, known as the Negro Fort, contained about 1,000 black Seminole. General Andrew Jackson demanded that Spain demolish the Negro Fort. When the Spanish governor refused, the United States invaded Florida and destroyed the fort.

Adams Buys Florida In 1818, Jackson again headed to Florida with a force of more than 3,000 soldiers. Spain protested but did little else. It was busy fighting rebels in Latin America and could not risk war with the United States.

In the end, Spain agreed to peace talks. Secretary of State John Quincy Adams worked out a treaty with Spain's foreign minister, Luis de Onís (LOO ess day oh NEES). In it, Spain agreed to give Florida to the United States in exchange for $5 million. The Adams-Onís Treaty took effect in 1821.

☑ READING CHECK **Identify Cause and Effect** What was the result of the Adams-Onís Treaty?

What Did the Monroe Doctrine State?

Americans cheered as Latin America won independence. The actions of European powers, however, worried Secretary of State Adams and President Monroe.

▼ Black Seminole were African Americans who had escaped slavery and lived peacefully alongside Seminole Indians in Florida.

In 1815, Prussia, France, Russia, and Austria formed an alliance aimed at crushing any revolution that sprang up in Europe. They seemed ready to help Spain regain its colonies in Latin America. In addition, Russia claimed lands on the Pacific coast of North America.

The British, too, worried about other European nations meddling in the Western Hemisphere. They feared that their profitable trade with the newly independent countries would be hurt if Spain regained control of its former colonies. Thus, they suggested that the United States and Britain issue a joint statement guaranteeing the freedom of the new nations of Latin America.

Monroe decided to act independently of Britain. In a message to Congress in 1823, he made a bold foreign policy statement known as the **Monroe Doctrine**. Monroe declared that the United States would not interfere in the affairs of European nations or existing colonies of the European nations. At the same time, he warned European nations not to attempt to regain control of the newly independent nations of Latin America.

The Monroe Doctrine stated that the United States would oppose any attempt to reclaim old colonies or build new colonies in the Americas. Monroe's message showed that the United States was determined to keep European powers out of the Western Hemisphere.

The United States did not have the military power to enforce the Monroe Doctrine. Britain, however, supported the statement. With its strong navy, it could stop Europeans from building new colonies in the Americas.

As the United States became stronger, the Monroe Doctrine grew in importance. On several occasions, the United States successfully challenged European **intervention**, or direct involvement, in Latin America. In the 1900s, Presidents also used the Monroe Doctrine to justify sending troops to Caribbean nations. Thus, Monroe's bold statement helped shape United States foreign policy for more than 100 years.

✓ READING CHECK **Identify Main Ideas** What was the purpose of the Monroe Doctrine?

What Was Daily Life Like in the Early Republic?

The government changed during the early years of the nation, and so did the daily lives of many Americans. The growth of industry was one reason. The country was still largely rural.

Analyze Political Cartoons In this political cartoon, Uncle Sam brandishes a big stick, labeled "Monroe Doctrine," as a warning to European nations not to attempt to re-colonize territory in the Americas. **Identify Cause and Effect** How do you think other nations reacted to this new U.S. foreign policy?

EXPANSION!
The western patrol's long stretch.

Many Americans worked on farms. But by the end of the period, factories had begun to sprout up. Many young women from farms in New England began to move to cities to work in textile factories.

Churches were centers of social life throughout the country. Protestant churches were most common, but Jews and Catholics were allowed to practice their religions under new state constitutions that required separation of church and state.

Free African Americans sometimes started their own churches, but they also formed many other organizations. These groups provided mutual aid and relief for those in need, such as widows and orphans.

Enslaved African Americans generally lived harsh, controlled lives. Families were broken up when members were sold. Many enslaved people turned to their own faith and customs for a sense of community.

Education Jefferson and others stressed the importance of education in a republican democracy. However, schools were mostly private. Americans received their education in different ways.

For example, a dame school was a small school run by a woman in her own home. She would teach young children the alphabet and numbers, as well as some reading and writing. Other Americans were educated in their own homes by family members or at church schools. The Bible was often used as a teaching tool for learning to read.

Wealthy Americans could subscribe to private membership libraries. Benjamin Franklin was an advocate for public libraries. In 1790 he donated books to a Massachusetts town that named itself Franklin after him. The residents voted for the books to be freely available for town members, forming a public library. As the number of public libraries increased, more and more Americans had access to books.

Art Wealthy, prominent Americans had their portraits painted. Gilbert Stuart's painting of George Washington is famous, as is Rembrandt Peale's portrait of Thomas Jefferson. Folk painters traveled around to paint portraits for less prominent rural Americans. However, formal painters and sculptors still looked to Europe, especially Britain, for training, style, and themes.

Useful household objects were often created with a sense of design. Furniture made in a style called Federal became popular. Newly wealthy merchants bought from the workshops of skilled craftspeople in New York or Philadelphia.

Analyze Images One-room schools such as this were common in rural areas in the early republic. **Compare and Contrast** What is the same and different about this classroom and those you use today?

Folk artists created samplers, weather vanes, ship's figureheads, and tavern and shop signs. They used many patriotic images in their craft, including likenesses of American hero George Washington.

Architecture also followed a style called Federal. Architects turned away from Britain and looked to the temples of ancient Greece for style. They used domes, pillars, and triangular roof lines for civic buildings.

Music People performed music in their homes for family and friends. British music was still enjoyed, and British entertainers toured the country. African Americans sang spirituals in their homes and churches, broadening American musical styles.

Literature The first American novel, *The Power of Sympathy*, was written by William Hill Brown in 1789. An original American voice in literature soon developed. Washington Irving's *The Sketch Book* included "The Legend of Sleepy Hollow" and "Rip Van Winkle," which was the first work by an American that won international popularity. James Fenimore Cooper wrote the extremely popular Leatherstocking Tales. The five novels tell of the wilderness adventures of a scout named Natty Bumppo.

Analyze Images Federal-style architecture for public buildings in the early 1800s resembled Greek temples in order to suggest the democratic ideals begun in ancient Greece. **Infer** How does this architecture reflect ancient Greek ideals of balance and harmony?

☑ READING CHECK **Draw Conclusions** Why do you think folk art of the early republic used patriotic images?

☑ Lesson Check

Practice Vocabulary

1. How did **sectionalism** affect the country in Monroe's term?

2. What was the **Monroe Doctrine**, and what was its purpose?

Critical Thinking and Writing

3. **Recognize Multiple Causes** After the War of 1812, British goods were again available in the United States. Why were these imported British goods less expensive than similar American goods?

4. **Generate Explanations** What was the principal reason the South rejected the American System, Henry Clay's plan to promote economic growth in all regions of the United States?

5. **Compare and Contrast** In what ways were the outcomes in *McCulloch* v. *Maryland* and *Gibbons* v. *Ogden* similar?

6. **Writing Workshop: Include Formatting and Graphics** Decide what graphics you can use to illustrate your information in the research paper you will write. What formatting will make your paper easy and interesting to read? Note these ideas in your 📓 Active Journal.

Construct a Timeline

Follow these steps to construct a timeline.

INTERACTIVE

Sequence

1 **Select key events of a time period and note the date of each.** The time period for this activity covers the first five presidencies. Some key events and their dates are noted below.

2 **Determine the beginning and ending dates of the period.** The timeline will span 1785 to 1825, a period of 40 years.

3 **Decide on how to break the line into time intervals. The intervals should be even.** Break your timeline into intervals of five years each. Draw a line on a piece of paper that can be broken evenly into eight sections of five years each. Mark the five-year intervals, beginning with 1785 and ending with 1825.

4 **Place a mark at the appropriate spot for each event and identify the year and the event.** Place the key events on the timeline. Then determine the dates of these events below and enter them on the timeline:

a. *Marbury* v. *Madison*

b. Burning of Washington, D.C., by the British

c. Washington's Farewell Address

Key Events of the First Five Presidencies

1789 Washington's inauguration

1794 Whiskey Rebellion

1797 Adams's inauguration

1798 Alien and Sedition Acts

1801 Jefferson's inauguration

1803 Louisiana Purchase

1809 Madison's inauguration

1812 Beginning of War of 1812

1817 Monroe's inauguration

1823 Monroe Doctrine

☑ Review and Assessment

VISUAL REVIEW

A Two-Party System

Federalists	Democratic Republicans
• Wanted a strong central government	• Wanted strong state governments
• Sympathetic to England	• Sympathetic to France
• Favored a national bank	• Opposed a national bank
• Thought the elite of society should control government	• Thought ordinary Americans should control the government
• Opposed to protection of individual liberties by law	• Wanted individual liberties to be protected by law
• Wanted an economy based on manufacturing and trade	• Wanted an economy based on agriculture

Five Presidencies

Washington
- Put down Whiskey Rebellion
- Political parties develop
- Foreign policy: neutrality

Adams
- Escalating conflict with France
- Alien and Sedition Acts

Jefferson
- Louisiana Purchase
- Lewis and Clark expedition
- *Marbury* v. *Madison* decision

Madison
- War of 1812

Monroe
- Era of Good Feelings
- Sectionalism arises
- Florida acquired
- The Monroe Doctrine

READING REVIEW

Use the Take Notes and Practice Vocabulary activities in your ◪ Active Journal to review the topic.

INTERACTIVE

Practice vocabulary using the Topic Mini-Games

Quest FINDINGS

Write your position paper, summarizing your chosen solution. Get help for writing your position paper in your ◪ Active Journal.

ASSESSMENT

Vocabulary and Key Ideas

1. **Define** What is **judicial review**?

2. **Describe** What is **sedition**, and what did the Alien and Sedition Acts do?

3. **Check Understanding** What role did **tariffs** play in early economic policy?

4. **Use** Use **interstate commerce** in a sentence about the Supreme Court.

5. **Identify Main Ideas** What were the causes of the War of 1812?

6. **Describe** How did the Louisiana Purchase change the boundaries of the United States?

7. **Check Understanding** Explain the Monroe Doctrine.

Critical Thinking and Writing

8. **Synthesize** How did the question of neutrality influence the early republic?

9. **Identify Cause and Effect** How did the conflict between Jefferson and Hamilton result in the development of two political parties?

10. **Evaluate** Was the Louisiana Purchase constitutional? Support your answer.

11. **Analyze** Why was education considered important in the early republic?

12. **Analyze** How did the government change during the early republic?

13. **Revisit the Essential Question** How was the question "How much power should the federal government have, and what should it do?" reflected in actions taken in the early republic?

14. **Writer's Workshop: Write a Research Paper** Using your notes in your 📓 Active Journal, write a paper describing the country's physical geography, political divisions, and expansion during the terms of its first four Presidents.

Analyze Primary Sources

15. Who is most likely the source of the quote?
    - **A.** Alexander Hamilton
    - **B.** John Marshall
    - **C.** John Adams
    - **D.** Thomas Jefferson

"It is emphatically the province and duty of the judicial department to say what the law is. Those who apply the rule to particular cases, must of necessity expound and interpret that rule. If two laws conflict with each other, the courts must decide on the operation of each."

Analyze Maps

16. What body of water made New Orleans important during the war?

17. Based on the blue lines, which show American troop movement, which was likely the first battle to have occurred?

18. The red lines and arrows show British movements. The blue bursts show American victories. Based on this information, which side was more successful during this part of the war?

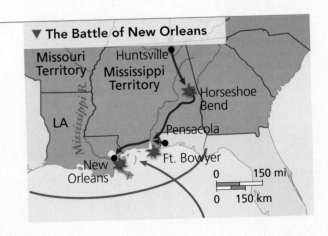

▼ **The Battle of New Orleans**

TOPIC

6

The Age of Jackson and Westward Expansion (1824–1860)

GO ONLINE
to access your
digital course

 VIDEO

 AUDIO

 ETEXT

 INTERACTIVE

 WRITING

 GAMES

 WORKSHEET

 ASSESSMENT

Go back to the early 1800s

and the **AGE OF JACKSON AND WESTWARD EXPANSION**. Why? Because it was during this time that Americans moved west, expanding the nation's borders—and forcing American Indians to leave their lands.

Explore
The Essential Question

Why do people move?

In the early 1800s, nearly all Americans lived east of the Appalachian Mountains. What led people to leave their homes and risk moving to the untamed West?

Unlock the Essential Question in your 📙 Active Journal.

Watch

NBC LEARN

BOUNCE TO ACTIVATE ▶ VIDEO

Narcissa Whitman and the Journey West

Learn what it was really like to be a pioneer moving west.

Read

about westward expansion and its impact on American Indians, the landscape, and American history.

Pioneers heading West on the Oregon Trail

The Age of Jackson and Westward Expansion (1824–1860)

Learn more about The Age of Jackson and Westward Expansion by making your own map and timeline in your 📓 Active Journal.

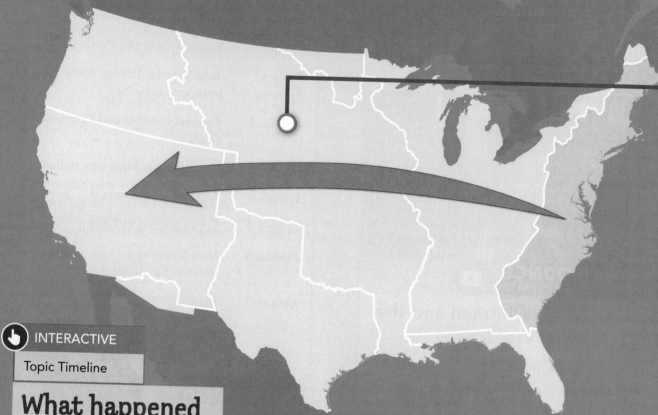

INTERACTIVE

Topic Timeline

What happened and when?

Growing democracy in America...settlers moving west...Explore the timeline to see some of what was happening during the Age of Jackson and westward expansion.

1830
Indian Removal Act leads to forced migration of American Indians

1828
Andrew Jackson elected president

1832
South Carolina passes Nullification Act

1837
Economic panic leads to depression

TOPIC EVENTS

1820

1830

WORLD EVENTS

1826
Friction match invented

1831
France invades and colonizes Algeria

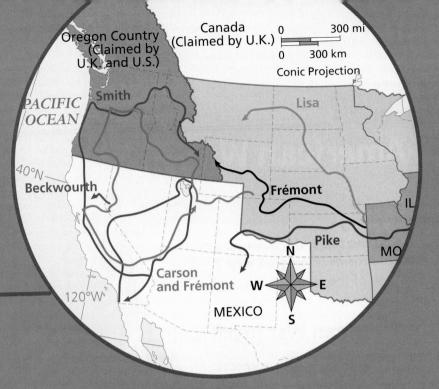

Oregon Country
(Claimed by
U.K. and U.S.)

Canada
(Claimed by U.K.)

0   300 mi
0   300 km
Conic Projection

PACIFIC
OCEAN

Smith

Lisa

40°N

Beckwourth

Frémont

IL

120°W

Carson
and Frémont

Pike

MO

MEXICO

N
W   E
S

 INTERACTIVE

Topic Map

How did the United States expand westward?

By the middle of the 1800s, the United States extended far to the west from the original 13 colonies on the East Coast, reaching from the Atlantic to the Pacific. As new lands were acquired, explorers paved the way for settlers from the East.

1848
Mexican-American War ends, United States takes control of California and New Mexico

1849
Gold discovered in California

1840

1850

1860

1848
Marx and Engels publish *The Communist Manifesto*

1850
Taiping Rebellion begins in China

Who will you meet?

Andrew Jackson, champion of the common people

James Beckwourth, mountain man freed from slavery

John Ross, leader of the Cherokee people

Quest

▼ American soldiers raise the flag during the Battle of Chapultepec.

The Mexican-American War

Quest KICK OFF

You are the leading historian on the topic of U.S. westward expansion. You're beginning the research for your next book on the Mexican-American War. One of the chapters in your book will focus on this question:

Was the Mexican-American War justified?

Be ready! Other historians will challenge your arguments. It's time to prepare!

1 Ask Questions

You are determined to know the best answer to the Guiding Question. Get started by making a list of questions about the Mexican-American War. Write the questions in your 📙 Active Journal.

2 Investigate

As you read the lessons in this Topic, look for **Quest CONNECTIONS** that provide information about the Mexican-American War. Collect examples in your 📙 Active Journal.

3 Examine Sources

Next, research primary sources about the Mexican-American War. Look for information that supports differing viewpoints about whether the war was justified. Capture notes in your 📙 Active Journal.

Quest FINDINGS

4 Discuss!

After you collect your clues and examine the sources, you will prepare to discuss this question: Was the Mexican-American War justified? You will use your knowledge as well as evidence from sources to make convincing arguments to answer YES or NO to the question. You may also come up with answers of your own.

LESSON 1

Jackson Wins the Presidency

BOUNCE TO ACTIVATE   ▶ VIDEO

GET READY TO READ

START UP

Look at the image of Jackson's 1828 inauguration celebration. What can you conclude about the kind of people who supported Jackson? Write a few sentences summarizing your ideas.

GUIDING QUESTIONS

- How did changes in suffrage affect political parties and elections?
- How did individual regions of the United States become both more similar and more different?
- What were the causes and effects of Jacksonian democracy?

TAKE NOTES

Literacy Skills: Identify Cause and Effect
Use the graphic organizer in your 📖 Active Journal to take notes as you read the lesson.

PRACTICE VOCABULARY

Use the Vocabulary Builder activity in your 📖 Active Journal to practice the vocabulary words.

Vocabulary

suffrage   Democratic Party
majority   spoils system
Whig Party

Academic Vocabulary

perceive
consequently

During the early 1800s, a growing spirit of democracy changed the political system and affected American ideas about social classes. The main cause stemmed from the influence of Andrew Jackson. He was an American politician during this time who supported expanding democratic rights. From the time of his first campaign for president in 1824 until his death in 1845, he dominated American politics. Jackson's policies had a significant effect on issues such as voting rights and the ways in which government functions. This period is often known as the Age of Jackson.

Democracy Expands

In the early 1800s, American democracy was a social outlook as well as a political system. Most Americans did not feel that the rich deserved special respect. Wealthy European visitors to the United States were surprised that servants in American households expected to be treated as equals. Others were amazed that butlers and maids refused to be summoned with bells, as in Europe.

Quick Activity

In your  Active Journal, compare Tocqueville's description of American life with American life at another time.

Alexis de Tocqueville A visitor from France, Alexis de Tocqueville, became especially well known for his observations on American democracy. He came to the United States in 1831 to study the American prison system. For several months, Tocqueville toured the United States. However, he observed much more than prisons. He observed a society that was becoming more and more democratic.

After his return to France, Tocqueville recorded his experiences and observations in a book titled *Democracy in America*. In it, he admired the American democratic spirit and the American goals of equality and freedom. He also observed that, while Americans expected to be treated as equals, equality only went so far. But overall, he found that the results of the social "revolution taking place" in America, while "still far from coming to an end," were "already incomparably greater than anything which has taken place in the world before."

Increased Suffrage During the 1820s, or the early years of the Age of Jackson, more Americans gained **suffrage**, or the right to vote. Others, however, were denied full participation in the growing democracy.

The United States was growing rapidly. New states were joining the Union. This growth fed some of the sectional divisions among states over taxes, trade, and other interests. People in the North, South, and West differed in their views on these issues.

Despite these disagreements, the regions grew more alike in their eagerness to expand voting rights to nearly all white men and to strengthen democracy. There were many citizens eager to participate in elections. Some of the first states to give voting privileges to white males who did not own property were in the West. In these states, any white man over age 21 could vote.

Class in America in 1830

Voting and Jury Rights	• White men
Unable to Vote, Unable to Serve on Juries	• All women • Enslaved African American men • Most free African American men • American Indian men
Property Rights	• White men • Some free African Americans • Single white women • American Indians
Unable to Own Land	• Married women • Enslaved African Americans • Some free African Americans

Analyze Images Class differences in the 1800s were reflected in unequal voting and property rights. **Draw Conclusions** Based on this chart, who ranked in the highest class in American society?

INTERACTIVE

Changing Voting Rights in Early America

Reformers in the East worked to expand suffrage in that region. By the 1830s, most eastern states had dropped the requirement that voters had to own land. In this way, laborers, artisans and craft workers, and shopkeepers gained the right to vote.

Throughout the country, growing numbers of Americans exercised their newly acquired right to vote. Before 1828, the turnout of eligible voters was never more than 27 percent. That low percentage rose to nearly 58 percent in the election of 1828. By 1840, voter turnout was nearly 80 percent.

Limits on Suffrage Despite the nation's growing democratic spirit, a great many Americans did not have the right to vote. These included women, Native Americans, and the vast majority of African Americans. Meanwhile, even through Jackson's presidency, a few states kept the requirement that only white male property owners were eligible to vote.

Although most white men had won suffrage, free African Americans had lost it. In the early years of the nation, most northern states and a few southern states allowed free African American men to vote. By the 1820s, however, many of these states had taken away that right. By 1830, only a few New England states permitted free African American men to vote on equal terms with white men. In New York, African American men had to own property in order to vote while white men did not. No state allowed enslaved African Americans to vote.

Analyze Images Nearly all white men gained the right to vote during the Age of Jackson, but still, most adults, including the enslaved African American men shown here, were not allowed to vote. **Infer** Why might people who were able to vote be reluctant to extend the vote to others?

☑ READING CHECK **Summarize** How did democracy expand during the Age of Jackson?

The Election of 1824 Leads to a "Bargain"

There were four candidates for president in 1824. All four were members of the old Republican Party. However, each had support in different parts of the country. John Quincy Adams was strong in New England. Henry Clay and Andrew Jackson had support in the West. William H. Crawford was favored in the South, but became too ill to campaign.

The Candidates John Quincy Adams of Massachusetts was the son of Abigail and John Adams, the second President. A graduate of Harvard University, the younger Adams had served as Secretary of State and helped end the War of 1812. People admired Adams for his intelligence and high morals. In 1821 as Secretary of State, he gave a Fourth of July speech before Congress. It set the tone for American foreign policy for decades to come. Adams, however, was uncomfortable campaigning among the common people. In fact, to most people he seemed hard and cold.

The Election of 1824

CANDIDATE	Andrew Jackson	John Quincy Adams	William Crawford	Henry Clay
HOME STATE	Tennessee	Massachusetts	Georgia	Kentucky
MAIN POSITIONS	Presents himself as the champion of the common man	Supports tariffs and spending on roads and canals to promote business	Supports states' rights	Supports tariffs and spending on roads and canals to promote business, compromise between North and South
POPULAR VOTE*	151,271	113,122	40,856	47,531
ELECTORAL VOTE	99	84	41	37
HOUSE VOTE BY STATE	7	13	4	Not on ballot

*The popular vote does not accurately measure candidates' popular support, because in several states there was no popular vote, and electors were chosen by state legislatures.

Analyze Images This chart shows information about the four candidates in the presidential election of 1824. **Compare** Which two candidates' positions were most similar, and how were they similar?

Henry Clay, a Kentuckian, was Speaker of the House of Representatives. He was a skillful negotiator and a shrewd politician. Despite his abilities, Clay was less popular than the other candidate from the West, Andrew Jackson.

William H. Crawford had served as treasury secretary, war secretary, and ambassador to France after the War of 1812, and as a senator from Georgia. Crawford's support was concentrated in the Southeast.

To many Americans, especially on the western frontier, Andrew Jackson was a hero. A general during the War of 1812, he had defeated the British and a group of Creek Indians who were allied with the British. He had gone on to defeat the Seminoles and the Spanish in Florida, gaining that territory for the United States. He was known as the "Hero of New Orleans" for his victory in the War of 1812. He also earned the nickname "Old Hickory" after a soldier said he was "tough as hickory." Jackson's fame as a general helped him launch a political career. Although he was a landowner and a slave owner, many saw him as a man of the people. Jackson had been born in a log cabin, and his parents had been poor farmers. He was admired by small farmers and others who felt left out of the growing economy in the United States. The expansion of the vote to white men without property helped account for Jackson's political popularity.

The "Corrupt Bargain" No clear winner emerged from the election of 1824. Jackson won the popular vote, but no candidate won a **majority**, or more than half, of the electoral votes. As a result, under the provisions of the Constitution, the House of Representatives had to choose the President from among the top three candidates. Because he had finished fourth, Clay was out of the running.

As Speaker of the House, though, Clay played an important role in influencing the results. He urged members of the House to vote for Adams. After Adams won the vote in the House and became President, he named Clay his secretary of state. In the past, secretaries of state had often gone on to become President.

Although the election was decided properly according to the Constitution, Jackson and his backers were furious. They accused Adams and Clay of making a "corrupt bargain" and stealing the election from Jackson. The anger of Jackson and his supporters seriously hampered President Adams's efforts to unify the nation.

☑ READING CHECK **Draw Conclusions** Why did some people refer to the 1824 election result as a "corrupt bargain"?

Academic Vocabulary

perceive • *v.*, notice or become aware of

The Presidency of John Quincy Adams

Adams **perceived** that the outcome of the election had angered many Americans. To "bring the whole people together," he pushed for a program of economic growth through internal improvements. His plan backfired, however, and opposition to him grew.

Promoting Economic Growth Like Alexander Hamilton and Henry Clay, Adams thought that the federal government should promote economic growth. He called for the government to pay for new roads and canals. These internal improvements would help farmers to transport goods to market.

Adams also favored projects to promote the arts and the sciences. He suggested building a national university and an observatory from which astronomers could study the stars. Most Americans objected to spending money on such programs. They feared that the federal government would become too powerful. Congress approved money for a national road and some canals but turned down most of Adams's other spending programs.

Origin of New Political Parties During the 1820s, nearly all politicians were members of Jefferson's Democratic-Republican Party. In the 1830s, however, new political parties took shape. These parties grew out of the conflict between John Quincy Adams and Andrew Jackson.

The Whig Party Democratic-Republicans who supported Adams and his programs for national growth called themselves National Republicans. In 1834, many of them joined a new party, organized by Henry Clay and known as the **Whig Party**.

Analyze Images John Quincy Adams, the sixth President of the United States, thought that the federal government should adopt policies and pay for projects that would help the economy. **Identify Main Ideas** How would building roads and canals help the economy?

Analyze Images Jackson drew wide support from small business people, farmers, laborers, and others. **Infer** Why do you think these people voted for Jackson?

Whigs wanted the government to act to help the economy. They wanted the federal government to promote business by paying for roads and canals. They also wanted the federal government to oversee banks. They believed that a stable banking system would encourage business. Whigs also wanted higher tariffs.

Tariffs are taxes or fees placed on imported goods. Because tariffs make imports more expensive, they help domestic producers. However, they may prompt foreign governments to counter with their own tariffs. This can harm exporters.

The Democratic Party Jackson and other Democratic-Republicans who supported him began to call themselves the **Democratic Party**. Today's Democratic Party traces its roots to Andrew Jackson's time. Like the Whig Party, Democrats also had a point of view. They called for more political power for ordinary white men and opposed privileges for the wealthy or educated. Democrats were opposed to a federal government role in the economy and to tariffs.

Democrats opposed high tariffs because farmers counted on being able to sell their goods overseas and did not want to risk retaliatory tariffs. Tariffs also protected American manufacturers from foreign competition. The result was higher prices for all kinds of goods that ordinary people needed. Democrats supported westward expansion to open up more land for frontier settlers.

Democrats were generally more tightly organized than Whigs. Members usually followed the direction set by party leaders.

Who Supported the Whigs and Democrats? The Whigs had their strongest support in the Northeast, with some support in cities and towns in the South and West. People from these places backed the Whigs because these places relied on manufacturing and commerce, and Whig policies aimed to help those parts of the economy.

INTERACTIVE

Political Parties in the Age of Jackson

Whig supporters included eastern factory owners and other businessmen, some southern planters, and many former Federalists. Whigs were often divided into factions, and not all of the party's members always followed the party's direction.

Democrats had strong support in the South and West, especially among laborers, artisans, and small farmers. These groups also supported Democrats in some parts of the Northeast. Small farmers and workers supported the Democrats because Democrats spoke up for them against bankers and Northeastern businessmen. While big business favored the Whigs, middle-class businesspeople and merchants lined up behind Jackson.

A Bitter Campaign In 1828, Adams faced an uphill battle for reelection. This time, Andrew Jackson was Adams's only opponent. The campaign was a bitter contest. Jackson supporters renewed charges that Adams had made a "corrupt bargain" after the 1824 election. They also attacked Adams as an aristocrat, or member of the upper class.

Adams supporters replied with similar attacks. They called Jackson a dangerous "military chieftain." If Jackson became president, they warned, he could become a dictator like Napoleon Bonaparte of France.

Jackson won the election easily. His supporters cheered the outcome as a victory for the common people. By common people, they meant white people who worked for a living, including farmers and city workers. For the first time since the Revolution, the politics of the common people were important.

✓ READING CHECK **Summarize** Why did Andrew Jackson win the election of 1828?

GEOGRAPHY **SKILLS**

This map shows the results of the 1828 presidential election.

1. **Movement** In which region of the country did most people vote for Jackson? Which region voted mostly for Adams?

2. **Use Visual Information** Which states were divided in their support of Jackson and Adams? Explain.

Election of 1828

KEY
- Andrew Jackson
- John Quincy Adams

Jacksonian Democracy

Jackson was a new kind of American politician. Unlike the polished, aristocratic easterners who preceded him, Jackson was a plainspoken frontiersman. His personality and point of view would influence American politics for years to come.

Andrew Jackson Growing Up Like many who admired him, Andrew Jackson was born in a log cabin on the frontier. His parents had left Ireland to settle in the Carolinas. Both died before Jackson was 15. **Consequently,** Jackson had to grow up quickly.

Although he was lean, he was a strong fighter. A friend who wrestled with him recalled, "I could throw him three times out of four, but he would never stay throwed."

Always determined, Jackson showed his toughness at 13 when he joined the American Revolution. He was captured by the British while carrying messages for the Patriots.

Jackson Prepares to Be President After the Revolution, Jackson studied law in North Carolina. He later moved to Tennessee and set up a successful law practice. Over time he became very wealthy by buying and selling land in Georgia and Alabama. While still in his twenties, he was elected to Congress. He served for just a few years before becoming a judge and a major general in the Tennessee militia.

Academic Vocabulary
consequently • *adv.,* as a result

Analyze Images Taken prisoner by the British at age 13, Andrew Jackson refused to clean a British officer's boots. The officer slashed Jackson with his sword, scarring him for life. **Draw Conclusions** What does this experience tell you about Andrew Jackson's character?

Jackson won national fame for his achievements during the War of 1812. He led American forces to a major victory over the British at the Battle of New Orleans. He was also known for his leadership during the Creek War. A group of Creeks, angered in part by white settlers moving onto their land, began to attack settlers. These Creeks massacred at least 250 people, including soldiers and their families, at Fort Mims, in present-day Alabama. Jackson led an army to stop the attacks. His victory at Horseshoe Bend forced the Creeks to give up vast amounts of land in what are now Georgia and Alabama.

Andrew Jackson was a complex person. He had led a violent and adventurous life. He was quick to lose his temper, and he dealt with his enemies harshly. When he became president, his opponents sarcastically called him "King Andrew." Jackson intended to be a strong president by expanding the powers of the presidency. At the same time, Jackson's supporters admired his ability to inspire and lead others. They considered him a man of his word and a champion of the common people.

Jackson's Inauguration As Jackson traveled to Washington to be inaugurated, large crowds cheered him along the way. For the first time, thousands of ordinary people flooded the capital to watch the President take the oath of office. After Jackson was sworn in, the crowd followed the new President to a reception at the White House. One onlooker described the scene with amazement:

KING ANDREW the FIRST

Analyze Images An artist drew this cartoon to criticize what he saw as Andrew Jackson's hunger for power. **Cite Evidence** What features of this cartoon suggest that Jackson was hungry for power?

Primary Source

"Country men, farmers, gentlemen, mounted and dismounted, boys, women and children, black and white. Carriages, wagons, and carts all pursuing [Jackson] to the President's house."

—Margaret Bayard Smith, *The First Forty Years of Washington Society*

The crowds were so huge, the observer continued, that the President was "almost suffocated and torn to pieces by the people in their eagerness to shake hands." Jackson's critics said the scene showed that "King Mob" was ruling the nation. Amos Kendall, a loyal Jackson supporter, saw the celebration in a more positive way: "It was a proud day for the people. General Jackson is their own President."

Causes of Jacksonian Democracy Andrew Jackson was elected in 1828 largely because white men without property could now vote. He drew much of his support from small farmers, laborers, artisans, and middle-class businessmen on the western frontier. The spread of political power to more people was part of what became known as Jacksonian democracy.

However, Jacksonian democracy was limited to select groups. In particular, Jackson owned slaves at his estate, The Hermitage, and opposed the antislavery movement.

Effects of Jacksonian Democracy Jackson was the first westerner to occupy the White House. His election marked a shift of political power to the West. He was seen as a daring individualist. His image helped shape an American consciousness focused on individual freedom and daring.

Another effect of Jacksonian democracy was the growth in political parties and in citizen participation in the political process. It was one thing to make it legal for nearly all white men to vote. It was another thing to convince them to vote.

Jackson's Democratic Party introduced political campaigns that appealed to common people and their concerns. These campaigns motivated white men to cast their vote for the Democrats.

✓READING CHECK **Draw Conclusions** Why was Andrew Jackson seen as a champion of the common people?

Analyze Images Jackson lived in this home he called The Hermitage from 1804 until his death in 1845. **Infer** Consider the kind of house Jackson lived in. Why do you think his supporters considered him a common man like themselves?

The Spoils System

One of the biggest effects of Jacksonian politics was the development of the **spoils system**. Spoils are loot or plunder. The spoils system was the practice of awarding government jobs to friends and supporters. As one Jackson supporter explained the system: "To the victor belong the spoils."

After taking office, Jackson fired many government employees. He replaced those employees with his supporters. Most other presidents had done the same, but Jackson did it on a much larger scale.

Critics said the spoils system was corrupt and unethical. They accused Jackson of rewarding his supporters instead of choosing qualified men. Jackson replied that giving government jobs to ordinary men would prevent a small group of wealthy men from controlling the government. He felt that most Americans could fill government jobs. "The duties of all public officers are . . . so plain and simple that men of intelligence may readily qualify themselves for their performance," he said.

✅ **READING CHECK** Draw Conclusions
Why did Jackson adopt the spoils system?

Analyze Images A cartoonist drew this cartoon in 1877 to criticize the spoils system, which survived long after Jackson introduced it. **Analyze Political Cartoons** How does the cartoon criticize the spoils system?

✅ Lesson Check

Practice Vocabulary

1. How did changes in **suffrage** affect the election of Andrew Jackson as President?

2. According to critics, what was wrong with the **spoils system** during Jackson's presidency?

3. Why did Jackson not win the 1824 presidential election even though he won the **majority** of the popular vote?

Critical Thinking and Writing

4. **Compare and Contrast** How did Andrew Jackson represent what Alexis de Tocqueville recognized as the American character?

5. **Explain an Argument** Why would Jackson's supporters oppose the economic programs proposed by Adams during his presidency?

6. **Writing Workshop: Introduce Characters** Write a short paragraph in your 📕 Active Journal from the point of view of a person who is moving westward during this time period. Tell your name, age, and where you come from, tell about your family and your life, and explain why you are moving west. You will use these details in an essay you will write at the end of the Topic.

John Quincy Adams, Speech on Independence Day

On July 4, 1821, U.S. Secretary of State John Quincy Adams gave a speech stating his view of the United States' role in the world. His ideas influenced American foreign policy for decades to come.

◀ John Quincy Adams, Secretary of State 1817–1825

Reading and Vocabulary Support

① What do you think Adams means by "modifications of internal government"?

② *Vicissitudes* means "unexpected changes."

③ *Consecrated* means made sacred or very special.

④ What does "abstained from interference" mean?

⑤ What do you think the word *dominion* means?

In the progress of forty years since the acknowledgement of our Independence, we have gone through many modifications of internal government ①, and through all the vicissitudes ② of peace and war, with other powerful nations. But never, never for a moment have the great principles consecrated ③ by the Declaration of this day been renounced or abandoned.

And . . . what has America done for the benefit of mankind? . . . America [has] proclaimed to mankind the inextinguishable rights of human nature and the only lawful foundations of government. America, in the assembly of nations, . . . has uniformly spoken among them, though often to heedless and often to disdainful ears, the language of equal liberty, of equal justice, and of equal rights. She has . . . respected the independence of other nations while asserting and maintaining her own. She has abstained from interference ④ in the concerns of others. . . . Wherever the standard of freedom and Independence has been or shall be unfurled, there will her heart . . . and her prayers be. But she goes not abroad in search of monsters to destroy. . . . She well knows that by once enlisting under other banners than her own, were they even the banners of foreign Independence, . . . [s]he might become the dictatress of the world, [but s]he would be no longer the ruler of her own spirit. . . .[America's] glory is not dominion ⑤, but liberty. Her march is the march of mind. She has a spear and a shield, but the motto upon her shield is, Freedom, Independence, Peace.

Analyzing Primary Sources

Cite specific evidence from the document to support your answers.

1. **Determine Author's Point of View** According to Adams, what should the United States do if other countries go to war?

2. **Analyze Information** What does Adams mean in saying that by "enlisting under other banners than her own . . . [s]he would be no longer the ruler of her own spirit"?

Political Conflict and Economic Crisis

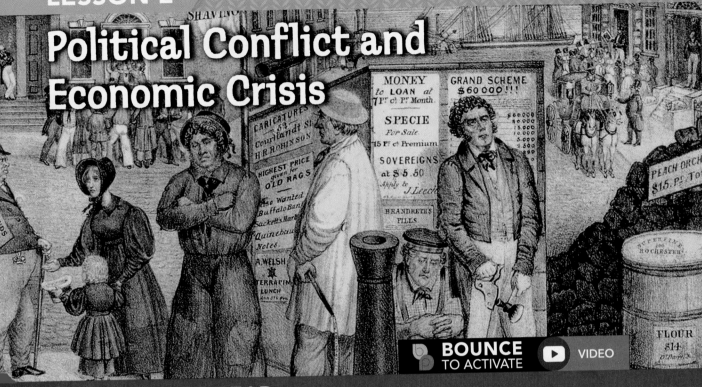

GET READY TO READ

START UP

This illustration shows people suffering from a nationwide economic downturn. How would you respond to an economic panic?

GUIDING QUESTIONS

- How did Andrew Jackson change the country?
- How did Jackson and his opponents clash over the issues of nullification and states' rights?
- Why did Americans disagree about the banking system?
- How did economic issues impact the election of 1840?

TAKE NOTES

Literacy Skills: Compare and Contrast
Use the Graphic Organizer in your 📓 Active Journal to take notes as you read the lesson.

PRACTICE VOCABULARY

Use the Vocabulary Builder activity 📓 Active Journal in your Journal to practice the vocabulary words.

Vocabulary

states' rights
Nullification Act
depression
caucus
nominating convention

Academic Vocabulary

implicit
speculation

During Jackson's two terms as President, conflicts and crises shook the nation. Some were thrust upon Jackson by the grinding of sectional rivalries. Others were events of his own making. The effects of his responses to these crises were felt throughout the nation for decades to come.

A Conflict Over States' Rights

The first crisis Jackson faced arose almost immediately after he entered office. It was an intense quarrel over **states' rights**, or the rights of states to exercise power independent of the federal government.

Regional Differences on the States' Rights Issue The conflict over states' rights divided the country along regional lines. The United States at the time was made up of three regions.

The North included the New England and Middle Atlantic states. Manufacturing and trade were very important to the economy of the North.

Analyze Images The
❶ North, **❷** South, and
❸ West had economies
based in different kinds
of work and businesses.
Identify Supporting Details
How did the different
regional economies depend
on each other?

👆 INTERACTIVE

Tariffs and Trade

The West was the region we now know as the Midwest. Its economy was based mainly on raising of livestock and farming food crops.

Finally, the South consisted of today's Southeast and South Central states. The South's people relied heavily on farming cash crops for export, such as cotton and tobacco.

Politically, northerners generally favored a strong federal government, which they saw as necessary to promote manufacturing and trade. Southerners feared the domination of the North and national policies that could hurt southern interests. Consequently, southerners tended to support stronger states' rights. These differences often made it hard for people from the North and South to agree on political issues.

Westerners sometimes sided with the North and sometimes with the South. For example, westerners wanted internal improvements for transportation, which most northerners supported. Westerners also wanted to be free to move into new territories, which southerners also wanted. Some westerners supported slavery, while others did not. In general, westerners agreed with northerners about tariffs.

Anger Over Tariffs In 1828, before Jackson took office, Congress passed the highest tariff in the history of the nation. Manufacturers, most of whom lived in the North, were helped by the tariff. It protected them from foreign competition.

Southern planters, however, called it the Tariff of Abominations. An abomination is something that is wrong and evil. Southerners sold much of their cotton to Britain and bought British manufactured goods in return. A high tariff would mean that southerners had to pay more for those British goods. Worse still, they feared that if the United States imposed a tariff on British manufactures, Britain would respond by imposing a tariff on American cotton. Many southerners thought the tariff was unconstitutional.

Debate Over Nullification A leader in the South's fight against the tariff was Vice President John Calhoun of South Carolina. He claimed that a state had the right to nullify, or cancel, a federal law that the state considered to be unconstitutional. This idea is called nullification. Calhoun believed that the states could nullify federal laws, because the states had joined together to form the federal government based on their understanding of the Constitution.

Daniel Webster, a senator from Massachusetts, disagreed. He made a speech in 1830 to the Senate attacking the idea of nullification. The Constitution, he said, united the American people, not just the states, as a nation. If states had the right to nullify federal laws, the nation would fall apart. The U.S. Supreme Court had also ruled against earlier attempts at nullification. The justices said that the provisions of Article III of the U.S. Constitution gave federal courts, not states, the right to decide on the constitutionality of federal laws. President Jackson agreed with the views of Webster and the Supreme Court. Because Calhoun strongly disagreed with Jackson, he resigned from the office of vice president. He was then elected senator from South Carolina. The debate over nullification would continue for years.

The Nullification Act Leads to Crisis Anger against the tariff increased in the South. Congress passed a new law in 1832 that lowered the tariff slightly. South Carolina was not satisfied. It passed the **Nullification Act**, declaring the new tariff illegal. It also threatened to secede, or withdraw, from the Union if challenged. Jackson was furious. He knew that nullification could lead to civil war.

▲ John Caldwell Calhoun of South Carolina served as representative, senator, secretary of war, secretary of state, and vice president twice.

Milestones in the States' Rights Debate

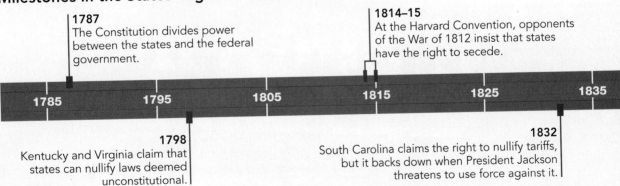

1787
The Constitution divides power between the states and the federal government.

1814–15
At the Harvard Convention, opponents of the War of 1812 insist that states have the right to secede.

1785   1795   1805   1815   1825   1835

1798
Kentucky and Virginia claim that states can nullify laws deemed unconstitutional.

1832
South Carolina claims the right to nullify tariffs, but it backs down when President Jackson threatens to use force against it.

Analyze Timelines As the timeline shows, the states' rights conflict began early in the nation's history. **Identify** an instance on the timeline of tension between a specific state and the federal government. How might sectionalism have contributed to this tension?

To defuse the crisis, Henry Clay, now a senator from Kentucky, proposed a lower, compromise tariff, which President Jackson supported. Jackson also asked Congress to pass the Force bill, which would allow the President to use the army, if necessary, to enforce the tariff. Daniel Webster sided with Jackson on the Force bill but opposed Clay's compromise tariff. However, Congress passed both the compromise tariff and the Force bill.

Faced with Jackson's firm stand, no other state chose to support South Carolina. When Calhoun supported the compromise tariff, South Carolina repealed its Nullification Act, and the Nullification Crisis passed. National identity had proven stronger than a state's claim to sovereignty.

While Jackson's actions kept South Carolina in the union and reinforced federal authority, they did not bring the quarrel to a close. In the years ahead, tensions between the North and South would lead to increased sectionalism.

☑ **READING CHECK** **Summarize** Why did Webster and Jackson oppose nullification?

The Bank War

In another political battle that had a long-term effect on the country, Jackson waged war against the Second Bank of the United States. Like many westerners, Jackson thought that the Bank was too powerful and needed to be eliminated. Jackson's Democratic Party opposed the Bank. The Whig Party, however, supported the Bank. Whigs believed that the Bank was needed to regulate lending by state banks to arrest the growth of debts that could not be repaid.

Analyze Images
Senator Daniel Webster defended the interests of his home state of Massachusetts by arguing that states could not nullify the Tariff of 1828.
Explain an Argument Why is it important for representatives to support their positions with good reasons?

FUNCTIONS OF THE SECOND BANK
OF THE UNITED STATES

BANK OF THE FEDERAL GOVERNMENT
- Holds the government's money
- Pays the government's bills

MONEY CREATOR
Issues paper money that people can use throughout the United States, unlike state money

REGULATOR
- Issues or redeems national money to keep economy stable
- Monitors amount of money from state banks

COMMERCIAL BANK
- Accepts deposits and makes loans
- Provides access to businesses and individuals at branches across the country

A Controversial Bank The Second Bank of the United States had been a subject of dispute since its early days. The Bank had great power because it controlled loans made by state banks. When the Bank's directors thought that state banks were owed too much money, they limited the amount these banks could lend. The cutbacks angered farmers and merchants, who often needed to borrow money to buy land or finance new businesses.

President Jackson and other leading Democrats saw the Bank as undemocratic. Although Congress created the Bank, it was run by private bankers. Jackson condemned these men as agents of "special privilege" who grew rich with public funds. He especially disliked Nicholas Biddle, president of the Bank since 1823.

With Biddle running the Bank, the U.S. economy had experienced stability and prosperity. However, Biddle was known to make loans to friends while turning down loans to people who opposed the Bank. Among these were many of Jackson's strongest supporters. Jackson felt that Biddle used the Bank to benefit the rich. He also resented Biddle's influence over certain members of Congress.

The Bank Applies for Renewal Biddle and other Whigs worried that the President might try to destroy the Bank. Two Whig senators, Henry Clay and Daniel Webster, thought of a way they might save the Bank and defeat Jackson in the upcoming election at the same time.

The Bank's charter was not due for renewal by Congress until 1836. However, Clay and Webster wanted to make the Bank an issue in the 1832 election. They persuaded Biddle to apply for renewal early. The Whigs believed that most Americans appreciated the role of the Bank in the nation's prosperity. If Jackson vetoed the bill to renew the charter, they felt sure that he would anger voters and lose the election.

Analyze Charts The Second Bank of the United States was founded to help the federal government manage its income and expenses. **Classify and Categorize** How was the Bank involved in the nation's economy?

INTERACTIVE

Disagreements Over the Bank

Analyze Images In this cartoon, President Jackson fights a snake representing the Bank and its branches. The largest head is Nicholas Biddle's. **Analyze Cartoons** How is Jackson trying to destroy the Bank?

Clay was able to push the charter renewal bill through Congress in 1832. Jackson was sick in bed when he heard that Congress had renewed the Bank's charter. "The Bank . . . is trying to kill me," Jackson fumed, "but I will kill it!"

Jackson Cuts Off the Bank In an angry message to Congress, Jackson vetoed the Bank bill. He gave two reasons for his veto. For one, he believed that the Bank helped aristocrats at the expense of the common people. He warned:

Primary Source

"When the laws undertake . . . to make the rich richer and the potent more powerful, the humble members of the society—the farmers, mechanics, and laborers—who have neither the time nor the means of [getting] like favors for themselves . . . have a right to complain of the injustices of their government."

—Andrew Jackson, Veto Message, July 10, 1832

Jackson's other reason for vetoing the bank bill was his belief that the Bank was unconstitutional. Like other Democrats, Jackson believed that the federal government could not charter a bank because the Constitution did not explicitly give it the power to do so.

Jackson had already lost this argument. In *McCulloch* v. *Maryland*, the Supreme Court had ruled that the "necessary and proper clause" of the

Constitution **implicitly** gave the federal government the right to create a bank. This clause states that the federal government has the power "To make all Laws which shall be necessary and proper for carrying into Execution the . . . Powers [already described], and all other Powers vested by this Constitution." However, Jackson did not accept the court's ruling. He continued to believe that only states had the right to charter banks.

As they had planned, the Whigs made the Bank a major issue in the election of 1832. They chose Henry Clay as their candidate to run against Andrew Jackson.

When the votes were counted, however, Jackson had won a stunning election victory. The common people had surprised the Whigs by supporting Jackson and rejecting the Bank of the United States.

The Bank Loses Its National Role Without a new charter, the Bank would have to close in 1836. Jackson refused to wait. He ordered Secretary of the Treasury Roger Taney to stop putting government money in the Bank. Instead, Taney deposited federal money in state banks. They became known as pet banks because Taney and his friends controlled many of them.

The loss of its federal deposits crippled the Second Bank of the United States. Its elimination as a national bank was another effect of Jackson's presidency—one that would have lasting impact. The end of the Bank contributed to an economic crisis that would have to be faced by the next President of the United States.

Without a national bank, responsibility for regulating banks fell to individual states. The period from the late 1830s until the 1860s is known as the state banking era. During this time, each state set its own rules for banks. Lax state regulations allowed banks to take risks.

☑ READING CHECK **Identify Supporting Details** What did Jackson do with the government's money after he ordered that it should no longer be deposited in the Second National Bank?

Academic Vocabulary
implicit • *adv.,* not expressed directly but able to be understood or inferred

Analyze Images During the state banking era, Americans relied on currency issued by state or private banks like that shown. Money from banks with poor reputations might not be accepted by other banks or merchants. **Infer** How might a person judge whether a bank's currency is trustworthy?

Economic Crisis and Political Changes

Following tradition, Andrew Jackson left office after two terms. Americans elected Martin Van Buren to succeed him as President. Although Van Buren did not have Jackson's popularity, he was clever and intelligent. As President, however, Van Buren needed more than sharp political instincts.

The Panic of 1837 Before leaving office, Jackson had been alarmed at wild **speculation**, or risky investment, in land. Since the Bank of the United States had closed, state banks were printing and lending money without limit. Speculators were borrowing more and more money to buy land and driving land prices up.

Analyze Images A debtor negotiates with a merchant (left), a customer wonders how he can pay his bill (center), and a man warms himself at a stove (right). **Draw Conclusions** How did the Panic of 1837 affect people differently?

To slow this process, Jackson had ordered that anyone buying public land had to pay for it with gold or silver. This sent speculators and others rushing to state banks to exchange their paper money for gold and silver. However, many banks had loaned too much money. If a bank did not have enough gold and silver to buy back the notes it had issued, it could go broke and be forced to close.

When Van Buren took office, the situation had only worsened. As more and more banks failed, the nation fell into a deep economic **depression**, a period when the economy shrinks and many people lose their jobs. This depression, known as The Panic of 1837, was the worst economic crisis the nation had yet known. It lasted five years. During the worst period, 90 percent of the nation's factories were closed. Unemployment was widespread. Hundreds of thousands of people were out of work.

Although many Americans blamed Van Buren and his policies for the economic depression, the roots of the problem lay in Jackson's administration. His closure of the Bank and his efforts to rein in land speculation both contributed to the crisis. Van Buren was not without fault, however. He believed in laissez-faire economics—the idea that government should play as small a role as possible in the economy. As the depression wore on, Van Buren became increasingly unpopular. His opponents called him "Martin Van Ruin."

▲ A national nominating convention

Party Caucuses and Conventions By the time of the next presidential election in 1840, Whigs and Democrats had developed more democratic ways to choose candidates for President. In the past, powerful members of each party had held a **caucus**, or private meeting, to choose their candidate. Critics called the caucus system undemocratic because only a few powerful people were able to take part in it.

In the 1830s, each party began to hold a national **nominating convention**, where delegates from all the states met to choose the party's candidate for President. Party leaders might still dominate a particular convention, but the people could now have some influence in the nominating process. Also, state nominating conventions encouraged citizen participation in elections. Once citizens learned about the events of the convention, they would work for their party's choices. Today, the major political parties still hold state and national conventions.

Democrats Lose the Election of 1840 Although Van Buren had lost support, the Democrats chose him to run for reelection in 1840. The Whigs chose William Henry Harrison of Ohio as their presidential candidate and John Tyler of Virginia as their vice presidential candidate. Their policies included creating a new Bank of the United States, improving roads and canals, and demanding a high tariff.

INTERACTIVE

Choosing a Presidential Candidate

Harrison was known as the hero of the Battle of Tippecanoe, which was fought between the American military and a Shawnee-led alliance in 1811. To appeal to voters, the Whigs focused on Harrison's war record. "Tippecanoe and Tyler too" became their campaign slogan. The Whigs created an image of Harrison as a "man of the people" from the western frontier. They presented him as a humble farmer and boasted that he had been born in a log cabin. In fact, Harrison was a wealthy, educated man who, at the time of the campaign, lived in a large mansion.

Harrison won the election. However, Whig hopes were dashed when, soon after taking office, President Harrison died of pneumonia. John Tyler then became President. President Tyler failed to live up to Whig expectations and opposed many Whig policies. In response, the Whigs threw Tyler out of their party just months after he took office.

Analyze Images In 1840, just as in the present time, political parties distributed campaign buttons, posters, flags, and other items to promote their party's candidate. **Synthesize Visual Evidence** What ideas from Harrison's campaign did these buttons represent?

☑ READING CHECK **Identify Supporting Details** How did President Jackson attempt to slow the land speculation that led to the Panic of 1837?

☑ Lesson Check

Practice Vocabulary

1. How was the **Nullification Act** justified by those who believed in **states' rights**?

2. How does an economic **depression** affect employment?

3. How is a **caucus** different from a **nominating convention**?

Critical Thinking and Writing

4. **Infer** Why do you suppose Andrew Jackson supported Henry Clay's proposed compromise over nullification even though they had been enemies previously?

5. **Understand Effects** Why was it such a disaster for the nation when Andrew Jackson crippled the Second National Bank?

6. **Writing Workshop: Establish Setting** Write three or four sentences in your 📓 Active Journal describing what you see, hear, feel, and smell on a journey west during this time period. You will use these details in the narrative you will write at the end of the Topic. These details will make your narrative vivid and real for your readers.

Interpret Economic Performance

Follow these steps to help you interpret economic performance.

INTERACTIVE

Analyze Data and Models

1 **Identify the type of statistics being presented** Economists use statistics called economic indicators. These statistics help them to determine if the economy is improving or declining. They include

- **Money supply:** total amount of money that a country has in circulation

- **GDP:** total market value of all goods and services produced by a country

- **Current Employment Statistics, or CES:** information on rates of employment, unemployment, and wages and earnings

- **Housing Starts:** number of new private homes and housing units being built

- **Consumer Price Index, or CPI:** measures changes in retail prices

- **Producer Price Index, or PPI:** measures the average selling price of goods and services that are produced in a country

- **Consumer Confidence Index, or CCI:** tracks how consumers feel about the state of the economy

- **Retail Numbers:** statistics measuring sales in retail and food service industries

- **Manufacturing Trade Inventories and Sales:** tracks production, trade sales, and shipments by manufacturers

- **Standard & Poor's 500 Stock Index, or S&P 500:** a list of 500 stocks that help economists and the financial industry measure how companies are performing

2 **Determine how the information is being presented** Is the information displayed in a line graph, a bar graph, a circle graph, or in some other type of figure?

3 **Evaluate what the graph or figure is displaying** Does the information show the relationship between two different economic factors? Is it showing an increase or a decrease?

Money Supply, 1832–1836

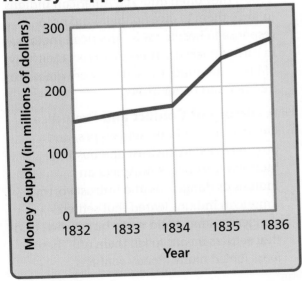

Price Levels, 1832–1836

Year	Index of Prices (year-to-year percentage change)	Total Value of Gold and Silver Coins (in millions of dollars)
1832	–	31
1833	4	41
1834	5	51
1835	20	65
1836	13	73

Conflict with American Indians

BOUNCE TO ACTIVATE ▶ VIDEO

GET READY TO READ

START UP

The U.S. Army captured these Seminole chiefs in 1824. Why did white Americans oust American Indians from their homes?

GUIDING QUESTIONS

- How did Indian removal change the country?
- What did the frontier mean to the nation in the first half of the nineteenth century?
- Describe the cultures of the American Indians living west of the Appalachians.

TAKE NOTES

Literacy Skills: Cite Evidence
Use the Graphic Organizer in your 📓 Active Journal to take notes as you read the lesson.

PRACTICE VOCABULARY

Use the Vocabulary Builder activity in your 📓 Active Journal to practice the vocabulary words.

Vocabulary

		Academic Vocabulary
frontier	Indian Territory	
Worcester v. Georgia	Trail of Tears	acquire
Indian Removal Act		exceedingly

When the first Europeans arrived in North America, they settled on lands that had belonged to American Indians. Although the two groups made attempts to cooperate, repeated conflicts brought tension, mistrust, and sometimes violence.

American Indians and the Frontier

As American settlers moved West in the early 1800s, they often attacked American Indians to force them to give up their land or in response to hostile raids. American Indians, in turn, attacked settlers to protect their way of life. Oftentimes the settlers were greater in number and better armed.

A History of Conflict and Prejudice

On both sides, biases, stereotypes, and prejudices led to mistrust and hostility. Most white settlers saw American Indians as dangerous and untrustworthy. American Indians feared that settlers' hunger for land could never be satisfied and that settlers meant to kill them off. These fears fueled many bloody conflicts.

As you have learned, before the Revolution, the British had made peace with American Indian groups by drawing the Proclamation Line of 1763 through the Appalachian Mountains. This line marked roughly the **frontier**, or edge, of white settlement. The frontier separated white settlers from the lands beyond, which they regarded as free and open to them.

The 1763 Proclamation forbade whites to settle west of the line. This gave American Indians some protection from settlers who wanted to take over their lands. Seeing the British as protectors, many American Indians had sided with them during the Revolutionary War.

After the war, Congress passed the Northwest Ordinance to bring order to white settlement of the Northwest Territory. One part of the ordinance provided a method for settlers to **acquire** land and eventually achieve statehood. The Ordinance fueled even more movement of people into the territory.

Believing their land and culture were at stake, American Indians attacked white settlements in the new Northwest Territory. The Battle of Tippecanoe, in Indiana in 1811, was a major defeat for Shawnee leader Tecumseh and his forces during this time of unrest.

When conflict between the United Kingdom and the United States broke out again in the War of 1812, many, but not all, American Indian groups again sided with the British. A group of Creek in present-day Georgia and Alabama formed an alliance with both Tecumseh and the British. Meanwhile, other Creeks and the neighboring Choctaw sided with the United States. As you have learned, forces led by Andrew Jackson defeated the Creeks allied with the British.

INTERACTIVE

Selected Native American Groups, 1820

GEOGRAPHY **SKILLS**

This map shows the territories of several American Indian groups in 1820.

1. **Location** With a partner, take turns describing the location of each group on the map.

2. **Draw Conclusions** Considering where these American Indian groups lived, what would happen to them as settlers continued to move west?

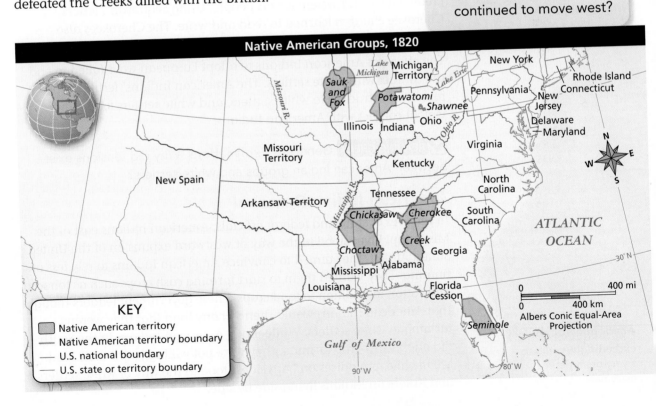

Native American Groups, 1820

KEY
- Native American territory
- Native American territory boundary
- U.S. national boundary
- U.S. state or territory boundary

Analyze Images Sequoyah, a Cherokee leader, developed and taught his people a new writing system for the sounds of the Cherokee language. **Draw Conclusions** Do you think Sequoyah's writing system helped ease conflicts with white settlers? Why, or why not?

The conflicts usually ended badly for the American Indians. They either lost in battle or signed treaties with the government that were soon broken. The first treaty between the U.S. government and American Indians was signed in 1778. Few promises made in that treaty with the Delaware were kept. Likewise, in 1794, the Pickering Treaty between the United States and the Iroquois was also broken. The treaty returned over a million acres to the Iroquois, but much of the land was taken again. American Indians were **exceedingly** distrustful of their white neighbors.

Efforts to Make Peace The Chickasaw, Choctaw, Creek, Seminole, and Cherokee nations lived in parts of what are now Mississippi, Alabama, Florida, Georgia, North Carolina, and Tennessee. The Shawnee, Potawatomi, Sauk, and Fox nations lived in parts of present-day Michigan, Ohio, Indiana, Illinois, and Wisconsin. Many hoped to live in peace with their white neighbors on the frontier.

The Choctaw believed they would be allowed to keep their land because they had sided with the United States during the War of 1812. Other tribes, like the Cherokee nation, adopted European customs, hoping this would help them to preserve their land. The Cherokee created a legal system and government that blended European and Cherokee traditions. In 1821, Sequoyah (suh KWOH yuh), a Cherokee man, created a writing system for his people. Using Sequoyah's letters, Cherokee children learned to read and write. The Cherokees also published a newspaper.

The efforts of American Indians to adopt European ways failed to end the conflict with white settlers. The American Indians' fertile land remained attractive to white settlers, and white settlers feared more violent conflict with American Indians.

✓ **READING CHECK** **Generate Explanations** Why did tensions exist between American Indian groups and white settlers?

American Indian Removal

In the eyes of state and federal officials, American Indians east of the Mississippi River stood in the way of westward expansion of the United States. At first, they aimed to convince American Indians to rely less on hunting. They wanted them to start farming cash crops such as tobacco and cotton in addition to food crops. These government leaders thought that American Indians would then sell any land that they weren't farming to white settlers. While many American Indians in the South did adopt cash-crop farming, they were not willing to sell their land. Meanwhile, prejudices on both sides stood in the way of white settlers and American Indians living side by side.

Academic Vocabulary
exceedingly • *adv.*, to a very great degree; extremely

Pressure on American Indians Increases In 1825, President James Monroe had suggested moving all American Indians living east of the Mississippi to land west of the river. At that time, nothing came of the plan. Yet, year by year, the pressure on the American Indians living along the frontier grew. Those in the North occupied land good for growing corn and wheat and raising livestock. The Northwest Ordinance had already marked this land for white settlers.

In the South, American Indians occupied land that was good for growing cotton. Around them, more and more white settlers arrived, many with enslaved African Americans, seeking to acquire land to grow cotton. Many white southerners were demanding that American Indians be removed by force.

In 1825 and 1827, the state of Georgia passed laws forcing the Creeks to give up most of their land. Laws such as these had previously been struck down by the Supreme Court in *Johnson* v. *M'Intosh* (1823). The ruling in this case stated that only the federal government could acquire land from American Indians, not individuals or state governments.

***Worcester* v. *Georgia* Decision Is Ignored** Georgia's actions were challenged in two suits that reached the Supreme Court. The decision in the first suit went against the Cherokees. In *Cherokee Nation* v. *Georgia* (1831), the Court decided that American Indian groups were not independent nations and so could not sue Georgia in court. The ruling meant the Cherokee could not stop Georgia from enforcing its law. But in **Worcester v. Georgia** (1832), the Court ruled that no state had the authority to enforce its laws within Indian territory. Only the federal government had authority over American Indian lands. Therefore, Georgia could not remove the Cherokee.

Analyze Images
Traditional Cherokee homes were made with woven twigs—seen here in the home's window—and daub plaster over a pole frame. **Summarize** Why were the Cherokee forced to leave their homes?

President Jackson disagreed with the ruling in *Worcester* v. *Georgia*. In the Nullification Crisis, Jackson had defended federal power. In the Cherokee case, however, he backed states' rights. Demonstrating that he was only willing to uphold the law when it suited his purpose, Jackson is reported to have said: "John Marshall has made his decision; now let him enforce it!" Instead, Jackson continued to displace American Indians from their homelands.

The Indian Removal Act At Jackson's urging, in 1830 Congress passed the **Indian Removal Act**. This law let the government take land from American Indians in exchange for land west of the Mississippi River. At the time, more than 100,000 American Indians still lived in the East.

Most white Americans, especially those in the South, supported the removal. They wanted the land for farming and new settlements. Some supported removal to protect the American Indians from conflicts with settlers. They assumed that the United States would never expand past the Mississippi, so American Indians could live there in peace. Some Americans believed the removal was cruel and unfair, but their protests were ignored.

The Indian Removal Act resulted in the expulsion of thousands of American Indians from their homes. In the North, the Ottawa, Potawatomi, Sauk, and Fox peoples all signed treaties to move west to Indian Territories in what are now Kansas and Oklahoma. While most members of these groups left, a few stayed behind in what are now Michigan and Wisconsin.

▲ John Ross was the principal chief, or highest leader, of the Cherokee people when they challenged Georgia in the Supreme Court and later when they were forced to move west.

Numbers Affected by American Indian Removal

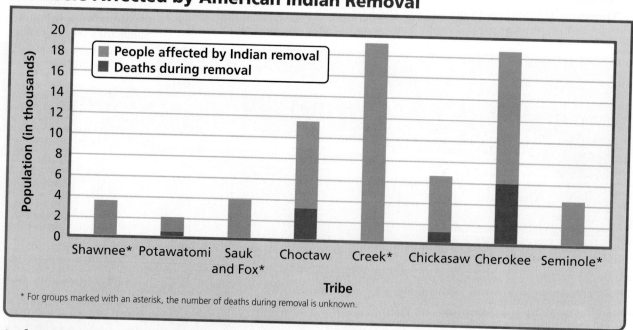

* For groups marked with an asterisk, the number of deaths during removal is unknown.

Analyze Images Several groups affected by American Indian removal are shown here. **Identify Patterns** Look at the groups whose number of deaths is known. About what proportion of those groups died during removal?

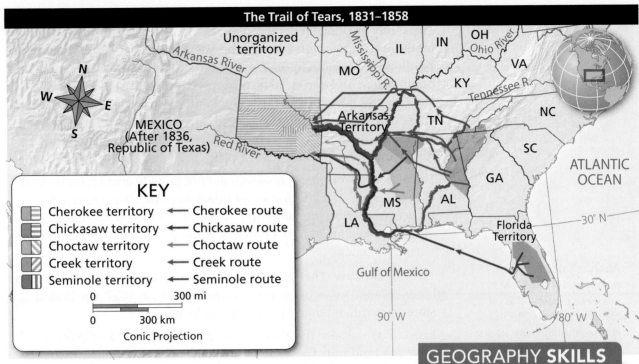

The Trail of Tears, 1831–1858

KEY

- Cherokee territory
- Chickasaw territory
- Choctaw territory
- Creek territory
- Seminole territory
- ← Cherokee route
- ← Chickasaw route
- ← Choctaw route
- ← Creek route
- ← Seminole route

0 — 300 mi
0 — 300 km
Conic Projection

Among the groups who tried to refuse to sign treaties were the Choctaw, Chickasaw, Cherokee, and Seminole. Ultimately, they were forced to sign and forced from their homelands.

Jackson's American Indian removal policy changed the country in several ways. First, it opened up vast areas of the South to white settlers. Many brought slaves with them. So by removing the American Indians, slavery expanded to new places and more states and became more entrenched.

Also because of Jackson's policy, few American Indians today live east of the Mississippi. As a result, most events in the contemporary United States involving American Indians take place in the West.

As well, the policy of taking rich, fertile, forested land from American Indians and restricting them to semi-arid areas in the far West had enormous consequences for American Indians. It impoverished them for generations, separated them from their ancestors' burial grounds, and all but ended their traditional ways of life.

READING CHECK **Explain** Why did Congress pass the Indian Removal Act?

Southern American Indians on the Trail of Tears

Faced with threats of military action, most American Indian leaders in the South saw no choice but to sign new treaties giving up their lands. They agreed to move to what was called the **Indian Territory**. Today, most of that area is in the state of Oklahoma.

GEOGRAPHY **SKILLS**

This map shows the routes and destinations of the American Indians forced from their homes in the East.

1. **Movement** With a partner, use the scale to estimate how far the Cherokee walked on the Trail of Tears.

2. **Identify Cause and Effect** How might the distance the Cherokee walked help explain why so many died on the journey?

INTERACTIVE

Southern Native Americans on the Trail of Tears

The Choctaw The Choctaw signed the first removal treaty in 1830. The Treaty of Dancing Rabbit Creek exchanged the Choctaw's tribal lands for a grant of land west of the Mississippi River. The people would be allowed to remain in their homeland if they gave up their tribal organization and agreed to be governed as citizens of Mississippi. A few Choctaw remained in Mississippi, but upwards of 15,000 people chose to leave so as to preserve some aspects of their culture. Between 1831 and 1833 the Choctaw made their way west, closely guarded by American soldiers.

The federal government, however, did not provide enough tents, food, blankets, shoes, winter clothes, or other supplies. Heavy rain and snow caused enormous suffering. An army lieutenant wrote that one group "walked for 24 hours barefoot through the snow and ice" before reaching shelter.

The Chickasaw The Chickasaw people held out for payment for their lands before they would agree to move. Finally, in 1837, the United States government agreed to pay them $3 million.

Expecting to receive this money, the Chickasaw spent $500,000 to purchase land from the Choctaw in what is now Oklahoma. The U.S. government, though, failed to pay the agreed amount for 30 years. As the Chickasaw trekked to their new land, many became ill and died.

Analyze Images The path of the Trail of Tears has been preserved as a National Historic Trail. It crosses through nine states, from Georgia to Oklahoma. **Synthesize Visual Information** What do you think you might learn from walking the actual route of the Trail of Tears?

Trail of Tears

TRAIL OF TEARS
NATIONAL HISTORIC TRAIL

Original Route

Woodhall's Depot (Westville), OK
60 miles

Fort Cass (Charleston), TN
720 miles

The Cherokee The Cherokee also tried to hold out. They were still on their land in 1836 when Jackson left office. A small group of Cherokee agreed to become citizens of North Carolina, and so were allowed to stay. Other Cherokee hid in remote mountain camps.

Finally, President Van Buren forced those Cherokee who had not made agreements and those who were not in hiding from their homes. In the winter of 1838–1839, the U.S. Army marched more than 15,000 Cherokee westward. They trekked hundreds of miles over a period of several months to reach Indian Territory. Thousands perished during the march, mostly children and the elderly.

The Cherokee's long, sorrowful journey west became known as the **Trail of Tears**. A soldier's description helps explain why:

Primary Source

"On the morning of November 17th, we encountered a terrific sleet and snow storm with freezing temperatures, and from that day until we reached the end of the fateful journey on March the 27th, 1839, the sufferings of the Cherokee were awful. The trail of the exiles was a trail of death."

—Memoirs of Private John G. Burnett, December 1890

The Seminole Resist In Florida, people of the Seminole nation also resisted removal. Led by Chief Osceola (ah see OH luh), they began fighting the United States Army in 1835. This conflict, known as the Second Seminole War, was the costliest war ever waged to gain Indian lands. Although most of the Seminole people were forced to leave Florida, starting in 1855, the United States waged a Third Seminole War to hunt down Seminoles who still resisted relocation.

While Jackson's Indian removal cleared the area east of the Mississippi River for white settlement, settlers already had their eyes on lands west of the Mississippi, too. These lands represented the new frontier. Although occupied by American Indians who had their own cultures and civilization, to white settlers, the term *frontier* meant wild and uncivilized. In their minds, it was free and theirs for the taking. In a few years more, settlers would be streaming into these new lands as they had recently streamed into the Northwest Territory and the South.

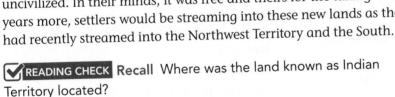

Analyze Images Seminoles began building chickee-style homes using palmetto thatch and a cypress log frame. **Use Visual Information** How did chickee-style homes help Seminoles to flee from the pursuing U.S. Army?

 **READING CHECK** **Recall** Where was the land known as Indian Territory located?

☑ Lesson Check

Practice Vocabulary

1. How did the **frontier** differ from the settled areas along the east coast?

2. How did the **Indian Removal Act** lead to the **Trail of Tears**?

3. What and where was the **Indian Territory**?

Critical Thinking and Writing

4. **Summarize** Why were white settlers and American Indians typically unable to live peacefully in neighboring areas?

5. **Draw Conclusions** What does *Worcester* v. *Georgia* demonstrate about the power of the judiciary?

6. **Writing Workshop: Organize Sequence of Events** In your 📓 Active Journal, list the main events you will tell about that take place on your journey west. Number them in the order you will write about them. You will follow this sequence of events in the narrative you will write at the end of the Topic.

LESSON 4

Westward Movement

BOUNCE TO ACTIVATE   ▶ VIDEO

GET READY TO READ

START UP
Examine this painting of wagons heading west. What might have gone through people's minds as they looked toward the wilderness before them?

GUIDING QUESTIONS
- What did the frontier mean to the nation in the first half of the nineteenth century?
- How did the Westward movement change family life?
- How did geography affect life in the West?

TAKE NOTES

Literacy Notes: Classify and Categorize
Use the Graphic Organizer in your 📓 Active Journal to take notes as you read the lesson.

PRACTICE VOCABULARY
Use the Vocabulary Builder activity in your 📓 Active Journal to practice the vocabulary words.

Vocabulary	Academic Vocabulary
revenue	extend
flatboat	despite
Clermont	
Erie Canal	
National Road	

English colonists began moving west almost as soon as they arrived in America in the 1600s. Westward expansion quickly became a tradition that helped define the nation.

Why Did Americans Move West?

As the population of the United States grew, land became more expensive, and some Americans began to feel crowded. By the early 1800s, the promise of new farmland and other work opportunities brought a flood of new emigrants from settled areas in the East to the lands west of the Appalachian Mountains.

Northwest Ordinance The Northwest Territory was the area north of the Ohio River and east of the Mississippi. Colonists had been moving into this area since before the American Revolution. When the United States acquired this land from the United Kingdom, the flow of settlers increased.

One of the first tasks of the new federal government was to organize how the territory was to be settled. In a series of three acts, passed between 1784 and 1787, Congress created the Northwest Ordinance. It applied specifically to the Northwest Territory at first. Later, the principles of the Ordinance were **extended** to other territories.

The Ordinance allowed individuals to buy land in 640-acre tracts. That much acreage was too expensive for most settlers. Soon, developers were buying land and dividing it into smaller parcels that were more affordable and more manageable.

The sale of land attracted settlers, but it also provided needed **revenue**, or income, for the U.S. government. The money was needed to pay off debt from the American Revolution.

In the past, people thought of territories as colonies. The Ordinance changed that. Settlers in these territories could now organize into states that would have all the rights of the original thirteen states. People moving into the territories were not leaving the United States, they were expanding it.

Another part of the Ordinance outlawed slavery in the territories. This provision would cause many sectional disputes.

Opportunities and Challenges Americans moved west for many reasons, but mostly they wanted the opportunity to own land, start businesses, and build new lives. Some people, like the Mormons, moved west to find religious freedom.

In 1803, President Jefferson made the Louisiana Purchase from France, doubling the size of the country. The Louisiana Purchase opened up a vast new territory with many valuable natural resources.

Academic Vocabulary
extend • v., to expand or apply further

INTERACTIVE

New Transportation Methods

GEOGRAPHY SKILLS

By 1819, the United States had grown to 23 states.

1 **Movement** What can the dates of statehood of the new states tell us about how settlers migrated into the western territories?

2 **Draw Conclusions** Based on this pattern of settlement, where will settlers move next?

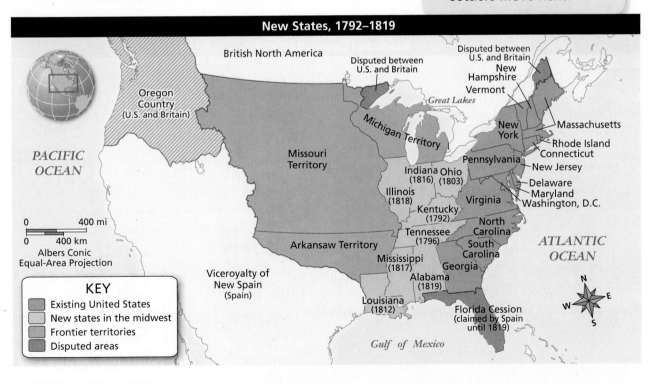

New States, 1792–1819

British North America

Disputed between U.S. and Britain

Disputed between U.S. and Britain

New Hampshire

Vermont

Great Lakes

Oregon Country (U.S. and Britain)

PACIFIC OCEAN

Michigan Territory

New York

Massachusetts

Rhode Island

Connecticut

Missouri Territory

Pennsylvania

New Jersey

Indiana (1816) Ohio (1803)

Delaware

Maryland

Washington, D.C.

Illinois (1818)

Kentucky (1792)

Virginia

North Carolina

Tennessee (1796)

Arkansaw Territory

South Carolina

ATLANTIC OCEAN

Mississippi (1817)

Georgia

0 — 400 mi
0 — 400 km
Albers Conic Equal-Area Projection

Viceroyalty of New Spain (Spain)

Alabama (1819)

Louisiana (1812)

Florida Cession (claimed by Spain until 1819)

Gulf of Mexico

N E W S

KEY
- Existing United States
- New states in the midwest
- Frontier territories
- Disputed areas

INTERACTIVE

New Technology:
The Steamboat

Some of the first people moving into the new territories were fur trappers. Beaver fur, in particular, was in high demand in the east and in Europe. Many of the trails forged by trappers were later used by settlers moving west.

READING CHECK **Summarize** In what ways did the Northwest Ordinance encourage settlement of the West?

Heading Into the West

When the United States formed its first government, it already controlled most of the land east of the Mississippi River. There was ample land for settlers. Very quickly though, the United States acquired more territory and expanded westward.

Expanded Territories Not all the new territories were gained by treaty. In 1818, the U.S. Army, led by General Andrew Jackson, invaded Florida. His action led to Spain's surrender of that territory. In the 1840s, the United States acquired the Oregon territory in a settlement with Britain that narrowly avoided a war. Victory in the Mexican-American war added lands in the Southwest and California. In less than 50 years, the United States expanded all the way to the Pacific Ocean.

Following the Rivers People wanted to settle these territories, but few easy routes led west. The best routes were often rivers.

Many people moving to the Northwest Territory traveled west along the Mohawk River and then sailed across Lake Erie. Others crossed the Appalachians to Pittsburgh. There, they loaded their animals and wagons onto **flatboats**, or flat-bottomed boats, and floated down the Ohio River.

GEOGRAPHY SKILLS

This map shows how roads and canals crisscrossed the United States.

1 **Movement** What routes could one take from Albany to Columbus?

2 **Draw Conclusions** Why might a traveler take the Great Valley Road from Lancaster to Louisville instead of traveling in more of a straight line?

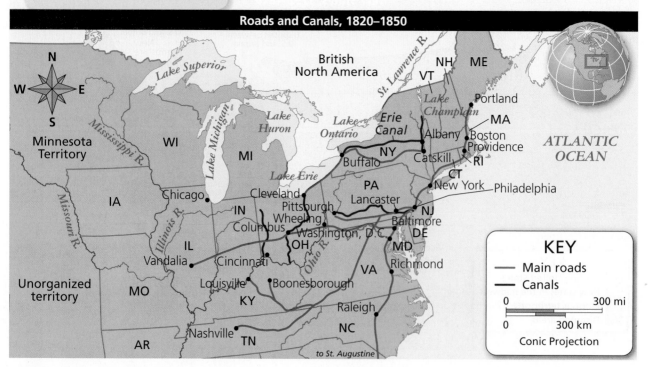

Roads and Canals, 1820–1850

KEY
— Main roads
— Canals

0   300 mi
0   300 km
Conic Projection

BENEFITS OF THE AMERICAN SYSTEM

CAUSES	EFFECTS
National Bank	Loans to expand investment
Tariffs	Funds for transportation improvements Protect industry from competition Promote industrial growth
Industrial Growth	Increased demand for raw materials, agricultural products
Increased Demand, Improved Transportation	Growth of agriculture Increased production of raw materials

FEDERAL FUNDING FOR TRANSPORTATION SYSTEM
- National Road
- Other Roads
- Canals
- River Development

RAW MATERIALS

MANUFACTURED GOODS — Exports

MANUFACTURED GOODS BLOCKED BY TARIFFS — Imports

As settlers journeyed west of the Mississippi, the rivers continued to play a key role. Lewis and Clark followed the Missouri River as they explored the Louisiana Purchase. Long sections of the Missouri are fast and unpredictable, so few settlers used it for transportation.

The Platte River, in Nebraska, was too shallow for shipping, but it was a reliable source of water in a dry region. Traders, settlers, and the U.S. Army built forts and settlements along the river. Settlers stocked up on supplies at these outposts as they traveled across the West.

The American System As the country expanded, Americans sought ways to develop the economy. Henry Clay promoted a plan known as the "American System." It was a government policy to benefit agriculture, merchants, and industry.

The American system had three main parts. First, tariffs would protect industry. Second, a national bank would make loans to promote business growth. Third, the tariffs and the sale of public lands would provide funds for the building of roads, canals, and other improvements. These transportation improvements would help farmers and manufacturers get their products to market. Finally, money from the payment of tariffs plus money from selling public lands would help pay for improvements.

Technology Speeds Transportation **Despite** its advantages, river travel presented problems. Moving upstream, for instance, was difficult. Technology, however, soon made travel faster and cheaper.

In 1807, Robert Fulton launched a steamboat, the **Clermont**, on the Hudson River. Soon steamboats plied the Ohio, Mississippi, and Missouri rivers. They carried passengers and gave farmers and merchants a cheap way to move goods.

Analyze Charts The American System aimed to take advantage of regional differences. **Use Evidence** Which region benefited most from tariffs?

Academic Vocabulary
despite • *prep.,* in spite of; notwithstanding

Another improvement was the **Erie Canal**. New York Governor DeWitt Clinton pushed for approval of this project. The legislature approved $7 million for the canal to link the Great Lakes to the Mohawk and Hudson rivers. The canal enabled timber and other goods to be shipped by barge from the Northwest Territory to New York Harbor. Soon other states as well as private investors were building canals that helped connect western farms and eastern cities.

The National Road Settlers faced difficult journeys when traveling west by land. Many roads were narrow dirt trails. They often plunged through muddy swamps. Tree stumps stuck up in the roads and broke wagon axles. The nation badly needed better roads.

Thomas Jefferson and others supported construction of a national road paid for by the government. Critics argued that the project was unconstitutional, as road-building is not an expressed power. Nevertheless, in 1806, Congress approved funds for the first national road-building project. By 1818, the **National Road** ran from Cumberland, Maryland, to the Ohio River at Wheeling, Virginia. Later, the road was extended into Illinois. As each new section of road was built, settlers eagerly drove their wagons farther and farther west.

✓ READING CHECK **Compare and Contrast** How was the landscape both an advantage and a disadvantage to settlers moving west?

Analyze Images
Although the Erie Canal no longer bustles with traffic as it once did, it is still in use today. **Cite Evidence** What in the picture shows that constructing the Erie Canal was a major undertaking?

State Populations, 1810–1840

STATE	POPULATION, 1810	POPULATION, 1840
New York	959,049	2,428,921
Ohio	230,760	1,519,467
Illinois	12,282	476,183
Louisiana	76,556	352,411
Tennessee	261,727	829,210

Source: U.S. Censuses of Population and Housing

Movement Changes the West and the Nation

Settling the West was a challenge for even the hardiest people. Settlers traveled long distances over rugged land for weeks or months. They lived outdoors in all kinds of weather. Sickness, hunger, and thirst were common. They confronted hostile American Indians, although few armed conflicts occurred.

Settlers Build New Lives When settlers finally arrived at their destination, the real work began. They found land that had never been plowed and was grown thick with trees, bushes, and dense grasses. The land was rich in natural resources, but it required extensive labor to use and develop them. Settlers created farms and built businesses and towns from the ground up.

Life in the West changed traditional roles for men and women. Women's roles were as necessary as those of men, and the two often overlapped. Few farms were run by a single man. It took two people to succeed, usually a husband and wife. Wives didn't just run the household as they had back east, they worked alongside their husbands at all sorts of jobs. They helped plant and harvest crops and care for livestock, as well as making clothing and household tools and furnishings. Children had chores, too. Everyone had to work hard to make and maintain a home on this new land.

It is not surprising that the lifestyle that developed in the West was somewhat different from that of the East. Women enjoyed greater equality in the West and, overall, there were fewer class distinctions. Most people were respected for their actions and their character rather than for who they were or how much money they had. Westerners also had a high regard for democracy.

Changing the Country By the early 1800s, Americans had settled many of the lands east of the Mississippi. By 1830, almost as many people lived west of the Appalachians as had lived in all of the United States in 1783. In the years that followed, the flood of people moved farther west to such places as Oregon, Texas, and California. The result was a rapid shift in population westward.

Analyze Images Over 30 years, many state populations exploded in size. **Analyze Charts** What caused each of these five states to grow so quickly in such a short time?

Analyze Images Starting from a young age, women in the West often took on jobs once regarded as work that only men did. **Synthesize Visual Information** What details in the illustration indicate how daily life in the West differed from daily life in an Eastern city?

As people moved westward, so did the frontier. Historian Frederick Turner described the frontier as "the outer edge of the wave—the meeting point between savagery and civilization." At each stage in westward movement, settlers learned how to survive in their new environment and how to use the available natural resources. They learned how to trade and cooperate with American Indians, and how to exploit and overcome them. They formed governments and disputed the slavery question. In these processes, they remade America.

While settlers were moving into the West, the rest of the country was still dealing with economic challenges and political disagreements. As you will read, sectional conflicts brewed through the first half of the 19th century as differences grew between the North and the South.

✔ **READING CHECK Draw Conclusions** Why did women experience greater equality in the West than in the East?

✔ Lesson Check

Practice Vocabulary

1. How did the United States government get **revenue** from the Northwest Ordinance?

2. How did settlers use **flatboats** on their journey's west?

3. How did the *Clermont* and the **Erie Canal** help unite the country?

Critical Thinking and Writing

4. **Revisit the Essential Question** Why do people move?

5. **Infer** How did technology help unify the nation?

6. **Writing Workshop: Use Narrative Techniques** In your 📓 Active Journal, write a brief description of your first day on your journey west. Use narrative techniques, such as dialogue, description, and similes. You will use this narration in the narrative you will write at the end of the Topic.

BOUNCE TO ACTIVATE   ▶ VIDEO

GET READY TO READ

START UP
This modern photograph of Oregon shows how the region might have appeared to settlers. In a few sentences tell what a landscape like this would have meant for the new arrivals.

GUIDING QUESTIONS
- What did the frontier mean to the nation in the first half of the nineteenth century?
- What challenges did the Oregon Trail present?
- How did mountain men help settle the Far West?
- What role did missionaries play in Oregon?

TAKE NOTES
Literacy Skills: Summarize
Use the Graphic Organizer in your 📓 Active Journal to take notes as you read the lesson.

PRACTICE VOCABULARY
Use the Vocabulary Builder in your 📓 Active Journal to practice the vocabulary words.

Vocabulary

Oregon Country   rugged
mountain man   individualist
                        Oregon Trail

Academic Vocabulary

varied
determination

By the 1820s, white settlers occupied much of the land between the Appalachians and the Mississippi River. Until this time, those lands were considered "the West." However, families searching for good farmland continued to move even farther west. In front of them were the Great Plains that stretched to the Rockies. Few settlers stopped on the plains, which were considered too dry for farming. Instead, most settlers headed to lands in the Far West. The movement to this distant region changed the meaning of the West for Americans. Now, it stretched all the way to the Pacific coast.

In Search of New Territory
Americans first learned about Oregon Country after Lewis and Clark explored the region in the early 1800s. **Oregon Country** was a huge area west of the Rocky Mountains. Today it includes the states of Oregon, Washington, Idaho, and parts of Wyoming, Montana, and western Canada.

Academic Vocabulary

varied • *adj.,* having many forms or types

INTERACTIVE

Oregon Country

Wild Country The geography of Oregon Country is **varied**. Along the Pacific coast, the soil is fertile. Temperatures are mild year round, and rainfall is plentiful.

Dense forest covered the Coastal Ranges and Cascade Mountains, which surrounded these lowlands. Beavers and other fur-bearing animals roamed these forests and the Rocky Mountains to the east. Between the Cascade Mountains and the Rockies is a dry plateau.

Guides to the West Fur trappers searching for beaver and other fur-bearing animals were the first people to enter Oregon Country. They followed American Indian trails through passes in the Rocky Mountains. Later, they used these trails and their knowledge of the land to guide settlers heading west. These men became known as **mountain men**.

Not all the mountain men were white. Manuel Lisa, a Latino fur trader, founded Fort Manuel, the first outpost on the upper Missouri. James Beckwourth, an African American freed from slavery, was a fur trader and lived among the Crow Indians. Beckwourth discovered a mountain pass that became a major route to California.

The U.S. government also sent expeditions to map and explore the new territories of the West. John C. Frémont (FREE mont), a young military officer, was commissioned to lead expeditions through many areas across the West, from Wyoming to California. The trapper and explorer "Kit" Carson served as a guide to Frémont. Later, Carson guided General Kearny on his campaign to take California from Mexico. Carson became a popular and legendary adventure hero.

BIOGRAPHY

5 Things to Know About

JOHN C. FRÉMONT
American Explorer (1813–1890)

- As a U.S. Army officer, he led three expeditions to explore the West, mapping much of the land between the Mississippi River and the West Coast.

- On his third expedition, Frémont helped capture California for the United States during the Mexican-American War.

- Frémont accepted the Mexican surrender and then declared himself governor of California. For these acts he was accused of mutiny and court-martialed, but the ruling was later dismissed.

- He became a multimillionaire when gold was discovered on land he had bought in California.

- He ran for President in 1856, but lost to James Buchanan.

Critical Thinking How was Frémont important to the development of California?

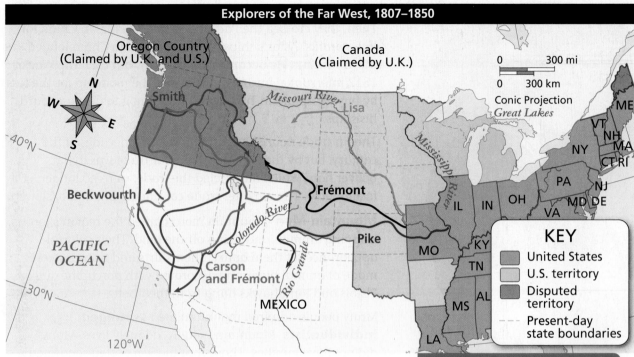

Explorers of the Far West, 1807–1850

Oregon Country (Claimed by U.K. and U.S.)

Canada (Claimed by U.K.)

Smith

Lisa

Missouri River

Beckwourth

Frémont

Colorado River

Carson and Frémont

Rio Grande

Pike

MO

KY

TN

MS

AL

LA

PACIFIC OCEAN

MEXICO

40°N

30°N

120°W

ME

VT

NH

NY

MA

CT RI

PA

NJ

IL IN OH

MD DE

VA

0   300 mi
0   300 km
Conic Projection
Great Lakes

KEY
- United States
- U.S. territory
- Disputed territory
- - - Present-day state boundaries

Nations Compete In the early 1800s, four countries claimed Oregon: the United States, Great Britain, Spain, and Russia. Of course, American Indian groups had lived there for centuries. However, the United States and European nations gave little thought to their rights.

In 1818, the United States and Britain agreed to occupy Oregon Country jointly. Citizens of each nation would have equal rights. Spain and Russia had few settlers there, so they withdrew their claims.

☑ READING CHECK **Predict Consequences** How might the arrival of many U.S. settlers affect the agreement between Britain and the United States about Oregon Country?

The Far West Fur Trade

The first Europeans and Americans who traveled to Oregon Country were fur traders. Fur was so valuable that it was sometimes referred to as "soft gold."

Trade in Sea Otter Fur John Jacob Astor was one of the most successful American traders. Astor started his first fur business in St. Louis, selling pelts collected in the American West and Canada to cities in the Northeast and Europe. But the most valuable furs came from sea otters that were hunted off the coast of the Oregon Country.

GEOGRAPHY SKILLS

Scouts and explorers traveled throughout the West before white settlers arrived from the East.

1. **Interaction** How were explorers important for westward movement?

2. **Infer** Why do you think some exploration routes were thousands of miles while others were much shorter?

Analyze Images James Beckwourth was a freed slave who became a fur trader and explorer. Later, he worked for the army and ran his own hotel and store. **Identify Main Ideas** What was the importance of the mountain men for the development of the nation?

Merchants came all the way from New England for the otters. Then, they crossed the Pacific and sold the furs in China for huge profits. Astor's ships regularly sailed to China loaded down with fur. He became very wealthy, but then the War of 1812 interrupted business. For a time, he made up for the loss by buying opium in Turkey and shipping it to China aboard his ships.

The fur trade flourished through the first decades of the century, but by the late 1830s, the fur trade was dying. Beaver hats, which had fueled the trade, were no longer fashionable. The sea otter trade continued, but it, too, slowed.

Mountain Men Mountain men roamed the region's forests, trapping animals and living off the land. Their colorful appearance set them apart. Their shirts and trousers were made of animal hides and decorated with porcupine quills. Pistols and tomahawks hung from their belts.

Many people admired mountain men as **rugged individualists**. Mountain men lived lonely lives. Many did not have families. Those that did were often separated from them for long periods of time. Based in part on the solitary lives of mountain men, a folklore of rugged American individualism developed. Today, it still influences our ideas of what America is and what makes an American.

Mountain men could make fine profits selling their furs, but their lives were hard and dangerous. Injuries, illness, and dangerous animals were a constant threat. Surviving alone, especially through the long, cold winters in the mountains, demanded special skills. "I have held my hands in an anthill until they were covered with ants, then greedily licked them off," one mountain man recalled.

✓ READING CHECK **Interpret** How did mountain men come to know so much about the Oregon Country?

The Oregon Trail

The first white Americans to settle permanently in Oregon Country were missionaries who began arriving in the 1830s. Among the first of these were Marcus and Narcissa Whitman. In 1836, they set out from their home in New York for Oregon Country, where they planned to convert American Indians to Christianity.

Missionaries Bring Settlers The Whitmans built their mission near the Columbia River and began to work with the Cayuse (kay-YOOS), setting up a mission school and a clinic. Soon, other missionaries and settlers arrived.

Eager for others to join them, the missionaries sent back glowing reports about the Oregon Country. By 1840, more Americans were making the journey west.

As settlers spread onto Cayuse lands, conflicts arose. Worse, the newcomers carried diseases that proved deadly for the Cayuse. In 1847, a measles outbreak killed many Cayuse children. Blaming the settlers, a band of angry Cayuse attacked the mission, killing the Whitmans and 12 others.

Wagons Ho! Despite such incidents, pioneers still set out for Oregon Country. Tales of wheat that grew taller than a person and turnips five feet around touched off a race to Oregon. Americans called it "Oregon fever." Soon, pioneers clogged the trails west.

Beginning in 1843, wagon trains left every spring for Oregon Country. They followed a route called the **Oregon Trail**. Families heading west would gather at Independence, Missouri, in the early spring. There, they formed wagon trains and hurried to start west by May. Along the way, travelers stopped near settlements where they might buy supplies or get care for the sick or injured.

Timing was important. Travelers had to reach the Oregon lowlands by early October, before the snow fell in the mountains. This meant they had to cover 2,000 miles in five months. In the 1840s, traveling 15 miles a day was making good time.

Life in a Wagon Train On the trail, families woke at dawn to a bugle blast. Breakfast was prepared and eaten. Horses and oxen were hitched to the wagons. By 6 A.M., the cry of "Wagons Ho!" rang across the plains.

At noon the wagon train stopped for a brief meal and then continued on until 6 or 7 P.M.

INTERACTIVE

The Oregon Trail

GEOGRAPHY **SKILLS**

By 1830, the United States had a claim to part of the Pacific Coast.

1. **Movement** Work with a partner to estimate the distance from the Oregon Country to the nearest state.

2. **Express Problems Clearly** Considering the distance of states and organized territories from Oregon Country, why might it have been difficult for the United States to control that region?

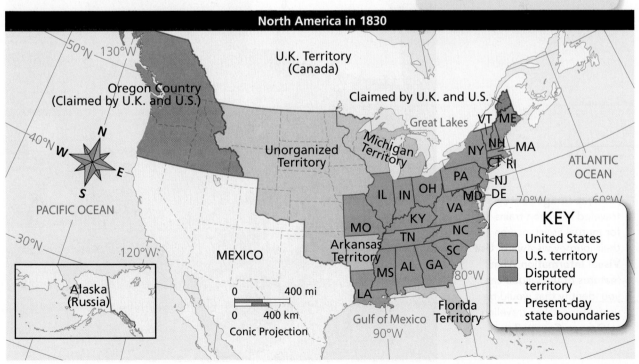

North America in 1830

Men and women took on their usual roles when a wagon train first began its journey. Men managed the teams and hunted. Women cooked, washed, and collected fire wood.

As time passed, though, women began driving wagons, hitching up teams, and loading wagons. Men occasionally even cooked and did other "women's work." People did what was needed to get to Oregon.

Daily life was not easy. Meals were cooked over open fires. Fuel for the fires was often scarce and took time to gather. Wind blew sand into people's food as they ate. At night, most people wrapped themselves in blankets and slept on the ground. If it rained, they got soaked, and the wagons might get stuck in the mud.

The trail west held many dangers. During the spring, travelers risked drowning as they crossed rain-swollen rivers. In summer, water sources dried up. People went thirsty, and livestock might die. The biggest threat was sickness. Cholera and other diseases could wipe out entire wagon trains.

Despite the many hardships, more than 50,000 Americans reached Oregon between 1840 and 1860.

Analyze Images Settlers traveled in wagon trains for mutual assistance on their journey westward. **Use Visual Information** What features of the wagon can you identify that would be useful for settlers traveling to Oregon Country?

Meeting the Locals As they moved west, pioneers met and often traded with American Indians. Hungry pioneers were grateful for the food that the locals supplied in return for clothing and tools. A traveler noted:

Primary Source

"Whenever we camp near any Indian village, we are no sooner stopped than a whole crowd may be seen coming galloping into our camp. The [women] do all the swapping."

—John S. Unruh, quoted in *The Plains Across: The Overland Emigrants and the Trans-Mississippi West, 1840–1860*

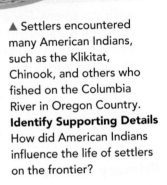

▲ Settlers encountered many American Indians, such as the Klikitat, Chinook, and others who fished on the Columbia River in Oregon Country. **Identify Supporting Details** How did American Indians influence the life of settlers on the frontier?

Journey's End By the 1840s, Americans outnumbered the British in Oregon Country. Many Americans wanted Oregon Country for the United States alone. After a long negotiation, the United States and United Kingdom signed a treaty dividing up the Oregon Country. Two years later, in 1848, Congress organized the Oregon Territory.

As the population of Oregon grew, it opened new markets for eastern merchants. But the significance of Oregon was not only economic. The Oregon Trail helped form America's national identify. It took courage and **determination** to complete the journey across the continent. The trail inspired Americans' faith that their nation can achieve anything.

Academic Vocabulary
determination • *n.*, personal drive to continue trying to achieve one's goal

☑ READING CHECK **Identify Cause and Effect** How did missionaries attract settlers?

☑ Lesson Check

Practice Vocabulary

1. Why did people go to **Oregon Country**?

2. In what way could **mountain men** be described as **rugged individualists**?

Critical Thinking and Writing

3. **Compare and Contrast** the lives of missionaries and mountain men in Oregon Country.

4. **Identify Main Ideas** Describe how settlers moving to Oregon Country made the trip from Independence, Missouri.

5. **Writing Workshop: Use Narrative Techniques** In your 📓 Active Journal, write about an important or unusual event that takes place during your journey west. Use narrative techniques, such as dialogue, flashback, or figurative language. You will use what you write here in the narrative you will write at the end of the Topic.

Distinguish Verifiable from Unverifiable Information

Follow these steps to distinguish verifiable from unverifiable information.

1 **Identify statements that could be verified** Historical sources may contain facts, or statements that can be proved true. What facts does the writer give you about the Red Buttes?

2 **Determine how you might verify these statements** Find ways to verify each statement. For example, you could compare a statement to an encyclopedia entry. How can you prove the statements about the Red Buttes are facts?

3 **Identify statements that cannot be verified** It is not possible to verify something like a person's opinion. Remember, though, that statements can be valuable even though they are not verifiable. Which statements in the journal entry for August 3 cannot be verified?

Primary Source

"July 25.— Since last date we camped at the ford where emigrants cross from the south to the north side of the Platte. . . . We stopped near the Red Buttes, where the hills are of a red color, nearly square and have the appearance of houses with flat roofs. . . . We also passed Independence Rock and the Devil's Gate, which is high enough to make one's head swim, and the posts reach an altitude of some 4 or 500 feet."

"Oregon, August 3. . . . Here the roads were so bad, as we went over the steep hills and clambered over the rocks, I could hardly hold myself in the wagon.

Sometimes the dust is so great that the drivers cannot see their teams at all though the sun is shining brightly, and it a great relief to the way-worn traveler to meet with some mountain stream, meandering through a valley. . . . One day we only made seven miles through a very deep sand. . . ."

"Monday, September 15th. . . . Mount St. Elias is in the distance, and is covered with snow, so you can imagine somewhat the beauty and grandeur of the scene. We are now among the tribe of Wallawalla Indians."

—Journal of a Trip to Oregon, Elizabeth Wood

New Spain and Independence for Texas

BOUNCE TO ACTIVATE   ▶ VIDEO

GET READY TO READ

START UP
The men in this painting were skilled with horses, roping, and caring for cattle. How are they similar to the American cowboy?

GUIDING QUESTIONS
- What were the causes and consequences of Texas independence?
- How did Mexican and American settlements affect the development of the Southwest?
- What was life like for the Spanish and American Indians who lived in California and New Mexico?

TAKE NOTES
Literacy Skills: Sequence
Use the Graphic Organizer in your 📓 Active Journal to take notes as you read the lesson.

PRACTICE VOCABULARY
Use the Vocabulary Builder in your 📓 Active Journal to practice the vocabulary words.

Vocabulary		Academic Vocabulary
Puebloan	vaquero	specify
Santa Fe Trail	dictator	generally
mission	Alamo	
self-sufficient	siege	

In the 1840s, New Mexico Territory included present-day Arizona, New Mexico, Nevada, and Utah, and parts of Colorado. California lay to the west. This huge region, ruled by Mexico, was southwest of the unorganized territory that the United States acquired through the Louisiana Purchase.

New Mexico Territory and California

The physical characteristics of the New Mexico Territory vary depending on location. Much of this region is hot and dry desert. There are also forested mountains. In some areas, thick grasses grow. Before the Spanish arrived, **Puebloans** (pweb LOH anz) farmed here using irrigation. Puebloans are American Indians who live in permanent towns made of mud, rock, and other materials. Other American Indians lived mainly by hunting and gathering.

Spain and New Mexico Territory The Spanish explorer Juan de Oñate (ohn YAH tay) claimed the region for Spain in 1598.

In the early 1600s, the Spanish founded the town of Santa Fe and made it the capital of the territory. With a bustling trade in horses, fur, and wool, Santa Fe grew into a busy trading center.

Some Americans were eager to settle in New Mexico. It was thinly populated but had good physical characteristics, including many natural resources. Spain, however, would not let Americans settle in Santa Fe or anywhere else in the territory. Only after Mexico became independent in 1821 were Americans welcome there.

William Becknell, a merchant and adventurer, was the first American to head for Santa Fe. In 1822, he led some traders from Franklin, Missouri, up the Arkansas River and across the plains to the New Mexico town. Other Americans soon followed Becknell's route, which became known as the **Santa Fe Trail**.

Spanish Settlements in California California, too, was ruled first by Spain and then by Mexico. In 1769, Captain Gaspar de Portolá led an expedition up the Pacific coast. With him was Father Junípero Serra (hoo NEE peh roh SEHR rah). Father Serra built his first mission at San Diego. He and other missionaries set up a string of 21 **missions** along the California coast. The Spanish built forts nearby.

Each mission complex included a church and the surrounding land. Each became **self-sufficient**, or able to produce enough for their needs. The missions had large herds of cattle and sheep as well as gardens and orchards. They produced enough food for their own needs and sometimes enough to supply neighboring forts and pueblos.

GEOGRAPHY **SKILLS**

Spain set up a series of missions, forts, and towns north of their earlier settlements in Mexico.

1. **Place** What common geographic feature do most of the Spanish settlements share?

2. **Draw Conclusions** Why do you think Spain built these settlements in these locations?

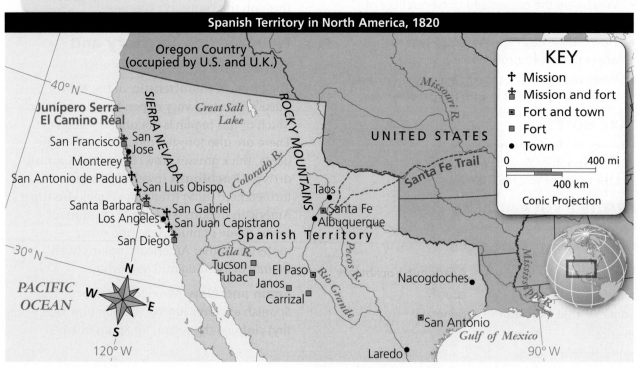

Spanish Territory in North America, 1820

Analyze Images Many of the missions built by the Spanish remain and can still be visited, like the Mission San Carlos Borromeo del Rio Carmelo in Carmel, California. Identify Main Ideas Why did the Spanish build missions in California?

Before the Spanish arrived, American Indians in California lived in small, scattered groups. As a result, they had little success resisting the Spanish soldiers who made them work on mission lands. They were forced to herd sheep and cattle and raise crops for the missions. In exchange they received no pay, only food and clothing. Many were forced to live at the missions and practice the Roman Catholic faith.

Mission life was harsh for the American Indians. They were forced to give up their culture. Families were often separated, and thousands of American Indians died from overwork and disease.

Culture and Tradition on Mexican Ranches In the 1820s, newly independent Mexico decided that California's economy was growing too slowly. Hoping to speed up growth, the government took land from the missions and gave it to individuals. These land grants were usually given to wealthy people. The landowners set up huge cattle ranches, called ranchos, and became rancheros, or ranch operators.

A new culture began to develop among the rancheros. Their lives centered on cattle raising and the selling of beef and hides. Cattle ranching grew to become the principal business in California. Rancheros gained great wealth and occupied a high social class. They married and socialized with other rancheros and with wealthy merchants.

A new culture also developed among some workers on the ranches—the culture of the **vaqueros**. Vaqueros were the Indian and Mexican cowhands who tended the cattle and other animals. They were excellent riders and ropers, and their traditions strongly influenced later cowhands throughout the West.

READING CHECK **Summarize** Who were the vaqueros?

Analyze Images Vaqueros were skilled with horses and managing livestock. **Synthesize Visual Information** How do this vaquero's clothing and equipment help him do his work?

Americans Colonize Mexican Texas

In the early 1800s, Texas was part of a Spanish province in the colony of New Spain, or Mexico. At that time, Texas had only about 4,000 Mexican settlers. As a result, Spain had difficulty keeping order, and settlers faced frequent raids by American Indian groups, such as the Comanche.

Spain Authorizes a Colony in Texas In 1820, Spain gave Moses Austin a land grant and permission to colonize Texas with 300 Catholic families. Although Austin died before he could set up a colony, his son, Stephen, took over the grant. Also around this time, in 1821, Mexico gained its independence from Spain.

Stephen Austin had no trouble finding settlers. By the 1820s, most of the land in the United States that was arable, or suitable for farming, was already occupied. There was a scarcity, or short supply, of affordable, fertile land, or land that is good for growing crops. When it was available, good farmland was expensive.

In Texas, by contrast, there was a large supply of fertile land that settlers could buy cheaply. Many Americans were eager to buy this land and settle in Texas.

Austin Founds a Colony Austin gathered the 300 families, and in late 1821, they began settling the colony. Many settlers came from the cotton country of the Southeast. Some built large cotton plantations and brought in enslaved African Americans to work the land.

Quest CONNECTIONS

How did the United States' relationship with Mexico develop after Mexican independence from Spain? Note your findings in your 📕 Active Journal.

As Austin's colony grew, Mexico gave Austin several more land grants. Grants were also given to other entrepreneurs like Austin to attract settlers to Texas. Some of these settlers were from Mexico, but the largest number came from the United States. By 1830, about 20,000 Americans had moved to Texas.

✓ READING CHECK **Identify Cause and Effect** Why were American settlers eager to move to Texas?

Conflict With the Mexican Government

In return for their land, the Mexican government **specified** that Austin and the original American settlers must become Mexican citizens and worship in the Roman Catholic Church. Later American settlers, however, felt no loyalty to Mexico. They spoke little or no Spanish, and most were Protestant. These and other differences led to conflicts between the settlers and the Mexican government.

Mexico Tightens Its Grip on Texas
In 1830, Mexico barred any more Americans from settling in Texas. Mexico feared that the Americans would try to make Texas a part of the United States. The United States had already tried twice to buy Texas from Mexico.

To assert its authority, Mexico sent troops to enforce laws requiring Texans to worship in the Catholic Church and banning slavery. American settlers opposed these laws. The law against slavery was a serious problem for them. Many had brought enslaved people with them and relied on enslaved workers to grow cotton.

INTERACTIVE

The Settlement of Texas

Academic Vocabulary

specify • *v.*, to name something exactly and in detail

Analyze Images This painting shows Stephen F. Austin rallying Texas colonists to fight Karankawa Indians. Austin's slave, Richmond, looks in through the window. **Identify Main Ideas** What role did the slavery question play in the conflict between Texas and Mexico?

Analyze Images As a young officer in the Spanish army, Antonio López de Santa Anna fought against Mexican independence. Later, he became president of Mexico. **Summarize** What was Santa Anna's role in Texas history?

INTERACTIVE

The Defenders of the Alamo

In 1833, General Antonio López de Santa Anna gained power in Mexico. He rejected the Mexican constitution and attempted to govern the nation as dictator. A **dictator** is a ruler with absolute power and authority.

Texans Rebel By October 1835, Americans in Texas decided that the time had come for action. They had the support of many Tejanos (teh HAH nohs), people of Mexican descent born in Texas. Tejanos did not necessarily want independence from Mexico. However, they did want to be rid of the dictator, Santa Anna.

In October 1835, Texan settlers in the town of Gonzales (gahn ZAH les) clashed with Mexican troops. Two months later, Texan settlers occupied the town of San Antonio. Determined to stamp out the rebellion, Santa Anna marched north with a large army.

☑ READING CHECK **Identify Cause and Effect** Why were U.S. settlers opposed to Mexican laws?

Independence for Texas

While Santa Anna was on the move, a group of Texans declared independence for the Republic of Texas on March 2, 1836. Sam Houston took command of its army. Volunteers from the United States and other nations, along with African Americans and Tejanos, joined the fight for Texan independence.

Siege at the Alamo By the time Santa Anna reached San Antonio, the Texans had taken up positions in an old Spanish mission called the **Alamo**. A young lieutenant colonel, William B. Travis, was in command. Among the volunteers at the Alamo were the famous frontiersmen Jim Bowie and Davy Crockett. Poorly equipped and badly outnumbered, the rebels waited for the Mexican attack.

On February 23, 1836, Mexican troops began the **siege** of the Alamo. In a siege, enemy forces try to capture a city or fort by surrounding and often bombarding it. The Texan defenders barely held out as cannons pounded the walls for 12 days.

At dawn on March 6, Mexican cannons finally shattered the mission walls. Thousands of Mexican soldiers poured over the broken walls, shouting *"Viva Santa Anna!"* ("Long live Santa Anna!"). In the end, about 180 Texans and almost 1,500 Mexicans lay dead. Most of the few Texans who survived were executed.

The Battle of San Jacinto The fall of the Alamo sparked Texan cries for revenge.

On April 21, 1836, the Texans caught their enemies by surprise camped near the San Jacinto (juh SIN toh) River. With cries of "Remember the Alamo!" Texans charged into battle.

Although the Texans were outnumbered, they were victorious. They captured Santa Anna and forced him to sign a treaty granting Texas independence.

☑ READING CHECK Identify Cause and Effect What was the key to the Texans' victory at San Jacinto?

The Republic of Texas Is Born

After winning independence, Texas declared itself a republic. A constitution was written using the United States Constitution as a model.

Issues Facing the New Country Texas's new constitution treated Mexicans in Texas harshly. It denied Mexicans citizenship and property rights if they could not prove that they had supported the revolution. Many chose to give up their lands and flee.

Analyze Images In this painting, Texans defend the Alamo against the Mexican siege. Twelve feet high and two feet thick, the Alamo walls were good protection but unable to endure days of bombardment. **Hypothesize** How might the defenders' confidence have changed during the siege?

INTERACTIVE

Texas: From Settlement to Statehood

The new country faced other problems. First, the government of Mexico refused to accept the treaty that Santa Anna had signed. Mexicans insisted that Texas was still part of Mexico. Second, Texas was nearly bankrupt.

Third, Comanche and other Indian groups threatened to attack small Texan communities. Most Texans thought that the best way to solve these problems was to become part of the United States.

The United States Considers Annexation In the United States, people were divided over whether to annex, or add on, Texas to the Union. The arguments reflected sectional divisions in the country. White southerners **generally** favored the idea. Many northerners opposed it. The main issue was slavery. By the 1830s, antislavery feeling was growing in the North. Because many Texans owned enslaved people, northerners feared that Texas would join the Union as a slave-owning state, strengthening support for slavery in the U.S. government.

In addition, President Andrew Jackson worried that annexing Texas would lead to war with Mexico. As a result, Congress refused to annex the Republic of Texas.

Academic Vocabulary

generally • *adv.*, in most cases

GEOGRAPHY SKILLS

After a brief yet bloody war, the Republic of Texas won its independence from Mexico.

1. **Movement** Describe the movement of Mexican and Texan forces after the battle at the Alamo.

2. **Use Visual Information** What disadvantage would Santa Anna's army have had in the Texas War?

The Texas War for Independence, 1836

Should the United States Annex Texas?

REASONS FOR	REASONS AGAINST
• Texans voted for annexation. • Statehood would guarantee defense against Mexican attacks and Native American raids. • The Republic would not survive for long as an independent nation. • The United States would benefit economically. • Britain might annex Texas if the United States did not.	• Tension between the North and South would increase if Texas were added as a slave state. • Mexico would see annexation as an act of war. • Annexation would heighten existing conflict between the Whig and Democratic parties. • Mexico might recognize Texas with the help of U.S. diplomacy, and the Republic of Texas could remain independent.

For the next nine years, leaders of the Republic of Texas worked to attract new settlers. The new Texas government encouraged immigration by offering settlers free land. During the Panic of 1837, thousands of Americans moved to Texas.

Settlers also arrived from Germany and Switzerland. They helped the new nation grow and prosper. By the 1840s, about 140,000 people lived in Texas, including many enslaved African Americans and some Mexicans. The Republic of Texas remained an independent country until the United States annexed it in 1845.

Analyze Images After gaining independence from Mexico, many Texans wanted to join the United States. **Evaluate Arguments** Do you think the argument for or against annexation was stronger? Why?

READING CHECK **Summarize** the three problems that faced the new Republic of Texas.

☑ Lesson Check

Practice Vocabulary

1. Why did Santa Anna lay **siege** to the **Alamo**?

2. In what way were the California **missions self-sufficient**?

Critical Thinking and Writing

3. **Identify Cause and Effect** Why did the Republic of Texas remain an independent country for nine years?

4. **Summarize** How did the arrival of the missionaries affect American Indians living in California?

5. **Writing Workshop: Use Descriptive Details and Sensory Language** In your 📓 Active Journal, revise one of the passages you have written about an event that occurs on your journey west. Include descriptive details and sensory language to make your narrative more vivid and specific.

LESSON 7

Manifest Destiny in California and the Southwest

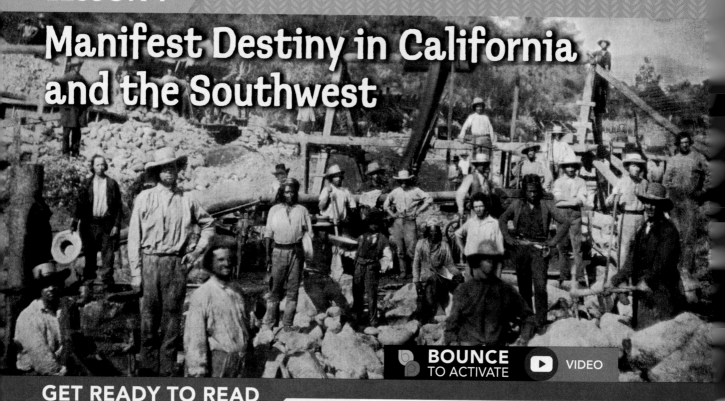

BOUNCE TO ACTIVATE   ▶ VIDEO

GET READY TO READ

START UP
Write three questions you might like to ask these miners at work during the California gold rush.

GUIDING QUESTIONS
- How did Manifest Destiny contribute to American expansion?
- What were the causes and consequences of the Mexican-American War?
- How did Utah and California grow?
- How did the gold rush and migration affect life in California?

TAKE NOTES
Literacy Skills: Identify Cause and Effect
Use the Graphic Organizer in your 📓 Active Journal to take notes as you read the lesson.

PRACTICE VOCABULARY
Use the Vocabulary Builder in your 📓 Active Journal to practice the vocabulary words.

Vocabulary		Academic Vocabulary
Manifest Destiny	Mexican Cession	allocation
Bear Flag Republic	forty-niner	consequently
Treaty of Guadalupe-Hidalgo		

In the mid-1840s, only about 700 people from the United States lived in California. Every year, however, more Americans were moving west.

Manifest Destiny

There were many economic, social, and political causes for this westward expansion. On several occasions, the United States government offered to buy California from Mexico. Some officials were eager to gain control of the ports at San Francisco and San Diego. Soon westward expansion became a major priority for the nation.

The Roots of Manifest Destiny In the 1840s, an editor named John L. O'Sullivan created the term **Manifest Destiny**. The term meant that the United States had the right to spread across the continent. *Manifest* means clear or obvious. *Destiny* means something that is fated to happen. The social roots of Manifest Destiny lay in the belief that Americans had the right and the duty to spread their culture across the continent all the way to the Pacific Ocean.

Americans who believed in Manifest Destiny thought that westward expansion would also open new opportunities. To many Americans, the fertile farmland and natural resources in the West were prime opportunities for economic growth.

Manifest Destiny and westward expansion had some negative effects, however. Many white Americans believed that they were superior to American Indians and Mexicans. They used this belief to justify taking lands belonging to people whom they considered inferior.

Polk and Westward Expansion The political roots of Manifest Destiny and westward expansion took hold during the election of 1844. The Whigs nominated the well-known national leader Henry Clay for President. Clay had opposed the annexation of Texas. The Democrats chose James Polk, a little-known candidate from Tennessee who wanted to add Texas and Oregon Country to the Union.

On Election Day, Americans showed their support for westward expansion by electing Polk president. Acting on his campaign promise, Polk reached an agreement with the United Kingdom in 1846 over Oregon Country. The two countries divided the territory at latitude 49°N. Britain got the lands north of the line, and the United States got the lands south of the line.

Texas proved a more difficult problem. The United States at first had refused to annex Texas. Senators feared that annexing Texas would cause a war with Mexico.

Roots of Manifest Destiny

Social	• Belief in America as an exceptional nation • Desire to spread American democracy and ideals • Belief that it was God's will for America to expand • View that white Americans were superior to American Indians
Political	• Monroe Doctrine warning against European colonization in the Western Hemisphere • Desire to acquire Oregon from Britain • Desire to acquire Texas from Mexico • Success of Democrats, who supported expansion, over Whigs, who did not
Economic	• Farmland for settlers • Access to rich resources • Land for southern crops such as cotton

Analyze Images People had different reasons for supporting Manifest Destiny. **Analyze Charts** How might people's values lead them to support Manifest Destiny?

◀ This election banner shows James Polk and his running mate George Dallas.

JAMES K. POLK.   GEO. M. DALLAS.

Meanwhile, Mexico feared the United States would go ahead with annexation. Out of desperation, Mexico offered a deal: It would accept the independence of Texas if Texas rejected annexation. Texans, however, would not give up on joining the union. They spread rumors that Texas might ally itself with the United Kingdom. This scared Congress into passing a joint resolution, in 1845, admitting Texas to the Union. The annexation of Texas set the stage for conflict with Mexico.

✔️**READING CHECK** Identify Main Ideas How did President Polk help fulfill America's Manifest Destiny?

Quest CONNECTIONS

What were the causes of the war? Note your ideas in your 📓 Active Journal.

The Mexican-American War

The annexation of Texas outraged Mexicans. They had not accepted Texan independence, much less annexation. They also worried that Americans might encourage rebellions in California and New Mexico as they had in Texas.

At the same time, Americans resented Mexico. They were annoyed when Mexico rejected President Polk's offer of $30 million to buy California and New Mexico. Many Americans felt that Mexico stood in the way of their country's Manifest Destiny.

The Clash Begins A border dispute finally caused war. Both the United States and Mexico claimed the land between the Rio Grande and the Nueces (noo AY says) River. In January 1846, Polk ordered General Zachary Taylor to set up posts in the disputed area. Polk knew the move might lead to war. In April 1846, Mexican troops crossed the Rio Grande and clashed with the Americans. At Polk's urging, Congress declared war on Mexico.

Americans were divided over the conflict. Many in the South and West were eager to fight, hoping to win new lands. Some northerners opposed the war. They saw it as a southern plot to add slave states to the Union. Still, the war was generally popular. When the army called for volunteers, thousands of recruits flocked to the cause.

Analyze Images The roots of the Mexican-American War lay in events that happened long before the war started. **Analyze Charts** How did land disputes lead to the war?

Causes of the Mexican-American War

Texas wins independence from Mexico.
Supporters of Manifest Destiny seek more U.S. territory in the West.
The United States annexes Texas, outraging Mexicans.
Mexico and Texas both claim an area of land.
Supporters of Manifest Destiny push to gain control of Mexican lands.
President Polk sends U.S. troops into the area claimed by both Mexico and Texas.
Mexican troops enter that area and clash with U.S. troops.

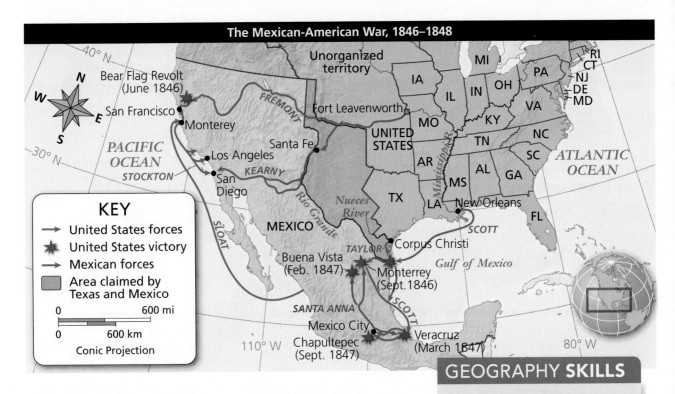

The Mexican-American War, 1846–1848

KEY
→ United States forces
✳ United States victory
→ Mexican forces
▨ Area claimed by Texas and Mexico

0   600 mi
0   600 km
Conic Projection

Fighting on Multiple Fronts During the Mexican-American War, the United States attacked on several fronts at once.

General Taylor crossed the Rio Grande into northern Mexico. In February 1847, he met Mexican General Santa Anna at the Battle of Buena Vista. The Americans were outnumbered more than two to one, but they were better armed and better led. After fierce fighting and intense artillery fire, they forced Santa Anna to retreat.

A second army under General Winfield Scott landed at the Mexican port of Veracruz. After a long battle, Scott took the city. He then headed toward Mexico City, the capital.

A third army, led by General Stephen Kearny, captured Santa Fe without firing a shot. Kearny then hurried on to San Diego. After several battles, he won control of southern California early in 1847.

Even before hearing of the war, Americans in northern California had begun a revolt against Mexican rule. The rebels declared California an independent republic on June 14, 1846. They nicknamed their new nation the **Bear Flag Republic**. Within a month, U.S. forces claimed California for the United States. Led by John C. Frémont, rebel forces drove the Mexican troops out of northern California.

By 1847, the United States controlled all of New Mexico and California, and Scott was headed for Mexico City. Blocking his way was the Mexican army in a well-protected position. But in the ensuing Battle of Cerro Gordo, American troops outmaneuvered the Mexicans, who suffered heavy losses and were forced to retreat.

GEOGRAPHY SKILLS

The Mexican-American War was fought over a vast amount of territory.

1. **Movement** What were the similarities between American land and sea strategies?

2. **Infer** Why do you think the Americans attacked Mexico by sea instead of sending the armies overland through Texas?

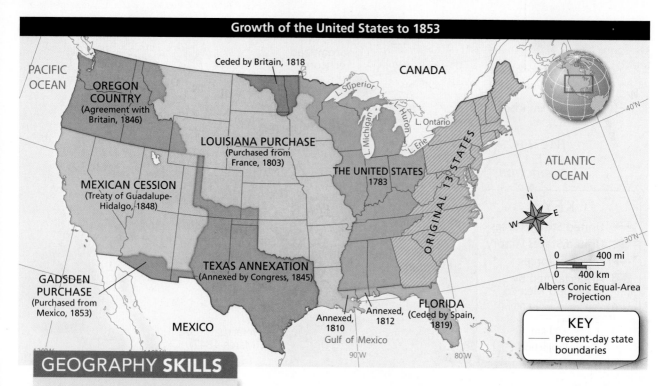

Growth of the United States to 1853

PACIFIC OCEAN

Ceded by Britain, 1818

CANADA

OREGON COUNTRY (Agreement with Britain, 1846)

LOUISIANA PURCHASE (Purchased from France, 1803)

L. Superior
L. Michigan
L. Huron
L. Ontario
L. Erie

THE UNITED STATES 1783

ORIGINAL 13 STATES

ATLANTIC OCEAN

MEXICAN CESSION (Treaty of Guadalupe-Hidalgo, 1848)

40°N

30°N

0   400 mi
0   400 km
Albers Conic Equal-Area Projection

TEXAS ANNEXATION (Annexed by Congress, 1845)

GADSDEN PURCHASE (Purchased from Mexico, 1853)

MEXICO

Annexed, 1810

Annexed, 1812

FLORIDA (Ceded by Spain, 1819)

Gulf of Mexico

90°W   80°W

KEY
— Present-day state boundaries

GEOGRAPHY SKILLS

By 1848, the United States extended from the Atlantic Ocean to the Pacific Ocean.

1. **Interaction** How would expansion of the United States across the continent change the character of the land?

2. **Identify Main Ideas** What was the impact of the Mexican-American War on the growth of the United States?

Then, at the edge of Mexico City, Scott's forces faced one last obstacle. Teenage Mexican cadets, or soldiers in training, made a heroic stand at Fort Chapultepec (chah POOL tuh pehk). Today, Mexicans honor those young cadets as heroes. At the battle's end, however, American forces captured Mexico City, and the war was essentially over. Scott's Mexico City campaign remains one of the most successful in U.S. military history.

The War Ends The Mexican-American War officially ended in 1848 when Mexico and the United States signed the **Treaty of Guadalupe-Hidalgo** (gwah duh LOOP ay hih DAHL goh). The treaty required Mexico to cede, or give up, all of California and New Mexico to the United States. These lands were called the **Mexican Cession**. In return, the United States paid Mexico $15 million.

In 1853, the United States paid Mexico an additional $10 million for a strip of land in present-day Arizona and New Mexico. Americans needed the land to complete a railroad. The land was called the Gadsden Purchase. With the Gadsden Purchase, many Americans felt that their dream of Manifest Destiny had been fulfilled.

✓ READING CHECK **Identify Cause and Effect** Why were Mexicans worried about the annexation of Texas by the United States?

Mormons Settle the Mexican Cession

Winning the Mexican-American War ushered in a new era of growth. New Mexico Territory, now the southwestern part of the United States, came to be known as the Southwest. After 1848, English-speaking settlers flocked to the Southwest. The largest group was the Mormons.

The Mormons Move West Mormons belonged to the Church of Jesus Christ of Latter-Day Saints. The church was founded in 1830 by Joseph Smith, a farmer in upstate New York.

Some of Smith's teachings differed from those of other Christian churches. These new teachings angered many non-Mormons, who forced the Mormons to leave New York.

The Mormons moved west and, in the 1840s, built a community they called Nauvoo on the banks of the Mississippi River in Illinois. Once again, the Mormons and their neighbors clashed. In 1844, an angry mob killed Joseph Smith, and Brigham Young was chosen as their new leader.

A New Home in Utah Young sought a place where Mormons would be safe from persecution. In 1847, he led an advance party into the valley of the Great Salt Lake. Soon, waves of Mormon families followed. For several years, Mormon wagon trains struggled across the plains and over the Rockies to Utah.

Young drew up plans for a large city, called Salt Lake City, to be built in the desert. The Mormon settlements in Utah grew, and eventually, in 1896, Utah became a state.

✓ **READING CHECK** **Identify Cause and Effect** Why did the Mormons go to Utah?

The 31st State

While the Mormons were moving to what would become Utah, thousands of other Americans were racing even farther west. The great California gold rush had begun.

Quest CONNECTIONS

What was the effect of the war? Note your ideas in your 📓 Active Journal.

Did you know?

Five companies of Mormon settlers walked all the way to Salt Lake City pushing their belongings in handcarts like the one shown here.

The Rush to California In 1848, John Sutter was having a sawmill built on the American River, north of Sacramento, California. Sutter had hired James Marshall to supervise the job. Early on January 24, Marshall was out making inspections. He later recalled the events of that day:

Primary Source

"As I was taking my usual walk, . . . my eye was caught with the glimpse of something shining in the bottom of the ditch. . . . I reached my hand down and picked it up; it made my heart thump, for I was certain it was gold."

—James Marshall, quoted in *Hutchings' Illustrated California Magazine*, 1857–1858

Analyze Images Two Chinese American forty-niners. **Use Visual Information** What difficulties did forty-niners face?

Sutter tried to keep the news a secret, but word spread quickly. Soon, thousands of Americans caught "gold fever," along with people from Europe, China, Australia, and South America. More than 80,000 people made the journey to California in 1849. They became known as **forty-niners**, a nickname created in reference to the year they arrived.

Very few miners actually struck it rich, and many went broke. In some cases, wives made more money at home than their husbands did in the mines. "I have made about $18,000 worth of pies," one woman boasted.

Many miners left the gold fields, but they stayed in California. In time, they found jobs or took up farming.

Conflicts Over Water While California has a variety of climates and landscapes, many areas of California are naturally dry, especially in the south. Not surprisingly, as the population grew, people quarreled over water **allocation**.

Two systems of water rights developed. One system, based in common law, gives water rights to the people who live in a place where water is. This system commonly gave first water rights to missions and pueblos, which were normally built near rivers or lakes.

> **INTERACTIVE**
>
> Growth of the West to 1860

Academic Vocabulary

allocation • *n.*, the dividing up of something for a special purpose

The other system of water rights developed in the gold rush mining areas. To the miners, water was like gold: whoever found it owned it. If your neighbor upstream took water from a river, there might not be any left for you. Conflicts over water rights led to legal and political battles between missions, ranchers, miners, and farmers.

Many conflicts involved farmers who needed water for their crops or missions that needed water for their residents. Farmers complained that the mining process polluted the water, making it unfit for agriculture. The conflicts over water were never completely resolved and continue to the present time.

Statehood for California The gold rush brought big changes to California. Almost overnight, San Francisco grew into a bustling city. In the gold fields, towns sprang up just as quickly. Greed led some forty-niners into crime. Murders and robberies plagued many mining camps.

Californians realized that they needed a strong government to stop such lawlessness. **Consequently**, in November of 1849, they drafted a state constitution and then asked to be admitted to the Union. Their request caused an uproar because of the slavery issue. After a heated debate, California was admitted to the Union as a free state as part of the Compromise of 1850. But the question of whether new states could allow slavery would continue to cause bitter disagreements that further divided the nation.

☑ READING CHECK **Sequence** How did California grow to statehood?

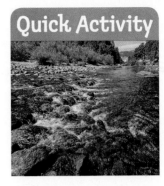

Quick Activity

Investigate ways in which rivers and streams helped determine where people settled in California.

Academic Vocabulary
consequently • *adv.,* as a result

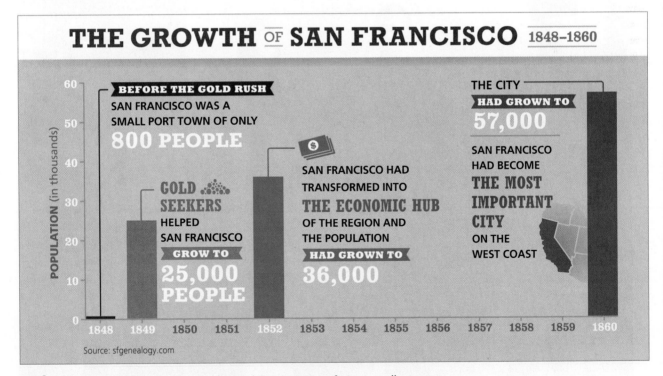

THE GROWTH OF SAN FRANCISCO 1848–1860

POPULATION (in thousands)

◄ BEFORE THE GOLD RUSH ►
SAN FRANCISCO WAS A SMALL PORT TOWN OF ONLY
800 PEOPLE

GOLD SEEKERS HELPED SAN FRANCISCO **◄ GROW TO ►** **25,000 PEOPLE**

SAN FRANCISCO HAD TRANSFORMED INTO **THE ECONOMIC HUB** OF THE REGION AND THE POPULATION **◄ HAD GROWN TO ►** **36,000**

THE CITY **◄ HAD GROWN TO ►** **57,000**

SAN FRANCISCO HAD BECOME **THE MOST IMPORTANT CITY** ON THE WEST COAST

1848 1849 1850 1851 1852 1853 1854 1855 1856 1857 1858 1859 1860

Source: sfgenealogy.com

Analyze Images The gold rush transformed San Francisco from a small port town into a major city. **Analyze Charts** How did immigration and migration impact the settlement of San Francisco?

 INTERACTIVE

The People of
California

The Effects of Migration to California

Westward expansion had many effects on the cultures and peoples of California. The gold rush brought diverse groups of people into contact with each other in the West.

A Mix of Cultures Most newcomers were white Americans from the East. Far more white men than women had joined the quest for gold. As a result, white men far outnumbered white women, making single women very sought after. This increased women's bargaining position and their stature, enabling them to achieve some rights that women elsewhere were denied.

The shortage of women also helped break down barriers between groups. In some areas, intermarriage between white men and Mexican women became more common.

California's mining camps included African Americans who had escaped from slavery in the South, free African Americans, and American Indians. There were also people from Hawaii, China, Peru, Chile, France, Germany, Italy, Ireland, and Australia.

Before the gold rush, California's population had included large numbers of Mexicans. Mexican Americans faced serious hardships. In the years following California statehood, many Mexican Americans lost land that their families had owned for generations.

Analyze Images People of all races came to California from across the country and around the world. **Identify Supporting Details** How did the gold rush change California's population?

American Indians fared even worse. Many were driven off the lands where they lived. Without any means to earn a living, large numbers died of starvation or disease brought by the newcomers. Others were murdered. In 1850, about 100,000 American Indians lived in California. By the 1870s, their population had dwindled to 17,000.

Lured by tales of a "mountain of gold," thousands of Chinese immigrants crossed the Pacific Ocean to California. At first, they were welcomed because California needed workers. When Chinese people staked claims in the gold fields, however, white miners often drove them off. Despite such injustice, many Chinese Americans stayed in California. Their contributions helped the state to grow. They shaped the environment by draining swamplands and digging irrigation systems to turn dry land into fertile farmland.

Free blacks also joined the gold rush. Some became well-off by starting and running businesses. By the 1850s, California had the wealthiest African American population of any state. Yet, African Americans faced discrimination and were denied certain rights.

Changes to the Region In spite of its problems, California continued to grow and prosper. Settlers from other states and immigrants from all over the world kept arriving. With their diverse backgrounds, the newcomers helped create California's identity. The economy grew as commerce and mining expanded. Agricultural production and the growth of the oil industry accounted for much of California's early economic growth. Cities and roads grew to accommodate the increase in people and goods.

Analyze Images This 1868 photo shows environmental damage near Dutch Flat, California, caused by hydraulic gold mining. **Sequence** Based on details in the photograph, describe how hydraulic mining damaged the environment.

☑ READING CHECK **Identify Cause and Effect** Why did so many American Indians die of disease as newcomers moved westward?

☑ Lesson Check

Practice Vocabulary

1. What happened to the **Bear Flag Republic**?

2. What did Mexico cede in the **Treaty of Guadalupe-Hidalgo**?

3. Who were the **forty-niners**?

Critical Thinking and Writing

4. **Identify Main Ideas** How were Americans influenced by the idea of Manifest Destiny?

5. **Draw Conclusions** Why do you suppose Brigham Young chose the isolated valley of the Great Salt Lake as a new home for the Mormons?

6. **Writing Workshop: End Strongly** In your 📓 Active Journal, write a final paragraph for your narrative. Bring it to an end in a way that will make it memorable for readers.

☑ Review and Assessment

VISUAL REVIEW

Events in the Age of Andrew Jackson

Social
- Tocqueville observes rising equality
- Life in the West expands women's roles
- American Indian removal
- Slavery extended in the South

Political
- Suffrage extended
- Common people support Jacksonian democracy
- Whigs and Democrats disagree about the role of government
- Nullification Crisis
- Jackson defies Supreme Court

EVENTS IN THE AGE OF ANDREW JACKSON

Military
- War for Texas Independence
- Mexican-American War
- Bear Flag Revolt

Economic
- Second Bank of the United States closes
- Development of steamboats, the National Road, and canals
- Panic of 1837
- California Gold Rush

Manifest Destiny

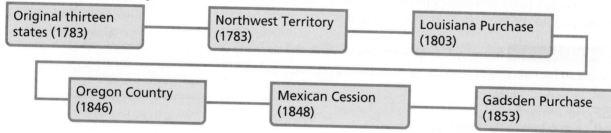

| Original thirteen states (1783) | Northwest Territory (1783) | Louisiana Purchase (1803) |
| Oregon Country (1846) | Mexican Cession (1848) | Gadsden Purchase (1853) |

READING REVIEW

Use the Take Notes and Practice Vocabulary activities in your 📕 Active Journal to review the topic.

 **INTERACTIVE**

Practice vocabulary using the Topic Mini-Games

Quest FINDINGS

Conduct Your Civic Discussion

Get help for conducting your discussion in your 📕 Active Journal.

ASSESSMENT

Vocabulary and Key Ideas

1. **Describe** How did **suffrage** change during the early years of the Age of Jackson?

2. **Check Understanding** Why did many people disapprove of the **spoils system**?

3. **Define** What was the **frontier**?

4. **Recall** What happens during a **depression**?

5. **Describe** How is a **caucus** different from a **nominating convention**?

6. **Use** What was the significance of the **National Road**?

7. **Check Understanding** What happened when Mexico signed the **Treaty of Guadalupe-Hidalgo**?

Critical Thinking and Writing

8. **Identify Point of View** Write a paragraph identifying the points of view the Whig Party and the Democratic Party held on major issues. What can you conclude about each party's point of view on the government's role in the economy?

9. **Explain an Argument** Explain how the issues of states' rights and nullification affected the nation during the Age of Jackson.

10. **Summarize** What is Manifest Destiny and how did this idea affect Americans and the people they encountered in the West?

11. **Revisit the Essential Question** Why did people move into the West? Think about the varied groups of people who settled in the West and their reasons for leaving their homes.

12. **Writing Workshop: Write a Narrative** Using the passages and notes you have written in your 📓 Active Journal, write a narrative from the perspective of a person moving westward during this time period. Tell about important or memorable events during your journey. Include description and sensory details to bring the narrative alive for readers. Create a strong opening and a memorable ending.

Analyze Primary Sources

13. The quotation presents one view of the conflict about
    A. the Second Bank of the United States.
    B. the Indian Removal Act.
    C. the "corrupt bargain."
    D. states' rights.

"When the laws undertake . . . to make the rich richer and the potent more powerful, the humble members of the society—the farmers, mechanics, and laborers—who have neither the time nor the means of [getting] favors for themselves . . . have a right to complain of the injustices of their government."

—President Andrew Jackson

Analyze Maps

Use the map to answer the following questions.

14. The Trail of Tears ended in which territory? Where did these American Indians live before they were relocated?

15. How did the Oregon Trail get its name? In which territory did the Oregon Trail begin?

16. Which territory did the United States acquire following the Mexican-American War? Which states were formed from this territory?

▼ **U.S. Growth to 1853**

GO ONLINE
to access your
digital course

 VIDEO

 AUDIO

 ETEXT

 INTERACTIVE

 WRITING

 GAMES

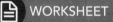 WORKSHEET

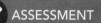 ASSESSMENT

Go back two centuries

to explore American SOCIETY AND CULTURE BEFORE THE CIVIL WAR. See how kids your age and younger worked in factories or picked cotton—10 to 14 hours a day. See how African Americans fought for their freedom and courageous women fought for their rights.

Explore
The Essential Question

Why is culture important?

Popular music, art, novels—all are important parts of our culture today. How did musicians, artists, and writers inspire Americans before the Civil War?

Watch

NBC LEARN

BOUNCE TO ACTIVATE   ▶ VIDEO

Lucy Larcom, Weaving Opportunity

Learn about Lucy Larcom's experience working in a textile mill.

Read

about the Industrial Revolution, the South's slave economy, social reform movements, and the art, music, and literature of this period.

TOPIC 7

Society and Culture Before the Civil War (1820–1860)

Learn more about the pre–Civil War era by making your own map and timeline in your 📖 Active Journal.

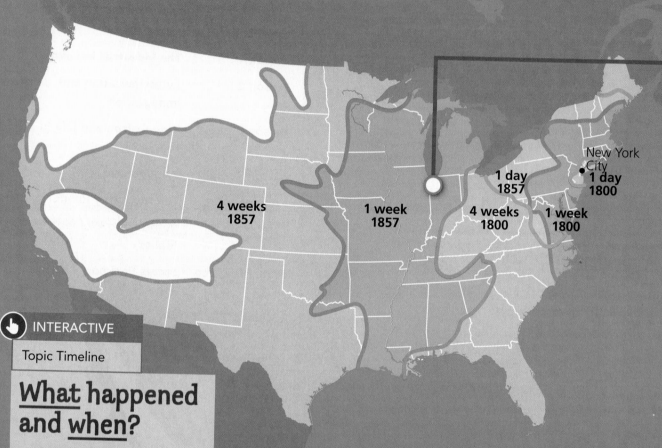

4 weeks
1857

1 week
1857

1 day
1857

New York
City
1 day
1800

4 weeks
1800

1 week
1800

👆 INTERACTIVE

Topic Timeline

What happened and when?

Noise and dust of the factory . . . women demanding equal rights . . . Explore the timeline to see some of what was happening in the United States and in the rest of the world.

1820
The Second Great Awakening begins.

TOPIC EVENTS

1810	1820	1830

WORLD EVENTS

1833
British Factory Act limits child labor.

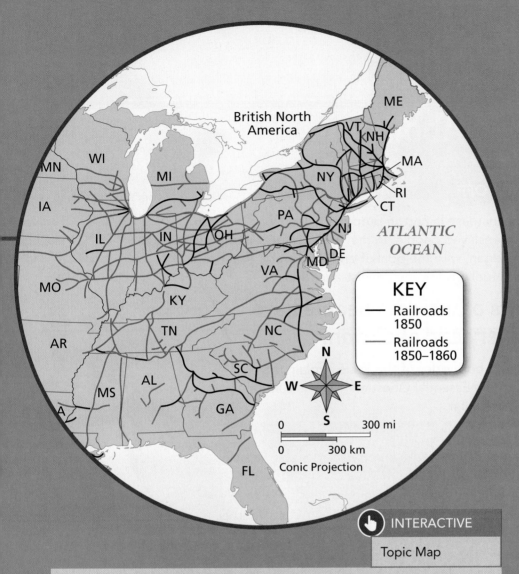

British North America

MN WI MI

IA IL IN OH

MO KY

AR TN

AL

MS

A

GA

FL

SC

NC

VA

PA NJ

MD DE

NY

VT NH

ME

MA

RI

CT

ATLANTIC
OCEAN

KEY
— Railroads 1850
— Railroads 1850–1860

N W E S

0   300 mi
0   300 km
Conic Projection

🖑 INTERACTIVE

Topic Map

How did the railroad change travel?

The growth of railroads greatly reduced travel time. Going from New York to Kentucky took a month in 1800. By 1857, travelers could go all the way to California in that time.

1844
Robert Morse patents the telegraph.

1848
Seneca Falls Convention

1854
Henry David Thoreau publishes *Walden*.

Eli Whitney, inventor of the cotton gin

Frederick Douglass, abolitionist

Susan B. Anthony, advocate for women's rights

Who will you meet?

1840   1850   1860   1870

1848
Revolutions shake Germany, Italy, and France.

1853
Great Exhibition displays products of the Industrial Revolution.

1858
Great Britain takes control of India.

Slavery and Abolition

▶ Once enslaved, Frederick Douglass became a leading abolitionist.

Quest KICK OFF

In the South, the increase in cotton production led to an increase in the number of enslaved people. In the 1830s, a movement called abolition began, with the goal of ending slavery. Americans expressed strong feelings for and against abolition.

What points of view did people have toward slavery and abolition?

How did people on both sides of this issue explain their position? Explore the Essential Question "Why is culture important?" in this Quest.

1 Ask Questions
What questions would you ask people on both sides of the slavery issue? Write your questions in your 📙 Active Journal.

2 Investigate
As you read the lessons in this topic, look for **Quest** CONNECTIONS that will help you understand differing points of view toward slavery and abolition. Record notes in your 📙 Active Journal.

3 Examine Primary Sources
Study the primary sources from the 1800s. They provide several points of view on both sides of the slavery issue. Record notes in your 📙 Active Journal.

Quest FINDINGS

4 Write Your Essay
The opinions that Americans expressed before the Civil War about slavery and abolition reflected both cultural differences and personal attitudes. At the end of the topic, you will use the primary sources and your own knowledge of history to write an essay stating your own conclusions about these opinions. Get help for this task in your 📙 Active Journal.

LESSON 1
The Industrial Revolution

BOUNCE TO ACTIVATE ▶ VIDEO

GET READY TO READ

START UP
Examine the illustration of workers in a textile mill. What would it be like to work here, in a large room filled with rapidly spinning machines?

GUIDING QUESTIONS
- How did work change between 1800 and 1850?
- What was family life like in different regions of the country during this period?

TAKE NOTES
Literacy Skills: Cite Evidence
Use the graphic organizer in your 📓 Active Journal to take notes as you read the lesson.

PRACTICE VOCABULARY
Use the vocabulary activity in your 📓 Active Journal to practice the vocabulary words.

Vocabulary

Industrial Revolution
capital
capitalist
scarcity
supply

interchangeable parts
Lowell girls
urbanization

Academic Vocabulary

profit
credit

In the early 1800s, busy factories and whirring machinery were part of a revolution that was spreading to the United States. Unlike the American Revolution, this one had no battles or fixed dates. The new revolution—the **Industrial Revolution**—was a long, slow process that completely changed the way goods were produced and where many people worked and lived.

The Industrial Revolution Begins

Before the 1800s, most Americans were farmers and most goods were produced by hand. As a result of the Industrial Revolution, this situation slowly changed. Machines replaced hand tools. New sources of power, such as steam, replaced human and animal power. While most Americans continued to farm for a living, the economy began a gradual shift toward manufacturing.

Technological Innovations The Industrial Revolution started in Britain in the mid-1700s. New machines transformed the textile industry.

Analyze Images The spinning jenny invented by James Hargreaves allowed workers to spin multiple spools of yarn at once. **Draw Conclusions** How did this invention affect the supply and cost of producing textiles?

Academic Vocabulary

profit • *n.*, the difference between the cost of a good and its selling price

Since the Middle Ages, workers had used spinning wheels to make thread. A spinning wheel, however, could spin only one thread at a time. In 1764, James Hargreaves developed the spinning jenny, a machine that could spin several threads at once. Other inventions sped up the process of weaving thread into cloth. In the 1780s, Edmund Cartwright built a loom powered by water. It allowed a worker to produce a great deal more cloth in a day than was possible before. These technological innovations would change how goods were made not only in Britain, but also in America and around the world.

New Ways to Produce Goods New inventions led to a new system of producing goods. Before the Industrial Revolution, most spinning and weaving took place in the home. Industrial production involved large machines, however, and these had to be housed in large mills near rivers. Water flowing downstream or over a waterfall turned a wheel that captured the power to run the machines.

To set up and operate a spinning mill required large amounts of **capital**, or invested money. Capitalists supplied this money. A **capitalist** is a person who invests in a business to make a **profit**. Capitalists built factories and hired workers to run the machines.

The new factory system brought workers and machinery together in one place to produce goods. Factory workers earned daily or weekly wages. They had to work a set number of hours each day.

In Britain, investors saw an opportunity. Because a single worker could produce much more with a machine than by hand, the cost of goods made by machine was much lower and more of those goods could be sold. If an investor built a factory that could produce cloth more cheaply, the investor could make a profit. Investors' desire to make a profit brought about rapid industrialization.

During the Industrial Revolution, the demand for factory-made products grew. In economics, demand is the readiness of people to purchase goods or services. The **supply**, or amount of goods available to sell, depended in part on the natural resources factories could get. To make products, factories needed raw materials, power, and laborers to run machinery. Some resources, such as cotton and iron, were in short supply. This **scarcity**, or limited supply, resulted in high prices. In response to high prices, farmers began to grow more cotton to supply spinning mills. Miners and others searched for new sources of iron and other materials used in machinery. The growing demand for products and for the supplies needed to make them led to a great change in standards of living.

☑ READING CHECK **Summarize** How did the Industrial Revolution affect the forces of supply and demand?

America's First Factories

Britain wanted to keep its technological innovations, or new technologies, secret. It did not want rival nations to copy the new machines. Therefore, the British Parliament passed a law forbidding anyone to take plans of the new machinery out of the country.

Slater Emigrates to the United States Samuel Slater soon proved that this law could not be enforced. Slater was a skilled mechanic in a British textile mill. He knew that his knowledge and skills would be in demand in the United States. In 1789, Slater boarded a ship bound for New York City. British officials searched the baggage of passengers sailing to the United States to make sure they were not carrying plans for machinery with them. Slater, however, did not need to carry any plans. Having worked in the British mills from an early age, Slater knew not only how to build the mills and machinery but also how to operate them.

The First American Mill Slater soon visited Moses Brown, a Quaker capitalist who had a mill in Pawtucket, Rhode Island. The mill was not doing well because its machinery constantly broke down. Slater set to work on improving the machinery. By 1793, in Pawtucket, he built what became the first successful textile mill in the United States that was powered by water.

Slater's factory was a huge success. Before long, other American manufacturers began using his ideas.

Interchangeable Parts American manufacturers also benefited from the pioneering work of American inventor Eli Whitney. Earlier, skilled workers made goods by hand. For example, gunsmiths spent days making the barrel, stock, and trigger for a single musket. Because the parts were handmade, each musket differed a bit from every other musket. If a part broke, a gunsmith had to make a new part to fit that particular gun.

INTERACTIVE

Early Textile Mill

Analyze Images A restored water wheel stands outside a New England mill. **Infer** Water wheels had been used for many years at grain mills. Did they differ significantly from those that powered textile mills?

Whitney wanted to speed up the making of guns by having machines manufacture each part. All machine-made parts would be alike—for example, one trigger would be identical to another. Identical parts would fit together with all other parts, and gunsmiths would not have build each gun from scratch. **Interchangeable parts** would save time and money.

Because the government bought many guns, Whitney went to Washington, D.C., to try to sell his idea. At first, officials laughed at his plan. Carefully, Whitney sorted parts for 10 muskets into separate piles. He then asked an official to choose one part from each pile. In minutes, the first musket was assembled. Whitney repeated the process until 10 muskets were complete.

In 1798, Whitney began producing muskets in the first factory to rely on interchangeable parts. The idea of interchangeable parts spread rapidly. Inventors designed machines to produce interchangeable parts for clocks, locks, and many other goods. With such machines, small workshops grew into factories.

Factories Spread The War of 1812 provided a boost to American industries. The British blockade cut Americans off from their supply of foreign goods. As a result, they had to produce more goods themselves. American merchants and bankers sought new ways to meet the increased demand. To profit from the efficiency provided by manufacturing, they built more factories. As American investors took advantage of new technologies and built more factories, the American economy grew.

Where Were Factories Built? The natural resources available to the people of a region shaped their economic activities. The first factories were built in the Northeast. Pennsylvania had abundant forests and iron ore. Lumbermen felled great swaths of forest for the timber used to make charcoal. Pennsylvania factories used the charcoal for power. These factories turned iron ore, which was mined and smelted locally, into machines, tools, and guns.

In New England, textile factories were built alongside the hilly region's numerous fast-moving streams. Falling water provided power for the mills. Humans also modified the landscape by building dams and canals to help power the mills. These modifications spurred economic growth. Wool and cotton produced in the South provided the raw materials for thread, yarn, and fabric. In Lynn, Massachusetts, businesses developed a step-by-step shoemaking process in the early 19th century. The large factories attracted new workers to the town, and the economy grew rapidly. New England became the first region in the United States to develop manufacturing on a wide scale.

The Market Economy and the Industrial Revolution In the United States, the Industrial Revolution took place in a period marked by the growth of a free enterprise, or market, economy. British restrictions on trade had been lifted. Hamilton's reforms had strengthened the banking system, and banks were able to lend more

▲ Eli Whitney's development of interchangeable parts, while making muskets, revolutionized manufacturing.

money. New access to **credit**, or borrowed money, allowed people to start mills and factories in cities and in rural places where swift streams provided power.

A market revolution was taking place. Mills and factories sprouted throughout the Northeast. New technologies, such as interchangeable parts and the steamboat, allowed for more efficient production and the transportation of goods. New roads and canals linked towns, expanding opportunities for commerce.

Businesses operated, for the most part, without much government control. Nor did the government own factories or intervene heavily in the market. The government, however, protected contracts and property. People could buy, sell, or use property as they saw fit.

Most Americans wanted the freedom to try new things. They believed in competition, which encouraged new inventions. In 1792, a group of 24 investors had started the New York Stock Exchange. This stock market raised private capital to pay for new ventures. Success meant profits and brought new wealth to investors. Profits led to new investment and further economic growth.

Low taxes allowed businesses to hold on to large amounts of capital and use it to expand and create even more wealth. The desire for profit and accumulated wealth sparked new ventures under new investors.

The Role of Market Forces Investors looked to the market to decide where to invest or what businesses to start. In a market economy, goods are bought and sold, and wages are determined, by the market. If a product is in high demand and the supply is limited,

Academic Vocabulary

credit • *n.,* an agreement or contract in which a borrower receives money or goods now, with an agreement to repay a greater amount later

Analyze Images The Pemberton Mill in Lawrence, MA, collapsed January 10, 1860, because the building's structure could not support the load placed on it. More than 145 workers, mostly women from Ireland, died in the collapse. **Draw Conclusions** What does this disaster tell you about the mill owners' attitude toward the mill's workers?

the price will be high. Entrepreneurs started businesses to supply high-priced or high-demand products. They abandoned businesses where the demand and price were low.

Workers faced the same market forces. People with skills that were in demand in factories could expect higher wages than those whose skills had less value in the market.

☑ READING CHECK **Understand Effects** How did transportation boost the market revolution in the early 1800s?

Daily Life in Factory Towns

Slater and Whitney's innovations were just the first steps in America's Industrial Revolution. During the early 1800s, entire cities began to emerge around factories.

Mills in Lowell During the War of 1812, Francis Cabot Lowell, a Boston merchant, found a way to improve on British textile mills. In Britain, one factory spun thread and a second factory wove it into cloth. Why not, Lowell wondered, combine spinning and weaving under one roof? The new mill that he built in Waltham, Massachusetts, had all the machines needed to turn raw cotton into finished cloth.

After Lowell's death, his partners took on a more ambitious project. They built an entire factory town and named it after him. In 1821, Lowell, Massachusetts, was a village of five farm families.

By 1836, it boasted more than 10,000 people. Visitors to Lowell described it as a model community composed of "small wooden houses, painted white, with green blinds, very neat, very snug, very nicely carpeted."

Analyze Images The town of Lowell was set up to be a factory town. **Compare and Contrast** Map ❶ shows Lowell in 1821, and map ❷ shows the town in 1845. What changes can you see?

❶

"Lowell Girls" To work in their new mills, the company hired young women from nearby farms. The **Lowell girls**, as they came to be called, usually worked for a few years in the mills before returning home to marry. These young women, and women like them in other mill towns, made an important economic contribution to American society by providing labor for the Industrial Revolution. Most sent their wages home to their families.

At first, parents hesitated to let their daughters work in the mills. To reassure parents, the company built boardinghouses, or buildings with many shared bedrooms and a kitchen that served meals. The company also made rules to protect the young women.

British author Charles Dickens toured Lowell in 1842. The Lowell girls impressed him. He later wrote:

Primary Source

"It is their station to work. And they do work. They labour in these mills, upon an average, twelve hours a day, which is unquestionably work, and pretty tight work too."

—Charles Dickens, *American Notes and Pictures from Italy*

Although factory work was often tedious, hard, and dangerous, many women valued the economic freedom they got from working in the mills. One worker wrote her sister Sarah back on a farm in New Hampshire:

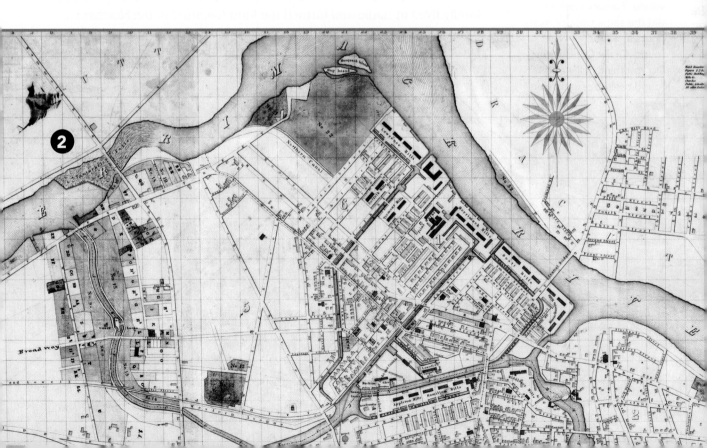

Primary Source

"Since I have wrote you, another pay day has come around. I earned 14 dollars and a half . . . I like it well as ever and Sarah don't I feel independent of everyone!"

— from *Lowell Offering: Writings by New England Mill Women*

In Lowell and elsewhere, mill owners hired mostly women and children. They did this because they could pay women and children half of what they would have had to pay men.

Child Labor Boys and girls as young as seven worked in factories. Small children were especially useful in textile mills because they could squeeze around the large machines to change spindles.

Today, most Americans look upon child labor as cruel. Yet in the 1800s, farm children also worked hard. Most people did not see much difference between children working in a factory or on a farm. Often, a child's wages were needed to help support the family.

Long Hours Working hours in the mills were long—12 hours a day, 6 days a week. True, farmers also put in long hours. However, farmers worked shorter hours in winter. Mill workers, in contrast, worked nearly the same hours all year round.

As industries grew and competition increased, employers took less interest in the welfare of their workers. Working conditions eventually declined.

Changes at Home The Industrial Revolution had a great impact on home life. Previously, most Americans worked in agriculture. The entire family lived at home and farmed the land together. In the Northeast, some families took part in cottage industries, making goods at home. Local merchants supplied them with materials, such as wool. Home workers, usually women and girls, would spin the wool into yarn and

Analyze Images Although farm work was hard, it varied. Factory workers did the same task for many hours at a time all year round. **Draw Conclusions** Do you think mill workers found their jobs satisfying?

weave it into cloth. Other cottage workers made shoes. As the factory system spread, the family economy gave way to industrial production. More family members left the home to earn a living.

These changes affected ideas about the role of women. In poorer families, women often had to go out to work. In wealthier families, husbands supported the family while wives stayed at home. For many husbands, having a wife who stayed at home became a sign of success. Men and women began to be viewed as fundamentally different, with distinct gender-based roles. Women were judged to be best suited to the domestic life, while men were expected to go out and earn a living in the world. As a result, women and men formed close bonds with one another inside their separate spheres, while at the same time were also expected to marry and raise a family.

Analyze Images In cottage industries, women were able to work at home and earn money for doing things such as weaving and spinning. **Infer** After factory work replaced cottage industry, how did family life change?

☑ **READING CHECK** **Draw Conclusions** How did competition and the quest for profit change working conditions in American mills?

How Did Cities Expand?

In 1800, nearly five million Americans lived in rural areas, compared to 322,000 who lived in cities. During the Industrial Revolution, many people left farms for cities, attracted by the job opportunities to be found in factories. As investors found that factories produced a profit, they invested those profits in building more factories, which attracted still more workers from farms. Older cities expanded rapidly, while new cities sprang up around factories. This movement of the population from rural areas to cities is called **urbanization**. Urbanization increased as industry grew.

Urbanization was a steady but gradual process. In 1800, only 6 percent of the nation's population lived in urban areas. By 1850, the number had risen to 15 percent. Not until 1920 did more Americans live in cities than in rural areas.

By today's standards, these early cities were small. A person could walk from one end of any American city to the other in as little as 30 minutes. Buildings were, at most, only a few stories tall. As the factory system spread, the nation's cities grew.

Problems in Cities Growing cities had numerous problems. Many of these resulted from the human modification of the environment. Dirt and gravel streets turned into mud-holes when it rained. Cities had no sewers, and people threw garbage into the streets. A visitor to New York reported that "The streets are filthy, and the stranger is not a little surprised to meet the hogs walking about in them, for the purpose of devouring the vegetables and trash thrown into the gutter."

Untreated sewage and garbage often seeped into wells or flowed into streams and rivers, polluting the water. The contaminated water spread disease. Epidemics of cholera (KAHL ur uh) raged through cities, killing thousands of people.

At about the same time, coal became an important source of industrial and home heating power. The smoke and soot from burning coal seriously modified the environment, polluting the air and dirtying cities. It also caused health problems.

Attractions Besides work opportunities, cities also had attractions. Theaters, museums, and circuses created an air of excitement. In cities, people could shop in fine stores that sold the latest fashions from Europe. Some offered modern "ready-to-wear" clothing. While most women continued to sew their own clothes, many enjoyed visiting hat shops, china shops, shoe stores, and "fancy-goods" stores.

✓ READING CHECK **Summarize** What were some drawbacks of urbanization?

New Inventions

Northern industry grew steadily in the mid-1800s. Most northerners still lived on farms. However, more and more of the northern economy began to depend on manufacturing and trade.

The 1800s brought a flood of new inventions in the North. "In Massachusetts and Connecticut," a European visitor exclaimed, "there is not a laborer who has not invented a machine or a tool." Americans of the period were a practical people. Americans, and especially northerners, looked to science for new and useful applications that could be put to work at once. They expected technology to bring economic development and to change the way people lived.

Technology refers to ways of doing things, sometimes involving advanced scientific knowledge, or tools that make use of advanced knowledge. Innovation is coming up with new ways of doing things.

New technologies during the colonial period, such as Franklin's lightning rod, had brought limited and modest changes to daily life in America. By comparison, the scientific and technological innovations of the 1800s transformed American life.

Analyze Images New stoves and new farm equipment were among the inventions of this era. **Draw Conclusions** How did inventions like these affect the way food was grown and prepared?

In 1834, Philo Stewart developed a cast-iron stove small enough for use in an average kitchen. His factory-built wood-burning stove was a great success. About 90,000 were sold. The cast-iron stove was only

one sign of the way northern factories were changing the lives of ordinary people.

Joseph Henry, a New Yorker, showed that electric current could be sent through a wire over long distances to ring a bell. His work paved the way for later inventions. Thomas Davenport, a blacksmith, invented an early type of electric motor in 1834.

Both inventions were adapted and marketed. Competition among inventors brought about more innovation.

Analyze Images Telegraph offices like this one were communication hubs. **Infer** When a telegram came in to such an office, how do you think it might have been handled?

In 1846, Elias Howe patented a sewing machine. A few years later, Isaac Singer improved on Howe's machine. Soon, clothing makers bought hundreds of the new sewing machines. Workers could now make dozens of shirts in the time it took a tailor to sew one by hand.

Farm Machines Some new inventions made work easier for farmers. In 1825, Jethro Wood began the manufacture of an iron plow with replaceable parts. John Deere improved on the idea when he invented a lightweight steel plow. Earlier plows made of iron or wood had to be pulled by oxen, which were strong but slow. A horse, less strong but faster than an ox, could pull a steel plow through a field more quickly.

In 1847, Cyrus McCormick opened a factory in Chicago that produced mechanical reapers. The reaper was a horse-drawn machine that cut and gathered wheat and other grains. McCormick's reaper could do the work of five people using hand tools.

Other farm machines followed. There was a mechanical drill to plant grain, a threshing machine to beat grain from its husk, and a horse-drawn hay rake. These machines helped farmers raise more grain with fewer hands. As a result, thousands of farmworkers left the countryside. Some went west to start farms of their own. Others found jobs in new factories in northern cities.

The Telegraph Connects the Nation Samuel F. B. Morse received a patent for a "talking wire," or telegraph, in 1844. The telegraph was a device that sent electrical signals along a wire. It was a new technology that was made possible by scientific discoveries about electricity. Morse also devised a code of dots, dashes, and spaces so messages could be sent. The dots stood for short tones, the dashes for long tones. This system of dots and dashes became known as the Morse code.

Congress gave Morse funds to run wire from Washington, D.C., to Baltimore. On May 24, 1844, Morse set up his telegraph in the Supreme Court chamber in Washington.

 INTERACTIVE

New Inventions Improve Life

As a crowd of onlookers watched, Morse tapped out a short message: "What hath God wrought!" A few seconds later, the operator in Baltimore tapped back the same message. The telegraph worked!

Morse's invention was an instant success. Telegraph companies sprang up everywhere. Thousands of miles of wire soon stretched across the country. News could now travel long distances in a few minutes.

The telegraph helped many businesses thrive. Merchants and farmers could have quick access to information about supply, demand, and prices of goods in different areas of the country. The availability of nearly instant information about markets changed the way goods were sold and contributed to the development of a nationwide market.

The telegraph connected the nation in a completely new way. Almost every American town eventually had a telegraph, providing rapid communication from coast to coast.

Ordinary people could communicate quickly with distant family and friends. The presence of telegraph offices in cities and towns was yet another of the many attractions that helped drive urbanization. The telegraph is an example of how scientific discoveries influenced daily life during the 1800s.

Analyze Images When something new was invented, other inventors started trying to improve it. A British inventor created this version of the telegraph. **Infer** Why might piano-style keys have been easier to use?

☑ **READING CHECK** Identify Implied Main Ideas How did the invention of new farm machines contribute to urbanization in the North?

☑ Lesson Check

Practice Vocabulary

1. What key role did **capitalists** play in the **Industrial Revolution**?

2. How would a **scarcity** of natural resources affect the **supply** of goods to a market?

Critical Thinking and Writing

3. **Identify Cause and Effect** How did the use of interchangeable parts contribute to the Industrial Revolution?

4. **Summarize** Explain how the willingness of factory owners to hire women and children changed family life.

5. **Writing Workshop: Introduce Characters** In your 📔 Active Journal, write a brief description of each character, including yourself, to appear in the narrative essay you will write at the end of the Topic. Include where each one lives, where they work, relationships, and any other interesting characteristics.

Detect Changing Patterns

Follow these steps to learn to identify causes of change in a society.

INTERACTIVE

Identify Trends

1 Gather information about the society. Look at different resources to learn about life in the society you are studying. What resources could help you find information about why and how United States society changed during the period 1820–1860?

2 Identify possible sources of change in the society. Sources of change can be economic, political, social, or cultural.

   a. What was the most revolutionary change during this period?

   b. Were there other sources of change linked to that major change—in other words, effects that themselves became agents of change?

3 Determine how the sources of change led to new patterns of living. What do the "before and after" images below tell you about a new pattern of living that resulted from the major change that you have identified?

4 Summarize what you discover. Use the information you have learned in order to make a general statement. What can you say about the effects on society of this major change?

Secondary Source

▲ The loom was an important tool used by the women and other family members who produced yarn and cloth at home for textile merchants.

Secondary Source

▲ Young women (often helped by children) operated complex machinery to produce yarn and cloth at a factory for the textile industry.

Industrialization and Immigration

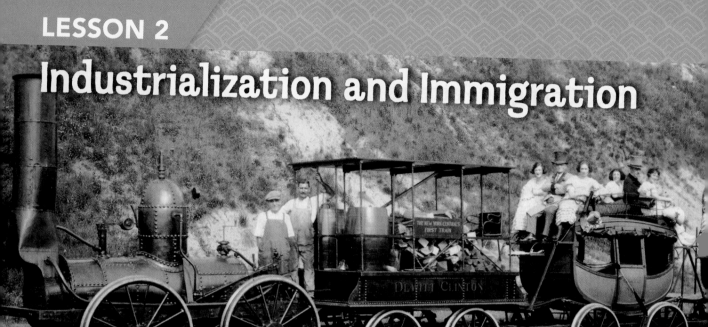

BOUNCE TO ACTIVATE   ▶ VIDEO

GET READY TO READ

START UP

Look at the photograph. What do you think Americans' reactions were to the first trains?

GUIDING QUESTIONS

- How did the use of steam power affect the Industrial Revolution?
- What was family life like in the growing cities?
- What was the impact of the Industrial Revolution on working conditions and social class?

TAKE NOTES

Literacy Skills: Identify Main Ideas

Use the graphic organizer in your 📓 Active Journal to take notes as you read the lesson.

PRACTICE VOCABULARY

Use the vocabulary activity in your 📓 Active Journal to practice the vocabulary words.

Vocabulary		Academic Vocabulary
artisan	nativist	
trade union	Know-Nothing Party	organize
strike	discrimination	immigrant
famine		

Where early industry had been powered by water, the Industrial Revolution went farther when it harnessed steam. Factory efficiency increased, and with improvements to locomotive technology, markets continued to expand.

What Changes Did the Age of Steam Power Bring?

At first, railroads were used to provide transportation to canals. Horses or mules pulled cars along wooden rails covered with strips of iron. Then, in 1829, an English family developed a steam-powered locomotive engine to pull rail cars. The engine, called the Rocket, barreled along at 30 miles per hour.

Early Difficulties Not all Americans welcomed the new railroads. Workers who moved freight on horse-drawn wagons feared that they would lose their jobs. People who had invested in canals worried that competition from the railroads might cause them to lose their investments.

There were problems with the early railroads. They were not always safe or reliable. Soft roadbeds and weak bridges often led to accidents. Locomotives often broke down. Even when they worked, their smokestacks belched thick black smoke and hot embers. The embers sometimes burned holes in passengers' clothing or set nearby buildings on fire.

Part of the problem was the way in which railroads were built. Often, instead of two tracks being laid—one for each direction—only one was set. Signals to control traffic on a single track did not yet exist. This increased the likelihood of a collision.

Another problem with early railroads was that there was no standard gauge, or distance between the rails. As a result, different railroads often used different gauges. To transfer from one railroad line to another, people and goods had to be moved off one train and then loaded onto another.

A Network of Railroads Gradually, railroad builders overcame problems and removed obstacles. Engineers learned to build sturdier bridges and solid roadbeds. They replaced wooden rails with iron rails. Railroads developed signaling systems and agreed on a standard gauge. Such improvements made railroad travel safer and faster.

By the 1850s, the American landscape had changed. A network of railroads crisscrossed the nation. The major lines were concentrated in the North and West. New York, Chicago, and Cincinnati became major rail centers. The South, less reliant on industry, had much less track than the North.

GEOGRAPHY SKILLS

This map shows the explosive growth of railroads between 1850 and 1860.

1. **Region** In which region were the most new rail lines?

2. **Infer** What does the increase in rail service tell you about the population of that region?

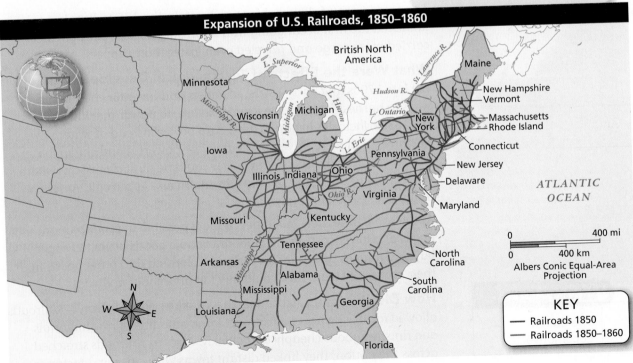

Expansion of U.S. Railroads, 1850–1860

KEY
— Railroads 1850
— Railroads 1850–1860

Railroads played an important role in urban growth. Cities with good rail connections attracted factories and other businesses. Railroads also made it possible for people to migrate more easily to new cities, increasing urban populations.

What Were Yankee Clippers?

Railroads increased commercial development in the United States. At the same time, trade with other nations also increased. At seaports in the Northeast, captains loaded their ships, the famed Yankee clippers, with cotton, fur, wheat, lumber, and tobacco. Then they set sail for other parts of the world.

Speed was the key to successful trade at sea. In 1845, an American named John Griffiths launched the *Rainbow*, the first of the clipper ships. These sleek vessels had tall masts and huge sails that caught every gust of wind. Their narrow hulls clipped swiftly through the water. These technological innovations traded cargo space for speed, which gave American merchants an advantage.

In the 1840s, American clipper ships broke every speed record. One clipper ship sped from New York to Hong Kong in 81 days, flying past older ships that took many months to reach China. The speed of the clippers helped the United States win a large share of the world's sea trade in the 1840s and 1850s.

The golden age of clipper ships was brief. In the 1850s, Britain launched the first oceangoing iron steamships. These sturdy vessels carried more cargo and traveled even faster than clippers.

What Were the Effects of Technological Developments?

In the late 1700s and early 1800s, scientists and inventors had found ways to harness heat, in the form of steam, to power machines. By the 1830s, factories began to use steam power instead of water power. Machines that were driven by steam were powerful and cheap to run. Also, factories that used steam power could be built almost anywhere, not just along the banks of swift-flowing rivers. As a result, American industry expanded rapidly.

At the same time, new machines made it possible to produce more goods at a lower cost. These more affordable goods attracted eager buyers. Families no longer had to make clothing and other goods in their homes. Instead, they could buy factory-made products.

How Did Railroads Advance the Market Revolution?

Railroads allowed factory owners to transport large amounts of raw materials and finished goods cheaply and quickly. Also, as railroads stretched across the nation, they linked distant towns with cities and factories.

INTERACTIVE

The Steam Locomotive

These towns became new markets for factory goods. Railroads greatly increased the size of the American marketplace and fueled even more factory production.

The growth of railroads also affected northern farming. Railroads brought cheap grain and other foods from the West to New England. New England farmers could not compete with this new source of cheap foods. Many left their farms to find new jobs in towns and cities as factory workers, store clerks, and sailors.

Rising Standards of Living The early rise of industrialization in the United States under a market economy brought striking economic and social benefits. Mass production lowered prices and raised Americans' purchasing power and standard of living. Wages increased for average workers. Food canned in factories improved peoples' year-round diets.

The use of stoves improved meals and home heating. Factory-made clothing was cheaper than homemade. Great numbers of newspapers and magazines reported regularly about the new inventions and advertised the new products. Along with these changes, though, there were also challenges.

☑ READING CHECK Draw Conclusions What was the principal advantage of steam power over water power?

How Did Workers Respond to Challenges?

Factories of the 1840s and 1850s differed greatly from the mills of the early 1800s. As industrialization grew, life changed for workers. The factories were larger, and they used steam-powered machines. Laborers worked longer hours for lower wages. Usually, workers and their families lived in dark, dingy houses in the shadow of the factory. Cramped quarters, poverty, and pollution made the lives of many of these families miserable.

Changing Roles The emphasis on mass production changed the way workers felt about their jobs. Before the growth of factories, skilled workers, or **artisans**, were proud of the goods they made. The factory owner, however, was more interested in how much could be produced than in how well it was made. Workers could not be creative. Furthermore, unlike the artisan who could have his or her own business, the factory worker was not likely to rise to a management position.

Families in Factories As the need for workers increased, entire families labored in factories. In some cases, a family agreed to work for one year. If even one family member broke the contract, the entire family might be fired.

The factory day began when a whistle sounded at 4 A.M. The entire family—father, mother, and children—headed off to work.

Analyze Images Workers tend machines in a mill. **Infer** How did work like this affect the workers' physical health?

Many factories, at that time, employed young children. The workday did not end until 7:30 P.M., when a final whistle sent the workers home.

Hazards at Work
Factory workers faced discomfort and danger. Few factories had windows or heating systems. In summer, the heat and humidity inside the factory were stifling. In winter, the extreme cold contributed to frequent sickness.

Factory machines had no safety devices, and accidents were common. There were no laws regulating factory conditions, and injured workers often lost their jobs.

Labor Organizations and Strikes
Poor working conditions and low wages led workers to organize into groups to improve their conditions. The first workers to organize were artisans. In the 1820s and 1830s, artisans in each trade united to form **trade unions**. Trade unions were part of a labor reform movement.

The concentration of workers in cities helped the formation of unions by allowing people working in the same industry for different companies to organize together. Their trade unions called for a shorter workday, higher wages, and better working conditions. Sometimes, unions went on strike to gain their demands. In a **strike**, union workers refuse to do their jobs until managers agree to address their concerns.

In the early 1800s, strikes were illegal in many parts of the United States. Strikers faced fines or jail sentences. Employers often fired strike leaders. Employers were politically opposed to workers organizing.

Progress for Artisans
Slowly, however, the labor reform movement made progress. In 1840, President Van Buren approved a ten-hour workday for government employees. Workers celebrated another victory in 1842 when a Massachusetts court declared that they had the right to strike.

Artisans won better pay because factory owners needed their skills. Unskilled workers, however, were unable to bargain for better wages since their jobs required little or no training. Because these workers were easy to replace, employers did not listen to their demands.

During the Industrial Revolution, a new awareness of class differences began to emerge. As a farming people, Americans had long viewed labor with deep respect. The changing conditions of factory labor and the gaps between the wages of unskilled workers, managers, and business owners led to a sense of people grouped in classes with shared interests. The interests of these classes were often different. By bringing together workers and managers in the same factories

Academic Vocabulary
organize • *v.*, to set up or establish a group, such as a labor union

Analyze Images Women, such as these working in a Massachusetts factory, received low pay although they worked long hours. **Identify Cause and Effect** Why would workers go out on strike?

and cities, urbanization led to a rise in conflicts resulting from differences in social class.

Women Organize The success of trade unions encouraged other workers to **organize**. Workers in New England textile mills were especially eager to protest cuts in wages and unfair work rules. Many of these workers were women.

Women workers faced special problems. First, they had always earned less money than men did. Second, most union leaders did not want women in their ranks. Like many people at the time, they believed that women should not work outside the home. In fact, the goal of many unions was to raise men's wages so that their wives could leave their factory jobs.

Despite these problems, women workers organized. They staged several strikes at Lowell, Massachusetts, in the 1830s. In the 1840s, Sarah Bagley organized the Lowell Female Labor Reform Association. The group petitioned the state legislature for a 10-hour workday.

☑ READING CHECK **Draw Conclusions** Why could artisans command higher wages while other workers could not?

Analyze Images Starving Irish people ransack a government potato store in 1845, during the potato famine. **Identify Cause and Effect** How did the failure of potato crops in Ireland affect immigration to the United States?

How Did Ethnic Minorities Fare in the North?

By the late 1840s, many factory workers in the North were **immigrants**. An immigrant is a person who enters a new country in order to settle there. In the 1840s and 1850s, about 4 million immigrants arrived in the United States. They were attracted, in large part, by the opportunities for farming the land or working in the cities. Economic opportunity, then, was a key "pull" factor—it pulled immigrants into the country. Among the new arrivals were immigrants from Britain who came to earn higher wages. There was a greater demand in the United States for skilled machinists, carpenters, and miners.

From Ireland and Germany In Ireland in the 1840s, a disease destroyed the harvest of potatoes, which were the main food of the poor people. Other crops, such as wheat and oats, were not affected. At the time, Ireland was under British rule and most Irish crops were exported to England. When a large part of the potato crop was lost to disease, British landowners continued to ship the wheat and oats to England. There was little left for the Irish to eat. This situation caused a **famine**, or severe food shortage. Thousands of people died of starvation.

Academic Vocabulary

immigrant • *n.*, a person who enters another country in order to settle there

Analyze Images Many German immigrants settled in the Midwest, including this Wisconsin town, which features a German heritage historic site. Infer How would the arrival of immigrants change these communities?

Nearly as many died from disease. This disaster became known as the "Great Irish Famine." Between 1845 and 1860, over 1.5 million Irish fled to the United States seeking freedom from hunger and British rule. Famine, then, was a "push" factor—it pushed the Irish to leave their country.

Meanwhile, many Germans were also arriving in the United States. Harsh weather conditions from 1829 to 1830 resulted in severe food shortages in Germany. By 1832, more than 10,000 Germans were coming to the United States every year, seeking fertile land to farm and a better life. In 1848, revolutions had broken out in several parts of Germany. The rebels fought for democratic reforms. When the revolts failed, thousands had to flee. Attracted by its democratic political system, many came to the United States.

Many other German immigrants came simply to make a better life for themselves. Between 1848 and 1860, nearly one million Germans arrived in the United States.

Immigrants Enrich the Nation Immigrants supplied much of the labor that helped the nation's economy grow. Although most of the Irish immigrants had been farmers, few had money to buy farmland. Many settled in the northern cities where low-paying factory jobs were available. Other Irish workers transformed the environment by helping to build many new canals and railroads. Irish women often worked as servants in private homes.

Immigrants from Germany often had enough money to move west and buy good farmland. These immigrants transformed the environment by turning prairie into farmland. Others were artisans and merchants. Cities of the Midwest such as St. Louis, Milwaukee, and Cincinnati had German grocers, butchers, and bakers.

A small minority of the immigrants from Germany were Jewish. German Jews began immigrating to the United States in the 1820s. By the early 1860s, there were about 150 communities in the United States with substantial Jewish populations.

✓ READING CHECK Compare and Contrast In what ways were Irish and German immigrants alike? Different?

A Reaction Against Immigrants

Not everyone welcomed the flood of immigrants. One group of Americans, called **nativists**, wanted to preserve the country for native-born, white citizens. Using the slogan "Americans must rule America," they called for laws to limit immigration. They also wanted to keep immigrants from voting until they had lived in the United States for 21 years. At the time, newcomers could vote after only 5 years in the country.

Did you know?

German Americans are the largest single ethnic group in the United States.

Some nativists protested that newcomers "stole" jobs from native-born Americans because they worked for lower pay. Furthermore, when workers went out on strike, factory owners often hired immigrant workers to replace them. Many distrusted the different languages, customs, and dress of the immigrants. Others blamed immigrants for the rise in crime in the growing cities. Still others mistrusted Irish newcomers because many of them were Catholics. Until the 1840s, most immigrants from Europe had been Protestants. As American cities attracted Catholic immigrants, these cities became centers of conflicts over religion.

By the 1850s, hostility to immigrants was so strong that nativists formed a new political party. Members of the party were anti-Catholic and anti-immigrant. Many meetings and rituals of the party were kept secret. It was called the **Know-Nothing Party** because members answered, "I know nothing," when asked about the party. The message of the party did gain supporters, but its support was limited to the North, where most immigrants settled. In 1856, Millard Fillmore, the Know-Nothing candidate for President, won 21 percent of the popular vote. Soon after, however, the party died out.

☑ READING CHECK **Infer** Why do you think the members of the Know-Nothing Party answered as they did?

African Americans Face Discrimination

During the nation's early years, slavery was legal in the North. By the early 1800s, however, all of the northern states had passed laws to bring an end to slavery. In some states, only the children of slaves gained freedom at first. Many did not completely abolish slavery until the mid-1800s. Still, thousands of free African Americans lived in the North, and their number grew steadily during the early 1800s.

Free African Americans in the North faced discrimination. **Discrimination** is a policy or an attitude that denies equal rights to certain groups of people. As one writer pointed out, African Americans were denied "the ballot-box, the jury box, the halls of the legislature, the army, the public lands, the school, and the church."

Even skilled African Americans had trouble finding good jobs. One African American woodworker was turned away by every furniture maker in Cincinnati. At last, a shop owner hired him. However, when he entered the shop, the other woodworkers dropped their tools. Either he must leave or they would, they declared. Similar experiences occurred throughout the North.

Some African Americans Find Success

Despite such obstacles, some northern African Americans achieved notable success in business.

Did you know?

Anti-Irish sentiment ran so high during this time that ads for jobs and housing would state bluntly, "No Irish need apply."

Quest CONNECTIONS

Find out how men like William Whipper and John Russwurm were involved in the abolitionist movement. Record your findings in your 📓 Active Journal.

Analyze Images Built in 1806, the African Meeting House in Boston is the oldest standing African American church in the United States. **Sequence** What other developments in the African American community followed the founding of this church?

Analyze Images
Freedom's Journal was the first newspaper owned by African Americans. **Infer** Do you think the editors of this paper were politically active? Why or why not?

William Whipper grew wealthy as the owner of a lumberyard in Pennsylvania. Henry Boyd operated a profitable furniture company in Cincinnati.

African Americans made strides in other areas as well. Henry Blair invented farm equipment. In 1845, Macon Allen became the first African American licensed to practice law in the United States. After graduating from Bowdoin College in Maine, John Russwurm edited *Freedom's Journal*, the first African American newspaper.

In the North, African Americans looked for ways to support one another. They set up schools to educate their youth. In 1852 in Philadelphia, an institute opened to train young African Americans for skilled jobs. Four years later, in Ohio, Wilberforce University was established. It was the first private university owned and run by African Americans.

The African Methodist Episcopal (AME) Church had purchased the land on which Wilberforce was built. Established in Philadelphia as an independent church in 1816 by Richard Allen, Absalom Jones, and others, the AME Church spread to major cities throughout the Northeast and Midwest. In these cities, the church worked to strengthen the African American community.

READING CHECK Identify Supporting Details Why did skilled African Americans have trouble finding jobs in the North?

☑ Lesson Check

Practice Vocabulary

1. Why were **artisans** the first to organize **trade unions** and launch **strikes**?

2. Why were the **Know-Nothings** considered a **nativist** party?

Critical Thinking and Writing

3. **Understand Effects** How did the construction of a large railroad network contribute to urban growth?

4. **Compare and Contrast** What "push" factors caused Irish and Germans to leave their homelands for the United States?

5. **Identify Supporting Details** How did schools and churches help strengthen African American communities?

6. **Writing Workshop: Establish Setting** Write a sentence in your 📓 Active Journal that identifies a setting related to the workers described in this lesson. You will use this setting or another appropriate setting in the essay you will write at the end of the Topic.

King Cotton and Life in the South

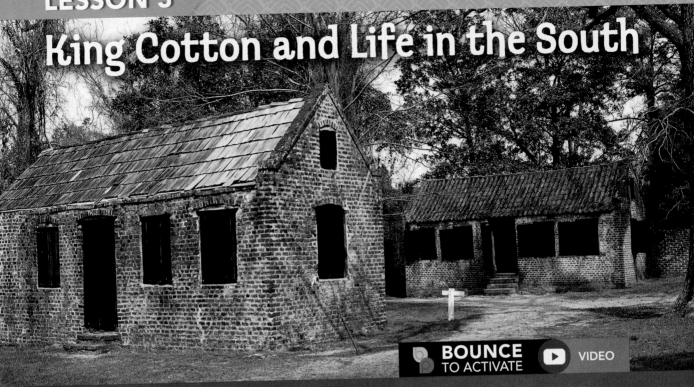

BOUNCE TO ACTIVATE   ▶ VIDEO

GET READY TO READ

START UP
Look at the cabins of enslaved people in the photograph. Describe what life might have been like for enslaved African Americans.

GUIDING QUESTIONS
- How did the invention of the cotton gin affect the Southern economy?
- What was the impact of slavery on the United States?
- What were the lives of enslaved people like?
- How did enslaved African Americans resist their enslavement?

TAKE NOTES
Literacy Skills: Compare and Contrast
Use the graphic organizer in your 📓 Active Journal to take notes as you read the lesson.

PRACTICE VOCABULARY
Use the vocabulary activity in your 📓 Active Journal to practice the vocabulary words.

Vocabulary

boom
cultivate
"cottonocracy"

slave code
extended family

Academic Vocabulary

cash crop
discrimination

During the 1800s, cotton continued to grow in importance in the South. It was so profitable that southerners did not even feel a need to invest in factories. Even though southerners grew other crops, cotton remained the region's leading export. Cotton plantations—and the slave system on which they depended—shaped the way of life in the South.

The South's Cotton Kingdom

The Industrial Revolution greatly increased the demand for southern cotton. Textile mills in the North and in Britain needed more and more cotton to make cloth. At first, southern planters could not meet the demand. They could grow plenty of cotton, because the South's soil and climate were ideal. However, removing the seeds from the cotton by hand was a slow process. Planters needed a better way to clean cotton.

Eli Whitney Invents the Cotton Gin
Eli Whitney, a young teacher from Connecticut, traveled to Georgia in 1793. He planned to be a tutor on a plantation.

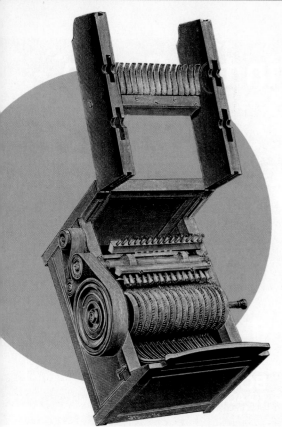

At that time, there were few public schools in the South. Whitney was also a tinkerer. He loved to fix things. When he learned of the planters' problem, he decided to build a machine to clean cotton.

In only ten days, Whitney came up with a model. His cotton engine, or gin, had two rollers with thin wire teeth. When cotton was swept between the rollers, the teeth separated the seeds from the fibers.

This machine led to a dramatic expansion of plantation agriculture across the South. A single worker using a cotton gin could do the work of 50 people cleaning cotton by hand. Planters could now grow cotton at a huge profit. As a result, this new technology brought economic growth.

The Cotton Kingdom and Slavery The cotton gin led to a **boom**, or swift growth, in cotton production. In 1792, planters grew only 6,000 bales of cotton a year. By 1850, they were producing more than 2 million bales.

In the southern states along the Atlantic coast, there was not enough farmland to meet demand. Cotton farmers needed new land to **cultivate**, or prepare for planting.

Analyze Images Workers fed cotton bolls through the gin's teeth and barbed roller to separate out the seeds and straighten the fibers. Using the gin, workers could produce much more cotton in a day. **Predict Consequences** How would this invention affect the demand for slaves?

INTERACTIVE

The Cotton Gin

After the War of 1812, cotton planters began to move west. They took enslaved African Americans with them. The huge demand for cotton, the efficiency offered by cotton gins, and southern planters' reliance on slave labor led to the growth of large plantations, each with many enslaved workers.

By the 1850s, cotton plantations extended in a belt from South Carolina to Texas. This area of the South became known as the Cotton Kingdom. Physical aspects of the environment in this part of the South, including rich soils, warm temperatures, and abundant rainfall, encouraged an economy focused on cotton farming.

Tragically, as the Cotton Kingdom spread, so did slavery. Even though cotton could now be cleaned by machine, it still had to be planted and picked by hand. The result was a cruel cycle in which slave labor brought profits to planters, who then used the profits to buy more land and more enslaved workers.

How Did the North and West Promote Slavery?

Slavery was a southern institution. However, northern and western factories, businesses, and banks indirectly promoted the enslavement of people through their commercial links with the South. Slave labor produced the cotton and other raw materials that fed the textile factories and other industries in the North and West. Slavery enabled those industries to thrive. When families in the North and West bought goods produced by enslaved workers, they too helped support the South's slave-based economy.

✓ READING CHECK **Identify Cause and Effect** How did the invention of the cotton gin lead to an increase in slavery in the South?

Reliance on Plantation Agriculture

Cotton was the South's most profitable **cash crop**. However, the best soils and climate for growing cotton could be found mostly in a belt stretching across inland South Carolina, Georgia, Alabama, Mississippi, Louisiana, and Texas. In other areas of the South, rice, sugar cane, and tobacco were major crops. In addition, southerners raised much of the nation's livestock. Characteristics of the physical environment in different regions of the South influenced what farmers in those regions produced.

Rice was an important crop along the coasts of South Carolina and Georgia. Sugar cane was important in Louisiana and Texas. Growing rice and sugar cane required expensive irrigation and drainage systems and a warm, moist climate, all found mainly along the coasts.

Cane growers also needed costly machinery to grind their harvest. Small-scale farmers could not afford such expensive equipment, however. As a result, rice and sugar farmers relied on the plantation system, just as cotton farmers did.

Tobacco had been an export of the South since 1619, and it continued to be planted in Virginia, North Carolina, Tennessee, and Kentucky. However, in the early 1800s, the large tobacco plantations of colonial days had given way to small tobacco farms. On these farms, a few field hands tended five or six acres of tobacco.

In addition to the major cash crops of cotton, rice, sugar, and tobacco, the South also led the nation in livestock production. Southern livestock owners profited from hogs, oxen, horses, mules, and beef cattle, raised on land unsuitable for crops.

Academic Vocabulary

cash crop • *n.,* a crop sold for money at market

Analyze Images African Americans enslaved on a plantation load rice onto a barge for transport on the Savannah River. **Infer** How long do you think it took to fill a barge with rice?

Livestock farming thrived in the woods of North Carolina and the hills of Georgia, western Virginia, Kentucky, Tennessee, and Arkansas. Kentucky developed a rural economy that included the breeding of horses.

Limited Southern Industry Because the South relied on agriculture, most of the industry in the South remained small and existed only to meet the needs of an agrarian society. This contrasted with the North, with its increasingly urban society and large and diverse industries. Southern factories made agricultural tools such as cotton gins, planters, and plows. They also made goods such as ironware, hoes, and jute or hemp cloth, which was used to make bags for holding bales of cotton. Cheap cotton cloth was made for use in enslaved workers' clothing. Some southerners wanted to encourage the growth of industry in the South. William Gregg, for example, modeled his cotton mill in South Carolina on the mills in Lowell, Massachusetts. Gregg built houses and gardens for his paid workers and schools for their children.

The South also developed a few other successful industries. In Richmond, Virginia, for example, the Tredegar Iron Works turned out railroad equipment, machinery, tools, and cannons. Flour milling was another important southern industry.

Even so, the South lagged behind the North in manufacturing. This difference had several causes. Rich planters invested their money in land and in purchasing enslaved African Americans rather than in factories.

Slavery also reduced the need for southern industry. In the North, most people had enough money to buy factory goods. In the South, however, millions of enslaved African Americans could not buy anything. As a result, the demand for manufactured goods in the South was not as great as it was in the North.

Analyze Data Although figures varied from state to state, all southern states had agricultural economies. **Use Visual Information** Why did the number of slaves in South Carolina increase even though its share of cotton production declined?

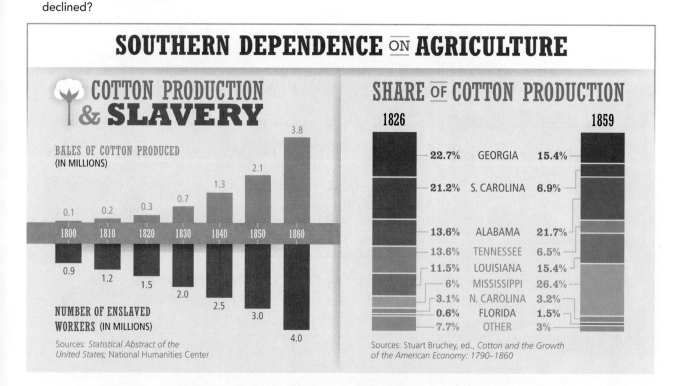

SOUTHERN DEPENDENCE ON AGRICULTURE

COTTON PRODUCTION & SLAVERY

BALES OF COTTON PRODUCED (IN MILLIONS)

1800	1810	1820	1830	1840	1850	1860
0.1	0.2	0.3	0.7	1.3	2.1	3.8

NUMBER OF ENSLAVED WORKERS (IN MILLIONS)

1800	1810	1820	1830	1840	1850	1860
0.9	1.2	1.5	2.0	2.5	3.0	4.0

Sources: *Statistical Abstract of the United States;* National Humanities Center

SHARE OF COTTON PRODUCTION

1826		1859
22.7%	GEORGIA	15.4%
21.2%	S. CAROLINA	6.9%
13.6%	ALABAMA	21.7%
13.6%	TENNESSEE	6.5%
11.5%	LOUISIANA	15.4%
6%	MISSISSIPPI	26.4%
3.1%	N. CAROLINA	3.2%
0.6%	FLORIDA	1.5%
7.7%	OTHER	3%

Sources: Stuart Bruchey, ed., *Cotton and the Growth of the American Economy: 1790–1860*

Southern Cities Although the South was mainly rural, there were some cities. The major ones were New Orleans, Louisiana; Charleston, South Carolina; and Richmond, Virginia. These cities had the same problems as northern cities, including poor housing and poor sanitation.

Fewer than 8 percent of white southerners lived in towns of more than 4,000 people. Many free African Americans lived in towns and cities.

Economically Dependent The South's lack of industry had a number of effects on the region. Because there were few industrial jobs, people in the South had few ways to escape the poverty of life on a small farm, whereas northern farmers could move to cities and take factory jobs. With little industry of its own, the South also came to depend more and more on the North and on Europe. Southern planters often borrowed money from northern banks. They also purchased much of their furniture, farm tools, and machines from northern or European factories.

Many southerners resented this situation. One described a burial to show how the South depended on the North for many goods:

Primary Source

"The grave was dug through solid marble, but the marble headstone came from Vermont. It was in a pine wilderness but the pine coffin came from Cincinnati. An iron mountain overshadowed it but the coffin nails and the screws and the shovel came from Pittsburgh. . . . A hickory grove grew nearby, but the pick and shovel handles came from New York. . . . That country, so rich in underdeveloped resources, furnished nothing for the funeral except the corpse and the hole in the ground."

—Henry Grady, Speech to the Bay Street Club, Boston, 1889

Agriculture in the South, 1860

KEY
- Cotton
- Rice
- Sugar
- Tobacco

GEOGRAPHY SKILLS

This map shows the major crops grown in various regions of the South in 1860.

1. **Region** What advantages did the South have in terms of the physical environment over the North?

2. **Use Visual Information** Which crop was grown in the most limited geographic area?

Quest CONNECTIONS

What does this reliance on other places for manufactured goods tell you about the South's stance on slavery?

✓ **READING CHECK** Draw Conclusions Why was the South dependent on the North and Europe for non-agricultural goods?

INTERACTIVE

Different Ways of
Life in the South

What Were the Characteristics of White Southern Society?

The Old South is often pictured as a land of vast plantations worked by hundreds of enslaved African Americans. Such grand estates did exist in the South. However, most white southerners were not rich planters. In fact, most whites owned no enslaved African Americans at all.

The "Cottonocracy" A planter was someone who owned at least 20 enslaved workers. In 1860, only one white southerner in 30 belonged to a planter family. An even smaller number—less than 1 percent—owned 50 or more enslaved workers. These wealthy families were called the **"cottonocracy"** because they made huge amounts of money from cotton. These rich planters lived mainly in the cotton belt of the lowland South and in coastal areas of South Carolina, Georgia, and Louisiana. Though few in number, their views and way of life dominated the South.

The richest planters built elegant homes and filled them with expensive furniture from Europe. They entertained lavishly. They tried to dress and behave like European nobility.

Because of their wealth and influence, many planters became political leaders. Planters hired white overseers to run day-to-day affairs on their plantations and to manage the work of enslaved people. Sometimes, enslaved African Americans, called drivers, were allowed to oversee their fellow workers.

Analyze Images Some wealthy white southerners lived in elegant homes on plantations, like this plantation home in Mississippi. **Use Visual Information** In what ways does this home resemble the homes of European nobility?

Small Farmers About 75 percent of southern whites lived on small family farms. These "plain folk" owned the land they farmed. They might also own one or two enslaved African Americans. Unlike planters, plain folk worked with their enslaved workers in the fields. Small farmers could be found in most parts of the South, but their numbers were fewer in the cotton belt and in coastal regions of the South, where plantation agriculture dominated.

Among these farm families, helping one another was an important duty. "People who lived miles apart counted themselves as neighbors," wrote a farmer in Mississippi. "And in case of sorrow or sickness, there was no limit to the service neighbors provided."

Poor Whites Lower on the social ladder were poor whites. These whites did not own enslaved African Americans. Many did not own the land they farmed. Instead, they rented it, often paying the owner with part of their crop. Many barely made a living.

Poor whites often lived in the hilly, wooded areas of the upland South, north and west of the cotton belt. They planted crops such as corn, potatoes, and other vegetables. They also herded cattle and pigs. Poor whites had hard lives, but they enjoyed rights that were denied to all black people, enslaved or free.

Analyze Images The lives of the white and the African American children in this image were vastly different. **Identify Supporting Details** Identify details in the image that support this statement.

Comparing Northern and Southern Whites Like northern whites, most southern whites were farmers. Most white farmers in both regions were small farmers. However, there were important differences in the white populations of the two regions. In the South, the wealthiest whites were planters who made their money from the work of enslaved African Americans. In the North, the wealthiest whites were capitalists who made their money from investing in industry. There were many white industrial workers and middle class people living in cities in the North. Relatively few southerners of any class lived in cities.

☑ READING CHECK **Summarize** Tell how the lives of white southerners differed.

What Was Life Like for African Americans in the South?

Both free and enslaved African Americans lived in the South. Their legal and political conditions were different. Although free under the law and with certain legal rights, free African Americans faced harsh **discrimination**. Enslaved African Americans had no rights at all.

Free African Americans Most free African Americans were descendants of enslaved people who were freed during and after the American Revolution. Others had bought their freedom. In 1860, more than 200,000 free blacks lived in the South. Most lived in Maryland and Delaware, where slavery was in decline. Others lived in cities such as New Orleans, Richmond, and Charleston.

Many free African Americans reached an impressive level of success. Working as farmers, laborers, and artisans, such as blacksmiths, carpenters, and cobblers, they contributed to and influenced southern life. Some ran their own businesses, such as inns and barbershops.

Academic Vocabulary
discrimination • *n.*, a policy or practice that denies equal rights to certain groups of people

A few became large plantation owners, growing cotton and owning enslaved workers.

White slave owners did not like free African Americans living in the South. They feared that free African Americans set a dangerous example, encouraging enslaved African Americans to rebel. Also, slave owners justified slavery by claiming that African Americans could not take care of themselves. Free African Americans proved this idea wrong.

To discourage free African Americans, southern states passed laws that limited their freedom and economic opportunities. Free African Americans were not allowed to vote or travel. In some southern states, they had to move out of the state or risk the chance of being kidnapped and enslaved.

Despite these limits, free African Americans were able to make a life for themselves and make valuable contributions to southern life. For example, Norbert Rillieux (RIHL yoo) invented a machine that revolutionized the way sugar was refined. Another inventor, Henry Blair, patented a seed planter.

Enslaved African Americans By 1860, enslaved African Americans made up one third of the South's population. Most worked as field hands on cotton plantations. Both men and women cleared new land and planted and harvested crops. Children helped by pulling weeds, collecting wood, and carrying water to the field hands. By the time they were teenagers, they worked between 12 and 14 hours a day. Daily labor in the fields bound enslaved workers into a community of people who tried to help and protect one another.

Analyze Images In 1849, Henry Brown thought of an ingenious way to escape slavery: He had himself mailed from Virginia to Philadelphia. **Infer** What do you think happened to the people in Virginia who helped Brown escape?

On large plantations, some enslaved African Americans had better positions. They might work as household servants or as skilled artisans, such as carpenters and blacksmiths. Such jobs might entitle workers to better food or clothing than field hands.

A few enslaved people worked in cities. Their earnings, however, belonged to their owners. Unlike free African Americans, enslaved African Americans could not easily start their own businesses.

Another major difference between the social circumstances of free and enslaved African Americans was that enslaved African American families could be broken up by their owners, with family members sold separately and to different owners. While they faced discrimination, free African American families were not forced to separate.

Analyze Images A child, a group of women and a man, probably enslaved African Americans, sit on the steps of the Florida Club in St. Augustine, Florida, in the mid-1800s. **Draw Conclusions** What role did the white woman standing behind them play in their lives?

☑ READING CHECK **Compare and Contrast** How was life in the South similar and different for free and enslaved African Americans?

Slavery in the South

The life of enslaved African Americans was determined by strict laws and the practices of individual slave owners. Conditions varied from plantation to plantation. Some owners made sure their enslaved workers had clean cabins, decent food, and warm clothes. Other planters spent as little as possible on their enslaved workers.

Slave Codes Southern states passed laws known as **slave codes** to keep enslaved African Americans from either running away or rebelling. Under the codes, enslaved African Americans were forbidden to gather in groups of more than three.

They could not leave their owner's land without a written pass from their owner. They were not allowed to own guns.

Slave codes also made it a crime for enslaved African Americans to learn how to read and write. Owners hoped that this law would make it hard for African Americans to escape slavery. They reasoned that uneducated enslaved African Americans who escaped their owners would not be able to use maps or read train schedules. They would not be able to find their way north.

Some laws were meant to protect enslaved African Americans, but only from the worst forms of abuse. However, enslaved African Americans did not have the right to testify in court. As a result, they were not able to bring charges against owners who abused them.

▶ INTERACTIVE

Lives of Free and Enslaved African Americans

Enslaved African Americans had only one real protection against mistreatment. Owners looked on their enslaved workers as valuable property. Most slave owners wanted to keep this human property healthy and productive. However, they would not hesitate to punish enslaved African Americans to keep them in line.

Frances Kemble, a British actress married to a southern slave owner, kept a journal about plantation life. She wrote about who had the right to whip an enslaved person:

Primary Source

"The common drivers are limited in their powers of chastisement, not being allowed to administer more than a certain number of lashes to their fellow slaves. Head man Frank, as he is called, has alone the privilege of exceeding this limit; and the overseer's latitude of infliction is only curtailed by the necessity of avoiding injury to life or limb. The master's irresponsible power has no such bound."

—Frances Anne Kemble, *Journal of a Residence on a Georgian Plantation in 1838–1839*

Hard Work Even the kindest owners insisted that their enslaved workers work long, hard days. Enslaved African Americans worked from "can see to can't see," or from dawn to dusk, up to 16 hours a day.

Analyze Images Music served as a source of solace and hope for enslaved African Americans. The spiritual is closely associated with the culture of slavery. **Infer** Why did people find hope in music?

Family Life It was hard for enslaved African Americans to keep their families together. Southern laws did not recognize slave marriages or slave families. As a result, owners could sell a husband and wife to different buyers. Children were often taken from their parents and sold.

On large plantations, many enslaved families did manage to stay together. For those African Americans, the family was a source of strength, pride, and love. Grandparents, parents, children, aunts, uncles, and cousins formed a close-knit group. This idea of an **extended family** had its roots in Africa.

Enslaved African Americans preserved other traditions as well. Parents taught their children traditional African stories and songs. They used folk tales to pass on African history and moral beliefs.

Religion Offers Hope By the 1800s, many enslaved African Americans were devout Christians. Planters often allowed white ministers to preach to their slaves. African Americans also had their own preachers and beliefs.

Religion helped African Americans cope with the harshness of slave life. Bible stories about how the ancient Israelites had escaped from slavery to freedom inspired a new type of religious song called a spiritual. Yet, enslaved African Americans had to be cautious even in their religious practice. While they sang of freedom in spirituals, the words of the spirituals suggested that this freedom would come after death, so as not to alarm slave owners.

✓ READING CHECK **Identify Supporting Details** Why was it difficult for enslaved African Americans to keep their families together?

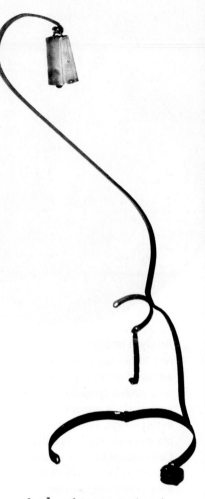

Analyze Images Enslaved people who tried to escape but were recaptured were forced to wear devices like this, which locked around their necks. **Use Visual Information** How would this device have affected a person wearing it?

How Did Enslaved African Americans Resist Their Enslavement?

Enslaved African Americans struck back against the system that denied them both freedom and wages. Some slowed the pace of their work, broke tools, destroyed crops, or pretended they were ill. Some passively resisted by learning to read and write. Others took much bolder action.

Many enslaved African Americans tried to escape to the North. Because the journey was long and dangerous, very few made it to freedom. Every county had slave patrols and sheriffs ready to question an unknown black person.

Because southern laws offered no means to resist slavery, a few African Americans turned to violence. Gabriel Prosser, an enslaved African American, organized an uprising in Richmond, Virginia, but it failed. Denmark Vesey, a free African American, planned a revolt in 1822. Vesey was betrayed before the revolt began. Both Prosser and Vesey were executed, along with dozens of their followers.

Other armed slave revolts took a toll on both blacks and whites. The Stono Rebellion in South Carolina in 1739 resulted in the deaths of some 30 enslaved African American rebels and a similar number of white colonists.

In 1831, an African American named Nat Turner led a major revolt. An enslaved worker on a plantation in Southampton County, Virginia, Turner believed his mission was to take revenge on plantation owners.

Turner led his followers through Virginia, killing more than 57 whites. For nearly two months terrified whites hunted the countryside looking for Turner. They killed many innocent African Americans before catching and hanging him.

Nat Turner's revolt increased southern fears of an uprising of enslaved African Americans. Whites now became even more suspicious of the African Americans, free or enslaved. Southern states reacted to the revolt by further limiting African Americans' rights. At first, the Virginia legislature seriously debated ending slavery in the state, but decided against it. Virginia then, like other southern states, increased its restrictions on African Americans.

Overall, organized slave revolts were rare. Because southern whites were well armed and kept careful track of African Americans, an uprising by African Americans had almost no chance of success.

Analyze Images In 1831, Nat Turner led other enslaved African Americans on a violent campaign against slave owners. In this image, Turner is planning an attack. **Predict Consequences** How would Turner's rebellion affect the lives of enslaved African Americans who did not rebel?

☑ READING CHECK **Draw Conclusions** What do the actions of leaders of slave revolts reveal about the conditions under which enslaved Africans were forced to live?

☑ Lesson Check

Practice Vocabulary

1. How did the **boom** in cotton production lead to the rise of the **"cottonocracy"**?

2. How did the physical characteristics of the environment affect a planter's decision about what crops to **cultivate**?

Critical Thinking and Writing

3. **Recognize Multiple Causes** What are three reasons that cotton became "king" in the South?

4. **Understand Effects** Why were there few factories in the South?

5. **Explain an Argument** Did their resistance to enslavement generally help or hurt enslaved African Americans? Explain.

6. **Writing Workshop: Organize Sequence of Events** Plan the events that you will describe in your narrative essay. In your 📓 Active Journal, write out those events in the order in which they will happen.

Abolitionism

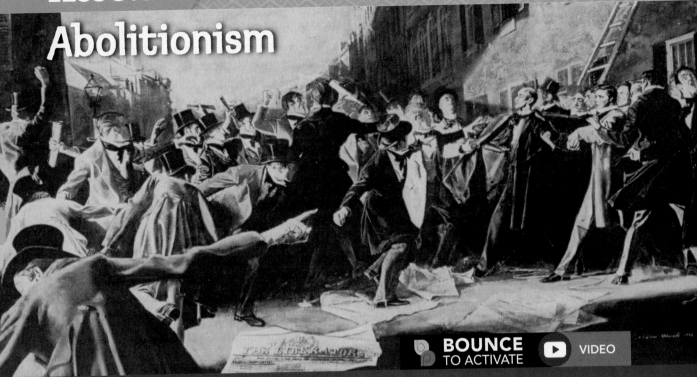

BOUNCE TO ACTIVATE ▶ VIDEO

GET READY TO READ

START UP

Look at the image of the abolitionist being attacked. Why was abolition such a volatile issue? Write a few sentences to explain your answer.

GUIDING QUESTIONS

- How did people work to end slavery?
- What opposition did those people face?
- How did the Underground Railroad function?

TAKE NOTES

Literacy Skills Summarize

Use the graphic organizer in your 📖 Active Journal to take notes as you read the lesson.

PRACTICE VOCABULARY

Use the vocabulary activity in your 📖 Active Journal to practice the vocabulary words.

Vocabulary

American Colonization Society

abolitionist

The Liberator

Underground Railroad

civil disobedience

Academic Vocabulary

public opinion

interest group

In the Declaration of Independence, Thomas Jefferson had written that "all men are created equal." Yet many Americans, including Jefferson himself, did not believe that this statement applied to enslaved African Americans. A growing number of reformers began to think differently.

What Form Did Early Opposition to Slavery Take?

Jefferson, owner of a slave plantation, may not have believed in the equality of whites and African Americans, but he did believe slavery should be ended. He wrote as much in his draft of the Declaration of Independence. The passage, which was later removed, criticized the existence of "a market where Men should be bought & sold."

In 1777, the constitution of the new state of Vermont banned slavery. Three years later, the Massachusetts constitution did the same, with the words "All men are born free and equal." In the years that followed, other northern states enacted policies aimed at eventually ending slavery.

Analyze Images This image of an enslaved African in chains was originally adopted as the seal of the Society for the Abolition of Slavery in England in the 1780s. **Draw Conclusions** Why do you think it took so long for slavery to become a major issue in the United States?

Religious beliefs led some Americans to oppose slavery. Since colonial times, Quakers had taught that it was a sin for one human being to own another. All people, they said, were equal in the sight of God. Benjamin Franklin, who owned two slaves, had a change of heart about slavery. He joined an early abolitionist society in Pennsylvania that was founded by Quakers. Later, during the Second Great Awakening, ministers such as Charles Grandison Finney called on Christians to join a massive effort to stamp out slavery.

In the North, with a population in 1800 of 50,000 enslaved African Americans, slavery was not very important to the economy. As growing numbers of northerners opposed it, slavery gradually came to an end in the North. By 1804, all the states from Pennsylvania through New England had ended slavery or promised to free their enslaved African Americans over time. The Northwest Ordinance of 1787 had banned slavery in the Northwest Territory, which became the Midwestern states north of the Ohio River and east of the Mississippi River. In 1807, Congress voted to end the slave trade. No more Africans could be enslaved and brought into the country.

These efforts to end slavery had little effect in the South, with its nearly one million slaves.

In fact, the South was growing ever more dependent on slavery. As you have learned, plantation agriculture expanded rapidly in the South in the early 1800s. As a result, there was little support in the South for ending slavery.

The Colonization Movement The **American Colonization Society** proposed to end slavery by setting up an independent colony in Africa for Africans and African Americans who had gained freedom from slavery. In 1822, President Monroe helped the society set up a colony in western Africa. This colony gained control over a territory that later became the nation of Liberia.

Some African Americans favored colonization, believing that they would never have equal rights in the United States. Most, however, opposed the movement. Nearly all, enslaved or free, had been born in the United States. They wanted to stay in their homeland. In the end, only a few thousand African Americans settled in Liberia.

✔ READING CHECK **Summarize** What early efforts attempted to end slavery?

How Did Abolitionism Gain Momentum?

A growing number of reformers, known as **abolitionists**, wanted to end slavery completely in the United States. Some abolitionists favored

INTERACTIVE

Opposing Views on Slavery

a gradual end to slavery. They expected slavery to die out if it was kept out of the western territories. Other abolitionists demanded that slavery end everywhere, at once. Almost all abolitionists were northerners. The abolitionist movement gradually gained strength from the 1820s through the 1840s. It grew more quickly during the 1850s.

A forceful voice for ending slavery was John Quincy Adams. A diplomat for many years, Adams served as President from 1824 to 1828. In the 1830s, he won election to the House of Representatives. There he proposed a constitutional amendment that would eventually end slavery by declaring all newborn children free. A few years earlier, however, southern members of Congress had agreed to abide by a "gag rule." They would not discuss anything having to do with slavery. As a result, Adams's proposal was ignored.

African American Abolitionists Free African Americans played a key role in the abolitionist movement by actively challenging the existence of slavery. Some tried to end slavery through lawsuits and petitions. In the 1820s, Samuel Cornish and John Russwurm set up an abolitionist newspaper, *Freedom's Journal*. They hoped to turn **public opinion** against slavery by printing stories about the brutal treatment of enslaved African Americans.

Other African American abolitionists called for stronger measures. In *An Appeal to the Colored Citizens of the World*, David Walker encouraged enslaved African Americans to free themselves by any means necessary:

Primary Source

"Now, I ask you, had you not rather be killed than to be a slave to a tyrant, who takes the life of your mother, wife, and dear little children? Look upon your mother, wife, and children, and answer God Almighty; and believe this, that it is no more harm for you to kill a man, who is trying to kill you, than it is for you to take a drink of water when thirsty."

—David Walker, *Walker's Appeal*, 1829

Quest CONNECTIONS

Who opposed slavery in the early years of the United States?

Academic Vocabulary
public opinion • *n.,* the views held by people, in general

Interpret Images William Lloyd Garrison's paper, *The Liberator*, was a leading abolitionist publication. **Use Visual Information** The illustration shows people being sold under a sign, "Horse-Market." What effect would that have had on someone who was seeing the paper for the first time?

THE LIBERATOR.

VOL. I.] WILLIAM LLOYD GARRISON AND ISAAC KNAPP, PUBLISHERS. [NO. 2?

BOSTON, MASSACHUSETTS.] OUR COUNTRY IS THE WORLD—OUR COUNTRYMEN ARE MANKIND. [SATURDAY, MAY 28, 1831.

Walker's friend Maria Stewart also spoke out against slavery. Stewart was the first American woman to make public political speeches.

Frederick Douglass The best-known African American abolitionist was Frederick Douglass. Douglass was born into slavery in Maryland. As a child, he defied the slave codes by learning to read.

Douglass escaped in 1838 and made his way to New England. One day at an antislavery meeting, he felt a powerful urge to speak. Rising to his feet, he talked about the sorrows of slavery and the meaning of freedom. The audience was moved to tears. Soon, Douglass was lecturing across the United States and Britain. In 1847, he began publishing an antislavery newspaper, which he called the *North Star*.

William Lloyd Garrison Speaks Out The most outspoken white abolitionist was a fiery young man named William Lloyd Garrison. To Garrison, slavery was an evil to be ended immediately. In 1831, Garrison launched **The Liberator**, the most influential antislavery newspaper. On the first page of the first issue, Garrison revealed his commitment:

Primary Source

"I will be as harsh as truth, and as uncompromising as justice. . . . I am in earnest. . . . I will not excuse—I will not retreat a single inch—and I WILL BE HEARD."

—William Lloyd Garrison, *The Liberator*, January 1831

A year later, Garrison helped to found the New England Anti-Slavery Society. Members included Theodore Weld, a young minister and follower of Charles Grandison Finney, who had preached against slavery. Weld brought the energy of a religious revival to antislavery meetings.

The Grimké Sisters Contribute to Reform Angelina and Sarah Grimké were the daughters of a South Carolina slaveholder. Hating slavery, they moved to Philadelphia to work for abolition. Their lectures drew large crowds.

Analyze Images Frederick Douglass escaped slavery and became a leading voice in the abolitionist movement. **Infer** Why could Douglass appeal to listeners in a unique way?

Some people, including other abolitionists, objected to women speaking out in public. "Whatsoever it is morally right for a man to do," replied Sarah Grimké, "it is morally right for a woman to do." As you will see, this belief helped spark a movement for women's rights.

INTERACTIVE

The Underground Railroad

Civil Disobedience and the Underground Railroad Some abolitionists formed the **Underground Railroad**. It was not a real railroad, but a network of abolitionists who secretly helped enslaved African Americans escape to freedom in the North or Canada.

"Conductors" guided runaways to "stations" where they could spend the night. Some stations were homes of abolitionists. Others were churches or even caves. Conductors sometimes hid runaways under loads of hay in wagons with false bottoms. It was illegal to help enslaved African Americans escape, but these conductors felt strongly about disobeying laws they considered unjust. Such acts of **civil disobedience** led thousands of enslaved people to freedom.

One daring conductor, Harriet Tubman, had escaped slavery herself. She felt deeply committed to freeing others from slavery. Risking her freedom and her life, Tubman returned to the South 19 times. She led more than 300 enslaved African Americans, including her parents, to freedom. Admirers called her the "Black Moses," after the biblical leader who led the Israelites out of slavery in Egypt. Slave owners offered a $40,000 reward for her capture.

Another escaped slave, Mary Pleasant, became a conductor on the Underground Railroad in the 1840s. In 1851, she feared being caught as a runaway and returned to slavery. She fled to California, a new state with a constitution that prohibited slavery. Pleasant became a successful businesswoman in San Francisco, where she worked to help other escaped slaves.

GEOGRAPHY SKILLS

The Underground Railroad provided routes African Americans fleeing slavery could take to reach the North or Canada.

1. **Movement** From which southern states did fugitives and their conductors travel by ship?

2. **Use Visual Information** After getting to Rochester, New York, what last physical obstacle did a fugitive face?

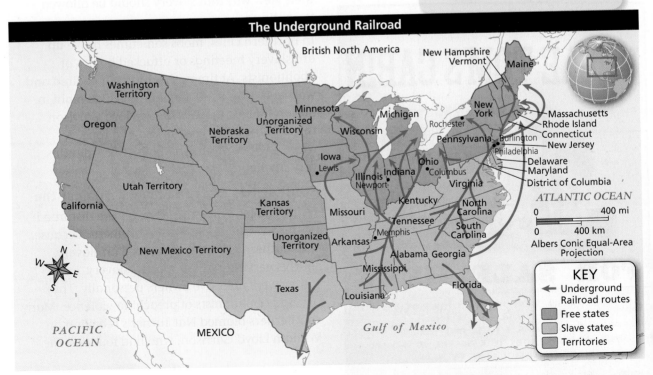

The Underground Railroad

KEY
⬅ Underground Railroad routes
Free states
Slave states
Territories

A Novel Promotes Abolitionism In 1852, a writer named Harriet Beecher Stowe published *Uncle Tom's Cabin*, a novel describing the suffering of enslaved African Americans.

The novel's characters were often unrealistic and stereotyped, or based on inaccurate assumptions and beliefs about supposed characteristics of African Americans. However, the novel sold widely and convinced many northerners during the 1850s that slavery was evil and should be outlawed.

As abolitionism spread during the 1850s, it had a powerful impact on the United States. It increased tensions between the North and the South and helped set the stage for the Civil War.

✓ READING CHECK **Use Evidence** Did the press play an important role in the abolition movement? Explain.

Who Opposed the Abolitionists?

By the mid-1800s, slavery existed only in the South. Still, abolitionists like Douglass and Garrison made enemies in the North as well.

Northerners Against Abolition As you have learned, abolitionists were one **interest group** in the controversy over slavery. Their view was that slavery had to end.

Academic Vocabulary

interest group • *n.*, people who have a certain concern or belief in common

However, northern mill owners, bankers, and merchants depended on cotton from the South. Some saw attacks on slavery as a threat to their livelihood. Some northern workers also opposed abolition. They feared that African Americans might come north and take their jobs by working for low pay.

These interest groups in the North took the view that slavery should be left up to individual states. Because few southerners opposed slavery, their view was that slavery should be allowed to continue.

▼ This advertisement promotes the abolitionist novel *Uncle Tom's Cabin*.

In northern cities, mobs sometimes broke up antislavery meetings or attacked homes of abolitionists. At times, the attacks backfired and won support for the abolitionists. One night, a Boston mob dragged William Lloyd Garrison through the streets at the end of a rope. A witness wrote, "I am an abolitionist from this very moment."

Southerners Defend Slavery Against the North Most white southerners were disturbed by the growing abolitionist movement. Because the southern economy depended on slavery, southerners strongly supported slavery, even if they were not slave owners personally. They accused abolitionists of preaching violence. Many southerners blamed Nat Turner's rebellion on William Lloyd Garrison, who had founded *The*

135,000 SETS, 270,000 VOLUMES SOLD.

UNCLE TOM'S CABIN

FOR SALE HERE.

AN EDITION FOR THE MILLION, COMPLETE IN 1 Vol. PRICE 37 1-2 CENTS.
"   "   IN GERMAN, IN 1 Vol. PRICE 50 CENTS.
"   "   IN 2 Vols. CLOTH, 6 PLATES, PRICE $1.50.
SUPERB ILLUSTRATED EDITION, IN 1 Vol. WITH 153 ENGRAVINGS,
PRICES FROM $2.50 TO $5.00.

The Greatest Book of the Age.

Analyze Images This engraving shows the burning of the print shop of Elijah P. Lovejoy, an abolitionist who published a newspaper opposed to slavery in Illinois. Anti-abolition rioters murdered Lovejoy during their attack on his shop. **Identify Implied Main Ideas** Why did some northerners resist abolition?

Liberator only a few months earlier. David Walker's call for a slave revolt seemed to confirm the worst fears of southerners.

Slave owners responded to the abolitionist effort by defending slavery even more. If enslaved African Americans were treated well, wrote one slave owner, they would "love their master and serve him . . . faithfully." Others argued that enslaved African Americans were better off than northern workers who labored long hours in dusty, airless factories.

Many southerners believed northern support for the antislavery movement was stronger than it really was. They began to fear that northerners wanted to destroy their way of life.

☑ READING CHECK **Summarize** Provide a summary of the reasons many northerners opposed abolition.

☑ Lesson Check

Practice Vocabulary

1. Do you think most **abolitionists** supported the **American Colonization Society**? Why or why not?

2. In what way was taking part in the **Underground Railroad** an act of **civil disobedience**?

Critical Thinking and Writing

3. **Use Evidence** Why was the movement to abolish slavery successful in the North but strongly opposed in the South?

4. **Infer** Why did William Lloyd Garrison, a white man, devote his professional life to the abolitionist movement?

5. **Draw Conclusions** What can you tell about Harriet Tubman from her actions?

6. **Writing Workshop: Use Narrative Techniques** How can you best tell your story to the reader? One way is to use the first person point of view—"I lived . . ." or "I saw . . ." In your 📓 Active Journal, identify your point of view, what tense you will use (present or past), and whether you will include dialogue.

Update an Interpretation

Follow these steps to learn ways to update interpretations of history, as new information is uncovered.

● INTERACTIVE

Draw Inferences

1 **Identify the interpretation that may need to change.** People in the South had long heard tales of runaway slaves living together in the Great Dismal Swamp, a wetland region in southeastern Virginia and northeastern North Carolina. But no evidence existed that the runaways had actually formed a community. Historians considered it a myth. According to the primary source, what was the existing interpretation of history regarding runaway slaves in the Great Dismal Swamp?

2 **Study new information about the subject.** Archaeologist Dan Sayers, a professor at American University, has found physical evidence of a community of runaways he thinks successfully lived in the swamp for 10 generations. Read the story below to learn what he discovered. What was Dan Sayers's key finding, and why was it important?

3 **Revise the interpretation, if needed, to reflect the new information.** As Dan Sayers once said, "Historical archaeology does require interpretation." Based on his discoveries in the Great Dismal Swamp, historians have revised their views. Most no longer question the ability of a community of escaped African Americans to adapt to an extreme environment in order to stay free. What part of the story about Dan Sayers confirms that the earlier interpretation of history has been updated?

Primary Source

[In the Great Dismal Swamp] Black men and women—escaped slaves— once scratched out lives, maybe even raised families, in what was once a 2,000-square-mile swamp, . . . The slaves established what historians call "Maroon Communities," . . .

Dan Sayers . . . has no doubts that escaped slaves lived in the swamp. . . . He wonders if researchers have shied away from searching for the Dismal's Maroons because they believe such a settlement couldn't exist in an era where the government and slave owners hunted down slaves who escaped. . . .

Sayers and a few volunteers surveyed likely settlement spots that took advantage of higher, drier ground. . . . Then, every 16 or so feet, he dug a careful hole no more than a foot wide and about 25 inches deep. . . . One of the very first pieces [he found], is the size of a quarter. . . . ceramic . . . Could it be that Maroons had [connected] with disenfranchised Native Americans and traded, or learned pottery-making skills? He hopes the context of this tiny piece will build and widen as he excavates more of the site.

—Kimberly Lenz, SunHerald.com, February 18, 2004

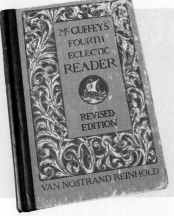

McGuffey Readers

The *McGuffey Readers* were widely used in American schools from the mid-1800s to the mid-1900s. They were filled with stories and poems that promoted religious values, proper behavior, and patriotism in children. Their moral and cultural influence helped shape the national character.

◀ The textbooks known as *McGuffey Readers* first appeared in 1836.

TRY, TRY AGAIN. 1. 'T is ① a lesson you should heed, Try, try again; If at first you don't succeed, Try, try again; ② Then your courage should appear, For, if you will persevere, ③ You will conquer, never fear; Try, try again. 2. Once or twice though you should fail, Try, try again; If you would at last prevail, ④ Try, try again; If we strive, 'tis no disgrace Though we do not win the race; What should you do in the case? Try, try again. 3. If you find your task is hard, Try, try again; Time will bring you your reward, ⑤ Try, try again. All that other folks can do, Why, with patience, should not you? Only keep this rule in view: Try, try again.

—William Holmes McGuffey, editor, *McGuffey's Fourth Eclectic Reader*

WORK. 1. Work, work, my boy, be not afraid; Look labor boldly in the face; Take up the hammer or the spade, And blush not for your humble place. 2. There's glory in the shuttle's song; There's triumph in the anvil's stroke; There's merit in the brave and strong Who dig the mine or fell the oak. 3. The wind disturbs the sleeping lake, And bids it ripple pure and fresh; It moves the green boughs till they make Grand music in their leafy mesh. 4. And so the active breath of life Should stir our dull and sluggard wills; For are we not created rife With health, that stagnant torpor kills? 5. I doubt if he who lolls his head Where idleness and plenty meet, Enjoys his pillow or his bread As those who earn the meals they eat. 6. And man is never half so blest As when the busy day is spent So as to make his evening rest A holiday of glad content.

—William Holmes McGuffey, editor, *McGuffey's Fifth Eclectic Reader*

Analyzing Primary Sources

Cite evidence from the introduction and the primary source to support your answers.

1. **Support Ideas with Examples** What "national character" traits do you think the *McGuffey Readers* helped shape?

2. **Analyze Style and Rhetoric** What effect do you think the repetition in these poems had on young readers?

Reading and Vocabulary Support

① A question in the *Reader* asks students, "What does the mark before 'T is' mean?" What does that mark stand for?

② The saying "If at first you don't succeed, try, try again" is still popular today. What does that say about the continuity of American culture?

③ The *Reader* defines perseverance as "continuance in anything once begun."

④ The *Reader* defines prevail as "overcome."

⑤ According to the *Reader*, your reward is "anything given in return for good or bad conduct."

Reform and Women's Rights

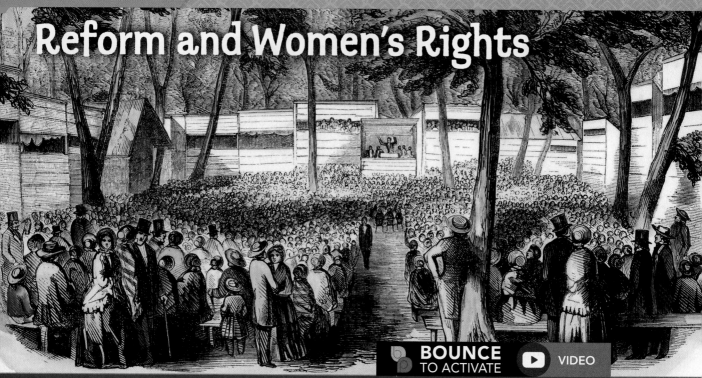

BOUNCE TO ACTIVATE ▶ VIDEO

GET READY TO READ

START UP
Look at the image. What could all those people be listening to? Write a list of ideas.

GUIDING QUESTIONS
- How did political and religious trends spark reform movements?
- How did family life change during this time?
- What effect did the women's rights movement have on opportunities for women?

TAKE NOTES
Literacy Skills: Draw Conclusions
Use the graphic organizer in your 📓 Active Journal to take notes as you read the lesson.

PRACTICE VOCABULARY
Use the vocabulary activity in your 📓 Active Journal to practice the vocabulary words.

Vocabulary

social reform
Second Great
  Awakening
debtor
temperance
  movement

Seneca Falls
  Convention
women's rights
  movement

**Academic
Vocabulary**

salvation
conservation

The period between 1815 and 1860 in the United States is sometimes called the Era of Reform because there were so many movements for social reform during this period. Reformers fought to end slavery, increase access to education, improve conditions in prisons, expand women's rights, and more.

The Era of Reform
Social reform is an organized attempt to improve what is unjust or imperfect in society. The impulse toward social reform had political, social, and religious causes.

Political Ideals Lead to Reform As you have read, during the Jacksonian era, politics was becoming more democratic. More people could vote and take part in government than ever before.

Still, some critics said American society was not living up to its ideals. They pointed to the promise of liberty and equality expressed in the Declaration of Independence. A society based on these ideals, they argued, would not allow slavery. Others asked why women had fewer rights than men. By changing such injustices, reformers hoped to move the nation closer to its political ideals.

Social Conditions Call for Reform As you have learned, the Industrial Revolution was changing the American economy and working conditions, especially in the North, and cities were growing rapidly. Crowded cities created new challenges for social well-being. At the same time, there was a growing need for an educated workforce. As American society changed, it required new institutions to meet its changing needs.

The Second Great Awakening and Its Causes During the colonial era, many American Protestant Christians believed in predestination. According to this idea, God decided in advance which people would attain **salvation** after death. This belief led many people to worry that they could do nothing to be saved.

Academic Vocabulary

salvation • *n.*, deliverance from sin

During the 1700s, Protestant thinkers in England and the colonies began to argue that salvation depended on a person's actions in this life. Its leaders stressed free will rather than predestination. They taught that individuals could choose to save their souls by their own actions. In the early 1800s, a dynamic religious movement known as the **Second Great Awakening** swept the nation. Arguments by religious thinkers were the main cause of this movement. Another cause was the democratic spirit of the Jacksonian era, which encouraged people to think independently and not blindly obey established religious authorities.

To stir religious feelings, preachers held revivals, huge outdoor meetings. Revivals might last for days and attract thousands of people. A witness recalled the excitement of a revival at Cane Ridge, Kentucky:

Analyze Charts The reform movement was an important part of the 1800s. **Use Visual Information** How did the reform movement reflect American culture at the time?

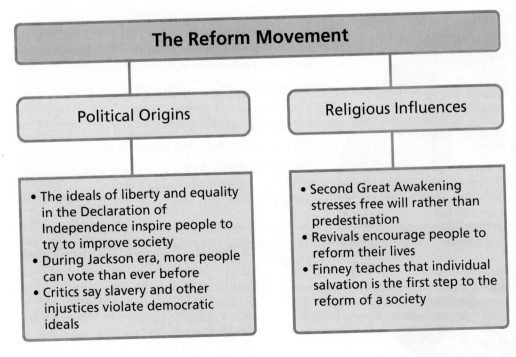

The Reform Movement

Political Origins

- The ideals of liberty and equality in the Declaration of Independence inspire people to try to improve society
- During Jackson era, more people can vote than ever before
- Critics say slavery and other injustices violate democratic ideals

Religious Influences

- Second Great Awakening stresses free will rather than predestination
- Revivals encourage people to reform their lives
- Finney teaches that individual salvation is the first step to the reform of a society

Primary Source

"The vast sea of human beings seemed to be agitated as if by storm. I counted seven ministers all preaching at once. . . . Some of the people were singing, others praying, some crying for mercy."

—James B. Finley, *Autobiography*

One leader of the Second Great Awakening was a minister named Charles Grandison Finney. A powerful speaker, Finney taught that individual salvation was the first step toward "the complete reformation of the whole world."

Such teachings had effects that changed the country, inspiring a number of new social reform movements. These ranged from equal education for women and African Americans to the abolitionist movement. Inspired by religion, these social reformers began a lasting tradition in American culture of working to improve society.

☑ **READING CHECK** **Identify Implied Main Ideas** What was the central premise on which the Second Great Awakening rested?

Social Reform Movements

The emphasis that the Second Great Awakening placed on improving society inspired many Americans. These Americans launched a number of reform movements, with far-reaching effects on prisons, care of the disabled, education, and attitudes toward slavery. Women often played a leading role in these reform movements.

One of the most vigorous social reformers was Dorothea Dix, a Boston schoolteacher whose strong religious beliefs spurred her to care for those less fortunate. She turned her attention to what one minister called the "outsiders" in society: criminals and the mentally ill.

Reforming Care of the Disabled In 1841, Dix visited a jail for women near Boston. She was outraged to discover that some of the prisoners were not criminals, but mentally ill.

Dix demanded to know why these women were locked in small, dark, unheated cells. The jailer replied that "lunatics" did not feel the cold.

During the next 18 months, Dix visited every jail, poorhouse, and hospital in Massachusetts. Her shocking reports helped persuade state legislators to fund a new mental hospital:

▼ Dorothea Dix, a former schoolteacher, became an advocate for social reform.

Primary Source

"I proceed, gentlemen, briefly to call your attention to the present state of Insane Persons confined . . . in cages, closets, cellars, stalls, pens! Chained, naked, beaten with rods, and lashed into obedience."

—Dorothea Dix, "Memorial to the State Legislators of Massachusetts"

Dix went on to inspect jails as far away as Louisiana and Illinois. Her reports persuaded most legislatures to treat the mentally ill as patients, not criminals.

The Impact of Prison Reform Dix also joined a growing movement to improve conditions in prisons. Men, women, and children were often crammed together in cold, damp rooms. When food supplies were low, prisoners went hungry—unless they had money to buy meals from jailers.

Five out of six people in northern jails were **debtors**, or people who could not pay money they owed. While behind bars, debtors had no way to earn money to pay back their debts. As a result, many debtors remained in prison for years.

Dix and others called for changes in the prison system. As a result, some states built prisons with only one or two inmates to a cell. Cruel punishments were banned, and people convicted of minor crimes received shorter sentences. Slowly, states stopped treating debtors as criminals.

The Impact of the Temperance Movement Alcohol abuse was widespread in the early 1800s. At political rallies, weddings, and funerals, men, women, and sometimes even children drank heavily. Men could buy whiskey in candy stores or barbershops.

The **temperance movement**, a campaign against alcohol abuse, took shape in the late 1820s. Women often took a leading role in the battle. They knew that "demon rum" could lead to the physical abuse of wives and children and the breakup of families.

As a teenager in Washington, D.C., Annie Bidwell took up the temperance cause. She continued to work for laws banning alcohol after she married and moved to California. Bidwell also actively promoted the causes of women's suffrage and **conservation**.

Some temperance groups urged people to drink less. Others sought to end drinking altogether. They won a major victory in 1851, when Maine banned the sale of alcohol.

Analyze Images Criminals, debtors, and the mentally ill were housed in terrible conditions. **Infer** Why do you think people were treated this way?

Academic Vocabulary
conservation • *n.*, the protection of natural resources

Analyze Images Students in a one-room schoolhouse recite for their teacher. **Compare and Contrast** How was a school of the mid-1800s different from today's schools? How was it similar?

Eight other states passed "Maine laws." Most were later repealed, but the temperance crusade would gain new strength in the late 1800s.

☑ **READING CHECK** **Summarize** Provide a summary of Dorothea Dix's legacy as a social reformer.

What Impact Did Reformers Have on Education?

In colonial times, children's education started in the home. Some children also received an education through their church or were privately taught. In Puritan New England, education focused mainly on religion, with the aim of ensuring salvation. In other regions, church-based schools added reading and writing. Wealthier students often had private tutors or attended "dame schools," run by a local teacher, usually a woman, in her home.

Several colonies and, later, states partly funded public grammar schools. The books used in these schools helped students gain reading skills, but they also had social and civic purposes. The *Columbian Orator*, a book of orations, or public speeches, was used in many schools. Its readings ranged from "A Dialogue on Learning and Usefulness" and "The Dignity of Human Nature" to "President Washington's Address to the People of the United States" and "Description of the First American Congress." The popular *McGuffey Readers* also provided students with numerous moral lessons.

Still, until the mid-1800s, few American children attended any school. In 1827, Massachusetts became the first state to require free community-supported public schools for all children. Teachers, however, were poorly trained and ill paid. Students of all ages crowded together in a single room.

As more men won the right to vote, reformers acted to improve education. They argued that a republic required educated citizens. They also believed that children should not spend their whole day working

in a factory. They belonged in school. In 1836, Massachusetts passed a law that required child laborers under age 15 to attend school at least three months of the year. Other states followed. Some of them limited children to a 10-hour day in the factory.

Education Reform Gives Rise to Public Schools Horace Mann became head of the Massachusetts Board of Education in 1837. A Unitarian inspired by the Second Great Awakening, Mann believed that education would help citizens become better Christians. He hounded legislators to provide more money for education. Under his leadership, Massachusetts built new schools, sorted children into grades by age, extended the school year, and raised teachers' pay. The state also opened three colleges to train teachers.

Other states followed the lead of Massachusetts. By the 1850s, most northern states had set up free tax-supported elementary schools. Schools in the South improved more slowly. In both the North and the South, schooling usually ended in the eighth grade. There were few public high schools.

Expanding Education for African Americans In most areas, African Americans had little chance to attend school. A few cities, like Boston and New York, set up separate schools for black students. However, these schools received less money than schools for white students. In the North, African American men and women often opened their own schools to educate their children.

Some attempts to educate African Americans met with hostility. In the 1830s, Prudence Crandall, a Connecticut Quaker, began a school for African American girls. Crandall continued to teach even as rocks smashed through the window. Finally, a mob broke in one night and destroyed the school.

Despite such obstacles, some African Americans went on to attend private colleges such as Middlebury, Dartmouth, and Oberlin. The first African American known to have earned a college degree was Alexander Lucius Twilight, who graduated from Middlebury College in Vermont in 1823. The first institute of higher learning for African Americans, the Institute for Colored Youth, was founded in Pennsylvania in 1837. It was later followed by Lincoln University, also in Pennsylvania (1854), and Wilberforce University in Ohio (1856).

Reforms for People With Disabilities Some reformers improved education for people with disabilities. In 1817, a Christian evangelical Thomas Gallaudet (gal uh DEHT) set up a school for the deaf in Hartford, Connecticut. Now in Washington, D.C., Gallaudet University is the world's only college that is free of barriers for deaf and hard-of-hearing students.

Analyze Images Alexander Lucius Twilight, below, was the first African American to graduate from college in the United States. **Infer** What do you think Twilight did after graduating from college?

Analyze Images Born into slavery but later freed, Isabella Van Wagener took the name "Sojourner Truth" because she believed God wanted her to travel, or sojourn, across the nation preaching abolition. **Draw Conclusions** Would she have been as effective a speaker if she had not changed her name? Why or why not?

Physician Samuel Gridley Howe founded the first American school for the blind in 1832. Howe was active in many reform movements spurred by the Second Great Awakening, working for improvements in public schools, prisons, and treatment of the disabled. Howe used a system of raised letters to enable students to read with their fingers. One of Howe's pupils, Laura Bridgman, was the first deaf and blind student to receive a formal education.

✅ **READING CHECK** **Identify Cause and Effect** Why did reformers insist that states set up publicly funded schools for their residents?

Early Calls for Women's Rights

Women had few political or legal rights in the mid-1800s. They could not vote or hold office. When a woman married, her husband became owner of all her property. If a woman worked outside the home, her wages belonged to her husband. A husband also had the right to hit his wife as long as he did not seriously injure her.

Many women, such as Angelina and Sarah Grimké, had joined the abolitionist movement. As these women worked to end slavery, they became aware that they lacked full social and political rights themselves. They and many other women felt limited by their gender when society was so dominated by men. Both white and African American abolitionists, men and women, joined the struggle for women's rights.

What Were the Contributions of Sojourner Truth? One of the most effective women's rights leaders was born into slavery in New York. After gaining freedom, she came to believe that God wanted her to fight slavery. Vowing to sojourn, or travel, across the land speaking the truth, she took the name Sojourner Truth.

Truth was a spellbinding speaker. Her exact words were rarely written down. However, her message spread by word of mouth. According to one witness, Truth ridiculed the idea that women were inferior to men by nature:

Primary Source

"I have as much muscle as any man, and can do as much work as any man. I have plowed and reaped and husked and chopped and mowed, and can any man do more than that?"

—Sojourner Truth, speech at Akron Women's Rights Convention, 1851

 INTERACTIVE

The Early Women's Rights Movement

The Contributions of Lucretia Mott and Elizabeth Cady Stanton Other abolitionists also turned to the cause of women's rights. The two most influential were Lucretia Mott and Elizabeth Cady Stanton. Lucretia Mott was a Quaker and the mother of five children. A quiet speaker, she won the respect of many listeners with her persuasive logic. Mott also organized petition drives across the North.

Elizabeth Cady Stanton was the daughter of a New York judge. As a child, she was an excellent student and an athlete. However, her father gave her little encouragement. Stanton later remarked that her "father would have felt a proper pride had I been a man."

Both women attended a series of classes in Boston known as "conversations." These women-only discussions were hosted by Margaret Fuller, a young literary critic. Fuller linked the advance of women's rights with a better understanding of liberty:

Primary Source

"It should be remarked that, as the principle of liberty is better understood, and more nobly interpreted, a broader protest is made in behalf of Woman. As men become aware that few men have had a fair chance, they are inclined to say that no women have had a fair chance."

—Margaret Fuller, *Woman in the Nineteenth Century*, 1844

In 1840, Stanton and Mott joined a group of Americans at a World Antislavery Convention in London. However, convention officials refused to let women take an active part in the proceedings. Female delegates were even forced to sit behind a curtain, hidden from view. After returning home, Mott and Stanton took up the cause of women's rights with new energy.

✓ **READING CHECK** **Draw Conclusions** How did their early experiences influence Sojourner Truth and Elizabeth Cady Stanton?

▼ Lucretia Mott used her persuasive logic and organizing skills to support the cause of women's rights.

Quick Activity

Explore the similarities between the Declaration of Sentiments and the Declaration of Independence in your 📓 Active Journal.

How Did the Women's Movement Start?

Even in London, Mott and Stanton had begun thinking about holding a convention to draw attention to the problems women faced. "The men . . . had [shown] a great need for some education on that question," Stanton later recalled. The meeting finally took place in 1848 in Seneca Falls, New York.

Different Views of Suffrage at the Seneca Falls Convention

About 200 women and 40 men attended the **Seneca Falls Convention**. Stanton's greatest contribution to the convention was the *Declaration of Sentiments*, which she had modeled on the Declaration of Independence. The delegates approved the declaration. It proclaimed, "We hold these truths to be self-evident: that all men and women are created equal."

The women and men at Seneca Falls voted for resolutions that demanded equality for women at work, at school, and at church. Only one resolution met with any opposition at the convention. It demanded that women be allowed to vote. Even the bold reformers at Seneca Falls hesitated to take this step. In the end, the resolution narrowly passed.

Analyze Images Elizabeth Cady Stanton addresses the Seneca Falls Convention. **Infer** Do you think public speaking was acceptable for women at this time?

Women Struggle for Justice The Seneca Falls Convention marked the start of an organized campaign for equal rights, or the **women's rights movement**. This movement was one of the most important reform movements of the Reform Era. In a speech the year after the convention, Lucretia Mott described what this movement would seek to gain:

Primary Source

"The question is often asked, 'What does woman want, more than she enjoys? What is she seeking to obtain? Of what rights is she deprived? What privileges are withheld from her?' I answer, she asks nothing as favor, but as right, she wants to be acknowledged a moral, responsible being."

—Lucretia Mott, "Discourse on Woman," 1849

New leaders took up the struggle. Susan B. Anthony built a close working partnership with Elizabeth Cady Stanton. While Stanton usually had to stay at home with her seven children, Anthony was free to travel across the country. Anthony was a tireless speaker. Even when audiences heckled her and threw eggs, she always finished her speech.

Around the country, Anthony campaigned for women's suffrage. She petitioned Congress repeatedly, and was even arrested in 1872 for trying to vote. After paying a $100 fine, she lashed out at the injustice:

Primary Source

"It was we, the people; not we, the white male citizens; nor yet we, the male citizens; but we, the whole people, who formed the Union. And we formed it, not to give the blessings of liberty, but to secure them; not to the half of ourselves and the half of our posterity, but to the whole people— women as well as men."

—Susan B. Anthony, "Women's Rights to the Suffrage," 1873

▲ Susan B. Anthony was probably the most powerful and influential leader of the women's rights movement during the 1800s.

In the years after 1848, women worked for change in many areas. They won additional legal rights in some states. For example, New York passed laws allowing married women to keep their own property and wages. Still, many men and women opposed the women's rights movement. The struggle for equal rights would last many years.

✓ READING CHECK **Identify Supporting Details** For what act of civil disobedience was Susan B. Anthony arrested in 1872?

Women Gain New Opportunities

The women at Seneca Falls believed that education was a key to equality. Elizabeth Cady Stanton said:

Primary Source

"The girl must be allowed to romp and play, climb, skate, and swim. Her clothing must be more like those of the boy—strong, loose-fitting garments, thick boots. . . . She must be taught to look forward to life of self-dependence and, like the boy, prepare herself for some [profitable] trade profession."

—Elizabeth Cady Stanton, Letter, 1851

Such an idea was startling in the early 1800s. Women from poor families had little hope of learning even to read. Middle-class girls who went to school learned dancing and drawing rather than science or mathematics. After all, people argued, women were expected to care for their families. Why did they need an education?

Opportunities for Women's Education Possibly the greatest impact of the women's movement in the mid-1800s was the creation of greater opportunities for women in education. Emma Willard opened a high school for girls in Troy, New York. Here, young women studied "men's" subjects, such as mathematics and physics.

Mary Lyon opened Mount Holyoke Female Seminary in Massachusetts in 1837. She did not call the school a college because many people thought it was wrong for women to attend college. In fact, however, Mount Holyoke was one of the first women's colleges in the United States.

New Employment Opportunities for Women At about this time, a few men's colleges began to admit women. As their education improved, women found jobs teaching, especially in grade schools.

A few women entered fields such as medicine. Elizabeth Blackwell attended medical school at Geneva College in New York. To the surprise of school officials, she graduated first in her class. Women had provided medical care since colonial times, but Blackwell was the first woman in the United States to earn a medical degree. She later helped found the nation's first medical school for women.

Women made their mark in other fields as well. Maria Mitchell was a noted astronomer. Sarah Josepha Hale edited *Godey's Lady's Book*, an influential magazine for women.

Analyze Graphs The infographic below shows some of the changes in women's lives in the first half of the 1800s. **Use Visual Information** What details in the graphs support the conclusion that women's educational opportunities expanded during the mid-1800s?

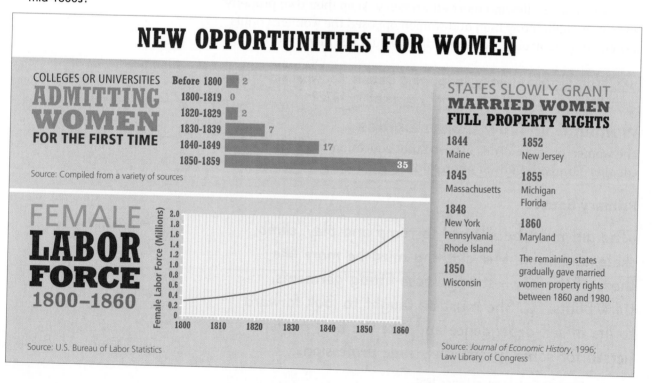

NEW OPPORTUNITIES FOR WOMEN

COLLEGES OR UNIVERSITIES ADMITTING WOMEN FOR THE FIRST TIME

Before 1800	2
1800-1819	0
1820-1829	2
1830-1839	7
1840-1849	17
1850-1859	35

Source: Compiled from a variety of sources

FEMALE LABOR FORCE 1800–1860

Female Labor Force (Millions)

Source: U.S. Bureau of Labor Statistics

STATES SLOWLY GRANT MARRIED WOMEN FULL PROPERTY RIGHTS

1844 Maine

1845 Massachusetts

1848 New York Pennsylvania Rhode Island

1850 Wisconsin

1852 New Jersey

1855 Michigan Florida

1860 Maryland

The remaining states gradually gave married women property rights between 1860 and 1980.

Source: *Journal of Economic History*, 1996; Law Library of Congress

Antoinette Blackwell became the first American woman ordained as a minister. She also campaigned for abolitionism, temperance, and women's right to vote.

The Struggle Continues

The struggle for women's rights continues today. As in the 19th century, different groups have differing points of view.

One issue on which women's groups differ today is whether companies or the government should be required to pay women on maternity leave, or a period away from their jobs to give birth and take care of babies. Some women's groups today, such as the National Organization for Women, believe that employers, including the government, should be required to pay women during maternity leave. They argue that women need this support. Other groups, such as the Independent Women's Forum, argue that requiring employers to pay for maternity leave might make them less willing to hire women.

Analyze Images Women began attending medical school during the 1800s. **Infer** Why would women have been good candidates for medical training?

☑ **READING CHECK** **Draw Conclusions** What effects did the women's movement have during the 1800s?

☑ Lesson Check

Practice Vocabulary

1. How did the teachings of the **Second Great Awakening** inspire movements for **social reform**?

2. What role did the **Seneca Falls Convention** play in the **women's rights movement**?

Critical Thinking and Writing

3. **Identify Main Ideas** What did social reformers believe was unjust about American society?

4. **Summarize** Summarize the changes in how children were educated from colonial times through the mid-1800s.

5. **Cite Evidence** Do you consider the women's rights movement in the mid-1800s successful or not? Explain.

6. **Writing Workshop: Use Descriptive Details and Sensory Language** Look around yourself right now. What do you see, what do you hear, what do you feel or smell? Write a few sentences in your ▰ Active Journal to describe these sensations. You will find that descriptive words and sensory language will add life and excitement to your narrative essay.

James Fenimore Cooper, "The Chainbearer"

James Fenimore Cooper wrote about life on the early American frontier. In this passage, the narrator is sailing up the Hudson River on his way to a frontier settlement in northern New York.

◀ Axes were essential for clearing forests.

Reading and Vocabulary Support

① A farmer was called a husbandman.

② The phrase *in their train* literally means "behind them," but its implied meaning is "as a result of."

③ Explain, in your own words, how Cooper's "conquests" of the axe "left civilization in their train" instead of destruction.

④ What is the war that Cooper is referring to here?

On the main-deck were six or eight sturdy, decent, quiet, respectable-looking labourers, who were evidently of the class of husbandmen. ① Their packs were lying in a pile, near the foot of the mast, and I did not fail to observe that there were as many axes as there were packs.

The American axe! It has made more real and lasting conquests than the sword of any warlike people that ever lived; but, they have been conquests that have left civilization in their train, ② instead of havoc and desolation. ③ More than a million of square miles of territory have been opened up from the shades of the virgin forest, to admit the warmth of the sun; and culture and abundance have been spread where the beast of the forest so lately roamed. . . . A brief quarter of a century has seen these wonderful changes wrought; and at the bottom of them all lies this beautiful, well-prized, ready, and efficient implement, the American axe!

It would not be easy to give the reader a clear notion of the manner in which the young men and men of all ages of the older portions of the new republic poured into the woods to commence the business of felling the forests, and laying bare the secrets of nature, as soon as the nation rose from beneath the pressure of war, ④ to enjoy the freedom of peace.

—James Fenimore Cooper, *The Chainbearer*

Analyzing Primary Sources

Cite specific evidence from this source to support your answers.

1. **Determine Author's Purpose** Why does Cooper glorify the axe?

2. **Determine Author's Point of View** How does Americans' image of the forest today differ from that of Cooper's time?

LESSON 6
Arts and Literature

BOUNCE TO ACTIVATE ▶ VIDEO

GET READY TO READ

START UP
Examine the painting by American artist Robert S. Duncanson. Write a sentence or two suggesting how this painting might reflect a theme common to writers and artists of this period.

GUIDING QUESTIONS
- What was life like in the early years of the republic?
- What themes did American painters pursue in the early to mid-1800s?
- What themes marked the works of writers during this period?
- How did transcendentalism affect American culture?

TAKE NOTES
Literacy Skills: Identify Cause and Effect
Use the graphic organizer in your 📓 Active Journal to take notes as you read the lesson.

PRACTICE VOCABULARY
Use the vocabulary activity in your 📓 Active Journal to practice the vocabulary words.

Vocabulary
Hudson River School
transcendentalist
individualism

Academic Vocabulary
idealize

Before 1800, most American painters studied in Europe. Benjamin West of Philadelphia was appointed historical painter to King George III. Many American painters journeyed to London to study with West. Two of them, Charles Wilson Peale and Gilbert Stuart, later painted famous portraits of George Washington.

A New American Art Style
By the mid-1800s, American artists began to develop their own style. The first group to do so became known as the **Hudson River School**. Artists such as Thomas Cole and Asher B. Durand painted vivid landscapes of New York's Hudson River region and other parts of the Northeast. African American painter Robert S. Duncanson depicted the beauty of nature.

Other artists painted scenes of hard-working country people in a natural setting. George Caleb Bingham of Missouri created a timeless picture of frontier life. George Catlin and Alfred Jacob Miller traveled to the Far West to record the daily life of American Indians.

Analyze Images John James Audubon's paintings of birds, like these Columbia jays, and other wildlife are still admired for their beauty and scientific accuracy. **Infer** Why did Audubon find endless subjects to paint in the United States?

🖐 INTERACTIVE

Painting America

Academic Vocabulary
idealized • v., to see in the best possible light

John James Audubon, a wildlife artist, traveled across the country painting birds and mammals. His collection of 435 life-size prints, titled *The Birds of America*, portrayed every bird known in the United States at the time.

American artists in the early and mid-1800s proved that the American landscape and people were worthy subjects of art. Their paintings portrayed the continuity in the American way of life—in the timelessness of the country's geography and in the patterns of farm work. They also showed the great changes that were underway in this new era. Artists depicted the effects of westward movement and the settlement of the frontier, capturing the nation's expansion and growth. In their attention to these themes, the work of these painters reflected American society in their day.

✅ **READING CHECK** **Identify Main Ideas** What were common themes in the works of American artists during the early to mid-1800s?

New Forms of Literature and Music

Like painters, early American writers also depended on Europe for their ideas and inspiration. In the 1820s, however, a new crop of poets and fiction writers began to write about American themes. At the same time, uniquely American forms of music began to emerge. These new forms of literature and music reflected American society in the early and mid-1800s.

American Poetry Henry Wadsworth Longfellow was the favorite poet of Americans in the mid-1800s. Longfellow based many of his poems on historical events. "Paul Revere's Ride" honored the Revolutionary War hero. "The Song of Hiawatha" **idealized** Native American life. His poems gave Americans a sense of where they came from and, in the process, helped establish a national identity.

Other poets spoke out on social issues. John Greenleaf Whittier, a Quaker from Massachusetts, and Frances Watkins Harper, an African American woman from Maryland, reflected change in American society as abolitionism gained supporters. They used their pens to make readers aware of the evils of slavery.

After a career as a journalist, Walt Whitman became a groundbreaking poet. His greatest work was *Leaves of Grass*. Like Longfellow, Whittier, and Harper, he focused on uniquely American themes. His poetry celebrated democracy. He wrote proudly of being part of a "nation of many nations":

🖱 INTERACTIVE

Early American Music and Literature

Primary Source

"At home on the hills of Vermont or in the woods of Maine, or the Texan ranch, comrade of Californians, comrade of free North-Westerners, . . . of every hue and caste am I, of every rank and religion."

—Walt Whitman, *Song of Myself*

Whitman was also one of the first modern poets to write about same-sex love. His romanticizing of same-sex friendship has given his work an important place in the modern gay rights movement.

Only seven of Emily Dickinson's more than 1,700 poems were published in her lifetime. A shy woman who rarely left her home, Dickinson called her poetry "my letter to the world / That never wrote to me." Her close friendship with her brother's wife, Susan, has led some scholars to speculate that the two women had a romantic relationship, although there is no definite evidence of this. Today, Dickinson is recognized as one of the nation's greatest poets.

Writers Begin to Tell American Stories One of the most popular American writers was Washington Irving, a New Yorker. Irving first became known for *The Sketch Book,* a collection of tales published in 1820. Two of his best-loved tales are "Rip Van Winkle" and "The Legend of Sleepy Hollow."

The exciting novels of James Fenimore Cooper were also set in the American past. Several of his novels, including *The Deerslayer* and *The Last of the Mohicans,* feature Natty Bumppo, a heroic model of a strong, solitary frontiersman. Cooper's novels gave an idealized view of relations between whites and Native Americans on the frontier.

Like Longfellow's poems, the stories of Cooper and Irving gave Americans a sense of the richness of their past. Their appeal went beyond the United States, however. Washington Irving was the first American writer to enjoy fame in Europe.

Later Writers In 1851, Herman Melville published *Moby-Dick*. The novel tells the story of Ahab, the crazed captain of a whaling ship. Ahab vows revenge on the white whale that years earlier bit off his leg. *Moby-Dick* had only limited success when it was first published. Today, however, critics rank it among the finest American novels.

Analyze Images Emily Dickinson, shown here in an early photograph, wrote poems that reflected the loneliness of her life. **Draw Conclusions** Why do you think Dickinson is still considered one of the greatest American poets?

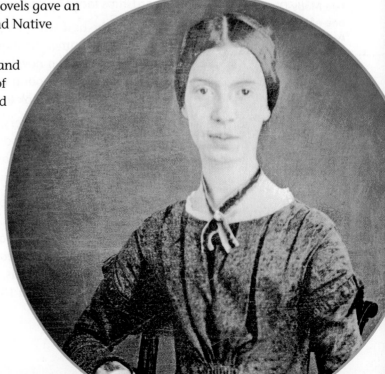

Nathaniel Hawthorne often drew on the history of New England in his novels and short stories. In *The Scarlet Letter,* published in 1850, Hawthorne explored Puritan notions of sin and salvation. The novel shows how a young man is consumed by guilt when he tries to hide his wrongdoing from the world.

Edgar Allan Poe became famous for his many tales of horror. His short story "The Tell-Tale Heart" is about a murderer, driven mad by guilt, who imagines he can hear his victim's heartbeat. Poe is also known as the father of the detective story for his mystery stories, such as "The Murders in the Rue Morgue."

William Wells Brown was the first African American to earn his living as a writer. He published *Clotel,* a novel about slave life, in 1853. Brown also wrote a play inspired by his own experiences as a fugitive slave and a conductor on the Underground Railroad. His lectures and readings drew large audiences in Europe as well as throughout the North.

▲ Whalers face the angry whale Moby-Dick in a scene from Herman Melville's epic tale *Moby-Dick,* considered one of the greatest American novels.

Women Writers Flourish Women wrote many of the best-selling novels of the period. Some novels told about young women who gained wealth and happiness through honesty and self-sacrifice. Others showed the hardships faced by widows and orphans.

Perhaps the best known of these women writers was Louisa May Alcott. Alcott wrote numerous short stories, poems, and books. Her most famous work was a novel written for girls, called *Little Women.* Centered on a strong-willed young woman who loves reading and writing, it remains a popular book today.

The novels of other writers, such as Catherine Sedgwick and Fanny Fern, have few readers today. Yet these writers earned far more than Hawthorne or Melville. Hawthorne complained about the success of a "mob of scribbling women."

American Music American classical music in the 1800s continued to follow European traditions. Yet, as American society changed and grew and different groups of people came into contact with one another, distinctly American musical forms began to emerge. Early songs were often patriotic or religious, such as "My Country Tis of Thee," written by Samuel Francis Smith in 1831, or "Amazing Grace," published in 1835.

Did you know?

The four sisters in *Little Women* were based on Alcott and her own sisters.

The 1800s saw the rise of a middle class interested in music that was entertaining and emotionally stirring. The songs of Stephen Foster, which drew on American themes, were especially popular. Although Foster was a northerner, many of his songs referred to southern traditions and were popular in the South. Another song popular in the South, "Dixie," was written by Ohio native Daniel Emmett. Western expansion, immigration, and migration mingled musical traditions together, creating new American sounds.

African American music in particular had a strong influence on the new forms that were developing. African American spirituals and work songs combined African and European musical traditions. During the 1800s, a new style of music now known as gospel music began to develop in African American religious congregations. These styles would later combine with European and American folk traditions to shape blues, jazz, country, and rock music.

READING CHECK **Draw Conclusions** What do many of the works of American literature of the early to mid-1800s have in common?

Transcendentalism Develops

In New England, a small but influential group of writers and thinkers emerged. They called themselves **transcendentalists**, because they believed that the most important truths in life transcended, or went beyond, human reason. They produced a unique body of literature reflecting transcendentalist thought. Transcendentalists valued the spark of deeply felt insights more than reason.

Analyze Images Although considered uniquely American, the banjo has roots in sub-Saharan Africa. **Cite Evidence** What other American musical traditions or instruments have African origins?

BIOGRAPHY
5 Things to Know About

LOUISA MAY ALCOTT
Author of *Little Women* (1832–1888)

- Her father was an educator, philosopher, abolitionist, and women's rights supporter.

- As a child, she spent time with her father's Boston-area friends Ralph Waldo Emerson and Henry David Thoreau.

- At the start of the Civil War, she served as a nurse at a Union hospital, where she contracted typhoid fever.

- She published two *Little Women* books, in 1868 and 1869, and their success allowed her to pay off her family's extensive debts.

- She wrote in her book *Little Men* (1871): "Money is the root of all evil, and yet it is such a useful root that we cannot get on without it any more than we can without potatoes."

Critical Thinking Why do you think Alcott immediately began a second *Little Women* book after publishing the first?

Did you know?

The land where Thoreau built his cabin was owned by Emerson and was about 20 minutes by foot from Thoreau's family home.

They believed that each individual should live up to the divine possibilities within. This belief influenced many transcendentalists to support social reform.

Emerson on the Importance of the Individual The leading transcendentalist was Ralph Waldo Emerson. Emerson was the most popular essayist and lecturer of his day. Audiences flocked to hear him talk on subjects such as self-reliance and character. Emerson believed that the human spirit was reflected in nature. Civilization might provide material wealth, he said, but nature exhibited higher values that came from God.

In his essays and lectures, Emerson stressed **individualism**, or the importance of each individual. In its individual focus, transcendentalism is unique to American culture. Individualism and individual responsibility are central to America's democracy. Each person, Emerson said, has an "inner light." He urged people to use this inner light to guide their lives and improve society. "Trust thyself," he wrote. "Every heart vibrates to that iron string."

Thoreau and Civil Disobedience Henry David Thoreau (thuh ROH), Emerson's friend and neighbor, believed that the growth of industry and the rise of cities were ruining the nation. He urged people to live as simply and as close to nature as possible. In *Walden,* his best-known work, Thoreau describes spending a year alone in a cabin on Walden Pond in Massachusetts.

Analyze Images This replica of Henry David Thoreau's cabin sits near the site of his original cabin beside Walden Pond in Concord, Massachusetts. **Understand Effects** How might living in a small cabin like this have inspired Thoreau?

Like Emerson, Thoreau believed that each individual must decide what is right or wrong. "If a man does not keep pace with his companions," he wrote, in *Walden,* "perhaps it is because he hears a different drummer. Let him step to the music he hears."

Thoreau's "different drummer" told him that slavery was wrong. He argued in favor of civil disobedience and once went to jail for refusing to pay taxes to support the U.S.-Mexican War, which he felt promoted slavery. Thoreau wrote an essay titled "Civil Disobedience" that explained why an individual may feel the need to break laws that are unjust without resorting to violence.

He argued, though, that anyone who chooses this course has to be prepared to be imprisoned or otherwise punished. This essay had a great impact on future leaders. Thoreau's ideas on civil disobedience and nonviolence later influenced Mohandas Gandhi, who led a struggle in India for independence from Britain, and Martin Luther King, Jr., an American civil rights leader during the mid-1900s.

▲ Ralph Waldo Emerson was one of the most influential of the transcendentalists.

☑ **READING CHECK** **Identify Main Ideas** What was the core belief of the transcendentalists?

☑ Lesson Check

Practice Vocabulary

1. What role did **individualism** play in the beliefs of the **transcendentalists**?

2. What distinguished the artists of **Hudson River School** from other artists?

Critical Thinking and Writing

3. **Summarize** How did writers in the 1800s contribute to social reform movements?

4. **Evaluate Arguments** How would you respond to the argument that American artists and writers explored common themes during this period?

5. **Generate Explanations** How did transcendentalism affect American culture?

6. **Writing Workshop: Prepare a Final Draft** Review your writing as you prepare to create your final draft. You may want to share it with a partner. Check your structure, spelling, and grammar. Have you said what you wanted to say?

☑ Review and Assessment

VISUAL REVIEW

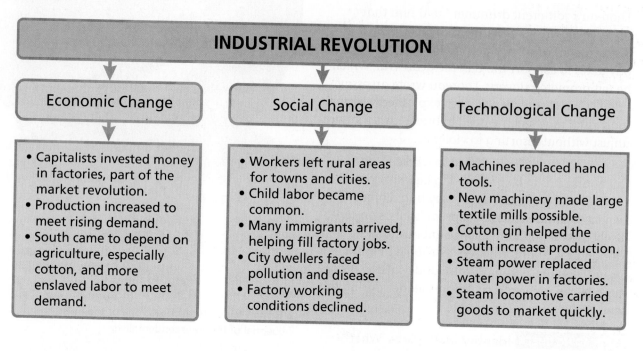

INDUSTRIAL REVOLUTION

Economic Change

- Capitalists invested money in factories, part of the market revolution.
- Production increased to meet rising demand.
- South came to depend on agriculture, especially cotton, and more enslaved labor to meet demand.

Social Change

- Workers left rural areas for towns and cities.
- Child labor became common.
- Many immigrants arrived, helping fill factory jobs.
- City dwellers faced pollution and disease.
- Factory working conditions declined.

Technological Change

- Machines replaced hand tools.
- New machinery made large textile mills possible.
- Cotton gin helped the South increase production.
- Steam power replaced water power in factories.
- Steam locomotive carried goods to market quickly.

Prisoners — Better treatment and health care — Disabled people

Mentally ill people

Temperance

SOCIAL REFORM MOVEMENTS

Women's rights and suffrage

Abolition

Better schools

Education

Colleges for women and African Americans

READING REVIEW

Use the Take Notes and Practice Vocabulary activities in your 📓 Active Journal to review the topic.

 **INTERACTIVE**

Practice vocabulary using the Topic Mini-Games.

Quest FINDINGS

Write Your Essay
Get help for writing your essay in your 📓 Active Journal.

ASSESSMENT

Vocabulary and Key Ideas

1. **Check Understanding** Why did the spread of the factory system rely on **capitalists**?

2. **Identify Supporting Details** How did work in a factory differ from farm work?

3. **Identify** Who were the people in the South said to make up the **"cottonocracy"**?

4. **Define** What was the **Underground Railroad**?

5. **Recall** What political advantage did the **Know-Nothing Party** gain by opposing Irish immigrants?

6. **Locate** Which state took the lead in reforming its educational system and establishing public schools?

7. **Identify** What philosophy is associated with **individualism** and reliance on nature?

Critical Thinking and Writing

8. **Compare and Contrast** How did interchangeable parts differ from the parts that had been used before in manufacturing products, and why did that matter?

9. **Draw Conclusions** Do you think social reforms such as the abolition of slavery would have been pursued even if the Second Great Awakening had not occurred? Why or why not?

10. **Sequence** How could the building of a factory along a river in the early 1800s lead eventually to the existence of a growing city?

11. **Infer** What role did the Seneca Falls Convention play in sparking the women's rights movement?

12. **Revisit the Essential Question** American writers, artists, and musicians of the 1800s focused on themes that were unique to American culture. Do you agree or disagree? Explain your answer.

13. **Writing Workshop: Write Narratives** Using the outline you created in your 📕 Active Journal, write a three-paragraph narrative from the point of view of a young person working in northern industry during this time period.

Analyze Primary Sources

14. Who was the author of this dialogue?
    A. Emily Dickinson
    B. Ralph Waldo Emerson
    C. Louisa May Alcott
    D. Herman Melville

"Well, sir, I want to see what whaling is. I want to see the world."

"Want to see what whaling is, eh? Have ye clapped eye on Captain Ahab?"

Analyze Maps

Use the map at right to answer the following questions:

15. What does the dark green area in Tennessee indicate?

16. Which state had the largest area devoted to producing sugar?

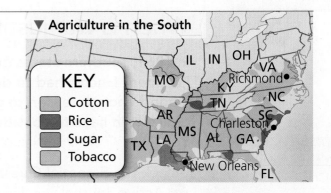

▼ Agriculture in the South

KEY
- Cotton
- Rice
- Sugar
- Tobacco

Sectionalism and Civil War
(1820–1865)

GO ONLINE
to access your
digital course

▶ VIDEO

◀)) AUDIO

📖 ETEXT

👆 INTERACTIVE

✏️ WRITING

🎮 GAMES

📄 WORKSHEET

☑️ ASSESSMENT

Go back to the 1820s

and the era of SECTIONALISM AND THE CIVIL WAR. Why? Because it was during this time that the seeds of the Civil War were sown. Learn what caused this terrible conflict.

Explore

The Essential Question

When is war justified?

In 1861, southern states quit the Union. President Lincoln had to decide if that was a good enough reason to go to war. What did Lincoln have to consider in making the decision?

Unlock the Essential Question in your 📔 Active Journal.

Read

about events leading up to the Civil War, the decisions leaders made, and the conflict that raged for four years.

Watch

NBC LEARN

BOUNCE TO ACTIVATE ▶ VIDEO

Robert E. Lee, the Marble Man

Learn about Robert E. Lee's leadership at the Battle of Chancellorsville.

▲ The Battle of Gettysburg, 1863

Sectionalism and Civil War

Learn more about Sectionalism and the Civil War by making your own map and timeline in your 📔 Active Journal.

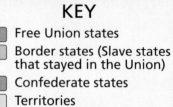

KEY
- Free Union states
- Border states (Slave states that stayed in the Union)
- Confederate states
- Territories

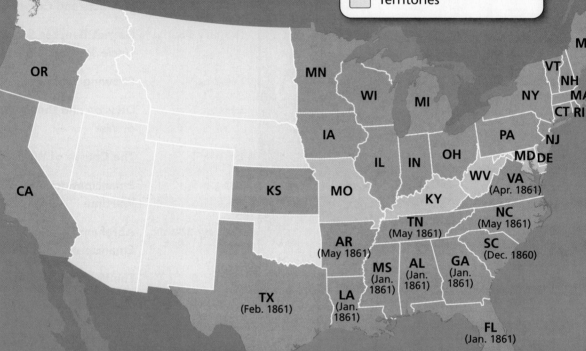

OR

MN

WI

MI

ME

VT

NH

NY   MA

CT RI

IA

PA

NJ

CA

KS

MO

IL   IN   OH

MD DE

WV   VA
(Apr. 1861)

KY

NC
(May 1861)

AR
(May 1861)

TN
(May 1861)

SC
(Dec. 1860)

TX
(Feb. 1861)

LA
(Jan. 1861)

MS
(Jan. 1861)

AL
(Jan. 1861)

GA
(Jan. 1861)

FL
(Jan. 1861)

👆 INTERACTIVE

Topic Timeline

What happened and when?

Tensions between states over slavery . . . compromises to keep the nation together . . . political divisions and courtroom drama. . . and then a long and bloody civil war. Explore the timeline to see some of what was going on in the United States and in the rest of the world.

1850
Compromise of 1850, Fugitive Slave Act

TOPIC EVENTS

1820	1830	1840

WORLD EVENTS

1820
African American colonists set sail for Liberia

1821
Mexico and most of Central America gain independence from Spain

Where was the Civil War fought?

The Civil War involved the whole United States, but most of the battles occurred in the Southern states that seceded from the Union and formed the Confederate States of America.

BY TELEGRAPH.
Sunday, April 14, 1861
Fort Sumpter Surrendered!
MAJ. ANDERSON
A PRISONER OF WAR
&c.   &c.   &c.

Who will you meet?

Abraham Lincoln, war President

Clara Barton, battlefield nurse

Jefferson Davis, leader of the Confederacy

1854
Kansas-Nebraska Act

1857
Dred Scott v. Sandford decision

1861
Shots fired at Ft. Sumter, Civil War begins

1865
Lee surrenders at Appomattox Court House

1850   1860   1870

1845
Great Famine begins in Ireland

1866
Transatlantic cable completed

Quest
Project-Based Learning Inquiry

A Lincoln Website

Quest KICK OFF

It is 1863, and you have come to hear President Lincoln dedicate a cemetery. As you listen to him speak, his words sound familiar.

How did Abraham Lincoln's writings and speeches relate to the Declaration of Independence?

With your team, explore the answer in this Quest, and then create a website to share your findings.

1 Ask Questions
In your 📖 Active Journal write questions about Lincoln and the Declaration of Independence to guide your Quest.

2 Investigate
As you read the lessons in this Topic, look for **Quest** CONNECTIONS to help you make connections between Lincoln's speeches and writings and the Declaration of Independence. Take notes about what you learn in your 📖 Active Journal.

3 Conduct Research
Now examine some of Lincoln's speeches and writings. In particular, read the Emancipation Proclamation (1863) Primary Source feature in Lesson 5, the "House Divided" speech (1858), the Gettysburg Address (1863), and the first and second inaugural addresses (1861, 1865). As you read, look for more connections.

Quest FINDINGS

4 Create a Web Site
Working with your team, create a two-page website so you can share your findings. Get help for this task in your 📖 Active Journal.

▲ President Lincoln, 1862

LESSON 1

Conflicts and Compromises

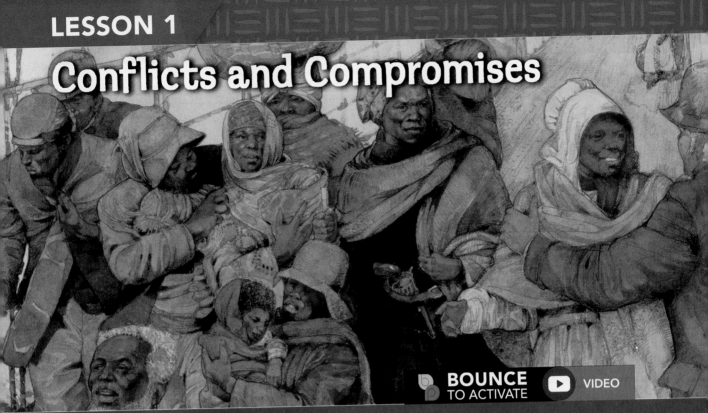

BOUNCE TO ACTIVATE ▶ VIDEO

GET READY TO READ

START UP

This picture shows enslaved people escaping to freedom. What kinds of risks did they face?

GUIDING QUESTIONS

- Why did conflict arise over the issue of slavery in the western territories?
- How did Congress try to resolve the issue of slavery?
- How did *Uncle Tom's Cabin* affect attitudes toward slavery?

TAKE NOTES

Literacy Skills Compare and Contrast

Use the Graphic Organizer in your 📖 Active Journal to take notes as you read the lesson.

PRACTICE VOCABULARY

Use the Vocabulary Builder in your 📖 Active Journal to practice these words.

Vocabulary		Academic Vocabulary
Missouri Compromise	fugitive	resolve
popular sovereignty	civil war	propose
Free-Soil Party	Compromise of 1850	
secede	Fugitive Slave Act	

In 1819, there were 11 free states in the North and 11 slave states in the South. The North and South had different economies, political views, and ideas about slavery. These differences created a growing sectionalism. Sectionalism is a rivalry or tension that develops between people who are loyal to their section, or region, of the country. This era of sectionalism lasted from the 1810s to the 1860s. As a result of sectionalism, there were many political conflicts over issues important to each region.

The Missouri Compromise

Before 1819, the equal number of slave and free states balanced the sectional divide. In that year, however, Missouri applied to join the Union as a slave state. Immediately, a crisis erupted. Missouri's admission would give the South a majority in the Senate. Determined not to lose power, northerners opposed letting Missouri enter as a slave state.

Missouri Compromise, 1820

British Territory

Oregon Country

Vermont
Maine

Michigan Territory

New Hampshire
Massachusetts
New York
Rhode Island
Connecticut
New Jersey
Delaware
Maryland

Unorganized territory

Pennsylvania

Indiana Ohio

Illinois

36°30'N

PACIFIC OCEAN

New Spain

Missouri

Virginia

Kentucky

Tennessee

North Carolina

South Carolina

ATLANTIC OCEAN

Arkansas Territory

Alabama

Georgia

Mississippi

Louisiana

Florida Territory

Gulf of Mexico

KEY
- Free states and territories
- Slave states and territories
- Missouri Compromise line

GEOGRAPHY SKILLS

The map shows how the Missouri Compromise divided the territories at latitude 36°30' N. All states that would be formed from the territory north of this line would be free states.

1. **Location** Based on the map, how was Missouri an exception to the terms of the Missouri Compromise?

2. **Analyze Maps** Based on the information in the map, how did the Missouri Compromise preserve a balance of power in the Senate?

The argument lasted many months. During the long debate, Maine had also applied for statehood. Finally, Senator Henry Clay suggested admitting Missouri as a slave state and Maine as a free state. His plan, the **Missouri Compromise**, kept the number of slave and free states equal.

Under the provisions of the Missouri Compromise, Congress drew an imaginary line extending the southern border of Missouri at latitude 36°30' N. Slavery was permitted in the part of the Louisiana Purchase south of that line. It was banned north of the line. The only exception was Missouri itself.

✓ READING CHECK **Check Understanding** Why did Missouri's application to join the Union as a slave state spark a crisis?

How Did Western Expansion Increase Tensions?

The Missouri Compromise applied only to the Louisiana Purchase. By 1846, however, there were rumblings of a war with Mexico, and the United States expected to gain vast new lands. Once again, the question of slavery in the territories arose.

The Wilmot Proviso Divides Congress Many northerners feared that the South would extend slavery into the West. Congressman David Wilmot of Pennsylvania called for a law to ban slavery in any territories won from Mexico. Southern leaders angrily opposed this Wilmot Proviso. They said that Congress had no right to ban slavery in the West.

The House passed the Wilmot Proviso in 1846, but the Senate defeated it.

Opposing Views As the debate over slavery heated up, people took sides. Abolitionists believed slavery was morally wrong and wanted it banned throughout the country. Southern slaveholders thought that slavery should be allowed in any territory. They also demanded that enslaved African Americans who escaped to the North be returned to them. Even white southerners who did not enslave African Americans generally agreed with these ideas.

Between these two extremes, some moderates argued that the Missouri Compromise line should be extended west all the way to the Pacific. Any new state north of the line would be a free state. Any new state south of the line could allow slavery. Other moderates felt that slavery should be allowed where it existed, but it should not be expanded to new territories.

Still others supported the idea of **popular sovereignty**, or the right of people to create their government. Under popular sovereignty, voters in a territory would decide for themselves whether or not to allow slavery.

✔ READING CHECK **Draw Conclusions** Why did the Missouri Compromise fail to solve the issue of slavery?

The Free-Soil Party Opposes Slavery in the West

By 1848, many northern Democrats and Whigs opposed the spread of slavery. However, with the presidential election ahead, leaders of both parties refused to take a stand for fear of losing southern votes. Some also feared that the slavery issue would split the nation.

In 1848, antislavery members of both parties met in Buffalo, New York. There, they founded the **Free-Soil Party**. The party's main goal was to keep slavery out of the western territories. Only a few Free-Soilers were abolitionists who wanted to end slavery in the South.

In the 1848 presidential campaign, Free-Soilers named former President Martin Van Buren as their candidate. Democrats chose Lewis Cass of Michigan. The Whigs selected Zachary Taylor, a hero of the 1848 Mexican-American War.

For the first time, slavery was an important election issue. Van Buren called for a ban on slavery in the Mexican Cession—the land ceded by Mexico after the 1848 war. Cass supported popular sovereignty. Taylor did not speak on the issue, but he was a slave owner from Louisiana, so many southern voters assumed that he supported slavery.

Analyze Images As Americans debated the issue of slavery, slave auctions, like this one in Virginia, continued in the South. **Infer** How did the slave system affect African American family life?

Presidential Election of 1848

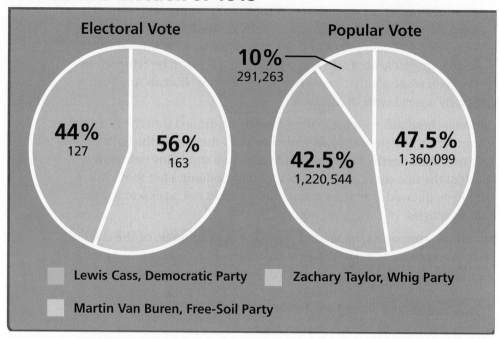

Electoral Vote

44% 127

56% 163

Popular Vote

10% 291,263

42.5% 1,220,544

47.5% 1,360,099

Lewis Cass, Democratic Party   Zachary Taylor, Whig Party

Martin Van Buren, Free-Soil Party

Analyze Graphs These graphs show the results of the 1848 presidential election. **Draw Conclusions** According to both pie graphs, what effect did Martin Van Buren's candidacy have on the other two candidates' electoral votes?

Zachary Taylor won the election. Still, Van Buren took 10 percent of the popular vote, and 13 other Free-Soil candidates won seats in Congress. The Free-Soil Party's success showed that slavery had become a national issue.

READING CHECK **Identify Central Issues** What was significant about the Free-Soil Party and the fact that slavery was a political issue for the first time?

California Reignites the Slavery Debate

For a time after the Missouri Compromise, both slave and free states entered the Union peacefully. However, when California requested admission to the Union as a free state in 1850, the balance of power in the Senate was once again threatened.

Conflict and Compromise In 1849, there were 15 slave states and 15 free states. Admitting California as a free state would upset the balance. Moreover, it seemed possible that Oregon, Utah, and New Mexico might also join the Union as free states.

Many southerners feared that the South would be hopelessly outvoted in the Senate. Some even suggested that southern states might want to **secede**, or remove themselves, from the United States. Northern congressmen, meanwhile, argued that California should enter the Union as a free state because most of the territory lay north of the Missouri Compromise line.

It was clear that the nation faced a crisis.

Conflicts Between Henry Clay and John C. Calhoun Henry Clay had won the nickname "the Great Compromiser" for working out the Missouri Compromise and the compromise Tariff of 1833, which **resolved** the Nullification Crisis. Now, decades later, the 73-year-old Clay was frail and ill. Still, he pleaded for the North and South to reach an agreement. If they failed to do so, Clay warned, the nation could break apart.

Senator John C. Calhoun of South Carolina had worked with Clay to pass the compromise Tariff of 1833, but now he opposed compromise over the extension of slavery to the West. He drafted a speech expressing his opposition.

Calhoun was dying of tuberculosis and could not speak loudly enough to address the Senate. He stared defiantly at his northern foes while Senator James Mason of Virginia read his speech.

Calhoun insisted that slavery be allowed in the western territories. In addition, he demanded that **fugitives**, or African Americans who had fled slavery, be returned to their owners. He wanted northerners to admit that slaveholders had the right to reclaim their "property."

Academic Vocabulary
resolve • v., to find an answer or solution to something

▼ The U.S. Senate debating California admission. ❶ Henry Clay thought northern and southern interests could be aligned. ❷ Daniel Webster feared the possibility of a civil war more than the spread of slavery. ❸ John C. Calhoun insisted on states' rights and preserving slavery.

Calhoun's demands were based on his belief in states' rights. He believed the federal government's power over the states was limited. As Calhoun saw it, states had chosen to give authority to the federal government; therefore, he believed, states had the right to decide how much authority to give, and they could cancel the agreement if they wished.

If the North rejected the South's demands, Calhoun told the Senate, "let the states . . . agree to part in peace. If you are unwilling that we should part in peace, tell us so, and we shall know what to do." Everyone knew what Calhoun meant. If an agreement could not be reached, the South would use force to leave the Union.

Daniel Webster Offers Compromise Daniel Webster of Massachusetts spoke next. He had opposed Clay's compromise Tariff of 1833. Now, he supported Clay's plea to save the Union. Webster stated his position clearly:

Primary Source

"I speak today not as a Massachusetts man, nor as a northern man, but as an American. . . . I speak today for the preservation of the Union. . . . There can be no such thing as a peaceable secession."

—Daniel Webster, Speech in the U.S. Senate, July 17, 1850

Webster opposed the concept of states' rights. He believed that in a union the federal authority was supreme. He feared that the states could not separate without suffering a bloody civil war. A **civil war** is a war between people of the same country.

Like many northerners, Webster viewed slavery as evil. The breakup of the United States, however, he believed was worse. To save the Union, Webster was willing to compromise. He would support southern demands that northerners be forced to return fugitives from slavery.

✔ READING CHECK **Check Understanding** Why did Daniel Webster, an avowed opponent of slavery, agree to support returning to their owners African Americans who had escaped slavery?

A Compromise Holds the Union Together

In 1850, as the debate raged, both Calhoun and President Taylor died. The new president was Millard Fillmore. Unlike Taylor, he encouraged Clay to seek a compromise.

The Compromise of 1850 Addresses Regional Concerns

Henry Clay gave more than 70 speeches in favor of a compromise. At last, Clay **proposed** the **Compromise of 1850**. By then, however, he had become too sick to continue. Stephen Douglas of Illinois took up the fight for him and guided Clay's plan through Congress.

Academic Vocabulary

propose • *v.*, to suggest something for people to consider

The Compromise of 1850 had five main provisions. First, it allowed California to enter the Union as a free state. There would be 16 free states and 15 slave states. Second, it divided the rest of the Mexican Cession into the territories of New Mexico and Utah. Voters in each state would decide the slavery question by popular sovereignty.

Third, it ended the slave trade in Washington, D.C., the nation's capital. Congress, however, declared that it had no power to ban the slave trade between slave states. Fourth, it included a strict fugitive slave law. Fifth, it settled a border dispute between Texas and New Mexico.

The Fugitive Slave Act Helps the South The **Fugitive Slave Act** of 1850 replaced the Fugitive Slave Act of 1793, which slave owners believed was too weak. Under the 1793 law, many northerners had refused to cooperate with slave owners who were trying to capture escapees and return them to slavery. The new law required all citizens to help catch African Americans trying to escape slavery. People who let fugitives escape could be fined $1,000 and jailed.

The Fugitive Slave Act also set up special courts to handle the cases of runaways. Suspects were not allowed a jury trial. Judges received $10 for sending an accused runaway to slavery but only $5 for setting someone free. Lured by the extra money, some judges sent African Americans to the South whether or not they were runaways.

Northern Anger Over the Fugitive Slave Act The Compromise of 1850 had the effect of holding the union together for a while longer. However, the conflict between the North and the South over the issues of slavery and its expansion remained. Many in the North and in the South were not satisfied with the compromise.

Analyze Graphs The graphic shows some effects of the Compromise of 1850. **Infer** Based on the information in the circle graph, what can you infer about the reason congressional representatives from slave states agreed to the Compromise of 1850?

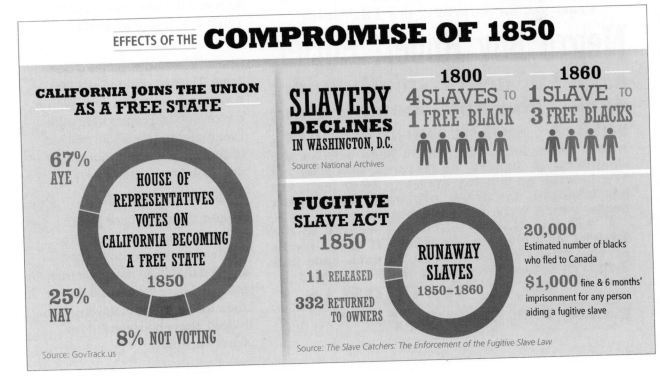

EFFECTS OF THE **COMPROMISE OF 1850**

CALIFORNIA JOINS THE UNION AS A FREE STATE

67% AYE

HOUSE OF REPRESENTATIVES VOTES ON CALIFORNIA BECOMING A FREE STATE 1850

25% NAY

8% NOT VOTING

Source: GovTrack.us

SLAVERY DECLINES IN WASHINGTON, D.C.

1800 — 4 SLAVES TO 1 FREE BLACK

1860 — 1 SLAVE TO 3 FREE BLACKS

Source: National Archives

FUGITIVE SLAVE ACT 1850

11 RELEASED

332 RETURNED TO OWNERS

RUNAWAY SLAVES 1850–1860

20,000 Estimated number of blacks who fled to Canada

$1,000 fine & 6 months' imprisonment for any person aiding a fugitive slave

Source: *The Slave Catchers: The Enforcement of the Fugitive Slave Law*

INTERACTIVE

The Fugitive Slave Act

Antislavery northerners were particularly angry about the Fugitive Slave Act. By forcing them to catch runaways, the law made northerners part of the slave system. Northerners found it harder to believe that slavery was a southern problem that they could ignore. In several northern cities, crowds protested by trying to rescue fugitives from their captors.

To counter the Fugitive Slave Act, many northern states passed personal liberty laws. These laws made it harder to recapture those accused of running away. The laws brought suspects before judges, provided jury trials, and prohibited kidnapping.

Some laws also gave legal assistance. One state, Vermont, declared free any enslaved person who entered the state. Southerners were outraged by these laws and called any interference with the Fugitive Slave Act unconstitutional.

Analyze Images This poster advertised a $100 reward for the capture and return of Robert Porter, who had escaped from enslavement. **Draw Conclusions** How did slavery affect people who lived in free states?

✓ **READING CHECK** **Generate Explanations** How did the Fugitive Slave Act of 1850 increase tensions between northerners and southerners?

A Book Sways the North Against Slavery

In 1852, Harriet Beecher Stowe of New England published a novel called *Uncle Tom's Cabin*. The novel shows the evils of slavery and the injustice of the Fugitive Slave Act.

100 DOLLS. REWARD.

RAN AWAY

From me, on Saturday, the 19th inst.,

Negro Boy Robert Porter, aged 19; heavy, stoutly made; dark chesnut complexion; rather sullen countenance, with a down look; face large; head low on the shoulders. I believe he entered the City of Washington on Sunday evening, 20th inst. He has changed his dress probably, except his boots. which were new and heavy.

I will give **$50** if taken and secured in the District of Columbia, or **$100** if taken north of the District, and secured in each case and delivered before the reward shall be good.

Dr. J. W. THOMAS.

Pomunky P. O., Charles Co., Md.

A Powerful Story Appeals to Northerners Stowe told the story of Uncle Tom, an enslaved African American known for his kindness and piety. Tom's world is shattered when he is bought by the brutal Simon Legree. When Tom refuses to reveal the whereabouts of two runaways, Legree whips him to death.

The novel quickly became a best seller. The first printing of 5,000 copies sold out in two days. Within a year, 300,000 copies were sold. Eventually, the book sold millions of copies and was translated into dozens of languages.

Nationwide Reaction Is Mixed Although *Uncle Tom's Cabin* was popular in the North, southerners objected to it. They claimed that it did not give a true picture of slave life and did not show the good side of slavery. Indeed, Stowe had seen little of slavery firsthand.

Despite such objections, *Uncle Tom's Cabin* helped change the way northerners felt about slavery. No longer could they ignore slavery as a political problem for Congress to settle. More and more northerners now saw slavery as a moral problem facing every American. For this reason, *Uncle Tom's Cabin* was one of the most important books in American history.

Analyze Images This painting shows a family attempting to escape from slavery. **Use Visual Information** What do you imagine each of these people is thinking?

☑ READING CHECK **Check Understanding** What was the political significance of *Uncle Tom's Cabin*?

 **INTERACTIVE**

Uncle Tom's Cabin

☑ Lesson Check

Practice Vocabulary

1. What did it mean when the **Compromise of 1850** allowed **popular sovereignty** to decide the slavery question?

2. Why did both John C. Calhoun and Daniel Webster suggest that a **civil war** would result if a state tried to **secede**?

3. Who were African American **fugitives**?

Critical Thinking and Writing

4. **Understand Effects** What were the long-term effects of the Missouri Compromise?

5. **Compare and Contrast** the actions of Northern states to nullify the Fugitive Slave Act with the actions of Southern states to nullify the tariff of 1832.

6. **Writing Workshop: Consider Your Purpose** You will be writing an informative essay on the differences between the North and South before, during, and after the Civil War. In your 📓 Active Journal, describe what you will need to do to satisfy the requirements of the task.

🔍 Primary Sources

Harriet Beecher Stowe, *Uncle Tom's Cabin*

Stowe's 1852 novel brought attention across the North to the evils of slavery. In this excerpt, Simon Legree explains to a stranger how he treats enslaved people.

◄ Harriet Beecher Stowe

Reading and Vocabulary Support

① Here, *constitution* refers to the health or physical condition of a person.

② Why does Simon say he doesn't try to "make 'em hold out"?

③ *Repressed* means to hold in feelings and not express them.

④ What do you think *humane* means?

⑤ *Sanction* means to approve or consent to. How is the planter sanctioning slavery?

"I don't go for savin' ['em]. Use up, and buy more, 's my way; . . . and I'm quite sure it comes cheaper in the end;" and Simon sipped his glass.

"And how long do they generally last?" said the stranger.

"Well, donno; 'cordin' as their <u>constitution</u> ① is. . . . I used to, when I fust begun, have considerable trouble fussin' with 'em and trying to <u>make 'em hold out</u> ②,—doctorin' on 'em up when they's sick, and givin' on 'em clothes and blankets, and what not, tryin' to keep 'em all sort o' decent and comfortable. . . . Now, you see, I just put 'em straight through, sick or well. When one [of 'em's] dead, I buy another. . . ."

The stranger turned away, and seated himself beside a gentleman, who had been listening to the conversation with <u>repressed</u> ③ uneasiness.

"You must not take that fellow to be any specimen of Southern planters," said he. . . . "[T]here are also many considerate and <u>humane</u> ④ men among planters."

"Granted," said the young man; "but, in my opinion, . . . if it were not for your <u>sanction</u> ⑤ and influence, the whole system could not keep foothold for an hour. If there were no planters except such as that one," said he, . . . "the whole thing would go down like a millstone. It is your respectability and humanity that licenses and protects his brutality."

Analyzing Primary Sources

Cite specific evidence from the document to support your answers.

1. **Identify Implied Main Ideas** How might Simon's dialogue about his enslaved workers make readers feel about slaveholders and slavery?

2. **Explain an Argument** According to the young man, how did "considerate and humane" planters keep slavery from dying out?

3. **Determine Author's Purpose** Based on this excerpt, why did Stowe write this novel?

Growing Tensions

BOUNCE TO ACTIVATE ▶ **VIDEO**

GET READY TO READ

START UP

Why do you think people, such as these Border Ruffians in Kansas, were so determined in their support of slavery?

GUIDING QUESTIONS

- What were the goals and outcomes of the Kansas-Nebraska Act?
- How did the Dred Scott case impact the nation?
- Why was the Republican Party founded, and how did Abraham Lincoln emerge as its leader?

TAKE NOTES

Literacy Skills Identify Cause and Effect

Use the graphic organizer in your 📕 Active Journal to practice the vocabulary words.

PRACTICE VOCABULARY

Use the vocabulary activity in your 📕 Active Journal to practice the vocabulary words.

Vocabulary

Kansas-Nebraska Act

Border Ruffian

guerrilla warfare

Dred Scott v. Sandford

Republican Party

arsenal

treason

martyr

Academic Vocabulary

denounce

maintain

The Compromise of 1850 dealt mainly with the Mexican Cession lands. It did not change the slavery policies for lands that had been part of the Louisiana Purchase—policies set by the Missouri Compromise. However, the Compromise of 1850 caused some people to question whether the Missouri Compromise needed to be changed.

Slavery in Kansas and Nebraska

In January 1854, Senator Stephen Douglas introduced a bill to set up a government for the lands in the northwestern part of the Louisiana Purchase. This territory stretched from present-day Oklahoma north to present-day Canada, and from Missouri west to the Rockies.

Congress Chooses Popular Sovereignty Douglas knew that white southerners did not want to add another free state to the Union. He proposed that this large region be divided into two territories, Kansas and Nebraska. The settlers in each territory would decide the issue of slavery by popular sovereignty.

Kansas-Nebraska Act, 1854

KEY
- Free states and territories
- Slave states and territories
- Open to slavery by popular vote, Compromise of 1850
- Open to slavery by popular vote, Kansas-Nebraska Act, 1854

GEOGRAPHY SKILLS

The Missouri Compromise of 1820 prohibited slavery in territory north of the 36' 30' parallel.

1. **Locate** Which territories were opened to popular vote for slavery as a result of the Compromise of 1850?

2. **Analyze Information** How did the Kansas-Nebraska Act of 1854 conflict with the Missouri Compromise of 1820?

INTERACTIVE

The Effects of the Kansas-Nebraska Act

Douglas's bill was known as the **Kansas-Nebraska Act.** The Kansas-Nebraska Act seemed fair to many people. After all, the Compromise of 1850 had applied popular sovereignty in New Mexico and Utah. Southern leaders especially supported the Kansas-Nebraska Act. They expected slave owners from neighboring Missouri would move with their enslaved African Americans across the border into Kansas, and that in time, Kansas would become a slave state.

President Franklin Pierce, a Democrat elected in 1852, also supported the bill. With the president's help, Douglas pushed the Kansas-Nebraska Act through Congress.

The Kansas-Nebraska Act Ignites Sectionalist Disputes

Douglas did not realize it at the time, but he had lit a fire under a powder keg. Sectionalist arguments over slavery once again erupted, this time bringing the nation closer to civil war.

Many northerners were unhappy with the new law. The Missouri Compromise had already banned slavery in Kansas and Nebraska, they insisted. In effect, the Kansas-Nebraska Act would repeal the Missouri Compromise.

The northern reaction to the Kansas-Nebraska Act was swift and angry. Opponents of slavery called the act a "criminal betrayal of precious rights." Slavery could now spread to areas that had been free for more than 30 years.

READING CHECK **Check Understanding** Why did northerners consider the Kansas-Nebraska Act a betrayal?

Violent Clashes in Kansas

Kansas now became a testing ground for popular sovereignty. Stephen Douglas hoped that settlers would decide the slavery issue peacefully. Instead, proslavery and antislavery forces sent settlers to Kansas to fight for control.

Activists Populate Kansas Most of the new arrivals were farmers from neighboring states. Their main interest in moving to Kansas was to acquire cheap land. Few of these settlers owned enslaved African Americans. At the same time, abolitionists brought in more than 1,000 settlers from New England.

Proslavery settlers moved into Kansas as well. They wanted to make sure that antislavery forces did not overrun the territory. Proslavery bands from Missouri often rode across the border. These **Border Ruffians**, as they were called, battled the antislavery forces in Kansas.

Rival Governments in Kansas In 1855, Kansas held elections to choose lawmakers. Hundreds of Border Ruffians crossed into Kansas and voted illegally. They helped to elect a proslavery legislature.

The new legislature quickly passed laws to support slavery. One law said that people could be put to death for helping enslaved African Americans escape. Another made speaking out against slavery a crime punishable by two years of hard labor. Refusing to accept these laws, antislavery settlers elected their own governor and legislature. With two rival governments, Kansas was in chaos.

Analyze Images Angry citizens in Boston protested an 1854 court order to return Anthony Burns to slavery in Virginia. **Sequence** How did the Fugitive Slave Act lead to violence in the North?

Open Fighting in Kansas In 1856, a band of proslavery men, including the town sheriff, raided the town of Lawrence. Lawrence was known as an antislavery stronghold. The attackers destroyed the Free State hotel as well as private homes and smashed the press of a Free-Soil newspaper.

John Brown, an abolitionist, decided to strike back. Brown and his five sons had moved to Kansas to help make it a free state. He claimed that God had sent him to punish supporters of slavery.

Three days after the Lawrence attacks, Brown rode with four of his sons and two or three other men to a settlement on Pottawatomie (paht uh WAHT uh mee) Creek. In the middle of the night, they dragged five proslavery settlers from their beds and murdered them.

The killings at Pottawatomie Creek led to even more violence. Both sides engaged in **guerrilla warfare**, or warfare in which small, informal military groups use surprise attacks and hit-and-run tactics. By late 1856, more than 200 people had been killed. Newspapers started calling the territory "Bleeding Kansas."

✓ READING CHECK **Understand Effects** How did events in Kansas foreshadow the looming Civil War?

Violence Over Slavery Breaks Out in the Senate

Even before John Brown's attack, the battle over Kansas had spilled into the Senate. Charles Sumner of Massachusetts was the leading abolitionist senator. In one speech, the sharp-tongued Sumner **denounced** the proslavery legislature of Kansas. He then viciously criticized his southern foes, singling out Andrew Butler, an elderly senator from South Carolina.

Butler was not in the Senate on the day Sumner spoke. A few days later, Butler's nephew, Congressman Preston Brooks, marched into the Senate chamber. Using a heavy cane, Brooks beat Sumner until he fell, bloody and unconscious, to the floor. Sumner did not fully recover from the beating for three years.

Many southerners thought Sumner got what he deserved. Hundreds of people sent canes to Brooks to show their support.

To northerners, however, the brutal act was more evidence that slavery led to violence. The violence in the Senate was another warning that the nation was veering toward a civil war over slavery.

READING CHECK Draw Conclusions What does the violence in the Senate tell you about the mood of the country in the late 1850s?

How Did the Dred Scott Case Affect the Nation?

With Congress in an uproar, many Americans looked to the Supreme Court to settle the slavery issue and restore peace. In 1857, the Court ruled on a case involving an enslaved man named Dred Scott. Instead of bringing harmony, however, the Court's decision further divided the North and the South.

Dred Scott had been enslaved for many years in Missouri. Later, he moved with his owner to Illinois and then to the Wisconsin Territory, where slavery was not allowed. After they returned to Missouri, Scott's owner died. Antislavery lawyers helped Scott to file a lawsuit, a legal case brought to settle a dispute between people or groups. Scott's lawyers argued that, because Dred Scott had lived in a free territory, he had become a free man.

The Supreme Court Rules on *Dred Scott v. Sandford*

In time, the case reached the Supreme Court as *Dred Scott v. Sandford*. The Court's decision shocked and dismayed Americans who opposed slavery. First, the Court ruled that Scott could not file a lawsuit because he was a slave, not a citizen. Also, the Court's written decision clearly stated that enslaved persons were considered to be property.

The Court's ruling did not stop there. Instead, the Justices went on to make a sweeping decision about the larger issue of slavery in the territories. According to the Court, Congress did not have the power to outlaw slavery in any territory. This meant that the Missouri Compromise was unconstitutional.

Academic Vocabulary

denounce • v., to publicly say that someone or something is wrong or bad

INTERACTIVE

The Dred Scott Case

Analyze Images Dred Scott, who had once lived in a free territory, appealed for his freedom after his owner died. **Predict Consequences** How did the Supreme Court ruling against Dred Scott challenge the Missouri Compromise?

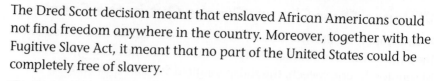

Quick Activity

How might an enslaved person planning an escape to the North have felt about the Dred Scott decision? Write a few sentences In your 📓 Active Journal examining this issue.

Academic Vocabulary

maintain • *v.*, to keep in an existing state

Analyze Images Frederick Douglass, who had once been enslaved, became a powerful spokesperson for abolition. **Infer** How do you think reactions to Frederick Douglass differed in the North and South?

The Dred Scott decision meant that enslaved African Americans could not find freedom anywhere in the country. Moreover, together with the Fugitive Slave Act, it meant that no part of the United States could be completely free of slavery.

The Democratic Party began to divide over the issue of slavery. The decision also increased support for abolition in the North.

Reactions to *Dred Scott v. Sandford* White southerners rejoiced at *Dred Scott v. Sandford*. It meant slavery was legal in all the territories.

African Americans responded angrily to the decision. In the North, many held public meetings to condemn the ruling. At one meeting in Philadelphia, a speaker hoped that the ruling would lead more whites to "join with us in our efforts to recover the long lost boon of freedom."

White northerners were shocked by the ruling. Many had hoped that slavery would eventually die out. Now, slavery could spread throughout the West. A newspaper in Cincinnati declared, "We are now one great . . . slaveholding community."

Abolitionist Frederick Douglass also spoke out against *Dred Scott v. Sandford*: "This infamous decision," he declared, "**maintains** that slaves . . . are property in the same sense that horses, sheep, and swine are property . . . that [people] of African descent are not and cannot be citizens of the United States." He told his listeners:

Primary Source

"All I ask of the American people is that they live up to the Constitution, adopt its principles, [take in] its spirit, and enforce its provisions. When this is done . . . liberty . . . will become the inheritance of all the inhabitants of this highly favored country."

—Frederick Douglass, *Collected Speeches*, 1857

☑ **READING CHECK** **Identify Main Ideas** What American values did the Dred Scott decision contradict?

The Republican Party Forms

By the mid-1850s, people who opposed slavery in the territories sought a new political voice. Neither Whigs nor Democrats, they maintained, would take a strong stand against slavery. "We have submitted to slavery long enough," an Ohio Democrat declared.

Birth of the Republican Party A group of Free-Soilers, northern Democrats, and antislavery Whigs gathered in Michigan in 1854. There they formed the **Republican Party**. While some Republicans hoped to completely abolish slavery throughout the country, the new party's main goal was to keep slavery from spreading to the western territories.

The Election of 1856 The new party grew quickly. In 1856, Republicans selected John C. Frémont to run for president. Frémont was a frontiersman who had fought for California independence. He had little political experience, but he opposed the spread of slavery.

Frémont's main opponent was Democrat James Buchanan of Pennsylvania. Many Democrats saw Buchanan as a "northern man with southern principles." Former President Millard Fillmore also ran as the candidate of the American, or "Know-Nothing," party. Fillmore, a strong supporter of the Union, feared that a Republican victory would split the nation apart.

Buchanan won the election with support from a large majority of southerners and many northerners. Still, the Republicans made a strong showing. Without the support of a single southern state, Frémont won one third of the popular vote. Southerners worried that their influence in the national government was fading.

READING CHECK Check Understanding Why was the Republican Party established in 1854?

Analyze Images American Party candidate Millard Fillmore separates Republican John Frémont (left) and Democrat James Buchanan (right) before they can harm one another. **Analyze Political Cartoons** What can you infer about Fillmore's view on sectional tensions?

▲ Abraham Lincoln had to teach himself to read by firelight.

How Did Abraham Lincoln Come to Lead the Republican Party?

The next chance for the Republican Party came in 1858 in Illinois. Abraham Lincoln, a Republican, challenged Democrat Stephen Douglas for his seat in the Senate. Because most Americans expected Douglas to run for president in 1860, the race captured the attention of the whole nation.

Lincoln's Early Career Abraham Lincoln was born on the Kentucky frontier. Like many frontier people, his parents moved often to find better land. The family lived in Indiana and later in Illinois. As a child, Lincoln spent only a year in school, but he taught himself to read.

After Lincoln left home, he opened a store in Illinois. There, he studied law on his own and launched a career in politics. He served eight years in the state legislature and one term in Congress.

Bitterly opposed to the Kansas-Nebraska Act, Abraham Lincoln decided to run for the U.S. Senate in 1858. When the race began, Lincoln was not a national figure. Still, people in Illinois knew him well and liked him. To them, he was "just folks"—someone who enjoyed picnics, wrestling contests, and all their favorite pastimes. His honesty, wit, and plain-spoken manner made him a good speaker.

Lincoln strongly opposed the Dred Scott decision and used his political platform to speak against it. In his "House Divided" speech, which he delivered upon being nominated for senator in 1858, he attacked the ruling. He expressed concern that popular sovereignty would lead to slavery throughout the country.

Lincoln continued to voice his opposition in debates with Stephen Douglas and later during his presidential campaign. He rallied Republicans to oppose the Court's decision.

Lincoln and Douglas Debate During the Senate campaign, Lincoln challenged Douglas to a series of debates. Douglas was not eager to accept, but he did. During the campaign, the question of slavery in the territories was the most important issue.

Douglas wanted to settle the slavery question by popular sovereignty, or a popular vote in each territory. He personally disliked slavery, but stated that he did not care whether people in the territories voted it "down or up."

Lincoln was not an abolitionist, either. He had no wish, he said, to interfere with slavery in the states where it already existed. And, like nearly all whites of his day, he did not believe in "perfect equality" between blacks and whites. He did, however, believe that slavery was wrong.

Primary Source

"There is no reason in the world why the negro is not entitled to all the natural rights [listed] in the Declaration of Independence, the right to life, liberty, and the pursuit of happiness. . . . In the right to eat the bread, without the leave of anybody else, which his own hand earns, he is my equal and the equal of Judge Douglas, and the equal of every living man."

—Abraham Lincoln, Speech at Ottawa, Illinois, August 21, 1858

Quest CONNECTIONS

Read the passage in the Declaration of Independence that explains the rights of all men. How do Lincoln's comments support the meaning expressed in the Declaration of Independence? Record your findings in your 📓 Active Journal.

Analyze Images In 1858, Abraham Lincoln and Stephen Douglas debated over the spread of slavery. **Draw Conclusions** What was the significance of the Lincoln-Douglas debates?

Since slavery was a "moral, social, and political wrong," said Lincoln, Douglas and other Americans should not treat it as an unimportant question to be voted "down or up." No one's liberty, he thought, should be subject to a popular vote, nor should it be decided by the sort of violence that arose in Kansas.

Lincoln Becomes a Leader Week after week, both men spoke nearly every day to large crowds. Newspapers reprinted their campaign speeches. The more northerners read Lincoln's words, the more they thought about the injustice of slavery.

In the end, Douglas won the election by a slim margin. Still, Lincoln was now known throughout the country. Two years later, the two rivals would again meet face to face—both seeking the office of president.

✓ READING CHECK Describe the contradiction in Lincoln's position on slavery.

John Brown Fights Slavery

In the meantime, more bloodshed inflamed divisions between the North and the South. In 1859, the radical abolitionist John Brown led a group of followers, including five African Americans, to the town of Harpers Ferry, Virginia.

There, Brown raided a federal **arsenal**, or weapons and ammunition warehouse. He thought that enslaved African Americans would join him there. He then planned to arm them and lead them in a revolt. No slave uprising took place, however. Instead, troops under the command of Robert E. Lee killed ten raiders and captured Brown.

John Brown's Raid Most people, in both the North and the South, thought that Brown's plan to lead a slave revolt was insane. First of all, there were few enslaved African Americans in Harpers Ferry to join a revolt. Furthermore, after seizing the arsenal, Brown did nothing further to encourage a slave revolt.

At his trial, however, Brown seemed perfectly sane. He sat quietly as the court found him guilty of murder and **treason**, or actions against one's country. Before hearing his sentence, he gave a moving defense of his actions. He showed no emotion as he was sentenced to death.

A Symbol of the Nation's Divisions Because he conducted himself with such dignity during his trial, Brown became a hero to many northerners. Some considered him a **martyr** because he was willing to give up his life for his beliefs. On the morning he was hanged, church bells rang solemnly throughout the North. In years to come, New Englanders would sing a popular song with the chorus: "John Brown's body lies a mold'ring in the grave, but his soul is marching on." When poet Julia Ward Howe heard the song, she was inspired to write the

Analyze Graphs The chart shows results of three votes in which slavery was a central issue. **Draw Conclusions** Did the Kansas-Nebraska Act influence the outcome of the Kansas election for territorial legislature in 1855? Explain.

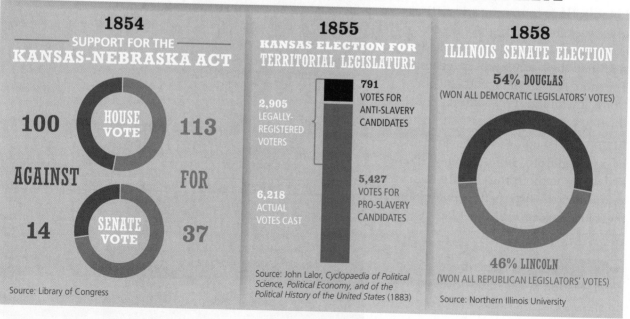

THE **CHANGING PERCEPTION** OF **SLAVERY**

1854
SUPPORT FOR THE
KANSAS-NEBRASKA ACT

100 AGAINST — HOUSE VOTE — 113 FOR

14 — SENATE VOTE — 37

Source: Library of Congress

1855
KANSAS ELECTION FOR TERRITORIAL LEGISLATURE

2,905 LEGALLY-REGISTERED VOTERS

6,218 ACTUAL VOTES CAST

791 VOTES FOR ANTI-SLAVERY CANDIDATES

5,427 VOTES FOR PRO-SLAVERY CANDIDATES

Source: John Lalor, *Cyclopaedia of Political Science, Political Economy, and of the Political History of the United States* (1883)

1858
ILLINOIS SENATE ELECTION

54% DOUGLAS
(WON ALL DEMOCRATIC LEGISLATORS' VOTES)

46% LINCOLN
(WON ALL REPUBLICAN LEGISLATORS' VOTES)

Source: Northern Illinois University

poem "The Battle Hymn of the Republic," which became a popular Civil War song set to the same tune.

To white southerners, the northern response to John Brown's death was outrageous. People were singing the praises of a man who had tried to lead a slave revolt. Many southerners became convinced that the North wanted to destroy slavery—and the South along with it. The nation was poised for a violent clash.

Analyze Images This illustration shows John Brown's band attacking the federal arsenal at Harpers Ferry. **Explain an Argument** Why did people say John Brown's raid was insane?

✔ READING CHECK **Check Understanding** Why were southerners outraged at the northern response to John Brown's execution?

☑ Lesson Check

Practice Vocabulary

1. Why was the **Republican Party** formed?

2. Why did a court decide John Brown had committed **treason**?

3. In what way was John Brown a **martyr**?

Critical Thinking and Writing

4. **Draw Conclusions** Some northerners were outraged by the passage of the Kansas-Nebraska Act. What did that outrage have to do with the location of the Kansas Territory?

5. **Summarize** the issue that was brought to the Supreme Court in *Dred Scott* v. *Sandford*.

6. **Identify Main Ideas** Neither Stephen Douglas nor Abraham Lincoln approved of slavery, so what disagreement did they have?

7. **Writing Workshop: Pick an Organizing Strategy** Begin thinking about how you will organize your essay on the differences between the North and South before, during, and after the Civil War. Take notes in your 📖 Active Journal.

Distinguish Relevant from Irrelevant Information

INTERACTIVE

Identify Evidence

Follow these steps to learn to distinguish relevant from irrelevant information.

1 Identify your focus or topic By clearly defining your topic, you can better determine which pieces of information will be relevant or irrelevant.

2 Locate sources and read about the topic Based on the topic you identified, select a number of sources that will likely offer information on this topic. You may find sources online or in your school's media center.

3 Identify the information that is relevant to your topic Scan your sources to find passages that may relate to your topic. Then, read these passages closely to determine whether or not they provide relevant information.

4 Identify the information that is irrelevant to your topic Irrelevant information, such as anecdotes, may be interesting, but not central to the topic. In the source, what passages are not relevant to the topic of attitudes toward popular sovereignty?

The letter below is historical fiction. In the letter, William, a farmer who had moved to Kansas Territory, writes to his brother Joseph in Vermont.

November 20, 1854

Dear Joseph,

I was pleased to receive your last letter. The success of your store is a great achievement. Our new farm continues to prosper and little Sarah has recovered from the fever that had sickened her for a month. Of course, the issue of the Kansas-Nebraska Act continues to trouble me. I do not agree with your support of Senator Stephen Douglas of Illinois; however, I enjoy reading his speeches. Those who oppose slavery, as I do, do not want that cruel system in place in a territory where it had been banned. Under the terms of the Kansas-Nebraska Act, it is up to the people to decide the issue peacefully by voting their hearts. Yet, settlers who are for and against slavery in the territory seem intent on using force, instead of the ballot box. The elections next year will settle the issue once and for all.

Your loving brother,

William

Division and the Outbreak of War

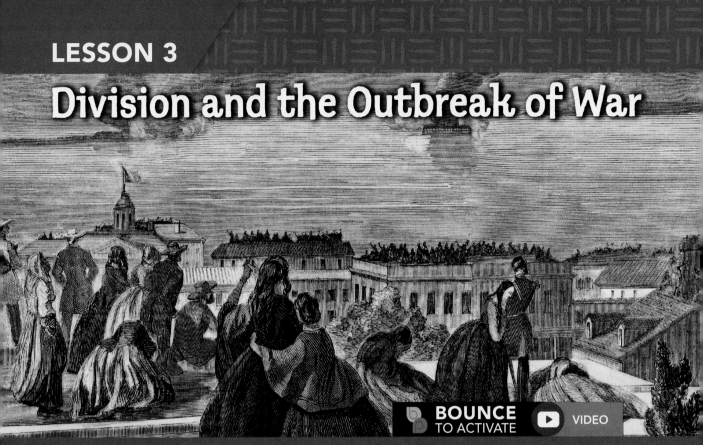

BOUNCE TO ACTIVATE   ▶ VIDEO

GET READY TO READ

START UP

Examine the civilians who have come to watch the bombardment of Fort Sumter. Why do you think these people have come, and what might they be thinking?

GUIDING QUESTIONS

- Why was there a Civil War?
- How did the 1860 election reflect sectional differences?
- Why did southern states secede from the Union following the election of 1860?
- What were the strengths and weaknesses of the North and South as the war began?

TAKE NOTES

Literacy Skills Compare and Contrast

Use the graphic organizer in your 🗐 Active Journal to take notes as you read the lesson.

Practice Vocabulary

Use the vocabulary activity in your 🗐 Active Journal to practice the vocabulary words.

Vocabulary

unamendable   border
acquiescence   state

Academic Vocabulary

comprise
conducive

The Republican National Convention for the presidential election of 1860 took place in Chicago, Illinois. Abraham Lincoln faced William Seward for the nomination. Seward was a U.S. senator for New York. Lincoln, whose fame had increased during the Lincoln-Douglas debates in 1858, won the nomination.

Why Did Abraham Lincoln Win the Election of 1860?

The Democrats held their convention in Charleston, South Carolina, where a lack of party unity proved costly. Southerners wanted the party to call for slavery in all new territories, but northern Democrats refused. In the end, the party split in two. Northern Democrats chose Stephen Douglas to run for president. Southern Democrats picked John Breckinridge of Kentucky.

Some Americans tried to heal the split between the North and the South by forming a new party. The Constitutional Union party chose John Bell of Tennessee to run for president. Bell was a moderate who wanted to keep the Union together.

Douglas was sure that Lincoln would win, but he believed Democrats "must try to save the Union." He urged southerners to stay with the Union, no matter who was elected.

When the votes were counted, Lincoln had won the election. He benefited from the division in the Democratic Party. Interestingly, southern votes did not affect the outcome, because Lincoln's name was not even on the ballot in ten southern states. Outnumbered and outvoted, many southerners lost hope that the national government would ever again serve their interests.

✓ READING CHECK Understand Effects How did the split in the Democratic Party in the 1860 election reflect the split in the country?

GEOGRAPHY SKILLS

The results of the 1860 election showed a nation deeply divided.

1. **Region** How did the electoral vote reflect sectional divisions?

2. **Synthesize Visual Information** Discuss with a partner: How might the election have turned out differently had Bell and Douglas not run for president?

A Move Toward Civil War

Lincoln's election brought a strong reaction in the South. A South Carolina woman described how the news was received:

Primary Source

"The excitement was very great. Everybody was talking at the same time. One . . . more moved than the others, stood up saying . . . 'No more vain regrets—sad forebodings are useless. The stake is life or death.'"

—Mary Boykin Chesnut, *A Diary From Dixie*, 1860

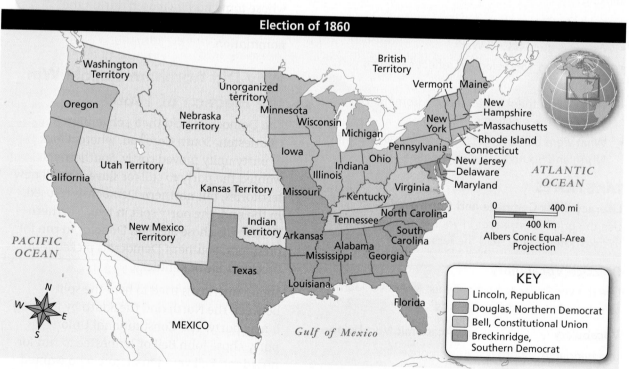

Election of 1860

KEY
- Lincoln, Republican
- Douglas, Northern Democrat
- Bell, Constitutional Union
- Breckinridge, Southern Democrat

Even before the election, South Carolina's governor had written to other southern governors. If Lincoln won, he wrote, it would be their duty to leave the Union. This sentiment revealed the strong currents of sectionalism running through the country. Many in the South felt stronger ties to their region than to the nation.

Secessionists leaving the Union.

The Nation Splits Senator John Crittenden of Kentucky made a last effort to save the Union. In December 1860, he proposed a package of legislation that he said would forever guarantee slavery south of the Missouri Compromise line and prohibit it north of the line. His proposal included a Constitutional amendment that he said would be **unamendable**, one that could not be changed.

The Crittenden Compromise received little support. Slavery in the West was no longer the issue. Many southerners believed the North had put an abolitionist in the White House and that secession was now their only choice. Most Republicans also were unwilling to surrender what they had won in the national election.

On December 20, 1860, South Carolina became the first state to secede. By late February 1861, Alabama, Florida, Georgia, Louisiana, Mississippi, and Texas had also seceded.

At a convention in Montgomery, Alabama, the seven states formed a new nation, the Confederate States of America. Jefferson Davis of Mississippi became its first president.

Causes Leading to War Now a new issue emerged: Did the Constitution allow states to secede? Most white southerners believed they had the right to secede. After all, the Declaration of Independence said that "it is the right of the people to alter or to abolish" a government that denies the rights of its citizens. Lincoln, they believed, would deny them the right to force African Americans to live and work as slaves.

For many southerners, secession was an issue of states' rights. According to this view, the Constitution created a Union **comprised** of sovereign states, and each state had the authority to make decisions without interference from the federal government. Any state could decide to leave the Union at any point and to join with others to form a new government, such as the Confederacy.

Lincoln disagreed. He maintained that the Constitution shared powers between national and state governments, but did not give states sovereignty that would allow them to secede. The causes of the looming Civil War thus included sectionalism, disagreement over slavery, and disagreement over the constitutionality of states' rights.

☑ READING CHECK Compare and Contrast the views of southerners and President Lincoln on the issues of state sovereignty and the right to secede from the Union.

Analyze Images In this cartoon, two secessionists are sawing off the branch of the tree upon which they are sitting. **Analyze Political Cartoons** What effect do you think the artist believes secession would have on the South?

Quest CONNECTIONS

The Declaration of Independence says people have the right to "alter or to abolish" a government. What does Lincoln say about this in his speeches? Record your findings in your 📓 Active Journal.

Academic Vocabulary
comprise • v., to be made up of

▲ Confederate troops, 1861

The Outbreak of War

When Lincoln took the oath of office on March 4, 1861, he faced a dangerous situation. Seven southern states had seceded from the United States and had joined together to form the Confederacy.

Lincoln's First Inaugural Address When he took office, Lincoln delivered an inaugural address. In the speech, Lincoln warned that "no state . . . can lawfully get out of the Union." Still, he pledged that there would be no war unless the South started it:

Primary Source

"In YOUR hands, my dissatisfied fellow-countrymen, and not in MINE, is the momentous issue of civil war. . . . We are not enemies, but friends. We must not be enemies. Though passion may have strained, it must not break our bonds of affection."

—Abraham Lincoln, First Inaugural Address, March 4, 1861

Lincoln's First Inaugural Address expressed ideas about union, liberty, equality, and government. Regarding union, Lincoln emphasized that the Constitution set limits on the actions of states, and that there was no provision in the Constitution for secession. That is, the Constitution required that the Union be preserved. On liberty, again, Lincoln emphasized that the states' liberty was constrained by their acceptance of the Constitution and did not include a right to secede.

Lincoln also stated his willingness to enforce the Fugitive Slave Act, but only if the liberty of free African Americans from kidnapping and enslavement could be ensured. Regarding equality, Lincoln assured Americans that he would provide government services and enforce federal law equally in all states, whether they were slave or free states.

Finally, Lincoln stated that government required **acquiescence**, or the willingness to accept laws whether or not a person agreed with those laws. The unwillingness of the South to accept his legal election under the Constitution, he implied, was a threat to government.

Jefferson Davis's Inaugural Address By the time Lincoln gave his address, the Confederate States of America had already sworn in Jefferson Davis as president. Davis's inaugural speech was very different from Lincoln's. Whereas Lincoln pledged to keep the Union together, Davis explained why the South had decided to secede from the Union. Davis said secession was based on "the desire to preserve our own rights and promote our own welfare."

Davis also said, "It is joyous, in the midst of perilous times, to look around upon a people united in heart, where one purpose of high resolve animates and actuates the whole—where the sacrifices to be made are not weighed in the balance against honor and right and liberty and equality."

For Davis, liberty and equality existed only between white men. Lincoln, in contrast, believed secession countered the principles of liberty and equality on which the nation was founded and its government was based. In a later speech, Lincoln would extend the idea of equality to all Americans.

Davis emphasized that government exists only with the consent of the governed. Since southerners no longer consented to this government, they had to break away and form a government to which they could consent. This was in contrast to Lincoln's argument that government sometimes requires citizens to acquiesce to, or obey, laws with which they disagree. He described secession as "the essence of anarchy."

Davis also argued that each state had the right to reclaim powers that it had given to the federal government. Lincoln disagreed. He argued that the Constitution was an agreement among all the states, and that no state could leave the Union without the agreement of the others.

Lincoln Faces War Lincoln said in his inaugural address that he did not want war, but Jefferson Davis had already ordered Confederate forces to begin seizing federal forts in the South. Lincoln faced a difficult decision. Should he let the Confederates take over federal property? If he did, he would seem to be admitting that states had the right to secede. Yet if he sent troops to hold the forts, he might start a civil war and lose the support of the eight slave states that had not yet seceded.

Analyze Timelines The timeline shows some important events that led up to the outbreak of the Civil War. **Identify Cause and Effect** How did the election of Lincoln as president contribute to the attack on Fort Sumter?

Events Leading Up to the Civil War

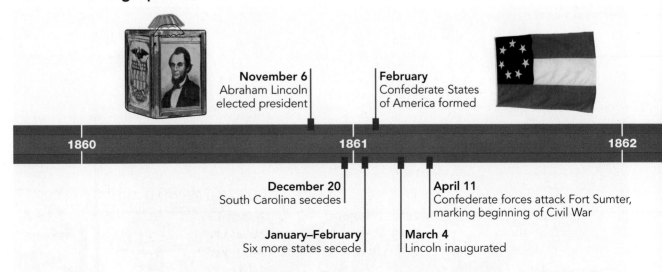

November 6
Abraham Lincoln elected president

February
Confederate States of America formed

1860   1861   1862

December 20
South Carolina secedes

April 11
Confederate forces attack Fort Sumter, marking beginning of Civil War

January–February
Six more states secede

March 4
Lincoln inaugurated

In April, the Confederacy forced Lincoln's hand. By then, Confederate troops controlled nearly all forts, post offices, and other federal buildings in the South. The Union held only three forts off the Florida coast and Fort Sumter in South Carolina. Fort Sumter was important to the Confederacy because it guarded Charleston Harbor.

Confederate Troops Attack Fort Sumter President Lincoln learned that food supplies at Fort Sumter were running low. He notified the governor of South Carolina that he was going to ship food to the fort. Lincoln promised not to send troops or weapons.

The Confederates refused to allow any shipments to the fort. On April 11, 1861, they demanded that Fort Sumter surrender. Major Robert Anderson, the Union commander, refused to give in, and Confederate guns opened fire. The Union troops quickly ran out of ammunition. On April 13, Anderson surrendered the fort.

The bombardment marked the start of the Civil War, which would last four terrible years, from 1861 to 1865.

✓ **READING CHECK** **Summarize** Lincoln's dilemma over southern states taking control of federal property.

How Did Americans Take Sides?

When the war began, each side was convinced that its cause was just. Southerners believed states had the right to leave the Union. In fact, they called the conflict the War for Southern Independence. White southerners wanted independence so that they could keep their traditional way of life—including the institution of slavery. They also believed the North had caused the war. Many southerners, therefore, also called it the War of Northern Aggression.

Northerners believed that they were fighting to save the Union. Abolishing slavery was not an official goal. In fact, many northerners,

Analyze Images This photograph shows one of a set of Civil War trading cards issued in 1887. **Identify Main Ideas** Why did Confederate troops attack Fort Sumter?

BOMBARDMENT OF FORT SUMTER.

Choosing Sides, 1860-1861

KEY
- Free Union states
- Border states (Slave states that stayed in the Union)
- Confederate states by April 1861
- States that joined the Confederacy after April 1861
- Territories

*Became a state in 1863

GEOGRAPHY **SKILLS**

1. **Location** Based on the map, why were Missouri, Kentucky, West Virginia, Maryland, and Delaware called border states?

2. **Analyze Maps** Based on the information in the map, approximately what percentage of Union states were slave states during the Civil War?

guided by feelings of racism, approved of slavery. Racism is the belief that one race is by nature superior to another.

In April 1861, eight slave states had not yet decided whether to remain in the Union. These states had more than half of the South's population and food crops and many of the South's factories. They would be important assets to whichever side they joined.

Four of these states—Virginia, North Carolina, Tennessee, and Arkansas—quickly joined the Confederacy. After some indecision, each of the four **border states**—Kentucky, Missouri, Maryland, and Delaware—decided to remain in the Union.

✅ READING CHECK **Understand Effects** Why were both the North and South trying to attract slave states outside the Confederacy to join their cause?

Strengths and Weaknesses of the North and South

Both sides during the Civil War had strengths and weaknesses. The South also had the advantage of fighting a defensive war. "We seek no conquest," said Confederate President Jefferson Davis. "All we ask is to be let alone." If the North did not move its forces into the South, the Confederacy would remain a separate country.

The South White southerners believed that they were fighting a war for independence, similar to the American Revolution. Defending their homeland and their way of life gave them a strong reason to fight. "Our men must prevail in combat," one Confederate said, "or they will lose their property, country, freedom—in short, everything."

Confederate soldiers also knew the southern countryside better. Friendly civilians aided them, often guiding soldiers along obscure roads that did not appear on maps.

The South, however, had serious weaknesses. These were the effects of economic and geographic differences between the North and the South.

The South had an agrarian, or farming, economy. Its fertile land, ample rainfall, and long growing season were **conducive** to growing cash crops, such as cotton and tobacco, rather than food crops.

Likewise, the South had few factories to produce weapons and other vital supplies, and few railroads to move troops and supplies. The railroads that it did have often did not connect to one another. Tracks simply ran between two points and then stopped.

The South had political problems as well. The Confederate constitution favored states' rights and limited the authority of the central government. As a result, the Confederate government often found it difficult to get things done. On one occasion, for example, the governor of Georgia insisted that only Georgian officers should command Georgian troops.

Analyze Graphs The graphic provides economic data comparing the North and the South at the start of the Civil War. **Compare and Contrast** Based on the information in the graphs, what advantages did the North have over the South?

Finally, the South had a small population of only 9 million people. Of these, one-third were enslaved African Americans. In comparison, the Union had 22 million people, including 3.8 million men of military age. In the South, just 1.1 million people were free men of military age, and it had to recruit 80 percent of them for the war. As a result, the South did not have enough people to serve as soldiers or to support the war effort.

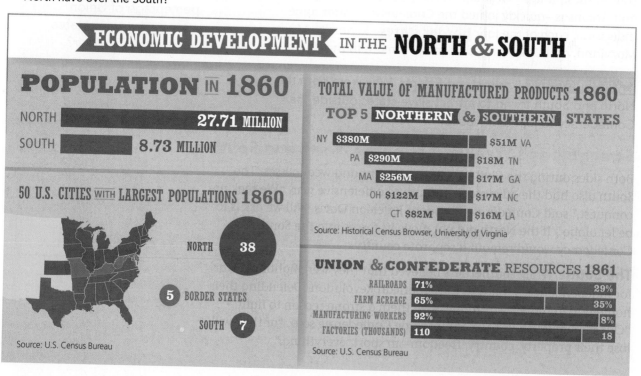

ECONOMIC DEVELOPMENT IN THE NORTH & SOUTH

POPULATION IN 1860

NORTH	27.71 MILLION
SOUTH	8.73 MILLION

50 U.S. CITIES WITH LARGEST POPULATIONS 1860

NORTH 38

5 BORDER STATES

SOUTH 7

Source: U.S. Census Bureau

TOTAL VALUE OF MANUFACTURED PRODUCTS 1860
TOP 5 NORTHERN & SOUTHERN STATES

NY	$380M	$51M	VA
PA	$290M	$18M	TN
MA	$256M	$17M	GA
OH	$122M	$17M	NC
CT	$82M	$16M	LA

Source: Historical Census Browser, University of Virginia

UNION & CONFEDERATE RESOURCES 1861

RAILROADS	71%	29%
FARM ACREAGE	65%	35%
MANUFACTURING WORKERS	92%	8%
FACTORIES (THOUSANDS)	110	18

Source: U.S. Census Bureau

Analyze Images As
these Union troops
marched through
Baltimore, Maryland,
on their way to defend
Washington, D.C.,
a pro-Confederate
mob attacked them.
**Identify Main
Ideas** What was the
significance of the
border states?

The North The North had many people to grow food and to work
in factories. But the war was unpopular among northerners, and
extremely high war casualties continued to make it unpopular.

The North's biggest advantage was its strong industrial economy.
Before the war, the North had ten times the industrial capacity of the
South. Once the war began, these factories began making guns, bullets,
cannons, boots, uniforms, and other supplies for the Union army. In
addition, the North had more than double the miles of railroad line,
which it used to transport both troops and supplies.

The geography of the North gave it another advantage. The prairie that
rolled from Ohio in the east to Iowa and beyond in the west produced
enormous food supplies. The South had nothing compared to it.

The North also benefited from a strong navy and a large fleet of
trading ships. With few warships and only a small merchant fleet, the
South was unable to compete with the North at sea.

The North had one other major advantage. West Point, the best
military academy in the country, was located in New York. While the
South had many West Point–trained officers, the Union could continue
to train officers throughout the war.

Despite these advantages, the North faced a difficult military challenge.
To force the South to rejoin the Union, northern soldiers had to conquer
a huge area. Instead of defending their homes, they were invading
unfamiliar land where their lines of supply would be long and open
to attack.

✓ READING CHECK **Summarize** how a weak economy and weak
industry can be problematic during wartime.

INTERACTIVE

Resources in the
North and South,
1860

Comparing Lincoln and Davis

Lincoln's Experience	Davis's Experience
• Self-taught lawyer • Eight years in Illinois state legislature • One term in U.S. Congress • Generally regarded as winner of Lincoln-Douglas debates	• Attended West Point Military Academy • Officer in the Mexican War • Secretary of War under President Pierce

Analyze Charts This chart compares the experience of Lincoln and Davis as they took office as presidents of the Union and Confederacy. **Cite Evidence** Why might people think Davis was better prepared than Lincoln to be president?

👆 INTERACTIVE

Abraham Lincoln and Jefferson Davis

How Did Lincoln and Davis Lead Their People?

Leadership was a crucial factor in the Civil War. President Davis, President Lincoln, and military leaders on both sides played key roles in determining the war's outcome.

Jefferson Davis Leads the South Many people had expected Davis to be a stronger leader than Lincoln. However, Davis did not want the presidency. As one observer stated:

Primary Source

"Mr. Davis's military instincts still predominate, and his eager wish was to have joined the army instead of being elected president."

—Arthur James Freemantle, from *The Freemantle Diary*

Davis's experience had prepared him for the position. He had attended the United States Military Academy at West Point and served as an officer in the Mexican-American War. Later, he was Secretary of War under President Franklin Pierce.

Davis was regarded as honest and courageous and was widely respected. However, he did not like to turn over to others the details of military planning. As a result, he spent much time worrying about small matters and arguing with advisers.

The Leadership Qualities of Abraham Lincoln At first, some northerners had doubts about Lincoln's ability to lead as President of the United States and commander-in-chief of the U.S. military. He had little experience in national politics or military matters. However, Lincoln proved to be a patient but strong leader and a fine war planner.

Day by day, Lincoln gained the respect of those around him. Many liked his sense of humor. They noted that Lincoln even accepted criticism with a smile. When Lincoln's Secretary of War, Edwin Stanton, called him a fool, Lincoln commented, "Did Stanton say I was a fool? Then I must be one, for Stanton is generally right, and he always says what he means."

The Role of Robert E. Lee, Military Leader As the war began, army officers in the South had to decide whether to stay in the Union army and fight against their home states, or join the Confederate forces.

Robert E. Lee of Virginia faced this dilemma when Lincoln asked him to command the Union army. He explained in a letter to a friend:

Primary Source

"If Virginia stands by the old Union, so will I. But if she secedes . . . , then I will still follow my native State with my sword and, if need be, with my life."

—Robert E. Lee, quoted in Carl Sandburg's *Abraham Lincoln*

Virginia did secede, and Lee refused Lincoln's offer. Later, Lee became commander of the Confederate army.

Many of the prewar United States Army's best officers served the Confederacy. As a result, President Lincoln had trouble finding generals to match those of the South.

Analyze Images This illustration shows how one artist imagined General Robert E. Lee of Virginia. **Infer** What impression of Lee do you think the artist was trying to convey?

☑ READING CHECK **Check Understanding** What advantages in leadership did the South have over the North?

Lesson Check

Practice Vocabulary

1. Why did Senator Crittenden say his proposed amendment on extending the Missouri Compromise line to the Pacific should be **unamendable**?

2. How were the **border states** different from the other states that stayed in the Union?

3. Why did Lincoln think government required **acquiescence**?

Critical Thinking and Writing

4. **Identify Main Ideas** What motivated the South to fight in the Civil War?

5. **Summarize** the principal disadvantages the North faced in fighting the Civil War.

6. **Writing Workshop: Develop Your Thesis** Begin to draft a thesis on the differences between the North and South before, during, and after the Civil War. Write your thesis in your 📓 Active Journal. You can revise your thesis statement as your essay develops.

Assess Credibility of a Source

Follow these steps to assess the credibility of a source.

INTERACTIVE

Analyze Primary and Secondary Sources

1 **Identify who created the source and when it was created**

   a. Who wrote and delivered the speech excerpted below?

   b. When was it delivered?

2 **Identify the topic** What is the main idea presented in this excerpt from the speech?

3 **Identify the facts, opinions, and possible inaccuracies or biases**

   a. What facts does Lincoln present in this speech?

   b. What opinions does he express?

   c. What inaccuracies or biases can you detect?

4 **Assess the credibility of the source**
When a source has credibility, it means it is believable and trustworthy. Are the ideas expressed by President Lincoln credible? Why do you think so?

Primary Source

On March 4, 1861, Abraham Lincoln delivered this speech at his first inauguration as President of the United States. Six weeks later, on April 12, the Civil War began.

Apprehension seems to exist among the people of the Southern States that by the accession of a Republican Administration their property and their peace and personal security are to be endangered. There has never been any reasonable cause for such apprehension. Indeed, the most ample evidence to the contrary has all the while existed and been open to their inspection. It is found in nearly all the published speeches of him who now addresses you. I do but quote from one of those speeches when I declare that—

I have no purpose, directly or indirectly, to interfere with the institution of slavery in the States where it exists. I believe I have no lawful right to do so, and I have no inclination to do so. . . .

[T]o the extent of my ability, I shall take care, as the Constitution itself expressly enjoins upon me, that the laws of the Union be faithfully executed in all the States. . . . I trust this will not be regarded as a menace, but only as the declared purpose of the Union that it will constitutionally defend and maintain itself.

— *President Abraham Lincoln, March 4, 1861*

The Course of War

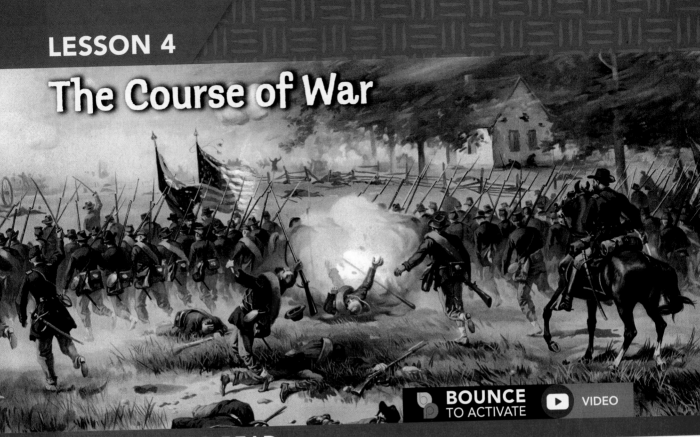

BOUNCE TO ACTIVATE   ▶ VIDEO

GET READY TO READ

START UP
How do you think fighting in battle would have changed a soldier's attitude toward the war? Write a few sentences expressing your ideas.

GUIDING QUESTIONS
- How was the Civil War conducted?
- How did the early battles of the war reflect broader patterns in the war?
- Which battles did the Confederacy and the Union win in the early years of the war?

TAKE NOTES
Literacy Skills Sequence
Use the graphic organizer in your 📓 Active Journal to take notes as you read the lesson.

PRACTICE VOCABULARY
Use the vocabulary activity in your 📓 Active Journal to practice the vocabulary words.

Vocabulary

Battle of Bull Run
Virginia
Monitor
Battle of Antietam

Battle of Fredericksburg
Battle of Chancellorsville
Battle of Shiloh

Academic Vocabulary

reluctant
demonstrate

As the war began, each side was confident that its strengths would lead it to victory.

How Did the Strategies of the North and South Differ?
The North and South had quite different strategies. The Union planned an aggressive, three-pronged campaign against the South.

The Union Strategy First, the Union planned to use its navy to blockade southern ports. This would cut off the South's supply of manufactured goods from Europe and its ability to earn money from cotton exports.

In the East, Union generals aimed to seize Richmond, Virginia, the Confederate capital. They thought they might end the war quickly by capturing the Confederate government.

In the West, the Union planned to seize control of the Mississippi River. This would prevent the South from using the river to supply its troops. It would also separate Arkansas, Texas, and Louisiana from the rest of the Confederacy.

Academic Vocabulary
reluctant • adj., not eager

🔘 **INTERACTIVE**

The Union's
Strategies to Win
the Civil War

The Confederate Strategy The South's strategy was simpler: The Confederate army would fight a defensive war until northerners tired of fighting. If the war became unpopular in the North, President Lincoln would have to stop the war and recognize the South's independence.

The Confederacy counted on European money and supplies. Southern cotton was important to the textile mills of England and other countries. Southerners thought that Europeans would recognize the Confederacy as an independent nation and that the South could continue to sell them cotton.

☑️ READING CHECK **Understand Effects** How was the Union plan for victory more aggressive than the Confederate plan?

Analyze Images Southern soldiers, like those shown here, prepared for a defensive war. **Identify Supporting Details** Why did the Confederates adopt a defensive strategy?

Early Battles

"Forward to Richmond! Forward to Richmond!" Every day for more than a month, the influential *New York Tribune* blazed this war cry across its front page. The Union army seemed **reluctant** to go on the offensive, however. At last, three months after the fall of Fort Sumter, Lincoln responded to public pressure and ordered an attack.

Stonewall Jackson Makes a Stand at Bull Run

The Confederate army was camped just 30 miles southwest of Washington, D.C. On July 21, 1861, Union troops set out from the nation's capital to attack the rebel forces. Hundreds of Washingtonians, in a festive mood, rode out along with the army to watch the battle. Many thought the Union army would crush the Confederates.

The Union troops had not gone far when they encountered Confederate troops near a small stream known as Bull Run, close by the town of Manassas, Virginia.

At first, Union forces succeeded in breaking up Confederate battle lines. "The war is over!" yelled some soldiers from Massachusetts. But General Thomas Jackson rallied the Virginia troops on a nearby hill. "Look!" cried a Confederate officer to his men, "There is Jackson standing like a stone wall! Rally behind the Virginians!"

From that day on, the general was known as "Stonewall" Jackson. Historians consider him one of the most gifted tactical commanders in the Civil War.

In the end, it was the Union troops who panicked and ran. "Off they went," reported one observer, "across fields, toward the woods, anywhere, everywhere, to escape."

The **Battle of Bull Run** (also referred to as the Battle of Manassas by the Confederates) showed how badly both Union and Confederate soldiers needed training. It also proved that the Confederate army could stand up to the Union, meaning the war would be long and bloody.

The Union Army Under George McClellan

Northerners were shocked by the disaster at Bull Run. Almost immediately, President Lincoln appointed General George McClellan as commander of the Union army of the East, known as the Army of the Potomac. McClellan was a superb organizer who transformed inexperienced recruits into battle-ready soldiers.

McClellan, however, was very cautious. Newspapers reported "all quiet along the Potomac" so often that the phrase became a national joke. President Lincoln lost patience. "If General McClellan does not want to use the army," the president snapped, "I would like to borrow it."

At last, in March 1862, McClellan and most of his troops left Washington. They sailed down the Potomac River and Chesapeake Bay and landed south of Richmond on the Virginia Peninsula. McClellan slowly moved toward the Confederate capital.

General Lee launched a series of counterattacks. At the same time, Lee sent Jackson north to threaten Washington, D.C. Lincoln was forced to retain troops in Washington to defend the capital. This prevented him from sending reinforcements to help McClellan. Cautious as usual, McClellan abandoned the attack and retreated. The Peninsula Campaign, as it became known, had failed.

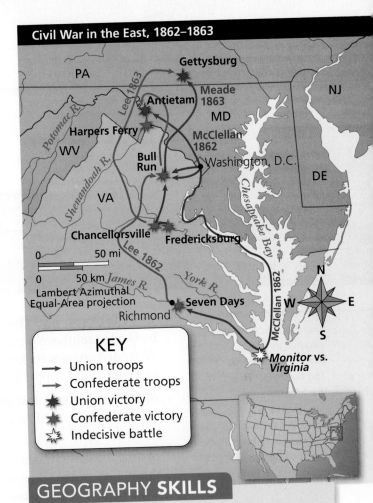

Civil War in the East, 1862–1863

KEY
→ Union troops
→ Confederate troops
✹ Union victory
✹ Confederate victory
☆ Indecisive battle

GEOGRAPHY SKILLS

This map shows the movement of troops and the major battles that took place from 1861 to 1862.

1. **Location** Using the scale of miles, measure the distance between the U.S. capital and the Confederate capital. How might the locations of the two capitals have influenced the battles and troop movements shown on the map?

2. **Synthesize Visual Information** Based on this map, which army seems to have had the advantage in the war during these years? Why?

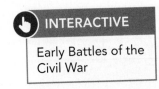

INTERACTIVE

Early Battles of the Civil War

Analyze Images The Confederate ship *Virginia* and the Union ship *Monitor* battled near Hampton Roads, Virginia, in 1862. **Draw Conclusions** The battle between the *Monitor* and the *Virginia* was a draw. What does this suggest about the advantages of ironclads?

Academic Vocabulary

demonstrate • *v.,* to prove something by being an example of it

Did you know?

In the 1970s, the USS *Monitor* was rediscovered 230 feet deep in the Atlantic Ocean. Some parts of the ship are now on display at the Mariner's Museum in Virginia.

The Blockade and the Ironclads Early in the war, Union ships blockaded southern ports. Because the South had few factories, it depended on imports for manufactured goods, such as weapons. A blockade could cripple the Confederate war effort.

At first, some small, fast ships slipped through the blockade. These "blockade runners" brought everything from matches to guns to the Confederacy.

In time, however, the blockade became more effective. Trade through southern ports dropped by more than 90 percent. The South desperately needed to break the Union blockade. One method it tried was the ironclad ship. *Clad* means *clothed*, or *covered*. Ironclad ships were covered with iron for protection.

Confederates modified an abandoned Union warship, the USS *Merrimack*. They covered it with iron plates and renamed it the **Virginia**. On its first day out in March 1862, the *Virginia* **demonstrated** the advantages of ironclads. It destroyed two Union ships and drove three more aground. Union cannonballs bounced harmlessly off the *Virginia's* metal skin.

The Union countered with its own ironclad, the **Monitor**. Soon, the two ships clashed near the mouth of Chesapeake Bay. This was the first time two ironclad warships battled one another.

Despite an exhausting battle, neither vessel seriously damaged the other, and both withdrew. Two months later, Confederates had to sink the *Virginia* when the Union captured Norfolk.

As ironclad ships became a standard part of naval forces, they changed naval warfare. The Union built 50 more ironclads during the Civil War and continued to build them for decades after. Other nations built them as well. They were later used in World War I.

Because of the North's ironclads, the South was never again able to mount a serious attack against the Union navy. The Union blockade held throughout the war.

The Battle of Antietam In September 1862, General Lee went on the offensive and marched his troops north into Maryland. He believed that a southern victory on northern soil would be a great blow to northern morale.

Luck was against Lee, however. At an abandoned Confederate campsite, a Union officer found a copy of Lee's battle plan. It was wrapped around three cigars, left behind by a careless general. General McClellan was overjoyed. "If I cannot whip 'Bobbie Lee,' I will be willing to go home," he boasted.

However, McClellan was slow to act. After a few days, he finally attacked Lee's main force near a creek called Antietam (an TEE tuhm) in the town of Sharpsburg, Maryland, on September 17. In the battle that followed, more than 23,000 Union and Confederate soldiers were killed or wounded—in one day. September 17, 1862, remains the bloodiest day in American military history.

On the night of September 18, Lee ordered his troops to slip back into Virginia. McClellan chose not to follow.

Neither side was a clear winner at the **Battle of Antietam** (also called the Battle of Sharpsburg by the Confederates). The battle was significant, however: Because Lee had withdrawn, the North was able to claim victory. As a result, northern morale improved. Still, President Lincoln was keenly disappointed. General McClellan had failed to follow up his victory by pursuing the Confederates. In November, Lincoln appointed General Ambrose Burnside to replace McClellan as commander of the Army of the Potomac.

✓ READING CHECK **Draw Conclusions** What conclusions can you draw from the first battles of the Civil War?

Analyze Images General George B. McClellan's Union forces met the Confederates at the Battle of Antietam. **Summarize** What was the significance of the Battle of Antietam?

Victories in the East for Confederate Forces

Two stunning victories for the Confederacy came in late 1862 and 1863. In December 1862, Burnside led Union forces once again toward Richmond. They soon confronted the Confederates outside Fredericksburg, Virginia. Lee's forces dug into the crest of a hill. There, in a strong defensive position, the outnumbered Confederates mowed down wave after wave of charging Union troops. The **Battle of Fredericksburg** was one of the Union's worst defeats. Soon after, Burnside was relieved of his command.

Half a year later, in May 1863, Lee, aided by Stonewall Jackson, again outmaneuvered Union forces. The **Battle of Chancellorsville** took place on thickly wooded ground near Chancellorsville, Virginia. Lee and Jackson defeated the Union troops in three days.

Victory came at a high price for the South, however. During the battle, nervous Confederate sentries fired at what they thought was an approaching Union soldier. The "Union soldier" turned out to be General Stonewall Jackson. Several days later, Jackson died, and the Confederacy lost one of its best generals.

Analyze Images These are some of the cannons used by Confederate forces. **Use Visual Information** Why were cannons dug into fortified positions?

☑ READING CHECK Draw Conclusions How might the Confederates have felt after the Battles of Fredericksburg and Chancellorsville?

Union Success in the West

In the West, Union forces had better results. As you have read, part of the Union strategy was to seize control of the Mississippi River. In February 1862, General Ulysses S. Grant attacked and captured Fort Henry and Fort Donelson in Tennessee. These forts guarded two important tributaries of the Mississippi.

Grant then pushed south to Shiloh, a village on the Tennessee River. There, on April 6, he was surprised by Confederate forces, who drove the Union troops back to the banks of the river.

Instead of retreating, Grant rushed reinforcements to the battle. That night, one of Grant's generals approached him. The officer thought Union forces should retreat. But, seeing Grant's stubborn face, the officer only said, "Well, Grant, we've had the devil's own day, haven't we?"

"Yes," Grant replied. "Lick 'em tomorrow, though."

And they did. On April 7, 1862, reinforcements arrived, and Grant's army beat back the Confederates and won the **Battle of Shiloh**. It was one of the bloodiest encounters of the Civil War. Because of the success at Shiloh, the Union was able to capture a crucial railroad crossing at Corinth.

Meanwhile, the Union navy moved to gain control of the Mississippi River. By June 1862, Union gunboats captured New Orleans, Louisiana, and Memphis, Tennessee. By capturing these ports, the Union controlled both ends of the southern Mississippi. The South could no longer use the river as a supply line.

Analyze Images General Ulysses S. Grant, pictured here, was Lincoln's most trusted general. **Draw Conclusions** How did individual personalities affect the conduct of the war?

☑ READING CHECK **Understand Effects** Why was the capture of Fort Henry and Fort Donelson critical to the Union's overall war strategy?

☑ Lesson Check

Practice Vocabulary

1. What was important about the *Virginia* and the *Monitor*?

2. What disaster happened at the **Battle of Chancellorsville**?

Critical Thinking and Writing

3. **Draw Conclusions** What can you conclude from the fact that spectators accompanied Union troops to Bull Run to watch the battle and were in a festive mood?

4. **Summarize** the problems that a successful blockade of southern ports would cause.

5. **Use Evidence** What do the battles and events that you have read about so far lead you to predict about the war?

6. **Writing Workshop: Support Thesis with Details** In your ▱ Active Journal, begin listing details about the differences between the North and South. You will use these details as you write the essay at the end of the Topic.

Emancipation and Life in Wartime

BOUNCE TO ACTIVATE ▶ VIDEO

GET READY TO READ

START UP

These men have just enlisted in the Union Army. Write three questions you would like to ask them.

GUIDING QUESTIONS

- How and why did the Civil War become a war to end slavery?
- In what ways did African Americans contribute to the Union war effort?
- What roles did women play in the war?

TAKE NOTES

Literacy Skills Summarize

Use the graphic organizer in your 📓 Active Journal to take notes as you read the lesson.

PRACTICE VOCABULARY

Use the vocabulary activity in your 📓 Active Journal to practice the vocabulary words.

Vocabulary

Emancipation Proclamation
54th Massachusetts Regiment
Fort Wagner

Copperhead
draft
habeas corpus
inflation
income tax

Academic Vocabulary

preliminary
essentially

The Civil War began as a war to restore the Union, not to end slavery. President Lincoln made this point clear in a letter that was widely distributed:

Primary Source

"If I could save the Union without freeing any slave, I would do it; and if I could save it by freeing all the slaves, I would do it; and if I could do it by freeing some and leaving others alone, I would also do that."

—Abraham Lincoln, August 22, 1862, quoted in Carl Sandburg, *Abraham Lincoln*

Lincoln's Emancipation Proclamation

Lincoln had a reason for handling the slavery issue cautiously. As you have read, four slave states remained in the Union, and the president did not want to do anything that might cause these states to join the Confederacy.

By mid-1862, however, Lincoln came to believe that he could save the Union only by broadening the goals of the war and emancipating, or freeing, the enslaved African Americans.

Lincoln Moves Slowly Lincoln knew that emancipation would weaken the Confederacy's ability to carry on the war. At the start of the war, Southerners held more than 3 million African Americans in slavery. They grew food that fed Confederate soldiers. They also worked in iron and lead mines that were vital to the South's war effort. Some served as nurses and cooks for the army.

However, Lincoln knew that many northerners opposed abolition. He hoped to introduce the idea of emancipation slowly, by limiting it to territory controlled by the Confederacy.

The President had another motive. Lincoln believed that slavery was wrong. When he felt that he could act to free enslaved African Americans without threatening the Union, he did so.

Lincoln needed a Union victory to announce his plan. He did not want Americans to think emancipation was a desperate effort to save a losing cause. On September 22, 1862, following the moderate success at Antietam, Lincoln announced a **preliminary** proclamation. He issued the formal **Emancipation Proclamation** on January 1, 1863.

The Emancipation Proclamation freed people enslaved in Confederate-held territory. It did not free enslaved African Americans in the four loyal slave states or those in Confederate lands that had already been captured by the Union, such as the city of New Orleans, Tennessee, and parts of Virginia.

Academic Vocabulary

preliminary • *adj.*, something that comes before or is introductory

GEOGRAPHY SKILLS

This map shows those parts of the United States that were under Union control and those parts that were controlled by the Confederacy in 1862.

1. **Interaction** Why might some southern regions have been exempted from the Emancipation Proclamation?

2. **Synthesize Visual Information** Where had the Union had its greatest successes?

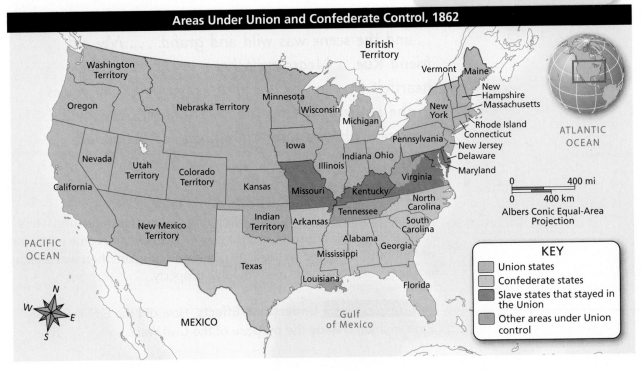

Areas Under Union and Confederate Control, 1862

British Territory

Washington Territory
Oregon
Nevada
California
Utah Territory
Colorado Territory
New Mexico Territory
Nebraska Territory
Minnesota
Wisconsin
Michigan
Iowa
Illinois
Indiana
Ohio
Kansas
Missouri
Kentucky
Indian Territory
Arkansas
Tennessee
Texas
Louisiana
Mississippi
Alabama
Georgia
Florida
South Carolina
North Carolina
Virginia
Pennsylvania
New York
Vermont
Maine
New Hampshire
Massachusetts
Rhode Island
Connecticut
New Jersey
Delaware
Maryland

ATLANTIC OCEAN
PACIFIC OCEAN
MEXICO
Gulf of Mexico

0   400 mi
0   400 km
Albers Conic Equal-Area Projection

N W E S

KEY
- Union states
- Confederate states
- Slave states that stayed in the Union
- Other areas under Union control

Analyze Images In this painting, Lady Liberty rides a chariot labeled EMANCIPATION, and Lincoln holds a scroll labeled PROCLAMATION.
Use Visual Information What does this painting say about the Emancipation Proclamation?

The Proclamation Changes the Purpose of the War Because the rebelling states were not under Union control, no African Americans actually gained their freedom on January 1, 1863. Still, the Emancipation Proclamation changed the war's purpose. Now, Union troops were fighting to end slavery as well as to save the Union.

The opponents of slavery greeted the proclamation with joy. Frederick Douglass witnessed a celebration in Boston:

Primary Source

"The effect of this announcement was startling . . . and the scene was wild and grand. . . . My old friend Rue, a Negro preacher, . . . expressed the heartfelt emotion of the hour, when he led all voices in the anthem, 'Sound the loud timbrel o'er Egypt's dark sea, Jehovah hath triumphed, his people are free!'"

—Frederick Douglass, *Life and Times of Frederick Douglass*

The proclamation also won the sympathy of Europeans, making it less likely that Britain or any other European country would come to the aid of the South. However, in the South, Lincoln's proclamation was seen as a "fiend's act" that destroyed valuable property.

✓ READING CHECK **Understand Effects** How did the Emancipation Proclamation change the purpose of the Civil War?

Why Did African Americans Fight for the Union?

When the war began, thousands of free African Americans volunteered to fight for the Union, but federal law forbade them to serve as soldiers. When Congress repealed that law in 1862, both free African Americans and African Americans who had escaped from slavery enlisted in the Union army.

Military Service The army assigned African American volunteers to all-black units, commanded by white officers. At first, the black troops served only as laborers. They performed noncombat duties such as building roads and guarding supplies. Black troops received only half the pay of white soldiers.

African American soldiers protested against this discrimination. Gradually, conditions changed. By 1863, African American troops were fighting in major battles. In 1864, the War Department announced that all soldiers would receive equal pay. By the end of the war, about 200,000 African Americans had fought for the Union. Nearly 40,000 lost their lives.

For the families of African American soldiers, the war was just as horrible as it was for the families of white soldiers. They struggled on without fathers, brothers, and sons. They worried if loved ones would come home.

Analyze Images This monument in Boston honors the 54th Massachusetts Regiment. **Draw Conclusions** Why were Union regiments segregated by race?

The 54th Regiment One of the most famous African American units in the Union army was the **54th Massachusetts Regiment**. The 54th accepted African Americans from all across the North. Frederick Douglass helped recruit troops for the regiment, and two of his sons served in it.

On July 18, 1863, the 54th led an attack on **Fort Wagner** near Charleston, South Carolina. Under heavy fire, troops fought their way into the fort before being forced to withdraw. Almost half the regiment was killed.

The courage of the African American regiments helped to win respect for African American soldiers. Sergeant William Carney of the 54th Massachusetts was the first of 16 African American soldiers to win the Congressional Medal of Honor in the Civil War. Secretary of War Stanton said such Union heroes had "proved themselves among the bravest of the brave."

Analyze Graphs The graph shows the numbers of free and enslaved African Americans in the North and in the South. **Use Evidence** Based on the information in the graph, approximately what percentage of enslaved African Americans from the South escaped to the North during the Civil War?

African American Population in the North and South, 1860

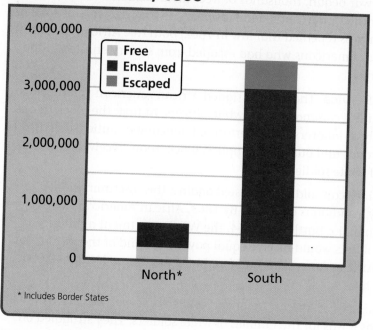

Free
Enslaved
Escaped

4,000,000

3,000,000

2,000,000

1,000,000

0

North*   South

* Includes Border States

Quick Activity

In your  Active Journal, explain how you can use a primary source to learn how the Civil War affected the lives of soldiers, African Americans, women, and others.

▶ INTERACTIVE

The Hardships of Soldiers

An Opportunity for Freedom Despite enslavement, many African Americans in the South contributed to the Union cause. To weaken the South's war effort, they worked more slowly or refused to work at all. They knew that when victorious Union troops arrived in their area, they would be free.

Thousands also took direct action to free themselves. Whenever a Union army moved into a region, enslaved African Americans fled across the Union lines to freedom. By the end of the war, about one-fourth of the South's enslaved population had escaped to freedom.

✓ READING CHECK **Identify Supporting Details** Why were many African Americans on plantations able to escape during the war?

The Horrors of War

On both sides, most soldiers were under the age of 21. As the death toll rose, age restrictions for soldiers were relaxed. The South drafted boys as young as 17 and men as old as 50. Boys learned to stand firm as cannon blasts shook the earth and bullets whizzed past their ears.

Soldiers drilled and marched for long hours. They slept on the ground even in rain and snow. Often their clothing was inadequate and uncomfortable. Many soldiers had no shoes, particularly in the Confederacy.

Outdated military tactics contributed to heavy casualties. For example, soldiers attacked in straight lines or bunched together. This made them easy targets for artillery and rifle fire.

Modern War Technology New technology added to the horror of war. Cone-shaped bullets and guns with rifling, or grooves cut on the inside of the barrel, made rifles twice as accurate. Improved cannons hurled exploding shells several miles and were much more deadly. Machine guns were introduced, and the first land mines brought unexpected horrors to war. Not surprisingly, soldiers began, for the first time, to dig trenches to escape gun and artillery fire. Even so, in most battles, one-fourth or more of the soldiers were killed or wounded.

Technology also brought the horror of modern warfare to civilians. Photographer Mathew Brady and his team of 20 battlefield photographers recorded the Civil War as had never before been done. Said one newspaper, "Mr. Brady has done something to bring home to us the terrible reality and earnestness of war."

The Civil War extended warfare into the skies and under water. Overhead, balloons gave commanders information about the enemy. It was the first war in which balloons were used extensively. At sea, submarines capable of sinking enemy ships were used for the first time.

Primitive Medical Technology Sick and wounded soldiers faced other horrors. Medical care was crude, especially on the battlefield. Surgeons routinely amputated injured arms and legs. Doctors did not know how germs cause infection and disease. As a result, minor wounds often became infected, and poor sanitary conditions in the army camps allowed disease to spread rapidly. Diseases such as pneumonia and malaria killed more men than guns or cannons did. Improper diet also caused sickness.

On both sides, prisoners of war faced horrifying conditions. At Andersonville, a prison camp in Georgia, many Union prisoners died of disease or starvation. The difficult life of soldiers led many to desert. One out of every seven Union soldiers and one out of every nine Confederate soldiers deserted.

✓ **READING CHECK** **Identify Main Ideas** How did disease affect Civil War troops?

 INTERACTIVE

Photography and the Civil War

Analyze Images This hospital was set up after the Battle of Fredericksburg. **Compare and Contrast** How does this battlefield hospital compare to a modern hospital?

PROVOST GUARD ATTACKING THE RIOTER'S

Analyze Images Rioters who opposed the draft law in New York City destroyed multiple buildings. **Identify Supporting Details** Why didn't all northerners support the war?

Other Challenges in the North and South

Many northerners opposed using force to keep the South in the Union. Supporters of the war called these people **Copperheads**, after the poisonous snake. Other northerners supported the war but opposed how Lincoln was conducting it.

Congress Imposes a Draft As the war dragged on, public support dwindled, and there was a shortage of volunteers for the Union army. In response, Congress passed a **draft** law in 1863. It required all able-bodied males between the ages of 20 and 45 to serve in the military if they were called.

A man could avoid the draft by paying $300 (about as much as an unskilled worker could earn in a year) or by hiring someone to serve in his place. Many people began to see the Civil War as "a rich man's war and a poor man's fight."

The Draft Leads to Riots Opposition to the draft led to riots in several northern cities. Because the law went into effect soon after Lincoln issued the Emancipation Proclamation, some white northerners believed that they were being forced to fight to end slavery. Many people in northern cities, especially recent immigrants, saw little reason for wanting slavery abolished. Freed African Americans, they thought, would compete with them for jobs and drive down wages. **Essentially**, they feared the draft would force them to fight against their self-interest.

Academic Vocabulary
essentially • *adv.,* basically, fundamentally, in essence

The worst riot occurred in New York City in July 1863. For four days, white workers attacked free African Americans along with rich New Yorkers who had paid to avoid serving in the army. At least 74 people were killed.

President Lincoln moved to stop the riots and other "disloyal practices." Several times, he suspended **habeas corpus** (HAY bee uhs KOR puhs), the right to be charged or have a hearing before being jailed. Lincoln argued that the Constitution allowed him to deny this right "when in the cases of rebellion or invasion, the public safety may require it." Eventually, nearly 14,000 people were arrested. However, most were never brought to trial.

A Draft Comes to the South President Jefferson Davis struggled to create a strong federal government for the Confederacy. Many southerners firmly believed in states' rights. They resisted paying taxes to a central government. At one point, Georgia even threatened to secede from the Confederacy.

Like the North, the South was forced to pass a draft law to fill its army. Men who owned or supervised more than 20 slaves were exempt. Southern farmers who had few or no slaves resented this law.

Near the end of the war, the South no longer had enough white men to fill the ranks. Desperate, the Confederate Congress enlisted enslaved African Americans in the military. The war ended, however, before more than a few thousand enslaved men fought for the Confederacy.

☑ READING CHECK **Identify** How did draft problems differ in the South and North?

Analyze Graphs As the war wore on, the Union blockade of southern ports began to have a greater and greater impact. **Summarize** Based on the information in the graph, what were the effects of the North blockading southern ports?

★ **BLOCKADE OF SOUTHERN PORTS** ★

$ PRICES $ FOR BASIC GOODS IN THE SOUTH
(IN CONFEDERATE DOLLARS)

Bacon	$8 a pound
Flour	$300 a barrel
Turkeys	$60 each
Milk	$4 a quart
Tea	$18 – $20 a pound
Sugar	$20 a pound

Source: *A Woman's Wartime Journal*

TRAVEL EXPENSES FOR ONE **ARMY OFFICER: RICHMOND TO ATLANTA, 1865**

March 11	Meal on the road	$20
March 20	Eyeglasses	$135
March 23	Coat, vest, pants	$2,700
March 30	Cavalry boots (1 pr)	$450
April 24	Matches	$25
April 24	Penknife	$125

Source: *The Nation: A Weekly Journal Devoted to Politics, Literature, Science, and Art,* Vol. 63

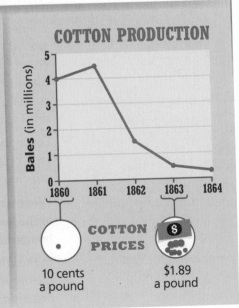

COTTON PRODUCTION

Bales (in millions)

1860 1861 1862 1863 1864

COTTON PRICES

10 cents a pound

$1.89 a pound

War Devastates the Southern Economy

The Civil War cost far more than any previous war. For the South, war brought economic ruin. The South struggled with the cost of the war, the loss of the cotton trade, and severe shortages brought on by the Union blockade.

A Weak Wartime Economy To raise money, the Confederacy imposed an income tax and a tax-in-kind. The tax-in-kind required farmers, who had little cash, to turn over one tenth of their crops to the government.

The South also printed paper money, which led to wild **inflation**. Inflation is a general rise in prices and a decrease in the value of money. By 1865, one Confederate dollar was worth only two cents in gold. In Richmond, a barrel of flour was $275 in early 1864, potatoes were $25 a bushel, and butter was $15 a pound.

Analyze Images This photo shows Charleston, South Carolina, in 1865. **Understand Effects** What would be the effects of such destruction across the South?

The war seriously damaged the cotton trade, the South's main source of income. Early in the war, President Davis halted cotton shipments to Britain. He offered to renew the shipments in exchange for Britain's support. But the tactic backfired when Britain bought its cotton from Egypt and India. Davis succeeded only in cutting the South's income.

The Union Blockade Creates Shortages The Union blockade created severe shortages in the South. Confederate armies sometimes waited weeks for supplies. With few factories of its own, the South bought many of its weapons in Europe. However, after the blockade cut off most deliveries, the Confederate government began building and running factories. Private manufacturers were offered contracts and draft exemptions for their workers if they produced war goods.

For civilians, the blockade brought food shortages. The production of food became critical to the economy. Many plantations switched from growing cotton to raising grain and livestock, or animals raised for food.

Widespread Destruction The impact of the war was everywhere in the South, where most of the fighting occurred. Many towns were bombarded. Homes and buildings were destroyed and burned.

In the countryside, trenches, defensive structures, cannon balls, and the debris of war spread across the land. Even where battles had not occurred, barns had been burned or stripped and fences torn down for firewood. Hungry armies destroyed fields of grain and seized livestock, mules, and other animals.

✓ **READING CHECK** **Identify Cause and Effect** What were the causes of wartime economic difficulties for the Confederacy?

How Did the War Affect the Northern Economy?

The Union used several strategies to pay for the war. In some ways, war helped the North's economy.

Taxation and Inflation To pay for the war, Congress established the nation's first **income tax**, or tax on people's earnings, in 1861. A new agency, the Internal Revenue Bureau, oversaw the collection process. The Union also issued bonds worth millions of dollars, and, like the Confederacy, it printed more than $400 million in paper money, which led to inflation. During the war, prices for goods nearly doubled in the North.

Economic Benefits of the War The war also helped the North's economy in several ways. As farmers went off to fight, there was a greater need for machines to plant and harvest crops. The purchase of reapers rose to nearly 165,000 during the war. As a result, farm production actually went up during the war.

The wartime demand for clothing, shoes, guns, and other goods helped many northern industries. Some manufacturers made fortunes by profiteering. Profiteers charged excessive prices for goods that the government desperately needed for the war.

✓ **READING CHECK** **Check Understanding** How did the Civil War strengthen the North's economy?

---

5 BIOGRAPHY Things to Know About **MARY EDWARDS WALKER**
Doctor during the Civil War (1832–1919)

- Walker served as assistant surgeon in battlefield hospitals for the Union Army.

- She was captured by the Confederate army and later exchanged for a Confederate prisoner of war.

- Walker lectured on women's rights, suffrage, and on reforming standards for acceptable female clothing.

- Walker did not support the suffrage amendment, saying women's right to vote was already included in the Constitution.

- She was the first woman to be awarded the Congressional Medal of Honor.

Critical Thinking Do you think Dr. Mary Walker was ahead of her time? Explain.

Women Contribute to the War Effort

Women in the North and South played vital roles during the war. As men left for the battlefields, women took over their jobs in industry and on farms. They also had to raise their families on their own.

In rare instances, some women disguised themselves as men and enlisted in the army. Others served as spies. Many served in army camps, choosing to accompany their husbands to war.

Women formed aid societies to help supply the troops with food, bedding, clothing, and medicine. Throughout the North, women held fairs and other fund-raising events to pay for supplies.

Analyze Images Clara Barton was one of the many women who cared for wounded soldiers at Union field hospitals. **Recognize Multiple Causes** How were women essential to the war effort?

Helping the Wounded Women on both sides worked as nurses. At first, doctors were unwilling to permit even trained nurses to work in military hospitals. When wounded men began to swamp army hospitals, however, this attitude changed. Women performed so well that nursing became an accepted occupation for women.

Dorothea Dix, famous for her work reforming prisons and mental hospitals, and Clara Barton, who later founded the American Red Cross, both became nurses for the Union army. Of her reasons for serving as a nurse, Clara Barton said, "What could I do but go with them [Civil War soldiers], or work for them and my country?" Mary Edwards Walker, an important advocate of women's rights, served as both a nurse and an assistant surgeon during the war.

Sojourner Truth, the African American antislavery leader, worked in Union hospitals and in camps for African Americans freed from slavery. In the South, Sally Tompkins set up a hospital in Richmond, Virginia.

☑ **READING CHECK** **Identify Main Ideas** What are some ways that women contributed to the war effort?

☑ Lesson Check

Practice Vocabulary

1. How did the **Emancipation Proclamation** change the purpose of the Civil War?

2. What did the **54th Massachusetts Regiment** accomplish at **Fort Wagner**?

3. What happens during a period of **inflation**?

Critical Thinking and Writing

4. **Draw Conclusions** Why did the roles of women change during the Civil War?

5. **Summarize** how the treatment of African American soldiers in the Union army changed as the war progressed.

6. **Writing Workshop: Write an Introduction** In your 📓 Active Journal, write an introduction to your essay about the differences between the North and South. Include your thesis statement in your introduction.

Abraham Lincoln, The Emancipation Proclamation

In 1863, in the midst of the Civil War, Abraham Lincoln believed it was necessary to give people more reasons to support the war. Until then, it had been about keeping the Union together. He chose to make it also about ending slavery.

▶ President Lincoln

That on the first day of January, in the year of our Lord one thousand eight hundred and sixty-three, all persons held as slaves within any State or designated ① part of a State, the people whereof shall then be in rebellion against the United States, shall be then, thenceforward ②, and forever free; and the Executive Government of the United States . . . will recognize and maintain the freedom of such persons, and will do no act or acts to repress ③ such persons, or any of them, in any efforts they may make for their actual freedom.

That the Executive will . . . designate the States and parts of States, if any, in which the people thereof, respectively, shall then be in rebellion against the United States; and the fact that any State, or the people thereof, shall on that day be, in good faith, represented in the Congress of the United States by members chosen thereto at elections wherein a majority of the qualified voters of such State shall have participated, shall, in the absence of strong countervailing testimony, be deemed . . . not then in rebellion against the United States.

Now, therefore I, Abraham Lincoln, President of the United States, . . . in time of actual armed rebellion against the authority and government of the United States, and as a fit and necessary war measure for suppressing ④ said rebellion, do. . . order and designate as the States and parts of States wherein the people thereof respectively, are this day in rebellion against the United States the following, to wit: Arkansas, Texas, Louisiana, . . . Mississippi, Alabama, Florida, Georgia, South Carolina, North Carolina, and Virginia.

Reading and Vocabulary Support

① *Designate* means "to name or point out for a particular purpose."

② What do you think the word *thenceforward* means?

③ *Repress* means "to control someone by force."

④ What does the word *suppressing* mean?

Analyzing Primary Sources

Cite specific evidence from the document to support your answers.

1. **Determine Author's Purpose** Why is Lincoln only freeing the slaves in certain states or parts of states?

2. **Summarize** According to Lincoln, what does a state have to do to prove it is not in rebellion?

3. **Cite Evidence** What reason does Lincoln give for freeing the enslaved people?

Quest CONNECTIONS

Read the passage in the Declaration of Independence that discusses the responsibility of governments to protect the safety and happiness of the people. How is that passage reflected in the Emancipation Proclamation? Record your findings in your 📓 Active Journal.

Recognize the Role of Chance, Oversight, and Error

INTERACTIVE

Interpret Sources

Follow these steps to recognize the role of chance, oversight, and error in shaping events.

1 Identify the topic When reading about an event, begin by focusing on what the passage is about. For example, is the passage about a military campaign or the rise of a new leader? Where did the event happen? Who were the key figures?

a. What event is the subject of Lee's letter?

b. What role did Lee play in the event?

2 Identify the goal or expected outcome Ask, "What was the leader trying to accomplish?" "What was expected to happen if everything had gone as planned?"

a. According to this letter, how did Lee expect the battle to progress?

b. What outcome did Lee expect?

3 Identify any unexpected outcomes As you consider the event or time period, ask, "Did events happen as the leader expected?" "Did something go wrong?" "Did key people achieve their stated goals?"

a. What happened that surprised Lee?

4 Analyze the cause of the unexpected outcomes Look for explanations for unexpected outcomes. Did something that nobody could have predicted go wrong—a storm or illness, for example? Did a person make a key mistake? Did someone forget some key step?

a. How did Lee explain what went wrong?

Primary Source

The following is a letter written by Confederate General Robert E. Lee to Jefferson Davis, president of the Confederacy.

Mr. President

Your note of the 27 [sic] enclosing a slip from the Charleston Mercury relative to the battle of Gettysburg is received. I much regret its general censure upon the operations of the army, as it is calculated to do us no good either at home or abroad. . . . No blame can be attached to the army for its failure to accomplish what was projected by me, nor should it be censured for the unreasonable expectations of the public. I am alone to blame, in perhaps expecting too much of its prowess & valor. . . . But with the knowledge I then had, & in the circumstances I was then placed, I do not know what better course I could have pursued. With my present knowledge, & could I have foreseen that the attack on the last day would have failed to drive the enemy from his position, I should certainly have tried some other course. What the ultimate result would have been is not so clear to me. Our loss has been heavy, that of the enemy's proportionally so. His crippled condition enabled us to retire from the country comparatively unmolested. The unexpected state of the Potomac was our only embarrassment.

— *Robert E. Lee, Letter to Jefferson Davis, July 31, 1863*

LESSON 6

The War's End

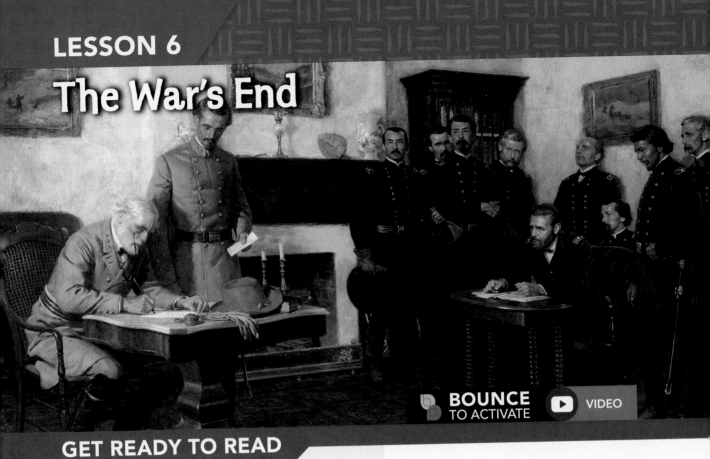

BOUNCE TO ACTIVATE

▶ VIDEO

GET READY TO READ

START UP

Lee (left) surrendered April 9, 1865. After all the bloodshed and destruction, how would the country heal? Write a few sentences stating your ideas.

GUIDING QUESTIONS

- How did the Civil War change the United States?
- What was the significance of Union victories at Vicksburg and Gettysburg?
- What was Grant's plan for ending the war?

TAKE NOTES

Literacy Skills Sequence
Use the graphic organizer in your 📕 Active Journal to take notes as you read the lesson.

PRACTICE VOCABULARY

Use the vocabulary activity in your 📕 Active Journal to practice the vocabulary words.

Vocabulary	Academic Vocabulary
siege	significant
Battle of Gettysburg	imply
Pickett's Charge	
Gettysburg Address	
Appomattox Court House	

Confederate armies won major battles at Fredericksburg in December 1862 and at Chancellorsville in May 1863. These were gloomy days for the North. Then, in July 1863, the tide of war turned against the South as Union forces won major victories in both the East and the West.

The Union Captures Vicksburg

In the West, by the summer of 1863, the Union had captured New Orleans and Memphis, giving them control of both ends of the southern Mississippi River. Still, the Confederates held Vicksburg, Mississippi.

Grant Targets Vicksburg Vicksburg was a crucial Mississippi River crossing, linking the eastern and western Confederate states. Vicksburg sat on a cliff high above the eastern shore of the river, which made it difficult to attack from the west.

Grant was desperate to capture Vicksburg, and the Confederates were desperate to keep it. Early in 1863, Grant's forces tried again and again but failed to seize Vicksburg.

At last, Grant devised a brilliant plan. Landing at an unguarded spot on the river, Grant marched inland eastward to launch a surprise attack on Jackson, Mississippi. Then, he turned back and attacked Vicksburg from the rear. On the side facing away from the river, no physical barriers protected Vicksburg.

The Siege of Vicksburg For more than six weeks, Grant's forces laid siege to Vicksburg. In a **siege**, a military force encircles an enemy position and blockades and bombards it in order to force it to surrender. Finally, on July 4, 1863, the Confederates surrendered Vicksburg.

On July 9, Union forces also captured Port Hudson, Louisiana, gaining control of the entire Mississippi River. The Confederacy was split in two. Cut off from the rest of the Confederacy, Texas, Arkansas, and Louisiana were no longer able to supply food, weapons, and other goods to the eastern Confederate states. This was a devastating blow.

☑ **READING CHECK** **Check Understanding** Why was Union control of the Mississippi River a blow to the Confederacy?

A Union Victory at Gettysburg

Meanwhile, in the East, after his victory at Chancellorsville, General Lee moved his army north into Pennsylvania. He hoped to take the Yankees by surprise. If he succeeded in Pennsylvania, Lee planned to swing south and capture Washington, D.C. The Union army followed the Confederates, making sure to remain between the Confederates and Washington.

The Battle Begins On June 30, 1863, the Union Army of the Potomac, now under command of General George C. Meade, met part of Lee's army at the town of Gettysburg, Pennsylvania. Both sides quickly sent in reinforcements. The three-day **Battle of Gettysburg** that followed was one of the most **significant** events of the Civil War.

On the first day of battle, July 1, the Confederates drove the Union forces out of Gettysburg. The Yankees, however, took up strong positions on Cemetery Ridge, overlooking the town. Union troops fortified these positions throughout the night.

The next day, Lee ordered an attack on both ends of the Union line, much of which was positioned on high ground, making the attacks difficult. Southern troops fought hard, but the Union army was well

Analyze Images For more than six weeks, General Grant's forces encircled Vicksburg, cutting off its supplies. **Synthesize Visual Information** Why did Grant circle around and approach Vicksburg from the East?

Academic Vocabulary
significant • *adj.*, very important

 **INTERACTIVE**

The Battle of Vicksburg

positioned. At the end of a day of savage fighting, Lee's forces had suffered heavy casualties but failed to dislodge the Union army.

Some of the Union's success lay in its use of the Spencer repeating rifle. It permitted soldiers to fire shot after shot very quickly. The Spencer became widely used by Union soldiers. The South lacked this technology. Rifles with similar repeating action became standard weapons in later wars.

A Disastrous Decision for the Confederacy Despite his losses, Lee attacked again. He wanted to "create a panic and virtually destroy the [Union] army." On July 3, he ordered General George Pickett to lead 15,000 men in a daring charge against the center of the Union line. This attack is known as **Pickett's Charge**. To reach their target, Pickett's men would have to march about 1,000 yards across sloping, open ground—all within clear view of the enemy.

When Pickett gave the order to charge, the Confederates marched forward, and Union guns opened fire. Row after row of soldiers fell to the ground, dead or wounded. The battle noise, one soldier recalled, was "strange and terrible, a sound that came from thousands of human throats . . . like a vast mournful roar."

Pickett's Charge failed. The steady barrage of bullets and shells kept all but a handful of Confederate soldiers from penetrating Union lines. The next day, a Union officer inspecting the battlefield found that "the dead and wounded lay too thick to guide a horse through them."

INTERACTIVE

The Battle at Gettysburg

Analyze Images
This photograph shows the cyclorama in the Museum and Visitor Center at Gettysburg National Military Park. **Explain an Argument** Why is it important to remember what happened at Gettysburg?

As the survivors limped back, Lee rode among them. "It's all my fault," he admitted gravely. Lee had no choice but to retreat. The Confederates would never invade the North again.

General Meade was proud of the victory. He had protected Pennsylvania and Washington, D.C. Lincoln, however, was disappointed. He felt that the Union army had once again allowed the Confederate troops to get away.

The Union victories at Vicksburg and Gettysburg marked the turning point of the Civil War. It seemed just a matter of time before the Confederacy would fall. However, the South was still determined to fight. The war would last another two years.

✓ READING CHECK Identify Main Ideas Why was the Union victory at Gettysburg significant?

Analyze Images This image shows President Lincoln with Union officers at a battlefield camp in 1862. **Draw Conclusions** What do Lincoln's visits to battlefields tell about him as a leader?

Academic Vocabulary

imply • v., to suggest without saying directly or plainly

Lincoln Delivers the Gettysburg Address

The Battle of Gettysburg left more than 50,000 dead or wounded. On November 19, 1863, there was a ceremony to dedicate a cemetery to the memory of those soldiers. President Lincoln delivered a speech now known as the **Gettysburg Address**. The speech exemplified Lincoln's leadership at a time of grief and crisis.

Lincoln said that the Civil War was a test of whether or not a democratic government could survive. This claim **implied** that the nation's survival depended on the integrity of the Union. He also reminded Americans that their nation was founded on the belief that "all men are created equal." Lincoln told the audience:

Primary Source

"We here highly resolve that these dead shall not have died in vain—that this nation, under God, shall have a new birth of freedom—and that government of the people, by the people, for the people, shall not perish from the earth."

—Abraham Lincoln, Gettysburg Address, November 19, 1863

Lincoln connected the phrases "all men are created equal," taken from the Declaration of Independence, and "a new birth of freedom." Coming so soon after the Emancipation Proclamation, this **implied** that equality for African Americans was a core purpose of the nation. While the entire speech was only ten sentences long and took about three minutes to deliver, it is still honored as a profound statement of American ideals.

✓ **READING CHECK** **Draw Conclusions** Lincoln said that the Civil War was a test. What was that test?

The Union Advances Into the South

Since the beginning of the war, Lincoln had searched for a general who could lead the Union to victory. More and more, he thought of Ulysses S. Grant.

General Grant Takes Charge General Ulysses S. Grant had led Union forces to victory at Shiloh. He developed an ingenious plan that led to the capture of Vicksburg. Then he continued to win battles in the West. In 1864, Lincoln appointed Grant commander of all Union forces. In this role, Grant would lead the final Union advance against the Confederacy.

Some questioned the choice of Grant, teasing that his initials stood for "Unconditional Surrender." But even back when Grant had been criticized for near disaster at the Battle of Shiloh, Lincoln had defended him: "I can't spare this man," Lincoln said. "He fights."

Grant's plan for ending the war was to destroy the South's ability to fight. To achieve this, Grant ordered his generals to wage total war. He wanted the Union army to destroy food, equipment, and anything else that might be useful to the enemy. At the start of the war, it was seen as an advantage of the Confederacy that the war would be fought on Southern soil, surrounded by Confederate supporters. Grant intended to turn this advantage into a liability. Confederate civilians would suffer hardship, and they would be unable to provide support to the military.

BIOGRAPHY

5 Things to Know About

ULYSSES S. GRANT
Commanding general of the Union army during the Civil War (1822–1885)

- A graduate of West Point, Grant served in the Mexican-American War under General Zachary Taylor.

- Grant resigned from the army in 1854 but rejoined at the start of the Civil War.

- President Lincoln appointed him General-in-Chief of the Union Army in 1864.

- Grant was elected 18th president of the United States, serving from 1869 to 1877.

- Near the end of his life, Grant wrote a memoir to pay off debts and provide for his family. It earned $450,000.

Critical Thinking In what ways do you think a military career prepares someone to be President?

Analyze Images Sherman's troops destroyed railroad tracks, farms, and other civilian property. **Infer** Why would Sherman order his troops to destroy civilians' property?

Sheridan Spreads Destruction in the Shenandoah To set his plan in motion, Grant sent General Philip Sheridan and his cavalry into the rich farmland of Virginia's Shenandoah Valley. He instructed Sheridan:

Primary Source

"Leave nothing to invite the enemy to return. Destroy whatever cannot be consumed. Let the valley be left so that crows flying over it will have to carry their rations along with them."

—Ulysses S. Grant, quoted in Bruce Catton, *Grant Takes Command*

In the summer and fall of 1864, Sheridan marched through the valley, destroying farms and livestock. His troops burned 2,000 barns filled with grain. There was nothing left for Lee's troops or for southern civilians.

Sherman's March to the Sea Grant ordered General William Tecumseh Sherman to capture Atlanta, Georgia, and then march to Savannah, on the Atlantic coast. Like Sheridan, Sherman had orders to destroy everything useful to the South. In Sherman's words, he would "make them so sick of war that generations would pass away before they would again appeal to it."

Sherman's troops captured Atlanta in September 1864. They began their campaign by turning the people of Atlanta out of their homes and burning a large part of the city. Then, Sherman began his March to the Sea.

As they marched through Georgia, Sherman's troops ripped up railroad tracks, killed livestock, and tore up fields. They burned barns, homes, bridges, and factories. Civilian lives were spared.

☑ **READING CHECK** **Summarize** Grant's concept of *total war.*

Contrasting Ideas of Liberty and Union

Lincoln ran for reelection in 1864. At first, his defeat seemed, in his own words, "exceedingly probable." Lincoln knew that many northerners were unhappy with his handling of the war.

The Democrats nominated General George McClellan to oppose Lincoln. They adopted a resolution demanding the immediate "cessation of hostilities" against the South. Although he had commanded the Union army, McClellan was willing to compromise with the Confederacy. If peace could be achieved, he would restore slavery.

Then, in September, Sherman took Atlanta, and the North rallied around Lincoln. Sheridan's victories in the Shenandoah Valley in October further increased Lincoln's popular support. In the election in November, the vote was close, but Lincoln remained President.

Lincoln's Second Inaugural In his Second Inaugural Address, Lincoln looked forward to the coming of peace:

Primary Source

"With malice toward none, with charity for all . . . let us strive . . . to bind up the nation's wounds . . . to do all which may achieve a just and a lasting peace among ourselves and with all nations."

—Abraham Lincoln, Second Inaugural Address

Lincoln's Second Inaugural Address, along with his First Inaugural and Gettysburg addresses, are landmark speeches in American history. Together, they present Lincoln's ideas about liberty, equality, union, and government.

In his First Inaugural, Lincoln emphasized the importance of the union of the states, which he viewed as "perpetual," or never-ending. In the Gettysburg Address, he emphasized the importance of maintaining the union of the country, especially since the country was based on freedom and equality. Lincoln's Second Inaugural highlighted slavery as a violation of equality and liberty, yet emphasized, again, the preservation of unity by urging people to "bind up the nation's wounds."

Analyze Images By the election of 1864, as this photograph clearly shows, the war had taken an emotional and physical toll on President Lincoln. **Draw Conclusions** What leadership qualities did Lincoln display?

Analyze Images Richmond, Virginia, shown here before (left) and after (right) the war, was the capital of the Confederacy. **Use Visual Information** What problems did the people of Richmond have to overcome after the war?

Two Contrasting Visions In Jefferson Davis's inaugural address, given four years earlier, the Confederate President had conveyed quite different views from Lincoln's. Davis explained the South's reasons for withdrawing from the Union as "a necessity, not a choice." Quoting the Declaration of Independence, Davis said:

Primary Source

"Our present condition . . . illustrates the American idea that governments rest upon the consent of the governed, and that it is the right of the people to alter or abolish governments whenever they become destructive of the ends for which they were established."

—President Jefferson Davis, First Inaugural Address, February 18, 1861

Lincoln had insisted in his First Inaugural Address that the Constitution required union. He had argued that "no state upon its own mere motion can lawfully get out of the Union." In the Emancipation Proclamation and the Gettysburg Address, Lincoln had extended the idea of liberty, enshrined in the nation's founding documents, to all Americans. While Lincoln's vision called for equality and liberty for enslaved African Americans, Davis called for the equality and liberty only of southern whites.

READING CHECK **Identify Main Ideas** What did the Union mean to Abraham Lincoln?

How Did the War Come to an End?

Grant began the drive to capture Richmond in May 1864. Throughout the spring and summer, he pursued Lee across eastern Virginia. Northerners read with horror that 60,000 men were killed or wounded in a single month at the Battles of the Wilderness, Spotsylvania, and Cold Harbor. Still, Grant pressed on with his Virginia Campaign. He knew that the Union could replace men and supplies. The South could not.

In June 1864, Lee dug in at Petersburg, near Richmond, and Grant began a siege. Nine months later, with a fresh supply of troops, Grant took Petersburg on April 2, 1865. The same day, Richmond fell.

The Confederacy Surrenders at Appomattox Lee withdrew his army to a small Virginia town called 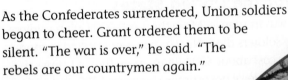**Appomattox Court House**. There, a week later, they were trapped by Union troops. Lee knew that his men would be slaughtered if he kept fighting. On April 9, 1865, Lee surrendered.

At Appomattox Court House, Grant offered generous terms of surrender. Officers were allowed to keep their pistols, and soldiers who had horses could keep them. Grant knew the animals would be needed for spring plowing. Finally, ordered Grant, "each officer and man will be allowed to return to his home, not to be disturbed by the United States authorities."

As the Confederates surrendered, Union soldiers began to cheer. Grant ordered them to be silent. "The war is over," he said. "The rebels are our countrymen again."

Honoring Those Who Served The war was over, but the people who lived through it would remember it all of their lives. On both sides, home towns honored returning veterans with ceremonies—even up to 75 years later.

During the war, President Lincoln had signed into law what would later become the Medal of Honor, the highest honor in the American military. Over 1,500 soldiers were awarded the Medal of Honor for their heroic actions during the Civil War.

INTERACTIVE

Key Battles of the Civil War

Analyze Images The Union Army took over this family's home in the town of Appomattox Court House, Virginia. There, Lee signed his formal surrender. **Understand Effects** How did the war affect civilians?

One Medal of Honor recipient was O.S. (ordinary seaman) Philip Bazaar, an immigrant from Chile who enlisted in the Union Navy. Although his rank was low, his actions proved him a hero. Bazaar earned the Medal of Honor carrying vital messages between commanders while serving on the USS *Santiago de Cuba* during the assault on Fort Fisher, North Carolina, on January 15, 1865:

Primary Source

"As one of a boat crew detailed to one of the generals on shore, O.S. Bazaar bravely entered the fort in the assault and accompanied his party in carrying dispatches at the height of the battle. He was 1 of 6 men who entered the fort in the assault from the fleet."

—Medal of Honor Citation for Philip Bazaar, June 22, 1865

Analyze Graphs The graphic organizer points out some of the immense costs that Americans paid for fighting the Civil War. **Analyze Data** Based on the information about the human costs of the war, which side had more casualties during the war?

☑ READING CHECK **Recall** What was significant about how General Grant treated Confederate soldiers after they surrendered?

A New Chapter for the United States

The cost of the Civil War was immense. More than 360,000 Union soldiers and 250,000 Confederate soldiers died. No war has ever resulted in more American deaths. The war cost about $20 billion, more than 11 times the entire amount spent by the federal government between 1789 and 1861.

★ COSTS OF THE CIVIL WAR ★

MONETARY COSTS (IN 1860 $)

$485.8 MILLION
Cost to state and local governments

$1.8 BILLION
Cost to the federal government

$3.4 BILLION
Total cost to the north

NORTH — Other costs

$1.48 BILLION
Loss in value of physical capital

$1 BILLION
Expenditures by the Confederate government and auxiliary state and local governments

$3.3 BILLION
Total cost to the South

SOUTH — Other costs

HUMAN COSTS

NORTHERNERS KILLED	360,000
NORTHERNERS WOUNDED	280,000
SOUTHERNERS KILLED	250,000
SOUTHERNERS WOUNDED	195,000

U.S. GROWTH VS. SOUTHERN AGRICULTURAL GROWTH
1874–1904

■ U.S. Gross National Product (GNP)
■ Gross Crop Output for the South

	1874–1884	1879–1889	1884–1894	1889–1899	1894–1904
GNP	2.79	1.91	0.96	1.15	2.30
Crop Output	1.57	1.14	1.51	0.97	0.21

POLITICAL COSTS

1864 to 1884 Republicans won **5 of 6** presidential elections:

1864	LINCOLN	Republican
1868	GRANT	Republican
1872	GRANT	Republican
1876	HAYES	Republican
1880	GARFIELD	Republican
1884	CLEVELAND	**Democrat**

Sources: *The Journal of Economic History,* Vol. 35, June 1975; *Explorations in Economic History,* Vol. 16, April 1979

The Civil War was a major turning point in American history. No longer would Americans speak of the nation as a confederation of states. Before the war, Americans referred to "*these* United States." After, they began speaking of "*the* United States." The idea that each state might secede if it chose was dead. At the same time, the power of the federal government grew.

The war also ended slavery in the United States. For years, Americans had debated whether slavery could exist in a nation dedicated to liberty and equality. By the war's end, millions of African Americans had gained their freedom. Millions more Americans, both northern and southern, began to think about what it meant to be free and equal.

To be sure, a long and difficult struggle for equality lay ahead. Yet, Lincoln's words at Gettysburg were prophetic: "We here highly resolve . . . that this nation, under God, shall have a new birth of freedom." From out of a cruel, bitter, heart-rending war, the United States emerged a stronger, freer nation.

 READING CHECK Identify Main Ideas In what ways was the Civil War significant?

Analyze Images The carnage of the Civil War forced Americans to invent a variety of contraptions for transporting the dead and wounded. **Identify Supporting Details** List the human costs of the war.

☑ Lesson Check

Practice Vocabulary

1. Why was Grant's attack on Vicksburg called a **siege**?

2. What were some of the main points of Lincoln's **Gettysburg Address**?

3. What occurred at **Appomattox Court House**?

Critical Thinking and Writing

4. **Use Evidence** What elements of total war do you see in General Sherman's March to the Sea?

5. **Identify Cause and Effect** How might General Lee's goal of capturing Washington, D.C., have led him to order Pickett's Charge at the Battle of Gettysburg?

6. **Writing Workshop: Draft Your Essay** Begin writing the essay about the differences between the North and South before, during, and after the Civil War. Use the details you have been gathering to develop your ideas. Write your paragraphs in your 📕 Active Journal.

VISUAL REVIEW

Major Events Leading to War

Missouri Compromise divided Louisiana Purchase into slave and free states	**Fugitive Slave Act** required citizens to capture runaways	**Compromise of 1850** admitted California as a free state	**Kansas-Nebraska Act** allowed settlers to decide slavery by popular sovereignty
IMPACT: Settled slavery issue in that territory	**IMPACT:** Made northerners feel they were supporting slavery	**IMPACT:** Kept Union from going to war	**IMPACT:** Opened territories to slavery; effectively repealed Missouri Compromise

Dred Scott* v. *Sandford established that African Americans could not be citizens	**John Brown's Raid** attacked a federal arsenal in Harpers Ferry	**Lincoln's Election** placed a northern Republican in the White House
IMPACT: No part of United States could be completely free of slavery	**IMPACT:** In the North, made Brown a martyr, won sympathy for the anti-slavery cause	**IMPACT:** Convinced southerners that they had no say in government

KEY EVENTS OF THE CIVIL WAR

Beginning	Middle	End
• Secession • Attack on Fort Sumter • Battle of Bull Run	• Battle of *Monitor* and *Virginia* • Battle of Antietam • Emancipation Proclamation	• Siege of Vicksburg • Battle of Gettysburg • Sherman's March • Virginia Campaign • Surrender at Appomattox Court House

READING REVIEW

Use the Take Notes and Practice Vocabulary activities in your 📓 Active Journal to review the topic.

INTERACTIVE

Practice vocabulary using the Topic Mini-Games

***Quest* FINDINGS**

Create Your Website

Get help for creating your website in your 📓 Active Journal.

ASSESSMENT

Vocabulary and Key Ideas

1. **Identify Main Ideas** How did the **Missouri Compromise** affect slavery in the territories?

2. **Recall** Why were many people in the North angry over the **Fugitive Slave Act**?

3. **Check Understanding** How did the court justify convicting John Brown of **treason**?

4. **Recall** How did the South's defeat at the **Battle of Gettysburg** affect the war?

5. **Identify Main Ideas** How did the **Emancipation Proclamation** treat the **border states** differently from the Confederate states?

6. **Identify Main Ideas** How did the Supreme Court's ruling in *Dred Scott* v. *Sandford* increase sectional tensions?

7. **Recall** What did General Grant do at **Appomattox Court House**?

Critical Thinking and Writing

8. **Compare and Contrast** What different views did John C. Calhoun and Henry Clay express during the conflict over the extension of slavery in 1850?

9. **Identify Main Ideas** How did economic issues during the war impact the North and the South?

10. **Identify Cause and Effect** How did states' rights help cause the Civil War?

11. **Revisit the Central Question** Was the North's participation in the Civil War justified?

12. **Writing Workshop: Write an Informative Essay** Complete writing the essay you have begun on the differences between the North and South before, during, and after the Civil War. Finalize your thesis and introduction. Revise the body paragraphs, using transitions to connect ideas. Then write a conclusion.

Analyze Primary Sources

13. Read the quotation. What does Lincoln most want to achieve?
    A. leave slavery just as it is
    B. keep the Union together
    C. free some enslaved persons
    D. free all enslaved persons

"If I could save the Union without freeing any slave, I would do it; and if I could save it by freeing all the slaves, I would do it; and if I could do it by freeing some and leaving others alone, I would also do that."

—Abraham Lincoln, August 22, 1862, quoted in Carl Sandburg, *Abraham Lincoln*

Analyze Maps

The map shows Union states in blue and Confederate states in gray. Use the map to answer the following questions.

14. Which states were the last to join the Confederacy?

15. For which side did Missouri fight during the Civil War? Why was it called a border state?

16. How many states made up the Confederacy? Which was the farthest west?

▼ **North and South, 1861–1865**

The Reconstruction Era (1865–1877)

Go back 150 years

to **THE RECONSTRUCTION ERA** following the Civil War. Why? The Union had survived, but big questions loomed: How would free African Americans fit into American society? How could the wounds of war be healed? How could the South be reconstructed?

Explore The Essential Question

How should we handle conflict?

The Reconstruction era was a time of uncertainty, distrust, and deep questioning. How did the United States find the answers?

Unlock the Essential Question in your 📓 Active Journal.

Read

how Americans met the challenges of the era and how the nation became one again.

Watch

 VIDEO

Born Into Slavery

Learn about life in slavery and the changes that came with emancipation.

The Reconstruction Era
(1865–1877)

Learn more about the Reconstruction Era by making your own map and timeline in your 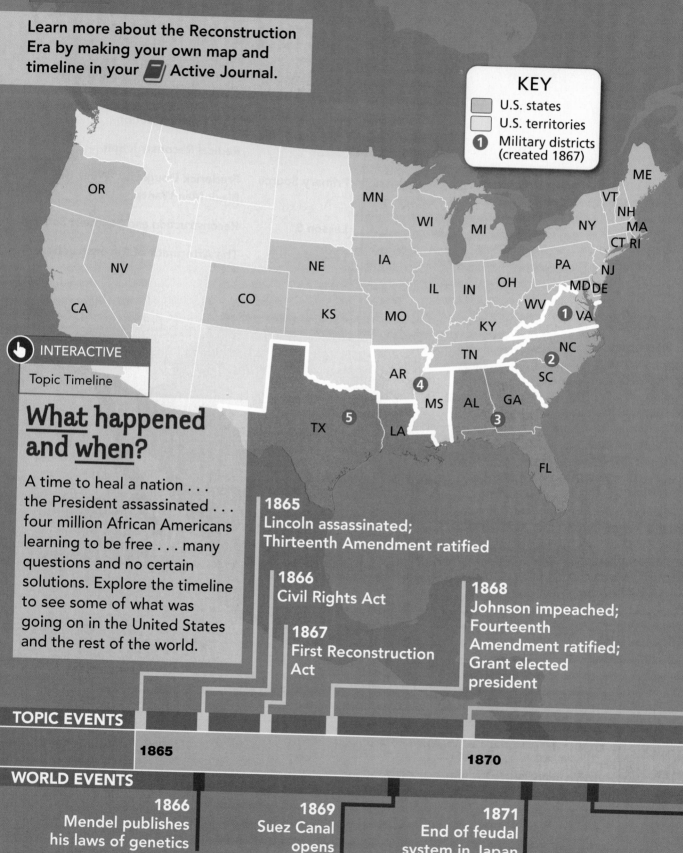 Active Journal.

KEY
- U.S. states
- U.S. territories
- 1 Military districts (created 1867)

INTERACTIVE

Topic Timeline

What happened and when?

A time to heal a nation . . . the President assassinated . . . four million African Americans learning to be free . . . many questions and no certain solutions. Explore the timeline to see some of what was going on in the United States and the rest of the world.

1865
Lincoln assassinated; Thirteenth Amendment ratified

1866
Civil Rights Act

1867
First Reconstruction Act

1868
Johnson impeached; Fourteenth Amendment ratified; Grant elected president

TOPIC EVENTS

1865

1870

WORLD EVENTS

1866
Mendel publishes his laws of genetics

1869
Suez Canal opens

1871
End of feudal system in Japan

Where did the Reconstruction Era have its greatest effect?

Reconstruction affected the whole nation, but its greatest impact was on the South. There, state governments had to be rebuilt, the states brought back into the Union, and a ruined economy restarted. And there were four million African Americans who had to discover life as a free people.

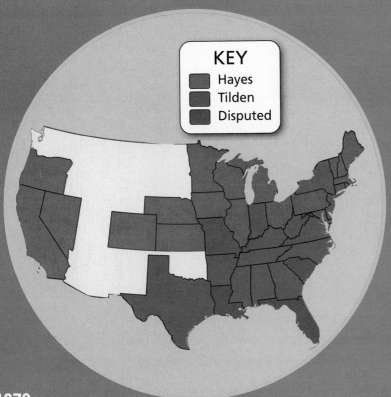

KEY
- Hayes
- Tilden
- Disputed

Who will you meet?

Andrew Johnson, president and opponent of strict Reconstruction

Thaddeus Stevens, representative and leader of the Radical Republicans

Blanche K. Bruce, U.S. senator born into slavery

1870
Fifteenth Amendment ratified

1876
Hayes-Tilden election

1875

1880

1872
Yellowstone—world's first national park

1876
Bell patents the telephone

549

Civic Discussion Inquiry

The End of Reconstruction

Quest KICK OFF

You are a leading scholar writing a multi-volume series on Reconstruction and its impact. Lately, you have been wrestling with a key question:

Should the United States have ended Reconstruction in 1877?

Be ready! Other historians will challenge your arguments. It's time to prepare!

1 Ask Questions

Get started by listing questions about the goals, the successes and failures, and the end of Reconstruction. Write the questions in your 📙 Active Journal.

2 Investigate

As you read this Topic, look for Quest Connections that provide information about Reconstruction. Collect your findings in your 📙 Active Journal.

3 Examine Sources

Next, explore primary sources that support differing viewpoints about Reconstruction. Capture notes in your 📙 Active Journal.

Quest FINDINGS

4 Discuss!

Next, prepare to discuss this question: Should the U.S. have ended Reconstruction in 1877? You will use your knowledge of Reconstruction as well as evidence from sources to make convincing arguments to support your answer.

▼ A Freedman's Bureau School classroom

Early Reconstruction

BOUNCE TO ACTIVATE ▶ VIDEO

GET READY TO READ

START UP

Examine this photograph showing the destruction suffered by the South. List three or four steps the South would have to take to begin rebuilding.

GUIDING QUESTIONS

- What economic, political, and social problems did the United States face after the Civil War?
- What steps were taken initially during Reconstruction?
- How did the assassination of Lincoln and the inauguration of a new President lead to conflict?

TAKE NOTES

Literacy Skills Identify Cause and Effect

Use the graphic organizer in your 📙 Active Journal to take notes as you read the lesson.

PRACTICE VOCABULARY

Use the vocabulary activity in your 📙 Active Journal to practice the vocabulary words.

Vocabulary		Academic Vocabulary
freedmen	Thirteenth Amendment	alternative
Reconstruction		intervene
amnesty		
Freedmen's Bureau		

At the end of the Civil War, the future looked bleak to many southerners. Across the South, cities and farms lay in ruins. All southerners, black or white, faced an unfamiliar new world. At the same time, a shattered nation had to find a way to become whole again.

The Effects of the Civil War

After four years of war, both northerners and southerners had to adjust to a changed world. The adjustment was far more difficult in the South.

Problems in the North Despite their victory, northerners faced a number of economic problems. Some 800,000 returning Union soldiers needed jobs. The government was canceling its war orders, and factories were laying off workers. Still, the North's economic disruption was temporary. Boom times quickly returned.

The North lost more soldiers in the war than the South did. However, only a few battles had taken place on northern soil.

Quest CONNECTIONS

What problems did the country face after the Civil War? What problems should Reconstruction be expected to solve? Record your findings in your ⬛ Active Journal.

INTERACTIVE

The Downfall of the Southern Economy

Analyze Images Like other major southern cities, Atlanta lay in ruins after the Civil War. **Use Visual Information** Examine the image and list the types of structures that were destroyed.

Northern farms and cities were hardly touched. One returning Union soldier remarked, "It seemed . . . as if I had been away only a day or two, and had just taken up . . . where I had left off." However, thousands of soldiers suffered wounds from the war, many of which included missing limbs and other painful injuries.

The North faced political problems, too. There was disagreement about how to bring the South back into the Union and what to do with newly freed African Americans. Many wanted to punish southerners for what they had done, while others wanted a more moderate approach.

Problems in the South Economic conditions in the South were far worse than in the North. Confederate soldiers had little chance of taking up where they had left off. In some areas, every house, barn, and bridge had been destroyed.

Two thirds of the South's railroad tracks had been turned into twisted heaps of scrap. The cities of Columbia, Richmond, and Atlanta had been leveled.

The war wrecked the South's financial system. After the war, Confederate money was worthless. People who had loaned money to the Confederate government were never repaid. Many southern banks closed, and depositors lost their savings.

The war changed southern society forever. Almost overnight, there was a new class of nearly four million people known as **freedmen**—men and women who had been freed from slavery. Under slavery, they could not own property or learn to read or write. What would become of them? How could the South cope with this drastic change?

These economic and social problems combined with political problems. It was unclear how the southern states would run their governments.

No legal systems were in place to protect African Americans, and many white southerners feared African Americans gaining political power. Also, many white politicians who had held office in the Confederacy were forbidden from politics.

Overall, the economic differences between the agrarian South and industrial North increased after the war. The northern economy picked up, while the South struggled to rebuild. Many southerners resented northerners coming in to "fix" southern problems. The ruined economy made recovery especially hard.

Environmental Damage from the War Because most of the fighting had been in the South, the region's physical environment suffered heavily from the war.

Many southern farms had become battlefields. Fields and buildings were destroyed, and battle debris littered the landscape. Other farms in the South were deliberately destroyed by Union troops.

Forests were destroyed as well. Soldiers cut down trees to build fortifications and campfires, and artillery and fires damaged other forests.

Animals also suffered. Mules and horses used in the war died by the thousands. Hungry soldiers captured livestock for food. Union soldiers killed the livestock they found as they swept through Georgia.

☑ READING CHECK **Summarize** the political, economic, and social difficulties faced by the South after the war.

Causes and Effects of Reconstruction

The era following the Civil War became known as **Reconstruction**, or the physical, political, and social rebuilding of the South. Lincoln wanted to make it easy for southerners to rejoin the Union. The sooner the nation was reunited, he believed, the faster the South could rebuild.

Lincoln's Plan for Reconstruction As early as 1863, Lincoln outlined his Ten Percent Plan for Reconstruction. Under this plan, a southern state could form a new government after 10 percent of its voters swore an oath of loyalty to the United States. The new government had to abolish slavery. Voters could then elect members of Congress and take part in the national government once again.

Lincoln's plan also offered **amnesty**, or a government pardon, to Confederates who swore loyalty to the Union. Amnesty would not apply to the former leaders of the Confederacy, however.

Analyze Images For this family, as for many other freedmen, life after emancipation still involved working in the fields for white people. **Draw Conclusions** After their emancipation, why did many freedmen continue to work as farm laborers?

 INTERACTIVE

Lincoln and Reconstruction

Quick Activity

What would a Congressional Republican in 1864 have said if asked why the Wade-Davis Bill was the best plan for Reconstruction?

Academic Vocabulary
alternative • *adj.,* offering a choice

Analyze Images
Freedmen's Bureau schools like this one aimed to provide skills needed for employment and civic life. **Infer** What do you think would be the most important skills and subjects to teach the former slaves?

Lincoln Rejects a Rival Proposal Many Republicans in Congress thought the Ten Percent Plan was too generous to the rebels. In 1864, they passed an **alternative** plan, the Wade-Davis Bill. It required a majority of white men in each southern state to swear loyalty to the Union. It also denied the right to vote or hold office to anyone who had volunteered for the Confederacy. Lincoln refused to sign the Wade-Davis Bill because he felt it was too harsh.

The Freedmen's Bureau Addresses Economic and Social Needs One month before Lee surrendered, Congress passed a bill creating the **Freedmen's Bureau**, a government agency to help former slaves. Lincoln signed the bill.

The Freedmen's Bureau gave food and clothing to former slaves. It also tried to find jobs for freedmen. The bureau helped poor whites as well. It provided medical care for more than one million people.

One of the bureau's most important tasks was to set up schools for freedmen. Most of the teachers were volunteers, often women from the North. Grandparents and grandchildren sat side by side in the classroom. Charlotte Forten, an African American volunteer from Philadelphia, wrote:

Primary Source

"It is wonderful how a people who have been so long crushed to the earth . . . can have so great a desire for knowledge, and such a capacity for attaining it."

—Charlotte Forten, article in the *Atlantic Monthly*

The Freedmen's Bureau laid the foundation for the South's public school system. It also created colleges for African Americans, including today's Howard University, Morehouse College, and Fisk University. Many graduates of these schools became teachers themselves. By the 1870s, African Americans were teaching in grade schools throughout the South.

✓ READING CHECK **Check Understanding** Why did President Lincoln want to make it easy for the South to rejoin the Union?

Abraham Lincoln Is Assassinated

President Lincoln hoped to persuade Congress to accept his Reconstruction plan. However, he never got the chance.

On April 14, 1865, just five days after Lee's surrender, President Lincoln attended a play at Ford's Theatre in Washington, D.C. A popular actor who supported the Confederate cause, John Wilkes Booth, crept into the President's box and shot Lincoln in the head. Lincoln died the next morning. Booth was later caught and killed in a barn outside the city.

The nation was plunged into grief. The assassination was significant because Lincoln was the first American President to be assassinated. Also, millions who had been celebrating the war's end now mourned Lincoln's death. His body was transported by train for burial in Springfield, Illinois, his hometown. Millions of Americans came to pay their respects along the route. "Now he belongs to the ages," commented Secretary of War Edwin Stanton.

Booth was part of a group of ten conspirators who had long been plotting to kill Lincoln, Vice President Andrew Johnson, and Secretary of State William Seward. None of the other assassinations took place, although Seward was attacked by one of the conspirators. Four of Booth's co-conspirators were hanged for their crimes, including Mary Surratt, the first woman executed by the United States.

READING CHECK Summarize the meaning behind Secretary of War Edwin Stanton's statement about Lincoln.

Analyze Images The first stage of Lincoln's funeral processed from the White House to the Capitol. **Compare and Contrast** How did Confederate and Union sympathizers feel about Lincoln's assassination?

Academic Vocabulary

intervene • *v.,* to interfere in order to stop or change something

President Johnson's Reconstruction Plan

Vice President Andrew Johnson was now President. Johnson had represented Tennessee in Congress. When his state seceded, Johnson had remained loyal to the Union.

The Thirteenth Amendment Changes Life in the United States

Republicans in Congress believed Johnson would support a strict Reconstruction plan. But his plan was much milder than expected. It called for a majority of voters in each southern state to pledge loyalty to the United States. Each state also had to ratify the **Thirteenth Amendment**, which banned slavery throughout the nation. (As you read, the Emancipation Proclamation did not free slaves in areas already under Union control.) Congress proposed the Thirteenth Amendment in January 1865. It was ratified in December that year.

The Thirteenth Amendment had a significant impact on life in the United States. Without slavery, the South developed new social and economic systems. Many newly freed African Americans were hired on plantations. Others moved to towns or to the North to find work. Many thousands searched for and reunited with the family members who had been torn away by slavery. For many, Reconstruction meant a chance to rebuild the kinship ties that slavery had severed. And African Americans founded churches, freeing them from another form of white dominance.

Politically, the amendment overturned previous state laws and Supreme Court decisions upholding slavery. The Thirteenth Amendment gave Congress the power to **intervene**, and later to pass additional legislation protecting civil rights.

Fighting in Congress

The southern states quickly met Johnson's conditions. While Congress was in recess, the President approved their new state governments in late 1865. Voters in the South then elected representatives to Congress. Many of those elected had held office in the Confederacy. For example, Alexander Stephens, the former vice president of the Confederacy, was elected senator from Georgia.

Analyze Images Although they had been freed, African Americans like this laborer had few opportunities and would struggle for many years to gain even the most basic civil rights. **Use Visual Information** What attitude does this man appear to express? Why do you think he posed for this picture?

Republicans in Congress were outraged. The men who had led the South out of the Union were being elected to the House and Senate. Plus, no southern state allowed African Americans to vote.

When the new Congress met, Republicans refused to let southern representatives serve. Instead, they set up a Joint Committee on Reconstruction to form a new plan for the South. The stage was set for a show-down between Congress and the President.

☑️ READING CHECK Compare and Contrast Which key difference between Lincoln's and Johnson's Reconstruction plans caused problems in 1865?

VIRGINIA ELECTIONS GEN: REBEL FOR CONGRESS. RE-UNION WITH THE U.S. GOVERNMENT

AN ACT TO SOUTHERN STATES

CONSTITUTIONAL AMENDMENT

PAROLE OF HONOR

THE VIRGINIA ELECTIONS.

PRESIDENT JOHNSON. "My good friend, don't sulk and swagger. We have done with all that. The United States mean no injustice to any man, white or black. They give you a chance. Let me advise you to use it wisely. Times have changed: if you can't change with them, the Government will help you."

Analyze Political Cartoons In this cartoon, President Johnson sympathizes with a former rebel while ignoring cruelty to a former slave. **Draw Conclusions** Which side of the debate between Johnson and Congress does the cartoonist support? How do you know?

☑️ Lesson Check

Practice Vocabulary

1. In what ways was **amnesty** an important part of **Reconstruction**?

2. Who were the **freedmen**, and what was the purpose of the **Freedmen's Bureau**?

3. What was the purpose of the **Thirteenth Amendment**?

Critical Thinking and Writing

4. **Identify Main Ideas** What problems did the South face after the Civil War that the North did not?

5. **Understand Effects** Why did Republicans in Congress refuse to let newly elected southern representatives take their seats?

6. **Writing Workshop: Generate Questions to Focus Research** You will be writing a research paper on the Freedmen's Bureau and its effects, and the restrictions placed on the rights and opportunities of African Americans in the Reconstruction-era South. In your 📓 Active Journal, write questions that will help you narrow your research on the topic.

LESSON 2
Radical Reconstruction

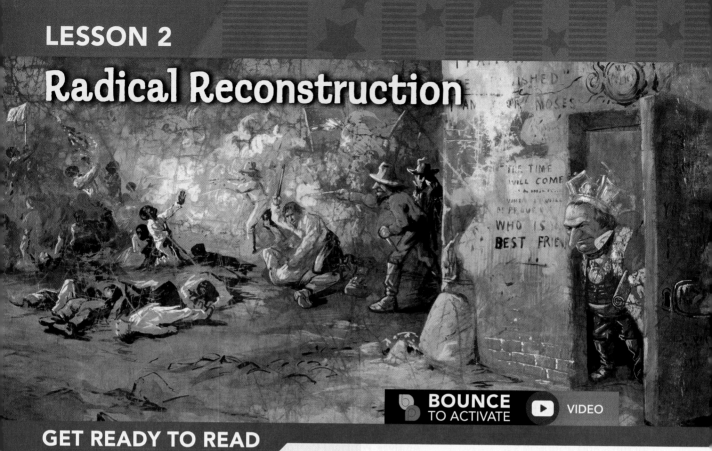

BOUNCE TO ACTIVATE   ▶ VIDEO

GET READY TO READ

START UP
According to the cartoon, what role did President Johnson (shown with a big, red nose) have in the 1866 New Orleans race riots?

GUIDING QUESTIONS
- How did Congress react to the black codes?
- Why was President Johnson impeached?
- How did Reconstruction redefine what it meant to be an American?

TAKE NOTES
Literacy Skills Identify Supporting Details
Use the graphic organizer in your 📓 Active Journal to take notes as you read the lesson.

PRACTICE VOCABULARY
Use the vocabulary activity in your 📓 Active Journal to practice the vocabulary words.

Vocabulary

		Academic Vocabulary
black codes	Reconstruction Act	capability
Radical Republicans	impeach	imposition
Fourteenth Amendment	Fifteenth Amendment	

Under Johnson's Reconstruction plan, most southern states promptly ratified the Thirteenth Amendment. However, southern legislatures also passed **black codes**, laws that severely limited the rights of freed African Americans. Their purpose was to preserve African Americans as an underclass and a source of cheap labor.

Continuing Conflict Over Reconstruction

The black codes did grant some rights. For example, African Americans could marry legally and own some kinds of property. Still, the codes were clearly meant to keep freedmen from gaining political and economic power.

Restrictions in the South Black codes forbade freedmen to vote, own guns, and serve on juries. In some states, African Americans were permitted to work only as servants or farm laborers. In others, they had to sign contracts for a year's work. Those without contracts could be arrested and sentenced to work on a plantation.

Reconstruction Turns Radical Republicans charged that Johnson's Reconstruction plan was so lenient that it had encouraged southern legislatures to pass the black codes. Republicans were also outraged by reports of violence against freedmen. In 1866, white police officers in Memphis, Tennessee, attacked African American Union soldiers, who fired back at the officers. A protest against the police ended in violence, and rioting broke out. Angry whites burned homes and schools in a black section of the city. Similar riots broke out in New Orleans when freedmen met to support the right to vote.

A report by the Joint Committee on Reconstruction accused the South of trying to "preserve slavery . . . as long as possible." When President Johnson ignored the report, members of Congress called **Radical Republicans** vowed to take control of Reconstruction.

INTERACTIVE

The Massacre of New Orleans

☑ READING CHECK **Understand Effects** Why were Radical Republicans outraged at President Johnson's approach to Reconstruction?

The Radical Reconstruction Congress

The Radicals were led by Thaddeus Stevens of Pennsylvania in the House and Charles Sumner of Massachusetts in the Senate. Radical Republicans had two main goals. First, they wanted to break the power of wealthy planters who had long ruled the South. Second, they wanted to ensure that freedmen received the right to vote.

Legislative Reform Radicals needed the support of moderate Republicans, the largest group in Congress. Moderates and Radicals disagreed on many issues, but they shared a strong political motive. Most southerners were Democrats. With southerners barred from Congress, Republicans could control both houses.

To combat the black codes, Congress passed the Civil Rights Act in April 1866. It gave citizenship to African Americans. When Johnson vetoed the bill, Congress overrode the veto.

▼ Senator Charles Sumner of Massachusetts

The Fourteenth Amendment Republicans feared that the Supreme Court might use its power of judicial review to declare the Civil Rights Act unconstitutional. To avoid such a ruling, Republicans supported the **Fourteenth Amendment**. It defines citizens as "all persons born or naturalized in the United States." Thus, the amendment voided the Dred Scott decision of 1857, in which Chief Justice Roger B. Taney wrote that African Americans were not and never could be citizens.

The Fourteenth Amendment guarantees citizens "equal protection of the laws" and forbids states to "deprive any person of life, liberty, or property without due process of law." Thus, states could not legally discriminate against a citizen on unreasonable grounds, such as race. The amendment did not apply to most American Indians.

Academic Vocabulary
capability • *n.*, ability, capacity

Under the Fourteenth Amendment, any state that denied any male citizen age 21 or older the right to vote would have its representation in Congress consequently reduced. Republicans believed that freedmen would have the **capability** to defend their rights if they could vote.

The Fourteenth Amendment was proposed by Congress in 1866. It was not ratified for another two years. Republicans hoped the amendment would secure basic political rights for African Americans in the South. That goal would take a century to achieve. In the 1950s, the Fourteenth Amendment's Equal Protection Clause became a powerful tool in the struggle for citizenship rights.

Analyze Images Thaddeus Stevens led the House in nullifying President Johnson's Reconstruction plan. **Draw Conclusions** What ideals motivated Stevens and the Radical Republicans?

✓ READING CHECK **Identify Cause and Effect** Why did Republicans believe that the Fourteenth Amendment was necessary?

New Rules for the South

President Johnson encouraged former Confederate states to reject the Fourteenth Amendment. He also decided to make the amendment an issue in the 1866 congressional elections.

Republicans Take Over Congress Across the North, Johnson urged voters to reject the Radicals. When a heckler yelled for Johnson to hang Jefferson Davis, Johnson shouted, "Why not hang Thad Stevens?"

In July, riots in New Orleans killed 34 African Americans who had gathered in support of a convention backing voting rights. White mobs attacked the crowd and fired into the convention. The violence convinced many northerners that stronger measures were needed. In the end, Republicans won majorities in both houses of Congress. African Americans were beginning to participate in elections. Almost all were Republicans and helped contribute to the Republicans' majority in Congress.

Rival Plans for Reconstruction

PLAN	TEN PERCENT PLAN	WADE-DAVIS BILL	JOHNSON PLAN	RECONSTRUCTION ACT
Proposed by	President Abraham Lincoln (1863)	Republicans in Congress (1864)	President Andrew Johnson (1865)	Radical Republicans (1867)
Conditions for Former Confederate States to Rejoin Union	• 10 percent of voters must swear loyalty to Union • Must abolish slavery	• Majority of white men must swear loyalty • Former Confederate volunteers cannot vote or hold office • Wartime debts by states will not be recognized	• Majority of white men must swear loyalty • Must ratify Thirteenth Amendment • Former Confederate officials may vote and hold office • Each state would be appointed a governor chosen by the president	• Must disband state governments • Must write new constitutions • Must ratify Fourteenth Amendment • African American men must be allowed to vote • Must disqualify former officials of the Confederacy from holding public office

Military Rule in the South In 1867, Republicans in Congress prepared to take charge of Reconstruction. With huge majorities in both houses, Congress could easily override vetoes. The period that followed is often called Radical Reconstruction.

Congress passed the first **Reconstruction Act** in March 1867. It threw out the state governments that had refused to ratify the Fourteenth Amendment—all the former Confederate states except Tennessee. The Military Reconstruction Acts of 1867 divided the southern states into five military districts, each governed by a military general.

Military rulers in these military districts had nearly unlimited power. They sometimes conducted trials without juries. Many southerners bitterly resented the **imposition** of military rule. They argued that the military occupation violated their rights because it was done without their consent or representation.

Congress, however, continued to impose new rules. To rejoin the Union, former Confederate states had to write new constitutions and ratify the Fourteenth Amendment. The Reconstruction Act also required that southern states allow African Americans to vote.

With the new constitutions in place, reconstructed states held elections to set up new state governments. The Fourteenth Amendment barred former Confederate officials from voting. Many other white southerners stayed away from the polls in protest. Protected by the army, freedmen proudly exercised their new right to vote. Most favored the Republican party, since it had supported their rights. As a result, Republicans gained control of all of the new southern state governments.

✓ READING CHECK **Generate Explanations** On what basis did the southern states argue against the Military Reconstruction Acts?

Analyze Charts Four plans for reconstructing the states that had seceded were proposed. **Compare and Contrast** In what ways did the Reconstruction Act of 1867 place more restrictions on former Confederate states than had previous plans?

Academic Vocabulary

imposition • *n.*, something applied or created based on authority

Political Problems and a New President

Congress passed other Reconstruction acts over Johnson's veto. As President, Johnson had a duty to execute, or carry out, the new laws. However, Johnson did what he could to limit their effect. For instance, he fired military commanders who supported Radical Reconstruction. Republicans in Congress decided to try to remove Johnson from office.

President Johnson on Trial On February 24, 1868, the House of Representatives voted to **impeach**, or bring formal charges against, Johnson. According to the Constitution, the House may impeach a president for "treason, bribery, or other high crimes and misdemeanors." The president is removed from office if found guilty by two thirds of the Senate.

During Johnson's trial, it became clear that he was not guilty of high crimes and misdemeanors. Even Charles Sumner, Johnson's bitter foe, admitted that the charges were "political in character." Despite intense pressure, seven Republican senators refused to vote for conviction. The Constitution, they said, did not allow Congress to remove a president just because they disagreed with him. In the end, the vote was 35 to 19—one vote shy of the two thirds needed to convict.

Grant Wins the Election of 1868 Johnson served out the few remaining months of his term. In May 1868, Republicans nominated the Union's greatest war hero, Ulysses S. Grant, for president.

In July 1868, the Fourteenth Amendment was ratified, granting citizenship to African Americans and guaranteeing equal protection of the laws. Former Confederate states were still required to ratify the amendment before they could be readmitted to the Union.

Analyze Graphs Once the Radical Republicans got into office, Congress's stand on protecting African Americans' rights was surprisingly consistent. **Summarize** How would you describe congressional support for the Fourteenth and Fifteenth Amendments?

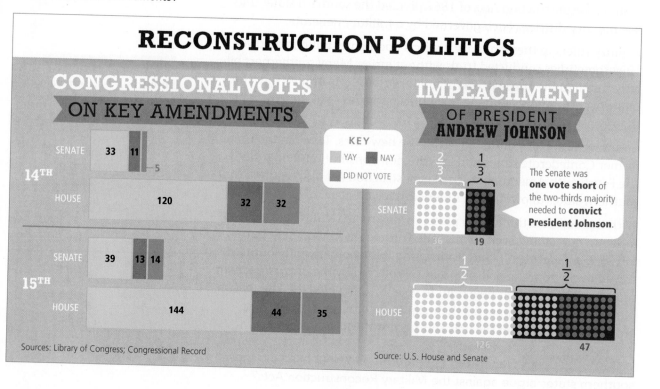

RECONSTRUCTION POLITICS

CONGRESSIONAL VOTES ON KEY AMENDMENTS

KEY
YAY — NAY
DID NOT VOTE

14TH
SENATE 33 | 11 | 5
HOUSE 120 | 32 | 32

15TH
SENATE 39 | 13 | 14
HOUSE 144 | 44 | 35

Sources: Library of Congress; Congressional Record

IMPEACHMENT OF PRESIDENT ANDREW JOHNSON

$\frac{2}{3}$ $\frac{1}{3}$

SENATE 36 | 19

The Senate was **one vote short** of the two-thirds majority needed to **convict President Johnson**.

$\frac{1}{2}$ $\frac{1}{2}$

HOUSE 126 | 47

Source: U.S. House and Senate

By election day, Texas, Mississippi, and Virginia had still not ratified the Fourteenth Amendment and were unable to vote. Most southern states had ratified the amendment and rejoined the Union, but some former Confederates in these states were still not allowed to vote. In addition, as required by the 1867 Reconstruction Act, the southern states allowed African American men to vote. About 500,000 blacks voted—nearly all of them for Grant. Grant won six states that had been part of the Confederacy. With support from most northerners as well, he easily won the election.

The Fifteenth Amendment In 1869, Congress proposed the **Fifteenth Amendment**. It forbids any state to deny any citizen the right to vote because of "race, color, or previous condition of servitude."

Republicans had moral and political reasons for supporting the Fifteenth Amendment. They remembered the great sacrifices made by African American soldiers in the Civil War. They also felt it was wrong to let African Americans vote in the South but not in the North. In addition, Republicans knew that if African Americans could vote in the North, they would help Republicans win elections there.

The Fifteenth Amendment was ratified in 1870. At last, all African American men over age 21 had the right to vote.

The Fifteenth Amendment was difficult to enforce, and southern conservatives were determined to find ways around it. It was not until the mid-1900s that new legislation began to effectively protect voting rights and the full impact of the amendment was felt.

☑ READING CHECK **Identify Cause and Effect** Why did some Republican senators refuse to vote to convict Johnson?

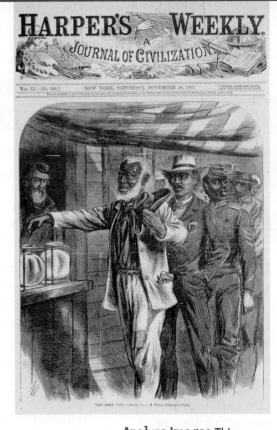

HARPER'S WEEKLY
JOURNAL OF CIVILIZATION

Vol. XI.—No. 568.] NEW YORK, SATURDAY, NOVEMBER 16, 1867.

Analyze Images This illustration shows African Americans voting for the first time in 1868. **Draw Conclusions** Why did the artist show different types of African American citizens?

☑ Lesson Check

Practice Vocabulary

1. What rights were secured for African Americans by the **Fourteenth Amendment** and the **Fifteenth Amendment**?

2. Why did Republicans **impeach** President Johnson?

Critical Thinking and Writing

3. **Generate Explanations** Why were the black codes so restrictive?

4. **Draw Conclusions** Why was the Republican plan for Reconstruction called Radical Reconstruction?

5. **Writing Workshop: Find and Use Credible Sources** Begin doing research on your paper on the Freedmen's Bureau. Look for reliable sources. Take notes on information you may use in your paper. Record web addresses and other source information in your 📓 Active Journal so you can find them again.

Frederick Douglass, "What the Black Man Wants"

In April 1865, millions of enslaved Americans were on the verge of being freed. White Americans wondered what to do with them. Douglass spelled out what the black man wanted.

◄ Frederick Douglass

Reading and Vocabulary Support

① *Deprivation* means the fact of having something valuable taken away.

② To "exercise the elective franchise" means to make use of the right to vote.

③ Benevolence is kindness.

④ What is the meaning of this metaphor about the apples?

We may be asked, I say, why we want [the right to vote]. I will tell you why we want it. We want it because it is our right, first of all. No class of men can, without insulting their own nature, be content with any deprivation ① of their rights. We want it, again, as a means for educating our race. Men are so constituted that they derive their conviction of their own possibilities largely from the estimate formed of them by others. If nothing is expected of a people, that people will find it difficult to contradict that expectation. By depriving us of suffrage, you affirm our incapacity to form an intelligent judgment respecting public men and public measures; you declare before the world that we are unfit to exercise the elective franchise ②, and by this means lead us to undervalue ourselves, to put a low estimate upon ourselves, and to feel that we have no possibilities like other men. . . .

What I ask for the negro is not benevolence ③, not pity, not sympathy, but simply justice. The American people have always been anxious to know what they shall do with us. . . . I have had but one answer from the beginning. Do nothing with us! Your doing with us has already played the mischief with us. Do nothing with us! If the apples will not remain on the tree of their own strength, if they are worm-eaten at the core, if they are early ripe and disposed to fall, let them fall! ④ . . . And if the negro cannot stand on his own legs, let him fall also. All I ask is, give him a chance to stand on his own legs! Let him alone! If you see him on his way to school, let him alone,—don't disturb him! If you see him going to the dinner-table at a hotel, let him go! If you see him going to the ballot-box, let him alone,—don't disturb him!

Analyzing Primary Sources

Cite specific evidence from the document to support your answers.

1. **Understand Effects** What effect does depriving black men of suffrage have on them?

2. **Determine Author's Point of View** What is Douglass's main message in this excerpt?

Quest CONNECTIONS

What did Frederick Douglass want Reconstruction to achieve? How did his goals for Reconstruction compare with those of others? Record your findings in your 📖 Active Journal.

Distinguish Essential from Incidental Information

INTERACTIVE

Identify Evidence

Follow these steps to help you distinguish essential from incidental information.

1 Identify a focus or topic. Set a purpose for your research. What exactly are you trying to find out? What key questions are you trying to answer? What idea or event are you trying to understand?

2 Locate your sources. The sources you choose will depend on your focus and topic.

3 Identify information that is essential to your topic. Based on your focus, what information will help you achieve your goal? What kinds of data will answer questions or increase your understanding?

4 Identify Information that is incidental to your topic. Remember the focus you have set for your research. Information that is not related to this focus is incidental. For example, suppose you want to use the information in the chart to learn about Andrew Johnson's plan for Reconstruction. Information about Johnson's impeachment might be accurate, but it is incidental to your topic. Which of the statements are incidental to your research? Which are essential?

President Andrew Johnson and Radical Reconstruction

Johnson supported a mild Reconstruction plan that called for a majority of voters in each southern state to pledge loyalty to the United States.

Johnson required states to ratify the Thirteenth Amendment as a condition of re-entering the union.

When southern states met his requirements for readmission to the Union, Johnson quickly approved their new state governments.

When President Lincoln was assassinated, Johnson became President. He took over the task of implementing Reconstruction.

Republicans were outraged when southern states that had been readmitted elected former Confederate officeholders to Congress.

The Radical Republicans were led in the House by Thaddeus Stevens of Pennsylvania and in the Senate by Charles Sumner of Massachusetts.

Republicans were angry when southern states enacted black codes that restricted the rights of freedmen.

Reconstruction and Southern Society

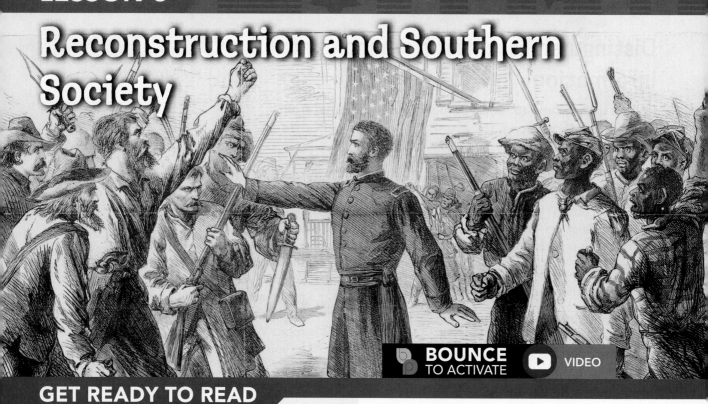

BOUNCE TO ACTIVATE   ▶ VIDEO

GET READY TO READ

START UP

In this image, a member of the Freedmen's Bureau holds off outraged white men. Look at other images and headings in this topic, then write two predictions of what you will read about.

GUIDING QUESTIONS

- How did conservatives resist Reconstruction?
- What economic, political, and social challenges faced Reconstruction governments?
- How did Reconstruction redefine what it meant to be an American?

TAKE NOTES

Literacy Skills Summarize

Use the graphic organizer in your ▤ Active Journal to take notes as you read the lesson.

PRACTICE VOCABULARY

Use the vocabulary activity in your ▤ Active Journal to practice the vocabulary words.

Vocabulary	Academic Vocabulary
scalawag	notorious
carpetbagger	anticipate
Ku Klux Klan	
sharecropper	

Before the Civil War, a small group of rich planters dominated politics in the South. During Reconstruction, however, new groups tried to reshape southern politics.

How Did New Political Groups Shape the South?

The state governments created during Radical Reconstruction were different from any governments the South had known before. The old leaders had lost much of their influence. Three groups stepped in to replace them.

White Southern Republicans One group to emerge consisted of white southerners who supported the new Republican governments. Many were businesspeople who had opposed secession in 1860. They wanted to forget the war and get on with rebuilding the South.

However, many whites in the South felt that any southerner who helped the Republicans was a traitor. They called the white southern Republicans **scalawags**, a word used for small, scruffy horses.

Northerners Many northerners came to the South after the war. White southerners accused the new arrivals of hoping to get rich from the South's misery. Southerners jested that these northerners were in such a hurry to move south that they had time only to fling a few clothes into carpetbags, a type of cheap suitcase. They became known as **carpetbaggers**.

In fact, northerners went south for various reasons. While a few did hope to profit as the South rebuilt, many more were Union soldiers who had grown to love the South's rich land. Others, both white and black, were teachers, ministers, and reformers who wanted to help the freedmen succeed in their new lives.

African Americans African Americans were the third major new group in southern politics. Before the war, they had no voice in government. During Reconstruction, they not only voted in large numbers, but they also ran for and were elected to public office. They became sheriffs, mayors, and legislators in the new state and local governments. As well, sixteen African Americans were elected to the United States Congress between 1869 and 1880.

Two African Americans, both representing Mississippi, served in the Senate. In 1870, Hiram Rhodes Revels, a clergyman and teacher, became the nation's first black senator. He completed the unfinished term of former Confederate president Jefferson Davis. In 1874, Blanche Kelso Bruce became the first African American elected to a full term in the Senate. Bruce served from 1875 to 1881.

INTERACTIVE

Reconstruction-Era Political Groups

Analyze Images This illustration shows the first seven African Americans to serve in Congress, including Hiram Revels (far left). **Identify Cause and Effect** What changes made it possible to elect freedmen to national office?

5 Things to Know About

BLANCHE K. BRUCE
First African American elected to a full term in the U.S. Senate
(1841–1898)

- Although born into slavery, Bruce received a good education as a child and attended Oberlin College for two years.

- At age 21 he won his freedom by escaping to Kansas.

- In 1864, he opened the first school for African American children in Missouri.

- The Mississippi legislature elected Bruce to the U.S. Senate in 1874, while the state was under military governance.

- As Senator, Bruce spoke out for fair treatment of African Americans and Native Americans.

Critical Thinking What was the significance of African Americans being elected to public office?

Revels's election was an important victory for African Americans. He served on the Committee on Education and Labor, where he opposed attempts to segregate, or separate, schools for African Americans and whites. He also promoted opportunities for African American workers.

Freedmen had less political influence than many whites claimed, however. Only in South Carolina did African Americans win a majority in one house of the state legislature. No state elected a black governor.

✓ **READING CHECK** **Describe** how politics in the South changed during Reconstruction.

Why Did Conservatives Resist Reform?

Most white southerners who had held power before the Civil War resisted Reconstruction. These conservatives resented the changes imposed by Congress and enforced by the military. Conservatives were willing to let African Americans vote and hold a few offices, but they were determined to keep real power in the hands of whites. A few wealthy planters tried to force African Americans back onto plantations. Many small farmers and laborers wanted the government to take action against freedmen, who now competed with them for land and power.

Most of these conservatives were Democrats. They declared war on anyone who cooperated with the Republicans. "This is a white man's country," declared one southern senator, "and white men must govern it."

The Ku Klux Klan Some white southerners formed secret societies to help them regain power. The most **notorious** was the **Ku Klux Klan**, or KKK. The Klan worked to keep African Americans and white Republicans out of office.

Dressed in white robes and hoods to hide their identities, Klansmen rode at night to the homes of African American voters, shouting

Did you know?
After Blanche Bruce's election in 1874, no African American was elected to the Senate until Edward Brooke, of Massachusetts, in 1966.

Academic Vocabulary
notorious • *adj.*, well known for some bad quality or effect

threats and burning wooden crosses. When threats did not work, the Klan turned to violence. Klan members murdered hundreds of African Americans and their white allies.

The Klan's Reign of Terror Many moderate southerners condemned the Klan's violence, but most did little to stop the reign of terror. Freedmen turned to the federal government for help. In Kentucky, African American voters wrote to Congress:

Primary Source

"We believe you are not familiar with the Ku Klux Klan's riding nightly over the country spreading terror wherever they go by robbing, whipping, and killing our people without provocation."

—Records of the U.S. Senate, April 11, 1871

In 1870, Congress made it a crime to use force to keep people from voting. Klan activities decreased, but the threat of violence remained. Some African Americans continued to vote and hold office, but others were frightened away from the ballot box.

✓ **READING CHECK** **Explain** the social and political impact of southern conservatives during Reconstruction.

How Did Political Problems Slow Progress?

Republican-dominated governments tried to rebuild the South. They made notable advances. They established the first publicly financed school systems in the South. These provided education for both black and white children.

Many states gave women the right to own property and otherwise expanded women's rights. In some cases, the legislatures provided debt relief for the poor.

In addition, Reconstruction governments rebuilt railroads, telegraph lines, bridges, and roads. Between 1865 and 1879, the South laid 7,000 miles of railroad track. However, progress was hindered by economic difficulties, white resistance to reform, and government corruption.

Analyze Political Cartoons Both the KKK and White League used violence to try to prevent freedmen from voting. **Infer** What does the phrase "worse than slavery" suggest about the effect of this violence on African American families?

Taxation and Voting Rights Before the war, southerners paid low taxes, but rebuilding the South cost money, and taxes rose sharply. This created discontent among many southern whites. Many former Confederate officers and officials resented being denied voting rights while people they considered inferior were allowed to vote. The tax increases also caused some landowners to lose their land.

Widespread Corruption Southerners were further angered by reports of widespread corruption in the Reconstruction governments. One state legislature, for example, voted $1,000 to cover a member's bet on a horse race. Other items billed to the state included hams, perfume, and a coffin.

Mixed Results for Legislative Reform State legislative reform in the South met with mixed success. New state constitutions allowed all adult men to vote, removed restrictions for holding office, and made public officials elected rather than appointed. Executive branches were given increased power to provide government services.

However, legislation to enroll voters was hindered by new restrictions that kept many African Americans from registering or voting. Many of the laws preventing former Confederates from voting and holding office did not last. In Georgia, African Americans were forced from the state legislature.

READING CHECK **Summarize** the problems that faced Reconstruction governments trying to rebuild the South.

Analyze Images This 1872 newspaper cartoon was titled "Lincoln, the Emancipator." **Synthesize Visual Information** What are the people in the cartoon doing? Why?

Economic Problems in the South

In the first months after the war, many freedmen left the plantations on which they had lived and worked. Some searched for family members. Others went in search of work. They found few opportunities, however.

Freedmen Have Limited Opportunities Some Radical Republicans talked about giving each freedman "40 acres and a mule" as a fresh start. This idea stemmed from a field order given by General William Tecumseh Sherman in 1865. Thaddeus Stevens suggested breaking up big plantations and distributing the land. Most Americans opposed the plan, however. In the end, former slaves received—in the words of a freedman—"nothing but freedom."

Through hard work or good luck, some freedmen did become land-owners. Most, however, felt they had little choice but to return to where they had lived in slavery. At the same time, some large planters found themselves with land but nobody to work it.

Rebuilding the South's Economy Before the Civil War, southern planters enjoyed prosperity because of strong demand for cotton, tobacco, and other farm products in the North and in Britain and Europe. During the war, a Union blockade cut off those markets. As a result, worldwide prices for those products rose, and suppliers in Latin America, India, and elsewhere began producing more tobacco, cotton, sugar cane, and rice. When the war ended and southern farmers returned to the market, they faced much greater competition from foreign producers. Predictably, according to the laws of supply and demand, this led to lower prices and less income. Some farmers went into debt and lost their land.

Analyze Images This photograph shows a group of freedmen in Richmond, Virginia. **Identify Main Ideas** Why did many freedmen have trouble finding jobs?

Meanwhile, the war had destroyed many of the South's cities and factories. Moreover, Southern planters had lost their enslaved workers, who were often a planter's main investment. As a result, the South had little money to invest in industry. It remained dependent on farming at a time when farming brought less income.

Poverty in the South During Reconstruction, many freedmen and poor whites became **sharecroppers** on plantations. As sharecroppers, they rented and farmed a plot of land in exchange for a share of the crop at harvest time. They also commonly purchased seed, fertilizer, and tools on credit, to be paid for with an additional share of their crop. To many freedmen, sharecropping offered a measure of independence. Many **anticipated** owning their own land one day.

In fact, this arrangement locked sharecroppers into a cycle of poverty. Each spring, they received supplies on credit. In the fall, they used their harvest to repay what they had borrowed. Since prices for farm products were low, the harvest often did not cover what they owed. Each year they fell further behind. Instead of rising toward independence, they sank deeper into debt.

Academic Vocabulary
anticipate • v., expect or look ahead to

⬇ **INTERACTIVE**

The Cycle of Poverty

Analyze Images This photograph shows freedmen planting sugar cane in Georgia in the late 1860s. **Identify Cause and Effect** What impact did sharecropping have on African Americans' economic status?

Sharecropping was not the only way freedmen could be trapped in peonage, or debt slavery. Under new laws against vagrancy, black men were stopped, arrested, and fined for being unemployed. Victims who could not pay the fine would be imprisoned and forced to work without pay. Sometimes, a local business owner would offer to pay the fine in exchange for a term of servitude. If the paperwork became lost, a victim might never regain his freedom.

☑ **READING CHECK** **Express Problems Clearly** What was the biggest problem with sharecropping?

☑ Lesson Check

Practice Vocabulary

1. What were the differences between **scalawags** and **carpetbaggers**?

2. What was the **Ku Klux Klan**, and what did it try to accomplish?

3. Why did **sharecroppers** often end up in debt?

Critical Thinking and Writing

4. **Summarize** why white southern conservatives resisted Reconstruction.

5. **Identify Main Ideas** What were the central challenges to rebuilding the South?

6. **Writing Workshop: Support Ideas With Evidence** Outline your research paper by writing your main ideas. Under each main idea, write facts and other evidence from your research that support that idea.

Interpret Thematic Maps

Follow these steps to review the ways to analyze a thematic map.

INTERACTIVE

Read Special-Purpose Maps

1 **Identify the type and general topic of the thematic map.** Often, the map title indicates both the general type of map and its specific topic. If it does not, look at the key to see what kind of information the map shows. After studying the map briefly, make a general statement about the topic of this map.

2 **Determine the place shown on the map.** Map titles often indicate the region shown. If not, look at the map. Do the colors give you any clues? Often, surrounding regions, states, or countries are shown in a single neutral color. Areas that are the main focus of the map may have colors that make them stand out. What do the colors used on the map suggest is the main area covered by the map?

3 **Determine the time period shown on the map.** If no dates are indicated in the map title or key, the map probably represents the present time. What time period is shown on this map?

4 **Explain what the map shows.** Use the key to analyze the information shown on the map. The key explains special symbols and colors used on the map and indicates what kinds of information you can find on the map. In a few sentences, summarize the information shown on this map.

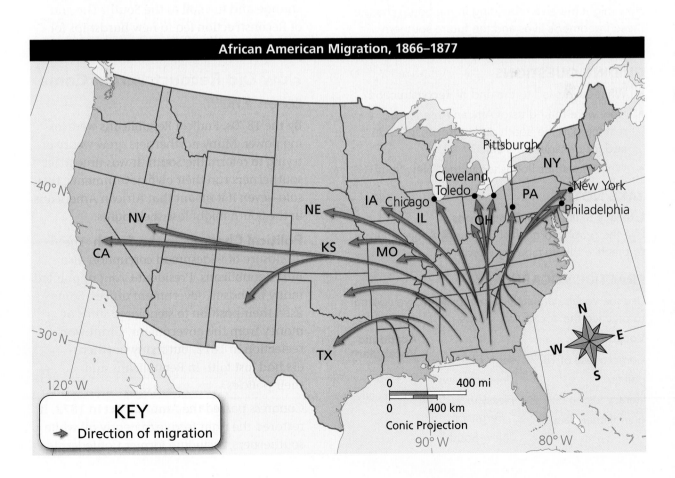

African American Migration, 1866–1877

KEY
→ Direction of migration

The Aftermath of Reconstruction

BOUNCE TO ACTIVATE ▶ VIDEO

GET READY TO READ

START UP

How might massive rebuilding in the South change these freedmen's lives and the future southern economy?

GUIDING QUESTIONS

- What events led to the end of Reconstruction?
- How were the rights of African Americans restricted in the South during Reconstruction and for decades afterward?
- What industries flourished in the "New South"?

TAKE NOTES

Literacy Skills Draw Conclusions
Use the graphic organizer in your ▱ Active Journal to practice the vocabulary words.

PRACTICE VOCABULARY

Use the vocabulary activity in your ▱ Active Journal to practice the vocabulary words.

Vocabulary

Compromise of 1877
poll tax
literacy test
grandfather clause

segregation
Jim Crow laws
Plessy v. *Ferguson*
"New South"

Academic Vocabulary

employ
specifically

Reconstruction had brought both positive change and turmoil to the South. The end of Reconstruction led to new hardships for African Americans in the South.

How Did Reconstruction Come to an End?

By the 1870s, Radical Republicans were losing power. Many northerners grew weary of trying to reform the South. It was time to let southerners run their own governments, they said—even if it meant that African Americans in the South might lose their rights.

Political Changes In the South The disclosure of widespread corruption also hurt Republicans. President Grant appointed many friends to government offices. Some used their position to steal large sums of money from the government. Grant won reelection in 1872, but many northerners had lost faith in Republicans and their policies.

Congress passed the Amnesty Act in 1872. It restored the right to vote to nearly all white southerners, including former Confederates.

These white southerners voted solidly Democratic. At the same time, they **employed** violence in order to prevent African Americans from voting. By 1876, only three southern states—South Carolina, Florida, and Tennessee—remained under Republican control.

A Disputed Election Leads to the End of Reconstruction The end of Reconstruction came with the election of 1876. The Democrats nominated Samuel Tilden, governor of New York, for president. The Republicans chose Ohio governor Rutherford B. Hayes. Both candidates vowed to fight corruption.

Tilden won the popular vote. However, he had only 184 electoral votes, one short of the number needed to win. The outcome of the election hung on 20 disputed electoral votes. Of the 20, 19 were from the three states that had not yet been reconstructed—South Carolina, Louisiana, and Florida. Democrats in these states accused Republican election officials of throwing out Democratic votes.

As inauguration day drew near, the nation still had no winner to swear in as president. The Republican-controlled Congress set up a special commission to settle the crisis. The commission, made up mostly of Republicans, gave all the disputed electoral votes to Hayes.

Southern Democrats could have fought the decision. Instead, they agreed to support the commission's decision in return for a promise by Hayes to end Reconstruction. This agreement is known as the **Compromise of 1877**. Once in office, Hayes removed all remaining federal troops from Louisiana, South Carolina, and Florida. Reconstruction was over.

GEOGRAPHY **SKILLS**

The 1876 presidential election between Tilden and Hayes was extremely close.

1. **Location** Why is the vote in New York, New Jersey, and Delaware surprising?

2. **Draw Conclusions** Based on the information in the map, why might Hayes's victory in the 1876 election have come as a surprise to some?

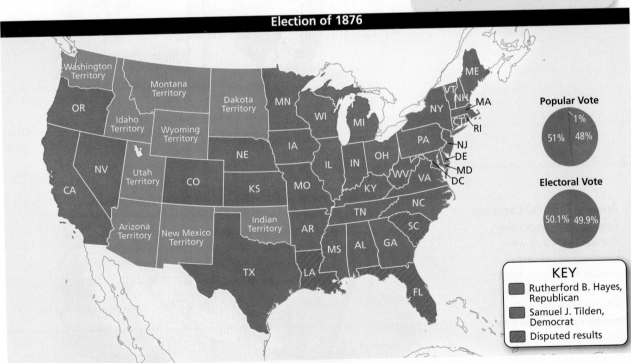

Election of 1876

Popular Vote: 51% 48% 1%

Electoral Vote: 50.1% 49.9%

KEY
- Rutherford B. Hayes, Republican
- Samuel J. Tilden, Democrat
- Disputed results

Reconstruction's Political Impact Reconstruction had a deep and lasting impact on southern politics. White southerners had bitter memories of Radical Republican policies and military rule. For the next hundred years, the South remained a stronghold of the Democratic party. At the same time, southern African Americans steadily lost most of their political rights.

✓ **READING CHECK** Sequence Explain the sequence of events that resulted in the end of Reconstruction.

New Restrictions on African American Rights

As federal troops withdrew from the South, conservative Democrats found new ways to keep African Americans from exercising their rights. Many of these were laws **specifically** intended to prevent African Americans from voting.

Academic Vocabulary
specifically • *adv.*, for a particular purpose

Southern States Limit Political Participation Over time, many southern states passed **poll taxes**, requiring voters to pay a fee each time they voted. As a result, freedmen could rarely afford to vote.

States also imposed **literacy tests** that required voters to read and explain a section of the Constitution. Since most freedmen had little education, such tests kept them from voting. Election officials also applied different standards to black and white voters. Blacks who were able to read often had to answer more difficult questions than whites.

Analyze Political Cartoons
This cartoon mocks the literacy tests that were intended to prevent African Americans from voting. **Synthesize Visual Information** How does this cartoon portray the new literacy tests?

Still, many poor whites could not have passed any literacy test. To increase the number of white voters, states passed **grandfather clauses**. These laws stated that if a voter's father or grandfather had been eligible to vote on January 1, 1867—a date after Johnson had restored rebels' right to vote—the voter did not have to take a literacy test. No African Americans in the South could vote before 1868, so the only effect of the grandfather clauses was to ensure that white men could vote.

Jim Crow Laws Separate Whites and African Americans

After 1877, **segregation**, or separation of races, became the law of the South. Blacks and whites were kept separate from each other in schools, restaurants, theaters, trains, streetcars, playgrounds, hospitals, and even cemeteries by **Jim Crow laws**. In some cases, African Americans were restricted to completely separate facilities. In others, facilities were divided, with favorable areas reserved for whites. Louisiana novelist George Washington Cable described segregation as

Analyze Images Jim Crow laws made racial segregation legal in places such as this theater. **Draw Conclusions** What impact did these laws have on the equality of educational opportunities for whites and African Americans?

Primary Source

"A system of oppression so rank that nothing could make it seem small except the fact that [African Americans] had already been ground under it for a century and a half."

—George Washington Cable, "The Freedman's Case in Equity"

African Americans brought lawsuits to challenge segregation. In 1896, in the case of **Plessy v. Ferguson**, the Supreme Court ruled that segregation was legal so long as facilities for blacks and whites were equal. In fact, facilities were rarely equal. For example, southern states spent much less on schools for blacks than for whites.

Despite such setbacks, the Constitution now recognized African Americans as citizens. Laws passed during Reconstruction—especially the Fourteenth Amendment—would become the basis of the civil rights movement almost 100 years later.

Freedmen Leave the South Their treatment as second-class citizens pushed many freedmen out of the South. They clung to the South because it was their home. Their families lived there. But they could also feel the pull of better opportunities elsewhere.

INTERACTIVE

Oppression of African Americans

Quest CONNECTIONS

Did Reconstruction successfully rebuild society? Record your ideas in your Active Journal.

African Americans in northern cities published newspapers to help their brethren in the South cope with their new challenges. They often encouraged freedmen to come north. Factories needed more workers and sent recruiters to the South. They promised jobs, better housing, freedom to vote, and freedom from fear. Many African Americans began leaving the South for cities in the North and West.

Some freedmen were permitted to join the U.S. Army. Congress authorized four regiments of African Americans, to be commanded by white officers. Nicknamed "buffalo soldiers," African Americans served protecting settlers and enforcing federal laws in the western territories. Fourteen buffalo soldiers earned the medal of honor.

✓ READING CHECK Summarize the ways in which southern governments restricted the rights of freedmen.

How Did the South Rebuild Its Economy?

During Reconstruction, the South made modest progress toward rebuilding its agricultural economy. By 1880, planters were growing as much cotton as they had in 1860.

After Reconstruction, a new generation of southern leaders worked to expand and diversify the economy. In stirring speeches, Atlanta journalist Henry Grady described a **"New South"** that used its vast natural resources to build up its own industry instead of depending on the North.

Old Industries Grow In 1880, the entire South still produced fewer finished textiles than Massachusetts. In the next decade, more communities built textile mills to turn cotton into cloth.

The tobacco industry also grew. In North Carolina, James Duke used new machinery to revolutionize the manufacture of tobacco products.

INTERACTIVE

Change in Southern Industry

Analyze Graphs The war set back the South's development by many years, but by 1880, its economy began improving rapidly. **Use Evidence** Cite evidence from the charts that the southern economy diversified after Reconstruction ended.

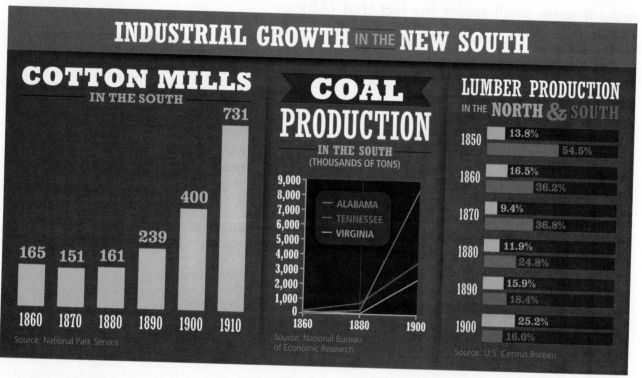

INDUSTRIAL GROWTH IN THE NEW SOUTH

COTTON MILLS IN THE SOUTH

Year	Mills
1860	165
1870	151
1880	161
1890	239
1900	400
1910	731

Source: National Park Service

COAL PRODUCTION IN THE SOUTH (THOUSANDS OF TONS)

— ALABAMA
— TENNESSEE
— VIRGINIA

9,000
8,000
7,000
6,000
5,000
4,000
3,000
2,000
1,000
0

1860   1880   1900

Source: National Bureau of Economic Research

LUMBER PRODUCTION IN THE NORTH & SOUTH

Year	North	South
1850	13.8%	54.5%
1860	16.5%	36.2%
1870	9.4%	36.8%
1880	11.9%	24.8%
1890	15.9%	18.4%
1900	25.2%	16.0%

Source: U.S. Census Bureau

Duke's American Tobacco Company eventually controlled 90 percent of the nation's tobacco industry.

The Environment Shapes New Industries The New South also used its natural resources to develop new industries other than those based on farming. With its large deposits of iron ore and coal, Alabama became a center of the steel industry. Oil refineries sprang up in Louisiana and Texas. Other states produced copper, granite, and marble.

By the 1890s, many northern forests had been cut down. The southern yellow pine competed with the northwestern white pine as a lumber source. Southern factories produced cypress shingles and hardwood furniture.

Factories, farming, and mining modified the South's physical environment. Clearing land and using the natural resources provided jobs and opportunities. The South's wood, steel, and other products were used in industry around the country.

The South had developed a more balanced economy by 1900. "We find a South wide awake with business," wrote a visitor, "eagerly laying lines of communication, rapidly opening mines, building furnaces, foundries, and all sorts of shops." Still, the South did not keep up with even more rapid growth in the North and the West.

Analyze Images This poster advertised "OUR NATIONAL INDUSTRIES: METHODS OF IRON MINING AT CARTER'S FURNACE." **Summarize** How were companies like Carter's important to rebuilding the South?

☑ READING CHECK **Compare and Contrast** the post-Reconstruction economy of the South with its pre-Civil War economy.

☑ Lesson Check

Practice Vocabulary

1. How did **poll taxes** and **literacy tests** make it hard for African Americans to vote?

2. What were **Jim Crow** laws?

3. What was the effect of the **Compromise of 1877**?

Critical Thinking and Writing

4. **Analyze Information** How was the decision in *Plessy* v. *Ferguson* inconsistent with reality?

5. **Compare and Contrast** What was life like for African Americans in the South after Reconstruction ended? How did it differ from life under slavery?

6. **Writing Workshop: Cite Sources** In your 📖 Active Journal, create citations on all the sources you have used. Include the name of the article or text, the author, the publisher, the date of publication, and the web address.

☑ Review and Assessment

VISUAL REVIEW

Causes and Effects of Reconstruction

Presidential Reconstruction: Southern states ratify Thirteenth Amendment; former Confederates swear loyalty to the Union.	President Johnson approves former Confederate states to rejoin Union.	Former Confederate leaders elected to government office. Southern states enact black codes.	Radical Republicans win majority in Congress and reject Presidential Reconstruction.

Civil Rights Act grants citizenship to African Americans. Southern states required to ratify Fourteenth Amendment and allow African Americans to vote. Congress establishes military districts.	African Americans elected to local, state, and federal offices. Schools established for black and white children.	Radical Republicans win majority in Congress and reject Presidential Reconstruction.

RADICAL RECONSTRUCTION AND ITS EFFECTS

Radical Reconstruction

- African American men gain right to vote.
- African Americans become citizens.
- African Americans gain right to own property.

After Reconstruction

- Poll taxes and literacy tests limit voting rights.
- Jim Crow laws enforce segregation.
- *Plessy* v. *Ferguson* endorses "separate but equal."
- Rise of the "New South."

READING REVIEW

Use the Take Notes and Practice Vocabulary activities in your 📓 Active Journal to review the topic.

 INTERACTIVE

Practice vocabulary using the Topic Mini-Games

Quest FINDINGS

Conduct your discussion

Get help for conducting your civic discussion in your 📓 Active Journal.

ASSESSMENT

Vocabulary and Key Ideas

1. **Identify Main Ideas** What was the significance of the **Thirteenth, Fourteenth**, and **Fifteenth Amendments**?

2. **Recall** Why were the **Radical Republicans** opposed to President Johnson's Reconstruction plan?

3. **Summarize** What was the **Ku Klux Klan**?

4. **Check Understanding** What was the **Compromise of 1877**, and what were the results?

5. **Identify Supporting Details** Why did the House of Representatives vote to impeach President Johnson, and why wasn't he convicted?

6. **Describe** How did the economy of the South change during Reconstruction?

7. **Identify Main Ideas** How did sharecropping affect African Americans?

Critical Thinking and Writing

8. **Identify Cause and Effect** How did the election of African Americans to public office impact freedmen?

9. **Identify Cause and Effect** What effects did the black codes and the reactions to them of Radical Republicans have on freedmen?

10. **Summarize** What is the Fifteenth Amendment, and what was its impact?

11. **Draw Conclusions** What lasting effects did Reconstruction have on the South?

12. **Revisit the Essential Question** How should people handle the kind of conflict that divided the country during Reconstruction?

13. **Writing Workshop: Write a Research Paper** Complete your research paper on the Freedmen's Bureau and its effects. Include a discussion of the limits placed on the rights and opportunities of African Americans. Finalize your introduction. Revise the body paragraphs, using transitions to connect ideas. Then write a strong conclusion that summarizes your main ideas.

Analyze Primary Sources

14. What system is George Washington Cable most likely referring to in this quotation?
    A. Radical Reconstruction
    B. Lincoln's plan for amnesty
    C. Jim Crow laws
    D. the economy of the "New South"

"A system of oppression so rank that nothing could make it seem small except the fact that [African Americans] had already been ground under it for a century and a half."

—George Washington Cable, "The Freedman's Case in Equity"

Analyze Maps

Use the map to answer the following questions. [Map Key: red = Hayes; blue = Tilden; red/blue = disputed]

15. Which candidate won more states?

16. From which part of the country did Samuel Tilden get most of his support?

17. For whom did Florida vote? Explain.

▼ **Election of 1876**

Declaration of Independence

Introduction

By signing the Declaration of Independence, members of the Continental Congress sent a clear message to Britain that the American colonies were free and independent states. Starting with its preamble, the document spells out all the reasons the people of the United States have the right to break away from Britain.

Primary Source

The Unanimous Declaration of the Thirteen United States of America

When in the Course of human events, it becomes necessary for one people to dissolve the political bands which have connected them with another, and to assume among the powers of the earth, the separate and equal station to which the Laws of Nature and of Nature's God entitle them, a decent respect to the opinions of mankind requires that they should declare the causes which impel [force] them to the separation.

We hold these truths to be self-evident, that all men are created equal, that they are endowed [gifted] by their Creator with certain unalienable [cannot be taken away] Rights, that among these are Life, Liberty and the pursuit of Happiness. That to secure these rights, Governments are instituted among Men, deriving their just powers from the consent of the governed. That whenever any Form of Government becomes destructive of these ends, it is the Right of the People to alter or to abolish it, and to institute new Government, laying its foundation on such principles and organizing its powers in such form, as to them shall seem most likely to effect their Safety and Happiness. Prudence [cautiousness], indeed, will dictate that Governments long established should not be changed for light and transient causes; and accordingly all experience hath shown that mankind are more disposed to suffer, while evils are sufferable, than to right themselves by abolishing the forms to which they are accustomed. But when a long train of abuses and usurpations [unjust uses of power], pursuing invariably the same Object evinces a design to reduce them under absolute Despotism [rule of absolute power], it is their right, it is their duty, to throw off such Government, and to provide new Guards for their future security.

Such has been the patient sufferance of these Colonies; and such is now the necessity which constrains them to alter their former Systems of Government. The history of the present King of Great Britain is a history of repeated injuries and usurpations, all having in direct object the establishment of an absolute Tyranny over these States. To prove this, let Facts be submitted to a candid world.

He has refused his Assent to Laws, the most wholesome and necessary for the public good.

He has forbidden his Governors to pass Laws of immediate and pressing importance, unless suspended in their operation till his Assent should be obtained; and when so suspended, he has utterly neglected to attend to them.

He has refused to pass other Laws for the accommodation of large districts of people, unless those people would relinquish [give up] the right of Representation in the Legislature, a right inestimable [priceless] to them and formidable to tyrants only.

He has called together legislative bodies at places unusual, uncomfortable, and distant from the depository of their public Records, for the sole purpose of fatiguing them into compliance with his measures.

He has dissolved Representative Houses repeatedly, for opposing with manly firmness his invasions on the rights of the people.

He has refused for a long time, after such dissolutions [closing down], to cause others to be elected; whereby the Legislative powers, incapable of Annihilation, have returned to the People at large for their exercise; the State remaining in the mean time exposed to all the dangers of invasion from without, and convulsions [riots] within.

He has endeavoured to prevent the population of these States; for that purpose obstructing the Laws for Naturalization of Foreigners; refusing to pass others to encourage their migrations hither, and raising the conditions of new Appropriations of Lands.

He has obstructed the Administration of Justice by refusing his Assent to Laws for establishing Judiciary powers.

He has made Judges dependent on his Will alone, for the tenure [term] of their offices, and the amount and payment of their salaries.

He has erected a multitude of New Offices, and sent hither swarms of Officers to harass our people, and eat out their substance.

He has kept among us, in times of peace, Standing Armies without the Consent of our legislatures.

He has affected to render the Military independent of and superior to the Civil power.

He has combined with others to subject us to a jurisdiction foreign to our constitution, and unacknowledged by our laws; giving his Assent to their Acts of pretended Legislation:

For quartering [lodging] large bodies of armed troops among us:

For protecting them, by a mock Trial, from punishment for any Murders which they should commit on the Inhabitants of these States:

For cutting off our Trade with all parts of the world:

For imposing Taxes on us without our Consent:

For depriving us in many cases, of the benefits of Trial by Jury:

For transporting us beyond Seas to be tried for pretended offences:

For abolishing the free System of English Laws in a neighbouring Province, establishing therein an Arbitrary government, and enlarging its Boundaries so as to render it at once an example and fit instrument for introducing the same absolute rule into these Colonies:

For taking away our Charters, abolishing our most valuable Laws, and altering fundamentally the Forms of our Governments:

For suspending our own Legislatures, and declaring themselves invested with power to legislate for us in all cases whatsoever.

He has abdicated Government here, by declaring us out of his Protection and waging War against us.

He has plundered our seas, ravaged our Coasts, burnt our towns, and destroyed the lives of our people.

He is at this time transporting large Armies of foreign Mercenaries [soldiers] to complete the works of death, desolation, and tyranny, already begun with circumstances of Cruelty and perfidy [dishonesty] scarcely paralleled in the most barbarous ages, and totally unworthy the Head of a civilized nation.

He has constrained our fellow Citizens taken Captive on the high Seas to bear Arms against their Country, to become the executioners of their friends and Brethren, or to fall themselves by their Hands.

He has excited domestic insurrections amongst us, and has endeavoured to bring on the inhabitants of our frontiers, the merciless Indian Savages whose known rule of warfare, is an undistinguished destruction of all ages, sexes and conditions.

In every stage of these Oppressions We have Petitioned for Redress [correction of wrongs] in the most humble terms: Our repeated Petitions have been answered only by repeated injury. A Prince, whose character is thus marked by every act which may define a Tyrant, is unfit to be the ruler of a free people.

Nor have We been wanting in attentions to our British brethren. We have warned them from time to time of attempts by their legislature to extend an unwarrantable jurisdiction over us. We have reminded them of the circumstances of our emigration and settlement here. We have appealed to their native justice and magnanimity [generosity], and we have conjured [begged] them by the ties of our common kindred, to disavow these usurpations, which would inevitably interrupt our connections and correspondence. They too have been deaf to the voice of justice and of consanguinity [relation by blood]. We must, therefore, acquiesce in the necessity, which denounces our Separation, and hold them, as we hold the rest of mankind, Enemies in War, in Peace Friends.

We, therefore, the Representatives of the United States of America, in General Congress, Assembled, appealing to the Supreme Judge of the world for the rectitude [justness] of our intentions, do, in the Name, and by Authority of the good People of these Colonies, solemnly publish and declare, That these United Colonies are, and of Right ought to be Free and Independent States; that they are Absolved from all Allegiance to the British Crown, and that all political connection between them and the State of Great Britain, is and ought to be totally dissolved; and that as Free and Independent States, they have full Power to levy War, conclude Peace, contract Alliances, establish Commerce, and to do all other Acts and Things which Independent States may of right do. And for the support of this Declaration, with a firm reliance on the protection of Divine Providence, we mutually pledge to each other our Lives, our Fortunes and our sacred Honor.

☑ Assessment

1. **Identify Cause and Effect** How might the ideas about equality expressed in the Declaration of Independence have influenced later historical movements, such as the abolitionist movement and the women's suffrage movement?

2. **Identify Key Steps in a Process** Why was the Declaration of Independence a necessary document for the founding of the new nation?

3. **Draw Inferences** English philosopher John Locke wrote that government should protect "life, liberty, and estate." How do you think Locke's writing influenced ideas about government put forth in the Declaration of Independence?

4. **Analyze Structure** How does the Declaration organize its key points from beginning to end?

Constitution Quick Study Guide

Preamble

Articles

Amendments

1st Amendment: **Freedom of Religion, Speech, Press, Assembly, and Petition**

2nd Amendment: **Right to Keep, Bear Arms**

3rd Amendment: **Lodging Troops in Private Homes**

4th Amendment: **Search, Seizures, Proper Warrants**

5th Amendment: **Criminal Proceedings, Due Process, Eminent Domain**

6th Amendment: **Criminal Proceedings**

7th Amendment: **Jury Trials in Civil Cases**

8th Amendment: **Bail; Cruel, Unusual Punishment**

9th Amendment: **Unenumerated Rights**

10th Amendment: **Powers Reserved to the States**

11th Amendment: **Suits Against the States**

12th Amendment: **Election of President and Vice President**

13th Amendment: **Slavery and Involuntary Servitude**

Section 1. Slavery and Involuntary Servitude Prohibited

Section 2. Power of Congress

14th Amendment: **Rights of Citizens**

Section 1. Citizenship; Privileges and Immunities; Due Process; Equal Protection

Section 2. Apportionment of Representation

Section 3. Disqualification of Officers

Section 4. Public Debt

Section 5. Powers of Congress

15th Amendment: **Right to Vote—Race, Color, Servitude**

Section 1. Suffrage Not to Be Abridged

Section 2. Power of Congress

16th Amendment: **Income Tax**

17th Amendment: **Popular Election of Senators**

Section 1. Popular Election of Senators

Section 2. Senate Vacancies

Section 3. Inapplicable to Senators Previously Chosen

18th Amendment: **Prohibition of Intoxicating Liquors**

Section 1. Intoxicating Liquors Prohibited

Section 2. Concurrent Power to Enforce

Section 3. Time Limit on Ratification

19th Amendment: **Equal Suffrage—Sex**

Section 1. Suffrage Not to Be Abridged

Section 2. Power of Congress

20th Amendment: **Commencement of Terms; Sessions of Congress; Death or Disqualification of President-Elect**

Section 1. Terms of President, Vice President, members of Congress

Section 2. Sessions of Congress

Section 3. Death or Disqualification of President-Elect

Section 4. Congress to Provide for Certain Successors

Section 5. Effective Date

Section 6. Time Limit on Ratification

21st Amendment: **Repeal of 18th Amendment**

Section 1. Repeal of Prohibition

Section 2. Transportation, Importation of Intoxicating Liquors

Section 3. Time Limit on Ratification

22nd Amendment: **Presidential Tenure**

Section 1. Restriction on Number of Terms

Section 2. Time Limit on Ratification

23rd Amendment: **Inclusion of District of Columbia in Presidential Election Systems**

Section 1. Presidential Electors for District

Section 2. Power of Congress

24th Amendment: **Right to Vote in Federal Elections—Tax Payment**

Section 1. Suffrage Not to Be Abridged

Section 2. Power of Congress

25th Amendment: **Presidential Succession; Vice Presidential Vacancy; Presidential Inability**

Section 1. Presidential Succession

Section 2. Vice Presidential Vacancy

Section 3. Presidential Inability

26th Amendment: **Right to Vote—Age**

Section 1. Suffrage Not to Be Abridged

Section 2. Power of Congress

27th Amendment: **Congressional Pay**

The Preamble states the broad purposes the Constitution is intended to serve—to establish a government that provides for greater cooperation among the States, ensures justice and peace, provides for defense against foreign enemies, promotes the general well-being of the people, and secures liberty now and in the future. The phrase We the People emphasizes the twin concepts of popular sovereignty and of representative government.

Legislative Department

Section 1. Legislative power; Congress

Congress, the nation's lawmaking body, is bicameral in form; that is, it is composed of two houses: the Senate and the House of Representatives. The Framers of the Constitution purposely separated the lawmaking power from the power to enforce the laws (Article II, the Executive Branch) and the power to interpret them (Article III, the Judicial Branch). This system of separation of powers is supplemented by a system of checks and balances; that is, in several provisions the Constitution gives to each of the three branches various powers with which it may restrain the actions of the other two branches.

Section 2. House of Representatives

▶ Clause 1. **Election** Electors means voters. Members of the House of Representatives are elected every two years. Each State must permit the same persons to vote for United States representatives as it permits to vote for the members of the larger house of its own legislature. The 17th Amendment (1913) extends this requirement to the qualification of voters for United States senators.

▶ Clause 2. **Qualifications** A member of the House of Representatives must be at least 25 years old, an American citizen for seven years, and a resident of the State he or she represents. In addition, political custom requires that a representative also reside in the district from which he or she is elected.

▶ Clause 3. **Apportionment** The number of representatives each State is entitled to is based on its population, which is counted every 10 years in the census. Congress reapportions the seats among the States after each census. In the Reapportionment Act of 1929, Congress fixed the permanent size of the House at 435 members with each State having at least one representative. Today there is one House seat for approximately every 700,000 persons in the population.

The words "three-fifths of all other persons" referred to slaves and reflected the Three-Fifths Compromise reached by the Framers at Philadelphia in 1787; the phrase was made obsolete, was in effect repealed, by the 13th Amendment in 1865.

---

* The blue words indicate portions of the Constitution altered by subsequent amendments to the document.

▶ Clause 4. **Vacancies** The executive authority refers to the governor of a State. If a member leaves office or dies before the expiration of his or her term, the governor is to call a special election to fill the vacancy.

PREAMBLE

We the People of the United States, in Order to form a more perfect Union, establish Justice, insure domestic Tranquility, provide for the common defence, promote the general Welfare, and secure the Blessings of Liberty to ourselves and our Posterity, do ordain and establish this Constitution for the United States of America.

Article I.

Section 1.

All legislative Powers herein granted shall be vested in a Congress of the United States, which shall consist of a Senate and House of Representatives.

Section 2.

▶ 1. The House of Representatives shall be composed of Members chosen every second Year by the People of the several States, and the Electors in each State shall have the Qualifications requisite for Electors of the most numerous Branch of the State Legislature.

▶ 2. No Person shall be a Representative who shall not have attained to the age of twenty-five Years, and been seven Years a Citizen of the United States, and who shall not, when elected, be an Inhabitant of that State in which he shall be chosen.

▶ 3. Representatives and direct Taxes* shall be apportioned among the several States which may be included within this Union, according to their respective Numbers, which shall be determined by adding to the whole Number of free Persons, including those bound to Service for a Term of Years, and excluding Indians not taxed, three fifths of all other Persons. The actual Enumeration shall be made within three Years after the first Meeting of the Congress of the United States, and within every subsequent term of ten Years, in such Manner as they shall by Law direct. The Number of Representatives shall not exceed one for every thirty Thousand, but each State shall have at Least one Representative; and, until such enumeration shall be made, the State of New Hampshire shall be entitled to choose three, Massachusetts eight, Rhode Island and Providence Plantations one, Connecticut five, New York six, New Jersey four, Pennsylvania eight, Delaware one, Maryland six, Virginia ten, North Carolina five, South Carolina five, and Georgia three.

▶ 4. When vacancies happen in the Representation from any State, the Executive Authority thereof shall issue Writs of Election to fill such Vacancies.

5. The House of Representatives shall choose their Speaker and other Officers; and shall have the sole Power of Impeachment.

Section 3.

1. The Senate of the United States shall be composed of two Senators from each State chosen by the Legislature thereof for six Years; and each Senator shall have one Vote.

2. Immediately after they shall be assembled in Consequences of the first Election, they shall be divided, as equally as may be, into three Classes. The Seats of the Senators of the first Class shall be vacated at the Expiration of the second Year; of the second Class, at the Expiration of the fourth Year; and of the third Class, at the Expiration of the sixth Year; so that one-third may be chosen every second Year; and if Vacancies happen by Resignation, or otherwise, during the Recess of the Legislature of any State, the Executive thereof may make temporary Appointments until the next Meeting of the Legislature, which shall then fill such Vacancies.

3. No Person shall be a Senator who shall not have attained to the Age of thirty Years, and been nine Years a Citizen of the United States, and who shall not, when elected, be an Inhabitant of that State for which he shall be chosen.

4. The Vice President of the United States shall be President of the Senate but shall have no Vote, unless they be equally divided.

5. The Senate shall choose their other Officers, and also a President pro tempore, in the Absence of the Vice President, or when he shall exercise the Office of President of the United States.

6. The Senate shall have the sole Power to try all Impeachments. When sitting for that Purpose, they shall be on Oath or Affirmation. When the President of the United States is tried, the Chief Justice shall preside: And no Person shall be convicted without the Concurrence of two thirds of the Members present.

7. Judgment in Cases of Impeachment shall not extend further than to removal from Office, and disqualification to hold and enjoy any Office of honor, Trust, or Profit under the United States: but the Party convicted shall nevertheless be liable and subject to Indictment, Trial, Judgment and Punishment, according to Law.

▶ Clause 5. **Officers; impeachment** The House elects a Speaker, customarily chosen from the majority party in the House. Impeachment means accusation. The House has the exclusive power to impeach, or accuse, civil officers; the Senate (Article I, Section 3, Clause 6) has the exclusive power to try those impeached by the House.

Section 3. Senate

▶ Clause 1. **Composition, election, term** Each State has two senators. Each serves for six years and has one vote. Originally, senators were not elected directly by the people, but by each State's legislature. The 17th Amendment, added in 1913, provides for the popular election of senators.

▶ Clause 2. **Classification** The senators elected in 1788 were divided into three groups so that the Senate could become a "continuing body." One-third of the Senate's seats are up for election every two years.
The 17th Amendment provides that a Senate vacancy is to be filled at a special election called by the governor; State law may also permit the governor to appoint a successor to serve until that election is held.

▶ Clause 3. **Qualifications** A senator must be at least 30 years old, a citizen for at least nine years, and must live in the State from which elected.

▶ Clause 4. **Presiding officer** The Vice President presides over the Senate, but may vote only to break a tie.

▶ Clause 5. **Other officers** The Senate chooses its own officers, including a president pro tempore to preside when the Vice President is not there.

▶ Clause 6. **Impeachment trials** The Senate conducts the trials of those officials impeached by the House. The Vice President presides unless the President is on trial, in which case the Chief Justice of the United States does so. A conviction requires the votes of two-thirds of the senators present.
No President has ever been convicted. In 1868 the House voted eleven articles of impeachment against President Andrew Johnson, but the Senate fell one vote short of convicting him. In 1974 President Richard M. Nixon resigned the presidency in the face of almost certain impeachment by the House. The House brought two articles of impeachment against President Bill Clinton in late 1998. Neither charge was supported by even a simple majority vote in the Senate, on February 12, 1999.

▶ Clause 7. **Penalty on conviction** The punishment of an official convicted in an impeachment case has always been removal from office. The Senate can also bar a convicted person from ever holding any federal office, but it is not required to do so. A convicted person can also be tried and punished in a regular court for any crime involved in the impeachment case.

Section 4. Elections and Meetings

▶ **Clause 1. Election** In 1842 Congress required that representatives be elected from districts within each State with more than one seat in the House. The districts in each State are drawn by that State's legislature. Seven States now have only one seat in the House: Alaska, Delaware, Montana, North Dakota, South Dakota, Vermont, and Wyoming. The 1842 law also directed that representatives be elected in each State on the same day: the Tuesday after the first Monday in November of every even-numbered year. In 1914 Congress also set that same date for the election of senators.

▶ **Clause 2. Sessions** Congress must meet at least once a year. The 20th Amendment (1933) changed the opening date to January 3.

Section 5. Legislative Proceedings

▶ **Clause 1. Admission of members; quorum** In 1969 the Supreme Court held that the House cannot exclude any member-elect who satisfies the qualifications set out in Article I, Section 2, Clause 2.

A majority in the House (218 members) or Senate (51) constitutes a quorum. In practice, both houses often proceed with less than a quorum present. However, any member may raise a point of order (demand a "quorum call"). If a roll call then reveals less than a majority of the members present, that chamber must either adjourn or the sergeant at arms must be ordered to round up absent members.

▶ **Clause 2. Rules** Each house has adopted detailed rules to guide its proceedings. Each house may discipline members for unacceptable conduct; expulsion requires a two-thirds vote.

▶ **Clause 3. Record** Each house must keep and publish a record of its meetings. The Congressional Record is published for every day that either house of Congress is in session, and provides a written record of all that is said and done on the floor of each house each session.

▶ **Clause 4. Adjournment** Once in session, neither house may suspend (recess) its work for more than three days without the approval of the other house. Both houses must always meet in the same location.

Section 4.

▶ 1. The Times, Places and Manner of holding Elections for Senators and Representatives, shall be prescribed in each State by the Legislature thereof; but the Congress may at any time by law make or alter such Regulations, except as to the Places of choosing Senators.

▶ 2. The Congress shall assemble at least once in every Year, and such Meeting shall be on the first Monday in December, unless they shall by Law appoint a different Day.

Section 5.

▶ 1. Each House shall be the Judge of the Elections, Returns and Qualifications of its own Members, and a Majority of each shall constitute a Quorum to do Business; but a smaller Number may adjourn from day to day, and may be authorized to compel the Attendance of absent Members, in such Manner, and under such Penalties, as each House may provide.

▶ 2. Each House may determine the Rules of its Proceedings, punish its Members for disorderly Behavior, and, with the Concurrence of two thirds, expel a Member.

▶ 3. Each House shall keep a Journal of its Proceedings, and from time to time publish the same, excepting such Parts as may in their Judgment require Secrecy; and the Yeas and Nays of the Members of either House on any question shall, at the Desire of one fifth of those Present, be entered on the Journal.

▶ 4. Neither House, during the Session of Congress, shall, without the Consent of the other, adjourn for more than three days, nor to any other Place than that in which the two Houses shall be sitting.

Section 6.

▶ 1. The Senators and Representatives shall receive a Compensation for their Services, to be ascertained by Law, and paid out of the Treasury of the United States. They shall in all Cases, except Treason, Felony, and Breach of the Peace, be privileged from Arrest during their Attendance at the Session of their respective Houses, and in going to and returning from the same; and for any Speech or Debate in either House, they shall not be questioned in any other Place.

▶ 2. No Senator or Representative shall, during the Time for which he was elected, be appointed to any civil Office under the Authority of the United States, which shall have been created, or the Emoluments whereof shall have been increased during such time; and no Person holding any Office under the United States, shall be a Member of either House during his Continuance in Office.

Section 7.

▶ 1. All Bills for raising Revenue shall originate in the House of Representatives; but the Senate may propose or concur with amendments as on other Bills.

▶ 2. Every Bill which shall have passed the House of Representatives and the Senate, shall, before it become a law, be presented to the President of the United States: If he approve, he shall sign it, but if not he shall return it, with his Objections to that House in which it shall have originated, who shall enter the Objections at large on their Journal, and proceed to reconsider it. If after such Reconsideration two thirds of the House shall agree to pass the Bill, it shall be sent, together with the Objections, to the other House, by which it shall likewise be reconsidered, and if approved by two thirds of that House, it shall become a Law. But in all such Cases the Votes of both Houses shall be determined by Yeas and Nays, and the Names of the Persons voting for and against the Bill shall be entered on the Journal of each House respectively. If any Bill shall not be returned by the President within ten Days (Sunday excepted) after it shall have been presented to him, the Same shall be a law, in like Manner as if he had signed it, unless the Congress by their Adjournment, prevent its Return, in which Case it shall not be a Law.

▶ 3. Every Order, Resolution, or Vote to which the Concurrence of the Senate and House of Representatives may be necessary (except on a question of adjournment) shall be presented to the President of the United States; and before the Same shall take Effect, shall be approved by him, or, being disapproved by him, shall be repassed by two thirds of the Senate and House of Representatives, according to the Rules and Limitations prescribed in the Case of a Bill.

Section 6. Compensation, Immunities, and Disabilities of Members

▶ **Clause 1. Salaries; immunities** Each house sets its members' salaries, paid by the United States; the 27th Amendment (1992) modified this pay-setting power. This provision establishes "legislative immunity." The purpose of this immunity is to allow members to speak and debate freely in Congress itself. Treason is strictly defined in Article III, Section 3. A felony is any serious crime. A breach of the peace is any indictable offense less than treason or a felony; this exemption from arrest is of little real importance today.

▶ **Clause 2. Restrictions on office holding** No sitting member of either house may be appointed to an office in the executive or in the judicial branch if that position was created or its salary was increased during that member's current elected term. The second part of this clause—forbidding any person serving in either the executive or the judicial branch from also serving in Congress—reinforces the principle of separation of powers.

Section 7. Revenue Bills, President's Veto

▶ **Clause 1. Revenue bills** All bills that raise money must originate in the House. However, the Senate has the power to amend any revenue bill sent to it from the lower house.

▶ **Clause 2. Enactment of laws; veto** Once both houses have passed a bill, it must be sent to the President. The President may (1) sign the bill, thus making it law; (2) veto the bill, whereupon it must be returned to the house in which it originated; or (3) allow the bill to become law without signature, by not acting upon it within 10 days of its receipt from Congress, not counting Sundays. The President has a fourth option at the end of a congressional session: If he does not act on a measure within 10 days, and Congress adjourns during that period, the bill dies; the "pocket veto" has been applied to it. A presidential veto may be overridden by a two-thirds vote in each house.

▶ **Clause 3. Other measures** This clause refers to joint resolutions, measures Congress often passes to deal with unusual, temporary, or ceremonial matters. A joint resolution passed by Congress and signed by the President has the force of law, just as a bill does. As a matter of custom, a joint resolution proposing an amendment to the Constitution is not submitted to the President for signature or veto. Concurrent and simple resolutions do not have the force of law and, therefore, are not submitted to the President.

Section 8. Powers of Congress

▶ **Clause 1.** The 18 separate clauses in this section set out 27 of the many expressed powers the Constitution grants to Congress. In this clause Congress is given the power to levy and provide for the collection of various kinds of taxes, in order to finance the operations of the government. All federal taxes must be levied at the same rates throughout the country.

▶ **Clause 2.** Congress has power to borrow money to help finance the government. Federal borrowing is most often done through the sale of bonds on which interest is paid. The Constitution does not limit the amount the government may borrow.

▶ **Clause 3.** This clause, the Commerce Clause, gives Congress the power to regulate both foreign and interstate trade. Much of what Congress does, it does on the basis of its commerce power.

▶ **Clause 4.** Congress has the exclusive power to determine how aliens may become citizens of the United States. Congress may also pass laws relating to bankruptcy.

▶ **Clause 5.** has the power to establish and require the use of uniform gauges of time, distance, weight, volume, area, and the like.

▶ **Clause 6.** Congress has the power to make it a federal crime to falsify the coins, paper money, bonds, stamps, and the like of the United States.

▶ **Clause 7.** Congress has the power to provide for and regulate the transportation and delivery of mail; "post offices" are those buildings and other places where mail is deposited for dispatch; "post roads" include all routes over or upon which mail is carried.

▶ **Clause 8.** Congress has the power to provide for copyrights and patents. A copyright gives an author or composer the exclusive right to control the reproduction, publication, and sale of literary, musical, or other creative work. A patent gives a person the exclusive right to control the manufacture or sale of his or her invention.

▶ **Clause 9.** Congress has the power to create the lower federal courts, all of the several federal courts that function beneath the Supreme Court.

▶ **Clause 10.** Congress has the power to prohibit, as a federal crime: (1) certain acts committed outside the territorial jurisdiction of the United States, and (2) the commission within the United States of any wrong against any nation with which we are at peace.

Section 8.

The Congress shall have Power

▶ 1. To lay and collect Taxes, Duties, Imposts and Excises to pay the Debts and provide for the common Defence and general Welfare of the United States; but all Duties, Imposts and Excises, shall be uniform throughout the United States;

▶ 2. To borrow Money on the credit of the United States;

▶ 3. To regulate Commerce with foreign Nations, and among the several States, and with the Indian Tribes;

▶ 4. To establish an uniform Rule of Naturalization, and uniform Laws on the subject of Bankruptcies throughout the United States;

▶ 5. To coin Money, regulate the Value thereof, and of foreign Coin, and fix the Standard of Weights and Measures;

▶ 6. To provide for the Punishment of counterfeiting the Securities and current Coin of the United States;

▶ 7. To establish Post Offices and post Roads;

▶ 8. To promote the Progress of Science and useful Arts, by securing, for limited Times to Authors and Inventors the exclusive Right to their respective Writings and Discoveries;

▶ 9. To constitute Tribunals inferior to the supreme Court;

▶ 10. To define and punish Piracies and Felonies committed on the high Seas, and Offences against the Law of nations;

11. To declare War, grant Letters of Marque and Reprisal, and make Rules concerning Captures on Land and Water;

▶ Clause 11. Only Congress can declare war. However, the President, as commander in chief of the armed forces (Article II, Section 2, Clause 1), can make war without such a formal declaration. Letters of marque and reprisal are commissions authorizing private persons to outfit vessels (privateers) to capture and destroy enemy ships in time of war; they were forbidden in international law by the Declaration of Paris of 1856, and the United States has honored the ban since the Civil War.

12. To raise and support Armies; but no Appropriation of Money to that Use shall be for a longer Term than two Years;
13. To provide and maintain a Navy;

▶ Clause 12 and 13. Congress has the power to provide for and maintain the nation's armed forces. It established the air force as an independent element of the armed forces in 1947, an exercise of its inherent powers in foreign relations and national defense. The two-year limit on spending for the army insures civilian control of the military.

14. To make Rules for the Government and Regulation of the land and naval Forces;

▶ Clause 14. Today these rules are set out in three principle statutes: the Uniform Code of Military Justice, passed by Congress in 1950, and the Military Justice Acts of 1958 and 1983.

15. To provide for calling forth the Militia to execute the Laws of the Union, suppress Insurrections and repel Invasions;
16. To provide for organizing, arming, and disciplining the Militia, and for governing such Part of them as may be employed in the Service of the United States, reserving to the States respectively the Appointment of the Officers, and the Authority of training the Militia according to the discipline prescribed by Congress;

▶ Clause 15 and 16. In the National Defense Act of 1916, Congress made each State's militia (volunteer army) a part of the National Guard. Today, Congress and the States cooperate in its maintenance. Ordinarily, each State's National Guard is under the command of that State's governor; but Congress has given the President the power to call any or all of those units into federal service when necessary.

17. To exercise exclusive Legislation in all Cases whatsoever, over such District (not exceeding ten Miles square) as may, by Cession of Particular States, and the Acceptance of Congress, become the Seat of the Government of the United States, and to exercise like Authority over all Places purchased by the Consent of the Legislature of the State in which the Same shall be, for the Erection of Forts, Magazines, Arsenals, Dockyards and other needful Buildings;—And

▶ Clause 17. In 1791 Congress accepted land grants from Maryland and Virginia and established the District of Columbia for the nation's capital. Assuming Virginia's grant would never be needed, Congress returned it in 1846. Today, the elected government of the District's 69 square miles operates under the authority of Congress. Congress also has the power to acquire other lands from the States for various federal purposes.

18. To make all Laws which shall be necessary and proper for carrying into Execution the foregoing Powers and all other Powers vested by this Constitution in the Government of the United States, or in any Department or Officer thereof.

▶ Clause 18. This is the Necessary and Proper Clause, also often called the Elastic Clause. It is the constitutional basis for the many and far-reaching implied powers of the Federal Government.

Section 9.

1. The Migration or Importation of such Persons as any of the States now existing shall think proper to admit, shall not be prohibited by the Congress prior to the Year one thousand eight hundred and eight, but a Tax or duty may be imposed on such Importation, not exceeding ten dollars for each Person.

Section 9. Powers Denied to Congress

▶ Clause 1. The phrase "such persons" referred to slaves. This provision was part of the Commerce Compromise, one of the bargains struck in the writing of the Constitution. Congress outlawed the slave trade in 1808.

Clause 2. A writ of habeas corpus, the "great writ of liberty," is a court order directing a sheriff, warden, or other public officer, or a private person, who is detaining another to "produce the body" of the one being held in order that the legality of the detention may be determined by the court.

Clause 3. A bill of attainder is a legislative act that inflicts punishment without a judicial trial. See Article I, Section 10, and Article III, Section 3, Clause 2. An ex post facto law is any criminal law that operates retroactively to the disadvantage of the accused. See Article I, Section 10.

Clause 4. A capitation tax is literally a "head tax," a tax levied on each person in the population. A direct tax is one paid directly to the government by the taxpayer—for example, an income or a property tax; an indirect tax is one paid to another private party who then pays it to the government—for example, a sales tax. This provision was modified by the 16th Amendment (1913), giving Congress the power to levy "taxes on incomes, from whatever source derived."

Clause 5. This provision was a part of the Commerce Compromise made by the Framers in 1787. Congress has the power to tax imported goods, however.

Clause 6. All ports within the United States must be treated alike by Congress as it exercises its taxing and commerce powers. Congress cannot tax goods sent by water from one State to another, nor may it give the ports of one State any legal advantage over those of another.

Clause 7. This clause gives Congress its vastly important "power of the purse," a major check on presidential power. Federal money can be spent only in those amounts and for those purposes expressly authorized by an act of Congress. All federal income and spending must be accounted for, regularly and publicly.

Clause 8. This provision, preventing the establishment of a nobility, reflects the principle that "all men are created equal." It was also intended to discourage foreign attempts to bribe or otherwise corrupt officers of the government.

Section 10. Powers Denied to the States

Clause 1. The States are not sovereign governments and so cannot make agreements or otherwise negotiate with foreign states; the power to conduct foreign relations is an exclusive power of the National Government. The power to coin money is also an exclusive power of the National Government. Several powers forbidden to the National Government are here also forbidden to the States.

Clause 2. This provision relates to foreign, not interstate, commerce. Only Congress, not the States, can tax imports; and the States are, like Congress, forbidden the power to tax exports.

2. The Privilege of the Writ of Habeas Corpus shall not be suspended, unless when in Cases of Rebellion or Invasion the public safety may require it.

3. No Bill of Attainder or ex post facto Law shall be passed.

4. No Capitation, or other direct, Tax shall be laid, unless in Proportion to the Census of Enumeration hereinbefore directed to be taken.

5. No Tax or Duty shall be laid on Articles exported from any State.

6. No Preference shall be given by any Regulation of Commerce or Revenue to the Ports of one State over those of another: nor shall Vessels bound to, or from, one State, be obliged to enter, clear or pay Duties in another.

7. No Money shall be drawn from the Treasury, but in Consequence of Appropriations made by Law; and a regular Statement and Account of the Receipts and Expenditures of all public Money shall be published from time to time.

8. No Title of Nobility shall be granted by the United States: And no Person holding any Office of Profit or Trust under them, shall, without the Consent of the Congress, accept of any present, Emolument, Office, or Title, of any kind whatever, from any King, Prince, or foreign State.

Section 10.

1. No State shall enter into any Treaty, Alliance, or Confederation; grant Letters of Marque and Reprisal; coin Money; emit Bills of Credit; make any Thing but gold and silver Coin a Tender in Payment of Debts; pass any Bill of Attainder, ex post facto Law, or Law impairing the Obligation of Contracts, or grant any Title of Nobility.

2. No State shall, without the Consent of the Congress, lay any Imposts or Duties on Imports or Exports, except what may be absolutely necessary for executing its inspection Laws; and the net Produce of all Duties and Imposts, laid by any State on Imports or Exports, shall be for the Use of the Treasury of the United States; and all such Laws shall be subject to the Revision and Control of the Congress.

3. No State shall, without the Consent of Congress, lay any Duty of Tonnage, keep Troops, or Ships of War in time of Peace, enter into any Agreement or Compact with another State, or with a foreign Power, or engage in War, unless actually invaded, or in such imminent Danger as will not admit of delay.

Article II

Section 1.

1. The executive Power shall be vested in a President of the United States of America. He shall hold his Office during the Term of four Years, and, together with the Vice President, chosen for the same Term, be elected as follows:

2. Each State shall appoint, in such Manner as the Legislature thereof may direct, a Number of Electors, equal to the whole Number of Senators and Representatives to which the State may be entitled in the Congress: but no Senator or Representative, or Person holding an Office of Trust or Profit, under the United States, shall be appointed an Elector.

3. The Electors shall meet in their respective States, and vote by Ballot for two Persons, of whom one at least shall not be an Inhabitant of the same State with themselves. And they shall make a List of all the Persons voted for, and of the Number of Votes for each; which List they shall sign and certify, and transmit sealed to the Seat of the Government of the United States, directed to the President of the Senate. The President of the Senate shall, in the Presence of the Senate and House of Representatives, open all the Certificates, and the Votes shall then be counted. The Person having the greatest Number of Votes shall be the President, if such Number be a majority of the whole Number of Electors appointed; and if there be more than one who have such Majority, and have an equal Number of Votes, then, the House of Representatives shall immediately choose by Ballot one of them for President; and if no Person have a Majority, then from the five highest on the List the said House shall in like Manner choose the President. But in choosing the President, the Votes shall be taken by States, the Representatives from each State having one Vote; a quorum for this Purpose shall consist of a Member or Members from two thirds of the States, and a Majority of all the States shall be necessary to a Choice. In every Case, after the Choice of the President, the Person having the greatest Number of Votes of the Electors shall be the Vice President. But if there should remain two or more who have equal Votes, the Senate shall choose from them by Ballot the Vice President.

▶ Clause 3. A duty of tonnage is a tax laid on ships according to their cargo capacity. Each State has a constitutional right to provide for and maintain a militia; but no State may keep a standing army or navy. The several restrictions here prevent the States from assuming powers that the Constitution elsewhere grants to the National Government.

Executive Department

Section 1. President and Vice President

▶ Clause 1. **Executive power, term** This clause gives to the President the very broad "executive power," the power to enforce the laws and otherwise administer the public policies of the United States. It also sets the length of the presidential (and vice-presidential) term of office; see the 22nd Amendment (1951), which places a limit on presidential (but not vice-presidential) tenure.

▶ Clause 2. **Electoral college** This clause establishes the "electoral college," although the Constitution does not use that term. It is a body of presidential electors chosen in each State, and it selects the President and Vice President every four years. The number of electors chosen in each State equals the number of senators and representatives that State has in Congress.

▶ Clause 3. **Election of President and Vice President** This clause was replaced by the 12th Amendment in 1804.

Clause 4. Date Congress has set the date for the choosing of electors as the Tuesday after the first Monday in November every fourth year, and for the casting of electoral votes as the Monday after the second Wednesday in December of that year.

Clause 5. Qualifications The President must have been born a citizen of the United States, be at least 35 years old, and have been a resident of the United States for at least 14 years.

Clause 6. Vacancy This clause was modified by the 25th Amendment (1967), which provides expressly for the succession of the Vice President, for the filling of a vacancy in the Vice Presidency, and for the determination of presidential inability.

Clause 7. Compensation The President now receives a salary of $400,000 and a taxable expense account of $50,000 a year. Those amounts cannot be changed during a presidential term; thus, Congress cannot use the President's compensation as a bargaining tool to influence executive decisions. The phrase "any other emolument" means, in effect, any valuable gift; it does not mean that the President cannot be provided with such benefits of office as the White House, extensive staff assistance, and much else.

Clause 8. Oath of office The Chief Justice of the United States regularly administers this oath or affirmation, but any judicial officer may do so. Thus, Calvin Coolidge was sworn into office in 1923 by his father, a justice of the peace in Vermont.

Section 2. President's Powers and Duties

Clause 1. Military, civil powers The President, a civilian, heads the nation's armed forces, a key element in the Constitution's insistence on civilian control of the military. The President's power to "require the opinion, in writing" provides the constitutional basis for the Cabinet. The President's power to grant reprieves and pardons, the power of clemency, extends only to federal cases.

▶ 4. The Congress may determine the Time of choosing the Electors, and the Day on which they shall give their Votes; which Day shall be the same throughout the United States.

▶ 5. No Person except a natural born Citizen, or a Citizen of the United States, at the time of the Adoption of this Constitution, shall be eligible to the Office of President; neither shall any person be eligible to that Office who shall not have attained to the Age of thirty-five Years, and been fourteen Years a Resident within the United States.

▶ 6. In Case of the Removal of the President from Office, or of his Death, Resignation, or Inability to discharge the Powers and Duties of the said Office, the Same shall devolve on the Vice President, and the Congress may by Law provide for the Case of Removal, Death, Resignation or Inability, both of the President and Vice President, declaring what Officer shall then act as President, and such Officer shall act accordingly, until the Disability be removed, or a President shall be elected.

▶ 7. The President shall, at stated Times, receive for his Services, a Compensation, which shall neither be increased nor diminished during the Period for which he shall have been elected, and he shall not receive within that Period any other Emolument from the United States, or any of them.

▶ 8. Before he enter on the Execution of his Office, he shall take the following Oath or Affirmation:
"I do solemnly swear (or affirm) that I will faithfully execute the Office of President of the United States, and will to the best of my Ability, preserve, protect and defend the Constitution of the United States."

Section 2.

▶ 1. The President shall be Commander in Chief of the Army and Navy of the United States, and of the Militia of the several States, when called into the actual Service of the United States; he may require the Opinion, in writing, of the principal Officer in each of the executive Departments, upon any Subject relating to the Duties of their respective Offices, and he shall have Power to Grant Reprieves and Pardons for Offences against the United States, except in Cases of Impeachment.

2. He shall have Power, by and with the Advice and Consent of the Senate, to make Treaties, provided two thirds of the Senators present concur; and he shall nominate, and by and with the Advice and Consent of the Senate, shall appoint Ambassadors, other public Ministers and Consuls, Judges of the supreme Court, and all other Officers of the United States, whose Appointments are not herein otherwise provided for, and which shall be established by Law: but the Congress may by Law vest the Appointment of such inferior Officers, as they think proper, in the President alone, in the Courts of Law, or in the Heads of Departments.

3. The President shall have Power to fill up all Vacancies that may happen during the Recess of the Senate, by granting Commissions which shall expire at the End of their next Session.

Section 3.

He shall from time to time give to the Congress Information of the State of the Union, and recommend to their Consideration such Measures as he shall judge necessary and expedient; he may, on extraordinary Occasions, convene both Houses, or either of them, and in Case of Disagreement between them, with Respect to the Time of Adjournment, he may adjourn them to such Time as he shall think proper; he shall receive Ambassadors and other public Ministers; he shall take Care that the Laws be faithfully executed, and shall Commission all the Officers of the United States.

Section 4.

The President, Vice President and all Civil Officers of the United States, shall be removed from Office on Impeachment for and Conviction of, Treason, Bribery, or other high Crimes and Misdemeanors.

Article III

Section 1.

The judicial Power of the United States, shall be vested in one supreme Court, and in such inferior Courts as the Congress may from time to time ordain and establish. The Judges, both of the supreme and inferior Courts, shall hold their Offices during good Behaviour, and shall, at stated Times, receive for their Services, a Compensation, which shall not be diminished during their Continuance in Office.

▶ **Clause 2. Treaties, appointments** The President has the sole power to make treaties; to become effective, a treaty must be approved by a two-thirds vote in the Senate. In practice, the President can also make executive agreements with foreign governments; these pacts, which are frequently made and usually deal with routine matters, do not require Senate consent. The President appoints the principal officers of the executive branch and all federal judges; the "inferior officers" are those who hold lesser posts.

▶ **Clause 3. Recess appointments** When the Senate is not in session, appointments that require Senate consent can be made by the President on a temporary basis, as "recess appointments." Recess appointments are valid only to the end of the congressional term in which they are made.

Section 3. President's Powers and Duties

The President delivers a State of the Union Message to Congress soon after that body convenes each year. That message is delivered to the nation's lawmakers and, importantly, to the American people, as well. It is shortly followed by the proposed federal budget and an economic report; and the President may send special messages to Congress at any time. In all of these communications, Congress is urged to take those actions the Chief Executive finds to be in the national interest. The President also has the power: to call special sessions of Congress; to adjourn Congress if its two houses cannot agree for that purpose; to receive the diplomatic representatives of other governments; to insure the proper execution of all federal laws; and to empower federal officers to hold their posts and perform their duties.

Section 4. Impeachment

The Constitution outlines the impeachment process in Article I, Section 2, Clause 5 and in Section 3, Clauses 6 and 7.

Judicial Department

Section 1. Judicial Power, Courts, Terms of Office

The judicial power conferred here is the power of federal courts to hear and decide cases, disputes between the government and individuals and between private persons (parties). The Constitution creates only the Supreme Court of the United States; it gives to Congress the power to establish other, lower federal courts (Article I, Section 8, Clause 9) and to fix the size of the Supreme Court. The words "during good behaviour" mean, in effect, for life.

Section 2. Jurisdiction

▶ Clause 1. **Cases to be heard** This clause sets out the jurisdiction of the federal courts; that is, it identifies those cases that may be tried in those courts. The federal courts can hear and decide—have jurisdiction over—a case depending on either the subject matter or the parties involved in that case. The jurisdiction of the federal courts in cases involving States was substantially restricted by the 11th Amendment in 1795.

▶ Clause 2. **Supreme Court jurisdiction** Original jurisdiction refers to the power of a court to hear a case in the first instance, not on appeal from a lower court. Appellate jurisdiction refers to a court's power to hear a case on appeal from a lower court, from the court in which the case was originally tried. This clause gives the Supreme Court both original and appellate jurisdiction. However, nearly all of the cases the High Court hears are brought to it on appeal from the lower federal courts and the highest State courts.

▶ Clause 3. **Jury trial in criminal cases** A person accused of a federal crime is guaranteed the right to trial by jury in a federal court in the State where the crime was committed; see the 5th and 6th amendments. The right to trial by jury in serious criminal cases in the State courts is guaranteed by the 6th and 14th amendments.

Section 3. Treason

▶ Clause 1. **Definition** Treason is the only crime defined in the Constitution. The Framers intended the very specific definition here to prevent the loose use of the charge of treason—for example, against persons who criticize the government. Treason can be committed only in time of war and only by a citizen or a resident alien.

▶ Clause 2. **Punishment** Congress has provided that the punishment that a federal court may impose on a convicted traitor may range from a minimum of five years in prison and/or a $10,000 fine to a maximum of death; no person convicted of treason has ever been executed by the United States. No legal punishment can be imposed on the family or descendants of a convicted traitor. Congress has also made it a crime for any person (in either peace or wartime) to commit espionage or sabotage, to attempt to overthrow the government by force, or to conspire to do any of these things.

Section 2.

▶ 1. The judicial Power shall extend to all Cases, in Law and Equity, arising under this Constitution, the Laws of the United States, and Treaties made, or which shall be made, under their Authority;— to all Cases affecting Ambassadors, other public ministers, and Consuls;— to all Cases of Admiralty and maritime Jurisdiction;— to Controversies to which the United States shall be a Party;— to Controversies between two or more States;— between a State and Citizens of another State;— between Citizens of different States;— between Citizens of the same State claiming Lands under Grants of different States, and between a State, or the Citizens thereof, and foreign States, Citizens, or Subjects.

▶ 2. In all Cases affecting Ambassadors, other public Ministers and Consuls, and those in which a State shall be a Party, the supreme Court shall have original Jurisdiction. In all the other Cases before mentioned, the supreme Court shall have appellate Jurisdiction, both as to Law and Fact, with such Exceptions, and under such Regulations as the Congress shall make.

▶ 3. The trial of all Crimes, except in Cases of Impeachment, shall be by Jury; and such Trial shall be held in the State where the said Crimes shall have been committed; but when not committed within any State, the Trial shall be at such Place or Places as the Congress may by Law have directed.

Section 3.

▶ 1. Treason against the United States shall consist only in levying War against them, or in adhering to their Enemies, giving them Aid and Comfort. No Person shall be convicted of Treason unless on the Testimony of two Witnesses to the same overt Act, or on Confession in open Court.

▶ 2. The Congress shall have Power to declare the Punishment of Treason, but no Attainder of Treason shall work Corruption of Blood, or Forfeiture except during the Life of the Person attainted.

Article IV

Section 1.

Full Faith and Credit shall be given in each State to the public Acts, Records, and judicial Proceedings of every other State. And the Congress may by general Laws prescribe the Manner in which such Acts, Records and Proceedings shall be proved, and the Effect thereof.

Section 2.

▶ 1. The Citizens of each State shall be entitled to all Privileges and Immunities of Citizens in the several States.

▶ 2. A Person charged in any State with Treason, Felony, or other Crime, who shall flee from justice, and be found in another State, shall on Demand of the executive Authority of the State from which he fled, be delivered up, to be removed to the State having Jurisdiction of the Crime.

▶ 3. No Person held to Service or Labor in one State, under the Laws thereof, escaping into another, shall, in Consequence of any Law or Regulation therein, be discharged from Service or Labor, but shall be delivered up on Claim of the Party to whom such Service or Labor may be due.

Section 3.

▶ 1. New States may be admitted by the Congress into this Union; but no new State shall be formed or erected within the Jurisdiction of any other State; nor any State be formed by the Junction of two or more States, or Parts of States, without the Consent of the Legislatures of the States concerned as well as of the Congress.

▶ 2. The Congress shall have Power to dispose of and make all needful Rules and Regulations respecting the Territory or other Property belonging to the United States; and nothing in this Constitution shall be so construed as to Prejudice any Claims of the United States, or of any particular State.

Section 4.

The United States shall guarantee to every State in this Union a Republican Form of Government, and shall protect each of them against Invasion; and on Application of the Legislature, or of the Executive (when the Legislature cannot be convened) against domestic Violence.

Relations Among States

Section 1. Full Faith and Credit

Each State must recognize the validity of the laws, public records, and court decisions of every other State.

Section 2. Privileges and Immunities of Citizens

▶ **Clause 1. Residents of other States** In effect, this clause means that no State may discriminate against the residents of other States; that is, a State's laws cannot draw unreasonable distinctions between its own residents and those of any of the other States. See Section 1 of the 14th Amendment.

▶ **Clause 2. Extradition** The process of returning a fugitive to another State is known as "interstate rendition" or, more commonly, "extradition." Usually, that process works routinely; some extradition requests are contested however—especially in cases with racial or political overtones. A governor may refuse to extradite a fugitive; but the federal courts can compel an unwilling governor to obey this constitutional command.

▶ **Clause 3. Fugitive slaves** This clause was nullified by the 13th Amendment, which abolished slavery in 1865.

Section 3. New States; Territories

▶ **Clause 1. New States** Only Congress can admit new States to the Union. A new State may not be created by taking territory from an existing State without the consent of that State's legislature. Congress has admitted 37 States since the original 13 formed the Union. Five States—Vermont, Kentucky, Tennessee, Maine, and West Virginia—were created from parts of existing States. Texas was an independent republic before admission. California was admitted after being ceded to the United States by Mexico. Each of the other 30 States entered the Union only after a period of time as an organized territory of the United States.

▶ **Clause 2. Territory, property** Congress has the power to make laws concerning the territories, other public lands, and all other property of the United States.

Section 4. Protection Afforded to States by the Nation

The Constitution does not define "a republican form of government," but the phrase is generally understood to mean a representative government. The Federal Government must also defend each State against attacks from outside its border and, at the request of a State's legislature or its governor, aid its efforts to put down internal disorders.

Provisions for Amendment

This section provides for the methods by which formal changes can be made in the Constitution. An amendment may be proposed in one of two ways: by a two-thirds vote in each house of Congress, or by a national convention called by Congress at the request of two-thirds of the State legislatures. A proposed amendment may be ratified in one of two ways: by three-fourths of the State legislatures, or by three-fourths of the States in conventions called for that purpose. Congress has the power to determine the method by which a proposed amendment may be ratified. The amendment process cannot be used to deny any State its equal representation in the United States Senate. To this point, 27 amendments have been adopted. To date, all of the amendments except the 21st Amendment were proposed by Congress and ratified by the State legislatures. Only the 21st Amendment was ratified by the convention method.

National Debts, Supremacy of National Law, Oath

Section 1. Validity of Debts

Congress had borrowed large sums of money during the Revolution and later during the Critical Period of the 1780s. This provision, a pledge that the new government would honor those debts, did much to create confidence in that government.

Section 2. Supremacy of National Law

This section sets out the Supremacy Clause, a specific declaration of the supremacy of federal law over any and all forms of State law. No State, including its local governments, may make or enforce any law that conflicts with any provision in the Constitution, an act of Congress, a treaty, or an order, rule, or regulation properly issued by the President or his subordinates in the executive branch.

Section 3. Oaths of Office

This provision reinforces the Supremacy Clause; all public officers, at every level in the United States, owe their first allegiance to the Constitution of the United States. No religious qualification can be imposed as a condition for holding any public office.

Ratification of Constitution

The proposed Constitution was signed by George Washington and 37 of his fellow Framers on September 17, 1787. (George Read of Delaware signed for himself and also for his absent colleague, John Dickinson.)

Article V

The Congress, whenever two thirds of both Houses shall deem it necessary, shall propose Amendments to this Constitution, or, on the Application of the Legislatures of two thirds of the several States, shall call a Convention for proposing Amendments, which, in either Case, shall be valid to all Intents and Purposes, as Part of this Constitution, when ratified by the Legislatures of three fourths of the several States, or by Conventions in three fourths thereof, as the one or the other Mode of Ratification may be proposed by the Congress; Provided that no Amendment which may be made prior to the Year One thousand eight hundred and eight shall in any Manner affect the first and fourth Clauses in the Ninth section of the first Article; and that no State, without its Consent, shall be deprived of its equal Suffrage in the Senate.

Article VI

Section 1.

All Debts contracted and Engagements entered into, before the Adoption of this Constitution, shall be as valid against the United States under this Constitution, as under the Confederation.

Section 2.

This Constitution, and the Laws of the United States which shall be made in Pursuance thereof; and all Treaties made, or which shall be made, under the Authority of the United States, shall be the supreme Law of the Land; and the Judges in every State shall be bound thereby, anything in the constitution or Laws of any State to the Contrary notwithstanding.

Section 3.

The Senators and Representatives before mentioned, and the Members of the several State legislatures, and all executive and judicial Officers, both of the United States and of the several States, shall be bound by Oath or Affirmation, to support this Constitution; but no religious Test shall ever be required as a Qualification to any Office or public Trust under the United States.

Article VII

The ratification of the Conventions of nine States, shall be sufficient for the Establishment of this Constitution between the States so ratifying the same.

Done in Convention by the Unanimous Consent of the States present the Seventeenth Day of September in the Year of our Lord one thousand seven hundred and Eighty-seven and of the Independence of the United States of America the twelfth. In witness whereof We have hereunto subscribed our Names.

Attest:

William Jackson,
Secretary
George Washington,
*President and Deputy
from Virginia*

New Hampshire

John Langdon
Nicholas Gilman

Massachusetts

Nathaniel Gorham
Rufus King

Connecticut

William Samuel Johnson
Roger Sherman

New York

Alexander Hamilton

New Jersey

William Livingston
David Brearley
William Paterson
Jonathan Dayton

Pennsylvania

Benjamin Franklin
Thomas Mifflin
Robert Morris
George Clymer
Thomas Fitzsimons
Jared Ingersoll
James Wilson
Gouverneur Morris

Delaware

George Read
Gunning Bedford, Jr.
John Dickinson
Richard Bassett
Jacob Broom

Maryland

James McHenry
Dan of St. Thomas Jenifer
Daniel Carroll

Virginia

John Blair
James Madison, Jr.

North Carolina

William Blount
Richard Dobbs Spaight
Hugh Williamson

South Carolina

John Rutledge
Charles Cotesworth
  Pinckney
Charles Pinckney
Pierce Butler

Georgia

William Few
Abraham Baldwin

Amendments

The first 10 amendments, the Bill of Rights, were each proposed by Congress on September 25, 1789, and ratified by the necessary three-fourths of the States on December 15, 1791. These amendments were originally intended to restrict the National Government—not the States. However, the Supreme Court has several times held that most of their provisions also apply to the States, through the 14th Amendment's Due Process Clause.

1st Amendment. **Freedom of Religion, Speech, Press, Assembly, and Petition**

The 1st Amendment sets out five basic liberties: The guarantee of freedom of religion is both a protection of religious thought and practice and a command of separation of church and state. The guarantees of freedom of speech and press assure to all persons a right to speak, publish, and otherwise express their views. The guarantees of the rights of assembly and petition protect the right to join with others in public meetings, political parties, interest groups, and other associations to discuss public affairs and influence public policy. None of these rights is guaranteed in absolute terms, however; like all other civil rights guarantees, each of them may be exercised only with regard to the rights of all other persons.

2nd Amendment. **Bearing Arms**

The right of the people to keep and bear arms was insured by the 2nd Amendment.

3rd Amendment. **Quartering of Troops**

This amendment was intended to prevent what had been common British practice in the colonial period; see the Declaration of Independence. This provision is of virtually no importance today.

4th Amendment. **Searches and Seizures**

The basic rule laid down by the 4th Amendment is this: Police officers have no general right to search for or seize evidence or seize (arrest) persons. Except in particular circumstances, they must have a proper warrant (a court order) obtained with probable cause (on reasonable grounds). This guarantee is reinforced by the exclusionary rule, developed by the Supreme Court: Evidence gained as the result of an unlawful search or seizure cannot be used at the court trial of the person from whom it was seized.

5th Amendment. **Criminal Proceedings; Due Process; Eminent Domain**

A person can be tried for a serious federal crime only if he or she has been indicted (charged, accused of that crime) by a grand jury. No one may be subjected to double jeopardy—that is, tried twice for the same crime. All persons are protected against self-incrimination; no person can be legally compelled to answer any question in any governmental proceeding if that answer could lead to that person's prosecution. The 5th Amendment's Due Process Clause prohibits unfair, arbitrary actions by the Federal Government; a like prohibition is set out against the States in the 14th Amendment. Government may take private property for a legitimate public purpose; but when it exercises that power of eminent domain, it must pay a fair price for the property seized.

1st Amendment

Congress shall make no law respecting an establishment of religion, or prohibiting the free exercise thereof, or abridging the freedom of speech, or of the press; or the right of the people peaceably to assemble, and to petition the Government for a redress of grievances.

2nd Amendment

A well-regulated Militia being necessary to the security of a free State, the right of the people to keep and bear Arms, shall not be infringed.

3rd Amendment

No Soldier shall, in time of peace be quartered in any house, without the consent of the Owner, nor, in time of war, but in a manner to be prescribed by law.

4th Amendment

The right of the people to be secure in their persons, houses, papers, and effects, against unreasonable searches and seizures, shall not be violated, and no Warrants shall issue, but upon probable cause, supported by Oath or affirmation, and particularly describing the place to be searched, and the persons or things to be seized.

5th Amendment

No person shall be held to answer for a capital, or otherwise infamous crime, unless on a presentment or indictment of a Grand Jury, except in cases arising in the land or naval forces, or in the Militia, when in actual service in time of War, or public danger; nor shall any person be subject for the same offence to be twice put in jeopardy of life or limb; nor shall be compelled in any criminal case to be a witness against himself, nor be deprived of life, liberty, or property, without due process of law; nor shall private property be taken for public use, without just compensation.

6th Amendment

In all criminal prosecutions, the accused shall enjoy the right to a speedy and public trial, by an impartial jury of the State and district wherein the crime shall have been committed, which district shall have been previously ascertained by law, and to be informed of the nature and cause of the accusation; to be confronted with the witnesses against him; to have compulsory process for obtaining witnesses in his favor, and to have the Assistance of Counsel for his defence.

7th Amendment

In Suits at common law, where the value in controversy shall exceed twenty dollars, the right of trial by jury shall be preserved, and no fact tried by a jury, shall be otherwise re-examined in any Court of the United States, than according to the rules of the common law.

8th Amendment

Excessive bail shall not be required, nor excessive fines imposed, nor cruel and unusual punishment inflicted.

9th Amendment

The enumeration in the Constitution, of certain rights, shall not be construed to deny or disparage others retained by the people.

10th Amendment

The powers not delegated to the United States by the Constitution, nor prohibited by it to the States, are reserved to the States respectively, or to the people.

6th Amendment. **Criminal Proceedings**

A person accused of crime has the right to be tried in court without undue delay and by an impartial jury; see Article III, Section 2, Clause 3. The defendant must be informed of the charge upon which he or she is to be tried, has the right to cross-examine hostile witnesses, and has the right to require the testimony of favorable witnesses. The defendant also has the right to be represented by an attorney at every stage in the criminal process.

7th Amendment. **Civil Trials**

This amendment applies only to civil cases heard in federal courts. A civil case does not involve criminal matters; it is a dispute between private parties or between the government and a private party. The right to trial by jury is guaranteed in any civil case in a federal court if the amount of money involved in that case exceeds $20 (most cases today involve a much larger sum); that right may be waived (relinquished, put aside) if both parties agree to a bench trial (a trial by a judge, without a jury).

8th Amendment. **Punishment for Crimes**

Bail is the sum of money that a person accused of crime may be required to post (deposit with the court) as a guarantee that he or she will appear in court at the proper time. The amount of bail required and/or a fine imposed as punishment must bear a reasonable relationship to the seriousness of the crime involved in the case. The prohibition of cruel and unusual punishment forbids any punishment judged to be too harsh, too severe for the crime for which it is imposed.

9th Amendment. **Unenumerated Rights**

The fact that the Constitution sets out many civil rights guarantees, expressly provides for many protections against government, does not mean that there are not other rights also held by the people.

10th Amendment. **Powers Reserved to the States**

This amendment identifies the area of power that may be exercised by the States. All of those powers the Constitution does not grant to the National Government, and at the same time does not forbid to the States, belong to each of the States, or to the people of each State.

11th Amendment. **Suits Against States**

Proposed by Congress March 4, 1794; ratified February 7, 1795, but official announcement of the ratification was delayed until January 8, 1798. This amendment repealed part of Article III, Section 2, Clause 1. No State may be sued in a federal court by a resident of another State or of a foreign country; the Supreme Court has long held that this provision also means that a State cannot be sued in a federal court by a foreign country or, more importantly, even by one of its own residents.

12th Amendment. **Election of President and Vice President**

Proposed by Congress December 9, 1803; ratified June 15, 1804. This amendment replaced Article II, Section 1, Clause 3. Originally, each elector cast two ballots, each for a different person for President. The person with the largest number of electoral votes, provided that number was a majority of the electors, was to become President; the person with the second highest number was to become Vice President. This arrangement produced an electoral vote tie between Thomas Jefferson and Aaron Burr in 1800; the House finally chose Jefferson as President in 1801. The 12th Amendment separated the balloting for President and Vice President; each elector now casts one ballot for someone as President and a second ballot for another person as Vice President. Note that the 20th Amendment changed the date set here (March 4) to January 20, and that the 23rd Amendment (1961) provides for electors from the District of Columbia. This amendment also provides that the Vice President must meet the same qualifications as those set out for the President in Article II, Section 1, Clause 5.

13th Amendment. **Slavery and Involuntary Servitude**

Proposed by Congress January 31, 1865; ratified December 6, 1865. This amendment forbids slavery in the United States and in any area under its control. It also forbids other forms of forced labor, except punishments for crime; but some forms of compulsory service are not prohibited—for example, service on juries or in the armed forces. Section 2 gives to Congress the power to carry out the provisions of Section 1 of this amendment.

11th Amendment

The Judicial power of the United States shall not be construed to extend to any suit in law or equity, commenced or prosecuted against one of the United States by Citizens of another State, or by Citizens or Subjects of any Foreign State.

12th Amendment

The Electors shall meet in their respective States and vote by ballot for President and Vice President, one of whom, at least, shall not be an inhabitant of the same State with themselves; they shall name in their ballots the person voted for as President, and in distinct ballots the person voted for as Vice President, and they shall make distinct lists of all persons voted for as President, and of all persons voted for as Vice President, and of the number of votes for each, which lists they shall sign and certify, and transmit sealed to the seat of the government of the United States, directed to the President of the Senate;— The President of the Senate shall, in the presence of the Senate and the House of Representatives, open all the certificates and the votes shall then be counted;— the person having the greatest Number of votes for President shall be the President, if such number be a majority of the whole number of Electors appointed; and if no person have such a majority, then, from the persons having the highest numbers not exceeding three on the list of those voted for as President, the House of Representatives shall choose immediately, by ballot, the President. But in choosing the President, the votes shall be taken by States, the representation from each State having one vote; a quorum for this purpose shall consist of a member or members from two thirds of the States, and a majority of all the States shall be necessary to a choice. And if the House of Representatives shall not choose a President whenever the right of choice shall devolve upon them, before the fourth day of March next following, then the Vice President shall act as President, as in case of death or other constitutional disability of the President. The person having the greatest number of votes as Vice President, shall be the Vice President, if such number be a majority of the whole number of Electors appointed, and if no person have a majority, then from the two highest numbers on the list, the Senate shall choose the Vice President; a quorum for the purpose shall consist of two thirds of the whole number of Senators, a majority of the whole number shall be necessary to a choice. But no person constitutionally ineligible to the office of President shall be eligible to that of Vice-President of the United States.

13th Amendment

Section 1. Neither slavery nor involuntary servitude, except as a punishment for crime whereof the party shall have been duly convicted, shall exist within the United States, or any place subject to their jurisdiction.

Section 2. Congress shall have power to enforce this article by appropriate legislation.

14th Amendment

Section 1. All persons born or naturalized in the United States and subject to the jurisdiction thereof, are citizens of the United States and of the State wherein they reside. No State shall make or enforce any law which shall abridge the privileges or immunities of citizens of the United States; nor shall any State deprive any person of life, liberty, or property, without due process of law; nor deny to any person within its jurisdiction the equal protection of the laws.

Section 2. Representatives shall be apportioned among the several States according to their respective numbers, counting the whole number of persons in each State, excluding Indians not taxed. But when the right to vote at any election for the choice of electors for President and Vice President of the United States, Representatives in Congress, the Executive and Judicial officers of a State, or the members of the Legislature thereof, is denied to any of the male inhabitants of such State, being twenty-one years of age and citizens of the United States, or in any way abridged, except for participation in rebellion, or other crime, the basis of representation therein shall be reduced in the proportion which the number of such male citizens shall bear to the whole number of male citizens twenty-one years of age in such State.

Section 3. No person shall be a Senator or Representative in Congress, or elector of President and Vice President, or hold any office, civil or military, under the United States, or under any State, who, having previously taken an oath, as a member of Congress, or as an officer of the United States, or as a member of any State legislature, or as an executive or judicial officer of any State, to support the Constitution of the United States, shall have engaged in insurrection or rebellion against the same, or given aid or comfort to the enemies thereof. But Congress may, by a vote of two thirds of each House, remove such disability.

Section 4. The validity of the public debt of the United States, authorized by law, including debts incurred for payment of pensions and bounties for services in suppressing insurrection or rebellion, shall not be questioned. But neither the United States nor any State shall assume or pay any debt or obligation incurred in aid of insurrection or rebellion against the United States, or any claim for the loss or emancipation of any slave; but all such debts, obligations and claims shall be held illegal and void.

Section 5. The Congress shall have power to enforce, by appropriate legislation, the provisions of this article.

14th Amendment. **Rights of Citizens**

Proposed by Congress June 13, 1866; ratified July 9, 1868. Section 1 defines citizenship. It provides for the acquisition of United States citizenship by birth or by naturalization. Citizenship at birth is determined according to the principle of jus soli—"the law of the soil," where born; naturalization is the legal process by which one acquires a new citizenship at some time after birth. Under certain circumstances, citizenship can also be gained at birth abroad, according to the principle of jus sanguinis—"the law of the blood," to whom born. This section also contains two major civil rights provisions: the Due Process Clause forbids a State (and its local governments) to act in any unfair or arbitrary way; the Equal Protection Clause forbids a State (and its local governments) to discriminate against, draw unreasonable distinctions between, persons.

Most of the rights set out against the National Government in the first eight amendments have been extended against the States (and their local governments) through Supreme Court decisions involving the 14th Amendment's Due Process Clause.

The first sentence here replaced Article I, Section 2, Clause 3, the Three-Fifths Compromise provision. Essentially, all persons in the United States are counted in each decennial census, the basis for the distribution of House seats. The balance of this section has never been enforced and is generally thought to be obsolete.

Section 3 limited the President's power to pardon those persons who had led the Confederacy during the Civil War. Congress finally removed this disability in 1898.

Section 4 also dealt with matters directly related to the Civil War. It reaffirmed the public debt of the United States; but it invalidated, prohibited payment of, any debt contracted by the Confederate States and also prohibited any compensation of former slave owners.

15th Amendment. **Right to Vote—Race, Color, Servitude**

Proposed by Congress February 26, 1869; ratified February 3, 1870. The phrase "previous condition of servitude" refers to slavery. Note that this amendment does not guarantee the right to vote to African Americans, or to anyone else. Instead, it forbids the States from discriminating against any person on the grounds of his "race, color, or previous condition of servitude" in the setting of suffrage qualifications.

16th Amendment. **Income Tax**

Proposed by Congress July 12, 1909; ratified February 3, 1913. This amendment modified two provisions in Article I, Section 2, Clause 3, and Section 9, Clause 4. It gives to Congress the power to levy an income tax, a direct tax, without regard to the populations of any of the States.

17th Amendment. **Popular Election of Senators**

Proposed by Congress May 13, 1912; ratified April 8, 1913. This amendment repealed those portions of Article I, Section 3, Clauses 1 and 2 relating to the election of senators. Senators are now elected by the voters in each State. If a vacancy occurs, the governor of the State involved must call an election to fill the seat; the governor may appoint a senator to serve until the next election, if the State's legislature has authorized that step.

18th Amendment. **Prohibition of Intoxicating Liquors**

Proposed by Congress December 18, 1917; ratified January 16, 1919. This amendment outlawed the making, selling, transporting, importing, or exporting of alcoholic beverages in the United States. It was repealed in its entirety by the 21st Amendment in 1933.

19th Amendment. **Equal Suffrage—Sex**

Proposed by Congress June 4, 1919; ratified August 18, 1920. No person can be denied the right to vote in any election in the United States on account of his or her sex.

15th Amendment

Section 1. The right of citizens of the United States to vote shall not be denied or abridged by the United States or by any State on account of race, color, or previous condition of servitude.

Section 2. The Congress shall have power to enforce this article by appropriate legislation.

16th Amendment

The Congress shall have power to lay and collect taxes on incomes, from whatever source derived, without apportionment among the several States, and without regard to any census or enumeration.

17th Amendment

The Senate of the United States shall be composed of two Senators from each State, elected by the people thereof, for six years; and each Senator shall have one vote. The electors in each State shall have the qualifications requisite for electors of the most numerous branch of the State legislatures.

When vacancies happen in the representation of any State in the Senate, the executive authority of such State shall issue writs of election to fill such vacancies: Provided, That the legislature of any State may empower the executive thereof to make temporary appointments until the people fill the vacancies by election as the legislature may direct.

This amendment shall not be so construed as to affect the election or term of any Senator chosen before it becomes valid as part of the Constitution.

18th Amendment

Section 1. After one year from the ratification of this article the manufacture, sale, or transportation of intoxicating liquors within, the importation thereof into, or the exportation thereof from the United States and all territory subject to the jurisdiction thereof for beverage purposes is hereby prohibited.

Section 2. The Congress and the several States shall have concurrent power to enforce this article by appropriate legislation.

Section 3. This article shall be inoperative unless it shall have been ratified as an amendment to the Constitution by the legislatures of the several States, as provided in the Constitution, within seven years of the date of the submission hereof to the States by Congress.

19th Amendment

The right of citizens of the United States to vote shall not be denied or abridged by the United States or by any State on account of sex.

Congress shall have power to enforce this article by appropriate legislation.

20th Amendment

Section 1. The terms of the President and Vice President shall end at noon on the 20th day of January, and the terms of Senators and Representatives at noon on the 3d day of January, of the years in which such terms would have ended if this article had not been ratified; and the terms of their successors shall then begin.

Section 2. The Congress shall assemble at least once in every year, and such meeting shall begin at noon on the 3d day of January, unless they shall by law appoint a different day.

Section 3. If, at the time fixed for the beginning of the term of the President, the President elect shall have died, the Vice President elect shall become President. If a President shall not have been chosen before the time fixed for the beginning of his term, or if the President-elect shall have failed to qualify, then the Vice President elect shall act as President until a President shall have qualified; and the Congress may by law provide for the case wherein neither a President elect nor a Vice President elect shall have qualified, declaring who shall then act as President, or the manner in which one who is to act shall be selected, and such person shall act accordingly until a President or Vice President shall have qualified.

Section 4. The Congress may by law provide for the case of the death of any of the persons from whom the House of Representatives may choose a President whenever the right of choice shall have devolved upon them, and for the case of the death of any of the persons from whom the Senate may choose a Vice President whenever the right of choice shall have devolved upon them.

Section 5. Sections 1 and 2 shall take effect on the 15th day of October following the ratification of this article.

Section 6. This article shall be inoperative unless it shall have been ratified as an amendment to the Constitution by the legislatures of three fourths of the several States within seven years from the date of its submission.

21st Amendment

Section 1. The eighteenth article of amendment to the Constitution of the United States is hereby repealed.

Section 2. The transportation or importation into any State, Territory, or possession of the United States for delivery or use therein of intoxicating liquors, in violation of the laws thereof, is hereby prohibited.

Section 3. This article shall be inoperative unless it shall have been ratified as an amendment to the Constitution by conventions in the several States, as provided in the Constitution, within seven years from the date of the submission hereof to the States by the Congress.

20th Amendment. **Commencement of Terms; Sessions of Congress; Death or Disqualification of President-Elect**

Proposed by Congress March 2, 1932; ratified January 23, 1933. The provisions of Sections 1 and 2 relating to Congress modified Article I, Section 4, Clause 2, and those provisions relating to the President, the 12th Amendment. The date on which the President and Vice President now take office was moved from March 4 to January 20. Similarly, the members of Congress now begin their terms on January 3. The 20th Amendment is sometimes called the "Lame Duck Amendment" because it shortened the period of time a member of Congress who was defeated for reelection (a "lame duck") remains in office.

This section deals with certain possibilities that were not covered by the presidential selection provisions of either Article II or the 12th Amendment. To this point, none of these situations has occurred. Note that there is neither a President-elect nor a Vice President-elect until the electoral votes have been counted by Congress, or, if the electoral college cannot decide the matter, the House has chosen a President or the Senate has chosen a Vice President.

Congress has not in fact ever passed such a law. See Section 2 of the 25th Amendment, regarding a vacancy in the vice presidency; that provision could some day have an impact here.

Section 5 set the date on which this amendment came into force.

Section 6 placed a time limit on the ratification process; note that a similar provision was written into the 18th, 21st, and 22nd amendments.

21st Amendment. **Repeal of 18th Amendment**

Proposed by Congress February 20, 1933; ratified December 5, 1933. This amendment repealed all of the 18th Amendment. Section 2 modifies the scope of the Federal Government's commerce power set out in Article I, Section 8, Clause 3; it gives to each State the power to regulate the transportation or importation and the distribution or use of intoxicating liquors in ways that would be unconstitutional in the case of any other commodity. The 21st Amendment is the only amendment Congress has thus far submitted to the States for ratification by conventions.

22nd Amendment. **Presidential Tenure**

Proposed by Congress March 21, 1947; ratified February 27, 1951. This amendment modified Article II, Section I, Clause 1. It stipulates that no President may serve more than two elected terms. But a President who has succeeded to the office beyond the midpoint in a term to which another President was originally elected may serve for more than eight years. In any case, however, a President may not serve more than 10 years. Prior to Franklin Roosevelt, who was elected to four terms, no President had served more than two full terms in office.

23rd Amendment. **Presidential Electors for the District of Columbia**

Proposed by Congress June 16, 1960; ratified March 29, 1961. This amendment modified Article II, Section I, Clause 2 and the 12th Amendment. It included the voters of the District of Columbia in the presidential electorate; and provides that the District is to have the same number of electors as the least populous State—three electors—but no more than that number.

24th Amendment. **Right to Vote in Federal Elections—Tax Payment**

Proposed by Congress August 27, 1962; ratified January 23, 1964. This amendment outlawed the payment of any tax as a condition for taking part in the nomination or election of any federal officeholder.

25th Amendment. **Presidential Succession, Vice Presidential Vacancy, Presidential Inability**

Proposed by Congress July 6, 1965; ratified February 10, 1967. Section 1 revised the imprecise provision on presidential succession in Article II, Section 1, Clause 6. It affirmed the precedent set by Vice President John Tyler, who became President on the death of William Henry Harrison in 1841.

Section 2 provides for the filling of a vacancy in the office of Vice President. The office had been vacant on 16 occasions and remained unfilled for the rest of each term involved. When Spiro Agnew resigned the office in 1973, President Nixon selected Gerald Ford per this provision; and, when President Nixon resigned in 1974, Gerald Ford became President and chose Nelson Rockefeller as Vice President.

22nd Amendment

Section 1. No person shall be elected to the office of the President more than twice, and no person who has held the office of President, or acted as President, for more than two years of a term to which some other person was elected President shall be elected to the office of the President more than once. But this Article shall not apply to any person holding the office of President, when this Article was proposed by the Congress, and shall not prevent any person who may be holding the office of President, or acting as President, during the term within which this Article becomes operative from holding the office of President or acting as President during the remainder of such term.

Section 2. This article shall be inoperative unless it shall have been ratified as an amendment to the Constitution by the legislatures of three fourths of the several states within seven years from the date of its submission to the States by the Congress.

23rd Amendment

Section 1. The District constituting the seat of Government of the United States shall appoint in such manner as the Congress may direct:

A number of electors of President and Vice President equal to the whole number of Senators and Representatives in Congress to which the District would be entitled if it were a State, but in no event more than the least populous State; they shall be in addition to those appointed by the States, they shall be considered, for the purposes of the election of President and Vice President, to be electors appointed by a State; and they shall meet in the District and perform such duties as provided by the twelfth article of amendment.

24th Amendment

Section 1. The right of citizens of the United States to vote in any primary or other election for President or Vice President, for electors for President or Vice President, or for Senator or Representative in Congress, shall not be denied or abridged by the United States or any State by reason of failure to pay any poll tax or other tax.

Section 2. The Congress shall have power to enforce this article by appropriate legislation.

25th Amendment

Section 1. In case of the removal of the President from office or of his death or resignation, the Vice President shall become President.

Section 2. Whenever there is a vacancy in the office of the Vice President, the President shall nominate a Vice President who shall take office upon confirmation by a majority vote of both Houses of Congress.

Section 3. Whenever the President transmits to the President pro tempore of the Senate and the Speaker of the House of Representatives his written declaration that he is unable to discharge the powers and duties of his office, and until he transmits to them a written declaration to the contrary, such powers and duties shall be discharged by the Vice President as Acting President.

Section 4. Whenever the Vice President and a majority of either the principal officers of the executive departments or of such other body as Congress may by law provide, transmit to the President pro tempore of the Senate and the Speaker of the House of Representatives their written declaration that the President is unable to discharge the powers and duties of his office, the Vice President shall immediately assume the powers and duties of the office as Acting President.

Thereafter, when the President transmits to the President pro tempore of the Senate and the Speaker of the House of Representatives his written declaration that no inability exists, he shall resume the powers and duties of his office unless the Vice President and a majority of either the principal officers of the executive department or of such other body as Congress may by law provide, transmit within four days to the President pro tempore of the Senate and the Speaker of the House of Representatives their written declaration that the President is unable to discharge the powers and duties of his office. Thereupon Congress shall decide the issue, assembling within forty-eight hours for that purpose if not in session. If the Congress, within twenty-one days after receipt of the latter written declaration, or, if Congress is not in session, within twenty-one days after Congress is required to assemble, determines by two-thirds vote of both Houses that the President is unable to discharge the powers and duties of his office, the Vice President shall continue to discharge the same as Acting President; otherwise, the President shall resume the powers and duties of his office.

26th Amendment

Section 1. The right of citizens of the United States, who are eighteen years of age or older, to vote shall not be denied or abridged by the United States or by any State on account of age.

Section 2. The Congress shall have the power to enforce this article by appropriate legislation.

27th Amendment

No law varying the compensation for the services of the Senators and Representatives, shall take effect, until an election of Representatives shall have intervened.

This section created a procedure for determining if a President is so incapacitated that he cannot perform the powers and duties of his office.

Section 4 deals with the circumstance in which a President will not be able to determine the fact of incapacity. To this point, Congress has not established the "such other body" referred to here. This section contains the only typographical error in the Constitution; in its second paragraph, the word "department" should in fact read "departments."

26th Amendment. **Right to Vote—Age**

Proposed by Congress March 23, 1971; ratified July 1, 1971. This amendment provides that the minimum age for voting in any election in the United States cannot be more than 18 years. (A State may set a minimum voting age of less than 18, however.)

27th Amendment. **Congressional Pay**

Proposed by Congress September 25, 1789; ratified May 7, 1992. This amendment modified Article I, Section 6, Clause 1. It limits Congress's power to fix the salaries of its members—by delaying the effectiveness of any increase in that pay until after the next regular congressional election.

Presidents of the United States

Name	Party	States	Entered Office	Age On Taking Office	Vice President(s)
George Washington (1732–1799)	Federalist	Virginia	1789	57	John Adams
John Adams (1735–1826)	Federalist	Massachusetts	1797	61	Thomas Jefferson
Thomas Jefferson (1743–1826)	Dem-Repb	Virginia	1801	57	Aaron Burr/George Clinton
James Madison (1751–1836)	Dem-Rep	Virginia	1809	57	George Clinton/Elbridge Gerry
James Monroe (1758–1831)	Dem-Rep	Virginia	1817	58	Daniel D. Tompkins
John Q. Adams (1767–1848)	Dem-Rep	Massachusetts	1825	57	John C. Calhoun
Andrew Jackson (1767–1845)	Democrat	Tennessee (SC)	1829	61	John C. Calhoun/ Martin Van Buren
Martin Van Buren (1782–1862)	Democrat	New York	1837	54	Richard M. Johnson
William H. Harrison (1773–1841)	Whig	Ohio (VA)	1841	68	John Tyler
John Tyler (1790–1862)	Democrat	Virginia	1841	51	none
James K. Polk (1795–1849)	Democrat	Tennessee (NC)	1845	49	George M. Dallas
Zachary Taylor (1784–1850)	Whig	Louisiana (VA)	1849	64	Millard Fillmore
Millard Fillmore (1800–1874)	Whig	New York	1850	50	none
Franklin Pierce (1804–1869)	Democrat	New Hampshire	1853	48	William R. King
James Buchanan (1791–1868)	Democrat	Pennsylvania	1857	65	John C. Breckinridge
Abraham Lincoln (1809–1865)	Republican	Illinois (KY)	1861	52	Hannibal Hamlin/Andrew Johnson
Andrew Johnson (1808–1875)	Democrat	Tennessee (NC)	1865	56	none
Ulysses S. Grant (1822–1885)	Republican	Illinois (OH)	1869	46	Schuyler Colfax/Henry Wilson
Rutherford B. Hayes (1822–1893)	Republican	Ohio	1877	54	William A. Wheeler
James A. Garfield (1831–1881)	Republican	Ohio	1881	49	Chester A. Arthur
Chester A. Arthur (1829–1896)	Republican	New York (VT)	1881	51	none
Grover Cleveland (1837–1908)	Democrat	New York (NJ)	1885	47	Thomas A. Hendricks
Benjamin Harrison (1833–1901)	Republican	Indiana (OH)	1889	55	Levi P. Morton
Grover Cleveland (1837–1908)	Democrat	New York (NJ)	1893	55	Adlai E. Stevenson

Name	Party	States[a]	Entered Office	Age On Taking Office	Vice President(s)
William McKinley (1843–1901)	Republican	Ohio	1897	54	Garret A. Hobart/ Theodore Roosevelt
Theodore Roosevelt (1858–1919)	Republican	New York	1901	42	Charles W. Fairbanks
William H. Taft (1857–1930)	Republican	Ohio	1909	51	James S. Sherman
Woodrow Wilson (1856–1924)	Democrat	New Jersey (VA)	1913	56	Thomas R. Marshall
Warren G. Harding (1865–1923)	Republican	Ohio	1921	55	Calvin Coolidge
Calvin Coolidge (1872–1933)	Republican	Massachusetts (VT)	1923	51	Charles G. Dawes
Herbert Hoover (1874–1964)	Republican	California (IA)	1929	54	Charles Curtis
Franklin Roosevelt (1882–1945)	Democrat	New York	1933	51	John N. Garner/ Henry A. Wallace/Harry S Truman
Harry S Truman (1884–1972)	Democrat	Missouri	1945	60	Alben W. Barkley
Dwight D. Eisenhower (1890–1969)	Republican	New York (TX)	1953	62	Richard M. Nixon
John F. Kennedy (1917–1963)	Democrat	Massachusetts	1961	43	Lyndon B. Johnson
Lyndon B. Johnson (1908–1973)	Democrat	Texas	1963	55	Hubert H. Humphrey
Richard M. Nixon (1913–1994)	Republican	New York (CA)	1969	56	Spiro T. Agnew/Gerald R. Ford
Gerald R. Ford (1913–2006)	Republican	Michigan (NE)	1974	61	Nelson A. Rockefeller
James E. Carter (1924–)	Democrat	Georgia	1977	52	Walter F. Mondale
Ronald W. Reagan (1911–2004)	Republican	California (IL)	1981	69	George H. W. Bush
George H.W. Bush (1924–)	Republican	Texas (MA)	1989	64	J. Danforth Quayle
William J. Clinton (1946–)	Democrat	Arkansas	1993	46	Albert Gore, Jr.
George W. Bush (1946–)	Republican	Texas	2001	54	Richard B. Cheney
Barack Obama (1961–)	Democrat	Illinois (HI)	2009	47	Joseph R. Biden
Donald J. Trump (1946–)	Republican	New York	2017	70	Michael R. Pence

[a] State of residence when elected; if born in another State, that State in parentheses.
[b] Democratic-Republican
[c] Johnson, a War Democrat, was elected Vice President on the coalition Union Party ticket.
[d] Resigned October 10, 1973.
[e] Nominated by Nixon, confirmed by Congress on December 6, 1973.
[f] Nominated by Ford, confirmed by Congress on December 19, 1974.

US: Political

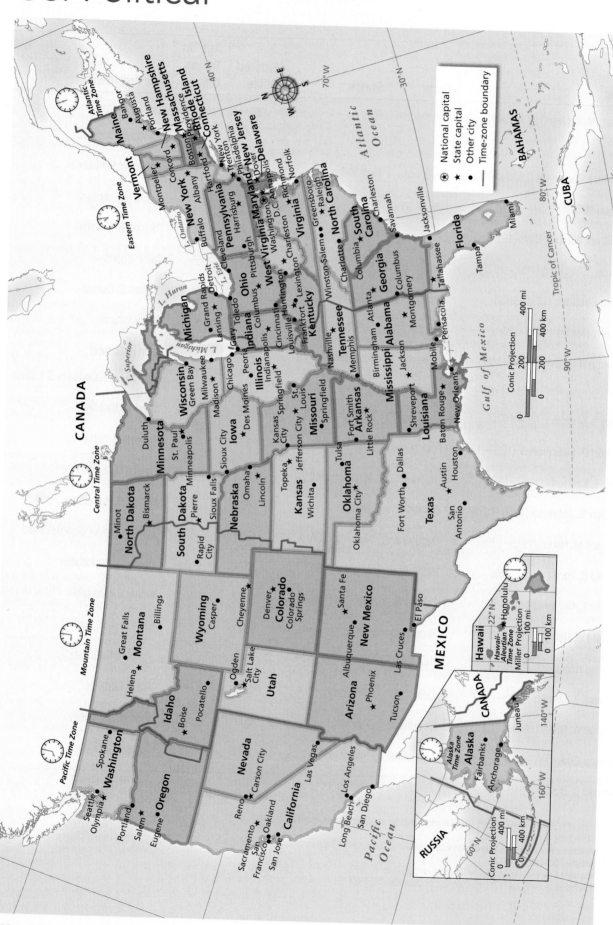

National capital ✪
State capital ★
Other city ●
Time-zone boundary —

Atlantic Time Zone
Eastern Time Zone
Central Time Zone
Mountain Time Zone
Pacific Time Zone

CANADA

Atlantic Ocean

BAHAMAS

CUBA

Gulf of Mexico

MEXICO

Pacific Ocean

RUSSIA

Conic Projection
400 mi
400 km
0   200   400

Hawaii
Honolulu
22°N
Hawaii-Aleutian Time Zone
Miller Projection
100 mi
100 km

CANADA
Juneau
140°W
Alaska Time Zone
Alaska
Fairbanks
Anchorage
160°W
60°N
Conic Projection
400 mi
400 km

Maine — Bangor, Augusta
New Hampshire — Portland, Concord
Vermont — Montpelier
Massachusetts — Boston
Rhode Island — Providence
Connecticut — Hartford
New York — Albany, Buffalo, New York
New Jersey — Trenton
Pennsylvania — Harrisburg, Philadelphia, Pittsburgh
Delaware — Dover
Maryland — Annapolis, Washington, D.C.
West Virginia — Charleston
Virginia — Richmond, Norfolk, Lexington
North Carolina — Raleigh, Greensboro, Winston-Salem, Charlotte
South Carolina — Columbia, Charleston
Georgia — Atlanta, Savannah, Columbus
Florida — Jacksonville, Tallahassee, Tampa, Miami
Ohio — Columbus, Cleveland, Toledo, Cincinnati
Michigan — Lansing, Detroit, Grand Rapids
Indiana — Indianapolis, Gary
Illinois — Springfield, Chicago, Peoria
Kentucky — Frankfort, Louisville
Tennessee — Nashville, Memphis
Alabama — Montgomery, Birmingham, Mobile
Mississippi — Jackson
Louisiana — Baton Rouge, New Orleans, Shreveport
Arkansas — Little Rock, Fort Smith
Missouri — Jefferson City, St. Louis, Kansas City, Springfield
Iowa — Des Moines, Sioux City
Wisconsin — Madison, Milwaukee, Green Bay
Minnesota — St. Paul, Minneapolis, Duluth
North Dakota — Bismarck, Minot
South Dakota — Pierre, Rapid City, Sioux Falls
Nebraska — Lincoln, Omaha
Kansas — Topeka, Wichita
Oklahoma — Oklahoma City, Tulsa
Texas — Austin, Dallas, Fort Worth, Houston, San Antonio, El Paso
Colorado — Denver, Colorado Springs
Wyoming — Cheyenne, Casper
Montana — Helena, Great Falls, Billings
Idaho — Boise, Pocatello
Washington — Olympia, Seattle, Spokane
Oregon — Salem, Portland, Eugene
Nevada — Carson City, Reno, Las Vegas
Utah — Salt Lake City, Ogden
New Mexico — Santa Fe, Albuquerque, Las Cruces
Arizona — Phoenix, Tucson
California — Sacramento, San Francisco, Oakland, San Jose, Los Angeles, Long Beach, San Diego

L. Superior
L. Huron
L. Michigan
L. Erie
L. Ontario

Tropic of Cancer

70°W 80°W 90°W 140°W 160°W
30°N 40°N 60°N

US: Physical

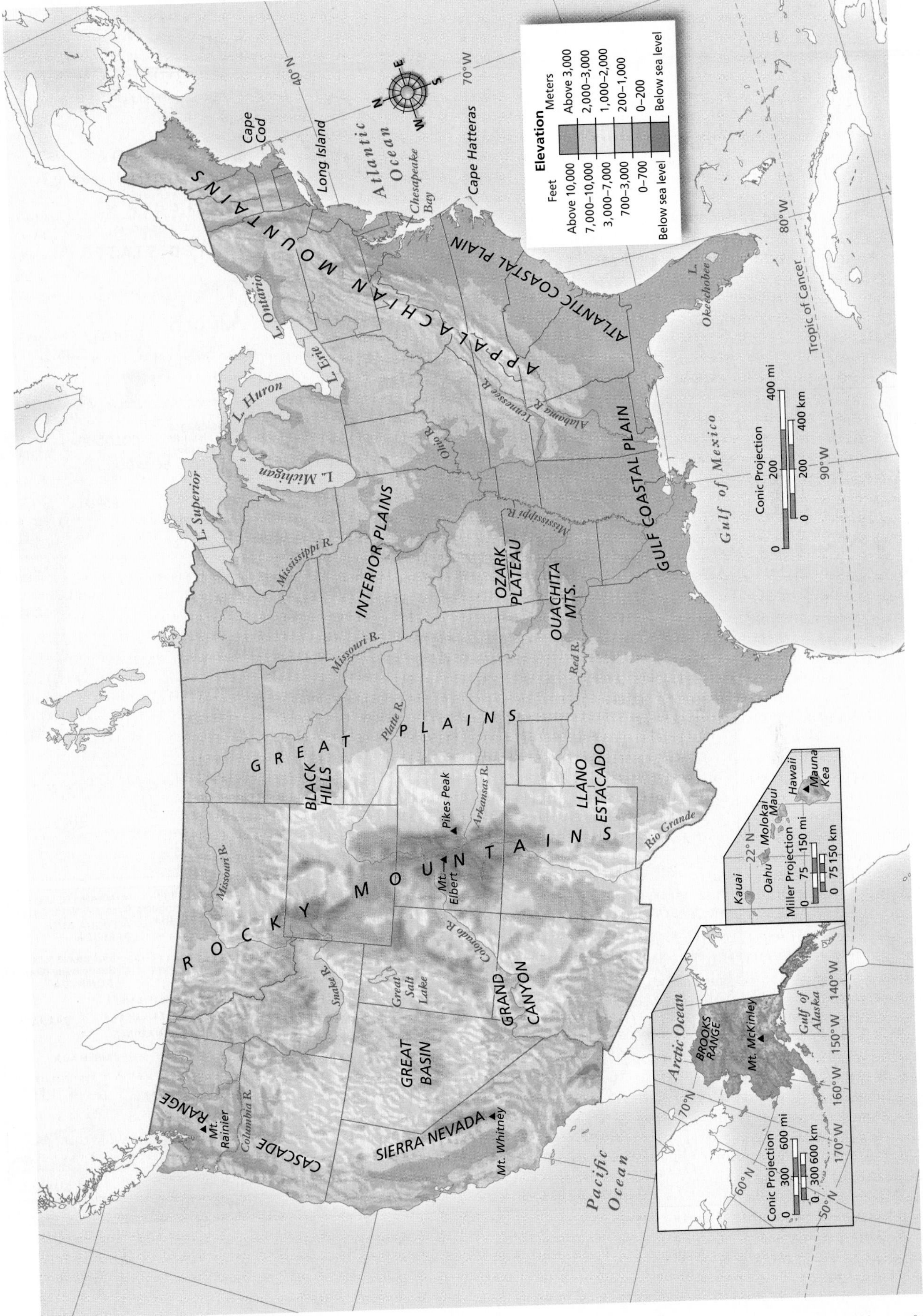

Elevation

Feet	Meters
Above 10,000	Above 3,000
7,000–10,000	2,000–3,000
3,000–7,000	1,000–2,000
700–3,000	200–1,000
0–700	0–200
Below sea level	Below sea level

40°N

70°W

Cape Cod

Long Island

Atlantic Ocean

Chesapeake Bay

Cape Hatteras

80°W

Tropic of Cancer

L. Okeechobee

APPALACHIAN MOUNTAINS

ATLANTIC COASTAL PLAIN

L. Ontario

L. Erie

L. Huron

L. Michigan

L. Superior

Tennessee R.

Ohio R.

Alabama R.

GULF COASTAL PLAIN

Gulf of Mexico

90°W

400 mi

400 km

200

200

0

0

Conic Projection

Mississippi R.

Mississippi R.

INTERIOR PLAINS

OZARK PLATEAU

OUACHITA MTS.

Red R.

Missouri R.

GREAT   P L A I N S

Platte R.

Arkansas R.

LLANO ESTACADO

Rio Grande

BLACK HILLS

Pikes Peak

R O C K Y   M O U N T A I N S

Mt. Elbert

Colorado R.

GRAND CANYON

Missouri R.

Snake R.

Great Salt Lake

GREAT BASIN

SIERRA NEVADA

Mt. Whitney

CASCADE RANGE

Columbia R.

Mt. Rainier

Pacific Ocean

Kauai

Oahu

Molokai

Maui

Hawaii

Mauna Kea

22°N

0   75   150 mi

0   75 150 km

Miller Projection

Arctic Ocean

BROOKS RANGE

Mt. McKinley

Gulf of Alaska

140°W

150°W

160°W

170°W

70°N

60°N

50°N

0   300   600 mi

0   300 600 km

Conic Projection

The World: Political

Alaska
(United States)

CANADA

NORTH
AMERICA

Chicago • Toronto
• New York
UNITED STATES ⊗ Washington, D.C.

Los Angeles •

Atlantic

Ocean

Houston •

Hawaii
(United States)   Tropic of Cancer

MEXICO

Mexico City ⊗

see inset below

Pacific
Ocean

Galápagos
Islands
(Ecuador)   COLOMBIA   ⊗ Bogotá

Equator   Line Islands
(United States)   ECUADOR   SURINAME

French Gui
(France)

BRAZIL

PERU   SOUTH

American Samoa
(United States)   AMERICA

SAMOA   BOLIVIA

French Polynesia
(France)   Rio de
Tropic of Capricorn   Janeiro
TONGA   Pitcairn Islands   PARAGUAY   • São P
(U.K.)
CHILE
ARGENTINA

⊗ Capital   URUGUAY
• Other city   Buenos Aires ⊗

Antarctic Circle   *Southern Ocean*

Gulf of Mexico   UNITED
STATES
B
A
Tropic of Cancer   H
A
M
A
S
CUBA
Turks and
Caicos Islands
(U.K.)   British Virgin
U.S. Virgin Islands   St. Martin (St. Maarten)
Islands (U.S.) (U.K.) Anguilla (France & Neth. Antilles)
MEXICO   (U.K.)   ANTIGUA AND
BARBUDA
Cayman Islands
(U.K.)   HAITI   Puerto Rico   Montserrat (U.K.)
BELIZE   JAMAICA   DOMINICAN (U.S.) ST. KITTS Guadeloupe (France)
REPUBLIC   AND NEVIS   DOMINICA
GUATEMALA
HONDURAS   *Caribbean Sea*   Martinique (France)
ST. LUCIA   • BARBADOS
EL SALVADOR   ST. VINCENT AND THE GRENADINES
NICARAGUA   Conic Projection
0   200   400 mi Aruba (Neth.)   GRENADA
Netherlands
0   200   400 km   Antilles   TRINIDAD
(Neth.)   AND TOBAGO
COSTA RICA   Caracas ⊗
Pacific   PANAMA   Lake   VENEZUELA
Ocean   COLOMBIA Maracaibo
SOUTH AMERICA   GUYANA

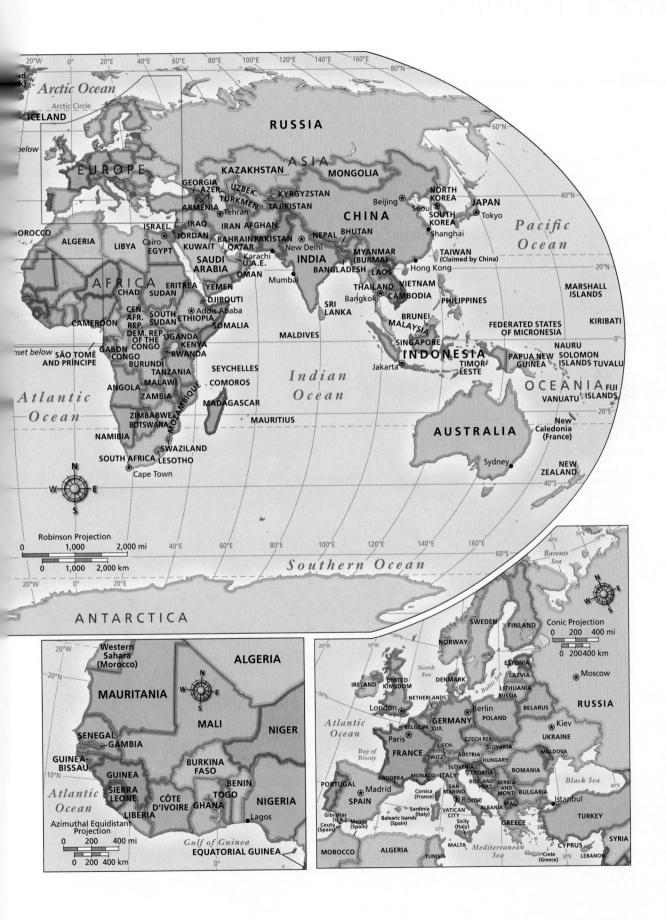

Africa: Political

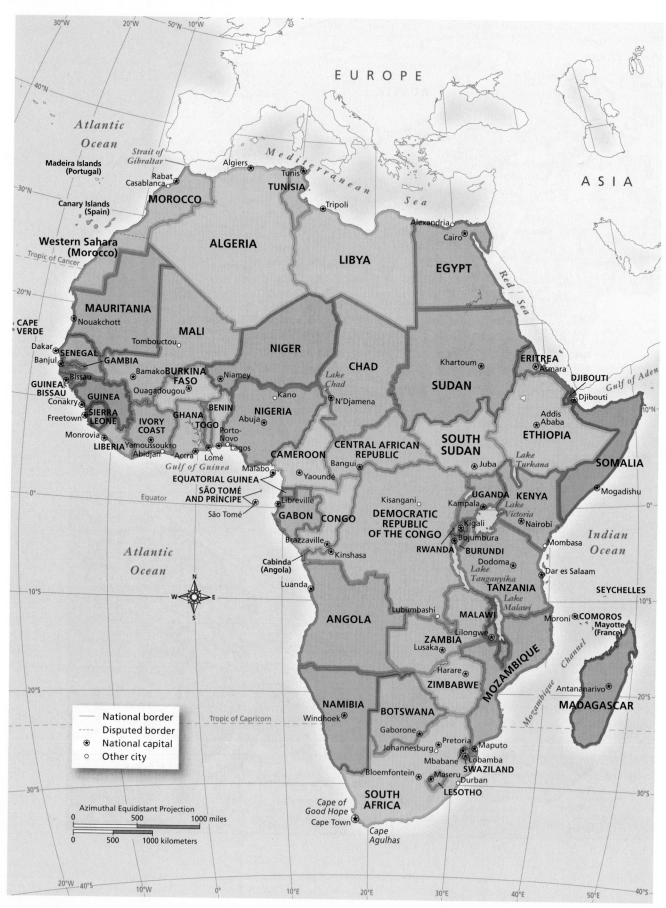

EUROPE

ASIA

Atlantic Ocean

Mediterranean Sea

Madeira Islands (Portugal)

Strait of Gibraltar

Algiers

Tunis ⊛

TUNISIA

Rabat ⊛
Casablanca ⊙

MOROCCO

Tripoli ⊛

Alexandria ⊙

Cairo ⊛

Red Sea

Canary Islands (Spain)

Western Sahara (Morocco)

Tropic of Cancer

ALGERIA

LIBYA

EGYPT

MAURITANIA

Nouakchott ⊛

MALI

Tombouctou ⊙

NIGER

CHAD

Khartoum ⊛

SUDAN

ERITREA

Asmara ⊛

DJIBOUTI

Gulf of Aden

CAPE VERDE

Dakar ⊛
Banjul ⊛

SENEGAL

GAMBIA

Bamako ⊛

BURKINA FASO

Niamey ⊛

Lake Chad

N'Djamena ⊛

Djibouti ⊛

Bissau ⊙

GUINEA-BISSAU

Ouagadougou ⊙

Kano ⊙

NIGERIA

Addis Ababa ⊛

ETHIOPIA

GUINEA

Conakry ⊛

SIERRA LEONE

Freetown ⊛

GHANA

BENIN

Abuja ⊛

CENTRAL AFRICAN REPUBLIC

SOUTH SUDAN

Juba ⊙

Lake Turkana

SOMALIA

IVORY COAST

TOGO

Porto-Novo ⊛

Monrovia ⊛

LIBERIA

Yamoussoukro ⊙

Abidjan ⊙

Accra ⊛

Lomé ⊛

Lagos ⊙

CAMEROON

Bangui ⊛

Malabo ⊛

Gulf of Guinea

EQUATORIAL GUINEA

Yaoundé ⊛

DEMOCRATIC REPUBLIC OF THE CONGO

Kisangani ⊙

Mogadishu ⊛

UGANDA

KENYA

Kampala ⊛

Lake Victoria

SÃO TOMÉ AND PRÍNCIPE

Libreville ⊛

GABON

CONGO

Nairobi ⊛

São Tomé ⊛

Equator

Kigali ⊛

Bujumbura ⊛

RWANDA

BURUNDI

Mombasa ⊙

Indian Ocean

Brazzaville ⊛

Kinshasa ⊛

Dodoma ⊙

Dar es Salaam ⊙

Cabinda (Angola)

Lake Tanganyika

TANZANIA

Atlantic Ocean

Luanda ⊛

Lubumbashi ⊙

Lake Malawi

SEYCHELLES

ANGOLA

MALAWI

Lilongwe ⊛

Moroni ⊛

COMOROS

Mayotte (France)

ZAMBIA

Lusaka ⊛

Mozambique Channel

Harare ⊛

ZIMBABWE

MOZAMBIQUE

Antananarivo ⊛

MADAGASCAR

NAMIBIA

BOTSWANA

Windhoek ⊛

Tropic of Capricorn

Gaborone ⊛

Pretoria ⊛

Maputo ⊛

Johannesburg ⊙

Mbabane ⊛

Lobamba ⊙

SWAZILAND

— National border
--- Disputed border
⊛ National capital
⊙ Other city

Bloemfontein ⊙

Maseru ⊛

Durban ⊙

LESOTHO

Cape of Good Hope

SOUTH AFRICA

Cape Town ⊛

Cape Agulhas

Azimuthal Equidistant Projection

0   500   1000 miles

0   500   1000 kilometers

Africa: Physical

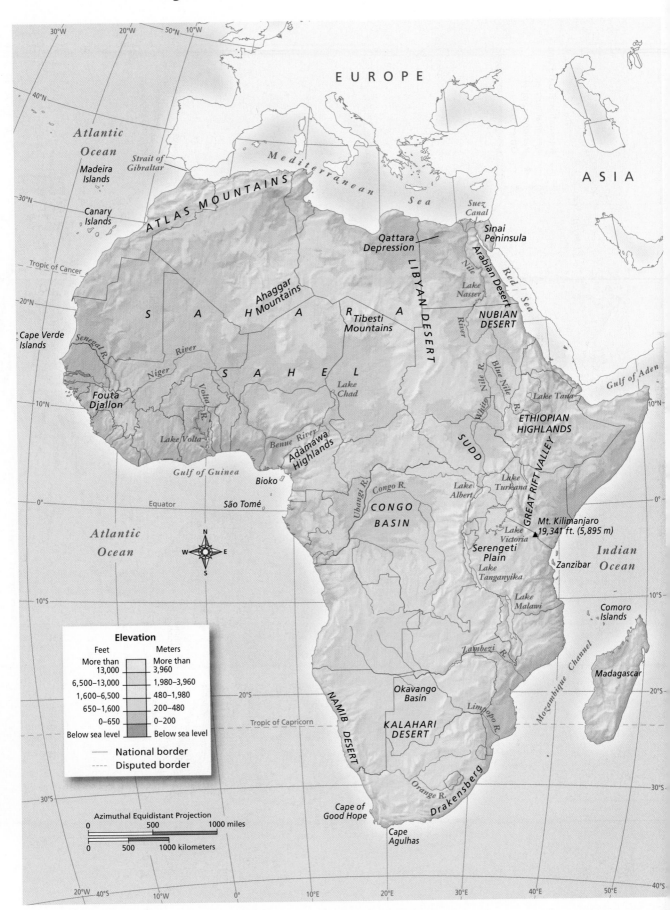

EUROPE

Atlantic Ocean

Madeira Islands

Strait of Gibraltar

Canary Islands

Tropic of Cancer

Cape Verde Islands

ATLAS MOUNTAINS

Mediterranean Sea

Qattara Depression

Suez Canal

Sinai Peninsula

ASIA

S A H A R A

Ahaggar Mountains

Tibesti Mountains

LIBYAN DESERT

Arabian Desert

Red Sea

Lake Nasser

Nile River

NUBIAN DESERT

Gulf of Aden

Senegal R.

Niger River

Volta R.

S A H E L

Lake Chad

White Nile R.

Blue Nile R.

Lake Tana

ETHIOPIAN HIGHLANDS

Fouta Djallon

Lake Volta

Benue River

Adamawa Highlands

Gulf of Guinea

Bioko

São Tomé

Equator

Atlantic Ocean

Ubangi R.

Congo R.

CONGO BASIN

SUDD

Lake Albert

Lake Turkana

GREAT RIFT VALLEY

Mt. Kilimanjaro
19,341 ft. (5,895 m)

Lake Victoria

Serengeti Plain

Lake Tanganyika

Zanzibar

Indian Ocean

Lake Malawi

Comoro Islands

Mozambique Channel

Madagascar

Zambezi R.

Okavango Basin

Limpopo R.

NAMIB DESERT

Tropic of Capricorn

KALAHARI DESERT

Orange R.

Drakensberg

Cape of Good Hope

Cape Agulhas

Elevation

Feet		Meters
More than 13,000		More than 3,960
6,500–13,000		1,980–3,960
1,600–6,500		480–1,980
650–1,600		200–480
0–650		0–200
Below sea level		Below sea level

— National border

--- Disputed border

Azimuthal Equidistant Projection

0   500   1000 miles

0   500   1000 kilometers

Asia: Political

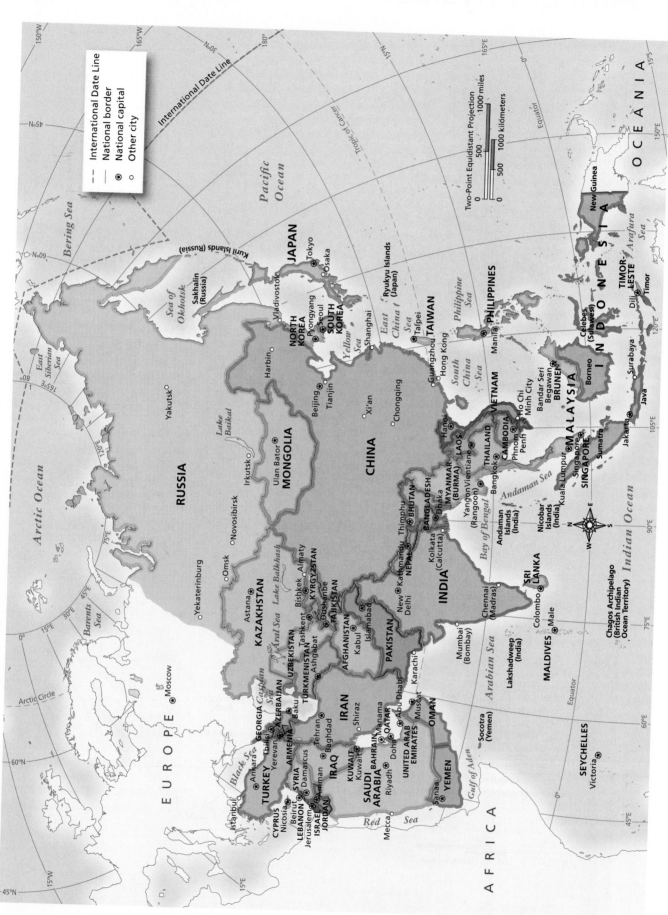

International Date Line
National border
⊛ National capital
○ Other city

International Date Line
International Date Line

Two-Point Equidistant Projection
1000 miles
500   1000 kilometers
500
0   0

Bering Sea

Pacific Ocean

East Siberian Sea

Arctic Ocean

Barents Sea

EUROPE

Moscow ⊛

Arctic Circle

RUSSIA

Yakutsk ○

Lake Baikal

Irkutsk ○

Ulan Bator ⊛

MONGOLIA

Novosibirsk ○

Omsk ○

Yekaterinburg ○

Astana ⊛

KAZAKHSTAN

Lake Balkhash

Aral Sea

Caspian Sea

Black Sea

Istanbul ○

Ankara ⊛ TURKEY

Tbilisi ⊛ GEORGIA
Yerevan ⊛ AZERBAIJAN
ARMENIA ⊛ Baku
CYPRUS
Nicosia ○
Beirut ○ SYRIA
LEBANON ⊛ Damascus
Jerusalem ⊛ ⊛ Amman
ISRAEL JORDAN
Baghdad ⊛
IRAQ
Mecca ○
Riyadh ⊛
SAUDI ARABIA
KUWAIT
Kuwait ⊛
BAHRAIN
Manama ⊛ QATAR
Doha ⊛
UNITED ARAB EMIRATES
Abu Dhabi ⊛

IRAN
Tehran ⊛
Shiraz ○

Sanaa ⊛
YEMEN

OMAN
Muscat ⊛

Red Sea

Gulf of Aden

Socotra (Yemen)

Arabian Sea

Baku

TURKMENISTAN
Ashgabat ⊛

UZBEKISTAN
Tashkent ⊛
Bishkek ⊛ Almaty ○
KYRGYZSTAN
Dushanbe ⊛
TAJIKISTAN
AFGHANISTAN
Kabul ⊛

Islamabad ⊛
PAKISTAN
Karachi ○

CHINA

Harbin ○

Beijing ⊛
Tianjin ○

Xi'an ○

Chongqing ○

Vladivostok ○

NORTH KOREA
Pyongyang ⊛
SOUTH KOREA
Seoul ⊛
Yellow Sea

Shanghai ○

JAPAN
Tokyo ⊛
Osaka ○

Sakhalin (Russia)

Sea of Okhotsk

Kuril Islands (Russia)

East China Sea

Ryukyu Islands (Japan)

TAIWAN
Taipei ⊛

Guangzhou ○
Hong Kong ○

South China Sea

Philippine Sea

PHILIPPINES
Manila ⊛

New Delhi ⊛
Delhi ○

Kathmandu ⊛
NEPAL
Thimphu ⊛
BHUTAN
BANGLADESH
Dhaka ⊛

INDIA

Mumbai (Bombay) ○

Kolkata (Calcutta) ○

Chennai (Madras) ○

Lakshadweep (India)

MALDIVES
Male ○

SRI LANKA
Colombo ⊛

Bay of Bengal

MYANMAR (BURMA)
Yangon (Rangoon) ⊛

Andaman Islands (India)

Nicobar Islands (India)

Andaman Sea

LAOS
Vientiane ⊛
THAILAND
Bangkok ⊛
CAMBODIA
Phnom Penh ⊛
VIETNAM
Hanoi ⊛
Ho Chi Minh City ○

MALAYSIA
Kuala Lumpur ⊛
SINGAPORE
Singapore ⊛

BRUNEI
Bandar Seri Begawan ⊛

Borneo

Celebes (Sulawesi)

INDONESIA

Sumatra

Java
Jakarta ⊛
Surabaya ○

TIMOR-LESTE
Dili ⊛ Timor

New Guinea

Arafura Sea

OCEANIA

Indian Ocean

Chagos Archipelago (British Indian Ocean Territory)

SEYCHELLES
Victoria ⊛

AFRICA

Equator

Tropic of Cancer

616   Atlas

Asia: Physical

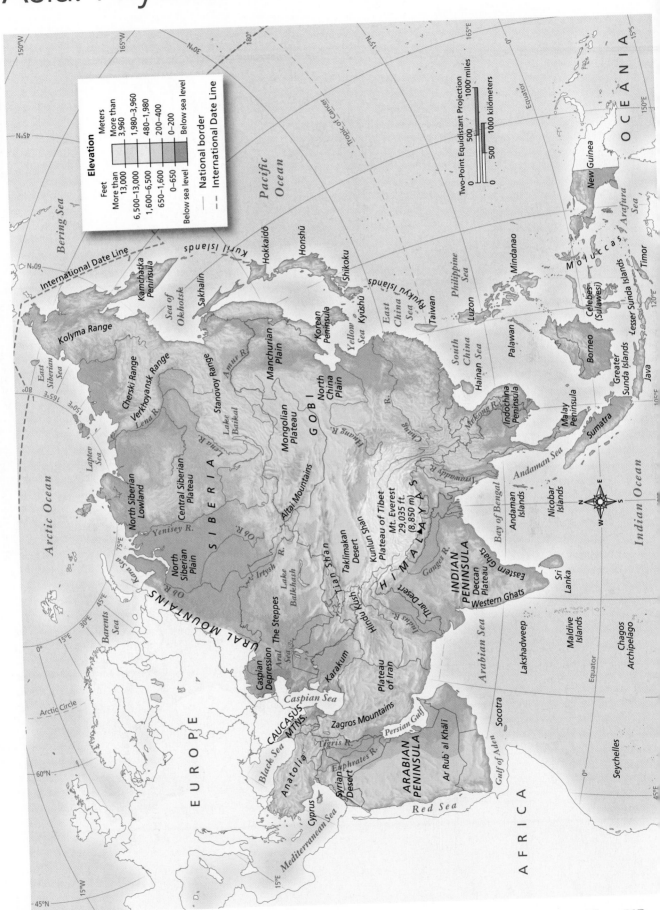

Europe: Political

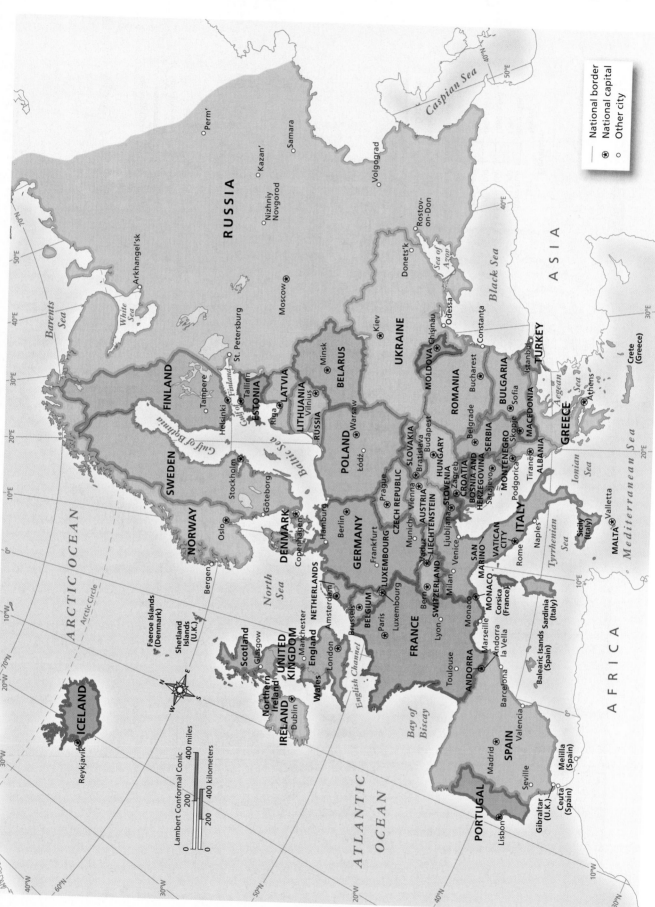

National border
National capital
○ Other city

RUSSIA

Perm'
Kazan'
Samara
Nizhniy Novgorod
Volgograd
Arkhangel'sk
Rostov-on-Don
Moscow
Donets'k
Sea of Azov
Caspian Sea
Black Sea

Barents Sea
White Sea

ASIA

St. Petersburg
Kiev
UKRAINE
Chişinău
Odessa
Constanţa
MOLDOVA

FINLAND
Tampere
Helsinki
Gulf of Finland
Tallinn
ESTONIA
Riga
LATVIA
LITHUANIA
Vilnius
Minsk
BELARUS
Warsaw
POLAND
Łódź
Prague
CZECH REPUBLIC

ROMANIA
Bucharest
Belgrade
SERBIA
Sofia
BULGARIA
Skopje
MACEDONIA
Tiranë
ALBANIA
MONTENEGRO
Podgorica
GREECE
Athens
Istanbul
TURKEY
Aegean Sea
Crete (Greece)

SWEDEN
Stockholm
Göteborg
Gulf of Bothnia
Baltic Sea

NORWAY
Oslo
Bergen

DENMARK
Copenhagen
Hamburg
Berlin
GERMANY
Frankfurt
LUXEMBOURG
Luxembourg
BELGIUM
Brussels
Amsterdam
NETHERLANDS

Munich
Vienna
AUSTRIA
Bratislava
SLOVAKIA
Budapest
HUNGARY
SLOVENIA
Ljubljana
Zagreb
CROATIA
BOSNIA AND HERZEGOVINA
Sarajevo
Vaduz
LIECHTENSTEIN
Bern
SWITZERLAND

North Sea

Faeroe Islands (Denmark)
Shetland Islands (U.K.)
ICELAND
Reykjavík

Scotland
Glasgow
Northern Ireland
IRELAND
Dublin
UNITED KINGDOM
Manchester
England
Wales
London
English Channel

FRANCE
Paris
Lyon
Toulouse
Marseille
MONACO
Monaco
ANDORRA
Andorra la Vella
Barcelona
Milan
Venice
SAN MARINO
VATICAN CITY
Rome
ITALY
Naples
Tyrrhenian Sea
Sicily (Italy)
MALTA
Valletta
Corsica (France)
Sardinia (Italy)
Balearic Islands (Spain)
Ionian Sea

Mediterranean Sea

AFRICA

Bay of Biscay

SPAIN
Madrid
Valencia
Seville
Melilla (Spain)
Gibraltar (U.K.)
Ceuta (Spain)
PORTUGAL
Lisbon

ATLANTIC OCEAN
ARCTIC OCEAN
Arctic Circle

Lambert Conformal Conic
400 miles
200
400 kilometers
200

Europe: Physical

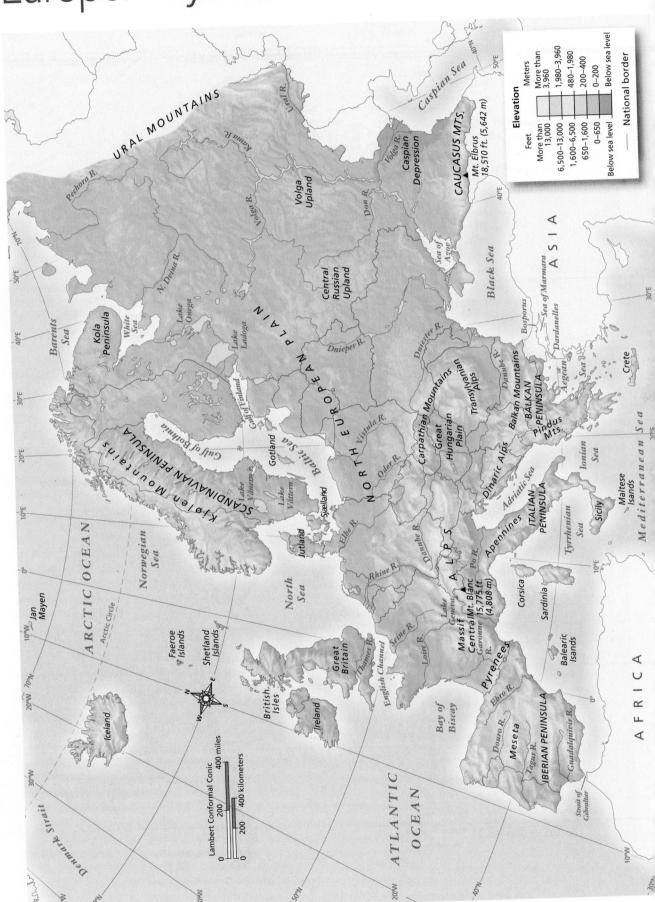

ARCTIC OCEAN

Denmark Strait

Iceland

Jan Mayen

Arctic Circle

Norwegian Sea

Faeroe Islands

Shetland Islands

British Isles

Ireland

Great Britain

North Sea

English Channel

Bay of Biscay

ATLANTIC OCEAN

Meseta

IBERIAN PENINSULA

Douro R.

Tagus R.

Guadalquivir R.

Ebro R.

Strait of Gibraltar

AFRICA

Pyrenees

Balearic Isands

Corsica

Sardinia

Garonne R.

Massif Central

Mt. Blanc 15,775 ft. (4,808 m)

Loire R.

Seine R.

Lake Geneva

A L P S

Rhine R.

Danube R.

Po R.

Apennines

ITALIAN PENINSULA

Tyrrhenian Sea

Sicily

Maltese Isands

Mediterranean Sea

Dinaric Alps

Adriatic Sea

Ionian Sea

BALKAN PENINSULA

Pindus Mts.

Aegean Sea

Crete

Sea of Marmara

Dardanelles

Bosporus

Balkan Mountains

Transylvanian Alps

Carpathian Mountains

Great Hungarian Plain

Thames R.

Elbe R.

Oder R.

Vistula R.

N O R T H   E U R O P E A N   P L A I N

Jutland

Sjælland

Baltic Sea

Gotland

Lake Vättern

Lake Vänern

SCANDINAVIAN PENINSULA

Kjølen Mountains

Gulf of Bothnia

Gulf of Finland

Lake Ladoga

Lake Onega

White Sea

Kola Peninsula

Barents Sea

Pechora R.

N. Dvina R.

Volga R.

Kama R.

Ural R.

URAL MOUNTAINS

A S I A

Volga Upland

Central Russian Upland

Dnieper R.

Dniester R.

Don R.

Volga R.

Caspian Depression

Caspian Sea

CAUCASUS MTS.

Mt. Elbrus 18,510 ft. (5,642 m)

Sea of Azov

Black Sea

Danube R.

Lambert Conformal Conic

0   200   400 miles

0   200   400 kilometers

Elevation

Feet	Meters
More than 13,000	More than 3,960
6,500–13,000	1,980–3,960
1,600–6,500	480–1,980
650–1,600	200–400
0–650	0–200
Below sea level	Below sea level

— National border

North & South America: Political

ASIA

Arctic Ocean

EUROPE

Bering Strait

Beaufort Sea

Greenland (Denmark)

Baffin Bay

180°

International Date Line

Alaska (United States)

Bering Sea

Great Bear Lake

Great Slave Lake

Gulf of Alaska

Nuuk

Davis Strait

Arctic Circle

0°

60°N

45°N

45°N

Hudson Bay

Labrador Sea

CANADA

Vancouver

Lake Winnipeg

Great Lakes

Ottawa

Toronto

Chicago

New York

Washington, D.C.

UNITED STATES

30°N

30°N

Atlantic Ocean

Los Angeles

Houston

Tropic of Cancer

MEXICO

Gulf of Mexico

Nassau

DOMINICAN REPUBLIC

Havana

BAHAMAS

Mexico City

CUBA

HAITI

Puerto Rico (United States)

15°N

JAMAICA

15°N

Belmopan

BELIZE

Kingston

Port-au-Prince

Santo Domingo

U.S. Virgin Islands (United States)

Guatemala City

HONDURAS

Guadeloupe (France)

GUATEMALA

Tegucigalpa

Caribbean Sea

Martinique (France)

San Salvador

NICARAGUA

DOMINICA

BARBADOS

EL SALVADOR

Managua

Caracas

TRINIDAD AND TOBAGO

San José

Panama

VENEZUELA

GUYANA

COSTA RICA

Georgetown

Paramaribo

PANAMA

Bogotá

French Guiana (France)

COLOMBIA

Cayenne

SURINAME

Equator

Quito

0°

0°

Galápagos Islands (Ecuador)

ECUADOR

Pacific Ocean

PERU

BRAZIL

Lima

Lake Titicaca

15°S

La Paz

Brasília

15°S

BOLIVIA

Tropic of Capricorn

Sucre

Rio de Janiero

PARAGUAY

São Paulo

Asunción

CHILE

ARGENTINA

30°S

URUGUAY

Santiago

Montevideo

Buenos Aires

Río de la Plata

Atlantic Ocean

30°S

National border
International Date Line
National capital
Other city

Lambert Azimuthal Equal-Area Projection
0   1000   2000 miles
0   1000   2000 kilometers

Falkland Islands (U.K.)

45°S

45°S

165°W   150°W   135°W   120°W   105°W   90°W   75°W   60°W   45°W   30°W   15°W

North & South America: Physical

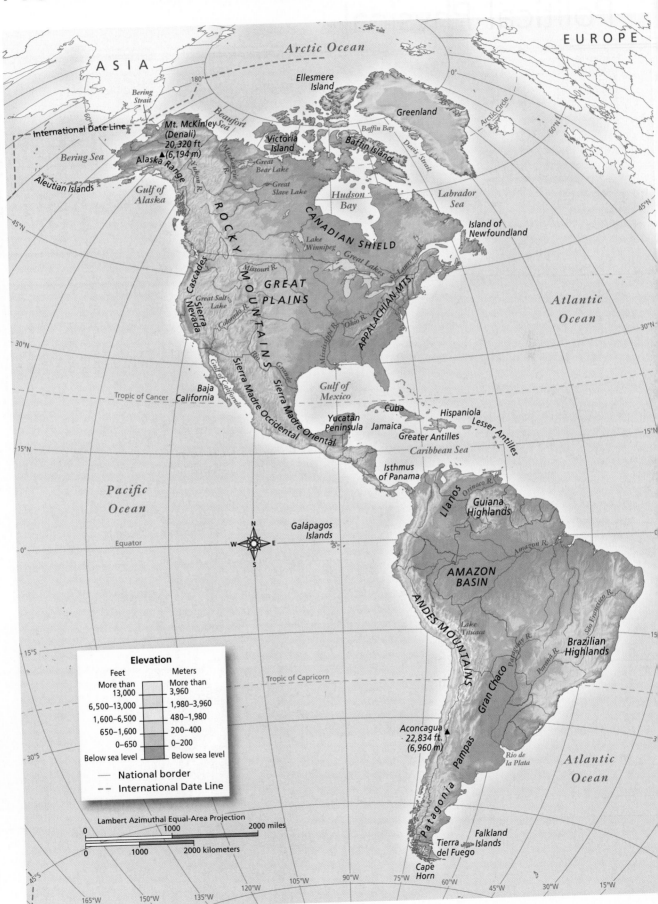

Elevation

Feet	Meters
More than 13,000	More than 3,960
6,500–13,000	1,980–3,960
1,600–6,500	480–1,980
650–1,600	200–400
0–650	0–200
Below sea level	Below sea level

—— National border
- - - International Date Line

Lambert Azimuthal Equal-Area Projection

0   1000   2000 miles
0   1000   2000 kilometers

Australia, New Zealand & Oceania: Political-Physical

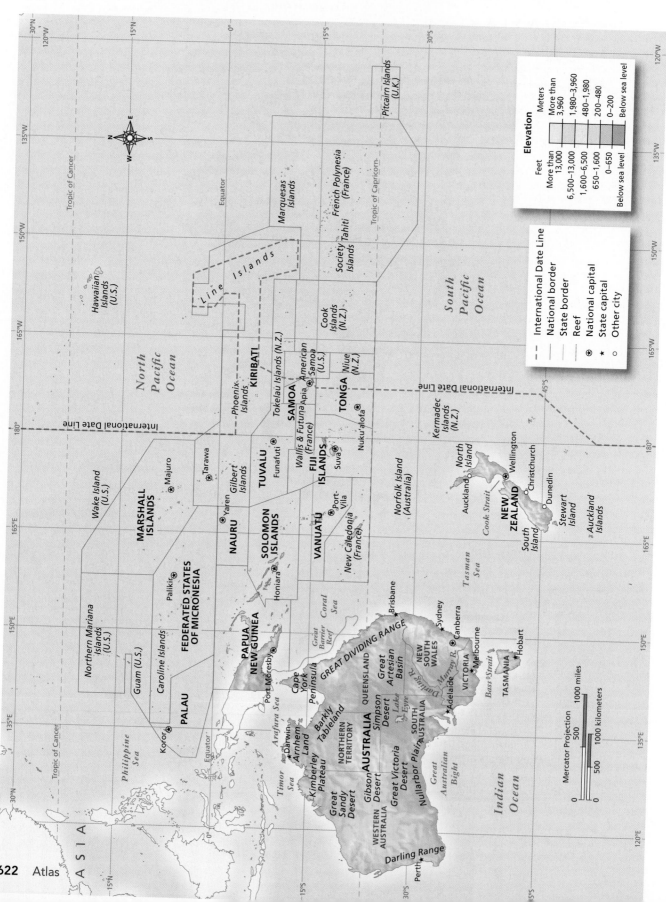

Elevation

Feet	Meters
More than 13,000	More than 3,960
6,500–13,000	1,980–3,960
1,600–6,500	480–1,980
650–1,600	200–480
0–650	0–200
Below sea level	Below sea level

- - - International Date Line
——— National border
——— State border
········· Reef
⊛ National capital
★ State capital
○ Other city

Mercator Projection

0 — 500 — 1000 miles
0 — 500 — 1000 kilometers

The Arctic: Physical

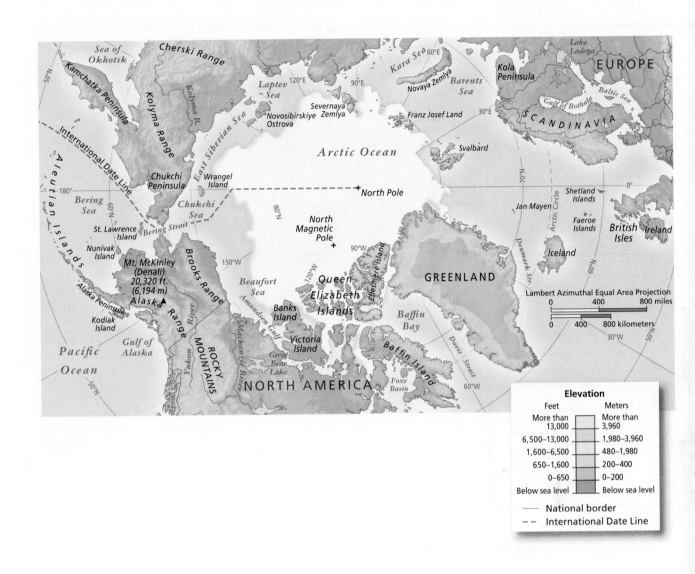

Elevation

Feet	Meters
More than 13,000	More than 3,960
6,500–13,000	1,980–3,960
1,600–6,500	480–1,980
650–1,600	200–400
0–650	0–200
Below sea level	Below sea level

—— National border
- - - International Date Line

Lambert Azimuthal Equal Area Projection

0   400   800 miles

0   400   800 kilometers

Antarctica: Physical

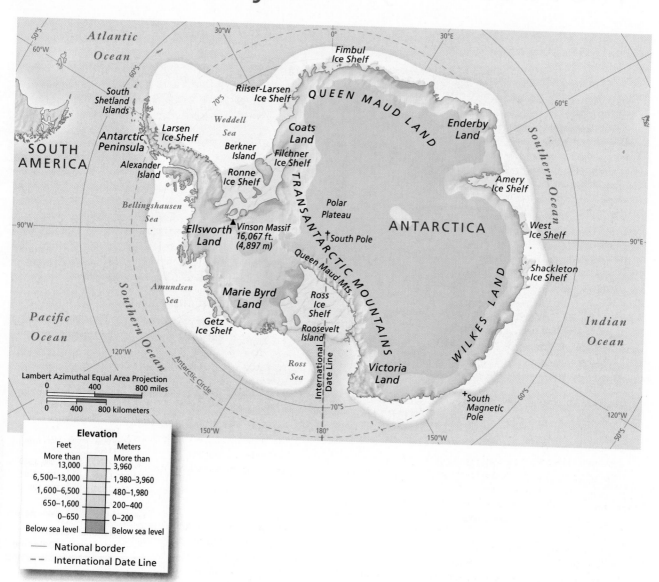

Atlantic Ocean

South Shetland Islands

SOUTH AMERICA

Antarctic Peninsula

Larsen Ice Shelf

Alexander Island

Weddell Sea

Riiser-Larsen Ice Shelf

Fimbul Ice Shelf

QUEEN MAUD LAND

Coats Land

Berkner Island

Filchner Ice Shelf

Ronne Ice Shelf

Enderby Land

Amery Ice Shelf

Southern Ocean

TRANSANTARCTIC MOUNTAINS

Polar Plateau

ANTARCTICA

West Ice Shelf

Bellingshausen Sea

Ellsworth Land

▲ Vinson Massif 16,067 ft. (4,897 m)

✝ South Pole

Shackleton Ice Shelf

Amundsen Sea

Queen Maud Mts.

Marie Byrd Land

Ross Ice Shelf

WILKES LAND

Pacific Ocean

Getz Ice Shelf

Roosevelt Island

Indian Ocean

Southern Ocean

Ross Sea

International Date Line

Victoria Land

✝ South Magnetic Pole

Antarctic Circle

Lambert Azimuthal Equal Area Projection

0   400   800 miles

0   400   800 kilometers

Elevation

Feet	Meters
More than 13,000	More than 3,960
6,500–13,000	1,980–3,960
1,600–6,500	480–1,980
650–1,600	200–400
0–650	0–200
Below sea level	Below sea level

—— National border

-- -- International Date Line

Glossary

54th Massachusetts Regiment an African American unit in the Union army

A

abolitionist a person who wanted to end slavery

according to *prep.*, as stated by

accordingly *adv.*, in a fitting or appropriate way

acquiescence agreeing or accepting something without arguing about it

acquire *v.*, to get (something)

Act of Toleration a 1649 Maryland law that provided religious freedom for all Christians

adobe sun-dried brick

advocate *n.*, a person who argues for or supports a cause or policy

Alamo an old Spanish mission building in Texas where Mexican forces under Santa Anna besieged Texans in 1836

Albany Plan of Union a proposal by Benjamin Franklin to create a unified government for the British colonies

alliance an agreement between nations to aid and protect one another

allocation *n.*, the dividing up of something for a special purpose

ally a nation that works with another nation for a common purpose

alternative *adj.*, offering a choice

amend to change

American Colonization Society an organization in the early 1800s that proposed to end slavery by helping African Americans to move to Africa

American System a program for economic growth promoted by Henry Clay in the early 1800s that called for high tariffs on imports

amnesty a government pardon

anticipate *v.*, expect or look ahead to

Antifederalist an opponent of a strong federal government

Appomattox Court House a Virginia town that was the site of the Confederate surrender in 1865

apprentice a person who learns a trade or craft from a master

arsenal a place where guns are stored

Articles of Confederation the first American constitution, passed in 1777, which created a loose alliance of 13 independent states

artisan a skilled worker

assumption *n.*, a belief held without proof

astrolabe a navigational instrument used to determine latitude, or location north or south of Earth's equator

B

Bacon's Rebellion a 1676 revolt of Virginia colonists against the colony's government

Battle of Antietam an 1862 Civil War battle in Maryland; also called the Battle of Sharpsburg

Battle of Bull Run the first major battle of the Civil War; fought in Virginia in 1861; also called the Battle of Manassas

Battle of Chancellorsville an 1863 Civil War battle in Virginia; important victory for the Confederacy

Battle of Fredericksburg an 1862 Civil War battle in Virginia; one of the Union's worst defeats

Battle of Gettysburg an 1863 Civil War battle in Pennsylvania that ended in a Union victory and stopped the Confederate invasion of the North

Battle of Shiloh an 1862 Civil War battle in Tennessee that ended in a Union victory

Bear Flag Republic the nickname for California after it declared independence from Mexico in 1846

bill a proposed law

bill of rights a list of key individual rights and freedoms

Bill of Rights the first ten amendments to the United States Constitution

black codes the southern laws that severely limited the rights of African Americans after the Civil War

blockade the shutting of a port to keep people or supplies from moving in or out

bond a certificate that promises to repay money loaned, plus interest, on a certain date

boom a period of rapid economic growth

Border Ruffians proslavery bands from Missouri who often battled antislavery forces in Kansas

border state a slave state that remained in the Union during the Civil War

boycott to refuse to buy or use certain goods or services

bribe *n.*, something valuable that is given in order to get someone to do something

burgess a representative to the colonial Virginia government

C

Cabinet the group of officials who head government departments and advise the President

capability *n.*, ability, capacity

capital money invested in a business venture

capitalist a person who invests in a business to make a profit

caravan a group of people who travel together for safety

carpetbagger an uncomplimentary nickname for a northerner who went to the South after the Civil War

cash crop *n.*, a crop sold for money at market

caucus a private meeting; often a political meeting

causeway a raised road made of packed earth

cavalry troops on horseback

cease *v.*, to stop; to end

cede to give up

characteristic *n.*, a distinguishing trait, quality, or property

charter a legal document giving certain rights to a person or company

circumnavigate to travel all the way around the Earth

citizen a person who owes loyalty to a particular nation and is entitled to all its rights and protections

city-state a political unit that controls a city and its surrounding land

civic *adj.*, having to do with being a citizen

civic virtue the willingness to work for the good of the nation or community even at great sacrifice

civil related to lawsuits involving the private rights of individuals

civil disobedience the refusal to obey unjust laws using non-violent means

civil war a war between people of the same country

civilian *adj.*, nonmilitary

civilization a society—or a people sharing a language, territory, and economy—that has certain basic features.

clan a group of two or more related families

Clermont the steamboat built in 1807 by Robert Fulton; first steamboat to be commercially successful in American waters

colony an area settled and ruled by the government of a distant land

Columbian Exchange the global exchange of goods and ideas resulting from the encounter between the peoples of the Eastern and Western hemispheres

commence *v.*, to begin

committee of correspondence a letter-writing campaign that became a major tool of protest in the colonies

commoner *n.*, a regular or average person

compel *v.*, force

complex *adj.*, composed of two or more parts

comprise *v.*, to be made up of

compromise a settlement or peaceful solution in which each side gives up some of its demands in order to reach an agreement or peaceful solution

Compromise of 1850 an agreement over slavery by which California joined the Union as a free state and a strict fugitive slave law was passed

Compromise of 1877 an agreement by Republican presidential candidate Rutherford B. Hayes to end Reconstruction in return for congressional Democrats accepting his inauguration as President after the disputed election of 1876

conducive *adj.*, making it easy for something to happen

confederation an alliance of independent states or nations, usually with a shared military command

conquistador a Spanish explorer who claimed lands in America for Spain

consequently *adv.*, as a result

conservation *n.*, the protection of natural resources

constitute *v.*, to set up; to establish

constitution a document that sets out the laws, principles, organization, and processes of a government

Constitutional Convention the gathering of state representatives on May 25, 1787 to revise the Articles of Confederation

constitutional initiative the power of citizens to call for votes to change state constitutions

continental divide a ridge that separates river systems flowing toward opposite sides of a continent

Copperhead a northerner who opposed using force to keep the southern states in the Union

cottonocracy a name for the wealthy planters who made their money from cotton in the mid-1800s

coureur de bois a French colonist who lived in the lands beyond French settlements as a fur trapper

credit *n.*, an agreement or contract in which a borrower receives money or goods now, with an agreement to repay a greater amount later

creole a person born in Spain's American colonies to Spanish parents

Crusades between 1100 and 1300, the series of wars fought by Christians to control Palestine, or the Holy Land

cultivate to prepare and work soil for planting and growing crops

culture an entire way of life developed by a people

culture region a region in which people share a similar way of life

currency money

D

dame school a school run by women, usually in their own homes

debtor a person who cannot pay money he or she owes

decisive *adj.*, clearly settling a dispute or question

decline *v.*, to draw to a close

Democratic Party a U.S. political party dating from the 1820s to the present that at first spoke out for small farmers and workers against moneyed businessmen and whose policies have changed over the years

Democratic Republican a member of the political party founded by Thomas Jefferson

demonstrate *v.*, to prove something by being an example of it

denounce *v.*, to publicly state that some action or person is wrong or bad

depression *n.*, a period when business activity slows, prices and wages fall, and unemployment rises

deprive *v.*, to take something away

despite *prep.*, in spite of; notwithstanding

determination *n.*, personal drive to continue trying to achieve one's goal

devise *v.*, to work out or create something

dictator a ruler with absolute power and authority over a country, usually through the use of violence

dictatorship a government in which one person or a small group holds complete authority

diffusion the process of spreading ideas from one culture to another

discrimination *n.*, a policy or practice that denies equal rights to certain groups of people

draft a law that requires people of a certain age to enlist in the military

Dred Scott v. Sandford an 1857 Supreme Court case that brought into question the federal power over slavery in the territories

E

Emancipation Proclamation an 1863 declaration by President Lincoln freeing enslaved African Americans in Confederate territory

embargo a ban on trade

employ *v.*, to make use of

English Bill of Rights a 1689 document that guaranteed the rights of English citizens

Enlightenment the movement in Europe in the 1600s and 1700s that emphasized the use of reason

ensure *v.*, to make certain; to secure

Erie Canal the artificial waterway opened in 1825, linking Lake Erie to the Hudson River

essentially *adv.*, having to do with the most important part of an idea or of something

ethical *adj.*, following accepted standards for conduct or behavior

evident *adj.*, obvious; apparent

exceed *v.*, to go above or beyond

exceedingly *adv.*, to a very great degree; extremely

expedition a long voyage of exploration

expel *v.*, to push or force out

export a trade product sent to markets outside a country

extend *v.*, to expand or apply further

extended family a family group that includes grandparents, parents, children, aunts, uncles, and cousins

extensive *adj.*, having a large area or scope

F

faction a party, or an opposing group within a party

famine a severe food shortage

Federalist a supporter of a strong federal government; a member of the party led by Alexander Hamilton that favored a strong federal government

Federalist Papers a series of essays by Federalists James Madison, Alexander Hamilton, and John Jay in support of ratifying the Constitution

feudalism a system of rule by lords who ruled their own lands but owed loyalty and military service to a monarch

Fifteenth Amendment an 1869 amendment to the United States Constitution that forbids any state to deny African Americans the right to vote because of race

flatboat a boat with a flat bottom used for transporting heavy loads on inland waterways

Fort Wagner a fort in South Carolina that was the site of an attack by the African American 54th Massachusetts Regiment in 1863

forty-niner a term to describe one of more than 80,000 people who joined the California Gold Rush in 1849

Fourteenth Amendment an 1868 amendment to the United States Constitution that guarantees equal protection of the laws

free enterprise *n.*, an economic system in which businesses compete freely with little government control

Free-Soil Party the bipartisan antislavery party founded in the United States in 1848 to keep slavery out of the western territories

freedmen the men and women who had been enslaved

Freedmen's Bureau a government agency founded during Reconstruction to help former slaves

French and Indian War a war that took place from 1754 to 1763 that led to the end of French power in North America

frontier a border, especially the border of an area of settlement; a line past which land is not settled

fugitive a runaway

Fugitive Slave Act one of two acts passed in 1793 and 1850 that provided for the capture and return of fugitive slaves

G

General Court the elected representative assembly of the Massachusetts Bay Colony

generally *adv.*, in most cases

gentry the highest social class in the English colonies

Gettysburg Address the speech made by President Lincoln in 1863 after the Battle of Gettysburg

glacier a thick sheet of ice

Glorious Revolution in 1688, the movement that brought William and Mary to the throne of England and strengthened the rights of English citizens

grandfather clause in the post-Reconstruction South, a law that excused a voter from a literacy test if his grandfather had been eligible to vote on January 1, 1867

Great Awakening a religious movement in the English colonies in the mid-1700s, also known as the First Great Awakening

Great Compromise a plan at the Constitutional Convention that settled the differences between large and small states

guerrilla a fighter who uses hit-and-run attacks

guerrilla warfare a type of warfare in which small, informal military groups use surprise attacks and hit-and-run tactics

Gullah a combination of English and West African languages spoken by African Americans in South Carolina and Georgia

H

habeas corpus the right not to be held in prison without first being charged with a specific crime

haven *n.*, a place where people are protected from danger and trouble

hesitate *v.*, to stop briefly because of nervousness

Hudson River School a group of American artists based in New York who developed a unique style of landscape painting in the mid-1800s

I

idealize *v.*, to see in the best possible light

immigrant a person who enters another country in order to settle there

impeach to bring charges of serious wrongdoing against a public official

implicit *adv.*, not expressed directly but able to be understood or inferred

imply *v.*, to suggest something without saying it directly or plainly

imports trade products brought into a country

imposition *n.*, something applied or created based on authority

impressment the practice of forcing people into military service

inauguration a ceremony in which the President publicly takes the oath of office

income tax a tax on people's earnings

incriminate to give evidence against

Indian Removal Act a law passed by Congress in 1830 setting up territories west of the Mississippi River where American Indians living in existing states could be relocated

Indian Territory a region set aside for the relocation of American Indians beginning with the Indian Removal Act, much of which later became part of the state of Oklahoma

indigo a plant used to make a valuable blue dye

individualism the belief in the uniqueness and importance of each individual

Industrial Revolution the change from manual production to machine-powered factory production that started in England in the late 18th century and spread to other places and brought a transformation in economy, society, and technology

inflation a rise in prices and a decrease in the value of money

influential *adj.*, having great influence or power; effective

infrastructure a system of transit lines, highways, bridges, and tunnels

infringe *v.*, to restrict or put limits on

innovation *n.*, a new method or idea

interchangeable parts identical, machine-made parts for a tool or an instrument

interest group *n.*, people who have a certain concern or belief in common

interstate commerce business that crosses state lines

intervene *v.*, to interfere in order to stop or change something

intervention interference in the affairs of another

invoke *v.*, to call on; to appeal to

Iroquois League the alliance of the Iroquois nations

J

Jim Crow laws laws that separated people of different races in public places in the South

judicial review the power of the Supreme Court to decide whether the acts of a President or laws passed by Congress are constitutional

jury duty the responsibility of every citizen to serve on a jury when called

K

Kansas-Nebraska Act an 1854 law that established the territories of Nebraska and Kansas, giving the settlers of each territory the right of popular sovereignty to decide on the issue of slavery

kinship a relationship between people who share a common ancestor, or a system of classifying such relationships

Know-Nothing party a political party of the 1850s that was anti-Catholic and anti-immigrant

Ku Klux Klan a secret society organized in the South after the Civil War to reassert white supremacy by means of violence

L

laissez faire the idea that government should play as small a role as possible in economic affairs

legacy *n.*, something received by a predecessor or from the past

legislature a group of people, usually elected, who have the power to make laws

libel the act of publishing a statement that may unjustly damage a person's reputation

liberty *n.*, freedom

literacy test an examination to see if a person can read and write; used in the past to restrict voting rights

local government a government on the county, parish, city, town, village, or district level

Lowell girls young women who worked in the Lowell Mills in Massachusetts during the Industrial Revolution

Loyalist a colonist who remained loyal to Britain

M

Magna Carta a British document signed in 1215 that contained two basic ideas: monarchs themselves have to obey the laws, and citizens have basic rights

maintain *v.*, to keep in an existing state

majority a group making up more than half of a larger group

Manifest Destiny the 1800s belief that Americans had the right to spread across the continent

manor an area ruled by a lord, including the lord's castle and the lands around it

martyr a person who dies for his or her beliefs

Mayflower Compact a 1620 agreement for ruling the Plymouth Colony

mercantilism the theory that a nation's economic strength came from selling more than it bought from other nations

mercenary a soldier who fights for pay, often for a foreign country

mestizo in Spain's American colonies, a person of mixed Spanish and Indian background

Mexican Cession the Mexican territories of California and New Mexico given to the United States in 1848

middle class in the English colonies, a class that included skilled craft workers, farmers, and some tradespeople

militia an army of citizens who serve as soldiers during an emergency

minutemen colonial militia volunteers who were prepared to fight at a minute's notice

mission a religious settlement run by Catholic priests and friars; a settlement that aims to spread a religion into a new area

Missouri Compromise an agreement, proposed in 1819 by Henry Clay, to keep the number of slave and free states equal

modification *n.*, a change

Monitor an ironclad Union warship

Monroe Doctrine President Monroe's foreign policy statement warning European nations not to interfere in Latin America

mountain man a trapper who explored and hunted in the American West in the early 1800s

N

National Road the first federally funded national road project, begun in 1811

nationalism a devotion to one's nation and its interests

nativist an American who sought to limit immigration and preserve the country for native-born, white Protestants

natural rights rights that belong to all people from birth

naturalize to grant citizenship to a person who has met official requirements for becoming a citizen

Navigation Acts a series of English laws beginning in the 1650s that regulated trade between England and its colonies

neutral not taking sides in a conflict

New Jersey Plan the plan at the Constitutional Convention, favored by smaller states, that called for three branches of government with a single-chamber legislature

"New South" a term used to describe the South in the late 1800s when efforts were being made to expand the economy by building up industry

nominating convention a meeting at which a political party chooses a candidate

Northwest Ordinance a 1787 law that set up a government for the Northwest Territory

northwest passage a waterway through or around North America

notorious *adj.*, well known for some bad quality or effect

Nullification Act an act passed by South Carolina that declared that the Tariff of 1832 was unconstitutional

nullify to cancel

O

Oregon Country a term used in the early 1800s for the region that includes present-day Oregon, Washington, and Idaho, as well as parts of Wyoming, Montana, and western Canada

Oregon Trail the route to the Oregon Country used by wagon trains in the 1800s

organize *v.*, to set up or establish a group, such as a labor union

override to overrule, as when Congress overrules a presidential veto

P

Patriot a colonist who favored war against Britain

patriotism a feeling of love and devotion to one's country

peninsular a person from Spain who held a position of power in a Spanish colony

Pennsylvania Dutch German-speaking Protestants who settled in Pennsylvania

perceive *v.*, notice or become aware of

persecution *n.*, the mistreatment or punishment of a group of people because of their beliefs

petition a formal written request to someone in authority that is signed by a group of people

Pickett's Charge the failed Confederate charge during the third day of the Battle of Gettysburg

Pilgrim an English settler who sought religious freedom in the Americas in the 1600s

pioneer someone who is one of the first people to move to and live in a new area

Plessy v. Ferguson an 1896 court case in which the Supreme Court ruled that segregation in public facilities was legal as long as the facilities were equal

poll tax a tax required before a person can vote

popular sovereignty government by consent of the governed

potlatch a ceremonial dinner held by some American Indians of the Northwest Coast to show off their wealth

preamble an introduction to a declaration, constitution, or other official document

precedent an act or decision that sets an example for others to follow

preliminary *adj.*, something that comes before or is introductory to something

presidio a fort where soldiers lived in the Spanish colonies

privatize *v.*, to put private individuals or companies in charge of something

profit *n.*, the difference between the cost of a good or service and its selling price

prohibit *v.*, to refuse to allow; to forbid

propose *v.*, to suggest something for people to consider

proprietary colony an English colony in which the king gave land to proprietors in exchange for a yearly payment

prosperous *adj.*, having success, usually by making a lot of money

public opinion *n.*, the views held by people, in general

pueblo a town in the Spanish colonies; a village or town of the Anasazi or other American Indian groups in the American Southwest

Puebloan One of a group of American Indian who live in the Southwest in flat-roofed houses in permanent towns

Puritans a group of English Protestants who settled the Massachusetts Bay Colony

Q

Quakers Protestant reformers who believe in the equality of all people

quarters *n.*, living accommodations

quipu a device made of cord or string with knots that stood for quantities; used by the Inca to keep accounts and records

R

racism the belief that one race is superior to another

Radical Republican a member of Congress during Reconstruction who wanted to take power from the wealthy southern plantation owners and ensure that freedmen received the right to vote

ratify to approve

Reconstruction the rebuilding of the South after the Civil War

Reconstruction Act an 1867 law that threw out the southern state governments that refused to ratify the Fourteenth Amendment

regulate *v.*, to make rules or laws that control something

religious tolerance the willingness to let others practice their own beliefs

reluctant *adj.*, not eager to do something

Renaissance the burst of learning in Europe from the late 1300s to about 1600

repeal to cancel, remove from law

representative government a political system in which voters elect representatives to make laws for them

republic a system of government in which citizens choose representatives to govern them

Republican Party a political party established in the United States in 1854 with the goal of keeping slavery out of the western territories

resident alien a person living in a country where he or she is not a citizen

resolve *v.*, to find an answer or solution to something

respect *n.*, understanding when something is serious and acting appropriately

responsibility *n.*, a duty or task one is expected to carry out

revenue money, especially money collected by a government for public use

royal colony a colony under direct control of the English crown

rugged individualist a person who follows his or her own independent course in life

S

salvation *n.*, deliverance from sin

Santa Fe Trail the route to Santa Fe, New Mexico, that was used by traders in the 1800s

scalawag a white southerner who supported the Republicans during Reconstruction

scarcity a shortage, lack, or insufficient supply

secede to withdraw from membership in a group

Second Great Awakening a widespread religious movement in the United States in the early 1800s

sectionalism loyalty to a state or section rather than to the whole country

sedition the act of stirring up rebellion against a government

segregation the legal separation of people based on racial, ethnic, or other differences

self-sufficient able to produce enough for one's own needs

Seneca Falls Convention an 1848 meeting at which activists called for equal rights for women, often seen as the birthplace of the women's rights movement

separation of powers a principle by which the powers of government are divided among separate branches

settlement a place or region newly settled

sharecropper a person who rents a plot of land from another person and farms it in exchange for a share of the crop

Shays' Rebellion a 1786 revolt in Massachusetts led by farmers in reaction to high taxes

shrewd *adj.*, clever

siege to surround and blockade an enemy town or position with troops to force it to surrender

significant *adj.*, very important

signify *v.*, to indicate or be a sign of

Silk Road a network of overland trade routes linking China to the Middle East

slave codes laws that controlled the lives of enslaved Africans and African Americans and denied them basic rights

smuggling the act of importing or exporting goods in violation of trade laws

social reform an organized attempt to improve what is unjust or imperfect in society

specifically *adv.*, for a particular purpose

specify *v.*, name something exactly and in detail

speculation *n.*, risky buying in hope of a large profit

speculator someone who invests in a risky venture in the hope of making a large profit

spoils system the practice of giving supporters government jobs

states' rights the rights and powers independent of the federal government that are reserved for the states by the Constitution

statute *n.*, a law or rule

strike the refusal by workers to do their jobs until their demands are met

subsidize *v.*, to help pay for the costs of something

suffrage the right to vote

supply the amount of goods or resources in stock, on hand, or available in the market to sell

surplus *n.*, an excess, or an extra amount

sustain *v.*, to undergo

T

tariff a tax on foreign goods brought into a country

temperance movement the campaign against alcohol consumption

terrace a wide shelf of land cut into a hillside

The Liberator the most influential antislavery newspaper; begun by William Lloyd Garrison in 1831

Thirteenth Amendment an 1865 amendment to the United States Constitution that banned slavery throughout the nation

Three-Fifths Compromise an agreement at the Constitutional Convention that three-fifths of the enslaved residents in any state be counted in its population

tolerant *adj.*, willing to accept beliefs that are different from your own

town meeting a meeting in colonial New England where settlers discussed and voted on local government matters

trade union association of workers in a specific trade, or line of work, formed to gain higher wages and better working conditions

Trail of Tears the forced migration by the Cherokee and other American Indian groups from their southeastern homelands to territories west of the Mississippi River

traitor a person who betrays his or her country

transcendentalist one of a group of New England writers and thinkers who believed that the most important truths transcended, or went beyond, human reason

treason a betrayal of or action against one's country

Treaty of Guadalupe-Hidalgo an 1848 treaty in which Mexico gave up California and New Mexico Territory to the United States for $15 million

Treaty of Paris a 1763 agreement between Britain and France that ended the French and Indian War and transferred much of North America from French to British control

triangular trade the colonial trade route between New England, Africa, and the West Indies

tribe a community of people that share common customs, language, and rituals

tribute a payment by a weaker party to a stronger party in return for protection

turning point a moment in history that marks a decisive change

U

unalienable rights rights that cannot be taken away

unamendable unable to be changed

unconstitutional not permitted by the Constitution

Underground Railroad a network of abolitionists who secretly helped African Americans to escape to freedom

unify *v.*, to bring together as one; to unite

urbanization the movement of population from farms to cities

V

vaquero a Spanish or Mexican cowhand

varied *adj.*, having many forms or types

veto to reject, as when the President rejects a law passed by Congress

Virginia an ironclad warship used by the Confederates in an attempt to break the Union blockade

Virginia Plan the plan at the Constitutional Convention that called for a strong national government with three branches and a two-chamber legislature

virtue *n.*, morally good behavior or character

vital *adj.*, extremely important

W

War Hawks the members of Congress from the South and the West who called for war with Britain prior to the War of 1812

Whig Party a political party organized by Henry Clay; they believed the federal government should help the economy and promote business

women's rights movement an organized campaign to win legal, educational, employment, and other rights for women

Worcester v. Georgia an 1832 Supreme Court ruling that proclaimed state laws do not apply within American Indian territory

writ of assistance a legal document that allowed British customs officers to inspect a ship's cargo without giving a reason

Y

Yankees a nickname for New Englanders

Glosario

54th Massachusetts Regiment > 54.o Regimiento de Massachusetts unidad del ejército de la Unión compuesta por afroamericanos

A

abolitionist > abolicionista persona que quería terminar con la esclavitud

according to > de acuerdo con según lo establecido por

accordingly > en consecuencia de una manera adecuada o apropiada

acquiescence > consentimiento acuerdo o aceptación de algo sin discutirlo

acquire > adquirir obtener algo

Act of Toleration > Ley de Tolerancia ley de Maryland de 1649 que garantizaba libertad religiosa para todos los cristianos

adobe > adobe ladrillo secado al sol

advocate > defensor persona que apoya o pelea a favor de una causa o política

Alamo > El Álamo edificio de un vieja misión española donde las fuerzas mexicanas, al mando de Santa Anna, sitiaron a los texanos en 1836

Albany Plan of Union > Plan de Unión de Albany propuesta de Benjamin Franklin para crear un gobierno unificado para las colonias británicas

alliance > alianza acuerdo entre naciones para ayudarse y protegerse mutuamente

allocation > asignación la división de algo con un propósito especial

ally > aliado nación que colabora con otra para alcanzar un objetivo en común

alternative > alternativo que ofrece una opción

amend > enmendar modificar

American Colonization Society > Sociedad Estadounidense de Colonización organización de comienzos del siglo XIX que proponía ayudar a los afroamericanos a trasladarse a África para terminar con la esclavitud

American System > sistema estadounidense programa de crecimiento económico promovido por Henry Clay a principios del siglo XIX, que proponía aranceles elevados sobre las importaciones

amnesty > amnistía indulto concedido por el gobierno

anticipate > anticipar esperar o prever algo

Antifederalist > antifederalista persona que se opone a un gobierno federal fuerte

Appomattox Court House > Appomattox Court House pueblo de Virginia donde tuvo lugar la rendición de la Confederación en 1865

apprentice > aprendiz persona que aprende un oficio de un maestro

arsenal > arsenal lugar donde se guardan armas

Articles of Confederation > Artículos de la Confederación primera constitución estadounidense, aprobada en 1777, que creó un principio de alianza de 13 estados independientes

artisan > artesano trabajador calificado

assumption > presunción creencia sostenida como cierta sin pruebas

astrolabe > astrolabio instrumento de navegación usado para determinar la latitud, es decir, la ubicación al norte o al sur del ecuador de la Tierra

B

Bacon's Rebellion > Rebelión de Bacon revuelta de los colonos de Virginia contra el gobierno de la colonia en 1676

Battle of Antietam > Batalla de Antietam batalla de la Guerra Civil que tuvo lugar en Maryland en 1862; también llamada Batalla de Sharpsburg

Battle of Bull Run > Batalla de Bull Run primera batalla importante de la Guerra Civil, que tuvo lugar en Virginia en 1861; también llamada Batalla de Manassas

Battle of Chancellorsville > Batalla de Chancellorsville batalla de la Guerra Civil que tuvo lugar en Virginia en 1863; importante victoria de la Confederación

Battle of Fredericksburg > Batalla de Fredericksburg batalla de la Guerra Civil que tuvo lugar en Virginia en 1862; una de las peores derrotas de la Unión

Battle of Gettysburg > Batalla de Gettysburg batalla de la Guerra Civil en Pennsylvania en 1863, que resultó en una victoria de la Unión y evitó que la Confederación invadiera el Norte

Battle of Shiloh > Batalla de Shiloh batalla de la Guerra Civil en Tennessee en 1862, que resultó en una victoria de la Unión

Bear Flag Republic > República de la Bandera del Oso apodo de California tras declarar su independencia de México en 1846

bill > proyecto de ley ley propuesta

bill of rights > carta de derechos lista escrita de libertades que el gobierno promete proteger

Bill of Rights > Carta de Derechos las primeras diez enmiendas de la Constitución de los Estados Unidos

black codes > códigos negros leyes de los estados sureños que limitaban seriamente los derechos de los afroamericanos después de la Guerra Civil

blockade > bloqueo cierre de un puerto con el fin de impedir la entrada y salida de personas y provisiones

bond > bono certificado que promete el pago de dinero que se ha prestado, más el interés, en una determinada fecha

boom > auge período de crecimiento económico acelerado

Border Ruffians > rufianes de la frontera bandas proesclavistas de Missouri que solían enfrentarse a las fuerzas antiesclavistas en Kansas

border state > estado fronterizo estado esclavista que permaneció en la Unión durante la Guerra Civil

boycott > boicot negarse a comprar o usar determinados bienes y servicios

bribe > soborno algo valioso que se le da a alguien para que haga algo

burgess > burgués representante del gobierno colonial de Virginia

C

Cabinet > gabinete grupo de funcionarios que dirigen departamentos gubernamentales y aconsejan al presidente

capability > capacidad habilidad, potencial

capital > capitalismo dinero con el que se inicia un negocio

capitalist > capitalista persona que invierte en un negocio con el fin de obtener una ganancia

caravan > caravana grupo de personas que viajan juntas para protegerse entre sí

carpetbagger > carpetbagger apodo ofensivo usado para describir a los norteños que se mudaban al Sur después de la Guerra Civil

cash crop > cultivo comercial cultivo que se vende en el mercado para obtener dinero

caucus > asamblea partidaria reunión privada; por lo general, reunión política

causeway > calzada elevada camino elevado hecho con tierra comprimida

cavalry > caballería tropas a caballo

cease > cesar detenerse; parar

cede > ceder renunciar

characteristic > característica rasgo distintivo, cualidad o propiedad

charter > cédula documento legal que otorga ciertos derechos a una persona o una compañía

circumnavigate > circunnavegar dar una vuelta completa a la Tierra en barco

citizen > ciudadano persona que debe lealtad a una nación en particular y a quien le corresponden todos sus derechos y protecciones

city-state > ciudad-estado unidad política que controla una ciudad y las tierras de sus alrededores

civic > cívico relacionado con ser un ciudadano

civic virtue > virtud cívica voluntad de trabajar por el bien de la nación o comunidad, incluso si eso implica un gran sacrificio

civil > civil relacionado con las demandas legales que involucran los derechos privados de los individuos

civil disobedience > desobediencia civil resistencia no violenta a acatar leyes que se consideran injustas

civil war > guerra civil guerra entre personas del mismo país

civilian > civil no militar

civilization > civilización una sociedad, es decir, un pueblo que comparte un idioma, un territorio y una economía, que tiene ciertas características básicas

clan > clan grupo de dos o más familias relacionadas

Clermont* > *Clermont barco a vapor construido en 1807 por Robert Fulton; fue el primer barco a vapor que tuvo éxito comercial en aguas estadounidenses

colony > colonia zona poblada y gobernada por el gobierno de un país distante

Columbian Exchange > intercambio colombino intercambio global de bienes e ideas que se dio como resultado del encuentro entre los pueblos de los hemisferios occidental y oriental

commence > comenzar empezar

committee of correspondence > Comité de Correspondencia campaña de intercambio de cartas que se convirtió en un importante instrumento de protesta en las colonias

commoner > plebeyo persona común

compel > forzar obligar

complex > complejo compuesto de dos o más partes

comprise > comprender estar formado por

compromise > acuerdo pacto en el que cada lado renuncia a parte de sus demandas con el fin de llegar a una solución pacífica

Compromise of 1850 > Acuerdo de 1850 acuerdo sobre la esclavitud por medio del cual California se sumaba a la Unión como estado libre y que incluía una estricta ley sobre esclavos fugitivos

Compromise of 1877 > Acuerdo de 1877 acuerdo del candidato presidencial republicano Rutherford B. Hayes en el que prometió dar fin a la Reconstrucción a cambio de que los congresistas demócratas aceptaran su toma de posesión del cargo de presidente tras la conflictiva elección de 1876

conducive > propicio que facilita que algo ocurra

confederation > confederación alianza de estados o naciones independientes que suele tener un mando militar compartido

conquistador > conquistador explorador español que tomaba posesión de tierras en las Américas en nombre de España

consequently > por consiguiente como resultado

conservation > conservación protección de los recursos naturales

constitute > constituir fundar; establecer

constitution > constitución documento que establece las leyes, los principios, la organización y los procesos de un gobierno

Constitutional Convention > Convención Constitucional reunión de representantes de los estados el 25 de mayo de 1787 para revisar los Artículos de la Confederación

constitutional initiative > iniciativa popular poder de los ciudadanos de solicitar una votación para modificar las constituciones estatales

continental divide > línea divisoria continental cadena de montañas que separa sistemas fluviales que corren en direcciones opuestas en un continente

Copperhead > cabeza de cobre norteño que se oponía a hacer uso de la fuerza para que los estados sureños permanecieran en la Unión

cottonocracy > aristocracia del algodón nombre dado a los plantadores ricos que ganaban dinero gracias al algodón a mediados del siglo XIX

coureur de bois > coureur de bois colono francés que vivía en las tierras más allá de los asentamientos franceses y era trampero de pieles

credit > crédito acuerdo o contrato en el que una persona recibe dinero o bienes ahora y se compromete a devolver más tarde una cantidad que es mayor a lo prestado

creole > criollo persona de padres españoles nacida en las colonias españolas de las Américas

Crusades > Cruzadas serie de guerras que libraron los cristianos para controlar Palestina, es decir, Tierra Santa, entre 1100 y 1300

cultivate > labrar preparar y trabajar el suelo para plantar y producir cultivos

culture > cultura forma de vida que lleva a cabo un pueblo

culture region > región cultural región donde las personas comparten una forma de vida similar

currency > moneda dinero

D

dame school > escuela de damas escuela dirigida por mujeres, habitualmente ubicada en sus propias casas

debtor > deudor persona que debe dinero y no puede pagarlo

decisive > concluyente que decide claramente el resultado de una disputa o una cuestión

decline > declinar acercarse al final

Democratic Party > Partido Demócrata partido político de los EE. UU. que data de la década de 1820 y continúa en la actualidad; en un principio, representaba a los pequeños granjeros y trabajadores frente a los empresarios adinerados; sus políticas cambiaron durante los años

Democratic Republican > demócrata republicano miembro del partido político fundado por Thomas Jefferson

demonstrate > demostrar probar algo sirviendo como ejemplo

denounce > denunciar declarar públicamente que una acción o persona es incorrecta o mala

depression > depresión período en el que disminuye la actividad de negocios, caen los precios y salarios y aumenta el desempleo

deprive > privar quitar algo

despite > a pesar aunque, no obstante

determination > determinación impulso personal para seguir intentando alcanzar los objetivos propios

devise > concebir desarrollar o crear algo

dictator > dictador gobernante que tiene poder y autoridad absolutos sobre un país, generalmente por medio de la violencia

dictatorship > dictadura sistema de gobierno en el que una persona o un grupo reducido tiene todo el poder

diffusion > difusión proceso de transmitir ideas de una cultura a otra

discrimination > discriminación política o práctica que niega la igualdad de derechos a ciertos grupos de personas

draft > conscripción ley que exige a las personas de determinada edad que realicen el servicio militar

***Dred Scott v. Sandford* > Dred Scott contra Sandford** caso de 1857 de la Corte Suprema que puso en duda el poder federal sobre la cuestión de la esclavitud en los territorios

E

Emancipation Proclamation > Proclamación de Emancipación declaración del presidente Lincoln presentada en 1863 en la que establecía la liberación de los afroamericanos esclavizados en el territorio confederado

embargo > embargo prohibición de comerciar

employ > emplear usar algo

English Bill of Rights > Declaración de Derechos inglesa documento de 1689 que garantizaba los derechos de los ciudadanos ingleses

Enlightenment > Ilustración movimiento europeo de los siglos XVII y XVIII que hizo hincapié en el uso de la razón

ensure > asegurar garantizar, afianzar

Erie Canal > canal del Erie vía artificial de navegación fluvial inaugurada en 1825, que conecta el lago Erie con el río Hudson

essentially > esencialmente relacionado con la parte más importante de una idea o de algo

ethical > ético que sigue las normas aceptadas de conducta o comportamiento

evident > evidente obvio, aparente

exceed > sobrepasar ir más allá

exceedingly > sumamente en un grado muy alto; extremadamente

expedition > expedición largo viaje de exploración

expel > expulsar echar o sacar por la fuerza

export > exportación producto comercial que es enviado a los mercados de otros países

extend > extender expandir o aplicar más allá

extended family > familia extensa grupo familiar que incluye abuelos, padres, hijos, tíos y primos

extensive > extenso que tiene una gran área o alcance

F

faction > facción partido o grupo opositor dentro de un partido

famine > hambruna severa escasez de alimentos

Federalist > federalista persona que apoya un gobierno federal fuerte

Federalist > federalista miembro del partido liderado por Alexander Hamilton que apoyaba un gobierno federal fuerte

Federalist Papers > ensayos de The Federalist serie de ensayos de los federalistas James Madison, Alexander Hamilton y John Jay a favor de ratificar la Constitución

feudalism > feudalismo sistema de gobierno en el que los señores gobiernan sus tierras, pero le juran lealtad y prestan ayuda militar a un monarca

Fifteenth Amendment > Decimoquinta Enmienda enmienda de la Constitución de los Estados Unidos, de 1869, que prohíbe a los estados negar el derecho al voto a los afroamericanos por motivo de raza

flatboat > barcaza embarcación con base plana, usada para transportar cargas pesadas a través de vías fluviales

Fort Wagner > fuerte Wagner fuerte de Carolina del Sur donde tuvo lugar un ataque liderado por el 54.° Regimiento de afroamericanos de Massachusetts

forty-niner > persona del 49 término que nombra a una de los más de 80,000 personas que en 1849 se unieron a la fiebre del oro

Fourteenth Amendment > Decimocuarta Enmienda enmienda de la Constitución de los Estados Unidos, de 1868, que garantiza igual protección de las leyes

free enterprise > libre empresa sistema económico en el que las empresas compiten libremente con poco control del gobierno

Free-Soil Party > Partido del Suelo Libre partido antiesclavista bipartito fundado en 1848 en los Estados Unidos para evitar que la esclavitud entrara en los territorios del Oeste

freedmen > liberto hombre o mujer que había sido esclavizado

Freedmen's Bureau > Oficina de Libertos agencia gubernamental fundada durante la Reconstrucción para ayudar a quienes habían sido esclavos

French and Indian War > Guerra contra la Alianza Franco-Indígena guerra que tuvo lugar entre 1754 y 1763, y que puso fin al dominio francés en América del Norte

frontier > frontera límite, especialmente el límite de un asentamiento; línea tras la cual no hay asentamientos

fugitive > fugitivo que huye

Fugitive Slave Act > Ley de Esclavos Fugitivos cada una de las dos leyes aprobadas en 1793 y 1850 que se ocupaban de la captura y el regreso de los esclavos fugitivos

G

General Court > Corte General asamblea de representantes electos en la colonia de la bahía de Massachusetts

generally > generalmente en la mayoría de los casos

gentry > clase alta clase social que estaba en la cima de la sociedad en las colonias inglesas

Gettysburg Address > Discurso de Gettysburg discurso que dio el presidente Lincoln en 1863 después de la Batalla de Gettysburg

glacier > glaciar capa gruesa de hielo

Glorious Revolution > Revolución Gloriosa movimiento de 1688 que llevó a Guillermo y María al trono de Inglaterra, y consolidó los derechos de los ciudadanos ingleses

grandfather clause > cláusula del abuelo en el Sur posterior a la Reconstrucción, ley que eximía a un votante de la prueba de alfabetización si su abuelo había calificado para votar el 1 de enero de 1867

Great Awakening > Gran Despertar movimiento religioso de las colonias inglesas a mediados del siglo XVIII, también conocido como Primer Gran Despertar

Great Compromise > Gran Concertación plan de la Convención Constitucional que resolvió las diferencias entre los estados grandes y pequeños

guerrilla > guerrilla combatiente que usa tácticas de ataque y huida

guerrilla warfare > guerra de guerrillas tipo de guerra en la que grupos militares reducidos e informales usan ataques sorpresivos y tácticas de ataque y huida

Gullah > gullah combinación del idioma inglés con idiomas de África occidental, hablado por los afroamericanos de Carolina del Sur y Georgia

H

habeas corpus > hábeas corpus el derecho a no ir a prisión sin antes ser acusado de un delito en particular

haven > refugio lugar donde las personas son protegidas del peligro y los problemas

hesitate > vacilar detenerse por un momento debido a los nervios

Hudson River School > Escuela de Hudson River grupo de artistas estadounidenses, con sede en Nueva York, que desarrollaron un estilo único de pintura de paisajes a mediados del siglo XIX

I

idealize > idealizar ver algo de la mejor manera posible

immigrant > inmigrante persona que ingresa a otro país con el objetivo de asentarse allí

impeach > enjuiciar políticamente presentar cargos contra un funcionario por ofensas graves

implicit > implícito no expresado directamente, pero que se puede entender o inferir

imply > implicar sugerir algo sin decirlo directamente

imports > importaciones producto comercial que se trae de otro país

imposition > imposición algo aplicado o creado basándose en la autoridad

impressment > reclutamiento forzado práctica de obligar a las personas a realizar el servicio militar

inauguration > toma de posesión ceremonia en la cual el presidente realiza públicamente el juramento de su cargo

income tax > impuesto sobre la renta impuesto sobre los ingresos de una persona

incriminate > incriminar presentar pruebas en contra de alguien

Indian Removal Act > Ley de Expulsión de Indígenas ley aprobada por el Congreso en 1830 que establecía tierras al oeste del río Mississippi para que los indígenas que vivían en los estados ya existentes se mudaran allí

Indian Territory > territorio indígena región establecida para la reubicación de los indígenas norteamericanos, que comenzó con la Ley de Expulsión de Indígenas; la mayor parte de esta región pasó a formar parte del estado de Oklahoma

indigo > añil planta usada para fabricar una valiosa tintura azul

individualism > individualismo creencia en la singularidad e importancia de cada individuo

Industrial Revolution > Revolución Industrial cambio de la producción manual a la producción hecha por máquinas en fábricas que comenzó en Inglaterra a fines del siglo XVIII y se expandió hacia otros lugares, y transformó la economía, la sociedad y la tecnología

inflation > inflación aumento de precios y disminución del valor del dinero

influential > influyente que tiene mucha influencia o poder; eficaz

infrastructure > infraestructura sistema de vías de tránsito, carreteras, puentes y túneles

infringe > infringir violar (leyes) o restringir (derechos)
innovation > innovación idea o método nuevo
interchangeable parts > piezas reemplazables piezas idénticas, hechas a máquina, de una herramienta o instrumento
interest group > grupo de interés personas que tienen una preocupación o una creencia en común
interstate commerce > comercio interestatal comercio que atraviesa los límites estatales
intervene > intervenir interferir para detener o cambiar algo
intervention > intervención interferencia en los asuntos de otros
invoke > invocar recurrir o apelar a algo
Iroquois League > Liga Iroquesa alianza formada por las naciones iroquesas

J

Jim Crow laws > Leyes de Jim Crow leyes que separaban a las personas según su raza en lugares públicos del Sur
judicial review > control de constitucionalidad poder de la Corte Suprema de decidir si los actos de un presidente o las leyes aprobadas por el Congreso son o no constitucionales
jury duty > servir como jurado responsabilidad de todos los ciudadanos de formar parte de un jurado cuando son convocados

K

Kansas-Nebraska Act > Ley Kansas-Nebraska ley de 1854 que estableció los territorios de Kansas y Nebraska y otorgó a los pobladores de cada territorio el derecho de soberanía popular para resolver el asunto de la esclavitud
kinship > parentesco relación entre personas que comparten un ancestro en común o sistema de clasificación de tales relaciones
Know-Nothing party > partido Know-Nothing partido político de la década de 1850 que era anticatólico y antiinmigrante
Ku Klux Klan > Ku Klux Klan sociedad secreta organizada en el Sur después de la Guerra Civil con el fin de reafirmar la supremacía de los hombres blancos usando la violencia

L

laissez faire > laissez faire idea de que el gobierno debe tener la menor participación posible en los asuntos económicos
legacy > legado algo recibido de un predecesor o del pasado
legislature > cuerpo legislativo grupo de personas, generalmente elegidos por medio del voto, que tienen la facultad de crear leyes
libel > difamación acto de publicar algo que puede dañar injustamente la reputación de otra persona
liberty > libertad condición de ser libre
literacy test > prueba de alfabetización prueba para comprobar si una persona puede leer y escribir; usada en el pasado para limitar el derecho al voto

local government > gobierno local gobierno a nivel del condado, feligresía, ciudad, pueblo, aldea o distrito
Lowell girls > chicas Lowell mujeres jóvenes que trabajaban en las hilanderías de Lowell en Massachusetts durante la Revolución Industrial
Loyalist > leal al rey colono que se mantuvo leal a Gran Bretaña

M

Magna Carta > Carta Magna documento británico firmado en 1215 que contenía dos ideas básicas: los monarcas debían obedecer las leyes y los ciudadanos tenían derechos básicos
maintain > mantener conservar un estado existente
majority > mayoría grupo que representa más de la mitad de un grupo más grande
Manifest Destiny > Destino Manifiesto en el siglo XIX, la creencia de que los Estados Unidos tenían el derecho de expandirse a través de todo el continente
manor > feudo área gobernada por un señor, incluyendo su castillo y las tierras a su alrededor
martyr > mártir persona que da la vida por sus ideales
Mayflower Compact > Pacto del Mayflower acuerdo de 1620 para gobernar la colonia de Plymouth
mercantilism > mercantilismo teoría que plantea que la fortaleza económica de una nación proviene de vender más de lo que compra a otras naciones
mercenary > mercenario soldado que lucha a cambio de un salario, generalmente para un país extranjero
mestizo > mestizo en las colonias españolas de las Américas, persona de mezcla de sangre española e indígena
Mexican Cession > Cesión Mexicana los territorios mexicanos de California y Nuevo México otorgados a los Estados Unidos en 1848
middle class > clase media en las colonias inglesas, clase que incluía a artesanos calificados, agricultores y algunos comerciantes
militia > milicia ejército de ciudadanos que prestan servicios como soldados durante una emergencia
minutemen > milicianos voluntarios de las milicias coloniales, que estaban preparados para luchar en cualquier momento
mission > misión asentamiento de sacerdotes y frailes católicos; asentamiento cuyo objetivo es difundir la religión en una nueva área
Missouri Compromise > Acuerdo de Missouri acuerdo propuesto en 1819 por Henry Clay para mantener la misma cantidad de estados libres y de estados esclavistas
modification > modificación cambio
Monitor > Monitor barco de guerra acorazado de la Unión
Monroe Doctrine > Doctrina Monroe declaración de la política exterior del presidente Monroe en la que advertía a las naciones europeas que no interfirieran en América Latina
mountain man > montañés trampero que exploraba y cazaba en el Oeste de los Estados Unidos a principios del siglo XIX

N

National Road > Carretera Nacional primer proyecto de construcción de una carretera nacional financiado por el gobierno federal, comenzado en 1811

nationalism > nacionalismo devoción por el país propio así como por sus intereses

nativist > nativista estadounidense que quería limitar la inmigración y conservar el país para los protestantes blancos nativos

natural rights > derechos naturales derechos que todas las personas tienen desde su nacimiento

naturalize > naturalizar otorgar la ciudadanía a una persona que ha cumplido con los requisitos oficiales para convertirse en ciudadano

Navigation Acts > Leyes de Navegación serie de leyes inglesas que regulaban el comercio entre Inglaterra y sus colonias a partir de la década de 1650

neutral > neutral que no toma partido en un conflicto

New Jersey Plan > Plan de Nueva Jersey plan de la Convención Constitucional, respaldado por los estados pequeños, que proponía tres poderes de gobierno y un cuerpo legislativo de una sola cámara

"New South" > "Nuevo Sur" término usado para describir al Sur a fines del siglo XIX, cuando se intentó expandir la economía a través de la construcción de industrias

nominating convention > convención de nominación reunión en la que un partido político elige a un candidato

Northwest Ordinance > Decreto del Noroeste ley de 1787 que estableció un gobierno para el territorio del Noroeste

northwest passage > paso del Noroeste vía navegable que atraviesa o bordea América del Norte

notorious > de mala reputación conocido por una mala cualidad o efecto

Nullification Act > Ley de Anulación ley aprobada por Carolina del Sur en 1832 que declaraba que el Arancel de 1828 era inconstitucional

nullify > invalidar cancelar

O

Oregon Country > Territorio de Oregón término usado a comienzos del siglo XIX para la región que incluye los actuales Oregón, Washington, Idaho y partes de Wyoming, Montana y el oeste del Canadá

Oregon Trail > Camino de Oregón ruta que conducía al Territorio de Oregón, usada por las caravanas de carretas en el siglo XIX

organize > organizar crear o establecer un grupo, como un sindicato

override > invalidar anular, como cuando el Congreso anula un veto presidencial

P

Patriot > patriota colono que estaba a favor de la guerra contra Gran Bretaña

patriotism > patriotismo sentimiento de amor y devoción hacia el propio país

peninsular > peninsular persona nacida en España que ocupaba una posición de poder en las colonias españoles

Pennsylvania Dutch > dutch de Pennsylvania protestante de habla alemana que se asentó en Pennsylvania

perceive > percibir notar o advertir algo

persecution > persecución maltrato o castigo de un grupo de personas por sus creencias

petition > petición demanda escrita y formal, dirigida a una autoridad y firmada por un grupo de personas

Pickett's Charge > Carga de Pickett ataque fallido de la Confederación en el tercer día de la Batalla de Gettysburg

Pilgrim > peregrino colono inglés que buscaba libertad religiosa en las Américas en el siglo XVII

pioneer > pionero persona que está entre los primeros en trasladarse a vivir a un área nueva

Plessy v. Ferguson **> Plessy contra Ferguson** caso de 1896 en el que la Corte Suprema decretó que la segregación era legal en los lugares públicos siempre que las instalaciones fueran iguales

poll tax > impuesto al voto impuesto que una persona debía pagar para poder votar

popular sovereignty > soberanía popular gobierno cuyo poder deriva del consentimiento de los gobernados

potlatch > potlatch cena ceremonial realizada por algunos indígenas de la costa del Noroeste para mostrar su riqueza

preamble > preámbulo introducción de una declaración, constitución u otro documento oficial

precedent > precedente acto o decisión que funciona como un ejemplo para otros

preliminary > preliminar algo que viene antes o sirve como introducción a algo

presidio > presidio fuerte donde vivían los soldados en las colonias españolas

privatize > privatizar poner a individuos privados o empresas a cargo de algo

profit > ganancia la diferencia entre el costo de un bien y su precio de venta

prohibit > prohibir negarse a permitir; impedir

propose > proponer sugerir algo para que la gente lo considere

proprietary colony > colonia de propietarios colonia inglesa en la que el rey entregaba tierras a una o más personas a cambio de un pago anual

prosperous > próspero que tiene éxito, generalmente por ganar mucho dinero

public opinion > opinión pública los puntos de vista de la gente, en general

pueblo > pueblo asentamiento en las colonias españolas; aldea de los anasazis u otros grupos de indígenas norteamericanos del Suroeste de los Estados Unidos

Puebloan > indígenas pueblo uno de los grupos de indígenas que vive en el Suroeste en casas de techo plano en asentamientos permanentes

Puritans > puritanos grupo de protestantes ingleses que se asentaron en la colonia de la bahía de Massachusetts

Q

Quakers > cuáqueros reformistas protestantes que creían en la igualdad de todas las personas

quarters > barracones alojamiento para trabajadores

quipu > quipu artefacto que consistía en una cuerda con nudos que representaban cantidades; era usado por los incas para llevar cuentas y registros

R

racism > racismo creencia según la cual una raza es superior a otra

Radical Republican > republicano radical durante la Reconstrucción, miembro del Congreso que quería someter a los adinerados dueños de plantaciones del Sur y garantizar que los libertos tuvieran derecho a votar

ratify > ratificar aprobar

Reconstruction > La Reconstrucción la restauración del Sur después de la Guerra Civil

Reconstruction Act > Ley de Reconstrucción ley de 1867 que rechazaba a los gobiernos de los estados sureños que se negaban a ratificar la Decimocuarta Enmienda

regulate > regular crear reglas o leyes para controlar algo

religious tolerance > tolerancia religiosa actitud de permitir que cada uno practique sus propias creencias

reluctant > reacio que no tiene la voluntad de hacer algo

Renaissance > Renacimiento auge de conocimiento en Europa que tuvo lugar desde fines del siglo XIV hasta comienzos del siglo XVII

repeal > derogar cancelar o anular una ley

representative government > gobierno representativo sistema político en el que los votantes eligen a representantes para que creen las leyes en su nombre

republic > república sistema de gobierno en el que los ciudadanos eligen representantes para que los gobiernen

Republican Party > Partido Republicano partido político establecido en los Estados Unidos en 1854 cuyo objetivo principal era evitar que la esclavitud se estableciera en los territorios del Oeste

resident alien > extranjero residente persona que vive en un país del que no es ciudadana

resolve > resolver hallar una respuesta o solución para algo

respect > respeto comprender cuando algo es serio y actuar apropiadamente

responsibility > responsabilidad deber o tarea que se espera que uno haga

revenue > ingresos dinero, especialmente el que recauda el gobierno para su uso público

royal colony > colonia de la corona colonia bajo control directo de la corona inglesa

rugged individualist > individualista extremo persona que sigue su propio camino independiente en la vida

S

salvation > salvación liberación del pecado

Santa Fe Trail > Camino de Santa Fe ruta que iba a Santa Fe, Nuevo México, usada por comerciantes en el siglo XIX

scalawag > sacalawag sureño blanco que apoyaba a los republicanos durante la Reconstrucción

scarcity > escasez falta de algo u oferta insuficiente

secede > separarse dejar de ser miembro de un grupo

Second Great Awakening > Segundo Gran Despertar amplio movimiento religioso en los Estados Unidos a principios del siglo XIX

sectionalism > seccionalismo lealtad a un estado o región antes que a todo el país

sedition > sedición acto de suscitar una rebelión en contra de un gobierno

segregation > segregación separación legal de las personas basada en diferencias raciales, étnicas u otras

self-sufficient > autosuficiente capaz de producir lo suficiente para satisfacer las propias necesidades

Seneca Falls Convention > Convención de Seneca Falls encuentro de 1848 en el que algunos activistas pidieron por la igualdad de derechos para las mujeres; considerado el origen del movimiento por los derechos de las mujeres

separation of powers > separación de poderes principio según el cual el gobierno se divide en poderes separados

settlement > asentamiento lugar o región recientemente poblado

sharecropper > aparcero persona que alquila una parcela de tierra a otra persona y la trabaja a cambio de una porción de los cultivos

Shays' Rebellion > Rebelión de Shays en 1786, levantamiento de granjeros en Massachusetts en contra de los altos impuestos

shrewd > astuto inteligente

siege > sitio situación en la que un ejército bloquea o rodea una ciudad o posición donde está un enemigo con el propósito de obligarlo a rendirse

significant > significativo muy importante

signify > significar indicar o ser el signo de algo

Silk Road > Ruta de la Seda red de rutas comerciales terrestres que unían China y Oriente Medio

slave codes > códigos de esclavos leyes que reglamentaban la conducta de los africanos y afroamericanos esclavizados y en virtud de las cuales les quitaron sus derechos humanos básicos

smuggling > contrabando acto de importar o exportar mercancías que viola las leyes de comercio

social reform > reforma social intento organizado de mejorar lo que es injusto o imperfecto en la sociedad

specifically > específicamente con un propósito en particular

specify > especificar nombrar algo exactamente y en detalle

speculation > especulación compra riesgosa con la expectativa de una gran ganancia

speculator > especulador alguien que invierte dinero en un negocio arriesgado con la expectativa de obtener grandes ganancias

spoils system > sistema de botines práctica de dar empleos en el gobierno a los partidarios de ese gobierno

states' rights > derechos de los estados derechos y facultades independientes del gobierno federal que se reservan para los estados según la Constitución

statute > estatuto ley o regla

strike > huelga negativa de los trabajadores a hacer su trabajo hasta que se satisfagan sus demandas

subsidize > subsidiar ayudar a pagar el costo de algo

suffrage > sufragio derecho al voto

supply > oferta cantidad de bienes o recursos que están disponibles en el mercado para su venta

surplus > superávit exceso o cantidad extra

sustain > padecer experimentar

T

tariff > arancel impuesto sobre los bienes extranjeros que ingresan a un país

temperance movement > movimiento por la templanza campaña contra el consumo de alcohol

terrace > terraza franja ancha de tierra escalonada en las laderas de las montañas

The Liberator > The Liberator el periódico antiesclavista más influyente del país; fundado en 1831 por William Lloyd Garrison

Thirteenth Amendment > Decimotercera Enmienda enmienda de la Constitución de los Estados Unidos de 1865, que prohibía la esclavitud en toda la nación

Three-Fifths Compromise > Acuerdo de los Tres Quintos acuerdo de la Convención Constitucional según el cual tres quintos de los residentes esclavizados de cada estado serían contados como parte de la población

tolerant > tolerante dispuesto a aceptar creencias que son diferentes de las propias

town meeting > reunión comunitaria en la Nueva Inglaterra colonial, reunión donde los colonos debatían y votaban sobre asuntos del gobierno local

trade union > sindicato asociación de trabajadores calificados formada con el fin de lograr salarios más altos y mejores condiciones laborales

Trail of Tears > Camino de Lágrimas migración forzada de los cheroquíes y otros grupos indígenas de sus hogares en el Sureste a los territorios al oeste del río Mississippi

traitor > traidor persona que traiciona a su país

transcendentalist > trascendentalista cada uno de los escritores y pensadores de Nueva Inglaterra que creían que las verdades más importantes de la vida trascienden la razón humana, es decir, la sobrepasan

treason > traición deslealtad o acciones contra el país propio

Treaty of Guadalupe-Hidalgo > Tratado de Guadalupe Hidalgo tratado de 1848 en el que México cedió California y el Territorio de Nuevo México a los Estados Unidos a cambio de 15 millones de dólares

Treaty of Paris > Tratado de París acuerdo de 1763 entre Gran Bretaña y Francia que puso fin a la Guerra contra la Alianza Franco-Indígena y estableció la transferencia de gran parte del territorio de América del Norte del control francés al británico

triangular trade > comercio triangular ruta comercial colonial entre Nueva Inglaterra, África y las Indias Occidentales

tribe > tribu comunidad de personas que comparten costumbres, un idioma y rituales

tribute > tributo pago de una parte débil a una más fuerte a cambio de protección

turning point > momento decisivo momento de la historia en el que se produce un cambio rotundo

U

unalienable rights > derechos inalienables derechos que no pueden ser quitados

unamendable > no enmendable que no se puede modificar

unconstitutional > inconstitucional no permitido por la Constitución

Underground Railroad > Tren Clandestino red de abolicionistas que ayudaban en secreto a los afroamericanos a escapar hacia la libertad

unify > unificar reunir a varias partes para formar una unidad; unir

urbanization > urbanización desplazamiento de la población de las granjas a las ciudades

V

vaquero > vaquero persona española o mexicana que se encargaba del ganado

varied > variado que tiene muchas formas o tipos

veto > veto rechazo, como cuando el presidente rechaza una ley aprobada por el Congreso

Virginia > Virginia acorazado que era un barco de guerra usado por la Confederación para atravesar el bloqueo de la Unión

Virginia Plan > Plan de Virginia plan de la Convención Constitucional que proponía un gobierno nacional fuerte con tres poderes y un cuerpo legislativo de dos cámaras

virtue > virtud buena conducta o carácter moral

vital > vital sumamente importante

W

War Hawks > Halcones miembros del Congreso provenientes del Sur y del Oeste que querían ir a la guerra con Gran Bretaña antes de la Guerra de 1812

Whig Party > Partido Whig partido político organizado por Henry Clay; estaba a favor de que el gobierno federal interviniera en la economía y estimulara los negocios

women's rights movement > movimiento por los derechos de las mujeres campaña organizada llevada a cabo con el fin de obtener derechos legales, educativos, laborales y de otro tipo para las mujeres

Worcester v. Georgia > Worcester contra Georgia fallo de 1832 de la Corte Suprema que estableció que las leyes estatales no regían en el territorio de los indígenas

writ of assistance > orden de asistencia documento legal que autorizaba a los soldados británicos a inspeccionar el cargamento de los barcos sin razón alguna

Y

Yankees > yankee apodo de los habitantes de Nueva Inglaterra

Index

The letters after some page numbers refer to the following: *c* = chart; *g* = graph; *m* = map; *p* = picture; *q* = quotation.

Great Mosque, 32
Great Plains, 375
    Indians of, 21
Great Wagon Road, 98, 105
Greece, 210
Green Corn Ceremony, 23
Greene, Nathanael, 184
Green Mountain Boys, 161, 167, 176
Grenville, George, 144–145, 145p, 147–148
Griffiths, John, 424
Griffitts, Hannah, 155q
Grimké, Angelina, 446–447, 458
Grimké, Sarah, 446–447, 458
Griswold, Roger, 276p
gross domestic product (GDP), 359
guerrilla warfare, 184, 492
Gullah, 112
gun ownership, 240
gunpowder, 36
Gutenberg, Johannes, 37

H
habeas corpus, 527
Hagar, Betsy, 180
Haiti, 41, 293
Hale, Nathan, 172
Hamilton, Alexander, 195p, 259p, 270, 287
    at Constitutional Convention, 205
    duel with Burr, 286, 286p
    facts about, 218
    Federalist Papers, 253
    Federalists and, 218, 223q, 277
    Madison and, 264–265
    political views of, 274c, 274–276
    "Report on Public Credit," 264
    as Treasury secretary, 263–266
Hancock, John, 169, 220
Hargreaves, James, 410
Harper, Frances Watkins, 466
Harpers Ferry, 498–499, 499p, 544g
harpsichord, 114p
Harrison, William Henry, 306q
    at battle of Tippecanoe, 306–307
    election of 1840 and, 357–358
    in War of 1812, 311, 315
Hartford Convention, 314
Harvard College, 113, 117
haven, 93
Hawthorne, Nathaniel, 467–468
Hayes, Rutherford B., 575
Hays, Mary Ludwig, 180, 181p
Henry, Joseph, 419
Henry, Patrick, 150, 151, 151p, 196p, 218q, 220, 222
Henry the Navigator, 37
Hermitage, 346p
hesitate, 57
Hessian mercenaries, 172p
Hiawatha, 5p
Hidalgo, Miguel, 323p, 324
higher education
    see also colleges and universities

for African Americans, 457, 554
    in colonies, 117
Hispaniola, 41
Historia Apologética, 65
historical points of view, 291
Hohokam, 14–15, 20
Holy Land, 29
Hooker, Thomas, 84, 84p
Hopewell Indians, 15
horses, 21p, 44, 44p, 57
Horseshoe Bend, Battle of, 311
House of Burgesses, 74–75, 74p, 123, 150, 213
House of Representatives, 206, 229
houses
    Anasazi, 15, 15p
    long, 24p
    in Middle Colonies, 98
housing starts, 359
Howard University, 554
Howe, Eias, 419
Howe, Julia Ward, 498
Howe, Samuel Gridley, 458
Howe, William, 166p, 167, 172, 175
Hudson River, 71
Hull, Isaac, 310
Hull, William, 310
human rights, 108–109, 170
hunters and gatherers, 16
Hurons, 71, 134, 135, 142
Hutchinson, Anne, 53p, 85–86
Hutchinson, Thomas, 155, 157
hydraulic mining, 401p
hymns, 114

I
ice ages, 7, 8
idealized, 466
immigrants, 248
    Chinese, 401
    contributions by, 428
    German, 98, 105–106, 427–428, 428p
    during Industrial Revolution, 427–429
    Irish, 427–429
    Jewish, 428
    reactions against, 428–429
    Scotch-Irish, 98, 105–106
    Spanish, 59
impeach, 236
impeachment, of Johnson, 562
implicitly, 355
imply, 536
imports, 121
imposition, 561c
impressment, 300p, 308
inauguration, 261
Inca empire, 12–13, 56–57
income tax, 529
incriminate, 240
indentured servants, 76, 111
Independence Hall, 192p–193p

independence movements, in Latin America, 324–325
Indiana Territory, 305–306
Indian Removal Act, 364–365, 364p
Indian Territories, 364, 365–366
Indian wars, 143, 311, 361–362, 367p
indigo, 102
individualism, 378, 470
individual rights, 229, 240
Indonesia, 31
industrialization, 327
    railroads and, 423–424
    roots of, 321g
    steam power and, 422–425
Industrial Revolution, 409–420, 472g
    beginning of, 409–411
    cotton demand and, 431
    factories, 411–414
    factory system, 410–411
    factory towns, 414–417
    home life and, 416–417
    immigrants during, 427–429
    inventions during, 409–410, 418–420, 418p
    market economy and, 412–413
    reforms and reform movements during, 453
    urbanization during, 417–418
industry
    cottage, 416–417, 417p
    lumber, 579
    in North, 509, 529
    shipping, 299–300, 424
    in South, 434, 508, 578–579
    textile, 320, 320p, 321g, 327, 409–410, 414–416, 431
    tobacco, 578–579
infectious diseases, 45, 57, 71, 108, 525
inflation, during Civil War, 528, 529
influential, 149
influenza, 45, 57
infographics, analyzing, 201g
informative/explanatory essays, ELA12–ELA13
infrastructure, 244
infringe, 239
Inglis, Charles, 164q
innovations
    see also inventions; technology
    Chinese, 35–36
    defined, 29
    effects of, 424
    during Industrial Revolution, 409–410, 418–420, 418p
    in navigation, 29, 35–36
    during Renaissance, 37
interchangeable parts, 411–412
interest groups, 448
Internal Revenue Service (IRS), 529
interstate commerce, 322–323
intervene, 556
intervention, 327
Intolerable Acts, 157–159
Inuit, 17–18, 18p, 39

inventions, 30–31, 35–36, 118–119, 320*p*, 409–410, 418–420, 418*p*, 431–432
invoke, 269
Ireland, potato famine in, 427–428, 427*p*
Irish immigrants, 98, 427–428, 429
ironclad warships, 516
iron plow, 419
iron stove, 119
Iroquois, 23–24, 71, 362
    culture of, 21
    in French and Indian War, 135, 138
    in Revolutionary War, 183
Iroquois Confederacy, 25
Iroquois League, 23–24, 46
Irving, Washington, 328, 467
Isabella (queen), 40, 41
Islam, 30–31

J

Jackson, Andrew, 335*p*, 337, 344*p*, 345*p*, 370, 402*g*
    annexation of Texas and, 390
    Bank War and, 352–355, 354*q*
    biography of, 344–345
    Democratic Party of, 342–343
    election of 1824 and, 340–341, 340*p*
    election of 1828 and, 343
    election of 1832 and, 355
    inauguration of, 345
    Indian policy of, 364–365
    Indian wars and, 311, 345
    invasion of Spanish Florida by, 325
    Nullification Crisis and, 351–352
    presidency of, 344–347, 349–356
    in War of 1812, 312–313, 315, 315*p*
Jackson, Stonewall, 514–515, 518
Jacksonian democracy, 344–346, 452–453
Jamaica, 41, 43
James I (king), 73
Jamestown colony, 72–77, 72*p*, 73*m*
    founding of, 73
    government of, 73, 74–75
    growth of, 76–77
    problems facing, 74
    reasons for, 73
    slavery in, 76, 76*p*, 77
    women in, 76
Jay, John, 186, 218, 262, 262*p*, 271
Jay's Treaty, 271–272, 271*p*, 281
Jefferson, Thomas, 131*p*, 150, 249, 252*q*, 277*q*, 278*c*
    on Alien and Sedition Acts, 283*q*, 284
    Articles of Confederation and, 200
    Democratic Republicans and, 277
    on education, 211*q*

election of 1796, 278*c*, 279
election of 1800, 285–286
on First Amendment, 222
foreign policy of, 292–293, 299–302
on French Revolution, 269
inauguration of, 287*p*
on Intolerable Acts, 158
on Lewis and Clark expedition, 295*q*
Louisiana Purchase and, 292–294, 294*q*, 369
on *Marbury* vs. *Madison*, 289–290, 289*q*
political views of, 274*c*, 274–276
portrait of, 328
presidency of, 286–290, 330
on states' rights, 284*q*
Virginia Statute for Religious Freedom by, 216, 222
writing of Declaration of Independence by, 168*p*, 169, 443
Jerusalem, 29
Jewish immigrants, 428
Jews, in Europe, 28
Jim Crow laws, 577
Jogues, Isaac, 70
John (king), 212, 212*p*
Johnson, Andrew, 236, 549*p*, 555, 560
    impeachment of, 562
    Radical Reconstruction and, 560–562
    Reconstruction plan of, 556–557, 561*c*
Johnson, Anthony, 76, 107
Johnson, William, 135
Johnson v. *M'Intosh*, 363
"Join, or Die" illustration, 171*p*
joint committees, 232
Jones, Absalom, 313
Jones, John Paul, 183*p*, 184
Judaism, 28
judicial branch, 215, 228, 228*c*, 233–235
judicial review, 234, 235, 289
judiciary, 213, 225
Judiciary Act of 1789, 233, 262, 289
Judiciary Act of 1801, 288
jury duty, 252, 338*c*

K

kachinas, 23
Kansas
    slavery in, 489–490
    violence in, 491–492
Kansas-Nebraska Act, 490, 490*m*, 496, 498*g*, 544*g*
Kearny, Stephen, 395
Kentucky, 433
Kentucky Resolution, 284*p*
Key, Francis Scott, 312
Kickapoos, 305

King, Rufus, 317
King Phillip's War, 87
Kino, Eusebio Francisco, 61
kinship, 34
Know-Nothing Party, 429, 495
Kosciusko, Thaddeus, 179
Ku Klux Klan, 568–569
Kwakiutl Indians, 22

L

labor
    see also factory workers; workers
    child, 416, 425–426, 457
labor organizations, 426–427
Lafayette, Marquis de, 179, 180*p*, 185, 269
laissez faire, 287, 357
Lake Erie, 311, 314*p*
Lake Texcoco, 11
land
    American Indian, 95, 134–135, 142–143, 305*m*, 362, 364–365
    conflicts over, 77, 142–143, 360–362
    dispute over Western, 199*m*, 199–200
    European claims on, 133–134
    manor, 28
    ownership, 338*c*
    privatization of western, 201
    speculation, 356
    in West, 368–369
land bridge, 7–8, 8*m*
land grants
    in Southern Colonies, 101, 103
    in Texas, 386–387
Land Ordinance of 1785, 201
La Salle, Robert de, 69
Las Casas, Bartolome de, 62, 63, 65
lateen sail, 32
Latin America
    independence in, 323–325
    map of, 324*m*
Laurens, Henry, 186
laws, obeying, 251
Laws of the Indies, 59, 61
Lee, Richard Henry, 168, 168*q*
Lee, Robert E., 475*p*, 511, 511*p*, 511*q*, 515, 517, 534–536, 541
legacy, 204, 205
legislative branch, 207*g*, 215, 228, 228*c*, 229–232
legislature, 123–124
    California, 241*p*
    two-house, 206
Le Jeune, Paul, 69
Leverett, Samuel, 180
Lewis, John, 230*p*
Lewis, Merriweather, 256–257*p*, 295
Lewis and Clark expedition, 256–257*p*, 295–299, 296*m*, 297*p*, 303, 371
Lexington, battle of, 131*p*, 159–161, 160*m*

Raleigh, Sir Walter, 72
rancheros, 385
ranches, Mexican, 385
Randolph, Edmund, 206, 209, 220
Randolph, John, 308
Rangel, Charles, 230p
Rankin, Jeannette, 227p
ratification
    of Constitution, 219–221
    debate over, of Constitution,
        217–219
ratified, 187
ratify, 217
reapers, 419
Reconstruction, 546–581, 548m
    African Americans during, 556,
        567–568
    aftermath of, 574–579
    causes and effects of, 553–554,
        580g
    end of, 550, 574–576
    Freedmen's Bureau, 554
    Johnson's plan for, 556–557
    Lincoln's plan for, 553–554
    politics of, 562g
    Radical, 558–563, 580g
    resistance to, 568–569
    rival plans for, 561c
    southern society and, 566–572
Reconstruction Act, 561c, 563
redcoats. See British soldiers
reforms and reform movements,
    453c, 472g
    education, 456–458
    era of, 452–454
    for people with disabilities,
        457–458
    political ideals leading to,
        452–453
    prison reform, 454–455
    social, 454–455
    social conditions leading to, 453
    temperance movement, 455–456
    women's rights, 458–459
regional differences, 350p
    on states' rights, 349–350
regulate, 319
Reign of Terror, 269
religion
    abolitionism and, 444
    African, 34–35
    American Indians, 22–23
    Aztec, 11–12
    in colonies, 88
    in Europe, 79
    Great Awakening, 114–116
    Islam, 30–31
    in medieval Europe, 28
    reforms, 66–67
    Second Great Awakening,
        453–454
    of slaves, 441
religious freedom, 78–80, 81, 94–95,
    222, 238–239, 369
religious persecution, 79
religious tolerance, 85, 101, 115

reluctant, 514
Renaissance, 36–38
repealed, 147
representative government, 75,
    123–125
republic, 210
republicanism, 210–211, 229
Republican Party, 231
    formation of, 494–495
    Lincoln as head of, 496–497
    in South, 566
Republic of Texas, 389–391
research skills, ELA15–ELA16
resident alien, 248
resolved, 483
respect, 249, 250
responsibilities, 249, 250
responsible citizenship, 250p,
    251–252
retail numbers, 359
Revels, Hiram Rhodes, 567–568,
    567p
revenue, 369
Revere, Paul, 159, 159p
revolts and rebellions
    Bacon's Rebellion, 76–77, 108
    Natchez Revolt, 69
    Shays' Rebellion, 203
    slave, 441–442, 448, 498
    Whiskey Rebellion, 267–268, 267p
Revolutionary Era, 130m
Revolutionary War, 162c, 163
    African Americans in, 181–183,
        182c
    American Indians in, 183
    battles of, 159–162, 160m, 165–167,
        172–176, 174p, 175m, 180,
        183–185, 185m, 189c
    beginning of, 159–161
    British strategy in, 174–175
    end of, 185–188
    Europeans in, 178–179
    events leading to, 146–151,
        154–159, 190
    French in, 176, 178–179, 187
    Loyalists in, 163, 167, 184, 187
    major figures of, 190
    mercenaries in, 167, 172p
    military tactics in, 184
    naval battles of, 183–184
    opposing sides in, 162c, 162–163
    reasons for American victory in,
        187–188
    in the South, 184, 185
    Spain and, 178, 187
    Treaty of Paris, 186–187, 187m
    Valley Forge, 179–180, 179f, 180p
    women during, 180–181, 181p
Rhode Island, 220–221
    colony of, 85
rice, 102, 433
Rillieux, Norbert, 438
riots
    colonial, 145
    draft, 526–527, 526p
    during Reconstruction, 559, 560

rivers, 370–371
roads, 321, 413
    1820–1850, 370m
    Great Wagon Road, 98, 105
    Inca, 13
    National Road, 372
    Silk Road, 32
Roanoke Island, 72
Rockefeller, John D., 495p
Rocky Mountains, 297, 375
Roman Catholic Church. See Catholic
    Church
Roman republic, 210–211, 211p
Ross, Betsy, 180
Ross, John, 335p
royal colony, 94
rudder, 35, 35p
rugged individualists, 378
rules, obeying, 251
Rush, Benjamin, 221
Russia, Oregon Country and, 377
Russwurm, John, 430

S

Sacajawea, 256–257p, 297, 297p
sailing ships, 31
sailor, impressment of U.S., 300
Salomon, Haym, 172–173, 173p
Salt Lake City, 397
salvation, 453
Samoset, 82
San Francisco, 399, 399c
San Jacinto, Battle of, 389
San Martín, José, 324–325
Santa Anna, Antonio López de, 388,
    388p
Santa Fe, 60, 384
Santa Fe Trail, 384
Santa Maria, 40
Santo Domingo, 41
Sapa Inca, 13
Saratoga, Battle of, 175–176
Sauk, 362, 364
savanna, 33
Savannah, Georgia, 102m, 103
scalawags, 566
scarcity, 411
The Scarlet Letter (Hawthorne),
    467–468
school boards, 245
schools
    see also education
    for African Americans, 457, 554p
    for the blind, 458
    dame, 117, 327, 456
    for deaf students, 457
    grammar, 456
    one-room, 116, 116p, 327p, 456p
    private, 116, 327
    public, 116, 457
Scotch-Irish immigrants, 98, 105–106
Scott, Dred, 493–494, 493p
Scott, Winfield, 395
sea navigation, 31

Acknowledgments

Photography

ELA 0 Hero Images Inc./Alamy Stock Photo; **ELA 1** Hero Images/ Getty Images; **ELA 9** Chassenet/BSIP SA/Alamy Stock Photo. **002–003** Dmitry Rukhlenko - Travel Photos/Alamy Stock Photo; **005T** Culture Club/Getty Images; **05CL** Mikael Utterström/Alamy Stock Photo; **005CR** Christopher Columbus (mosaic), Salviati, Antonio (1816–90)/ Palazzo Tursi, Genoa, Italy/Peter Newark American Pictures/ Bridgeman Art Library; **005B** Colport/Alamy Stock Photo; **006** Bjorn Landstrom/National Geographic/Getty Images; **007** Jan Wlodarczyk/ Alamy Stock Photo; **009** Avalon/World Pictures/Alamy Stock Photo; **010** HIP/Art Resource, NY; **011** Felix Lipov/Alamy Stock Photo; **012** PhotoStock-Israel/Alamy Stock Photo; **013** Zoonar GmbH/Alamy Stock Photo; **014** Tom Till/Alamy Stock Photo; **015** imageBROKER/Alamy Stock Photo; **018** Louise Murray/Robertharding/Alamy Stock Photo; **019T** Bettmann/Getty Images; **019B** Buyenlarge/Getty Images; **020T** Male head, Natchez, 1200–1500 (stone), Mississippian culture (c.800–1500)/Private Collection/Photo Dirk Bakker/Bridgeman Art Library; **020B** Franke Keating/Science Source/Getty Images; **021** The Last of the Buffalo, c.1888 (oil on canvas), Bierstadt, Albert (1830– 1902)/Corcoran Collection, National Gallery of Art, Washington D.C., USA/Gift of Mary (Mrs. Albert) Bierstadt/Bridgeman Art Library; **022** Sissie Brimberg/National Geographic/Getty Images; **023** Nancy Carter/North Wind Picture Archives; **024** Philip Scalia/ Alamy Stock Photo; **025** Fototeca Storica Nazionale/Hulton Archive/ Getty Images; **027** World History Archive/Alamy Stock Photo; **029** Lebrecht Music and Arts Photo Library/Alamy Stock Photo; **031** Art Directors & TRIP/Alamy Stock Photo; **032** Mansa Kankan Musa I, 14th century king of the Mali empire (gouache on paper), McBride, Angus (1931–2007)/Private Collection/Look and Learn/Bridgeman Art Library; **033** Abraham Cresques/Getty Images; **034** African Village, published 1806 (lithograph), Alexander, W. (19th century) (after)/Private Collection/Ken Welsh/Bridgeman Art Library; **035** Mariner's compass in an ivory case, probably Italian, c.1570/ National Maritime Museum, London, UK/Bridgeman Art Library; **036** Ivy Close Images/Alamy Stock Photo; **037** Al Schaben/Los Angeles Times/Getty Images; **039** Mikael Utterström/Alamy Stock Photo; **040T** Christian Kober/Robertharding/Alamy Stock Photo; **040B** Tupungato/Shutterstock; **041** Florilegius/SSPL/Getty Images; **043** Colport/Alamy Stock Photo; **044** Erich Lessing/Art Resource, NY; **045** Incamerastock/Alamy Stock Photo; **046** North Wind Picture Archives/Alamy Stock Photo; **047** Greg Balfour Evans/Alamy Stock Photo. **050–051** A View of Charleston, South Carolina (oil on canvas), Mellish, Thomas (18th century)/Ferens Art Gallery, Hull Museums, UK/Bridgeman Art Library; **053T** Portrait of Anne Hutchinson (1591–1643), American School, (20th century)/ Schlesinger Library, Radcliffe Institute, Harvard University/ Bridgeman Art library; **053CL** North Wind Picture Archives/ Alamy Stock Photo; **053CR** Colport/Alamy Stock Photo; **053B** Dbimages/Alamy Stock Photo; **054** Timewatch Images/Alamy Stock Photo; **055** Ipsumpix/Corbis Historical/Getty Images; **056** Library of Congress Prints and Photographs Division Washington [LC-USZC4-741]; **057** World History Archive/Alamy Stock Photo; **059** America/Alamy Stock Photo; **061** The Purebred Gentleman and his Spanish Wife Springs the Young Spaniard (oil on canvas), Spanish School, (18th century)/Museo de America, Madrid, Spain/Index/ Bridgeman Art Library; **062** V&A Images/Alamy Stock Photo; **064** World History Archive/Alamy Stock Photo; **065** North Wind Picture Archives/Alamy Stock Photo; **066** North Wind Picture Archives/Alamy Stock Photo; **067** Prisma Archivo/Alamy Stock Photo; **069** Bpk Bildagentur/Art Resource, NY; **071** North Wind Picture Archives/ Alamy Stock Photo; **072** Ira Block/National Geographic/Getty Images; **074** De Luan/Alamy Stock Photo; **076** Everett Collection Inc/ Alamy Stock Photo; **077** North Wind Picture Archives/Alamy Stock Photo; **078** North Wind Picture Archives/Alamy Stock Photo; **079** Brenda Kean/Alamy Stock Photo; **080** North Wind Picture Archives/ Alamy Stock Photo; **081** The Signing of the Mayflower Compact, c.1900 (oil on canvas), Moran, Edward Percy (1862–1935)/Pilgrim Hall Museum, Plymouth, Massachusetts/Bridgeman Art Library; **082** Marka/UIG/Getty Images; **083** Niday Picture Library/Alamy Stock Photo; **084** The NYC collection/Alamy Stock Photo; **086** Portrait of Anne Hutchinson (1591–1643), American School, (20th century)/ Schlesinger Library, Radcliffe Institute, Harvard University/ Bridgeman Art library; **089** Prisma Archivo/Alamy Stock Photo; **090** The Signing of the Mayflower Compact, c.1900 (oil on canvas), Moran, Edward Percy (1862–1935)/Pilgrim Hall Museum, Plymouth, Massachusetts/Bridgeman Art Library; **091** Anonymous Person/AKG Images; **093** Peter Mross/Alltravek/Alamy Stock Photo; **094** Andrew F. Kazmierski/Shutterstock; **095** Niday Picture Library/Alamy Stock Photo; **096** Ken Howard/Alamy Stock Photo; **097** Courthouse, Philadelphia (oil on canvas), Smith, Russell William Thompson (1812–98)/Philadelphia History Museum at the Atwater Kent,/ Courtesy of Historical Society of Pennsylvania Collection,/Bridgeman Art Library; **099** North Wind Picture Archives/Alamy Stock Photo; **100** North Wind Picture Archives/Alamy Stock Photo; **102T** Wildlife GmbH/Alamy Stock Photo; **102B** Everett Historical/Shutterstock; **103** Lanmas/Alamy Stock Photo; **104** North Wind Picture Archives/ Alamy Stock Photo; **105** North Wind Picture Archives/Alamy Stock Photo; **108** Pictorial Press Ltd/Alamy Stock Photo; **109** Everett Historical/Shutterstock; **110** North Wind Picture Archives; **111** MPI/ Getty Images; **112** Planetpix/Alamy Stock Photo; **113** Governor Peter Stuyvesant (1592–1672), c.1660 (oil on panel), Couturier, Hendrick (fl.1648–d.c.1684) (attr.)/Collection of the New-York Historical Society, USA/Bridgeman Art Library; **114** CSP_AlienCat/AGE Fotostock; **115** Lebrecht Music and Arts Photo Library/Alamy Photo Stock; **116** Gene Ahrens/Alamy Stock Photo; **117** North Wind Picture Archives/Alamy Stock Photo; **118** North Wind Picture Archives; **119** Dbimages/Alamy Stock Photo; **120** North Wind Picture Archives/ Alamy Stock Photo; **121** RMN-Grand Palais/Art Resource, NY; **123** Scala/Art Resource, NY; **125** North Wind Picture Archives. **128–129** Painting/Alamy Stock Photo; **131T** GL Archive/Alamy Stock Photo; **131CL** Photo Researchers, Inc/Alamy Stock Photo; **131CR** IanDagnall Computing/Alamy Stock Photo; **131B** Lebrecht Music and Arts Photo Library/Alamy Stock Photo; **132** Christian Delbert/Shutterstock; **133** Archive Images/Alamy Stock Photo; **135** Native American trading furs, 1777 (coloured engraving), American School, (18th century)/ Private Collection/Peter Newark American Pictures Bridgeman Images; **136** Pat & Chuck Blackley/Alamy Stock Photo; **138** 19th era/ Alamy Stock Photo; **139** Oronoz/Album/SuperStock; **142** North Wind Picture Archives; **143** North Wind Picture Archives/Alamy Stock Photo; **145** George Grenville (1712–70) (litho), Houston, Richard (1721–75)/Leeds Museums and Galleries (Leeds Art Gallery) U.K./ Bridgeman Art Library; **147** DeAgostini/SuperStock; **148** Historical/ Corbis/Getty Images; **149** North Wind Picture Archives; **150** North Wind Picture Archives/Alamy Stock Photo; **151T** Stock Montage/Getty Images; **151B** Archive Photos/Getty Images; **153L** North Wind Picture Archives/Alamy Stock Photo; **153R** North Wind Picture Archives/Alamy Stock Photo; **154** Photo Researchers, Inc/Alamy Stock Photo; **155** Debu55y/Shutterstock; **156** North Wind Picture Archives; **157** Revere, Paul (1735–1818) (after)/Private Collection/Bridgeman Images; **158** Roberts H. Armstrong/ClassicStock/Alamy Stock Photo; **159** Vlad G/Shutterstock; **161** Lebrecht Music and Arts Photo Library/ Alamy Stock Photo; **163** North Wind Picture Archives/Alamy Stock Photo; **165** North Wind Picture Archives/Alamy Stock Photo; **166** North Wind Picture Archives/Alamy Stock Photo; **167** Digital Image Library/Alamy Stock Photo; **168** GraphicaArtis/Getty Images; **169** Lawcain/Fotolia; **170** Loren File/Alamy Stock Photo; **171** Encyclopaedia Britannica, Inc./Library of Congress/Universal Images Group North America LLC/Alamy Stock Photo; **172** North Wind Picture Archives/Alamy Stock Photo; **173** DomonabikeUSA/Alamy Stock Photo; **174T** General John Stark at the Battle of Bennington, Vermont, 1902 (colour litho), Yohn, Frederick Coffay (1875–1933) (after)/Private Collection/Bridgeman Art Library; **174B** North Wind Picture Archives; **176** Heritage Image Partnership Ltd/Alamy Stock Photo; **177** Photo Researchers, Inc/Alamy Stock Photo; **178** George Washington at Valley Forge, preliminary sketch, 1854 (oil on canvas), Matteson, Tompkins Harrison (1813–84)/Private Collection/Photo Christie's Images/Bridgeman Images; **179** North Wind Picture Archives; **180** North Wind Picture Archives/Alamy Stock Photo; **181T** Kean Collection/Getty Images; **181B** Photo Researchers, Inc/Alamy Stock Photo; **182** The Massacre of Wyoming Valley in July 1778 (colour litho) (detail), Chappel, Alonzo (1828–87) (after)/Private Collection/Peter Newark American Pictures/Bridgeman Art Library; **183** North Wind Picture Archives/Alamy Stock Photo; **184** Visual Arts Library/The Art Gallery Collection/Alamy Stock Photo; **186** North Wind Picture Archives/Alamy Stock Photo; **188** The Museum of the City of New York/Art Resource, NY. **192–193** F11photo/Shutterstock; **195T** IanDagnall Computing/Alamy Stock Photo; **195C** North Wind Picture Archives/Alamy Stock Photo; **195B** Albert Knapp/Alamy Stock Photo; **196** The Metropolitan Museum of Art/Art Resource, NY; **197** Virginia Constitutional Convention of 1829–30 (oil on panel), Catlin, George (1796–1872)/Virginia Historical Society, Richmond, Virginia, USA/Bridgeman Art Library; **198** State of Massachusetts in Convention, State Constitution, 16th June 1780 (litho), American School, (18th century)/Gilder Lehrman Collection, New York, USA/Bridgeman Images; **200** Lebrecht Music and Arts Photo Library/Alamy Stock Photo; **202** North Wind Picture Archives/Alamy Stock Photo; **203** North Wind Picture Archives/Alamy Stock Photo; **204** North Wind Picture Archives/Alamy Stock Photo; **205** SuperStock; **206** World History Archive/Alamy Stock Photo; **209** North Wind Picture Archives/Alamy Stock Photo; **210** SuperStock/Getty Images; **211** Culture Club/Getty Images; **212** SuperStock/Alamy Stock Photo; **213** The Bill of Rights presented to William and Mary (engraving), English School, (19th century)/Private Collection/Look and Learn/Bridgeman Images; **214** World History Archive/Alamy Stock Photo; **215** Lebrecht Music and Arts Photo Library/Alamy Stock Photo; **216** GraphicaArtis/Archive Photos/Getty Images; **217** The Metropolitan Museum of Art/Art Resource, NY; **218** Albert Knapp/Alamy Stock Photo; **219** Courtesy of the New York Public Library; **220** National Archives and Records Administration; **221** North Wind Picture Archives; **222** Hulton Archive/MPI/Getty Images; **223** Courtesy of the New York Public Library; **225** Michael Ventura/Alamy Stock Photo; **226** Sean Rayford/Images News/Getty Images; **227** Ken Cedeno/Corbis/Getty Images; **229** Orhan Cam/Shutterstock; **230** Tom Williams/CQ Roll Call/Newscom; **231** Kim Warp The New Yorker Collection/The Cartoon Bank; **232** Bastiaan Slabbers/Alamy Stock Photo; **234** Roger L. Wollenberg/Pool/Corbis/Getty Images; **236** Artley Cartoons; **237** Jim West/Alamy Stock Photo; **239** SuperStock; **241** Ian G Dagnall/Alamy Stock Photo; **242** Andrew Cullen/Reuters/Alamy Stock Photo; **243** David Wall/Alamy Stock Photo; **244** Marmaduke St. John/Alamy Stock Photo; **245** National Geographic Creative/Alamy Stock Photo; **247** Kevin Shields/Alamy Stock Photo; **248** Roger Bacon/Reuters/Alamy Stock Photo; **249** Spencer Grant/Alamy Stock Photo; **250** RosaIreneBetancourt 1/Alamy Stock Photo; **252** Kaisar Andreas/Alamy Stock Photo; **253** Albert Knapp/Alamy Stock Photo. **256–257** Lewis & Clark on the Lower Columbia River, 1905 (oil on canvas), Russell, Charles Marion (1865–1926)/Private Collection/Peter Newark American Pictures/Bridgeman Art library; **259T** IanDagnall Computing/Alamy Stock Photo; **259CL** North Wind Picture Archives/Alamy Stock Photo; **259CR** IanDagnall Computing/Alamy Stock Photo; **259B** North Wind Picture Archives/Alamy Stock Photo; **260** White House Photo/Alamy Stock Photo; **261** Science Source; **262** World History Archive/Alamy Stock Photo; **265** Everett Collection Inc/Alamy Stock Photo; **266** Trekandshoot/Shutterstock; **267** Whiskey rebels escorting a tarred and feathered tax collector from his burning homestead (colour litho), American School, (18th century) (after)/Private Collection/Peter Newark American Pictures/Bridgeman Art Library; **268** Lanmas/Alamy Stock Photo; **271** The Print Collector/Glow Images; **272** Everett Collection Historical/Alamy Stock Photo; **273** Sipley/ClassicStock/Alamy Stock Photo; **274L** GL Archive/Alamy Stock Photo; **274R** IanDagnall Computing/Alamy Stock Photo; **275L** North Wind Picture Archives/Alamy Stock Photo; **275R** North Wind Picture Archives/Alamy Stock Photo; **276** Library of Congress Prints and Photographs Division Washington [LC-DIG-ppmsca-31832]; **278** Kean Collection/Getty Images; **279** IanDagnall Computing/Alamy Stock Photo; **281** North Wind Picture Archives/Alamy Stock Photo; **282** Satirising the XYZ Affair, 1797 (colour litho), American School, (18th century)/Archives du Ministere des Affaires Etrangeres, Paris, France/Archives Charmet/Bridgeman Images; **283** National Portrait Gallery, Smithsonian Institution/Art Resource, NY; **284** Jefferson, Thomas/Library of Congress Prints and Photographs Division Washington; **286** Bettmann/Getty Images; **287T** North Wind Picture Archives/Alamy Stock Photo; **287B** GL Archive/Alamy Stock Photo; **288** North Wind Picture Archives/Alamy Stock Photo; **289** Wiskerke/

Alamy Stock Photo; **290** Irene Abdou/Alamy Stock Photo; **292** Bettmann/Getty Images; **293** Bettmann/Getty Images; **294** View of New Orleans from the Plantation of Marigny, 1803 (oil on canvas), Woiseri, J. L. Bouquet de (fl.1797–1815)/Chicago History Museum, USA/Bridgeman Art Library; **297T** North Wind Picture Archives/Alamy Stock Photo; **297B** Witold Skrypczak/Alamy Stock Photo; **299** The Hongs at Canton, before 1820 (oil on ivory), Chinnery, George (1774–1852) (follower of)/Ferens Art Gallery, Hull Museums, UK/Bridgeman Images; **300** North Wind Picture Archives/Alamy Stock Photo; **302** Stevemart/Shutterstock; **303** North Wind Picture Archives/Alamy Stock Photo; **304** North Wind Picture Archives/Alamy Stock Photo; **306** JT Vintage/Glasshouse Images/Alamy Stock Photo; **307** Kurz & Allison/Library of Congress Prints and Photographs Division Washington [LC-DIG-pga-01891]; **308** Cosmo Condina North America/Alamy Stock Photo; **309** Stock Montage/Getty Images; **310** Bettmann/Getty Images; **311** Everett Collection Historical/Alamy Stock Photo; **312** Our Flag was still there, War of 1812; The Defense of Fort McHenry. September 13–14, 1814, 2012 (oil on canvas), Troiani, Don (b.1949)/Private Collection/Bridgeman Art Library; **314** Carol M Highsmith/Library of Congress Prints and Photographs Division Washington[LC-DIG-highsm-09904]; **315** Ken Welsh/Design Pics/Newscom; **316** Niday Picture Library/Alamy Stock Photo; **317** North Wind Picture Archives/Alamy Stock Photo; **318L** North Wind Picture Archives/Alamy Stock Photo; **318C** Classic Image/Alamy Stock Photo; **318R** Stock Montage/Getty Images; **319** CPC Collection/Alamy Stock Photo; **320** Mansell/The LIFE Picture Collection/Getty Images; **322** North Wind Picture Archives/Alamy Stock Photo; **323** Interfoto/Alamy Stock Photo; **325** Everett Collection Historical/Alamy Stock Photo; **326** Bettmann/Getty Images; **327** Bob Pardue – SC/Alamy Stock Photo; **328** Bank of Pennsylvania, c.1804 (oil on canvas), American School, (19th century)/Philadelphia History Museum at the Atwater Kent,/Courtesy of Historical Society of Pennsylvania Collection/Bridgeman Art Library. **332–33** World History Archive/Alamy Stock Photo; **335T** Everett Collection Inc/Alamy Stock Photo; **335C** MPI/Getty Images; **335B** Newberry Library/SuperStock; **336** World History Archive/Alamy Stock Photo; **337** Everett Collection Inc/Alamy Stock Photo; **338** Heritage Image Partnership Ltd/Alamy Stock Photo; **339** North Wind Picture Archives; **340L** Everett Collection Inc/Alamy Stock Photo; **340CL** SuperStock/Getty Images; **340CR** Kean Collection/Staff/Getty Images; **340R** Stock Montage/Getty Images; **341** Library of Congress Print and Division [LC-DIG-pga-06984]; **342** Francis G. Mayer/Corbis Historical/Getty Images; **344** Library of Congress Prints and Photographs Division [LC-USZ62-2340]; **345** North Wind Picture Archives; **346** Danita Delimont/Alamy Stock Photo; **347** North Wind Picture Archives; **348** IanDagnall Computing/Alamy Stock Photo; **349** Everett Collection Historical/Alamy Stock Photo; **350L** North Wind Picture Archives/Alamy Stock Photo; **350C** North Wind Picture Archives/Alamy Stock Photo; **350R** The Print Collector/Alamy Stock Photo; **351** Niday Picture Library/Alamy Stock Photo; **352** ClassicStock/Alamy Stock Photo; **354** 'Jackson slaying the many headed monster', 1828 (colour litho), American School, (19th century)/Private Collection/Peter Newark American Pictures/Bridgeman Images; **355** Herbert Orth/The LIFE Picture Collection/Getty Images; **356** Bettmann/Getty Images; **357** Old Paper Studios/Alamy Stock Photo; **358** Bygone Collection/Alamy Stock Photo; **360** North Wind Picture Archives/Alamy Stock Photo; **362** National Portrait Gallery, Smithsonian Institution/Art Resource, NY; **363** Nancy Carter/North Wind Picture Archives; **364** Newberry Library/SuperStock; **366** Terry Smith Images/Alamy Stock Photo; **367** Willard R. Culver/National Geographic/Getty Images; **368** W H Jackson/MPI/Getty Images; **372** Ian Dagnall/Alamy Stock Photo; **374** North Wind Picture Archives/Alamy Stock Photo; **375** Leon Werdinger/Alamy Stock Photo; **376** Everett Collection Inc/Alamy Stock Photo; **378** Jim Beckwourth (engraving) (b/w photo), Janet, Ange-Louis (Janet-Lange) (1815–72) (after)/Bibliotheque des Arts Decoratifs, Paris, France/Archives Charmet/Bridgeman Art Library; **380** Witold Skrypczak/Alamy Stock Photo; **381** North Wind Picture Archives/Alamy Stock Photo; **383** Interfoto/History/Alamy Stock Photo; **385** Ian Shaw/Alamy Stock Photo; **386** North Wind Picture Archives/Alamy Stock Photo; **387** Carol M. Highsmith/Library of Congress Prints and Photographs Division [LC-DIG-highsm-27900]; **388** World History Archive/Alamy Stock Photo; **389** Bettmann/Getty Images; **392** Huntington Library/SuperStock; **393** Everett Collection Historical/

Alamy Stock Photo; **397** North Wind Picture Archives/Alamy Stock Photo; **398** Hulton Archive/Getty Images; **399** Robin Runck/Alamy Stock Photo; **400** Underwood Archives/Archive Photos/Getty Images; **401** Everett Collection Historical/Alamy Stock Photo. **404–405** Port of New Orleans, engraved by D.G. Thompson (coloured engraving), Waud, Alfred Rudolph (1828–91) (after)/Bibliotheque Nationale, Paris, France/Bridgeman Art Library; **407T** Stock Montage/Archive Photos/Getty Images; **407C** GL Archive/Alamy Stock Photo; **407B** VCG Wilson/Historical/Corbis/Getty Images; **408** GL Archive/Alamy Stock Photo; **409** Bettmann/Getty Images; **410** Chronicle/Alamy Stock Photo; **411** Frank Vetere/Alamy Stock Photo; **412** M841 Mississippi Contract Rifle by Eli Whitney/Private Collection/Photo Don Troiani/Bridgeman Art Library; **413** Historical/Contributor/Corbis Historical/Getty Images; **414** Library of Congress Prints and Photographs Division Washington; **415** Library of Congress Prints and Photographs Division Washington; **416** Weaving on Power Looms, Cotton factory floor, engraved by James Tingle (fl.1830–60) c.1830 (litho), Allom, Thomas (1804–72) (after)/Private Collection/Ken Welsh/Bridgeman Art Library; **417** Stock Montage/Archive Photos/Getty Images; **418L** Interfoto History/Alamy Stock Photo; **418R** Photo Researchers, Inc/Alamy Stock Photo; **419** De Agostini Picture Library/De Agostini Editore/AGE Fotostock; **420** Telegraphe de Hughes/Photo CCI/Bridgeman Art Library; **421L** Stock Montage/Archive Photos/Getty Images; **421R** Bettmann/Getty Images; **422** Everett Collection Inc/CSU Archives/Alamy Stock Photo; **424** Photo Researchers, Inc/Alamy Stock Photo; **425** UIG/Underwood Archives/Akg-images; **426** Frances/Everett Collection/Newscom; **427** Attack on a Potato Store in Ireland, c.1845 (engraving) (b&w photo), English School, (19th century)/Private Collection/Bridgeman Art Library; **428** Don Smetzer/Alamy Stock Photo; **429** Vespasian/Alamy Stock Photo; **430** Courtesy of the New York Public Library; **431** Ball Miwako/Alamy Stock Photo; **432** North Wind Picture Archives/Alamy Stock Photo; **433** North Wind Picture Archives/AP Images; **436** Franz Marc Frei/Look Die Bildagentur der Fotografen Gmbh/Alamy Stock Photo; **437** North Wind Picture Archives/Alamy Stock Photo; **438** Library of Congress Prints and Photographs Division Washington [LC-DIG-pga-04518]; **439** Hulton Archive/Staff/Getty Images; **440** North Wind Picture Archives/The Image Works; **441** Slave harness with bell (b/w photo), American School/Philadelphia History Museum at the Atwater Kent,/Courtesy of Historical Society of Pennsylvania Collection/Bridgeman Art Library; **442** Stock Montage/Getty Images; **443** Herbert Orth/The LIFE Picture Collection/Getty Images; **444** American Anti-Slavery Society/Library of Congress Rare Book and Special Collections Division Washington [LC-USZC4-5321]; **445** North Wind Picture Archives/Alamy Stock Photo; **446** Bailey-Cooper Photography/Alamy Stock Photo; **448** Niday Picture Library/Alamy Stock Photo; **449** North Wind Picture Archives; **451** Robert Martin/Alamy Stock Photo; **452** North Wind Picture Archives/Alamy Stock Photo; **454** MPI/Getty Images; **455** North Wind Picture Archives; **456** North Wind Picture Archives/Alamy Stock Photo; **457** Collection of the Orleans County Historical Grammar Schools; **458** Bettmann/Getty Images; **459** Akg-images/Newscom; **460** Bettmann/Getty Images; **461** VCG Wilson/Historical/Corbis/Getty Images; **463** Everett Collection Inc./AGE Fotostock; **464** North Wind Picture Archives/Alamy Stock Photo; **465** Niday Picture Library/Alamy Stock Photo; **466** Liszt Images/Artokoloro Quint Lox Limited/Alamy Stock Photo; **467** IanDagnall Computing/Alamy Stock Photo; **468** Moby Dick, English School, (20th century)/Private Collection/Look and Learn/Bridgeman Images; **469T** Travelib history/Alamy Stock Photo; **469B** Glasshouse Images/Newscom; **470** Zachary Frank/Alamy Stock Photo; **471** Photo Researchers, Inc/Alamy Stock Photo. **474–475** John Parrot/Stocktrek Images, Inc./Alamy Stock Photo; **477T** Hesler, Alexander/Library of Congress Prints and Photographs Division [LC-DIG-ppmsca-23723]; **477CL** Ames F. Gibson/Buyenlarge/Getty Images; **477C** Everett Collection Inc/Alamy Stock Photo; **477CR** World History Archive/Alamy Stock Photo; **477B** Photo Researchers, Inc/Alamy Stock Photo; **478** Abraham Lincoln with Allan Pinkerton and Major General John A. McClernand, 1862 (b/w photo), Gardner, Alexander (1821–82)/Collection of the New-York Historical Society, USA/Bridgeman Art Library; **479** Jerry Pinkney/National Geographic Creative/Alamy Stock Photo; **481** North Wind Picture Archives/Alamy Stock Photo; **483** Picture History/Newscom; **484** North Wind Picture Archives/Alamy Stock Photo; **486** Fotosearch/Stringer/Getty Images; **487** Bettmann/Getty Images; **488** North Wind Picture Archives/Alamy Stock Photo; **489** North Wind Picture Archives/Alamy Stock Photo; **491** North Wind Picture Archives/Alamy Stock Photo; **492** Photo Researchers, Inc./Alamy Stock Photo; **493** Pictorial Press Ltd/Alamy Stock Photo; **494** North Wind Picture Archives/Alamy Stock Photo; **495** Library of Congress Prints and Photographs Division Washington [LC-DIG-ds-00859]; **496** When They Were Young: Abraham Lincoln, Jackson, Peter (1922–2003)/Private Collection/Look and Learn/Bridgeman Art Library; **497** Abraham Lincoln (1809–65) in public debate with Stephen A. Douglas (1813–61) in Illinois, 1858 (colour litho), American School, (19th century)/Private Collection/Peter Newark American Pictures/Bridgeman Art Library; **499** Photo Researchers, Inc/Alamy Stock Photo; **501** North Wind Picture Archives; **503** The New York Historical Society/Contributor/Getty Images; **504** Pictorial Press Ltd/Alamy Stock Photo; **505L** Lincoln Lantern used for Presidential Campaign, 1864 (tin and glass with paint), American School, (19th century)/Collection of the New-York Historical Society, USA/Bridgeman Art Library; **505R** Nancy Carter/North Wind Picture Archives; **506** Popperfoto/Getty Images; **509** The Lexington of 1861, pub. by Currier & Ives, c.1861 (colour litho), American School, (19th century)/American Antiquarian Society, Worcester, Massachusetts, USA/Bridgeman Images; **510L** Hesler, Alexander/Library of Congress Prints and Photographs Division [LC-DIG-ppmsca-23723]; **510R** Photo Researchers, Inc./Alamy Stock Photo; **511** Glasshouse Images/JT Vintage/Alamy Stock Photo; **513** John Parrot/Stocktrek Images/Alamy Stock Photo; **514** Library of Congress Prints and Photographs Division [LC-DIG-ppmsca-35625]; **516T** GL Archive/Alamy Stock Photo; **516B** Mai/The LIFE Images Collection/Getty Images; **517** Niday Picture Library/Alamy Stock Photo; **518** Kean Collection/Archive Photos/Getty Images; **519** North Wind Picture Archives/Alamy Stock Photo; **520** 'Come and Join Us Brothers', Union recruitment poster aimed at black volunteers (colour litho), American School, (19th century)/Private Collection/Peter Newark American Pictures/Bridgeman Art Library; **522** H. Armstrong Roberts/ClassicStock/Alamy Stock Photo; **523** Pete Cutter/Alamy Stock Photo; **524** Two Amputee Officers, 4th Vermont Vols. wounded at Petersburg, VA/Private Collection/Photo Don Troiani/Bridgeman Art Library; **525** The Protected Art Archive/Alamy Stock Photo; **526** Bettmann/Getty Images; **528** Glasshouse Images/Alamy Stock Photo; **529** Everett Collection Historical/Alamy Stock Photo; **530** Clara Barton tending wounded during the American Civil War (colour litho), American School, (19th century)/Private Collection/Peter Newark American Pictures/Bridgeman Art Library; **531** Fotosearch/Stringer/Getty Images; **533** Tom Lovell/National Geographic Creative/Alamy Stock Photo; **534** The Print Collector/Alamy Stock Photo; **535** Tim Sloan/APF/Getty Images; **536** Abraham Lincoln with Union Officers 1862/Universal History Archive/UIG/Bridgeman Art Library; **537** Niday Picture Library/Alamy Stock Photo; **538** Fototeca Gilardi/Hulton Archive/Getty Images; **539** Everett Collection Inc/Alamy Stock Photo; **540L** Courtesy U.S. National Archives; **540R** American Civil War (1861–1865): view of the ruins in Richmond, Virginia, after fall of the city april-june 1865, photo by Alexander Gardner/Photo PVDE/Bridgeman Art Library; **541** Timothy H. O'Sullivan/U.S. Library of Congress/Handout/Getty Images; **543** Ivy Close Images/Alamy Stock Photo. **546–547** George N. Barnard/George Eastman House/Getty Images; **549T** Prisma Archivo/Alamy Stock Photo; **549C** Pictorial Press Ltd/Alamy Stock Photo; **549B** Everett Collection/Newscom; **550** North Wind Picture Archives/Alamy Stock Photo; **551** LOC Photo/Alamy Stock Photo; **552** Hulton Archive/Getty Images; **553** Lightfoot/Getty Images; **554** Historical/Corbis/Getty Images; **555** Photo Researchers, Inc/Alamy Stock Photo; **556** Library of Congress Prints and Photographs Division Washington [LC-DIG-ppmsca-11312]; **557** Courtesy The New York Public Library; **558** Niday Picture Library/Alamy Stock Photo; **559** Charles Sumner (1811–74), US Senator; photo by George Warren, Boston (albumen print), American Photographer, (19th century)/American Antiquarian Society, Worcester, Massachusetts, USA/Bridgeman Art Library; **560** North Wind Picture Archives/Alamy Stock Photo; **563** MPI/Getty Images; **564** Universal Images Group North America LLC/Encyclopaedia Britannica, Inc./Library of Congress/Alamy Stock Photo; **566** Library of Congress [LC-USZ62-105555]; **567** Pictorial

Press Ltd/Alamy Stock Photo; **568** Everett Collection/Newscom; **569** GL Archive/Alamy Stock Photo; **570** Old Paper Studios/Alamy Stock Photo; **571** Bettmann/Getty Images; **572** Hulton Archive/Getty Images; **574** Hulton Archive/Getty Images; **576** North Wind Picture Archives/Alamy Stock Photo; **577** Courtesy of the New York Public Library; **579** Artokoloro Quint Lox Limited/Alamy Stock Photo. **584** Steve Gottlieb/Stock Connection Blue/Alamy Stock Photo.

Text

Academy of Achievement Interview with Rosa Parks. Copyright © by American Academy of Achievement. **Alfred A. Knopf, Inc.** Berlin Diary by William L. Shirer. Copyright © by Alfred a. Knopf. **Daily Press** A Dismal Refuge by Kimberly Lenz. Daily Press, February 08, 2004. Copyright © Daily Press. **Ferrell, Melvin B** Men of D-Day by Melvin B. Ferrell. Copyright © Gail Ferrell. **Harper & Brothers** Giants in the Earth: A Saga of the Prairie by O E Rolvaag. Copyright © 1927 by Harper & Brothers. **Harper Collins Publishers** Little Town on the Prairie by Laura Ingalls Wilder. Copyright © by Harper Collins Publishers. **Harper's Magazine** Race prejudice and the Negro artist by James Weldon Johnson. Copyright © Harper's Magazine 1928. **Langston Hughes** The Negro Speaks of Rivers by Langston Hughes. Copyright © Langston Hughes. Reprinted by permission. **McKay, Claude, Estate** If We Must Die by Claude McKay. Copyright © McKay Estate. **Nabokov, Peter** Native American Testimony by Peter Nabokov. Copyright © Peter Nabokov. **Nelson Mandela Foundation** Inaugural Speech, Pretoria, "HOPE AND GLORY" by Nelson Mandela. Copyright by Nelson Mandela Foundation. Reprinted by permission. **Penguin Random House Canada** The Good Old Days—They Were Terrible! by Otto Bettmann. Copyright Otto L. Bettmann. Published by Penguin Random House. **Southern Christian Leadership Conference** SCLC Statement. Copyright 1957 by Southern Christian Leadership Conference **The New York Times Magazine** Sandra Day O'Connor's Interview by Deborah Salomon, March 16, 2009. Copyright © 2017 The New York Times. **Writers House** I Have a Dream, Speech by Martin Luther King, Jr. Reprinted by arrangement with The Heirs to the Estate of Martin Luther King Jr., c/o Writers House as agent for the proprietor New York, NY. Copyright Dr. Martin Luther King 1963; Copyright renewed Coretta Scott King (1991). Reprinted by permission. **Writers House** Speech by Martin Luther King, Jr. Reprinted by arrangement with The Heirs to the Estate of Martin Luther King Jr., c/o Writers House as agent for the proprietor New York, NY. Copyright Dr. Martin Luther King 1963; Copyright renewed Coretta Scott King (1991). Reprinted by permission.